# OXFORD LIBRARY OF AFRICAN LITERATURE

*General Editors*

E. E. EVANS-PRITCHARD
G. LIENHARDT
W. H. WHITELEY

# Oxford Library of African Literature

SELECTION OF AFRICAN PROSE
I. Traditional Oral Texts.  II. Written Prose
W. H. WHITELEY
(*Two volumes*)

THE HEROIC RECITATIONS OF THE
BAHIMA OF ANKOLE
H. F. MORRIS

SOMALI POETRY.  An Introduction
B. W. ANDRZEJEWSKI *and* I. M. LEWIS

PRAISE-POEMS OF TSWANA CHIEFS
I. SCHAPERA

THE GLORIOUS VICTORIES
OF 'ĀMDA ṢEYON, KING OF ETHIOPIA
together with THE HISTORY OF THE EMPEROR AND CEƠN
OTHERWISE CALLED GÂBRA MAZCÂL BY PERO PAEZ
G. W. HUNTINGFORD

A SELECTION OF HAUSA STORIES
H. A. S. JOHNSTON

THE CONTENT AND FORM OF YORUBA IJALA
S. A. BABALOLA

AKAMBA STORIES
JOHN S. MBITI

LIMBA STORIES AND STORYTELLING
RUTH FINNEGAN

THE MEDICINE MAN: *SWIFA YA NGUVUMALI*
PETER LIENHARDT

IZIBONGO: ZULU PRAISE POEMS
TREVOR COPE

THE ZANDE TRICKSTER
E. E. EVANS-PRITCHARD

SHINQIṬĪ FOLK LITERATURE AND SONG
H. T. NORRIS

LITTÉRATURE DE COUR AU RWANDA
A COUPEZ *and* TH. KAMANZI

# ORAL LITERATURE
# IN AFRICA

RUTH FINNEGAN

OXFORD
AT THE CLARENDON PRESS
1970

*Oxford University Press, Ely House, London W. 1*

GLASGOW   NEW YORK   TORONTO   MELBOURNE   WELLINGTON
CAPE TOWN   SALISBURY   IBADAN   NAIROBI   DAR ES SALAAM   LUSAKA   ADDIS ABABA
BOMBAY   CALCUTTA   MADRAS   KARACHI   LAHORE   DACCA
KUALA LUMPUR   SINGAPORE   HONG KONG   TOKYO

PRINTED IN GREAT BRITAIN

# PREFACE

WHEN I first became interested in research into one particular form of African oral literature in 1961, I found to my surprise that there was no easily accessible work to which I could turn to give me some idea of what was known in this field, the various publications available, or the controversies and problems that demanded further investigation. In fact, I gradually discovered, there was an immense amount in print—but most of it was not easy to find, it was not systematic, and there was relatively little treatment of contemporary forms. It was true that there was plenty of work on *written* African literature (which has received a lot of publicity in recent years) and, of a rather speculative kind, on 'primitive mentality' or 'mythopœic imagination'. But on the oral side or on the actual literary products of such minds much less was said.

There therefore seemed a place for a general work on oral literature in Africa, an introductory survey which could sum up the present knowledge of the field and serve as a guide to further research. It seemed likely that others too besides myself had felt the need to consult an introduction of some kind to this subject. It is hoped that the resulting book will be useful not only to those intending to do specific research on African oral literature but also to those with a general interest either in Africa or in literature generally.

The aim in presenting the material has been to strike a balance between general discussion and actual instances. It has been necessary to include rather more detailed descriptions and quotations than might be the case with a book on European literatures, as the majority of African examples are not readily accessible and too abstract a discussion would give little idea of the intricacy and artistic conventions of many of the oral forms. It is also an intrinsic part of the book to consider some of the social background as well as the more purely aesthetic and stylistic features. With African as with other literature it is essential to treat both literary and social facets (if indeed these two are ultimately distinguishable at all) for a full appreciation, a point too often neglected by writers on this subject.

This book is based only on the more obvious sources and is intended as an introduction, not as a comprehensive account. Only some examples are given from a huge field and experts in particular areas will be able to point to exceptions and omissions. Some of my conclusions too may turn out to be controversial; indeed one of my hopes is to stimulate further publications and study. On each chapter and each section more research could—and I trust will—take the subject very much further. But in spite of these limitations, the general purpose of the book will, I hope, be fulfilled—to show that African oral literature is, after all, a subject worthy of study and interest, and to provoke further research in this fascinating but too often neglected field.

*Ibadan* 1968

# ACKNOWLEDGEMENTS

I HAVE many thanks to express. All the editors of the 'Oxford Library of African Literature' have helped me in many ways; in particular Professor Wilfred Whiteley has worked through the whole book and made many helpful suggestions and criticisms; his serial letters on the subject over several months were a highlight of 1967/8 and I am more grateful to him than I can say. The following have also read and commented on parts of the book: Dr. G. Innes, Mr. D. K. Rycroft, and Mrs. Agnes Finnegan. I have greatly appreciated and profited from their advice (even where I have not taken all of it). I have also had a number of most helpful discussions with Mr. Robin Horton and with my husband, Dr. David Murray. I have obviously used the writings of a great number of people, but would like to mention in particular the stimulus I have received from work by Bascom, Berry, Bowra, Babalola, and, above all, Nketia; I have not always agreed with them or even referred much directly to their work, but have constantly found them illuminating. Finally, the dedication is a serious one. Anything that is of interest in this book is ultimately due to the many people over many years who have taught me—and I do not mean only those who have taught me about Africa or about anthropology.

I would also like to thank the staff of libraries where I have collected the material used here: especially the library of the (then) University College of Rhodesia and Nyasaland (in particular for allowing me access to the Doke Collection of works on Bantu studies); the library of the University of Ibadan (especially the Africana and reference librarians); and the library of the Institute of Social Anthropology, Oxford. I am also most grateful to the Institute of African Studies, Ibadan, for a grant towards the cost of obtaining photocopies of articles not locally available.

I would like to thank the following authors and publishers for permission to quote from the published works mentioned:

Mr. Wande Abimbọla (The Odu of Ifa, *African notes* 1, 3, 1964).
Oba Adetoyese Laoye I, The Timi of Ede (*The orikis of 13 of the Timis of Ede*, 1965).

x *Acknowledgements*

Dr. Ethel M. Albert and the American Anthropological Association ('Rhetoric', 'logic', and 'poetics' in Burundi, reproduced by permission of the American Anthropological Association from the *American Anthropologist*, vol. 66, no. 6, Pt. 2 (1964), pp. 35–54).

Professor R. G. Armstrong (Talking drums in the Benue-Cross River region of Nigeria, *Phylon* 15, 1954).

Professor William Bascom (The sanctions of Ifa divination, *J. roy. anthrop. institute* 71, 1941; The forms of folklore: prose narratives, *J. American folklore* 78, 1965).

Professor Robin Horton and the International African Institute (The Kalabari *Ekine* society: a borderland of religion and art, *Africa* 33, 1963).

Abbé Alexis Kagame (*La poésie dynastique au Rwanda*, Institut royal colonial belge, Mem. 22, 1, 1951).

Professor E. J. Krige and Shuter and Shooter (Pty.) Ltd. (*The social system of the Zulus*, 1936).

Mr. L. S. B. Leakey and Methuen & Company Ltd. (*Defeating Mau Mau*, 1954).

Mbari publications (B. Gbadamosi and U. Beier, *Yoruba poetry*, 1959; H. Owuor, Luo songs, *Black Orpheus* 19, 1961).

Professor J. H. Nketia (*Funeral dirges of the Akan people*, 1955; Akan poetry, *Black Orpheus* 3, 1958; Drum proverbs, *Voices of Ghana*, Accra, Ministry of Information and Broadcasting, 1958; *African music in Ghana*, 1962; *Drumming in Akan communities of Ghana*, 1963.)

Professor Willard Rhodes (Music as an agent of political expression, *African studies bulletin* 5, 2, 1962).

Professor M. G. Smith and the International African Institute (The social functions and meaning of Hausa praise-singing, *Africa* 27, 1957).

Father F. Theuws (*Textes Luba*, Bulletin du centre d'étude des problèmes sociaux indigènes (C.E.P.S.I.) 27, 1954).

Dr. Hugh Tracey ('*Lalela Zulu*', *100 Zulu lyrics*, 1948).

Professor A. N. Tucker (Children's games and songs in the Southern Sudan, *J. roy. anthrop. institute* 63, 1933).

M. Pierre Verger (*Notes sur le culte des Orisa*, Mem. I.F.A.N. 51, 1957).

Witwatersrand University Press (extracts from the following articles in *Bantu studies* and *African studies* on the pages mentioned: E. W. Grant, The Izibongo of the Zulu chiefs, *Bantu studies* 13, 1927–9, pp. 211–13, 227; S. K. Lekgothoane, Praises of animals in Northern Sotho, *Bantu studies* 12, 1938, pp. 193–5; P. A. W. Cook, History and Izibongo of the Swazi chiefs, *Bantu studies* 5, 1931, p. 193; F. Laydevant, The praises of the divining bones among the Basotho,

# CONTENTS

# Contents

# ABBREVIATIONS

| | |
|---|---|
| *AA* | *African Abstracts*. London. |
| *Afr.* (in journal title) | African/africain(e)(s). |
| *Afr. u. Übersee* | *Afrika und Übersee*. Berlin. |
| *Am. Anthrop.* | *American Anthropologist*. Menasha, Wisconsin. |
| *AMRAC* | *Musée royal de l'Afrique centrale. Annales (sciences humaines)*. Tervuren. |
| *AMRCB* | *Musée royal du Congo belge. Annales (sciences humaines)*. Tervuren. |
| *AMRCB-L* | *Musée royal du Congo belge. Annales (sciences de l'homme, linguistique)*. Tervuren. |
| *Ann. et mém. Com. ét. AOF* | *Annuaire et mémoires du Comité d'études historiques et scientifiques de l'AOF*. Gorée. |
| *Anth. Ling.* | *Anthropological Linguistics*. Indiana. |
| *Anth. Quart.* | *Anthropological Quarterly*. Washington. |
| *ARSC* | *Académie royale des sciences coloniales (sciences morales). Mémoires*. Brussels. |
| *ARSOM* | *Académie royale des sciences d'outre-mer. Mémoires*. Brussels. |
| *ARSOM Bull.* | *Académie royale des sciences d'outre-mer. Bulletin des séances*. Brussels. |
| *BSO(A)S* | *Bulletin of the School of Oriental (and African) Studies*. London. |
| *Bull. Com. ét. AOF* | *Bulletin du Comité d'études historiques et scientifiques de l'AOF*. Paris. |
| *Bull. IFAN* (B) | *Institut français d'Afrique noire. Bulletin (série B)*. Dakar, Paris. |
| *Cah. étud. afr.* | *Cahiers d'études africaines*. Paris. |
| *CEPSI* | *Bulletin trimestriel du Centre d'étude des problèmes sociaux indigènes*. Élisabethville. |
| IAI | International African Institute. London. |
| IFAN | Institut français d'Afrique noire. Dakar. |
| *IRCB Bull.* | *Institut royal colonial belge. Bulletin des séances*. Brussels. |
| *IRCB Mém.* | *Institut royal colonial belge. Mémoires*. Brussels. |
| *JAF* | *Journal of American Folklore*. Richmond, Virginia. |
| *JRAI* | *Journal of the Royal Anthropological Institute*. London. |
| *J. Soc. africanistes* | *Journal de la Société des africanistes*. Paris. |
| *Mém. IFAN* | *Institut français d'Afrique noire. Mémoires*. Dakar. |

# *Abbreviations*

| | |
|---|---|
| *Mitt. Inst. Orientforsch.* | *Mitteilungen des Instituts für Orientforschung.* Berlin. |
| MSOS | *Mitteilungen des Seminars für orientalische Sprachen zu Berlin.* |
| OLAL | Oxford Library of African Literature. Oxford. |
| *Rass. studi etiop.* | *Rassegna di studi etiopici.* Roma. |
| SOAS | School of Oriental and African Studies. University of London. |
| *SWJA* | *Southwestern Journal of Anthropology.* Albuquerque. |
| *TMIE* | *Travaux et mémoires de l'Institut d'ethnologie.* Paris. |
| *Trans. Hist. Soc. Ghana* | *Transactions of the Historical Society of Ghana.* Legon. |
| *ZA(O)S* | *Zeitschrift für afrikanische (und oceanische) Sprachen.* Berlin. |
| ZES | *Zeitschrift für Eingeborenen-Sprachen.* Berlin. |
| ZKS | *Zeitschrift für Kolonial-Sprachen.* Berlin. |

# NOTE ON SOURCES AND REFERENCES

ONLY the more obvious sources have been used. Where I have come across unpublished material I have taken account of it but have not made a systematic search. The sources are all documentary with the exception of some comments arising from fieldwork among the Limba of Sierra Leone and a few points from personal observation in Western Nigeria; gramophone recordings have also occasionally been used. In general, I have tried not to take my main examples from books that are already very easily accessible to the general reader. I have, for instance, given references to, but not lengthy quotations from, the 'Oxford Library of African Literature' series or the French 'Classiques africains'.

In time, I have not tried to cover work appearing after the end of 1967 (though references to a few 1968 publications that I happen to have seen are included). This means that the book will already be dated by the time it appears, but obviously I had to break off at some point.

References are given in two forms: (1) the general bibliography at the end, covering works I have made particular use of or consider of particular importance (referred to in the text merely by author and date); and (2) more specialized works not included in the general bibliography (full references given ad loc.). This is to avoid burdening the bibliography at the end with too many references of only detailed or secondary relevance. With a handful of exceptions I have seen the works I cite. Where this is not so, I have indicated it either directly or by giving the source of the reference in brackets. Where I have seen an abstract but not the article itself, this is shown by giving the volume and number of *African Abstracts* (*AA*) in brackets after the reference.

The bibliography and references are only selective. It would have been out of the question to have attempted a comprehensive bibliography.

# I · INTRODUCTION

## 1

## THE 'ORAL' NATURE OF AFRICAN UNWRITTEN LITERATURE

*The significance of performance in actualization, transmission, and composition. Audience and occasion. Implications for the study of oral literature. Oral art as literature.*

AFRICA possesses both written and unwritten traditions. The former are relatively well known—at any rate the recent writings in European languages (much work remains to be publicized on earlier Arabic and local written literatures in Africa). The unwritten forms, however, are far less widely known and appreciated. Such forms do not fit neatly into the familiar categories of literate cultures, they are harder to record and present, and, for a superficial observer at least, they are easier to overlook than the corresponding written material.

The concept of an *oral* literature is an unfamiliar one to most people brought up in cultures which, like those of contemporary Europe, lay stress on the idea of literacy and written tradition. In the popular view it seems to convey on the one hand the idea of mystery, on the other that of crude and artistically undeveloped formulations. In fact, neither of these assumptions is generally valid. Nevertheless, there are certain definite characteristics of this form of art which arise from its oral nature, and it is important at the outset to point to the implications of these. They need to be understood before we can appreciate the status and qualities of many of these African literary forms.

It is only necessary here to speak of the relatively simple oral and literary characteristics of this literature. I am not attempting to contribute to any more ambitious generalized theory of oral literature in terms of its suggested stylistic or structural characteristics[1] or of the particular type of mentality alleged to go with reliance on oral rather than written communication.[2] These larger questions I leave on one side to concentrate on the more obvious properties of unwritten literature.[3]

I

There is no mystery about the first and most basic characteristic of oral literature—even though it is constantly overlooked in collections and analyses. This is the significance of the actual performance. Oral literature is by definition dependent on a performer who formulates it in words on a specific occasion—there is no other way in which it can be realized as a literary product. In the case of *written* literature a literary work can be said to have an independent and tangible existence in even one copy, so that questions about, say, the format, number, and publicizing of other written copies can, though not irrelevant, be treated to some extent as secondary; there is, that is, a distinction between the actual creation of a written literary form and its further transmission. The case of oral literature is different. There the connection between transmission and very existence is a much more intimate one, and questions about the means of actual communication are of the first importance—without its oral realization and direct rendition by singer or speaker, an unwritten literary piece cannot easily be said to have any continued or independent existence at all. In this respect the parallel is less to written literature than to music and dance; for these too are art forms which in the last analysis are actualized in and through their performance and, furthermore, in a sense depend on repeated performances for their continued existence.

The significance of performance in oral literature goes beyond a mere matter of definition: for the nature of the performance itself can make an important contribution to the impact of the

---

[1] On which see e.g. Jousse 1924; A. B. Lord, *The Singer of Tales*, Cambridge, Mass., 1960; V. Propp, *Morphology of the Folktale* (Eng. tr.), Bloomington, 1958; cf. Olrik's 'epic laws' (discussed in Thompson 1946, pp. 455 ff.).

[2] e.g. C. Lévi-Strauss, *The Savage Mind* (Eng. tr.), London, 1966; cf. also the discussion and references in Goody and Watt 1963.

[3] For the general discussion in this chapter see particularly the valuable brief article by Bascom in *JAF* 1955, also Chadwicks 1932–40 (especially vol. iii) and Chadwick 1939. Some of the more detailed theories which have affected the study of African oral literature are discussed in Ch. 2.

particular literary form being exhibited. This point is obvious if we consider literary forms designed to be delivered to an audience even in more familiar literate cultures. If we take forms like a play, a sermon, 'jazz poetry', even something as trivial as an after-dinner witty anecdote—in all these cases the actual delivery is a significant aspect of the whole. Even though it is true that these instances may *also* exist in written form, they only attain their true fulfilment when actually performed.

The same clearly applies to African oral literature. In, for example, the brief Akan dirge

> Amaago, won't you look?
> Won't you look at my face?
> When you are absent, we ask of you.
> You have been away long: your children are waiting for you.[1]

the printed words alone represent only a shadow of the full actualization of the poem as an aesthetic experience for poet and audience. For, quite apart from the separate question of the over-tones and symbolic associations of words and phrases, the actual enactment of the poem also involves the emotional situation of a funeral, the singer's beauty of voice, her sobs, facial expression, vocal expressiveness and movements (all indicating the sincerity of her grief), and, not least, the musical setting of the poem. In fact, all the variegated aspects we think of as contributing to the effectiveness of performance in the case of more familiar literary forms may also play their part in the delivery of unwritten pieces—expressiveness of tone, gesture, facial expression, dramatic use of pause and rhythm, the interplay of passion, dignity, or humour, receptivity to the reactions of the audience, etc., etc. Such devices are not mere embellishments superadded to the already existent literary work—as we think of them in regard to written literature —but an integral as well as flexible part of its full realization as a work of art.

Unfortunately it is precisely this aspect which is most often over-looked in recording and interpreting instances of oral literature. This is partly due, no doubt, to practical difficulties; but even more to the unconscious reference constantly made by both re-corders and readers to more familar written forms. This model leads us to think of the *written* element as the primary and thus

[1] Nketia 1955, p. 184.

somehow the most fundamental material in every kind of literature—a concentration on the *words* to the exclusion of the vital
and essential aspect of performance. It cannot be too often emphasized that this insidious model is a profoundly misleading one in
the case of oral literature.

This point comes across the more forcibly when one considers
the various resources available to the performer of African literary
works to exploit the oral potentialities of his medium. The
linguistic basis of much African literature is treated in a later
chapter;[1] but we must at least note in passing the striking consequences of the highly tonal nature of many African languages.
Tone is sometimes used as a structural element in literary expression and can be exploited by the oral artist in ways somewhat
analogous to the use of rhyme or rhythm in written European
poetry. Many instances of this can be cited from African poetry,
proverbs, and above all drum literature. This stylistic aspect is
almost completely unrepresented in written versions or studies of
oral literature, and yet is clearly one which can be manipulated
in a subtle and effective way in the actual process of delivery.[2] The
exploitation of musical resources can also play an important part,
varying of course according to the artistic conventions of the
particular genre in question. Most stories and proverbs tend to be
delivered as spoken prose. But the Southern Bantu praise poems,
for instance, and the Yoruba hunters' *ijala* poetry are chanted in
various kinds of recitative, employing a semi-musical framework.
Other forms draw fully on musical resources and make use of
singing by soloist or soloists, not infrequently accompanied or
supplemented by a chorus or in some cases instruments. Indeed,
much of what is normally classed as poetry in African oral literature is designed to be performed in a musical setting, and the
musical and verbal elements are thus interdependent. An appreciation, therefore, of these sung forms (and to some extent the chanted
ones also) depends on at least some awareness of the musical
material on which the artist draws, and we cannot hope fully to
understand their impact or subtlety if we consider only the bare
words on a printed page.

In addition the performer has various visual resources at his
disposal. The artist is typically face to face with his public and can

---

[1] Ch. 3.
[2] For further details on the significance of tone see Ch. 3, pp. 69 ff.

take advantage of this to enhance the impact and even sometimes the content of his words. In many stories, for example, the characterization of both leading and secondary figures may appear slight; but what in literate cultures must be written, explicitly or implicitly, into the text can in orally delivered forms be conveyed by more visible means—by the speaker's gestures, expression, and mimicry. A particular atmosphere—whether of dignity for a king's official poet, light-hearted enjoyment for an evening story-teller, grief for a woman dirge singer—can be conveyed not only by a verbal evocation of mood but also by the dress, accoutrements, or observed bearing of the performer. This visual aspect is sometimes taken even further than gesture and dramatic bodily movement and is expressed in the form of a dance, often joined by members of the audience (or chorus). In these cases the verbal content now represents only one element in a complete opera-like performance which combines words, music, and dance. Though this extreme type is not characteristic of most forms of oral literature discussed in this volume, it is nevertheless not uncommon; and even in cases where the verbal element seems to predominate (sometimes in co-ordination with music), the actual delivery and movement of the performer may partake of something of the element of dancing in a way which to both performer and audience enhances the aesthetic effectiveness of the occasion.

Much more could be said about the many other means which the oral performer can employ to project his literary products—his use, for instance, of vivid ideophones or of dramatized dialogue, or his manipulation of the audience's sense of humour or susceptibility (when played on by a skilled performer) to be amazed, or shocked, or moved, or enthralled at appropriate moments. But it should be clear that oral literature has somewhat different potentialities from written literature, and additional resources which the oral artist can develop for his own purposes; and that this aspect is of primary significance for its appreciation as a mode of aesthetic expression.

The detailed way in which the performer enacts the literary product of his art naturally varies both from culture to culture and also among the different literary genres of one language. Not all types of performance involve the extremes of dramatization. Sometimes indeed the artistic conventions demand the exact opposite—a dignified aloof bearing, and emphasis on continuity of delivery rather than on studied and receptive style in the exact choice of words. This is so, for instance, of the professional reciter of historical Rwanda poetry, an official conscious of his intellectual superiority over amateurs and audience alike:

Contrairement à l'amateur, qui gesticule du corps et de la voix, le récitant professionnel adopte une attitude impassible, un débit rapide et monotone. Si l'auditoire réagit en riant ou en exprimant son admiration pour un passage particulièrement brillant, il suspend la voix avec détachement jusqu'à ce que le silence soit rétabli.[1]

This might seem the antithesis of a reliance on the arts of performance for the projection of the poem. In fact it is part of this particular convention and, for the audience, an essential part. To this kind of austere style of delivery we can contrast the highly emotional atmosphere in which the southern Sotho praise poet is expected to pour out his panegyric. Out of the background of song by solo and chorus, working up to a pitch of excitement and highly charged emotion,

the chorus increases in its loudness to be brought to a sudden stop with shrills of whistles and a voice (of the praise poet) is heard: 'Ka-mo-hopola mor'a-Nyeo!' (I remember the son of so-and-so!) Behind that sentence lurks all the stored up emotions and without pausing, the name . . . is followed by an outburst of uninterrupted praises, save perhaps by a shout from one of the listeners: 'Ke-ne ke-le teng' (I was present) as if to lend authenticity to the narration. The praiser continues his recitation working himself to a pitch, till he jumps this way and that way while his mates cheer him . . . and finally when his emotion has subsided he looks at his mates and shouts: 'Ntjeng, Banna' (lit. Eat me, you men). After this he may burst again into another ecstasy to be stopped by a shout from him or from his friends: 'Ha e nye bolokoe kaofela!' or 'Ha e nye lesolanka!' a sign that he should stop.[2]

Different again are the styles adopted by story-tellers where there tends to be little of this sort of emotional intensity, but where the vividness and, often, humour of the delivery add drama and meaning to the relatively simple and straightforward wording. The Lamba narrator has been particularly well described:

It would need a combination of phonograph and kinematograph to reproduce a tale as it is told. . . . Every muscle of face and body spoke, a swift gesture often supplying the place of a whole sentence. . . . The

---

[1] Coupez and Kamanzi 1962, p. 8.  [2] Mofokeng 1945, p. 137.

animals spoke each in its own tone: the deep rumbling voice of Momba, the ground hornbill, for example, contrasting vividly with the piping accents of Sulwe, the hare . . .[1]

Even within the same culture there may be many set styles of performance designed to suit the different literary genres recognized in the culture. Indeed these genres are sometimes primarily distinguished from each other in terms of their media of performance rather than their content or purpose. In Yoruba poetry, for instance, the native classification is not according to subject-matter or structure but by the group to which the reciter belongs and, in particular, by the technique of recitation and voice production. Thus there is *ijala* (chanted by hunters in a high-pitched voice), *rara* (a slow, wailing type of chant), and *ewi* (using a falsetto voice), and even though the content of various types may often be interchangeable, a master in one genre will not feel competent to perform a different type: he may know the words but cannot manage the necessary subtleties of tone and style and the required type of voice production.[2] Many other cases could also be cited where the mode of performance is as significant for the native critic as actual content or structure.

So far we have been speaking of the importance of performance in all types of oral literature and of the way in which techniques of delivery can be variously exploited and evaluated by performer or audience. But there is a further, related, characteristic of oral literature to which we must now turn. This is the question of improvisation and original composition in general. In other words, something more may be involved in the delivery of an oral piece than the fact of its actualization and re-creation in and through the performance, aided by a technique of delivery that heightens its artistic effectiveness. There are also the cases when the performer introduces variations on older pieces or even totally new forms in terms of the detailed wording, the structure, or the content.

The extent of this kind of innovation, of course, varies with both genre and individual performer, and the question of original composition is a difficult one. It is clear that the process is by no means the same in all non-literate cultures or all types of oral literature,[3]

---

[1] Smith and Dale ii, 1920, p. 336.

[2] Gbadamosi and Beier 1959, pp. 9–10; Babalọla 1966, pp. vi, 23.

[3] On some of the many variations in the forms of composition (including musical composition) among different peoples see Nettl 1954*b* and 1956, esp. pp. 12 ff.

and between the extremes of totally new creation and memorized reproduction of set pieces there is scope for many different theories and practices of composition. There are, for instance, the long-considered and rehearsed compositions of Chopi singers, the more facile improvisation of a leader in a boat- or dance-song, the combination and recombination of known motifs into a single unique performance among Limba story-tellers. There are also occasional cases, like the Rwanda poet just mentioned, where there is interest in the accuracy and authenticity of the wording (at least in outline) and where memorization rather than creation is the expected role of the performer.

In spite of the very real significance of these variations, one of the striking characteristics of oral as distinct from written literature is its verbal variability. What might be called the 'same' poem or prose piece tends to be variable to such an extent that one has to take some account at least of the original contribution of the artist who is actualizing it—and not simply in terms of the technique of delivery. Take for instance the case of Ankole praise poems. Since the ideas expressed in these poems are stereotyped and repetitive, the *omwevugi* (poet/reciter) must change the wording to obtain variety.

[He] has to rely to a great extent upon the manner in which he expresses these ideas in order to give beauty and interest to his poem. Herein lies the art of the accomplished *omwevugi* who, by the ingenious choice of his vocabulary, can repeat identical themes time and time again, always with a different and startling turn of phrase.[1]

Again, there is the production of stories among the Thonga. It is worth quoting Junod's excellent description of this at some length. Having postulated the 'antiquity' of Thonga tales, he goes on:

This antiquity is only relative: that is to say they are constantly transformed by the narrators and their transformations go much further than is generally supposed, further even than the Natives themselves are aware of. After having heard the same stories told by different story-tellers, I must confess that I never met with exactly the same version. First of all *words* differ. Each narrator has his own style, speaks freely and does not feel in any way bound by the expressions used by the person who taught him the tale. It would be a great error to think that, writing a story at the dictation of a Native, we possess the recognized standard form of the tale. There is no standard at all! . . .

[1] Morris 1964, p. 25.

The same can be said with regard to *the sequence of the episodes*; although these often form definite cycles, it is rare to hear two narrators follow exactly the same order. They arrange their material as they like, sometimes in a very awkward way. . . .

I go further: *New elements* are also introduced, owing to the tendency of Native story-tellers always to apply circumstances of their environment to the narration. This is one of the charms of Native tales. They are living, viz., they are not told as if they were past and remote events, in an abstract pattern, but considered as happening amongst the hearers themselves. . . . So all the new objects brought by civilisation are, without the slightest difficulty, made use of by the narrator. . . .

Lastly, my experience leads me to think that, in certain cases, the *contents of the stories* themselves are changed by oral transmission, this giving birth to numerous versions of a tale, often very different from each other and sometimes hardly recognisable.[1]

The scope of the artist to improvise or create may vary, but there is almost always *some* opportunity for 'composition'. It comes out in the exact choice of word and phrase, the stylistic devices like the use of ideophones, asides, or repetitions, the ordering of episodes or verses, new twists to familiar plots or the introduction of completely new ones, improvisation or variation of solo lines even while the chorus remains the same—as well, of course, as all the elaborations and modifications to which the musical aspect is subject. Such additions and changes naturally take place within the current literary and cultural conventions—but what is involved, nevertheless, is some degree of individual creativity.[2] With only a few exceptions, this process is likely to enter into the actualization of any piece of oral literature, which thus becomes in one sense a unique literary work—the work rendered on one particular occasion.

The variability typical of oral literary forms has tended to be overlooked by many writers. This is largely because of certain theoretical assumptions held in the past about the verbatim handing down of oral tradition supposedly typical of non-literate societies. The model of written literature has also been misleading in this context, with its concept of exact transmission through manuscripts or printing press. It must therefore be stressed yet

[1] Junod 1913, ii, pp. 198–200. The whole of this passage is worth consulting.

[2] For instances of this see the various examples in Parts II and III and in particular the discussion in Ch. 9, pp. 266 ff.

again that many of the characteristics we now associate with a written literary tradition do not always apply to oral art. There is not necessarily any concept of an 'authentic version', and when a particular literary piece is being transmitted to an audience the concepts of extemporization or elaboration are often more likely to be to the fore than that of memorization. There is likely to be little of the split, familiar from written forms, between composition and performance or between creation and transmission. A failure to realize this has led to many misconceptions—in particular the presentation of one version as *the* correct and authentic one—and to only a partial understanding of the crucial contribution made by the performer himself.

A further essential factor is the audience, which, as is not the case with written forms, is often directly involved in the actualization and creation of a piece of oral literature. According to convention, genre, and personality, the artist may be more or less receptive to his listeners' reactions—but, with few exceptions,[1] an audience of some kind is normally an essential part of the whole literary situation. There is no escape for the oral artist from a face-to-face confrontation with his audience, and this is something which he can exploit as well as be influenced by. Sometimes he chooses to involve his listeners directly, as in story-telling situations where it is common for the narrator to open with a formula which explicitly arouses his audience's attention; he also often expects them to participate actively in the narration and, in particular, to join in the choruses of songs which he introduces into the narrative.[2] The audience can be exploited in similar ways in the performance of poetry, particularly in sung lyrics where it is common practice for the poet to act as leader, singing and improvising the verse line, while the audience performs as a chorus keeping up the burden of the song, sometimes to the accompaniment of dancing or instrumental music. In such cases the close connection between artist and audience can almost turn into an identity, the chorus directly participating in at least certain parts of the performance.

Even in less formalized relationships the actual literary expression can be greatly affected by the presence and reactions of the audience. For one thing, the type of audience involved can affect

---

[1] e.g. the solitary working songs, some herding songs, sometimes individual rehearsals for later performance, and perhaps some of the lullabies.

[2] For further details on audience participation in stories see Ch. 13, pp. 385 ff.

the presentation of an oral piece—the artist may tend, for instance, to omit obscenities, certain types of jokes, or complex forms in the presence of, say, children or missionaries (or even foreign students) which he would include in other contexts. And direct references to the characteristics, behaviour, or fortunes of particular listeners can also be brought in with great effectiveness in a subtle and flexible way not usually open to written literature. Members of the audience too need not confine their participation to silent listening or a mere acceptance of the chief performer's invitation to participate—they may also in some circumstances break into the performance with additions, queries, or even criticisms. This is common not only in the typical and expected case of story-telling but even in such formalized situations as that of the complex Yoruba *ijala* chants. A performance by one *ijala* artist is critically listened to by other experts present, and if one thinks the performer has made a mistake he cuts in with such words as

> I beg to differ; that is not correct.
> You have deviated from the path of accuracy . . .
> Ire was not Ogun's home town.
> Ogun only called there to drink palm-wine . . .

to which the performer may try to defend himself by pleading his own knowledge or suggesting that others should respect his integrity:

> Let not the civet-cat trespass on the cane rat's track.
> Let the cane rat avoid trespassing on the civet-cat's path.
> Let each animal follow the smooth stretch of its own road.[1]

This possibility of both clarification and challenge from members of the audience and their effect on the performance is indeed one of the main distinctions between oral and written literary pieces. As Plato put it long ago: 'It is the same with written words [as with painting]. You would think they were speaking as if they were intelligent, but if you ask them about what they are saying and want to learn [more], they just go on saying one and the same thing for ever.'[2] This leads on to a further important characteristic of oral literature: the significance of the actual occasion, which can directly affect the detailed content and form of the piece being performed. Oral pieces are not composed in the study and later

---

[1] Babalọla 1966, pp. 64, 62.       [2] *Phaedrus*, 275 d.

transmitted through the impersonal and detached medium of print, but tend to be directly involved in the occasions of their actual utterance. Some of the poetry to be discussed in this volume is specifically 'occasional', in that it is designed for and arises from particular situations like funerals, weddings, celebrations of victory, soothing a baby, accompanying work, and so on; again, with certain prose forms (like, for instance, proverbs), appropriateness to the occasion may be more highly valued by local critics than the verbal content itself. But even when there is not this specific connection, a piece of oral literature tends to be affected by such factors as the general purpose and atmosphere of the gathering at which it is rendered, recent episodes in the minds of performer and audience, or even the time of year and propinquity of the harvest. Many oral recitations arise in response to various social obligations which, in turn, are exploited by poet and narrator for his own purposes. The performer of oral pieces could thus be said to be more involved in actual social situations than the writer in more familiar literate traditions.

II

These characteristic qualities of oral literary forms have several implications for the study of oral literature. It is always essential to raise points which would seem only secondary in the case of written literature—questions about the details of performance, audience, and occasion. To ignore these in an oral work is to risk missing much of the subtlety, flexibility, and individual originality of its creator and, furthermore, to fail to give consideration to the aesthetic canons of those intimately concerned in the production and the reception of this form of literature.

This is easy enough to state—but such implications are exceedingly difficult to pursue. Not only is there the seductive model of written literature which constantly tempts one to set aside such questions for the more familiar textual analysis; there are also practical difficulties to surmount. The words themselves are relatively easy to record (even though this is often not done with much scholarly rigour): one can use dictation, texts written by assistants, or recordings on tape. But for the all-important aspect of the actual performance—how is one to record this? Even more difficult, how is one to convey it to readers not themselves acquainted with this art form? In the days before the availability of the portable tape-recorder this problem was practically insuperable.[1] The general tendency was thus for the early scholars to rely only on written records of the oral literature they collected. In many cases, further-more, they were using quite inadequate sources, perhaps second-hand (so that they themselves had not direct experience of the actual performance involved), or in synopsis only with the artistic elaborations or repetitions omitted. This in itself goes a long way to account for the very simplified impression of African oral literature we often receive from these collections (particularly when it is remembered that they emphasized prose narrative rather than the more elaborate and difficult poetic forms). This was all the more unfortunate because the common practice of concen-trating on the texts only encouraged others to follow the same pattern even when it became open to them to use new media for recording.

By now there is an increasing, though by no means universal, reliance on the tape-recorder by serious students of African oral literature. This medium has helped immensely in solving some of the problems of recording details of the performance. But the visual effects produced by the artist still tend to elude record. Furthermore, the problem of communicating the style of per-formance to a wider audience is still a real one: few if any pub-lishers are prepared to include recordings with their collections of published texts. Thus the public is still given the impression of African oral literature as a kind of written literature *manqué*—apparently lacking the elaboration of wording and recognizability of associations known from familiar forms, and without the particu-lar stylistic devices peculiar to oral forms being made clear.

Even when the importance of performance is stressed in general terms, more needs to be said to convey the particular style and flavour of any given genre. A full appreciation must depend on an analysis not only of the verbal interplay and overtones in the piece, its stylistic structure and content, but also of the various detailed devices which the performer has at his disposal to convey his pro-duct to the audience, and the varying ways these are used by

[1] A few early observers speak of recording certain of their texts on 'the phonograph'. See e.g. Torrend 1921 (Northern Rhodesian stories, including songs); N. W. Thomas, *Anthropological Report on the Edo-speaking Peoples of Nigeria*, London, 1910, vol. ii; Lindblom iii, 1934, p. 41 (Kamba songs, recorded about 1912).

different individuals. Something also needs to be said of the role
and status of the composer/performer who is the one to communicate this oral art directly to his public, the variant forms that
arise according to audience and occasion, the reactions and participation likely to be forthcoming from his listeners and spectators,
the respective contributions, if any, of musical or balletic elements,
and finally the social contexts in which this creation and re-creation
takes place.

All these factors are far more difficult to discover and describe
than a mere transcription of the texts themselves, followed by
their leisured analysis. It is not surprising that most editions of
oral art concentrate on the textual aspect and say little or nothing
about the other factors. But, difficult or not, without the inclusion
of some consideration of such questions we have scarcely started
to understand its aesthetic development as a product of literary
artistry.

Various questionable assumptions about the nature of oral
tradition and so-called 'folk art' among non-literate people have
not made matters any easier. Several of these theories are discussed
in some detail in later chapters, but briefly they include such ideas
as that 'oral tradition' (including what we should now call oral
literature) is passed down word for word from generation to
generation and thus reproduced verbatim from memory throughout the centuries; or, alternatively, that oral literature is something
that arises communally, from the people or the 'folk' as a whole,
so that there can be no question of individual authorship or
originality. It can be seen how both these assumptions have
inevitably discouraged interest in the actual contemporaneous
performance, variations, and the role of the individual poet or
narrator in the final literary product. A related assumption was that
oral literature (often in this context called 'folklore') was relatively
undeveloped and primitive; and this derogatory interpretation was
applied to oral literature both in completely non-literate societies
and when it coexisted with written literary forms in 'civilized'
cultures. This opinion received apparent confirmation from the
appearance of bare prose texts in translation or synopsis, and
people felt no need to enter into more profound analysis about,
say, the overtones and artistic conventions underlying these texts,
far less the individual contribution of performer and composer.
There was thus no need for further elucidation, for it was assumed

in advance that little of real interest could emerge from this 'inherently crude' oral medium.

There are also various other special difficulties about the presentation of African oral literature—how, for instance, to delimit literary from everyday speech forms or convey the subtleties or overtones which only emerge fully to one familiar with the cultural and literary traditions of the society. But these do not arise directly from the *oral* nature of African literature and will thus be more suitably discussed later. The main point I want to reiterate here, the more emphatically because of the way it has so often been overlooked in the past, is that in the case of oral literature, far more extremely than with written forms, the bare words can *not* be left to speak for themselves, for the simple reason that in the actual literary work so much else is necessarily and intimately involved. With this type of literature a knowledge of the whole literary and social background, covering these various points of performance, audience, and context, is, however difficult, of the first importance. Even if some of the practical problems of recording and presenting these points sometimes appear insoluble, it is at least necessary to be aware of these problems from the outset, rather than, as so commonly happens, substituting for an awareness of the shallowness of our *own* understanding an imaginary picture of the shallowness in literary appreciation and development of the peoples we are attempting to study.

### III

So far we have been concentrating on the *oral* aspect of African unwritten literature—the implications of this for the nature of such literature and the difficulties of presentation and analysis to which it gives rise. Little has yet been said about the *literary* status of these oral products, and we have indeed been begging the question of how far these can in fact be regarded as a type of literature at all.

Various positions have been taken up on this question. A number of the scholars who have carried out extensive studies of the oral art of non-literate peoples are quite dogmatic about the suitability of the term 'literature'. N. K. Chadwick, for one, is explicit on this point:

In 'civilised' countries we are inclined to associate literature with writing; but such an association is accidental. . . . Millions of people throughout Asia, Polynesia, Africa and even Europe who practise the art of literature have no knowledge of letters. Writing is unessential to either the composition or the preservation of literature. The two arts are wholly distinct.[1]

This general view is supported, by implication at least, by the many writers who have referred to their collections or descriptions of oral forms by such terms as 'oral literature', 'unwritten literature', or sometimes 'popular' or 'traditional literature'.[2] The opposite viewpoint, however, also seems to carry weight. There is, for one thing, the association, both popular and etymological, between 'literature' and letters or writing. The fact, furthermore, that oral art depends for its creation on the actual (and thus ephemeral) performance of it seems to some to disqualify it from true literary status, so that other terms like 'folk art', 'folklore', or 'verbal art' appear more accurate designations. Added to this is the alleged practicality so often supposed to be the root of 'primitive art forms'. According to this view, even if some primitive formulation, say a story, might seem in outward form, style, or content to present a superficial resemblance to a written work of fiction, in essentials, being fundamentally pragmatic rather than aesthetic, it is something wholly different. Finally, individual authorship is often presumed not to be in question in the case of oral forms, being replaced, according to current fashions, by such supposed entities as 'the group mind', 'the folk', 'social structure', or simply 'tradition', all of which equally result in a finished product with a totally different basis and orientation from that of written literature. This kind of view, then, would draw a basic distinction between, on the one hand, the products of a written literary tradition and, on the other, most if not all of the instances of verbal art included in this and similar volumes.

In this controversy, my own position is clearly implied in both my title and the discussion so far. It is that, despite difficulties of exact delimitation and presentation, the main body of the material I discuss and illustrate in this volume falls within the domain of literature (the class of literature I call 'oral literature'); and that it is misleading as well as unfruitful to attempt to draw a strict line between the verbal art of literate and of non-literate cultural traditions.

---

[1] Chadwick 1939, p. 77.
[2] For some reference to early approaches of this kind in Africa see Ch. 2, pp. 30 f.

In part this approach is an arbitrary one. It is, after all, open to anyone to produce a wide enough definition of 'literature' for all the examples produced here to fit within its limits—or a narrower one to exclude them. But it is also adopted because it has been found that to approach instances of oral art as *literary* forms and thus proceed to ask about them the same kind of questions we might raise in the case of written literature, has in fact been a productive approach leading to both further appreciation of the oral forms and a deeper understanding of their role in society. Such an approach then is in principle its own justification—how justifiable it in fact turns out to be in leading to greater insight can be left to the readers of this book to judge.[1] But there is also more to this view than whether or not it is a fruitful one. It seems to me to bear more relation to the empirical facts than its opposite in that many of the apparent reasons for the supposed cleavage between oral and written forms have in fact rested on mistaken assumptions. So, even though I am not attempting to put forward any new definition or theory of literature—an attempt likely to raise as many difficulties as it solves—some of these misleading points should be clarified at this stage.[2]

The first point can be easily disposed of. The etymological connections between literature and writing may seem at first a clear validation for limiting the term to literate cultures. But even if we are prepared to be coerced by etymologies (and why should we, unless to rationalize already held assumptions?), we must admit that this association by no means exists in all languages—we need only mention the German *Wortkunst* or Russian *slovesnost*[3]—so it can hardly be said to have universal validity.

The fact of a positive and strongly held popular association between writing and literature is more difficult to deal with. Current prejudices may be false, but they go deep. And this is especially so when they are securely rooted in particular historical and cultural experiences, so that the familiar and traditional forms of a given culture come to be regarded as the natural and universal ones, expected to hold good for all times and places. This kind of

[1] Or, better, to the readers of such original and detailed studies as e.g. Nketia 1955, etc., Babalǫla 1966, Kagame 1951*b*.
[2] Several of them are more fully elaborated in later chapters, particularly Ch. 2.
[3] Pointed out in R. Wellek and A. Warren, *Theory of Literature*, London, 1949, p. 11.

ethnocentric preconception has had to be revised by scholars in other spheres such as, for instance, the study of modes of political organization or religious practices, as they are viewed in the light of wider research and thus greater comparative perspective. This, it seems now, may also be the case with the study of literature. In spite of the natural reluctance to regard very different verbal forms as of ultimately the same nature as our own familiar types, we have at least to consider the possibility that the literary models of (in effect) a few centuries in the Western world, which happen to be based on writing and more especially on printing, may not in fact exhaust all the possibilities of literature.

This possibility can be rendered more intelligible by considering further the relationship between oral and written literature. It becomes clear that this is a difference of degree and not of kind: there are many different gradations between what one could take as the oral and the printed ideal types of literature. It is perhaps enough to allude to the literature of the classical world which, as is well known, laid far more stress on the oral aspect than does more recent literature. Even laying aside the famous and controversial question of the possible oral composition of Homer's great epics (universally passed as 'literature'), we can see that the presence of writing can coexist with an emphasis on the significance of performance as one of the main means of the effective transmission of a literary work. For the Greeks there was a close association between words, music, and dance—one which seems much less obvious to a modern European—and Aristotle, still accepted as one of the great literary critics, can give as his first reason for considering tragedy superior to epic the fact that it makes an additional impact through music and visual effects.[1] Throughout much of antiquity even written works were normally read aloud rather than silently, and one means of transmitting and, as it were, 'publishing' a literary composition was to deliver it aloud to a group of friends. In such cases the relationship of the performance and transmission of literary works to the content is not totally dissimilar from that in African oral literature.

What is true of classical literature is also true of many cultures in which writing is practised as a specialist rather than a universal art and, in particular, in societies without the printing-press to make the multiplication of copies feasible. We are so accustomed,

[1] *Poetics*, 1462[a].

at our present stage of history, to associate the written word with
print that we tend to forget that the mere fact of *writing* does
not necessarily involve the type of detachment and relatively
impersonal mode of transmission that we connect with printing.
Transmission by reading aloud or by performing from memory
(sometimes accompanied by improvisation) is not at all incompatible with some reliance on writing—a situation we find not only in
earlier European societies[1] but also in a few of the African instances
described later.[2] Here again the contrast between fully oral forms
on the one hand and the impersonal medium of print on the other
is clearly only a relative one: we would hardly suggest that works
written and, in part, orally transmitted before the advent of printing were therefore not literature, any more than we would be prepared to state dogmatically that the Homeric epics—or an African
poem—only became literature on the day they were first written
down.

Even in a society apparently dominated by the printed word the
oral aspect is not entirely lost. Perhaps because of the common
idea that written literature is somehow the highest form of the
arts, the current significance of oral elements often tends to be
played down, if not overlooked completely. But we can point to
the importance of performance and production in a play, the idea
held by some at least that much poetry can only attain its full
flavour when spoken aloud, or the increasing but often underestimated significance of the oral reproduction and dissemination
of classic literary forms (as well as wholly new compositions) through
radio and television. Add to this the interplay between the oral and
the written—the constant interaction in any tradition between the
written word and, at the least, the common diction of everyday
speech (an interaction which may well be heightened by the
spreading reliance on radio and television channels of transmission), as well as the largely oral forms like speeches, sermons,

[1] Cf. for instance H. J. Chaytor's pertinent comment on medieval vernacular
literature: 'In short, the history of the progress from script to print is a history
of the gradual substitution of visual for auditory methods of communicating and
receiving ideas. . . . To disregard the matter and to criticise medieval literature
as though it had just been issued by the nearest circulating library is a sure and
certain road to a misconception of the medieval spirit' (*From Script to Print,
an Introduction to Medieval Vernacular Literature*, Cambridge, 1945, p. 4). The
oral aspects of manuscript culture are further discussed in M. McLuhan, *The
Gutenberg Galaxy*, Toronto, 1962.
[2] See Ch. 3, pp. 49 ff. and, in particular, Ch. 7, pp. 169 f., 172.

children's rhymes, satires depending in part on improvisation, or many current pop songs, all of which have both literary and oral elements—in view of all this it becomes clear that even in a fully literate culture oral formulations can play a real part, however unrecognized, in the literary scene as a whole.

Even so brief an account suggests that our current preoccupation with written, particularly printed, media may give only a limited view and that the distinction between oral and written forms may not be so rigid and so profound as is often implied. It is already widely accepted that these two media can each draw on the products of the other, for orally transmitted forms have frequently been adopted or adapted in written literature, and oral literature too is prepared to draw on any source, including the written word. To this interplay we can now add the fact that when looked at comparatively, the two forms, oral and written, are not so mutually exclusive as is sometimes imagined. Even if we picture them as two independent extremes we can see that in practice there are many possibilities and many different stages between the two poles and that the facile assumption of a profound and unbridgeable chasm between oral and written forms is a misleading one.

Some further misconceptions about the nature of oral forms must be mentioned briefly here; they will be taken up further in the main body of the book. First, the idea that all primitive (and thus also all oral) art is severely functional, and thus basically different from art in 'civilized' cultures. To this it must be replied that this whole argument partly arises from a particular and temporary fashion in the interpretation of art (the rather unclear idea of 'art for art's sake'); that since there is little detailed empirical evidence on the various purposes of particular genres of oral literature—it was much easier to write down texts and presume functions than to make detailed inquiries about the local canons of literary criticism—this assertion rests as much on presupposition as on observed fact; and, finally, that the whole argument is partly just a matter of words. How far and in what sense and for whom a given piece of literature is 'functional' and just how one assesses this is as difficult a question in non-literate as in literate cultures. Certainly we can say that even when we can find a clear social purpose (and the 'occasional' aspect in oral literature varies according to genre, composer, and situation just as it does in written literature), this by no means necessarily excludes an interest in aesthetic as well as functional considerations. The question of authorship in oral literature has already been mentioned in the context of performance and of the composition that arises from this. By now, few people probably take very seriously the concept of the 'group mind' or the 'folk mind' as an empirical entity to which the authorship of particular literary pieces could be assigned. But in the case of the oral literature of basically unfamiliar cultures this idea acquires an apparent validity mainly from ignorance of the actual circumstances involved. Again, this is a large question that cannot be pursued in detail here. But it can be said categorically that while oral literature—like all literature—in a sense arises from society and, being oral, has the extra facet of often involving more direct interplay between composer and audience, nevertheless it is totally misleading to suggest that individual originality and imagination play no part. The exact form this takes and the exact degree of the familiar balance between tradition and creativity naturally vary with the culture, the genre, and the personalities involved. But it will be clear from the instances in this volume that the myth attributing all oral literature either to the 'community' alone or, alternatively, to one particular portion of it ('the folk') is not true to the facts; and that the whole picture is much more complex than such simplified and speculative assumptions would suggest.

A final point which has, I think, wrongly deterred people from the recognition of oral forms as a type of literature has been the idea that they have only resulted in trivial formulations without any depth of meaning or association. This impression has, it is true, been given by the selection and presentation of much of the African verbal art that reaches the public—the emphasis on animal tales and other light-hearted stories (relatively easy to record) rather than the more elaborate creations of the specialist poets; and the common publication of unannotated texts which give the reader no idea whatsoever of the social and literary background which lies behind them, let alone the arts of the performer. Quite apart from mere problems of translation, the difficulties of appreciating the art forms of unfamiliar cultures without help are well known. We need only consider—to take just one example—how much our appreciation of

Like as the waves make towards the pebbled shore,
So do our minutes hasten to their end . . .

depends, among other things, on our knowledge of the particular
art form used, its whole literary setting, the rhythm, phrasing, and
music of the line, and, not least, on the emotive overtones of such
familiar words as 'waves', 'minutes', 'end' which bring us a whole
realm of associations, sounds, and pictures, all of which can be said
to form an essential part of the meaning of the line. This is obvious—
but it is often forgotten that exactly the same thing applies in oral
literature:

Grandsire Gyima with a slim but generous arm
(Nana Gyima abasateaa a adɔeɛ wɔ mu)[1]

is the first line of an Akan dirge, and seems of itself to have little
poetic force or meaning. But its significance appears very different
when we know the overtones of the concept of generosity, metaphorically expressed here through the familiar concept of the dead
man's 'arm'; the particular style and structure, so pleasing and
acceptable to the audience; the rhythm and quasi-musical setting
of the line; the familiarity and associations of the phrasing; the
known fact that this is a mother singing for her dead son whom
she is calling her 'grandsire' in the verse; and the grief-laden and
emotional atmosphere in which these dirges are performed and
received—all this makes such a line, and the poem that follows
and builds on it, something far from trivial to its Akan listeners.
Akan dirges are among the few African literary genres that have
as yet been subject to any full treatment along these lines,[2] but
there is reason to suppose that similar discussions of other genres
would also reveal ample evidence that the charge of triviality in
oral literature as a whole rests far more on ignorance and unfamiliarity than on any close acquaintance with the facts.

There is one further problem that should be mentioned here.
This is the difficult question of how to distinguish in wholly oral
communication between what is to count as literature and what is
not. Are we to include, say, speeches by court elders summing
up cases, an impromptu prayer, non-innovatory genres like some
formulaic hunting-songs, formal words of welcome, or the dramatic
reporting of an item of news?

---

[1] Nketia 1955, pp. 195, 245.　　[2] Nketia 1955; cf. also Ch. 6 below.

This is a real problem to which there is no easy solution. However, it has to be said at once that despite first impressions there is no difference *in principle* here between written and unwritten literature. In written forms too there are problems in delimiting what is truly 'literature'. It is largely a matter of opinion, for example, as to whether we should include science fiction, certain newspaper articles, or the words of popular songs. Opinions differ, furthermore, not only between different individuals and different age and social groups, but at different periods of history. The problem, clearly, is not unique to oral literature.

In considering this question, the criteria used in relation to oral literature are much the same as in the case of written literature. First, some cases are clear-cut. These are instances when the accepted characteristics of 'literature'[1] are clearly applicable, or where the African examples are clearly comparable with literary genres recognized in familiar European cultures. In other words, once the concept of an oral literature is allowed, there will be no dispute over such cases as panegyric poetry, lyrics for songs, fictional narratives, or funeral elegies. Other cases are not so clear. Here at least one criterion must be the evaluation of the particular societies involved—we cannot assume *a priori* that their definitions of 'literary' will necessarily coincide with those of English culture. Since the evaluation of some form as literature is, as we have seen, a matter of opinion, it seems reasonable at least to take seriously the *local* opinions on this. Thus when we are told that among the Ibo 'oratory . . . calls for an original and individual talent and . . . belongs to a higher order [than folk-tales]', this ought to incline us to consider including at least some rhetorical speeches as a part of Ibo oral literature (although among other societies with less interest in oratory this may not be the case). Again, proverbs are sometimes locally thought to be as serious and 'literary' as more lengthy forms—and in some cases are even expanded into long proverb-poems, as with the 'drum proverbs' of the Akan. Finally we have verbal forms that are clearly marginal: obviously not 'literature' in their own right, and yet not irrelevant to literary formulation and composition. We could instance metaphorical names, elaborate greeting forms, the serious art of conversation, and, in some cases, proverbs or rhetoric. As described in Chapter 16, these show an appreciation of the artistic aspect of

[1] See below, p. 24.

language and a rich background from which more purely literary forms arise—a relationship perhaps particularly obvious in the case of oral literature, but not unknown to literate cultures. The plan of the central portion of this book[1] is to proceed from the clearly 'literary' forms through more questionable cases like proverbs or riddles to the marginally relevant forms like names or word-play. There is no one point at which I would draw a definite dividing line, even though one extreme is clearly literary, the other not.

Earlier I made the negative point that many of the assumptions that seem to set oral forms totally apart from written literature are in fact questionable or false. The same point can be put more positively. Oral literary forms fall within most definitions of 'literature' (save only for the point about writing as a medium, not always included in such definitions), and the problems arising from most of these apply to oral as well as to written literary forms. In other words, though I am not putting forward any one particular definition of 'literature', it seems clear that the elements out of which such definitions tend, variously, to be constructed are also recognizable in oral forms, often with exactly the same range of ambiguities. The basic medium is words—though in both cases this verbal element may be supplemented by visual or musical elements. Beyond this, literature, we are often told, is expressive rather than instrumental, is aesthetic and characterized by a lack of practical purpose—a description equally applicable to much oral art. The exploitation of form, heightening of style, and interest in the medium for its own sake as well as for its descriptive function can clearly be found in oral literary forms. So too can the idea of accepted literary conventions of style, structure, and genre laid down by tradition, which are followed by the second-rate and exploited by the original author. The sense in which literature is set at one remove from reality is another familiar element: this too is recognizable in oral literature, not merely in such obvious ways as in the use of fiction, satire, or parable, but also through the very conventionality of the literary forms allied to the imaginative formulation in actual words. If we prefer to rely on an ostensive type of definition and list the kind of genres we would include under the heading of 'literature', this procedure gives us many analogies in oral literature (though we may find that we have to add

---

[1] In particular Parts II and III.

a few not familiar in recent European literature). Among African oral genres, for instance, we can find forms analogous to European elegies, panegyric poetry, lyric, religious poetry, fictional prose, rhetoric, topical epigram, and perhaps drama. Whichever approach we adopt we shall run into some difficulties and unclear cases— in the case of *oral* literature the problem of delimiting literary from everyday spoken forms is a peculiarly difficult one which I do not think I have solved successfully here—but the point I want to stress is that these difficulties are fundamentally the same as those that arise in the study of any kind of literature.[1]

This argument tends to the conclusion that there is no good reason to deny the title of 'literature' to corresponding African forms just because they happen to be oral. If we do treat them as *fundamentally* of a different kind, we deny ourselves both a fruitful analytic approach and, furthermore, a wider perspective on the general subject of comparative literature. We need of course to remember that oral literature is only one type of literature, a type characterized by particular features to do with performance, transmission, and social context with the various implications these have for its study. But for all these differences, the view that there is no essential chasm between this type of literature and the more familiar written forms is a basic assumption throughout this book.

---

[1] For some further discussion of the question of African oral forms as 'literature' see Whiteley 1964, pp. 4 ff. and references given there.

# 2

# THE PERCEPTION OF AFRICAN
# ORAL LITERATURE

Nineteenth-century approaches and collections. Speculations
and neglect in the twentieth century. Recent trends in
African studies and the revival of interest in oral literature.

A CONSIDERABLE amount of work has been published on the
subject of African oral literature in the last century or so. But the
facts are scattered and uneven, often buried in inaccessible journals,
and their significance has not been widely appreciated. The popular
image of Africa as a land without indigenous literary traditions
retains its hold; even now, it is still sometimes expressed in a form
as crude as that criticized by Burton a century ago:

'The savage custom of going naked', we are told, 'has denuded
the mind, and destroyed all decorum in the language. Poetry there is
none. . . . There is no metre, no rhyme, nothing that interests or soothes
the feelings, or arrests the passions . . .' [1]

Even those who would immediately reject so extreme a view are still
often unconsciously influenced by fashionable but questionable
assumptions about the nature of literary activity among non-literate
peoples, which determine their attitude to the study of African
oral literature. We still hear, for instance, of the 'savage' reliance
on the 'magical power of the word', of the communal creation
of 'folktales' with no part left for the individual artist, or of the
deep 'mythic' consciousness imagined to be characteristic of non-
literate society. All in all, there is still the popular myth of Africa
as a continent either devoid of literature until contact with civilized
nations led to written works in European languages, or possessing
only crude and uninteresting forms not worthy of systematic study
by the serious literary or sociological student.

In fact, there is a strong indigenous tradition of both unwritten

[1] Burton 1865, p. xii.

and, in some areas, written literature in Africa.[1] The oral literature in particular possesses vastly more aesthetic, social, and personal significance than would be gathered from most general publications on Africa. Far more, too, has been published on this subject than is usually realized even by many of the students who have recently taken some interest in the subject. But because much of the detailed research this century has been carried out by individuals working in isolation or, at best, by various schools of researchers out of touch with the work of other groups, the subject as a whole has made little progress over the last generation or so, whether in consolidating what is already known, in criticizing some of the earlier limiting preconceptions, or in publicizing the results to date.

This introductory chapter traces briefly the history of the study of African oral literature over the last century. The purpose of the chapter is twofold. First, there have been so many assumptions and speculations about both Africa and oral literature that it is necessary to expose these to clear the way for a valid appreciation of our present knowledge of the subject.[2] Second, the various sources we have for the study of African oral literature need to be assessed and put in historical perspective. For though there are far more collections of African oral art than is usually realized, they are of very uneven quality and their usefulness depends on a knowledge of the theoretical preconceptions of the collector.

I

The European study of oral literature in Africa begins about the middle of the last century. There had been a few isolated efforts before then, notably Roger's retelling of Wolof fables from Senegal (1828) and an increasing awareness of the written Arabic tradition. But until the mid-century there was no available evidence to refute the popular European image of Africa as totally without literary pretensions. By about the 1850s the position changed. African linguistic studies were emerging as a specialist and scholarly field,

[1] Written literature, mainly on Arabic models, is further mentioned in Ch. 3, pp. 49 ff.; cf. also Ch. 7, pp. 168 ff.

[2] For more detailed accounts of the study of oral literature in general (usually under the name of 'folklore') see Thompson 1946; Jacobs 1966; A. H. Krappe, *The Science of Folk-lore*, London, 1930; R. M. Dorson, *The British Folklorists*, vol. i, London, 1968; and the more general essays in von Sydow 1948.

and this in turn led to a fuller appreciation of the interest and subtleties of African languages. The main motive of many of these linguistic studies was to aid the evangelization of Africa, and grammars, vocabularies, and collections of texts appeared by and for missionaries. There was close collaboration between linguists and missionaries, and many of the great collections of texts in the nineteenth century were a result of professional or amateur linguists working in full sympathy with the missionary movement and published under its auspices.[1] A further stimulus was the general interest in comparative studies. This was revealed not only in linguistic work and in the comparative analysis of social and political institutions, but also in the field of literature: in the school of comparative mythology and in the impetus to collection arising from the publications of the Grimm brothers in Germany.

The result of these various influences was the publication of many lengthy collections of African texts and translations in the second half of the nineteenth century.[2] These contain narratives of various kinds (including stories about both animals and humans), historical texts, proverbs, riddles, vernacular texts describing local customs, sometimes additional vernacular compositions by the collector, and very occasionally songs or poems. There is of course some variation in size and quality, but by and large these editions compare favourably with many more recent publications. Most include complete texts in the vernacular with a facing translation usually into English or German, and occasionally a commentary (most often linguistic).

The main emphasis in these collections was, it is true, linguistic (or, in some cases, religio-educational, preoccupied with what it was thought fitting for children to know). There was little attempt to relate the texts to their social context, elucidate their literary significance, or describe the normal circumstances of their recitation. There are many questions, therefore, which these texts cannot

---

[1] On this period see Curtin 1965, pp. 392 ff.; Greenburg 1965, pp. 432 ff.

[2] e.g. Casalis 1841 (Sotho), Koelle 1854 (Kanuri), Schlenker 1861 (Temne), Burton 1865 (a re-publication of the collections of others), Bleek 1864 (Hottentot), Callaway 1868 (Zulu), Steere 1870 (Swahili), Christaller 1879 (Twi), Bérenger-Féraud 1885 (Senegambia), Schön 1885 (Hausa), Theal 1886 (Xhosa), Jacottet 1895, 1908 (Sotho), Taylor 1891 (Swahili), C. G. Büttner, *Anthologie aus der Suaheli-Litteratur*, 2 vols., Berlin, 1894, Chatelain 1894 (Kimbundu), Junod 1897 (Ronga), Dennett 1898 (Fjort), Velten 1907 (Swahili). For further references to works currently considered relevant, see introductions to Chatelain 1894, Jacottet 1908; also Seidel 1896, Basset 1903.

answer. Nevertheless, the very size of many of these collections, presenting a corpus of literature from a single people, often throws more light on the current literary conventions among a given people than all the odd bits and pieces which it became so fashionable to publish later. And the linguistic and missionary motive was not always so narrow as to exclude all interest in the wider relevance of these collections. A number of scholars noted the connections between their work and the progress in comparative studies in Europe. Bleek, for instance, significantly entitles his collection of Hottentot stories *Reynard the Fox in South Africa*, to bring out the parallelism between African and European tales. Although at first some people refused to believe that tales of such striking similarity to European folk-stories and fairy-tales could really be indigenous to Africa, this similarity of content gradually became accepted. By the end of the century, Chatelain could assert with confidence in his authoritative survey that many myths, characters, and incidents known elsewhere also occur in African narratives, and that African folklore is thus a 'branch of one universal tree'.[1]

The cultural implications of these collections were not lost on their editors. There was a general recognition, often accompanied by some slight air of surprise, that the negro too was capable of producing works which manifested depth of feeling and artistry and showed him to be human in the fullest sense of the word. Both the climate of opinion to which he felt he had to address himself and his own conclusions on the basis of his study of the language come out clearly in the preface to the early work by Koelle, *African Native Literature, or Proverbs, Tales, Fables and Historical Fragments in the Kanuri or Bornu Language*, published in 1854. It is illuminating to quote this eloquent and early statement at some length:

It is hoped that the publication of these first specimens of a Kanuri literature will prove useful in more than one way. Independently of the advantages it offers for a practical acquaintance with the language, it also introduces the reader, to some extent, into the inward world of Negro mind and Negro thoughts, and this is a circumstance of paramount importance, so long as there are any who either flatly negative the question, or, at least, consider it still open, 'whether the Negroes are a genuine portion of mankind or not'. It is vain to speculate on this

---

[1] Chatelain 1894, p. 20. Chatelain's introduction gives an excellent summary of the publications and conclusions on African oral literature to that date.

question from mere anatomical facts, from peculiarities of the hair, or the colour of the skin: if it is *mind* that distinguishes man from animals, the question cannot be decided without consulting the *languages* of the Negroes; for language gives the *expression* and *manifestation* of the mind. Now as the Grammar proves that Negro languages are capable of expressing human thoughts,—some of them, through their rich formal development, even with an astonishing precision—so specimens like the following 'Native Literature' show that the Negroes actually have thoughts to express, that they reflect and reason about things just as other men. Considered in such a point of view, these specimens may go a long way towards refuting the old-fashioned doctrine of an essential inequality of the Negroes with the rest of mankind, which now and then still shows itself not only in America but also in Europe.[1]

By the end of the century the same point could be stated more dogmatically and succinctly; as Seidel has it in his description of the impact of African oral literature, 'Und alle sahen mit Erstaunen, daß der Neger denkt und fühlt, wie wir selbst denken und fühlen';[2] but the point has been made—and often with a similar air of discovery—at intervals ever since.[3]

The appreciation of the cultural relevance of the collected texts was taken further by the emerging tradition that a general study of any African people could suitably include a section on their unwritten literature. Even in the nineteenth century some general volumes appeared in which the literary creations of African peoples were set in the context of their life in general.[4]

One of the striking contributions of these early collectors— missionaries, linguists, ethnographers—is the frequent recognition that the texts they recorded could be truly regarded as a type of literature, fundamentally analogous to the written fiction, history, and poetry of European nations. This point is worth making. Recent scholars of the subject too often give the impression that they are the first to recognize the true nature of these texts as literature (although it must indeed be admitted that not only has it been difficult for this approach to gain popular acceptance, but

[1] Koelle 1854, pp. vi–vii.
[2] Seidel 1896, p. 3.
[3] See e.g. McLaren 1917 ('how human the Bantu peoples are!', p. 332); Smith and Dale ii, 1920 ('man's common human-heartedness is in these tales . . . across the abysses we can clasp hands in a common humanity', p. 345); Junod 1938 ('proof that the *Umuntu* has a soul, and that under his black skin beats a genuine human heart . . .', p. 57; cf. p. 83); etc.
[4] e.g. Macdonald 1882 (Yao), Ellis, 1890 (Ewe) 1894 (Yoruba).

for much of this century it has for various reasons been overlooked by professional students of Africa). Many of those working in this field in the nineteenth century, however, were quite clear on the point. The term 'literature' appears in the titles of books or sections,[1] and Chatelain expressed a fairly common attitude among collectors when he stressed the importance of studying 'their unwritten, oral literature'.[2] One of the earliest clear statements is that of Bleek in the preface to his famous collection of Namaqa Hottentot tales. These fables, he writes, form

[an] extensive . . . mass of traditional Native literature amongst the Namaqa. . . . The fact of such a literary capacity existing among a nation whose mental qualifications it has been usual to estimate at the lowest standard, is of the greatest importance; and that their literary activity . . . has been employed almost in the same direction as that which had been taken by our own earliest literature, is in itself of great significance.[3]

By the end of the century, then, the subject was fairly well recognized by a limited group of scholars. A certain amount had been both recorded and published—in special collections, in general surveys of particular peoples, and as appendices and illustrations in grammatical works. Though few were working in this field, they tended to be in touch and to be aware of each other's research, so that by the 1890s serious comparative and general accounts could be produced, drawing on the published works of others.[4] It is true that a certain air of condescension was at times discernible; but this attitude in fact often seems less noticeable in these nineteenth-century sources than in many produced later. There was a general appreciation of the cultural implications of the studies: the fact that Africa could no longer be treated as an area totally without its own cultural traditions, that these could be looked at comparatively in the context of European as well as of African studies, and, finally, that the texts recorded by linguists, missionaries, and others could be treated as at least analogous to parallel written forms. Needless to say, this more liberal approach

[1] e.g. Koelle 1854; Macdonald 1882, i, ch. 2 and pp. 47–57.
[2] Chatelain 1894, p. 16. Cf. also Burton 1865, pp. xii ff.; M. Kingsley in introduction to Dennett 1898, p. ix; Seidel 1896 (introduction); Cronise and Ward 1903, p. 4.
[3] Bleek 1864, pp. xii–xiii.
[4] e.g. Chatelain's introductory sections in 1894 and Seidel's general survey in 1896. Cf. also Jacottet 1908 (introduction).

met with little popular recognition. The works were obscurely published and intended for specialist reading, and—perhaps even more important—the common myth that saw the African as uncultivated and un-literary was too firmly established to allow for easy demolition.[1] But at least among a small group of scholars, in particular the German and English linguists, there was a sense that the subject had been established as one worthy of study and one which had even made a certain amount of progress.

This serious interest was consolidated by the group of German scholars working together towards the end of the nineteenth and during the first decades of the twenthieth century—and also, to a lesser extent, later. Linguistic studies were considered to include African languages, and a series of specialist journals were published, some short-lived, others still continuing today, in which systematic work on various aspects of African languages, including oral literature, appeared.[2] University chairs were established in Bantu or African languages (at Hamburg and Berlin) before any similar appointments in the English-speaking academic world.[3] The linguistic interests of these scholars were by no means strictly limited to grammatical or syntactical analysis, but included both the recording of literary texts and a general appreciation of African literature as a suitable object of scholarship. Comparative surveys appeared which, though in some respects dated, are still among the best available.[4] Drawing on the various published sources for African texts (both large and small), the authors called attention to the literary status of many of them, and pointed not only to the obvious prose forms recorded from Africa but also—a far less common recognition even now—to the various categories of poetry. Seidel, for instance, lists love songs, satirical songs, war songs, epic, dirges, religious songs, and didactic poems as among African

---

[1] See Curtin 1965, p. 397.
[2] *Zeitschrift für afrikanische Sprachen* (Berlin, 1887–90), edited by C. G. Büttner; *Zeitschrift für afrikanische und oceanische Sprachen* (Berlin, 1895–1903), edited by A. Seidel; *Zeitschrift für Kolonial-Sprachen* (Berlin), founded in 1910 and, under its present title of *Afrika und Übersee*, still in continuation (at some periods entitled *Zeitschrift für Eingeborenen-Sprachen*). Material on African literature is also included in *Mitteilungen des Seminars für orientalische Sprachen zu Berlin* (1898–), *Zeitschrit für Ethnologie* (Berlin, 1869–), and *Anthropos* (Salzburg, Vienna, and Fribourg, 1906–); cf. also *Mitteilungen des Instituts für Orientforschung* (Berlin, 1953–).
[3] Pointed out by McLaren 1917, p. 330.
[4] Especially Seidel 1896, Meinhof 1911.

literary forms, and even makes some attempt to discuss their formal structure.[1] To this general recognition of the subject was added a tradition of systematic empirical research. The extension of the German empire further stimulated the interest in African studies, and many texts were recorded and analysed by scholars publishing in German, above all in the areas under German rule— South-West Africa, German East Africa (covering Tanganyika and Ruanda-Urundi), Kamerun, and Togo.[2] Between them these collectors recorded or discussed such forms as prose narratives, proverbs, riddles, names, drum literature, and, more unusually in the subject as a whole, different kinds of poems and songs, sometimes accompanied by the recording and analysis of the music, in keeping with the early German interest in ethnomusicology.[3]

As far as the sheer provision of basic sources goes, these German collections are among the most valuable, and their number and quality seem surprisingly underestimated by recent English-speaking writers. Even though their interests were primarily linguistic, and more purely literary or social aspects were little pursued, they established the subject as one worthy of serious study (thus demanding systematic empirical research) and recognized that the texts they recorded were a form of literature.

In the first couple of decades of this century the study of African

---

[1] Op. cit., pp. 8 ff.

[2] See, among many others, C. G. Büttner, 'Märchen der Herero', *ZAS* 1888; B. Gutmann 1914, 1928; also *Dichten und Denken der Dschagganeger*, Leipzig, 1909, and 'Grußlieder der Wadschagga', *Festschrift Meinhof*, Gluckstadt, 1927, etc.; A. Seidel, 'Sprichwörter der Wa-Bondei in Deutsch-Ostafrika', *ZAOS* 4, 1898; 5, 1900, etc.; E. von Hornbostel, 'Wanyamwezi-Gesänge', *Anthropos* 4, 1909; H. Fuchs, *Sagen, Mythen und Sitten der Masai*, Jena, 1910; E. Bufe, 'Die Poesie der Duala-Neger in Kamerun', *Archiv für Anthropologie* 13. 1, 1914; P. Hecklinger, 'Dualasprichwörter', *ZES* 11, 1920/1; F. Ebding, 'Dualarätsel aus Kamerun', *MSOS* 14. 3, 1911; 'Duala-Märchen', *Mitt. Ausland-Hochschule* 41. 3, 1938 (not seen); and, with J. Ittmann, 'Religiöse Gesänge aus dem nördlichen Waldland von Kamerun', *Afr. u Übersee* 39, 1955; 40, 1956; C. J. Bender, 'Die Volksdichtung der Wakweli', *ZES*, Beiheft 4 (not seen); P. A. Witte 1906, etc. (Ewe); C. Spiess, 'Bedeutung der Personennamen der Ewe-Neger', *Archiv für Anthropologie* 16, 1918, and 'Fabeln über die Spinne bei den Ewe', *MSOS* 21. 3, 1918; 22. 3, 1919; G. Härtter, 'Aus der Volkslitteratur der Evheer in Togo', *ZAOS* 6, 1902. German scholars also worked on Hausa and Kanuri in Northern Nigeria, e.g. R. Prietze 1904, 1916a, 1916b, 1917, 1918, 1927, 1931 (Hausa), 1914 (Kanuri), also 'Bornusprichwörter', *MSOS* 18. 3, 1915; 'Bornu-Texte', *MSOS* 33. 3, 1930; J. Lukas 1937 (Kanuri), also 'Aus der Literatur der Bádawi-Kanúri in Bornu', *ZES* 26, 1935. See also some of the collections mentioned above, p. 28.

[3] See discussion of this school in Nettl 1956, ch. 3.

oral literature could in some ways be said to have reached its peak as a recognized and closely studied academic subject. Then German interest in Africa waned with the loss of their imperial interests; a number of valuable studies continued to be made by German writers and to appear in scholarly German journals,[1] but there was no longer the same stimulus to research and the solid foundations laid earlier were hardly built upon. To some extent the place of the Germans was taken by the South African linguistic school, where there is a strong tradition of informed research in a wide sense;[2] and Werner's work in England also resulted in some contact being kept between the German linguistic tradition and the very much weaker English school.[3] But in general German linguists became isolated from the French and English professional scholars who were now coming to the fore in African studies, concentrating more on aspects of social institutions than on linguistic matters. Much of the earlier ground was therefore lost, and until very recently the study of African oral literature has been relatively neglected as a subject of research in its own right.

## II

Various factors have contributed to the relative lack of interest in oral literature in this century. To understand these, it is necessary to include some account of the history of anthropology, for

[1] e.g. the work by Ittmann and Ebding on Duala and other Cameroons languages, or Dammann on Swahili; cf. also the rather different series of publications by Frobenius 1921–8.

[2] Cf. the early university recognition of African languages and Bantu studies generally, and in particular the influence of C. M. Doke, famous both as linguist and as collector and analyst of oral literature. The South African journal *Bantu Studies*, later entitled *African Studies* (Johannesburg 1921–), is one of the best sources for scholarly and well-informed articles in English on oral literature (mainly but not exclusively that of southern Africa). On the contribution of South African universities to linguistic studies see Doke in *Bantu Studies* 7, 1933, pp. 26–8.

[3] Till recently, not very developed in England, especially as concerns the oral literature aspect. The School of Oriental Studies (later Oriental and African Studies) of the University of London, founded in 1916, was the main centre of what African linguistic studies there were, but in the early years the African side was little stressed. Some of the better of the articles on African oral literature produced in England in the first half of this century have tended to appear in the Bulletin of this school (e.g. Green 1948), but, in spite of some work by missionaries (e.g. by UMCA on Swahili), the intensity of research was less than in the earlier period in Germany.

during much of the first half of the twentieth century it was anthropologists who tended to monopolize the professional study of African institutions and culture. The various assumptions of anthropology in this period both directed research into particular fields and also dictated the selection of texts and the particular form in which they were to be recorded.

A number of the theories that held sway at this time were almost fatal to the serious study of oral literature. This so far had fortunately been free from over-speculative theorizing, for in spite of the dominance in some circles of Muller's particular theories of 'comparative mythology', they seem to have had little effect on studies in the field; the general interest in comparison had thus acted more as a stimulus than as a strait jacket. But the rise first of the evolutionist and diffusionist schools and later of the British structural-functional approach resulted in certain definite limitations being placed on the study of oral art.[1]

The evolutionist approach to the study of society, so influential in the later nineteenth and early twentieth centuries, was a complex movement that took many different forms. Its central tenets, however, were clear. They included the belief in the concept of unilinear and parallel stages of social and cultural evolution through which all societies must pass; a concentration on the *origins* of any institution as being of the first importance; and, finally, the implicit and evaluative assumption that the direction of evolution was upwards—a progress from the crude communal stage of primitive life towards the civilized and differentiated culture of contemporary Europe. Speculative pseudo-history and totally unverified assumption were asserted as proven fact. Many generalizations too were authoritatively pronounced about how 'primitive man must have felt' or 'probably imagined', which drew on little more evidence than the writer's own introspection or his belief that what he most valued in his own, civilized, society were just those elements surely lacking in primitive life. 'Primitive', furthermore, was interpreted to mean both early in history (or prehistory) and low and undeveloped generally in the scale of evolution. The stage of development attained by non-literate peoples could thus be equated and evaluated as the same as that once traversed by the prehistoric ancestors of European nations.

[1] For a fuller discussion of the effect of these theories on the interpretation of prose narratives, see Ch. 12.

This approach clearly has implications for the study of oral literature and in the early twentieth century these were increasingly explored, mainly by scholars writing in England.[1] The concentration was on the idea of origins and evolution: questions asked (and confidently answered) concerned which type of literature came first in the prehistory of man, the survivals into the present of more primitive stages of life and culture in the form of 'folk literature' or 'folk-lore', and the supposed nature of the early primitive stage, still allegedly that of present-day 'savages'.

Current preconceptions about the nature both of oral literature and of primitive society could be fitted into this conceptual framework. Such literature was, for instance, supposed to be the work of communal consciousness and group authorship rather than, as in civilized communities, of an individual inspired artist; it was handed down word for word 'from the dim before-time' or 'far back ages', for no individual creativity or imagination could be expected of primitive peoples; it was basically similar among all peoples at the same stage of evolution, so that one could generalize about, say, 'the primitive' or 'the African' without having to consider the particular history or culture of a given area, much less the individual composer; and finally, although it might ultimately evolve into something higher, at the moment such oral literature was radically different from that of higher civilizations with their emphasis on originality, innovation, and the written word. The exact stage assigned to various non-literate peoples varied, but there was general agreement that most African peoples belonged to an early and low stage, and that their art, if any, would be correspondingly primitive. They were variously described as dominated by the idea of magic, by totemism, or by their failure to distinguish between themselves and the animal world round them. And all these ideas could be presumed to come out in their oral literature or 'folk-lore'.

These theories were not in fact often applied in detail to African

[1] e.g. the general works by J. A. MacCulloch (*The Childhood of Fiction: a Study of Folk Tales and Primitive Thought*, London, 1905), G. L. Gomme (*Folklore as an Historical Science*, London, 1908), A. S. MacKenzie (*The Evolution of Literature*, London, 1911—quite a perceptive account, in spite of its evolutionist framework, including some treatment of African oral literature), E. S. Hartland (*The Science of Fairy Tales*, London, 1891), J. G. Frazer (*Folklore in the Old Testament*, London, 1918), and (in some respects a later survival of evolutionist assumptions) Bowra 1962. Though the detailed theories differ considerably, all share the same basically evolutionist approach.

oral literature. Nevertheless, they had a direct effect on its study. First, the evolutionist movement gave an apparently 'scientific' validation to certain current prejudices about the nature of oral art which naturally affected the attitude of those working in the field (and has to some extent continued to do so, particularly among those with little first-hand knowledge of unwritten literature).[1] It has also dictated the selection of oral literature recorded or the kind of interpretation thought suitable. Because such oral literature was 'communal', for instance, variant forms were not recorded or looked for and no questions were raised about individual authorship, which was presumed not to exist. Because items of oral literature could also be regarded as 'survivals' of yet more primitive stages, an acceptable interpretation would be in terms of hypothetical earlier customs, such as 'primitive matriarchy' or 'totemism', rather than of its literary effectiveness or acceptability. Because primitive tribes were supposed to be preoccupied with tradition rather than innovation, 'traditional' tales were sought and 'new' ones ignored or explained away. Because interest was focused on broad evolutionary stages, few questions were asked about the idiosyncratic history, culture, or literary conventions of a particular people. Finally because origins and early history assumed such importance in people's minds, there was little emphasis on the *contemporary* relevance of a piece of literature, so there seemed every excuse for collecting and publishing bits and pieces without attempting to relate them to their particular social and literary context. The interest of anthropologists was turned away from the systematic collection or analysis of detailed literary texts and concentrated on generalized theory.

The main outlines and many of the details of this approach are now rejected by the majority of professional anthropologists as either false or unproven. But as it was not just a matter of esoteric academic interest but a reflection and apparent validation of many popular views, its rejection by professionals by no means implies the end of its influence. Many of these assumptions can still be found in the writings of non-anthropologists, in particular among some of the self-styled English 'folklorists'. They have also been

[1] And not just those. See, for example, the contradictions Cope runs into in his otherwise excellent treatment of Zulu praise poetry because of his assumption (undiscussed) that 'traditional literature' must be due to 'communal activity' (compare pp. 24 and 33, also pp. 53–4, in Cope 1968).

lent apparent support by the actual selection and treatment of sources presented to the public.

By the 1930s anthropologists were turning to more empirical and first-hand studies of African societies, with the consequent promise of more systematic collection of oral literature. The so-called structural-functional school of British anthropology, associated in its most rigid form with the name of Radcliffe-Brown, concentrated on *function*, in particular on the function of stabilizing or validating the current order of things. This approach was naturally applied to literature as to other social data. The idea that certain types of oral literature could have a utilitarian role was, of course, not new;[1] nor was the related but more extreme hypothesis that, in contrast to the idea of 'art for art's sake' supposedly characteristic of civilized nations, the oral literatures of Africa had a severely practical rather than aesthetic aim. But, while chiming in with these notions, structural-functional anthropology took a particular form of its own. Its central theoretical interest was, at root, the functional integration and maintenance of society: and items of oral literature were regarded as relevant only in so far as they could be fitted into this framework.

The fact that this approach has till recently held sway among British anthropologists—those who in other spheres have made the greatest contribution to the empirical study of African institutions—has several implications for the study of oral literature. Most important is the implicit assumption that oral literature is not worthy of study as a subject in its own right and that it can be ignored except for passing references which fit in with a particular interpretation of society. The result is that over the last generation or so practically no collections or analyses of oral literature have been made by British scholars. When oral literature *was* mentioned, the fashion was to play down the aesthetic aspect in favour of the functional and to stress 'traditional' material even to the extent of sometimes refusing to record anything that seemed to smack of innovation. Prose narrative was more often referred to than sung poetry, since it was easier to make a quick record of it and since it was more suitable, particularly in the form of 'myths', for use in functional analysis. Altogether the emphasis was on brief synopsis or paraphrase rather than a detailed recording of literary forms as actually delivered. The well-known British tradition of empirical

[1] e.g. A. Van Gennep, *La Formation des légendes*, Paris, 1910.

and painstaking field work in Africa has therefore borne little fruit in the field of oral literature. And the dominance of this functional approach, following on the more speculative evolutionist framework of earlier years, helps to explain why the study of oral literature has made so little progress in this century.

The interest in diffusion—the geographical spread of items of material and non-material culture—has also had its repercussions. In both the nineteenth and the twentieth centuries, curiosity about the geographical origin and subsequent history of particular stories encountered in different parts of the world has been considerable. This has been most specifically expressed in the Scandinavian or 'historical-geographical' school of folklore, which for much of this century has been trying to discover the 'life history' of stories of various kinds, by means of systematic classification and an elaborate indexing of comparative references.[1] This approach is also prevalent in America, where it has to some extent blended with the less ambitious and more liberal diffusionist approaches pioneered by Boas and his followers.[2] It has had relatively few adherents in Britain, largely because of the dominance of the theories just described, but it has had some wider influence through its association with the international folklore movement.[3]

The main consequence of these diffusionist approaches was the focusing of interest on the *subject-matter* of oral literature—for it is this that must be considered when attempting to trace its historical and geographical diffusion.[4] Detailed investigations of the actual social and literary role of forms of oral literature in

[1] See Thompson 1955–8 for the best-known general reference work and, for African material, Klipple 1938 and Clarke 1958. Detailed comparative analyses of particular motifs or plots from African materials, mainly published in Uppsala (Studia ethnographica Upsaliensia), include H. Abrahamsson, *The Origin of Death: Studies in African Mythology*, Uppsala, 1951; H. Tegnaeus, *Le Héros civilisateur*, Uppsala, 1950; E. Dammann, 'Die "Urzeit" in afrikanischen Verschlingemythen', *Fabula* [Berlin] 4, 1961. Cf. also the South African branch of this school, e.g. S. C. Hattingh, 'Die Teer-popsprokie in Afrika', *Tydskrif vir volkskunde en volkstaal* (Johannesburg) 1. 1, 1944 (*AA* 5. 356); Mofokeng 1955.

[2] Cf. Boas's early works on (mainly American-Indian) oral literature, and more recent work relevant to Africa by Herskovits (1936 and 1958) and Bascom (1964, etc.). Some of the best collections of African literature have been published by the American Folk-lore Society (Chatelain 1894, Doke 1927).

[3] Cf. Thompson 1946, pp. 396 ff.

[4] Cf. the excellent critical accounts of this approach in von Sydow 1948, M. Jacobs 1966.

particular cultures were thus not called for. Similarly there was no onus on collectors to provide laborious and detailed transcriptions when all that was needed was a synopsis of the content: unskilled assistants could be employed to write down 'texts' and summaries. The emphasis was naturally on prose tales whose motifs could be traced, and once again attention was focused away from poetry.

As a result of these varied theories there was a turning away from the more systematic and empirical foundations laid earlier in the century towards a more limited approach to the subject. Different as the theories are in other respects, they all share the characteristics of playing down interest in the detailed study of *particular* oral literatures and, where such forms are not ignored altogether, emphasize the bare outline of content without reference to the more subtle literary and personal qualities. In many cases, the main stress is on the 'traditional' and supposed static forms, above all on prose rather than poetry. The detailed and systematic study of oral literature in its social and literary context has thus languished for much of this century.

This is not to say that there were no worthwhile studies made during this period. A number of gifted writers have produced valuable studies, often the fruit of long contacts with a particular culture and area,[1] and many short reports have appeared in various local journals. But with the exception of a handful of American scholars and of the well-founded South African school,[2] most of these writers tended to work in isolation, their work not fully appreciated by scholars.

Another apparent exception to this general lack of concern with oral literature was the French interest associated with the *négritude* movement and the journal (and later publishing-house) *Présence africaine*.[3] But this, though profoundly important in influencing general attitudes to African art, was primarily a literary and quasi-political movement rather than a stimulus to exact recording or

[1] e.g. Equilbecq 1913–16, Junod 1912–13, Smith and Dale 1920, Rattray 1930, etc., Green 1948, Carrington 1949b, etc., Verger 1957. Cf. also the mammoth general survey by the Chadwicks (1932–40).

[2] See particularly the many publications of Doke, and a series of valuable articles in *Bantu Studies* (later *African Studies*); there are also a number of as yet unpublished theses (especially Mofokeng 1955).

[3] Paris, 1947–; cf. also many articles in *Black Orpheus* and some in the various IFAN journals; Senghor 1951, etc.; and generalized descriptions such as that in J. Jahn, *Muntu, an Outline of Neo-African Culture* (Eng. tr.), London, 1961, ch. 5.

analysis. It rests on a mystique of 'black culture', and a rather glamorized and general view is put forward of the moral value or literary and psychological depth of both African traditional literature and its contemporary counterparts in written form. Thus, though a few excellent accounts have been elicited under the auspices of this movement, mainly by local African scholars,[1] many of its publications are somewhat undependable as detailed contributions to the study of oral literature. Its romanticizing attitudes apart, however, this school has had the excellent effect of drawing interest back to the *literary* significance of these forms (including, this time, poetry). But it cannot be said that this interest did very much to reverse the general trend away from the recognition of African oral literature as a serious field of scholarship.

### III

By the late 1950s and 1960s, however, the situation started to change. There was a rapidly increasing interest in African studies as a whole, expressed both in the recognition of Africa as a worthwhile field of academic study and in a marked proliferation of professional scholars concerned with different aspects of African life. Work became increasingly specialist. With the new boom in African studies, those who before were working in an isolated and limited way, or in only a local or amateur context, found their work gradually recognized. Some of the earlier work was taken up again,[2] and the interests of certain professional students of Africa widened —not least those of British anthropologists, who for long had held a near monopoly in African studies but who were now turning to previously neglected fields. The result has been some renewal of interest in African oral literature, though—unlike most branches of African studies—it can hardly yet be said to have become consolidated as a systematic field of research.

To mention all the contributory streams in the present increasing interest in African verbal art would be tedious and nearly impossible. But certain of the main movements are worth

[1] e.g. A. Hampaté Ba (Bambara and Fulani), G. Adali-Mortti (Ewe), Laşebikan (Yoruba), perhaps A. Kagame (Ruanda); cf. also the more general accounts by Colin 1957, Traoré 1958.
[2] Notably the Chadwicks' great comparative study of oral literature which had previously had surprisingly little impact on African studies.

mentioning, not least because each tends to have its own pre-conceptions and methods of research, and because in several cases groups are out of touch with others working on the same basic subject from a different viewpoint.

The musicologists represent a very different approach from all those mentioned previously. Though their primary interest is, of course, musical, this involves the recording and study of innumerable songs—that is, from another point of view, of poetry. It is true that the words of songs are not always recorded or published with the same meticulous care as the music itself. But in a number of cases the words do appear, and this approach has had the invaluable effect of drawing attention to the significance of poetic forms so neglected in most other approaches. The musicologists furthermore have provided a much needed corrective to earlier emphases on the traditional rather than the new and topical, by giving some idea of the great number of ephemeral and popular songs on themes of current interest. The African Music Society in particular, centred in Johannesburg, has built up a systematic and scholarly body of knowledge of African music, mainly that of southern and central Africa but with interests throughout the continent. Its main stimulus has come from Tracey, who has taken an interest in oral art as well as music for many years,[1] but its activities are now finding a wider audience not least through its issue of large numbers of records in the *Music of Africa* series.[2] Altogether it can be said that the musicologists, and above all the African Music Society, have done more both to co-ordinate scientific study and to publicize the results in the field of sung oral literature than any other group in this century.

Another significant contribution is that made by a small group of American anthropologists working closely together, and publishing much of their work in the *Journal of American Folklore*, an academic publication which has taken an increasing interest in Africa in recent years.[3] There has always been a tradition of

[1] e.g. Tracey 1929, 1933, 1948*b*, etc.

[2] See its journal, *African Music* (1954–), and the earlier *Newsletter* (1948–); a library of African music has been built up in Johannesburg; cf. also the work of such scholars as Rhodes and Merriam, and various publications in the journal *Ethnomusicology*. Other musicologists less closely associated with this school but carrying out similar studies include A. M. Jones, Rouget, Nketia, Blacking, Belinga, Carrington, Rycroft, Wachsmann, and Zemp.

[3] Some of their work also appears in the main anthropological journals in America.

serious interest in oral literature among American anthropologists,[1] unlike the British, but this has recently gained further momentum and there are now a number of American scholars engaged in the serious study of African oral art.[2] Their main field of interest is the southerly part of West Africa and they seem to have less acquaintance with the work, say, of the South African school; but their general aspiration is to establish the study of oral literature over the continent as a whole. This group has to some extent been influenced by the contributions of the historical-geographical school, but takes a wider approach and, consonant with its anthropological interests, is concerned not only to record oral art (including poetry) but also to relate it to its social context rather than just analyse and classify the types and motifs of narrative. They point out the importance of considering individual inspiration and originality as well as the 'traditional' 'tribal' conventions, the role of poet and audience as well as subject matter. Though they have not always managed to pursue these topics very far in practice, the points they make about the direction of further research are so valid and, at the same time, so unusual in the study of African oral literature that this group assumes an importance in the subject out of all proportion to its size.

Some of the most original work has come from the growing numbers of Africans carrying out scholarly analyses of oral literature in their own languages. These writers have been able to draw attention to many aspects which earlier students tended to overlook either because of their theoretical preconceptions or because they were, after all, strangers to the culture they studied. Writers like Kagame on Rwanda poetry, Babalọla on Yoruba hunters' songs, or, outstanding in the field, Nketia on many branches of Akan music and literature, have been able to explore the overtones and imagery that play so significant a part in their literature and to add depth through their descriptions of the social and literary context. They

[1] e.g. the well-known work of anthropologists like Boas, Benedict, or Reichard (mainly on American Indian peoples), and more recently Herskovits on Africa and elsewhere. See also the general discussion in Greenway 1964.

[2] See especially the bibliographic and other survey articles by Bascom, who is probably doing more than any other single scholar at the present to consolidate the subject as a recognized branch of scholarship, e.g. Bascom 1964, 1965a, 1965b; cf. also Herskovits 1958, 1961, etc.; Messenger 1959, 1960, 1962; Simmons 1958, 1960a, etc. Berry's useful survey of West African spoken art (1961) draws largely on the findings of this group.

have been among the few scholars to pay serious and detailed
attention to the role of the poet, singer, or narrator himself. Not
all such writers, it is true, have been saved even by their close
intimacy with language and culture from some of the less happy
assumptions of earlier generalizing theorists. But with the general
recognition in many circles of African studies as a worthwhile
field of research, an increasing number of local scholars are both
turning to detailed and serious analysis of their own oral literature
and beginning to find some measure of encouragement for publication of their results.[1] And it is from this direction above all
that we can expect the more profound and detailed analyses of
particular oral forms to come.[2]

Other groups or individuals need only be mentioned briefly;
many of them have mainly localized or idiosyncratic interests. The
strong South African school has already been mentioned and continues to take an interest in oral literature (both prose and intoned
praise poetry) in Bantu Africa as a whole. In the Congo a number
of scholars have for some years been working closely together,
though relatively little in touch with the work of other groups.[3]
They tend to concentrate on the provision and analysis of *texts*,
some on a large scale, but with perhaps rather less concern for
social background and imaginative qualities; there have, however,
been a few striking studies on style, particularly on the significance
of tone.[4] Swahili studies too continue to expand, mainly focused,
however, on traditional written forms, with less interest in oral
literature. Traditional written literature in African languages
generally is gaining more recognition as a field of academic research; strictly, this topic is outside the scope of this book, but is
none the less relevant for its impact on attitudes to indigenous
African literature as a whole.

[1] That this has not yet gone as far as it might is shown by the very limited
recognition of the material of so original a scholar as Nketia, much of whose
work has appeared only in local publications.
[2] These local scholars include, to mention only a selection, Laṣebikan
(Yoruba), Abimbola (Yoruba), Owuor (alias Anyumba) (Luo), Mofokeng
(Sotho), Nyembezi (Zulu), Hampaté Ba (Fulani), Adali-Mortti (Ewe), Okot
(Acholi and Lango).
[3] e.g. Stappers, Van Caeneghem, Van Avermaet, Boelaert, Hulstaert, de Rop,
publishing mainly in such periodicals as *Aequatoria, Zaïre, Kongo-Overzee*, and
the various publications of the *Musée / Académie / Institut royal(e) de Congo belge /
de l'Afrique centrale* (and various similar titles).
[4] e.g. Van Avermaet 1955.

Oral literature, like any other, has been and is subject to all the rising and falling fashions in the criticism and interpretation of literature and the human mind. Thus with African literature too we have those who interpret it in terms of, for instance, its relevance for psychological expression,[1] 'structural characteristics' beyond the obvious face value of the literature (sometimes of the type that could be fed into computers),[2] its social functions,[3] or, finally and most generalized of all, its 'mythopœic' and profoundly meaningful nature.[4] All these multifarious approaches, to oral as to written literature, can only be a healthy sign, even though at present there are the grave drawbacks of both lack of reliable material and lack of contact between the various schools.

All this has had its effect on the older established disciplines within African studies. The linguists, for instance, who have in any case been taking an increasingly systematic interest in Africa recently,[5] have been widening their field to include a greater appreciation of the literary aspect of their studies.[6] The British social anthropologists, influenced by increasing contacts with colleagues in France and America and by co-operation with linguists, are also beginning to take a wider view of their subject,[7] and French scholars too have recently produced a number of

[1] e.g. the somewhat Freudian approaches in Rattray 1930 and Herskovits 1934, or Radin's more Jungian turn (1952, etc.).

[2] See the influential and controversial article by C. Lévi-Strauss, 'The Structural Study of Myth', *JAF* 68, 1955 (not directly concerned with African oral literature but intended to cover it among others); A. Dundes, 'From etic to emic Units in the Structural Study of Folktales', *JAF* 75, 1962; I. Hamnett, 'Ambiguity, Classification and Change: the Function of Riddles', *Man*, N.S. 2. 3, 1967. For a useful critique of this approach see M. Jacobs 1966.

[3] An extension both of the functionalist school mentioned earlier and of the 'structuralist' approach; see e.g. Beidelman 1961, 1963 (and a number of other articles on the same lines).

[4] See Lévi-Strauss, op. cit., some of the writings of a group of French scholars including Dieterlen, Griaule, Calame–Griaule, and the speculations of a number of English literary critics not themselves directly concerned with African studies.

[5] Cf. the newly founded journals *African Language Studies* (1960–), *Journal of African Languages* (1962–), *Journal of West African Languages* (1964–), and the local but excellent *Sierra Leone Language Review* (1962–) (later = *African Langauge Review*).

[6] Cf. e.g. Arnott 1957, Berry 1961, Andrzejewski 1965, etc., Whiteley 1964, and other work under the auspices of the School of Oriental and African Studies in the University of London.

[7] The Oxford Library of African Literature, for instance (mainly devoted to oral literature), is edited by two anthropologists and a linguist.

detailed and imaginative studies.[1] Besides these direct studies, there is a growing awareness by other groups of the significance of oral literature as an ancillary discipline: historians discuss its reliability as a historical source,[2] creative writers turn to it for inspiration,[3] governments recognize its relevance for propaganda or as a source in education.[4] Much of this does not, perhaps, amount to systematic study of the literature as such—but it at least reflects an increasing recognition of its existence.

There are, then, growing signs of a fuller appreciation of the extent and nature of African oral literature. But even now it is only beginning to be established as a systematic and serious field of study which could co-ordinate the efforts of all those now working in relative isolation. The desultory and uneven nature of the subject still reflects many of the old prejudices, and even recent studies have failed to redress the inherited over-emphasis on bare prose texts at the expense of poetry, or provide any close investigation of the role of composer/poet and the social and literary background. The idea is still all too prevalent—even in some of the better publications—that even if such literature is after all worthy of study, this can only be so in a 'traditional' framework. The motive, then, for the study is partly antiquarian, and haste is urged to collect these items before they vanish or are 'contaminated' by new forms. These 'new' forms, it is frequently accepted without question, are either not significant enough in themselves to deserve record or, if they are too obvious to evade notice, are 'hybrid' and

[1] Notably de Dampierre, Lacroix, and others in the new *Classiques africains* series; cf. also a number of excellent studies in the journal *Cahiers d'études africaines* (Paris, 1960–) and the Unesco series of African texts which has involved the collaboration of a number of scholars, many of them French. As this type of approach interacts with the already established tradition of Islamic and Arabic scholarship in parts of Africa, we may expect further interesting studies in these areas. This has already happened to some extent for indigenous written literature (see e.g. Lacroix 1965, Sow 1966 on Fulani poetry).

[2] See especially Vansina 1965, and the general interest in recording texts for primarily historical purposes, e.g. the series of Central Bantu Historical Texts (Rhodes–Livingstone Institute, Lusaka).

[3] Though written literature and its relation to oral themes are beyond the scope of this book, it is interesting to note in passing the number of original writers who have also worked as amateurs or professionals on the study of oral literature—e.g. Kagame, Vilakazi, Bereng, Mqhayi, Mofokeng, Dhlomo, Dipumba, Okot, and a number of the *Négritude* group of writers.

[4] A number of school textbooks use material from traditional orally transmitted prose (mainly narrative, also sometimes proverbs and riddles). On propaganda, see Ch. 10.

somehow untypical. How misleading a picture this is is obvious when one considers the many topical songs recorded by, for instance, the African Music Society, the modern forms of praise poems or prose narratives, oral versions embroidered on Christian hymns, or the striking proliferation of political songs in contemporary Africa—but the old assumptions are still tenacious and time after time dictate the selection and presentation of African oral literature with all the bias towards the 'traditional'. In keeping with this approach too is the still common idea that African literature consists mainly of rather childish stories, an impression strengthened by the many popular editions of African tales reflecting (and designed to take advantage of) this common idea. Even now, therefore, such literature is often presented and received with an air of condescension and slightly surprised approval for these supposedly naïve and quaint efforts. Most prevalent of all, perhaps, and most fundamental for the study of African oral literature is the hidden feeling that this is not really *literature* at all: that these oral forms may, perhaps, fulfil certain practical or ritual functions in that supposedly odd context called 'tribal life', but that they have no aesthetic claims, for either local people or the visiting scholar, to be considered as analogous to proper written literature, let alone on a par with it. The idea continues to hold ground that it is *radically* different from real (i.e. written) literature and should even have its own distinctive name ('folklore' perhaps) to make this clear. The fact, however, that oral literature can also be considered on its own terms, and, as pointed out in the last chapter, may have its *own* artistic characteristics, analogous to but not always identical with more familiar literary forms, is neglected in both popular conceptions and detailed studies.

The poetic, the topical, and the literary—all these, then, are aspects which still tend to be overlooked. It is indeed hard for those steeped in some of the earlier theories to take full account of them. But what the subject now demands is further investigation of these aspects of African oral art, as well as the whole range of hitherto neglected questions which could come under the general heading of the sociology of literature; and a turning away from the generalized assumptions of earlier theoretical and romanticizing speculators and of past (or even present) public opinion.

# 3

# THE SOCIAL, LINGUISTIC, AND LITERARY BACKGROUND

*Social and literary background. The linguistic basis—the example of Bantu. Some literary tools. Presentation of the material. The literary complexity of African cultures*

I

In Africa, as elsewhere, literature is practised in a society. It is obvious that any analysis of African literature must take account of the social and historical context—and never more so than in the case of oral literature. Some aspects of this are discussed in the following chapter on poetry and patronage and in examples in later sections. Clearly a full examination of any one African literature would have to include a detailed discussion of the particularities of that single literature and historical period, and the same in turn for each other instance—a task which cannot be attempted here. Nevertheless, in view of the many prevalent myths about Africa it is worth making some general points in introduction and thus anticipating some of the more glaring over-simplifications about African society.

A common nineteenth-century notion that still has currency today is the idea of Africa as the same in culture in all parts of the continent (or at least that part south of the Sahara); as non-literate, primitive, and pagan; and as unchanging in time throughout the centuries. Thus 'traditional' Africa is seen as both uniform and static, and this view still colours much of the writing about Africa.

Such a notion is, however, no longer tenable. In the late nineteenth or earlier twentieth centuries (the period from which a number of the instances here are drawn) the culture and social forms of African societies were far from uniform. They ranged—and to some extent still do—from the small hunting bands of the Bushmen of the Kalahari desert, to the proud and independent pastoral peoples of parts of the Southern Sudan and East Africa, or the elaborate and varied kingdoms found in many parts of the continent, above all in western Africa and round the Great Lakes in the east. Such kingdoms provided a context in which court poetry and court poets could flourish, and also in some cases a well-established familiarity with Arabic literacy. Again, in the economic field, almost every gradation can be found from the near self-sufficient life of some of the hunting or pastoral peoples to the engagement in far-reaching external trade based on specialization, elaborate markets, and a type of international currency, typical of much of West Africa and the Arab coast of East Africa. The degree of specialization corresponding to these various forms has direct relevance to the position of native composers and performers of oral literature—in some cases leading to the possibility of expert and even professional poets, and of a relatively leisured and some-times urban class to patronize them. In religion again, there are many different 'traditional' forms: the older naïve pictures of Africa as uniformly given up to idol-worshipping, fetishes, or totemism are now recognized as totally inadequate. We find areas (like the northerly parts of the Sudan region and the East Coast) where Islam has a centuries-long history; the elaborate pantheons of West African deities with specialized cults and priests to match; the interest in 'Spirit' issuing in a special form of monotheism among some of the Nilotic peoples; the blend between belief in the remote position of a far off 'High God' and the close power of the dead ancestors in many Bantu areas—and so on. This too may influence the practice of oral art, sometimes providing the context and occasion for particular forms, sometimes the need for expert religious performers.

In some areas we also find a long tradition of Arabic literacy and learning. The east coast and the Sudanic areas of West Africa have seen many centuries of Koranic scholarship and of specialist Arabic scribes and writers using the written word as a tool for correspondence, religion, and literature. To an extent only now being fully realized, these men were responsible for huge numbers of Arabic manuscripts in the form of religious treatises, historical chronicles, and poetry.[1] In fact, even for earlier centuries a

[1] A great number of these Arabic manuscripts have been collected and catalogued in recent years. See e.g. V. Monteil, 'Les manuscrits historiques arabo-africains', *Bull. IFAN* (B) 27–9, 1965–7; J. O. Hunwick, 'The Influence of Arabic in West Africa', *Trans. Hist. Soc. Ghana* 7, 1964; A. D. H. Bivar and M. Hiskett, 'The Arabic Literature of Nigeria to 1804, a provisional account',

nineteenth-century writer on Arabic literature in the Sudan region as a whole can sum up his work:

> On peut conclure que, pendant les XIVᵉ, XVᵉ et XVIᵉ siècles, la civilisation et les sciences florissaient au même degré sur presque tous les points du continent que nous étudions; qu'il n'existe peut-être pas une ville, pas une oasis, qu'elles n'aient marquée de leur empreinte ineffaçable, et surtout, que la race noire n'est pas fatalement reléguée au dernier échelon de l'espèce humaine. . . .[1]

Not only was Arabic itself a vehicle of communication and literature, but many African languages in these areas came to adopt a written form using the Arabic script. Thus in the east we have a long tradition of literacy in Swahili and in the west in Hausa, Fulani, Mandingo, Kanuri, and Songhai. With the exception of Swahili,[2] the native written literature in these languages has not been very much studied,[3] but it seems to be extensive and to include historical and political writings in prose, theological treatises, and long religious and sometimes historical poems. The literary models tend to be those of Arabic literature, and at times paraphrase or even translation seem to have been involved. In other cases local literary traditions have been built up, like the well-established Swahili literature, less directly indebted to Arabic originals but still generally influenced by them in the form and subject-matter of their writings.

In stressing the long literate tradition in certain parts of Africa, we must also remember that this was the preserve of the specialist few and that the vast majority even of those peoples whose languages adopted the Arabic script had no direct access to the written word. In so far as the writings of the scholars reached them at all, it could only be by *oral* transmission. Swahili religious

---

BSOAS 25, 1962; C. E. J. Whitting, 'The Unprinted Indigenous Arabic Literature of Northern Nigeria', *J. Royal Asiatic Society*, 1943; W. E. N. Kensdale, 'Field Notes on the Arabic Literature of the Western Sudan', *J. Royal Asiatic Society*, 1955, 1956; T. Hodgkin, 'The Islamic Literary Tradition in Ghana' (in I. M. Lewis (ed.), *Islam in Tropical Africa*, London, 1966); G. Vajda, 'Contribution à la connaissance de la littérature arabe en Afrique occidentale', *J. Soc. africanistes* 20, 1950.

[1] A. Cherbonneau, *Essai sur la littérature arabe au Soudan d'après le 'Tekmilet-ed-dibadje' d'Ahmed-Baba, le Tombouctien*, Constantine, 1856, p. 42.

[2] See the work of e.g. Werner, Dammann, Allen, Harries, and Knappert.

[3] Though see recent work by Hiskett and Paden on Hausa poetry and the production of various texts in Fulani (e.g. by Lacroix and Sow).

poems were publicly intoned for the enlightenment of the masses,[1] Fulani poems were declaimed aloud,[2] and Hausa compositions were memorized as oral forms and sung by beggars[3] or chanted on the streets at night (or, nowadays, on the radio).[4] The situation was thus totally unlike the kind of mass literacy accompanied by the printing-press with which we are more familiar.

Besides Arabic forms, there are a few other instances of literate traditions in Africa. These include the now obsolete *tifinagh* script of the Berber peoples of North Africa, among them the Tuareg of the Sahara. Here the written form was probably little used for literary composition, but its existence gave rise to a small lettered class and the interplay between written and oral traditions. Most often it was the women, staying at home while the men travelled, who composed the outstanding panegyric, hortatory, and love poetry of this area.[5] More important is the long written tradition of Ethiopia. This is the literature of a complex and ancient civilization whose association with Christianity probably dates back to about the fourth century. Though probably never in general use, writing was used from an early period. It occurs particularly in a Christian context, so that the history of Ethiopic written literature coincides pretty closely with Christian literature, much of it based on translation. There are chronicles (generally taking the Creation of the World as their starting-point), lives of the saints, and liturgical verse. In addition there are royal chronicles which narrate the great deeds of various kings.[6] The few other

---

[1] Harries 1962, p. 24.

[2] Lacroix i, 1965, p. 25.

[3] e.g. the 'song of Bagaudu' (M. Hiskett, *BSOAS* 27, 1964, p. 540).

[4] Paden 1965, pp. 33, 36.

[5] The Tuareg are marginally outside the area covered in this work and are only touched on in passing. For an account of their written and oral literature see Chadwicks iii, 1940, pp. 650 ff. and references to date given there. Among more recent works on Tuareg see F. Nicolas 1944; H. Lhote, 'La documentation sonore (chant, musique et poésie) établie chez les Touaregs du Hoggar en 1948', *Cahiers Foucauld* [Paris] 27. 3, 1952 (*AA*. 4. 310); also de Foucauld 1925–30. The North African Berbers are excluded here.

[6] Cf. the recent English translation of the fourteenth-century chronicle *The Glorious Victories of 'Āmda Ṣeyon, King of Ethiopia* (OLAL) by G. W. B. Huntingford, Oxford, 1965 (and bibliography given there). On Ethiopian literature in general (particularly oral) see Chadwicks iii, 1940, pp. 503 ff., and bibliography to date there; also (mainly on written literature): E. Cerulli, *Storia della letteratura etiopica*, Milan, 1956; D. Lifchitz, *Textes éthiopiens magico-religieux*, *TMIE* 38, 1940; E. Ullendorf, *The Ethiopians*, London, 1960, ch. 7 (and bibl.); C. Conti Rossini, *Proverbi, tradizioni e canzoni Tigrine*,

minor instances of indigenous scripts for local languages, such as Vai, are of little or no significance for literature and need not be pursued.

The common picture, then, which envisages all sub-Saharan Africa as totally without letters until the coming of the 'white man' is misleading. Above all it ignores the vast spread of Islamic and thus Arabic influences over many areas of Africa, profoundly affecting the culture, religion, and literature. It must be repeated, however, that these written traditions were specialist ones unaccompanied by anything approaching mass literacy. The resulting picture is sometimes of a split between learned (or written) and popular (or oral) literature. But in many other cases we find a peculiarly close interaction between oral and written forms. A poem first composed and written down, for instance, may pass into the oral tradition and be transmitted by word of mouth, parallel to the written form; oral compositions, on the other hand, are sometimes preserved by being written down. In short, the border-line between oral and written in these areas is often by no means clear-cut.

The earlier belief that Africa had no history was due to ignorance. Africa is no exception to the crowded sequence of historical events, even though it is only recently that professional historians have turned their attention to this field. The early impact and continuing spread of Islam, the rise and fall of empires and kingdoms throughout the centuries, diplomatic or economic contacts and contracts within and outside Africa, movement and communication between different peoples, economic and social changes, wars, rebellions, conquests, these are all the stuff of history. No doubt too there have been in the past, as in the present, rising and falling literary fashions, some short-lived, others long-lasting; some drawing their inspiration from foreign sources, others developing from existing local forms. Examples in this volume may give a rather static impression, as if certain 'traditional' forms have always been the same throughout the ages; but such an impression is misleading and arises more from lack of evidence than from any necessary immobility in African oral art. Unfortunately there are few if any African societies whose oral literature has been thoroughly studied and recorded even at one period of time, let alone at several

Verbania, 1942; A. Klingenheben, 'Zur amharischen Poesie', *Rass. studi etiop.* 15, 1959 and various articles in *J. Ethiopian Studies* and *Rass. studi etiop.*

periods.[1] But with increasing interest in oral art it may be hoped that enough research will be undertaken to make it feasible, one day, to write detailed literary and intellectual histories of particular cultures.

A further consequence of the facile assumptions about lack of change in Africa until very recently is to lead one to exaggerate the importance of these more recent changes. To one who thinks African society has remained static for, perhaps, thousands of years, recently induced changes must appear revolutionary and upsetting in the extreme. In fact, recent events, important as they are, can be better seen in perspective as merely one phase in a whole series of historical developments. As far as oral literature and communication are concerned, the changes over the last fifty or hundred years are not so radical as they sometimes appear. It is true that these years have seen the imposition and then withdrawal of colonial rule, of new forms of administration and industry, new groups of men in power, and the introduction and spread of Western education accompanied by increasing reliance on written forms of communication. But the impact of all this on literature can be over-emphasized. For one thing, neither schools nor industrial development have been evenly spread over the area, and many regions have little of either. There is nowhere anything approaching mass literacy. Indeed it has been estimated that something like eight out of ten adults still cannot read or write,[2] and even where mass primary education is the rule it will take years to end adult illiteracy. Bare literacy, furthermore, in what is often a foreign language (e.g. English or French) may not at all mean that school leavers will turn readily to writing as a form of communication, far less as a vehicle of literary expression. Literacy, a paid job, even an urban setting need not necessarily involve repudiation of oral forms for descriptive or aesthetic communication.

There is a tendency to think of two distinct and incompatible types of society—'traditional' and 'modern', for instance—and to assume that the individual must pass from one to the other by some sort of revolutionary leap. But individuals do not necessarily feel torn between two separate worlds; they exploit the situations

[1] An exception is the interesting but controversial discussion of different periods in Zulu praise poetry in Kunene's unpublished thesis (1962), summarized in Cope 1968, pp. 50 ff.

[2] *The World Year Book of Education*, London, 1965, p. 443 (possibly an exaggeration, but it is clear that the number is still very high).

in which they find themselves as best they can. There is, indeed, nothing to be surprised at in a continuing reliance on oral forms. Similarly there is nothing incongruous in a story being orally narrated about, say, struggling for political office or winning the football pools, or in candidates in a modern election campaign using songs to stir up and inform mass audiences which have no easy access to written propaganda. Again, a traditional migration legend can perfectly well be seized upon and effectively exploited by nationalist elements for their own purposes—to bring a sense of political unity among a disorganized population, as in Gabon in the late 1950s.[1] Or university lecturers can seek to further their own careers and standing by hiring praise singers and drummers to attend the parties given for their colleagues and to panegyricize orally the virtues of hosts and guests.

Such activities may appear odd to certain outside observers— as if having 'modern' competence in one sphere must necessarily involve an approximation to Western cultural modes in others. But the complexity of the facts contradicts this view, which in part still derives from nineteenth-century ideas about evolutionary stages. In fact, many different forms of literature are possible and exist, and if most of the examples in this volume appear to deserve the term 'traditional', this is perhaps more a function of the outlook and interests of previous collectors than an indication that certain forms of oral art cannot coexist with some degree of literacy.[2]

One of the main points of this section is to emphasize that the African world is not totally different from that of better-known cultures. It is true that much remains to be studied, that the special significance of the oral aspect must be grasped, and that one of the difficulties of appreciating African literature arises from the unfamiliarity of much of its content or context. But—and this is the crucial point—the unfamiliarities are on the whole those of detail, not of principle. Far from being something totally mysterious or blindly subject to some strange force of 'tradition', oral literature in fact bears the same kind of relation to its social background as does written literature. In each case it is necessary to study in

[1] See the detailed description of this in Fernandez 1962.

[2] Cf. for instance the political songs, Christian lyrics, work songs, topical songs, and children's singing games described later, as well as the increasing use of radio.

detail the variations bound up with differing cultures or historical periods, and to see the significance of these for the full appreciation of their related literary forms. In neither case are these studies necessarily easy. But it is a disservice to the analysis of comparative literature to suggest that questions about African oral literature are either totally simple (answered merely by some such term as 'tribal mentality' or 'tradition') or so unfamiliar and mysterious that the normal problems in the sociology of literature cannot be pursued.

II

African literature, like any other, rests on the basis of language. Something must now therefore be said about this. Though a full account could only be given by a linguist and this description only tries to convey a few points and illustrations, the topic is so important for the appreciation of African oral literature that some treatment must be attempted here.

Linguistically Africa is one of the complex areas in the world. The exact number of languages to be found is a matter of dispute, but the most often cited figure is 800, if anything an underestimate.[1] These, let it be stressed, are languages in the full sense of the term and not mere 'dialects'. They can, however, be grouped together into larger language families. The exact composition and relationships of these are, again, a matter of controversy, but the over-all picture is clear. The best-known group is that made up of the Bantu languages (these include such languages as Zulu, Swahili, and Luba), which extend over a vast area, practically all of south and central Africa. In the opinion of some recent scholars, even this large Bantu group is only one sub-division within a much larger family, the 'Niger–Congo' group, which also includes most of the languages of West Africa.[2] Another vast family is the Afro-Asiatic (also called Hamito-Semitic), a huge language group which not only includes Arabic but also, in the form of one language or another, covers most of North Africa, the Horn of East Africa (including Ethiopia), and an extensive area near Lake Chad (where

[1] J. H. Greenberg, 'Africa as a Linguistic Area', in W. R. Bascom and M. J. Herskovits (eds.), *Continuity and Change in African Cultures*, Chicago, 1962; cf. also J. H. Greenberg, *Languages of Africa*, Indiana, 1963.

[2] Including the sub-families of West Atlantic, Mandingo, Gur, Kwa, Ijaw, Central, and Adamawa-Eastern (Greenberg, op. cit., 1962, p. 17).

it includes the well-known and widely spoken example of Hausa). The Central Saharan and Macrosudanic families are two further groupings, the former covering a large but mostly sparsely inhabited region north and east of Lake Chad (including Kanuri), the latter various Sudanic languages around the Nile–Congo divide and eastwards in the Nilotic and Great Lakes region of East Africa.[1] Finally there is the Click (or Khoisan) family covering the Bushman and Hottentot languages which, in the south-west of Africa, form a separate island in an area otherwise dominated by Bantu.[2] Besides these indigenous languages we should also mention the more recently arrived language of Arabic and, more recently still, European languages like English, French, or Afrikaans.

In spite of the differentiation into separate language families, there are nevertheless certain distinctive features which the indigenous languages tend to have in common. These, Greenberg writes,

> result from later contacts among the languages of the continent, on a vast scale and over a long period. Practically none of the peculiarities listed . . . as typical are shared by all African languages, and almost every one is found somewhere outside of Africa, but the combination of these features gives a definite enough characterization that a language, not labeled as such for an observer, would probably be recognized as African.[3]

Some of the detailed characteristics in the realm of phonetics or semantics are not worth lingering over in the present context, but the significance of tone must be mentioned. Outside the Afro-Asiatic family, tone (pitch) as an element in the structure of the language is almost universal in Africa and is particularly striking in several of the West African languages. Even some of the Afro-Asiatic languages (in the Chad sub-group) seem to have developed tonal systems through the influence of neighbouring languages. Complex noun-classifications are also widespread though not universal. The best-known instance of this is the system of classes,

---

[1] It includes among others the Nilotic and 'Nilo-Hamitic' languages.

[2] The once-held view that certain languages outside the Afro-Asiatic family (as now recognized) are wholly or partly 'Hamitic' (e.g. Fulani, Bushman, Masai) and that the history of these and other areas in Africa could therefore be explained by successive incursions of 'Hamites' (racially white) is now rejected by professional scholars of Africa.

[3] Greenberg, op. cit., 1962, p. 22.

characterized by prefixes, into which all nouns are divided in the Bantu languages; but similar morphological forms are also to be found elsewhere. Series of derivations built up on the verb are also common and express such concepts as causative, reciprocal, reflexive, passive, or applicative. As will be seen later, all these features have direct relevance for the student of oral literature.

Contrary to earlier views based on either ignorance or speculation about the supposed primitive nature of non-literate language, it is now clear that African languages are neither simple in structure nor deficient in vocabulary. They can, indeed, be exceedingly complex. Some, for instance, make complicated and subtle use of varying tones to express different lexical and grammatical forms. Others have a system of affixes which have been compared in scope to those of Russian, Hungarian, or ancient Greek.[1] In these and many other ways each language has its own genius, its own individual resources of structure and vocabulary on which the native speaker can draw for both everyday communication and literary expression.

A full appreciation of these points can naturally only be gained through a detailed study and knowledge of a particular language and its various forms of expression. But a general discussion of the single example of the Bantu group of languages may serve to illustrate better than mere assertion the kinds of factors that can be involved in the constant interplay in any African language between its linguistic and literary features.

The literary resources of the Bantu languages have been vividly described by Doke. He writes:

> Great literary languages have a heritage of oral tradition which has influenced the form of the earliest literary efforts: in many cases this early heritage has had to a great extent to be deduced; but we are in the fortunate position of being able to observe the Bantu languages at a stage in which their literature is still, in the vast majority of cases, entirely oral. . . .[2]

The linguistic basis from which Bantu oral literature has developed and on which further written forms may be built emerges clearly from his description.

---

[1] Andrzejewski 1965, p. 96.
[2] Doke 1948, p. 284; the following account is largely based on this classic article; cf. also Lestrade 1937.

In the first place, the literary potentialities of these languages include their large and 'remarkably rich' vocabularies. Languages like Zulu or Xhosa, for instance, are known to have a vocabulary of over 30,000 words (excluding all automatic derivatives), the standard Southern Sotho dictionary (20,000 words) is definitely not exhaustive, and Laman's great Kongo dictionary gives 50,000–60,000 entries. A large percentage of this vocabulary, furthermore, is employed in daily use by the 'common people'.[1] While they naturally did not include traditional terms for objects and ideas outside indigenous cultural forms, Bantu languages have, both earlier and more recently, shown themselves peculiarly adaptable in assimilating foreign terms; and in the range of 'the fields of experience with which Bantu thought is familiar, the extent of Bantu vocabulary tends to be rather larger than that of the average European language'.[2]

Vocabulary, however, is not just a matter of the number of words. It also concerns the way in which they are used. In this respect, the picturesque and imaginative forms of expression of many Bantu languages are particularly noticeable. These are often applied to even the commonest actions, objects, and descriptions. The highly figurative quality of Bantu speech comes out in some of these terms—*molalatladi*, the rainbow, is literally 'the sleeping-place of the lightning'; *mojalefa*, the son and heir of a household, is 'the eater of the inheritance'; *bohlaba-tšatši*, the east, is 'where the sun pierces'.[3] This also comes out in compound nouns. In Kongo, for instance, we have *kikolwa-malavu*, a drunken person (lit. 'being stiff with wine'), or *kilangula-nsangu*, a slanderer (lit. 'uprooting reputations'), and in Bemba *icikata-nsoka*, a courageous person (lit. 'handling a snake'), and *umuleka-ciwa*, ricochet (lit. 'the devil aims it').[4] Besides the praise forms mentioned later, figurative expression is also commonly used to convey abstract ideas in a vivid and imaginative way. The idea of 'conservatism', for instance, is expressed in Zulu by a phrase meaning literally 'to eat with an old-fashioned spoon', 'dissimulation' by 'he spoke with two mouths', while in Southern Sotho idiom, the idea of 'bribery' is conveyed by 'the hand in the cloak'.[3]

---

[1] Doke 1948, p. 285.
[2] Lestrade 1937, pp. 303–4.                              [3] Ibid., p. 304.
[4] J. Knappert, 'Compound Nouns in Bantu Languages', *J. Afr. Languages* 4, 1965, pp. 221, 223–4.

The flexible way in which this vocabulary can be deployed can only be explained with some reference to the characteristics of Bantu morphology. One of the most striking features of its structure is the wealth of derivative forms which it is possible to build up on a few roots through the use of affixes, agglutination, and at times internal vowel changes. By means of these derivatives it is feasible to express the finest distinctions and most delicate shades of meaning.

The verb system in particular is extraordinarily elaborate. There are of course the normal forms of conjugation of the type we might expect—though these forms are complex enough and exhibit a great variety of moods, implications, aspects, and tenses. Zulu, for instance, has, apart from imperative and infinitive forms, five moods, three implications (simple, progressive, and exclusive), three aspects, and a large number of tenses built up both on verbal roots and through a system of deficient verbs forming compound tenses.[1] But in addition there is also a wealth of derivative verbal forms which provide an even more fertile source on which the speaker can draw. There is an almost endless variety of possibilities in this respect, with full scope for *ad hoc* formation according to the speaker's need or mood, so that stereotyped monotony is easily avoided.

The extent of these derivative verbal forms can be illustrated from the case of Lamba, a Bantu language from Central Africa. For this one language, Doke lists seventeen different formations of the verb, each expressing a different aspect. These comprise:

1. Passive (suffix *-wa*).

2. Neuter (intransitive state or condition, suffix *-ika* or *-eka*).

3. Applied (action applied on behalf of, towards, or with regard to some object, suffix *-ila*, *-ina*, *et al.*), e.g. *ima* (rise) > *imina* (rise up against).

4. Causative (various suffixes), e.g. *lāla* (lie down) > *lālika* (lay down).

5. Intensive (intensity or quickness of action, suffix *-isya* or *-esya*), e.g. *pama* (beat) > *pamisya* (beat hard).

6. Reciprocal (indicating action done to one another, suffix *-ana* or (complex form) *-ansyanya*), e.g. *ipaya* (kill) > *ipayansyanya* (indulge in mutual slaughter).

[1] Doke 1948, pp. 292–3.

7. Associative (indicating action in association, suffix *-akana* or *-ankana*), e.g. *sika* (bury) > *sikakana* (be buried together).

8. Reversive (indicating reversal of the action, various suffixes with different meanings), e.g. *loŋga* (pack) > *loŋgoloka* (come unpacked), *loŋgolola* (unpack), and *loŋgolosya* (cause to be in an unpacked state).

9. Extensive (indicating an action extended in time or space, various suffixes), e.g. *pama* (strike) > *pamāla* (beat).

10. Perfective (of action carried to completion or perfection, various suffixes), e.g. *leka* (leave) > *lekelela* (leave quite alone).

11. Stative (state, condition, or posture, in *-ama*).

12. Contactive (indicating contact, touch, in *-ata*).

13. Frequentative (by reduplicating the stem), e.g. *-ya* (go) > *-yayaya* (go on and on and on).

There are a few other forms which occur only sporadically:

14. Excessive (in *-asika*), e.g. *pema* (breathe) > *pemasika* (pant).

15. Contrary (in *-ŋgana*), e.g. *seleŋgana* (be in confusion).

16. Reference to displacement, violent movement (*-muka* and various other suffixes), e.g. *cilimuka* (rush off).

17. Reference to extension, spreading out (suffix *-alala*), e.g. *andalala* (spread out at work).[1]

Lamba is perhaps particularly rich in these verbal derivatives, but similar formations could be cited for each of the Bantu languages. In the rather different case of Mongo, for instance, Hulstaert lists eighty different forms of the verb in his table of verbal 'conjugation', each with its characteristic format and meaning.[2] Madan sums up the 'extraordinary richness' of the Bantu verb when he writes:

. . . any verb stem . . . can as a rule be made the base of some twenty or thirty others, all reflecting the root idea in various lights, sometimes curiously limited by usage to a particular aspect and limited significance, mostly quite free and unrestrained in growth, and each again bearing

---

[1] Doke 1948, pp. 290–2.
[2] G. Hulstaert, *Grammarie du Lɔmɔ́ŋgɔ, II. Morphologie, AMRAC* 57, 1965, table at end of vol., also chs. 5–6.

the whole luxuriant super-growth of voices, moods, tenses, and person-forms, to the utmost limits of its powers of logical extension.[1]

In this way, then, a constant and fertile resource is provided on which a composer can draw according to his wishes and skill.

A second subtle linguistic instrument is provided by the system of nouns and noun-formation. The basic structure is built up on a kind of grammatical class-gender, with concordial agreement. In Bantu languages, that is, there are a number of different classes, varying from twelve or thirteen to as many as twenty-two (in Luganda), into one or other of which all nouns fall. Each class has a typical prefix which, in one or another form, is repeated throughout the sentence in which the noun occurs (concordial agreement). A simple example will make this clear. The Zulu term for horses, *amahhashi*, is characterized by the prefix *ama-* which must re-appear in various fixed forms (*a-*, *ama-*) in the relevant phrase. Thus 'his big horses ran away' must be expressed as 'horses they-his they-big they-ran-away' (*amahhashi akhe amakhulu abalekile*).[2] The precision of reference achieved through this grammatical form dispels the vagueness and ambiguity sometimes inherent in equi-valent English forms, and at the same time provides possibilities— which are exploited—for alliteration and balance in literary formu-lations.

Each of these noun classes tends to cover one main type of referent, though there are variations between different languages. In general terms we can say that names of people tend to pre-dominate in classes 1 and 2, names of trees in classes 3 and 4, names of animals in classes 9 and 10, abstract terms in class 14, verb infinitives in class 15, and locatives in classes 16, 17, and 18.[3] There are effective ways of using this system. Sometimes by changing the prefix (and thus class) of a particular word it is possible to put it into a new class and so change its meaning or connotation. In Tswana, for instance, *mo/nna*, man (class 1) takes on new meaning when transferred to other classes, as *se/nna*, manliness, *bo/nna*, manhood; while in Venda we have *tshi/thu*, thing, *ku/thu*, tiny thing, and *di/thu*, huge thing.[4] Besides such straightforward and accepted instances, the transference of noun class is sometimes exploited in a vivid and less predictable way in

---

[1] A. C. Madan, *Living Speech in Central and South Africa, an Essay Intro-ductory to the Bantu Family of Languages*, Oxford, 1911, p. 53.
[2] Doke 1948, p. 289.          [3] So ibid., p. 288.          [4] Loc. cit.

the actual delivery of an oral piece. We can cite the instance of a Nilyamba story about the hare's wicked exploits which ends up with the narrator vividly and economically drawing his conclusion by putting the hare no longer in his own noun class but, by a mere change of prefix, into that normally used for monsters![1]

Besides the basic noun class system, there is the further possibility of building up a whole series of different noun formations to express exact shades of meaning—humour, appraisement, relationships, and so on. This system is far too complex to be treated briefly, but a few instances may serve to show the kind of rich flexibility available to the speaker.

There are special forms which by the use of suffixes or prefixes transform the root noun into a diminutive, into a masculine or feminine form, or into a term meaning the in-law, the father, the mother, the daughter, and so on of the referent. Personification is particularly popular. It can be economically effected by transferring an ordinary noun from its usual class to that of persons. Thus in Zulu, for instance, we have the personified form *uNtaɓa* (Mountain) from the common noun for mountain, *intaɓa*; and *uSikhotha*, from the ordinary *isikhotha*, long grass.[2] This is a type of personification sometimes found in stories where the name of an animal is transferred to the personal class and thus, as it were, invested with human character. A further way of achieving personification is by a series of special formations based, among other things, on special prefixes, derivations from verbs or ideophones, reduplication, or the rich resources of compounding.

Several of these bases are also used to form special impersonal nouns. Such nouns built up on verbal roots include instances like, say, a verb stem modified by a class 4 prefix to indicate 'method of action' (e.g. the Kikuyu *mūthiīre*, manner of walking, from *thiī*, walk), or by a class 7 prefix suggesting an action done carelessly or badly (e.g. Lamba *icendeende*, aimless walking about, from *enda*, walk; or Lulua *tshiakulakula*, gibberish, from *akula*, talk), and many others.[3] Reduplication is also often used in noun formation. In Zulu we have the ordinary form *izinhloɓo*, kinds, becoming *izinhloɓonhloɓo*, variety of species, and *imimoya*, winds, reduplicated to give *imimoyamoya* with the meaning of 'constantly changing winds'.[4]

---

[1] F. Johnson, 'Kiniramba Folk Tales', *Bantu Studies* 5, 1931, p. 330.
[2] Doke 1948, p. 295.          [3] Ibid., p. 296.          [4] Ibid., p. 297.

Compound nouns above all exhibit the great variety of expression open to the speaker of a Bantu language. These are usually built up on various combinations of verbs (compounded with e.g. subject, object, or descriptive) or nouns (compounded with other nouns, with a qualitative, or with an ideophone). Thus we get the Lamba *umwēnda-ŋandu*, a deep ford (lit. 'where the crocodile travels'), *icikoka-mabwe*, the klipspringer antelope (lit. 'rock-blunter'); the Xhosa *indlulamthi*, giraffe (lit. 'surpasser of trees'), or *amaɓona-ndenzile*, attempts (lit. 'see what I have done'); or, finally, the Ila name for the Deity, *Ipaokubozha*, with the literal meaning 'He that gives and rots'.[1] To these must be added the special 'praise names' described later which add yet a further figurative aspect to those already mentioned.

In these various formations and derivatives of noun and verb, Bantu languages thus have a subtle and variable means of expression on which the eloquent speaker and composer can draw at will. In addition there is the different question of style and syntax as well as the actual collocation of the vocabulary used, all of which vary with the particular literary genre chosen by the speaker. In general, apart from the rhetorical praise poems of the southern areas, Bantu syntax gives the impression of being relatively simple and direct. This impression can however be a little misleading: the syntactical relationships of sentences are more complex than they appear at first sight. What seems like co-ordination of simple sentences in narrative in fact often conceals subtle forms of sub-ordination through the use of subjunctive, sequences of historic tenses, or conditionals. In this way the fluent speaker can avoid the monotony of a lengthy series of parallel and conjunctive sentences—though this is the form in which such passages tend to appear in English translations. Furthermore, Bantu expression generally is not limited, as is English, by a more or less rigid word-order: because of its structure there are many possible ways in which, by changes in word-order or terminology, delicate shades of meaning can be precisely expressed which in English would have to depend on the sometimes ambiguous form of emphatic stress. All in all, Doke concludes, 'Bantu languages are capable of remarkable fluency. . . . They provide a vehicle for wonderful handling by the expert speaker or writer.'[2]

Besides the basic structure of Bantu languages in vocabulary

----

[1] Ibid., pp. 297–8.    [2] Ibid., p. 285.

and morphology, there are some further linguistic features which add to its resources as a literary instrument. Perhaps most important among these is the form usually called the *ideophone*.[1] This is a special word which conveys a kind of idea-in-sound and is commonly used in Bantu languages to add emotion or vividness to a description or recitation. Ideophones are sometimes onomatopœic, but the acoustic impression often conveys aspects which, in English culture at least, are not normally associated with sound at all—such as manner, colour, taste, smell, silence, action, condition, texture, gait, posture, or intensity. To some extent they resemble adverbs in function, but in actual use and grammatical form they seem more like interjections. They are specifically introduced to heighten the narrative or add an element of drama. They also come in continually where there is a need for a particularly lively style or vivid description and are used with considerable rhetorical effect to express emotion or excitement. An account, say, of a rescue from a crocodile or a burning house, of the complicated and excited interaction at a communal hunt or a football match—these are the kinds of contexts made vivid, almost brought directly before the listener's eyes, by the plentiful use of ideophones:

They are used by accomplished speakers with an artistic sense for the right word for the complete situation, or its important aspects, at the right pitch of vividness. To be used skilfully, I have been told, they must correspond to one's inner feeling. Their use indicates a high degree of sensitive impressionability.[2]

The graphic effect of these ideophones is not easy to describe in writing, but it is worth illustrating some of the kinds of terms involved. The Rhodesian Shona have a wide range of ideophones whose use and syntax have been systematically analysed by Fortune.[3] Among them are such terms as

*k'we*—sound of striking a match.
*gwengwendere*—sound of dropping enamel plates.
*nyiri nyiri nyiri nyiri*—flickering of light on a cinema screen.
*dhabhu dhabhu dhabhu*—of an eagle *flying slowly*.
*tsvukururu*—of finger millet *turning quite red*.

[1] Sometimes also called 'mimic noun', 'intensive noun', 'descriptive', 'indeclinable verbal particle', etc.
[2] Fortune 1962, p. 6, on Shona ideophones.
[3] Op. cit.

*go, go, go, ngondo ngondo ngondo, pxaka pxaka pxaka pxaka pxaka*—the chopping down of a tree, its *fall*, and *the splintering of the branches.*

Again we could cite the following Zulu instances:

*khwi*—turning around suddenly.
*dwi*—dawning, coming consciousness, returning sobriety, easing of pain, relief.
*ntrr*—birds flying high with upward sweep; aeroplane or missile flying.
*bekebe*—flickering faintly and disappearing.
*khwibishi*—sudden recoil, forceful springing back.
*fafalazi*—doing a thing carelessly or superficially.
*ya*—perfection, completion.[1]

The ideophone often appears in a reduplicated form. This is common with many of its uses in Thonga to give a vivid impression of gait and manner of movement:

A tortoise is moving *laboriously—khwanya-khwanya-khwanya!*
A butterfly in the air—*pha-pha-pha-pha.*
A frog jumps into a pond, after three little jumps on the ground—*noni-noni-noni-djamaaa.*
A man runs *very slowly—wahlé-wahlé-wahlé.*
    „    „    *with little hurried steps—nyakwi-nyakwi-nyakwi.*
    „    „    *at full speed—nyu-nyu-nyu-nyu-nyuuu.*
He walks *like a drunkard—tlikwi-tlikwi.*
A tired dog—*fambifa-fambifa-fambifa.*
A lady *with high-heeled shoes—peswa-peswa.*[2]

Using this form, a Thonga writer can describe vividly and economically how a man was seized, thrown on the thatched roof of a hut, came down violently and fell on the ground:

*Vo nwi!* <u>*tshuku-tshuku!*</u> *o tlhela a ku:* <u>*shulululuuu!*</u> *a wa hi matimba a ku:* <u>*pyakavakaa.*</u>[3]

In Thonga as in other Bantu languages ideophones are constantly being invented anew, demonstrating the richness and elasticity of the language. For the Thonga, this form

---

[1] D. Fivaz, *Some Aspects of the Ideophone in Zulu* (Hartford Studies in Linguistics 4), Hartford, Connecticut, 1963 (mimeographed).
[2] Junod 1938, pp. 31–2.      [3] Ibid., p. 31.

expresses in a little word, a movement, a sound, an impression of fear, joy or amazement. Sensation is immediate and is immediately translated into a word or a sound, a sound which is so appropriate, so fitting, that one sees the animal moving, hears the sound produced, or feels oneself the very sensation expressed.[1]

In the ideophone, therefore, speakers of Bantu languages have a rhetorical and emotive tool whose effectiveness cannot be over-emphasized. In vivid and dramatic passages 'to use it is to be graphic; to omit it is to be prosaic',[2] and, as Burbridge wrote of it earlier:

> In descriptive narration in which emotions are highly wrought upon . . . the vivid descriptive power of *kuti* [ideophone] is seen, and *the human appeal* is made, and the depths of pathos are stirred by this medium of expression of intensely-wrought emotion without parallel in any other language. The ideophone is the key to Native descriptive oratory. I can't imagine a Native speaking in public with intense feeling without using it.[3]

Also very striking are the praise names of Bantu languages. These are terms which pick out some striking quality of an object and are used for inanimate objects, birds, animals, and finally, in their fullest form, as names for people. We meet compound names that could be translated as, for instance, 'Forest-treader', 'Little animal of the veld', 'Crumple-up-a-person-with-a-hardwood-stick', or 'Father of the people'. Other examples are the Ankole 'He Who Is Not Startled', 'I Who Do Not Tremble', 'He Who Is Of Iron', 'He Who Compels The Foe To Surrender', or 'He Who Is Not Delirious In The Fingers' (i.e. who grasps his weapons firmly),[4] and the Zulu 'He who hunted the forests until they murmured', 'With his shields on his knees' (i.e. always ready for a fight), or 'Even on branches he can hold tight' (i.e. able to master any situation).[5] Sometimes the reference is to more recent conditions and formulations, a type which occurs in Kamba praise names for girls in popular songs. These include *Mbitili* (from

---

[1] Junod 1938, pp. 30–1.    [2] Doke 1948, p. 301.
[3] A. Burbridge, *Bantu Studies* 12, 1938, p. 243, quoted in Doke 1948, p. 287. For some other discussions of ideophones in Bantu languages see A. A. Jaques, 'Shangana–Tsonga Ideophones and their Tones', *Bantu Studies* 15, 1941; D. P. Kunene, 'The Ideophone in Southern Sotho', *J. Afr. Languages* 4, 1965; G. Hulstaert, 'Les idéophones du Lomongo', *ARSOM Bull.* 8. 4, 1962. On ideophones in non-Bantu languages see below, p. 71.
[4] Morris 1964, pp. 19 ff.    [5] Cope 1968, p. 72.

English 'battery'): car-batteries are said to provide heat just as the girl's attractiveness heats up her admirers; *Singano* (needle), praising the sharpness of the girl's breasts; and *Mbyuki* (from English 'Buick'): as Buicks are famous for their high-gloss black finish, this is effective praise of the beauty of the girl's skin.[1] Praise names, it is clear, provide a figurative element in the literature in which they appear and, like the Homeric epithet in Greek epic, add colour and solemnity. In panegyric poetry the use of praise names is one of the primary characteristics,[2] but in all contexts the use of praise names can add an extra dimension to speech or literature and continue to flourish amidst new conditions.[3]

A few further features should be mentioned briefly. One is the sound system. There is the 'dominantly vocalic quality of the Bantu sound-system, the absence of neutral and indeterminate vowels, and the general avoidance of consonant-combinations'.[4] Bantu languages differ in the use they make of this system. Shona, for instance, is definitely staccato, Swahili to some extent so, and the tonal systems also vary. Some use a regular long syllable, as in the Nguni languages of the south (including Zulu and Xhosa):

> Strongly-marked dynamic stresses, occurring in more or less regular positions in all words of the same language, and the fairly regular incidence of long syllables also usually in the same positions, give to Bantu utterance a rhythmic quality and a measured and balanced flow not met with in languages with irregular stresses and more staccato delivery.[5]

The particular genius of each language gives rise to various possibilities in the structure of verse. The type of 'prosody' often used exploits the grammatical and syntactical possibilities of the language, which is not, as in English, bound by a fixed word order. Alliterative parallelism is easily achieved. Thus in the Zulu proverb

> *Kuhlwíle | phambíli || kusíle | emíva*
> It is dark / in front // it is light / behind (i.e. 'it is easy to be wise after the event')[6]

[1] W. H. Whiteley, 'Loan-words in Kamba', *Afr. Language Studies* 4, 1963, p. 165.                    [2] See Ch. 5.
[3] For some further comments on praise names see Ch. 16, pp. 475 ff.
[4] Lestrade 1937, p. 302.                    [5] Ibid., p. 303.
[6] Quoted by Lestrade 1937, p. 307. Zulu proverbs frequently exhibit a type of metrical form.

there is perfect parallelism, idea contrasting to idea in corresponding position, identical parts of speech paralleling each other (verb
for verb, and adverb for adverb), and, finally, number of syllables
and dynamic stress exactly matching each other. Similar effects
are produced by 'cross-parallelism' (chiasmus) where the correspondence is to be found crosswise and not directly, and by 'linking', the repetition of a prominent word or phrase in a previous
line in the first half of the next one. The kind of balance may even
extend to correspondence in intonation and, though very different
from more familiar 'metrical' forms, is felt to provide perfect
balance and rhythm by native speakers of the language.[1]

To these linguistic resources on which the Bantu speaker can
draw we must also add the whole literary tradition that lies behind
his speech. There is, for one thing, the interest in oratory and in
the potentialities of the language which is typical of many Bantu
peoples. 'They have the germ of literary criticism in their very
blood', writes Doke, and discussions of words and idioms, and
plays on tone, word, and syllable length 'all provide hours of
entertainment around the hearth or camp fire in Central Africa'.[2]
There is the rich fund of proverbs so often used to ornament both
everyday and literary expression with their figurative and elliptical
forms. There are the 'praise names' that occur so commonly in
Bantu languages, forming on the one hand part of the figurative
resources of Bantu vocabulary and word-building, and on the
other a form of literary expression in its own right, often elaborated
in the south into full praise verses of complex praise poetry.[3] To
all these literary resources we must, finally, add the formal genres
of Bantu literature—prose narration, proverb, riddle, song, praise
poetry. In each of these the artist can choose to express himself,
drawing both on the resources of the language and on the set
forms and styles placed at his disposal

. . . from the artless discursiveness and unaffected imagery of the folktales to the stark economy of phrasing and the elaborate figures of
speech in the ritual chants, from the transparent simplicity and highly-
charged emotion of the dramatic songs to the crabbed allusiveness and
sophisticated calm of the proverb, and from the quiet humour and
modest didacticism of the riddle to the high seriousness and ambitious
rhetorical flight of the praise-poem.[4]

[1] Lestrade 1937, pp. 307–8.     [2] Doke 1948, p. 284.
[3] See Ch. 5.     [4] Lestrade 1937, p. 305.

I have written at some length about the basis for oral literature in the single Bantu group in order to illustrate from one well-documented example the kind of resources which may be available in an African language. Other languages and language groups in Africa have other potentialities—some in common with Bantu, some very different—but a similar kind of analysis could no doubt be made in each case. There is no reason, in short, to accept the once common supposition that African languages, unlike those of Europe, could provide only an inadequate vehicle for the development of literature. This point is made here in general terms and will not be repeated constantly later, but it is necessary, in the case of each analysis of a single literary form, to remember the kind of literary and linguistic resources that, though unmentioned, are likely to lie behind it.[1]

III

It is necessary to examine briefly the general relevance of certain other elements, particularly tone, metre and other prosodic forms, and music.

The significance of tone in literary forms has been most fully explored in West African languages, though it is not confined to them. In these languages tone is significant for grammatical form and for lexical meaning. In, for instance, Yoruba, Ibo, or Ewe, the meaning of words with exactly the same phonetic form in other respects may be completely different according to the tone used—it becomes a different word in fact. The tense of a verb, case of a noun, even the difference between affirmative and negative can also sometimes depend on tonal differentiation. Altogether, tone is something of which speakers of such languages are very aware, and it has even been said of Yoruba that a native speaker finds it easier to understand someone who gets the sounds wrong than someone speaking with incorrect tones.

This awareness of tone can be exploited to aesthetic effect. Not only is there the potential appreciation of unformalized tonal patterns and the interplay of the tones of speech and of music in sung verse,[2] but tones also form the foundation of the special

---

[1] This point is particularly important to bear in mind since in most cases it has only been possible to include translations of the literary examples quoted.
[2] See Ch. 9, p. 264.

literary form in which words are transmitted through drums.[1] In addition tone is apparently sometimes used as a formal element in the structure of certain types of orally delivered art. In Yoruba not only do tonal associations play a part in conveying overtones and adding to the effectiveness of literary expression, but the tonal patterning is also part of the formal structure of a poem. One light poem, for instance, is based on the tonal pattern of high, mid, low, mid, with its reduplicate of low, low, mid, low:

> Jó báta—bata o gb'ônà àbàtà (2)
> Ojó báta—bàta (2)
> Opa b'ó ti mo jó lailai.

Dancing with irregular steps you are heading for the marsh (2),
If you will always dance with those irregular steps, you [? will] never be a good dancer.[2]

Another, in more serious vein, gives a vivid description of a great battle, adding a note of authenticity with the author's claim to have been an eye-witness:

> Ìjà kan, ìjà kàn ti nwọn jà l'Ọfà nkó—
> Ojú tal'ó tó diẹ ḿbẹ?
> Gbogbo igi t'ó ṣ'ojú è l'ó wọ 'wé,
> Gbogbo ikàn t'ó ṣ'ojú è l'ó w'ẹwù èjè
> Ọgọrọ̀ àgbọnrín t'ó ṣ'ojú ẹ l'o hù'wo l'óju ọdẹ;
> Ṣugbọn ó ṣ'oju mi pã kete n'ilé we nibi nwọn bí mi l'ọmọ;
> Àgbà ni ng ò tĩ dà, mo kuro l'ọmọde àgbékọ́ruǹ r'oko.

What about a great fight that was fought at Ofa—
Is there anyone here who witnessed a bit of it?
Although the trees that saw it here all shed their leaves,
And the shrubs that saw it were all steeped with blood,
And the very stags that saw it grew fresh horns while the hunters looked on,
Yet I saw every bit of it, for it was fought where I was born.
I do not claim to be old, but I'm no more a child that must be carried to the farm.[3]

Laṣebikan comments on the tonal structure of this poem. It falls into four distinct divisions: 'How are these divisions marked out? Not by means of rhymes as in English poems, but by the tone of

---

[1] See Ch. 17.
[2] Laṣebikan 1956, p. 48. The conventional tone marks are used: ´ for a high tone, ` for low, and no mark for mid.
[3] Laṣebikan 1955, pp. 35–6.

the last syllable of the division.' He shows how the actual words used are carefully chosen to fit this tonal structure, for possible alternatives with the same meaning and syllable number have tonal compositions that 'would spoil the cadence of the poem'.[1]

A similar but more detailed analysis has been made by Babalọla of the way tonal patterning is a characteristic feature of the structure of Yoruba hunting poetry (*ijala*). The musical and rhythmic effect of this poetry arises partly from tonal assonance—specific short patterns of syllabic tones repeated at irregular intervals—or, alternatively, from tonal contrast which 'seems to . . . increase the richness of the music of the ijala lines by adding to the element of variety in successive rhythm-segments'.[2]

In other forms and areas too we sometimes see tonal correspondence. There is sometimes tonal parallelism between question and answer in 'tone riddles' or within the balanced phrases of some proverbs.[3] The use of tone correspondence in some poetry is so striking as to have been called a species of 'rhyme'.[4]

Some of the detailed analyses of the significance of tone in literature are controversial, and little enough work has as yet been done on this formal aspect. But as linguists increasingly stress the general importance of tone in African languages throughout the continent, so we can expect many more studies of this aspect of literature.

Ideophones and other forms of sound association are so important in non-Bantu as well as Bantu languages that they are worth mentioning again at this point. Thus there are the important sound associations in Yoruba which connect, for instance, a high toned nasal vowel with smallness, or low toned plosives with huge size, unwieldiness, or slow movement, often intensified by reduplication;[5] the connection in Ewe and Gbeya with the vowel /i/ and a lateral resonant consonant in ideophones for 'sweet', or the common use of back rounded vowels for ideophones indicating 'dark, dim, obscure, foggy', etc.[6] In many cases ideophones

---

[1] Ibid., p. 36.

[2] Babalọla 1965, pp. 64–5; cf. Babalọla 1966, appendix A *passim*.

[3] See e.g. Simmons 1958 (Efik); Van Avermaet 1955 (Luba).

[4] e.g. the 'tonal rhyme' of Efik, Ganda, and possibly Luba poetry (Simmons 1960*a*; Morris 1964, p. 39; Van Avermaet 1955, p. 5; Stappers 1952).

[5] Lạṣẹbikan 1956, p. 44.

[6] W. J. Samarin, 'Perspective on African Ideophones', *Afr. Studies* 24, 1965, p. 120.

constitute a high proportion of the lexical resources of the language. In Gbeya, in the Central African Republic, about 1,500 ideophones have been recorded. A number of African languages are said to have twenty, thirty, or even forty ideophones just to describe different kinds of 'walking'.[1] Indeed it has been suggested by one authority that 'ideophones by count constitute, next to nouns and verbs, a major part of the total lexicon of African languages'.[2]

Many different instances of these graphic ideophones could be added to the earlier (Bantu) examples we have cited. We have, for instance, the Yoruba representation of water draining out drop by drop (*tó tó tó*), a lady in high heels (*kó kò kó kò, kó*), or a stalwart in heavy boots (*kò, kà, kò*);[3] The Zande ideophones *digbidigbi* (boggy, oozy, slushy), *guzuguzu* (fragrantly, sweet smelling), *gangbugangbu* (listlessly), *degeredegere* (swaggeringly), and *gbaraga-gbaraga* (quarrelsome-ly).[4] The effectiveness of such forms for descriptive and dramatic formulations and the poetic quality they can add to ordinary language need not be re-emphasized except to say that this point constantly reappears in detailed analyses of African oral art.

Then there is the topic of prosodic systems in African verse. This is a difficult question which, apart from one classic article by Greenberg[5] (largely devoted to Arabic influence), has received relatively little attention. It is clear that many different forms are possible which can only be followed up in detailed accounts of particular literary genres. Broadly, however, one can say[6] that six main factors can be involved: rhyme, alliteration, syllable count, quantity, stress, and tone. Of these, the last three can only be used when there is a suitable linguistic basis. Tone, for instance, can only perform a prosodic function in tonal languages; and this influence of language on form can be seen in the way Hausa has

---

[1] W. J. Samarin, op. cit., pp. 117, 118.

[2] Ibid., p. 121.                                    [3] Laṣebikan 1956, p. 44.

[4] Evans-Pritchard 1962, p. 143; cf. also E. E. Evans-Pritchard, 'A Note on Bird Cries and Other Sounds in Zande', *Man* 61, 1961. For other discussions of ideophones in non-Bantu languages see e.g. Equilbecq i, 1913, pp. 100–2 (West Africa); Finnegan 1967, pp. 80–1 (Limba); M. H. I. Galaal and B. W. Andrzejewski, *Hikmad Soomaali* (SOAS Annotated African Texts 4), London, 1956, p. 94 ('imitative words' in Somali), as well as many passing references in collections of stories, etc.

[5] Greenberg 1960; cf. also two earlier articles by Greenberg: 'Swahili prosody', *J. Am. Oriental Soc.* 67, 1947; 'Hausa verse prosody', ibid. 69, 1949).

[6] Here and throughout this section I draw mainly on Greenberg 1960.

been able to keep to the quantitative form of its Arabic verse models, whereas in Swahili, equally or more dominated by the Arabic tradition, the nature of the language has precluded the use of quantitative metres and instead turned interest to rhyme and syllable count.[1]

The Arabic influences on African prosody have been summarized by Greenberg and need not be repeated in detail here. In spite of various difficulties and uncertainties the Arabic-based styles are somewhat easier to analyse than some other forms of African poetry, partly because, for one familiar with the Arabic forms, the parallel African ones are ultimately recognizable, partly because they appear in local *written* forms in which the evidence tends to be somewhat more plentiful and accurate than for oral African poetry. Classical Arabic prosody is a source of verse forms in several African languages, particularly the *qaṣīdah* (ode) based on quantity and rhyme. This occurs, for example, in learned Fulani poetry, and in learned (and sometimes in popular and oral) Hausa poetry; in both cases there is the retention of quantitative features made feasible by the forms of these two languages. The post-classical *tasmīt* has also influenced African forms. Again it uses quantity and rhyme, but with more stress on rhyme. It occurs in several West African languages (Hausa, Kanuri), but has reached its highest development in Swahili where 'it is by far the most common form in both learned and popular poetry, whether sung or recited'.[2] Since Swahili does not possess vowel quantitative distinctions, this principle has been replaced by that of syllable count accompanied by rhyme. Its most popular form is the four-line stanza (each line containing eight syllables), with the basic rhyme scheme aaab/cccb/dddb/ . . ., but five-line stanzas (*takhmis*) also sometimes occur.[3]

The instances so far are unmistakable cases of direct Arabic influences. Certain other examples are not so clear, though Arabic influence seems likely. In the Horn of Africa (Ethiopia and Somali, etc.) rhyme is a frequent prosodic principle (sometimes in combination with other features), to such an extent that Greenberg speaks of this region as the 'East African rhyming area'.[4] In

[1] Greenberg 1960, pp. 927, 935; cf. also other articles by Greenberg cited above and Knappert 1966, pp. 136 ff.    [2] Greenberg 1960, p. 935.

[3] Ibid., pp. 934–6; cf. also Harries 1962, pp. 9 ff., Greenberg, op. cit., 1947, *passim*; also W. Hichens, 'Swahili Prosody', *Swahili* 33, 1962/3.

[4] Greenberg 1960, pp. 937 ff.

various ways, this use of rhyme is exploited in—to give just a few instances—early Ge'ez verse (classical Ethiopic), the Amharic royal songs, Galla strophic poetry, and Tigre verse. A few indications of possible Arabic influence can also be detected among the Muslim Nubians of the Nile Valley and the Berbers (particularly the Tuareg) where, again, rhyme is used.[1] As Greenberg sums it up:

> The outstanding impression in the historic dimensions is the vast reach of certain, and in many cases highly probable, Arabic influence in the northern part of Africa—an influence well documented for many other aspects of the culture of the area.[2]

For the forms of African prosody which cannot be thus traced to ultimate Arabic influence, the picture is much less clear—indeed little work has been done on this. It seems that rhyme and regular metre are uncommon or non-existent. Sometimes alliteration seems to be a marked feature. There are, for example, the very rigid rules of alliteration in Somali poetry in which each line in the whole poem must contain a word beginning with the same sound.[3] There is also the much less formalized alliteration arising from parallelism in Southern Bantu praise poetry.[4] As was mentioned earlier, tone is also sometimes a formal characteristic of some African poetry, though its analysis has not as yet proceeded very far. In Nkundo poetry, on the other hand, tone seems to be of less significance, if we accept Boelaert's contention that stress (*accent dynamique*) is the basic characteristic of the prosodic system.[5] The same point might be made about the dynamic stress in Southern Bantu praise poems[6] and in Ankole recitations.[7] In other cases again, it seems that either the musical setting or such features as repetition, linking, or parallelism perform certain of the functions we normally associate with metre or rhyme. But the whole question is a difficult one, and there seem to be many cases when, either out

---

[1] De Foucauld i, 1925, p. xiii.

[2] Greenberg 1960, p. 947. On Arabic influences see also A. I. Sow, 'Notes sur les procédés poétiques dans la littérature des Peuls du Fouta-Djalon', *Cah. étud. afr.* 19, 1965. Cf. also the interesting analysis of a Fulani poem by C. Seydou, ' "Majaaɓo Alla gaynaali", poème en langue peule de Fouta-Djalon', *Cah. étud. afr.* 24, 1966.

[3] Greenberg 1960, pp. 928–9; Andrzejewski and Lewis 1964, pp. 42–3.

[4] See above, pp. 67–8; and Ch. 5, pp. 131–2.

[5] E. Boelaert, 'Premières recherches sur la structure de cinq poésies lonkundo', *IRCB Bull.* 23. 2, 1952.

[6] See Ch. 5, pp. 129–30.          [7] Morris 1964, pp. 32 ff.

of ignorance or from the nature of the material, the observer finds
it difficult to isolate any clear prosodic system in what he calls
'poetry'. Thus in Southern Bantu literature, to quote Lestrade
again:

> The distinction between prose and verse is a small one . . . the
> border-line between them is extremly difficult to ascertain and define,
> while the verse-technique, in so far as verse can be separated from
> prose, is extremely free and unmechanical. Broadly speaking, it may be
> said that the difference between prose and verse in Bantu literature is
> one of spirit rather than of form, and that such formal distinction as
> there is is one of degree of use rather than of quality of formal elements.
> Prose tends to be less emotionally charged, less moving in content and
> full-throated in expression than verse; and also—but only in the second
> place—less formal in structure, less rhythmical in movement, less
> metrically balanced.[1]

The analysis of indigenous African prosody is thus clearly by no
means a simple matter, and apart from the work of musicologists
on the rhythm of fully musical forms,[2] relatively little study has
apparently yet been made of this aspect of African literature.[3]

This brings us to the final point—the significance of music.
Clearly this is not a feature of *all* African literary forms. It occurs
seldom in what is normally classified as 'prose'—stories, narrations, riddles, proverbs, or oratory.[4] In 'poetry' it is more common.
In fact the occurrence of music or of a sung mode of expression
has sometimes been taken as one of the main differentiating marks
between prose and verse. Even here, however, there is a wide
range of possibilities. On the one hand, in much panegyric and
some religious verse the verbal element is markedly predominant
over the musical, and such forms are, at most, delivered in a kind
of recitative or intoned form. Then there are other types in
which the music is progressively more important, until we reach
the extreme choric form (often with leader and chorus) with

---

[1] Lestrade 1937, p. 306.          [2] On which see Ch. 9 below.

[3] For some further references to questions of prosody see Coupez and Kamanzi
1957, and 1962, pp. 8–9; A. Coupez 1958 and idem., 'Rythme quantitatif dans
les berceuses Rundi', *Folia Scientifica Africae Centralis* [Bukavu], 5. 3, 1959 (on
the quantitative element in Rundi and Ruanda verse); A. Klingenheben, 'Zur
amharischen Poesie', *Rass. studi etiop.* 15, 1959 (argues from Amharic popular
songs that metre is based on accent rather than, according to the usual view, on
syllabic numbering).

[4] Except for songs within stories, on which see Chs. 9, pp. 244 ff.; 13,
pp. 385 ff.

instrumental accompaniment and even dance, like the 'symphonic poems' of the Chopi.[1] In such cases the music, however closely intertwined with the words, may come to dominate them and we can no longer assume that, as seems so often to be taken for granted in Western culture, verbally expressed literature can be taken as self-evidently the 'top art'. In some cases, indeed, it is clear that musical expression (or even sometimes the dance) may be the object of greater interest, critical appreciation, and specialized performance. This is a central question in any assessment of the position of oral literature within a particular cultural tradition, for even in less extreme cases the musical aspect may still be a very important one. Though it may appear secondary to one basically interested in literature, it is clearly something which cannot be ignored, above all in lyric forms.

As in the case of the more purely linguistic basis, I will not keep drawing attention to the significance of music in the case of every single relevant form.[2] But to allow ourselves to forget the importance music may assume in certain cases of African poetry is to minimize the intricacy and full aesthetic appeal of these instances of oral literature.

## IV

Before proceeding to the main part of the book, there are a few general points to make about presentation and the nature of the literature involved.

First, there is the question of the categories I have used to present the material. An immediate problem is how to differentiate between 'prose' and 'poetry'. Though some cases seem to fall clearly under one or the other heading, the distinction between the two is not always self-evident. I have in fact begged the question by making a firm division between the parts devoted to 'prose' and to 'poetry' respectively. This however has been done more for convenience than in an attempt to make a definite typology. The kinds of factors which it has seemed helpful to consider include: musical setting (most sung forms can reasonably be regarded as poetry); the intensity and emotion of expression; sometimes (but not always) rhythm, and tonal or syllabic rhyme (the latter

---

[1] Tracey 1948*a*.
[2] Some further points are made on this subject in Ch. 9.

infrequent except under Arabic influence); special vocabulary, style, or syntactical forms; local evaluation and degree of specialism (more marked with poetry than with prose); and, finally, the native classifications themselves. Such factors give some kind of indication of the form involved, though none is either necessary or sufficient. At best they are only a matter of degree and in many cases can provide no rigid distinctions.[1] There is clearly a large amount of overlap, like the introduction of songs into stories (in some cases so marked that the 'story' becomes swamped in the singing) or the 'poetic' form of proverbs which are nevertheless usually classified as prose. But this kind of overlap and lack of clear differentiation need not worry us too much (unless, that is, our main preoccupation is the building of typologies), particularly when we recall the recent blurring of the traditional prose/verse distinctions in more familiar literatures.

One obvious way to present the evidence might have seemed to be by geographical area, describing the different oral forms characteristic of different regions or peoples. But there are serious difficulties about such an approach. One is its tendency to become a mere catalogue—and a repetitive one at that, since such forms as stories, proverbs, or work songs are very wide-spread, and perhaps universal. A more serious obstacle is the fact that so far there has only been the most haphazard sampling of the apparently huge oral literary resources of the continent. The selection has all too often depended not only on geographical accessibility and historical accident, but also on the preconceptions of the observer or the ease of recording, rather than on the evaluation of the people involved. Hence we have a vast number of proverbs, riddles, and stories but relative neglect of poetry or oratory. Only the literature of very few peoples has ever been at all adequately covered,[2] and for some whole areas little serious work appears to be available.[3] It is thus extremely difficult to draw any well-founded conclusion about the different forms recognized by a people at a given time.

[1] Since a clear distinction between prose and poetry seems to be associated with writing (and more particularly with printing), it is not surprising that the difference is somewhat blurred in non-literate cultures.

[2] Among them perhaps some of the Southern Bantu languages, Swahili, Fulani, Hausa, Dogon, and some of the Kwa groups of the West African coast; but even in these cases there has not been systematic or rigorous coverage.

[3] e.g. from Portuguese Africa, South West Africa, or the Central African republics.

G

One can make a few broad generalizations: the significance of Arab-influenced forms in the north and east in such languages as Fulani, Hausa, or Swahili; the importance of elaborate panegyric among the Southern in contrast to some of the Central Bantu; the spread of drum literature over the tropical forest areas of West and West Central Africa (including the Congo); and the probability (yet to be fully explored) that some languages and cultures are more interested in certain forms of artistic expression than are others.[1] But beyond this one can give little of an over-all picture. In this unsystematically covered field the *argumentum ex silentio* is not a good one and at present there is not enough evidence for a geographical approach.

There are also drawbacks to the type of presentation I have adopted, i.e. grouping the material according to broad literary genres. A 'religious song', for instance, or a 'praise poem' may be very different in form, in relationship to other genres, or even in function in different areas, and an over-rigid insistence on the categories I am using could be misleading. Suffice it to say that the chapter headings I use here seem satisfactory enough for a brief introductory survey and have arisen fairly naturally from the material at present available; but that they are likely to prove inadequate for future detailed research. In fact local classifications of poetry in particular would seem normally to be far more complex than the handful of categories I employ.

This leads on to a further point. To read about, say, the hunting songs of the Ambo, Christian lyrics of the Fante, proverbs of the Jabo, or stories of the Limba may give the impression that each of these are the most valued or even the only forms of oral art in the society concerned. In fact all the available evidence suggests that this would be misleading. In general terms, poetry seems to be more highly valued and specialized than prose—the opposite of the impression given in many of the numerous collections of African stories. It is also common for many different literary genres to be recognized in any one society. Among the

[1] e.g it has been observed (by R. Horton) that Yoruba seems to be an intensely 'verbal' culture with particular emphasis on poetry as against, say, Ibo or Kalabari where the main stress is rather on drama (including drumming and dancing) and perhaps oratory. (On Yoruba, cf. Babalọla (1966, p. v) on their 'tonal, metaphor-saturated language which in its ordinary prose form is never far from music in the aural impression it gives and which has produced an extensive variety of spoken art'.)

Akan-speaking peoples of Ghana, for instance, a large number of different poetic forms have been distinguished by Nketia.[1] In terms of the mode of delivery, there are four broad classes of Akan poetry, each including many different types in detail: (1) spoken poetry, which covers many of the poems to do with chiefship, like the praises delivered at state functions; (2) recitative, poetry half spoken, half sung, like funeral dirges, elegies by court musicians, and hunters' poetry; (3) lyric (i.e. sung) poetry, a large category comprising many different types of song each with its own conventions—among them songs of insult, heroic songs, sung interludes in stories, maiden songs, love songs, songs of prayer, exhilaration and incitement, cradle songs, and warrior songs; and finally (4) poetry expressed through the medium of horns or drums, in lyric, eulogistic, or proverbial vein. These instances, furthermore, are only selective (and cover only poetry, not prose), and many others could have been added in a more comprehensive catalogue.[2] A similar account could be given of Yoruba literature from Western Nigeria. In prose there are stories of various kinds, riddles, proverbs, and praise appellations. In poetry, the variety can be sufficiently illustrated by merely listing some of the vernacular terms that describe different verse forms; *eṣa, ewi, ijala, rara, ọfọ, ogede, oriki, ogbere, ege, arofo, odu ifa*.[3] Poetic forms have probably been studied in more detail in West African languages than elsewhere, and it is possible that some of these languages may be particularly rich in poetic forms. There is no reason, however, to suppose that this kind of poetic diversity is without parallels in other parts of the continent. We hear, for instance, of many different forms among the Ngoni of Malawi, Ila and Tonga of Zambia, Luba of the Congo, Rwanda of Ruanda, Somali of North-East Africa, and many others.[4] And further research will without doubt reveal similar instances throughout the continent.

This kind of literary complexity can be assumed to lie behind many of the actual examples which are mentioned in this volume

---

[1] In his classic article in *Black Orpheus* 3, 1958 (Nketia 1958*b*).

[2] Cf. for instance the sung forms mentioned in Nketia 1962, chs. 2, 3, and *passim*; and 1963*a*, *passim*.

[3] See Babalọla 1966, p. vi; Laṣebikan 1956, pp. 46, 48; Gbadamosi and Beier 1959, *passim*.

[4] Read 1937; A. M. Jones 1943; Kalanda 1959, pp. 77–9, and Burton 1943; Kagame 1947, 1951*b*, etc.; Andrzejewski and Lewis 1964.

(and elsewhere). It needs to be remembered that practically all accounts to date give only a tiny selection from the manifold literary genres of any one society. The present exceedingly simple impression of African literature can be seen to rest more on lack of research than on lack of actual material. A real understanding of the oral literature of any single African people will only be possible with further detailed research and collection. More information is required not only of actual texts but also of the nature and inter-relationships of all their literary genres: their conventional forms, content, occasions, exponents, and expected audience.

# 4

## POETRY AND PATRONAGE

*Variations in the poet's position. Court poets. Free-lance and
wandering poets. Part-time poets*

THIS chapter is intended to give some account of the conditions
in which African oral poets produce their works, and the audiences
to which they address themselves. However, even the most summary account of this topic is a matter of great difficulty. This is
partly because of sheer lack of data. Even those who have spent
time and care recording African texts have frequently taken next
to no interest in the position of the authors or reciters. A related
but more profound cause of confusion lies in the popular images
which underlie the work of many commentators on African oral
literature, images which suggest some general and simple pattern
to which these poets are expected to conform.

One commonly held view of the position of the poet among
unlettered peoples seems ultimately to derive from the picture of
the rhapsodist of the Homeric age. The bard is depicted as standing before the gathered lords to chant the heroic lays handed down
through the generations, rewarded with honour and rich gifts. It
seemed to some earlier writers natural to assume that African
societies were at a certain evolutionary stage, one long since passed
by Indo-European peoples, and that the type of poetry and of
patronage apparently once found in the latter would be discover-
able in the former. This image of the bard delivering his rude but
stirring verses to barbaric audiences has gained a profound hold
on the popular imagination from its vivid representation in literature as well as in scholarly works inspired by the concept of 'the
heroic age'.

There is another common image which presents an opposite picture. In this the poetry of non-literate peoples is seen as in some way arising directly and communally from the undifferentiated folk. In this case song is its own reward and the specialized role of the poet has not yet made its appearance.

In fact neither picture fits the varied nature of poetry in Africa. This will be immediately obvious: as soon as the question is raised it is self-evident that any study of the conditions and background of poetry in Africa can no longer afford to rely on such half-consciously held generalizations but must proceed to a much more rigorous and detailed investigation of the actual position of poets in the various societies. Some poets, it is clear already, are associated with royal courts and receive reward as professionals. Others depend on private enterprise, perhaps wandering from patron to patron and living on their wits. Others gain their basic livelihood from farming or cattle-keeping (or whatever the local basis of subsistence may be), but are marked out by their expert skill on special occasions. Finally, in some contexts poets are not set apart from their fellows in terms of training, reward, or position. Indeed, almost every category of relationship between poet and audience can be found in Africa in one context or another. These differences are not confined to different geographical areas but can be discovered even within a single society. Even in one culture (Hausa or Fulani, for instance, or, to a lesser exent, Ashanti) one can sometimes see the coexistence of a learned and a more popular tradition, and it is common for many different genres of poetry to be recognized simultaneously, each with its own type of performer, reward, and occasion. No single picture can cover all these variations and even the most cursory account of poetry in Africa must begin by insisting on the variety before going on to discuss certain common patterns.

I

The practice of poetic composition and performance as a specialist art is not uncommon in Africa. Poetry is, by and large, differentiated from prose as being marked by greater specialism. The most specialized genres of poetry occur in association with royal courts. The other familiar form of patronage—religion—is also relevant, but in an organized form it is less significant.

In the traditional kingdoms of Africa, with their royal courts and clearly marked differences in wealth, power, and leisure, court poetry flourished. Poets were attached to the courts of powerful kings, to the retinues of nobles or lesser chiefs, and to all those who had pretensions to honour and thus to poetic celebration in their society. The speciality of these court poets was, of course, panegyric, a form illustrated in the following chapter. One can cite the elaborate praise poems of the Zulu or Sotho in southern Africa, the poems of the official singers of the ruler of Bornu, the royal praises of the Hausa emirs, the eulogies addressed to rulers in the various kingdoms of the Congo, and many others. In all these areas the ruling monarchs and their ancestors were glorified in poems, and real and ideal deeds were attributed to them in lofty and effusive language. The court poets sometimes had other functions too. Preservation of the historical record and of genealogies, for example, was often a part of their art, and it is sometimes suggested that this was at times a distinctive activity carried on in its own right. But in spite of repeated assertions about this,[1] there are few details about the actual performance or expression of historical poetry as distinct from panegyric, and we have to content ourselves with vague generalizations.[2] It is clear, at least, that a knowledge of accepted history in the sense of the glorification of the great deeds of royal ancestors or present rulers was a necessary part of the cultivation of panegyric poetry, and that praise poems are a fruitful source of the currently authorized interpretations of certain historical events and genealogies. What we always come back to in the productions of these court poets is the adulatory aspect, giving rise to poetry of profound political significance as a means of political propaganda, pressure, or communication.

The actual position and duties of these court poets vary in different areas. In some cases a poet holds a single clearly recognized office among a ruler's entourage. This was so with the Zulu and other Bantu kingdoms of southern Africa where not only the paramount king but also every chief with any pretensions to political power had, wherever possible, his own *imbongi* or praiser.

[1] e.g. on the Yoruba (S. Johnson, *The History of the Yorubas*, London, 1921, p. 125), Fon (Herskovits 1958, pp. 20–1), and the general comments in *Notes and Queries on Anthropology*, London, 6th ed., 1951, p. 204, and Vansina 1965, pp. 148–9.

[2] On the question of 'epic' and historical poetry generally see Note on pp. 108 ff.

This was an official position at the court, important enough to the rulers to have survived even the eclipse of much of their earlier power. The *imbongi*'s profession was to record the praise names, the victories, and the glorious qualities of the chief and his ancestors, and to recite these in lengthy high-sounding verse on occasions which seemed to call for public adulation of the ruler. The poet had two duties: to remember and to express the appropriate eulogies. Though these praises tended to have a set and recognized form (particularly those of dead rulers), the poet's task did not consist of mere memorizing. The praises had no absolute verbal immutability, and emotional and dramatic force in actual recitation was expected of a successful *imbongi*. The lofty strain of these Zulu eulogies and the impressiveness of their delivery can be pictured from a few lines taken from the praises of a Zulu king; they glorify the swiftness and completeness of his victory over the foe:

> Faster-than-the-sun-before-it-has-risen!
> When it rose the blood of men had already been shed.
> The Bush, 'the Buck-catcher', caught the men of Sekwayo's.
> He made men swim who had forgotten how,
> Yes! even in the pools! . . .
> The tobacco fields rotted even to pulp!
> The wrapping-mats were finished at Banganomo;
> At (the kraal) of Kuvukuneni,
> At that at Mdiweni, even Vimbemsheni's,
> At that at Bukledeni,
> At that at Panyekweni.[1]

In many West African kingdoms the pattern is more complicated. A whole band of poets is often involved, the various members making their own specialist contributions to the performance. Musical as well as verbal elements play a part, so that the skills of many different performers are necessary. Among the Ashanti, for instance, there were not only minstrels (*kwadwumfo*) to recount the deeds of past kings whenever the living king appeared in public, but also royal horn-blowers and a band of court drummers specially appointed as part of the ruler's formal entourage and over whose performances he held a kind of monopoly. On state occasions these drummers provided both music and the type of 'drum poems' described in a later chapter—the drum-beats or notes

[1] Grant 1927, p. 227.

of the horn being heard as actual words, praising the ruler and his predecessors and commemorating the glorious victories of the past. Such performances were an essential part of state occasions: at state receptions at the palace or out of doors; in processions to display the regalia or visit some sacred spot; and at national festivals, state funerals, and political functions like the installations of new chiefs or the swearing of oaths of allegiance by subchiefs.[1] Again, in the old and powerful kingdom of Dahomey there was not just one but a series of royal orchestras charged with praising the power of the royal dynasty, the high deeds of past kings, and the glory of the present ruler. Every morning in Abomey concerts were held by the main state orchestra before the royal palace, and when the king went out it accompanied him to sing his praises.[2] A final well-known West African example is that of the *maroka* teams of praisers still associated with the wealthy and cultivated Islamic emirates of the Hausa of Northern Nigeria. These highly specialized teams are attached permanently to the office of the king, and, to a lesser extent, to that of District Heads. Smith describes the king's team:

The king's musicians and *maroka* form an organized group containing one or more titular series and effective authority hierarchies. The group is both more numerous and specialized in its musical functions, and more permanently attached to the title, than are the teams linked to District headships, which are similarly organized. Many of the royal *maroka* proudly describe themselves as royal slaves, and point to the fact that their ancestors held titles as royal musicians under earlier kings. It seems that there is at least a core of such *maroka* hereditarily attached to the throne. The king's musical troupe is also peculiar in containing one *marokiya* (female praiser), who formerly had the title of *Boroka* in Zaria, but is nowadays known as *Zabiya* (the guinea-hen) from the shrill ululating sound which it is her function to let out at odd moments, such as during the king's address to his assembled subjects after *Sallah*. Other specialized musical functions in the royal troupe include blowing on the long silver horns or shorter wooden ones, playing on the *taushe* (a small hemispherical drum), and singing the royal praises in Fulani, the last being the task of *maroka* recruited from among the Bombadawa Fulani. Royal *maroka* are in constant attendance at the palace, and

---

[1] Nketia 1963*b*, ch. 10; cf. E. L. R. Meyerowitz, *Akan Traditions of Origin*, London, 1952, pp. 19–20. Similar musical groups are found in the retinues of other Ghanaian chiefs (e.g. Ga, Adangme, or Ewe), charged with the duty of performing praise chants as well as processional and dancing music (Nketia 1962, pp. 18–19). [2] Da Cruz 1954, p. 12, ch. 3.

announce the arrival of distinguished visitors such as the Resident, Divisional Officer, District Chiefs, and the like, by trumpet fanfares, drumming, and shouting. They also salute the king on the Sabbath eve and nightly during the annual fast of *Ramadan*, when the royal drums (*tambari*) are regularly played. The king's *maroka* address no one except their master, unless to herald visitors into his presence. They are allocated compounds, farm-lands, and titles by the king, who may also give them horses and frequently provides them with clothes, money, or assistance at weddings as well as with food. . . . As befits their position, the royal *maroka* are unique within the state and work only as a team.[1]

In spite of differences in status and medium of expression, there are obvious similarities in the positions of all these court poets. They all depended on royal or chiefly patronage, given them in an official capacity and often implying exclusive rights over their services. Their performances were public with the emphasis, it appears, on their ceremonial functions rather than their entertainment value. And their audiences were primarily those who attended either the royal court or state occasions in the royal capital. To some extent this type of poetry must also have filtered down to other levels of society, with every local chief and leader attempting to follow the model of the ruler. But it seems that it was at the centre that court poetry and music were cultivated in their most specialized and exclusive form.

Many of these court poets seem to have been true professionals in the sense that they gained their livelihood from their art. Their official position at court presumably gave them a share in the greater luxury and leisure of court life, though the degree must have varied from area to area—more marked, say, in the wealthy and specialized Hausa emirates than in the kingdoms of southern Africa. However, the exact economic position of court poets is obscure. There is little detailed evidence about, for instance, the relative wealth of specialized poet and ordinary subject, or how

[1] Smith 1957, p. 31. Nothing has been said about the Interlacustrine Bantu kingdoms of East Africa: there is in fact surprisingly little evidence about any formal office of court poet(s) there, though the Chadwicks report a personal communication by Roscoe about a chief at the Ganda royal court responsible for the recitation in poetical form of royal genealogies (Chadwicks iii, 1940, p. 576; cf. also J. Roscoe, *The Baganda*, London, 1911, p. 35). It is possible that some of the functions of court poets, such as adding pomp and ceremony to the king's public appearances, were in East Africa fulfilled by musical performances with less stress on the verbal element, e.g. by the Ganda royal drummers described in Roscoe, op. cit., pp. 25 ff., etc.

far court poets could count on steady economic support as distinct from occasional lavish gifts. The whole subject merits further investigation.

The question of specialized training is also not very clear. That apprenticeship in some sense was involved is obvious, but this was probably sometimes of an informal kind, perhaps particularly when, as with the Hausa or the Yoruba, there was some hereditary tendency. In the case of highly specialized skills, however, there must also be a certain amount of quite formal training. This is so with Ashanti players of the speaking drums,[1] for instance, the Fang *mvet* singers,[2] or the highly specialized bards of Ruanda.

It is worth considering the Rwanda school of poetry and its complex corporation of poets in some detail. They are among the few official poets of Africa whose life and learning have been described at all fully and they provide a striking instance of the specialized and learned artistic tradition which can develop in a once-termed 'simple' society.[3]

In the highly centralized traditional kingdom of Ruanda, the royal poets had their own association and were officially recognized as holding a privileged position within the state. They were in charge of the delivery and preservation of the dynastic poems whose main object was to exalt the king and other members of the royal line. This was only one branch among the three main types of Rwanda poetry (dynastic, military, and pastoral) which corresponded to the three pivots of their society (king, warrior, and cattle). It was in turn divided into three sub-types, different genres through which the king's praises could be declaimed.

A court poet was known as *umúsízí w'Umwâmi* (dynastic poet of the king). This category included a number of poets, both those with the inspiration and skill to compose original works, and those (the bards) who confined themselves to learning and reciting the compositions of others. The court poets have always had their own association—the *Umútwé w'Ábásizi*, 'band of dynastic poets' —comprising those families officially recognized as poetic. The office of president of this band, the *Intébé y'Ábásizi*, was previously restricted to a member of the clan that was first traditionally associated with the profession of poet. More recently the president has been the most conspicuous of the royal poets, a role that has

---

[1] Nketia 1963*b*, pp. 156–7.     [2] Towo-Atangana 1965, p. 172.
[3] The account here is based mainly on Kagama 1951*b*, esp. pp. 22 ff.

tended over the last few generations to become a hereditary one. The president had the responsibility of organizing the poetry officially needed by the royal court for any particular occasion, including both ceremonial affairs and discussions on points of tradition. This he was in a position to do because of the attachment of a number of official poets to the court. Each of the recognized families of the poetic association had to be permanently represented there, if not by a creative poet, at least by a bard capable of reciting the poems particularly known by that group. In the reign of Yuhi V Musînga, for example, there were nine royal poets holding such official positions, each on duty for a month. In addition there were a number of unofficial bards, also members of poetic families, who gathered in large numbers around the court and could be called on if necessary.

Both the poets themselves and the recognized poetic families had a privileged position in Rwanda society. They held hereditary rights like exemption from the jurisdiction of the civil chiefs and from certain servile duties. This applied even to ordinary bards and individual amateurs—so long as they were able to recite certain poems by heart, they were automatically regarded as direct servants of the crown. The exact economic position of the official court poets is not fully described; but the presentation of a poem to the king normally earned the gift of a cow—perhaps more—and in a society in which economic, social, even political worth was measured in terms of cattle, this was no mean reward.

The poems themselves were exceedingly elaborate and sophisticated, with a specialized mode of expression mastered only by the corporation of poets and the intelligentsia of the society. The style was full of archaisms, obscure language, and highly figurative forms of expression.[1] The sort of sentiments and phraseology involved, elevating the king as the centre and ideal of Rwanda society, can be glimpsed from a few lines extracted from a long dynastic praise poem of the *impakanizi* genre:

> Il me vient à l'esprit une autre parole du Roi,
> Lui Source intarissable, fils de la Souveraine,
> Je me suis rappelé que ce Refuge devait introniser un Roi,
> Lequel deviendrait l'objet de mes hommages dès qu'investi.

[1] Cf. Kagame 1951b, pp. 14 ff. on the three main types of figurative language which he designates, respectively, as *synonymique, homonymique,* and *métonymique.*

Il n'y a pas d'époque où le Rwănda n'éprouve des perplexités,
O Artisan-des-lances, souche du Chef des Armées:
Personne ne jugera à l'encontre de ta décision.
En ce jour-là des préparatifs minutieux,
O Empoigneur-d'arc, descendance du Svelte,
Ta marche a brûlé les étapes accoutumées.
Un conflit armé dans le palais même s'était déclanché,
L'Irréprochable seul luttant en personne,
Nous, hommes, la terre faillit nous engloutir vivants. . . .[1]

The poems are clearly the conscious product of a learned and specialist intellectual tradition.

The skilled and separate nature of this poetry is further evident from the existence of specialist training, particularly in the skill of recitation. Among the Rwanda, somewhat unusually, part of the production of their oral literature was through memorization of received versions of the poems, and the attribution of personal authorship was the rule rather than the exception. The praise poems were often repeated by bards with little change from one occasion to the next, and there seems to have been a conscious effort to preserve the exact words of the text. From an early age, children of the recognized poetic families had to learn poems by heart. Though this took place within the family, at first at least, it was under the general supervision of the president of the association of poets who was ultimately responsible. Local representatives of the president called frequent gatherings in the open air at which the youths of the privileged poets' families exhibited their art in recitation. Those who showed themselves to good advantage were given a reward by their family, perhaps even a cow as 'récompense de félicitation'. In this way future court poets and reciters underwent a long and rigorous apprenticeship, one necessary both for the mastery of the actual poems already extant and for acquiring the vocabulary, imagery, and subject-matter which formed the traditional basis of any future composition.

In Ruanda then we see the development of a strikingly specialized class of court poetry, one designed not for everyday recitation to the people at large, but for performance among other members of this specialist group, and, above all, for the king himself. The royal court was the centre of patronage—in fact in most important genres of Rwanda poetry the court held a near

---

[1] Ibid., pp. 117–18.

monopoly—and the Rwanda assumed it to be basic to the production of specialist poetry, being both its central stimulus and its most valued context.

Clearly not all African court poetry took so highly specialized and restricted a form. But it can serve as an extreme instance of one important type of patronage for the poet in traditional Africa. It must be added, however, that this particular patronage—the royal court—is in many areas increasingly a thing of the past. This is not because of any decline of interest in poetry or in praise, for both continue to flourish in different contexts and with new patrons. Praise poems crop up as flattery of political leaders or party candidates, and can be heard on the radio or at political meetings; they can be seen in written form in newspapers; and they even appear under the auspices of commercial recording companies. But often the older royal courts with their official retinues and monopoly of the most highly professionalized poetry have become less attractive as political and economic centres, and many of the traditional court poets have either abandoned their art or turned to other more lucrative patrons.

II

Unlike court patronage, religious patronage in Africa is relatively limited. Islam, it is true, has in certain areas played a potent role in the stimulation of verse on religious and historical topics. But this has not been through the direct patronage of an organized church so much as through the historical association of Islam with Arabic culture in general, so that Islamic scholars were also sometimes engaged in the transmission within their own societies of local compositions based on Arabic models.[1] These were primarily designed for the academic few, qualified by learning to produce or appreciate such pieces, and were often written down, though wider dissemination in other spheres of society sometimes took place orally. Among such peoples as the Swahili, Fulani, or Hausa it appears that such composers held honoured positions (and presumably also economic resources) primarily because of their Koranic learning, their association with royal courts, or, in some cases their noble birth.[2]

[1] For further comments on Islamic religious poetry see below, Ch. 7, pp. 168–57.

[2] e.g. the Cameroons Fulani *modibbo*, who was at once an official writer, a narrator, and a court poet (Mohamadou 1963, p. 68).

Ethiopia is one important exception. Here there is a long history of patronage of the arts by the Coptic Christian Church. This includes a vast amount of literature which, being in every sense a written one, falls outside the scope of this book. There was also, however, a certain amount of oral ecclesiastical poetry by the *dabteras* or professional religious poets. Besides long written poems their work also included oral compositions like extemporized hymns at church festivals and similar occasions. Their most famous product was the *qene*, a short witty poem, highly artificial, of which there were said to be at least ten different types. These were marked by great obscurity of style, extreme condensation, delight in the use of puns, and an abundance of metaphors and religious allusions. In keeping with their highly specialized nature the *qene* demanded prolonged intellectual training for their mastery, and we hear of schools of rhetoric designed to train poets in the art of *qene* composition. We may also suppose that their audiences were correspondingly restricted. Indeed it seems to be the other important class of professional Ethiopian poets, the non-religious *azmaris*, who were found among all classes of society and thus reached wider audiences,[1] while the *dabteras* preserved their specialist and intellectual type of versification.

More recently, Christian missions have made their contribution to the encouragement of oral literature. As yet, this seems mainly to be of the more or less extempore type—a worshipper declaiming or leading the singing in the course of a service—and has probably not produced any highly specialized poets.[2] But much more may yet come of this type of religious patronage, and it is possible that this might be one of the growing points in the further development of oral literature in Africa.[3]

Apart from the patronage of these larger religious movements, we also find poetry evoked by more localized cults. This is particularly marked in the non-Islamic parts of West Africa where there are specialized cults to the deities of the various West African pantheons. Priests of some of the gods among, say, the Yoruba of Nigeria or Fon of Dahomey seem to be fully professional, and

---

[1] Chadwicks iii, 1940, pp. 524 ff.

[2] Or so it seems from the sources. But much more investigation needs to be made of the role of the local preacher in this respect (and of course in the sphere of oratory many of these preachers make their own contributions to oral art week after week).

[3] Cf. Ch. 7, pp. 184 ff.

sometimes to have undergone many years of training. This is true in particular of the priests of Ifa (described in Chapter 7) who spend at least three years as apprentices learning the lengthy verses and stories pertaining to this oracle-god. The gods each have their own lengthy and allusive praises which must be mastered by their priests, who are, it seems, responsible for both their recitation and, ultimately, their composition. Such professional priests receive direct or indirect recompense in virtue of their religious office and in this way have a certain amount of leisure to devote to the practice of poetry. However, fully professional priests are by no means the rule in these societies; they seem to be more typical of the highly organized and wealthy kingdoms, like those of the Akan, Fon, or Yoruba. But even in these areas priests are often only part-time experts who also rely on other means of subsistence. Their relationship to their public is more like that discussed in section IV below: they are experts who only appear on particular occasions when they display their art in return for direct reward.

In spite of some exceptions, one cannot really speak of religion as having the same outstanding connection with the arts in Africa as it has sometimes held elsewhere. In terms of specialization of the poet's role or of the complexity of the verse itself, it does not seem to be anything like as important as royal and courtly patronage. The interpretation of poetry which connects it directly with the religious role of the seer[1] would not, therefore, in its obvious sense at least, derive much support from the data on oral literature in Africa.

### III

Another large category among oral poets in Africa is that of the free-lance specialist, a poet who moves from place to place according to where he can find a wealthy patron or audience prepared to reward him in return for his poems. This type of poet may shade into the official court poet, but even if he spends a certain amount of time at the courts he does not hold an official and exclusive position. He relies on occasional rather than permanent employment. Such independent professional poets are particularly common in West Africa, the coastal areas of East Africa, and Ethiopia,

[1] As in N. K. Chadwick, *Poetry and Prophecy*, Cambridge, 1942.

where both the degree of specialization and the existence of relatively large quantities of movable wealth from which poets can
be subsidized make it feasible for them to gain a livelihood in this
manner. The existence of court poets may actually facilitate the
development of this type of free-lance professional tradition. Court
poetry is what local chieflets or wealthy commoners would like to
hear declaimed around them; and many of these wandering singers
and poets have found lucrative patrons in men who wish to hear
addressed to themselves some semblance of the praises ultimately
due to the rulers. It is not surprising then to find frequent instances of the coexistence in one society of both official poets at
court and roving poets in other spheres of the kingdom. This is
true, for instance, of the Hausa roaming singers, the counterparts
of the royal praise bands already mentioned. Among the Nzakara
of the Sudan the trained professional poet, a singer accompanying
his words on the harp, gains his livelihood either at the court of
a prince or, alternatively, by moving from village to village, ready
to vilify a chief who does not entertain him up to the standard of
his expectations, or singing the glorious ancestry of one who does.[1]
Such singers can exploit the hierarchy of political power without
an official permanent attachment to any one individual.

For these unattached poets, generosity and economic resources
are as great an attraction as the political power connected with state
office. Thus where there is a distinction between the distribution
of wealth and that of aristocratic political power, the former may
be a particular focus for poetic activity. We hear, for instance, of the
wealthy but low-born Hausa man who is a prey to poets who sing
of his high descent—or at least significantly omit any oblique suggestion of commoner birth[2]—in return for large rewards. Poets
naturally turn to the patronage of well-off men. In Pemba, an
area in which the development of verse is probably unequalled
along the whole of the East African coast, there have until recently
been large numbers of poets, each with his band of pupils, esteemed
and patronized by the wealthy Arab landowners. These poets
lived in or around the main centres or by the clove plantations and
delighted their patrons with poems expressed in the traditional
mainland forms on subjects inspired by local events.[3] Nowadays
another lucrative source can be found in commercial concerns—

[1] de Dampierre 1963, p. 17.  [2] Smith 1957, p. 31.
[3] Whiteley 1958.

record companies and broadcasting in particular—and in some areas these are now becoming a potent if erratic source of patronage to the free-lance poets.

The poet's reliance on their art and their wits for a livelihood also affects the subject-matter of their compositions. Overt begging, innuendo, and even threats towards individual patrons are much more marked a feature of this poetry than in the praises and occasional verse associated with state ceremonials, the normal context of the official court poetry. The element of entertainment rather than formal pomp is perhaps also more to the fore. Whatever their individual media, at any rate, it is certain that some of these poets have been able to amass large fortunes and have sometimes gained the general reputation of being avaricious and mercenary.[1] Unlike court poets, their performances are not at the service of one exclusive patron, and they can move on (or threaten to move on) to another patron who is prepared to give them a better price.

It is not surprising that these poets have sometimes been the object of fear and suspicion as well as of admiration, and the reward given to a poet by his temporary patron may seem to be more like a buying off than any positive appreciation of his talents. This comes out very clearly in, for instance, Smith's description of the arts of the roving solo singer among the Hausa.[2] The singer arrives at a village and finds out the names of the important and wealthy individuals in the area. Then he takes up his stand in public and calls out the name of the individual he has decided to apostrophize. He proceeds to his praise songs, punctuated by frequent and increasingly direct demands for gifts. If they are forthcoming in sufficient quantity he announces the amount and sings his thanks in further praise. If not, his innuendo becomes gradually sharper, his delivery harsher and more staccato. This is practically always effective—all the more so as the experienced singer knows the utility of choosing a time when all the local people are likely to be within hearing, in the evening, the early morning before they have left for the farm, or on the occasion of a market which leaves no escape for the unfortunate object singled out for these 'praises'. The result of this public scorn is normally the victim's surrender. He attempts to silence the singer with gifts of money or, if he has

---

[1] e.g. among the Khassonke (C. Monteil, *Les Khassonké*, Paris, 1915, p. 137) and Wolof (D. P. Gamble, *The Wolof of Senegambia*, London, 1957, p. 45).

[2] Smith 1957, p. 38.

no ready cash, with clothes or a saleable object like a new hoe. Similar types of pressure are used by groups of Hausa praise singers in the towns. Here they mainly address themselves to the *nouveaux riches*, relatively wealthy men like builders, commission agents, and the larger farmers. People with officially recognized high status through noble birth, religious position, or high government employment are not attacked in this way, but people from other areas or local people of low birth are picked on even if they are in government pay. Again the declamation begins as praise, but failure to pay soon leads to a hostile tone. Instead of laudatory remarks about his ancestry, prosperity, and political influence, the victim soon hears innuendo on all these themes, as well as derogatory references to his occupation, reputation, political integrity—and, of course, his meanness. There is never open mention of 'the ultimate insult—imputation of ambiguous paternity', but this lies behind the increasing pressures on the man addressed.[1] In view of the effectiveness of this type of poetic pressure—the extraction of money by virtual blackmail—it is small wonder that attempts have been made in some Hausa kingdoms recently to forbid or limit the activities of these singers.[2]

Though there are few other such detailed accounts of the pressures of professional poets, it is clear that this pattern is not uncommon in West Africa. Similar powers have been exercised by the well-known Mande musicians, for instance, or the Senegalese 'griots'. The forceful way in which their counterparts in some of the more southerly areas too can sing *at* a chosen patron has to be seen to be believed. The praisers direct their verses and their music with such vehemence and volume that until they are placated with a gift or by the intervention of some recognized authority, no business can go forward.

From one point of view the power of free-lance poets can be increased if they are regarded as foreign or at any rate set apart from the patrons to whom they address themselves. This can add to the fearsome quality of their words while at the same time making them free from the obligations which are binding on other members of the society. We find that this is the case with some

[1] Ibid., p. 39.
[2] Ibid., p. 38. That all free-lance poets are not equally conventional, however, is apparent from Gidley's account of Hausa comedians who satirize and parody the usual praise songs (Gidley 1967, esp. pp. 64–9).

free-lance poets in the further western area of West Africa. The Mande-speaking musicians sometimes known in West African English as 'jellemen' (from Mandingo *dyalo*) are found (sometimes as professional, sometimes as part-time experts) throughout a wide area of the country outside their original home area. Throughout this region they exploit their abilities and extract rewards for their songs from wealthy and powerful families.[1]

An even more striking example are the 'griots' of Senegambia, poets belonging to a special low caste in the society. In view of the wide currency of this word in both French and English, it is worth saying a little more about the particular poets to whom it refers. In fact the term 'griot' gives a totally false impression of precision. Though it was presumably originally a translation of the Fulani *gaoulo* (wandering poet or praiser) or Wolof *gewɛl* (poet and musician), it is now popularly used as a term to refer to almost any kind of poet or musician throughout at least the French-speaking areas of West Africa.[2] In the process it has acquired a kind of quasi-technical ring which, it seems, is felt to absolve those using it from any further detailed description of the status of these artists. But clearly not all poets throughout this wide area answer to the more precise description of the term: they do not all belong to special castes and are not necessarily regarded as of inferior status.[3]

Those that concern us here, the poets of Senegambia and of the Western Fulani, were so regarded, however. Among the various castes into which society was divided, those of the poets and musicians came near the bottom. They were thus set apart from

[1] Cf. Zemp 1964. I came across a number of these musicians in northern Sierra Leone in 1961 plying their trade in the non-Mandingo communities of the country, as did Laing over a century earlier (A. G. Laing, *Travels in the Timannee, Kooranko and Soolima Countries*, London, 1825, pp. 132–3).

[2] It has also been suggested that the term is connected with the Arabic *oawwal* (narrator of the Soufi sect) (by D. S. Blair in B. Diop, *Tales of Amadou Koumba* (Eng. tr.), London, 1966, p. xix). It apparently first entered French through the early French travellers to Senegal in the eighteenth century (see Zemp 1964, p. 375), and, as is well known, has since been taken up by the *Négritude* French literary movement. But a full study of the history and usage of this word in European languages, let alone its referents in West Africa, seems never to have been made (though see the discussion in Colin 1957, ch. 3; Rouget n.d., pp. 225–7) and should be well worth pursuing.

[3] In particular this seems not to apply to the authors of Muslim poetry, who, among some of the Fulani at least, tend to be of noble birth (Ba 1950, pp. 173–4; Lacroix i, 1965, pp. 31, 35–6). See also Belinga 1965, pp. 116 ff. on the *mbôm-mvet* of Cameroun.

those to whom they addressed themselves and not unexpectedly
met with a somewhat ambiguous attitude among other members
of society—at once feared, despised, and influential. Some of
these Senegambian griots specialized in shouting praises and reciting genealogies and had some kind of attachment to the various
freeborn lineages; others sang praises of chiefs and leading men
at public functions and could gain great influence with local rulers.
Traditionally a Wolof *gewel* had the power to insult anyone and,
as in other areas, could switch to outspoken abuse if no sufficient
reward was forthcoming. Their membership of the special poetic
caste gave them impunity, so that together with their low status
they at the same time had freedom from the sanctions that deterred
other members of society from open insult of their fellows. Here
too some legal attempts have been made to limit their power, and
it is significant that as the old caste system breaks down, thus in a
sense raising the low status of the poet, this brings with it a decrease in his previous power to mock with impunity.[1]

The free-lance professionals clearly have more scope than the
court poets, who are exclusively employed, as it were, by the state.
The poet can, indeed must, think about himself as well as his
patron; he can more easily vary conventional styles and motifs
than his official counterpart. There is no premium on verbal
accuracy or even near accuracy as in the case of some of the
politically sanctioned court poetry, and there is not the distinction
between reciter and composer that was just discernible in some of
the court poetry discussed. The audiences, too, tend to be wider,
and there is a corresponding lack of a highly specialized or esoteric
style. The public is still chosen from among the wealth and
powerful, but depends more on entertainment and on communication and less on formal pomp.

It is through poets like these that the poetry of a certain culture
can become diffused over a wide area, even one covering different
sub-cultures and languages. For instance, one of the characteristic
results of the professional free-lance poets (*azmaris*) in Ethiopia

---

[1] For some further details of this rather complex organization in Senegambia
see Gamble, op. cit., esp. p. 45; O. Silla, 'Persistance des castes dans la société
wolof contemporaine', *Bull. IFAN* (B) 28, 1966, esp. pp. 764–7; in Haut-
Sénégal and Niger, M. Delafosse, *Haut-Sénégal-Niger*, Paris, 1912, vol. iii,
pp. 117–18; for the Toucouleur of Senegal, A. B. Diop, *Société toucouleur et
migration*, Dakar, 1965, pp. 23 ff. A useful bibliography is given in H. Zemp,
'La légende des griots malinké', *Cah. étud. afr.* 24, 1966.

was that poets were found everywhere, from the courts to the poorer houses, to the roads, or to public gatherings, commenting on their audiences or on local events, a kind of *gazette chantante* in their reflection of contemporary public opinion. Their persons were sacrosanct and they were received honourably everywhere. In the opinion of the Chadwicks it was this which to a large extent led to the uniformity of Ethiopian poetry.[1] The same general point holds good for certain areas of West Africa. In parts of Senegambia, Guinea, and Sierra Leone, the cultural uniformities stretching over a wide area of differing societies and languages can be put down in part to the long history of wandering poets who could apparently travel unmolested even in wartime.[2] Such poets give an international as well as a national currency to the conventions of their poetry in a way that formally appointed court poets or localized experts could never have done.

### IV

So far we have been dealing with professionals or semi-professionals, those who are known first and foremost as poets and who depend primarily on their art. But there are also many less specialized poets to consider. These practitioners are sometimes found coexisting with their more professional colleagues, but they also sometimes appear as the most skilled proponents of the poetic art in cultures which, as in many of the traditionally uncentralized societies of Africa, do not possess full-time literary specialists. At these less professional levels women are often mentioned. Certain kinds of poetry are typically delivered or sung by women (particularly dirges, lullabies, mocking verses, and songs to accompany women's ceremonies or work), and each culture is likely to have certain genres considered specially suitable for women.[3] However, references to men seem to occur even more often and, with a few striking exceptions,[4] men rather than women tend to be the bearers of the poetic tradition.

[1] Chadwicks iii, 1940, p. 525.

[2] See S. H. Walker, *Mission in Western Africa*, Dublin, 1845, p. 14.

[3] e.g. the Fon wives' choruses praising chiefs (M. J. Herskovits, *Dahomey*, New York, 1938, vol. ii, p. 322), the Hottentot sarcastic 'reed songs' (T. Hahn, *Tsuni-‖Goam, the Supreme Being of the Khoi-Khoi*, London, 1881, p. 28), Somali *buraambur* (Andrzejewski and Lewis 1964, p. 49), or certain named dancing songs at Limba memorial ceremonies.

[4] Notably the Tuareg (see Chadwicks iii, 1940, pp. 658 ff.).

Very often these poets earn their living in some other way, supplementing their incomes by their art. At times the poet's main reward may be in terms of honour rather than of more tangible goods, but usually some material return is forthcoming from his audience or temporary patron. These poets are often not equally expert in the whole field of oral art. Usually a poet becomes known for his exposition of a single genre of sung or spoken verse, one perhaps associated with a particular occasion when the poet-singer comes forward from the mass of his fellows to exhibit his art.

Within this general category there are naturally many different degrees of expertise. Some poets hold a relatively specialized status, differing only in degree from that of the professionals discussed earlier. This seems to be true of some of the West African poets usually lumped together under the general name of 'griot',[1] or the non-professional poets of the Somali who build up an entourage of admirers in competition with others and hear their poems transmitted further by reciters who learn them by heart.[2] It is also true, although to a lesser degree, of the Luo *nyatiti* (lyre) player who generally acts as an entertainer in this uncentralized society of East Africa. As we have some detailed evidence[3] about these particular singers, it is worth giving a fairly full description to illustrate the kind of part the poet may play in such a society.

The great forte of the Luo *nyatiti* singer is the lament song. Funerals are celebrated on a grand scale and one essential part is the songs of the *nyatiti* player. He needs no special invitation for he is always welcome once the noise and bustle of the actual burial have subsided. From the singer's point of view there are various reasons why he puts in an appearance: he may come from sorrow at the loss of a friend or relative; to do his duty to a neighbour; to take advantage of the food and drink profusely available at funerals; and finally—a not insignificant motive—to make money from a large and admiring audience (here he may have to contend with a rival). He takes up his stance, singing at the top of his voice to the accompaniment of his lyre and the rattling of his ankle-bells. He sweats profusely with the effort, and consumes vast quantities of beer. Before him lies a plate into which those who accost him can drop their pennies. He is frequently called on to sing about the dead person, and, in preparation for this, he has

[1] e.g. some of the Ivory Coast singers mentioned in Zemp 1964.
[2] Andrzejewski and Lewis 1964, pp. 4, 44–6.     [3] Anyumba 1964.

a tune ready from his normal repertoire which can be modified to suit the occasion. He adds 'an uncle here and a grandfather there, together with any knowledge he may possess of the attributes of the deceased. . . . The skill and beauty with which the musician is able to improvise at such moments is a measure of his musical and poetic stature.'[1]

These songs, involving the arts both of composition and of performance, are in fact usually soon forgotten after serving the purpose of the moment. Others, however, arise from more studied composition in preparation for the funeral. This is usually when the singer himself is deeply moved by the death or has some specially close link with the deceased. Here he creates a new song. He must consider and weigh up both the suitable melodic patterns and also the words and names to go with them. The process takes time and concentration, but the tune itself sometimes comes to the singer at an inspired moment. After some trials on his lyre, he then, on the actual occasion, sings with so much intensity and meaning that large gifts are showered on him. Indeed the song may gain such favour that he is begged to sing it later by his fans— and, after the due deposit of a few coins on his plate, he agrees. By then 'the song being freed from the solemnity of a funeral may rove from the fate of a particular individual to that of other people, and finally to the mystery of death itself'.[2]

If the *nyatiti* singer's prime function is that of the lament, his art also extends to other spheres and occasions. He is called on to praise friends or relatives, to recount his personal experiences, to exalt kindness, hospitality, or courage, and to comment on current affairs. In all these he is judged by the degree to which he can unite the art of the musician/performer and that of the poet/composer; he is 'judged as much by his skill on the instrument as by his ability to weave a story or meditate on human experience. In this lies the real fascination of the nyatiti player.'[3]

This account of the *nyatiti* singer illustrates the kind of role which the part-time poet/musician can play in a non-literate society. His art is practised partly to fulfil social obligations and to share in ceremonies which are also open to others, but also partly for direct material reward. Some of his performances arise out of the ceremonial occasion itself, with his audience directly involved in the occasion; but others, particularly those by the

[1] Anyumba 1964, pp. 189–90.  [2] Ibid., p. 190.  [3] Ibid., pp. 187–8.

most skilled singers, are specifically given at the request of admirers who patronize him and reward his performance. Finally, there are some occasions (and for some singers these may be in the majority) when the song produced is uninspired and stale, in spite of cleverly introduced modifications; while on other occasions the song is the product, and recognized as such, of the truly creative imagination of the singer.

The position of the poet in many other African societies is unfortunately not often described in even the detail given in Anyumba's short article.[1] But it seems that the position and conditions of many of the more expert (but non-professional) poets are not unlike those of the Luo *nyatiti* singer. We frequently meet the same kind of balance between the social and the profit motive, the more and the less specifically 'artistic' occasion, the greater and lesser personal inspiration of the poet.

Other African poets, however, have less general recognition than Luo singers. But there are still many specific occasions when they can exhibit their poetic skills. One frequent context is at meetings of the specialized associations characteristic of many parts of West Africa. The Yoruba, Akan, and others have hunters' societies each with their own special hunting songs. These are performed on festive occasions, at funerals of members of the group, and at other meetings of the association. The poets are there in their capacity as hunters, but one aspect of their craft, for some members at least, is skill in poetic composition and performance.[2] These very part-time poets, then, are patronized by fellow-hunters and also at times by the public at large, as when the Yoruba *ijala* poet is specially invited to perform as a general entertainer on non-hunting occasions. Similar connections between specialist association and a specific genre of poetry exist among the Akan military associations, cults of particular deities among the Yoruba and others, secret societies, local churches, and some of the more formally organized co-operative work groups. In all these cases the primary context is that of the association, and the poet is fulfilling his social obligations as a member (though he may acquire a material profit in addition); special performances to wider audiences or for more direct reward seem to be secondary and in many cases not to occur at all.

The various crucial points in the human life cycle also provide

[1] But see the excellent description of Yoruba *ijala* singers in Babalọla 1966, esp. ch. 4.    [2] For examples and further discussion see Ch. 8, pp. 224–6.

contexts for festivity and thus for artistic performance. Occasions such as initiations, weddings, or funerals provide fertile stimuli for poetic exhibition. Here again the range is wide—from occasions when those most intimately involved sing just as part of their general social obligations in the ceremony, to special appearances of famous artists or bands. Even within one society, different rituals may have different degrees of expertise considered appropriate to them. A good example of this can be seen in the contrast between the initiation ceremonies of boys and of girls among the Limba. An important part of the boys' ceremony consists of the all-night session during which the boys must demonstrate their skill and endurance in the dance before hundreds of interested spectators. A number of singer-drummers must be present. Therefore the best (part-time) artists in the boys' village or group of villages are called on to attend and are booked several weeks in advance. They receive numerous small monetary gifts during their performance, and the amount earned, when all the several contributions from the boys' relatives and the audience are counted up, may come to as much as a fifth or quarter of the average labourer's wage for a month. By contrast the girls' ceremony is a less celebrated affair. The singers are merely those who are in any case directly involved in the occasion, with no special reward due to them for their songs. Other Limba occasions provide yet another contrast. In their large-scale memorial rituals the most famous singers in the whole chiefdom area or beyond are begged to come to display their specialist art; they usually have no direct relationship to the principals in the ceremony—or if they have this is irrelevant—but take time off from their everyday pursuits to attend as specialists in return for the very large gifts their hosts undertake to provide.

In some areas weddings are occasions for much singing and dancing, sometimes by those directly involved, sometimes by specially invited expert teams. Thus Hausa weddings, elaborate and complex affairs, require the presence of specialist *maroka* teams. These are independent and unattached bands who gain their livelihood partly from their craft and partly from subsistence farming.[1] They attend weddings largely for profit, and they are the principal beneficiaries of the costly gifts that are made publicly on these occasions.

[1] Smith 1957, pp. 30–1, 32.

The kind of performance that can take place at funerals—another common context for poetry—has already been illustrated from the case of the Luo lament singer. A rather different type is provided by the Akan dirge singers. Every Akan woman is expected to have some competence in the dirge, and though some singers are considered more accomplished than others, nevertheless every woman mourner at a funeral is expected to sing—or run the risk of strong criticism, possibly even suspicion of complicity in the death.[1] Thus they perform as part of their general social responsibilities and their audiences hear and admire their performances as one aspect of the funeral rituals which they are attending, rather than as a specialist aesthetic occasion which demands direct recompense to the artist. Yet that even this relatively low degree of specialization can result in elaborate literary compositions, valued alike for their aesthetic merits and their social functions, should be clear from the detailed account of these dirges given by Nketia.[2]

Besides such occasional poetry at the crucial points in the life cycle, there are other contexts in which the element of entertainment is foremost. Sometimes these actually hinge on organized competitions by poets, as used to be the case in several areas of East Africa. In Tanganyika, for instance, two singers of the same type of song, each leading his own group of members, sometimes decide to compete on an agreed day. In the interval they teach their followers new songs of their own composition. Then on the day the two groups sing in turn at a little distance from each other. The victor is the singer who draws the greatest number of spectators to his side. Sometimes these competitions are arranged by the Sultan who also acts as umpire between the two insulting sides—for insults are also in order, and as each side has taken the trouble to find out their opponents' songs in advance, they have prepared suitably sarcastic replies to them.[3] In other types of entertainment, the element of competition is absent and the emphasis is on the skill and expertise with which the artists make their specialized contribution to the occasion. At social gatherings among the Ila and Tonga of Zambia, for instance, a woman who is skilled in the

[1] Nketia 1955, p. 18.  [2] Nketia 1955 (summarized in Ch. 6 below).
[3] Koritschoner 1937, pp. 57–9; see also the Pemba competitions mentioned in Whiteley 1958, and the rather different Somali use of poetic combat as a means of publicity in war and peace (B. W. Andrzejewski and M. H. I. Galaal, 'A Somali Poetic Combat', *J. Afr. Languages* 2, 1963).

special type of solo termed *impango* stands up and sings from her own personal repertoire. If she has close friends or relatives present, they too stand up to praise her song and present her with small gifts like tobacco or a sixpence.[1] Some of the West African entertainments draw on more complex teams, with singer, drummers, and sometimes wind-instruments—like the Hausa teams who sometimes play for the young peoples' recreational associations,[2] or the Akan popular bands who perform for pure entertainment, often for dancing in the evenings. Their purpose is social and recreational, but they make some economic profit from their performances.[3]

This discussion of the various occasions and forms of poetry finally brings us to the times when there is practically no degree of specialization at all. This is particularly true of certain general categories of song in any society—in work songs,[4] children's verse, lullabies, or the chorus parts of antiphonal songs. There are also the times when every member of a society (or every member who falls into a certain category) is expected to have some competence in certain types of verse. Sotho boys, for instance, were all required to demonstrate proficiency in praise poetry as part of their initiation ceremonies, and had to declaim the praises of their own achievements and expectations before the crowd gathered to welcome them after their seclusion;[5] while among some of the Zambian peoples a young man had to sing a song of his own composition on the occasion of his marriage.[6] Not all contexts are as formal as this. We hear of the Nuer youth leading his favourite ox round the kraal in the evenings, in pride and joy, leaping before it and singing its praises, or, again, of young Nuer or Dinka boys chanting their songs in the lonely pastures;[7] the lullabies which mothers in numberless societies sing to their babies; the spontaneous outburst of song over a pot of palm wine or millet beer in a Ghanaian village; the lyrics sung by Somali lorry drivers to shorten the tedium of their long journeys;[8] or the ability of the

---

[1] Jones 1943, p. 11.   [2] Smith 1957, p. 37.
[3] Nketia 1963*b*, ch. 6, p. 157.
[4] Though even there the common African practice of balancing soloist and chorus gives scope for a certain degree of expertise by the leader.
[5] Laydevant 1930, p. 524.
[6] A. M. Jones 1943, p. 11.
[7] E. E. Evans-Pritchard, *The Nuer*, Oxford, 1940, pp. 46 ff.; G. Lienhardt, *Divinity and Experience, the Religion of the Dinka*, Oxford, 1961, pp. 13, 18 f.
[8] Andrzejewski 1967, p. 12.

Congolese Mabale, or Rhodesian Shona, or West African Limba, or countless others to join in the choruses of songs led by their more expert fellows. In all these cases poetic facility has become no longer a specialist activity, but one which in some degree or other all individuals in the society are expected to have as a universal skill.

It would clearly be impossible to relate all the occasions and audiences that there are for poetry, or all the roles that can be played by the African poet. But enough has been said to show that it is not only in societies in which there is courtly, aristocratic, or religious patronage, or marked cleavages of wealth or power, that the poet finds opportunity to exercise his skills. There are many egalitarian societies too, often those with little specialism in any sphere of life, in which nevertheless poetry can flourish—like the Ibo, the Somali, the Nilotic peoples of the Sudan, and many others. It is true that it does seem to be in court poetry, and occasionally in religious poetry, that we find the highest degree of specialism, and the longest and, in a sense, most intellectual poems. But they do not necessarily reflect a more sensitive understanding of language and of experience than, say, a Dinka youth's praise of his ox, which to him represents both his own role and 'the whole world of beauty around him',[1] a lyric to accompany the dance, or the lullaby in which an Akan mother verbalizes her joy in her child in the world she knows:

Someone would like to have you for her child
But you are my own.
Someone wished she had you to nurse you on a good mat;
Someone wished you were hers: she would put you on a camel blanket;
But I have you to rear you on a torn mat.
Someone wished she had you, but I have you.[2]

## V

We have assumed that there is a conjunction, characteristic of oral poetry, between the performer and the composer. It is often futile, therefore, to ask about the circulation of a *particular* piece—for those who 'circulate' it are themselves poets of a kind and make their contributions and modifications. It may be that many of them are not particularly good or original poets even in terms of their

[1] Francis Deng in G. Lienhardt 1963, p. 828.    [2] Nketia 1958*b*, p. 18.

own culture, and make more of a contribution to the performance than to the composition. But the fact remains that this too is an essential part of the poetic skill of the oral practitioner, and that poems cannot reach their public without the interposition of such artists.

There are, however, a few exceptions to the joint role of the poet which should be mentioned in conclusion. In some of the most highly specialized or technically complex poetry—Rwanda dynastic poetry, Yoruba Ifa literature, or Somali *gabay*—reciters may be distinguished from creative poets: the former are responsible for transmitting the poems of others, and for preserving the authoritative tradition for political or religious motives. Thus even if in fact the reciter does modify a poem, this aspect is played down and the poem is supposed to be merely transmitted by reciters in the traditional form. Thus certain poems may circulate in their own right, sometimes even with named authors (as in Ruanda or Somaliland).

Another and very different class of poems where performance may be so much to the fore that the element of composition seems to vanish is that of dance songs, work songs, or songs accompanying children's games. Here the song is merely the background to some other activity, and repetition of known verses is more noticeable than poetic originality. Songs of this kind can become popular and spread over a wide area with incredible speed, to be supplanted after a time by new ones. Yet, as will appear in later chapters, even in these cases there can be modification and additions either in the musical aspects or in the words. Even if, for instance, the chorus remains more or less the same so that a superficial observer may be pardoned for considering it just another performance of the same old song, the soloist who leads the song and supplies the verses may in fact be making his own original musical and verbal contribution.

A more accurate case of the true circulation of a poem independently of its composer is to be found in the areas where the existence of writing has led to the concept of a *correct* version which, can be copied or learnt in an exact form. For indigenous African verse the writing is most often in Arabic script, and we find—as in Swahili, Hausa, or Fulani—a tradition both of the circulation of definitive versions of poems and of remembering the original authors by name. Such poems may also circulate by oral means, for actual literacy is often confined to the few, but they differ from fully oral compositions in that the roles of composer and reciter can be clearly distinguished.

In many cases it is difficult to assess how much emphasis should be laid on the two aspects of composition and of delivery. It is not easy to tell, for instance, how far the verse in any single instance is the product just of a performer reproducing well-known and prescribed forms with little contribution of his own, and how far it can also be put down to the arts of the creative poet; or how much one can attribute to the stimulation and participation of the audience or the emotion of the occasion itself. Many investigators have particularly emphasized the aspect of the second-hand reproducing of known traditional forms; and this interpretation has of course been especially popular with those very impressed by the concepts of communal creation or of the 'typical' poem and so on.

In African literature one can of course encounter both the second-rate technician and the inspired artist—oral art is no exception in this. But when the role of the poet or singer is analysed in some detail, we are left wondering whether creative composition (either the spontaneous creation of the accomplished and sensitive artist or conscious long-drawn-out composition in preparation for later display) may not be rather more important than is often realized; and we may suspect that the playing down of this factor may be due as much to lack of investigation as to any basis in the facts. Without Anyumba's analysis, for instance, we could hardly appreciate the care and conscious art with which some Luo singers sometimes compose their songs, and would be more likely, in a common search for 'the typical lament' of the Luo, to omit any consideration of the individuality of the inspired Luo poet. The actual circumstances of composition and the personality and skill of individual poets deserve fuller consideration than they have yet received.[1]

To others, as to me, this chapter must seem unbearably sketchy and impressionistic. A few of the points raised are explored a little further in later chapters which deal with some of the different genres of poetry and their exponents in various cultures. But the

---

[1] For some further remarks on composition see Ch. 9, pp. 266 ff. A partial exception, with the main emphasis on the musical aspect, is Nketia's *African Music in Ghana*, 1962. See also (besides references given earlier) Lacroix 1965 (on Adamawa Fulani), de Dampierre 1963 (Nzakara), Andrzejewski and Lewis 1964 (Somali), Babalǫla 1966 (Yoruba).

main reason for the gaps is ignorance, not lack of space. This must be in part because I have not read far enough in the sources to discover the answers to many of the questions I want to raise. But it is also that such factors as the general position of the poet, his poetic training, his economic situation, his relation to his audience, his patron, other poets, or the general culture of his time, his modes of composition and inspiration—all these have seemed to be of little interest to investigators, even those who have published excellent accounts of other aspects of oral literature. We know enough to be able to guess at the variety that can be found and that the simplicist pictures we opened with are not sufficient; but in practically no African society have these points been fully explored. This is the sphere above all in which there is the widest need and scope for further investigation.

## A NOTE ON 'EPIC'[1]

EPIC is often assumed to be the typical poetic form of non-literate peoples, or at least of non-literate peoples at a certain stage. Surprisingly, however, this does not seem to be borne out by the African evidence. At least in the more obvious sense of a 'relatively long narrative poem', epic hardly seems to occur in sub-Saharan Africa apart from forms like the (written) Swahili *utenzi* which are directly attributable to Arabic literary influence.

The term 'epic' appears in the titles of several collections or discussions of African oral literature[2] (perhaps partly because of the

---

[1] This is admittedly a large subject to discuss in such a note, but some brief apologia seemed due to explain the non-appearance of the term in a work of this kind. For a helpful introduction to this rather controversial subject see Knappert in Andrzejewski and Messenger 1967.

[2] e.g. D. A. Puplampu, 'The National Epic of the Adangme', *Afr. Affairs* 50, 1951; T. J. Larson, 'Epic Tales of the Mbukushu', *Afr. Studies* 22, 1963; J. Jacobs, 'Les épopées de Soundjata et de Chaka: une étude comparée', *Aequatoria* 25, 1962; D. Biebuyck and J. Jacobs, *Littérature épique d'Afrique noire*, Paris (forthcoming); H. Ba and L. Kesteloot, 'Les épopées de l'Ouest africain', *Abbia* 14/15, 1966 (also in *Présence afr.* 58, 1966); C. Meillassoux *et al.*, *Légende de la dispersion des Kusa* (*épopée Soninké*), *IFAN*, Dakar, 1967; D. T. Niane, *Soundjata ou l'épopée mardingue*, Paris, 1960; R. Cornevin, 'Les poèmes épiques africains et la notion d'épopée vivante', *Présence afr.* 60, 1966; M. Konate, 'Une épopée malienne: Da Monzon de Ségou', *Abbia*, 14/15, 1966; A. H. Ba and L. Kesteloot, 'Da Monzon et Karta Thiéma', *Abbia* 14/15, 1966; see also J. P. Clark, 'The Azudu Saga', *Afr. notes* 1. 1, 1963; T. Papadopoullos, *Poésie dynastique du Ruanda et épopée akritique*, Paris, 1963; J. de Vries, *Heroic*

common expectation that it is likely to be a wide-spread art form). But almost all these works in fact turn out to be in prose, not verse—and often only brief prose tales at that. There are only a very few in verse form.[1] Many of the lengthy praise poems, particularly those in South Africa, do contain some epic elements and provide the nearest common parallel to this form in Africa. Nevertheless, as will emerge in the following chapter, panegyric poetry concentrates far more on the laudatory and apostrophic side than on the narrative and cannot really qualify as 'epic' poetry in the normal sense of the word.

The most frequent mentions come from the equatorial areas of the Congo, particularly among the Mongo-Nkundo peoples where 'epics' have been referred to by many scholars.[2] But even these cases are somewhat doubtful. For one thing, many of these narratives seem quite clearly to be in prose merely interspersed with some sung pieces in the regular manner of African stories,[3] and there is no reason to believe that they differ radically in form from such prose tales.[4] And even if one waives the verse criterion, as is done in some definitions of epic, the Congo instances are still rather ambiguous. Take the most famous case of all, the 'Lianja epic'.[5] In its most fully published form it runs to about 120 pages of print for both text and translation—the sort of scale which might qualify—and covers the kinds of events we tend to associate with epic or heroic poetry: the birth and tribulations of the hero, his travels and leadership of his people, finally his death. But how far was this conceived of and narrated as a unity prior to its recording (and perhaps elaboration) in written form? It is not at all certain that the traditional pattern was not in fact a very loosely related bundle of separate episodes, told on separate occasions and not necessarily thought of as one single work of art (though recent and sophisticated narrators say that ideally it should be told at one sitting).[6] By now, of course, its circulation as a composite written narrative among sophisticated audiences has, in a

*Song and Heroic Legend* (Eng. tr.), London, 1963 (ch. 7, 'The Epic Poetry of Non-Indo-European Nations', pp. 159 ff., speaks of the 'epic poetry of the Fulbe', based on the (? prose) texts in Frobenius, *Atlantis* vi, 1921).

[1] See especially the discussion in Cornevin, op. cit., and the poems in Coupez and Kamanzi 1962.

[2] e.g. Boelaert, de Rop, Biebuyck, Jacobs. For full references see Bibliography and n. 5 below.

[3] See Ch. 13, pp. 385.

[4] In spite of Bascom's description of the Lianja narrative of the Nkundo as a 'remarkable epic poem' (1964, p. 18), examination of the actual text suggests that seven-eighths or more is in prose.

[5] Edited or discussed in, among other sources, Boelaert 1949 and 1957–8; A. de Rop, 'Het epos van de Nkundo Mongo', Band 18, 1959 (*AA* 11. 323); idem., 'L'épopée des Nkundo; l'original et la copie', *Kongo-Overzee* 24, 1958 (with bibliography); ibid. 1964.

[6] de Rop 1964, p. 17.

sense, established 'The Tale of Lianja' as a kind of (prose) epic in its own right, and this and similar forms in the Congo are well worth study —but it does not follow that we have discovered the existence of an *oral* epic tradition even in prose, much less in verse.

A better case might be made out for the less celebrated *mvet* literature further to the west in Gabon, Spanish Guinea, and the Southern Cameroons (particularly among the Fang peoples). In this area many different kinds of songs are sung to the accompaniment of the *mvet* (a type of lyre), and these seem to include some historical poetry not unlike epic.[1] It has been described as 'art musical, art chorégraphique, art théâtral même, mais surtout art de la parole qui retrace avec tant d'habileté la société de nos pères pahouins'.[2] However there is as yet little published material readily available about this type of narrative poetry, and further study is needed before we can come to any conclusion about whether or not it can truly be described as 'epic'.

All in all, epic poetry does not seem to be a typical African form. Some exceptions can of course be found (in addition to the controversial cases already mentioned), nearly all of which need further published elucidation;[3] and we must not forget the many Arabic-influenced historical narratives in the northerly areas of the continent and the East Coast.[4] Certain *elements* of epic also come into many other forms of poetry and prose. But in general terms and apart from Islamic influences, epic seems to be of remarkably little significance in African oral literature, and the *a priori* assumption that epic is the natural form for many non-literate peoples turns out here to have little support.

[1] e.g. S. Awona, 'La guerre d'Akoma Mba contre Abo Mama (épopée du mvet)', *Abbia* 9/10, 1965, 12/13, 1966 (a narrative poem of about 2,800 lines); Towo-Atangana 1965 (discusses the various types of *mvet* songs, including the Angon Mana, a 'type of epic'); Towo-Atangana 1966; Echegaray 1955 (on 'primitive epic poetry' in Spanish Guinea); Belinga 1965, ch. 4 (on Pahouin-Bantu of Cameroun).

[2] Towo-Atangana 1965, p. 178.

[3] e.g. the 'magnificent traditional sung historical . . . chants' of the Nigerian Idoma (R. Armstrong, personal communication), the Haya 'sung legend' (Tracey 1954*a*, 238), or the Igala 'chanted stories' (J. Boston, personal communication).

[4] Cf. above, p. 90 and Ch. 7, pp. 168 ff.

# 5

## PANEGYRIC

Introductory: nature and distribution; composers and reciters; occasions. Southern Bantu praise poetry: form and
style; occasions and delivery; traditional and contemporary
significance

I

In its specialized form panegyric is *the* type for court poetry and
is one of the most developed and elaborate poetic genres in Africa.
It seems to go with a particular ethos, a stress on royal or aristocratic power, and an admiration for military achievement. It is
true that praises (including self-praises) also occur among non-
centralized peoples, particularly those who lay stress on the
significance of personal achievement in war or hunting (such as the
Galla or Tuareg), and also that the use of 'praise names' is nearly
universal. But the most specialized forms, and those which will
primarily be considered here, are the formalized praises which
are directed publicly to kings, chiefs, and leaders, and which are
composed and recited by members of a king's official entourage.

First, something must be said about the 'praise names' which
often form the basis of formal praise poetry. These are most often
given to people but may also describe clans, animals, or inanimate
objects, and they are usually explicitly laudatory. The Zulu king
Shaka is praised in one of his names as 'The Ever-ready-to-meet-
any-challenge',[1] a Hausa chief as 'Fearful and terrible son of Jato
who turns a town into ashes', or an Ankole warrior as 'He who
Does Not Fear Black Steel'.[2] Such words or phrases occur frequently within the more complex form of a complete poem. Other
'praise' names are derogatory or concerned more with insight into
inherent qualities than with praise. The Hausa 'praise names'
(*kirari*), which in fact are often whole sentences and may refer to
inanimate objects, illustrate this well. The stock praise name of
*molo* (three-stringed guitar) goes 'Molo, the drum of intrigue; if

---

[1] Grant 1927, p. 211.　　　　　[2] Morris 1964, p. 48.

it has not begun it is being arranged' (in reference to the common association between the *molo* and immorality);[1] of the wind 'O wind you have no weight, but you cut down the biggest trees'.[2] Similar stock descriptions are used of people or animals: a butterfly is 'O Glistening One, O Book of God, O Learned One open your book' (i.e. the wings, compared to the Koran); a lion 'O Strong One, Elder Brother of the Forest'; while an old woman is addressed as 'O Old Thing, you are thin everywhere except at the knee, of flesh you have but a handful, though your bones would fill a basket'.[3] These generalized and derogatory 'praise' names seem characteristic of some West African societies and appear in proverbs and riddles as well as conversation. They do not replace the more laudatory comments, however, for, also among the Hausa, every celebrated man has his own praise name which is used as a basis for prolonged praises by what Tremearne describes as 'professional flatterers'.[4] Similarly among the Yoruba the *oriki* or praise names are permanent titles held by individuals, given to them by friends or, most often, by the drummers. Some individuals have several of these names, so that a collection of them, recited together, resembles a loosely constructed poem (also called *oriki* ) about the person praised.[5]

In eastern and southern Africa cattle form a popular subject in praise poetry, and inanimate things like divining implements or even a train or bicycle are also praised. In West Africa, apparently unlike other areas, formal praises are addressed to supernatural beings. Hausa *bori* spirits for instance, each have their own praise songs (*taki, kirari*). When the spirit is to be called, its praise songs are played through one after another until it takes possession of one of its worshippers.[6] The Yoruba praise poems to deities in Nigeria and Dahomey (as well as from the Yoruba in Brazil) are particularly famous.[7] Each of the many Yoruba deities (*orisha*) has a series of praises expressed in figurative and obscure language, sung by the priest. Here, for instance, is a praise poem about Ogun, the god of iron; he is one of the most powerful deities and is worshipped particularly by warriors, hunters, and blacksmiths:

---

[1] Fletcher 1912, p. 48.
[2] G. Merrick, *Hausa Proverbs*, London, 1905, p. 76.
[3] Tremearne 1913, pp. 174–6.                          [4] Ibid., p. 177.
[5] Gbadamosi and Beier, 1959, p. 7. Some further discussion of names and their significance can be found in Ch. 16, pp. 470 ff.
[6] Smith 1957, p. 33.          [7] The largest collection is that in Verger 1957.

Ogun kills on the right and destroys on the right.
Ogun kills on the left and destroys on the left.
Ogun kills suddenly in the house and suddenly in the field.
Ogun kills the child with the iron with which it plays.
Ogun kills in silence.
Ogun kills the thief and the owner of the stolen goods.
Ogun kills the owner of the slave—and the slave runs away.
Ogun kills the owner of thirty 'iwofa' [pawns]—and his money, wealth
    and children disappear.
Ogun kills the owner of the house and paints the hearth with his
    blood.
Ogun is the death who pursues a child until it runs into the bush.
Ogun is the needle that pricks at both ends.
Ogun has water but he washes in blood.

Ogun do not fight me. I belong only to you.
The wife of Ogun is like a tim tim [decorated leather cushion].
She does not like two people to rest on her.

Ogun has many gowns. He gives them all to the beggars.
He gives one to the woodcock—the woodcock dyes it indigo.
He gives one to the coucal—the coucal dyes it in camwood.
He gives one to the cattle egret—the cattle egret leaves it white.

Ogun is not like pounded yam:
Do you think you can knead him in your hand
And eat of him until you are satisfied?
Ogun is not like maize gruel:
Do you think you can knead him in your hand
And eat of him until you are satisfied?
Ogun is not like something you can throw in your cap:
Do you think you can put on your cap and walk away with him?

Ogun scatters his enemies.
When the butterflies arrive at the place where the cheetah excretes,
They scatter in all directions.

The light shining on Ogun's face is not easy to behold.
Ogun, let me not see the red of your eye.

Ogun sacrifices an elephant to his head.
Master of iron, head of warriors,
Ogun, great chief of robbers.
Ogun wears a bloody cap.
Ogun has four hundred wives and one thousand four hundred
    children.
Ogun, the fire that sweeps the forest.
Ogun's laughter is no joke.

Ogun eats two hundred earthworms and does not vomit.
Ogun is a crazy orisha [deity] who still asks questions after 780 years.
Whether I can reply, or whether I cannot reply,
Ogun please don't ask me anything.

The lion never allows anybody to play with his cub.
Ogun will never allow his child to be punished.
Ogun do not reject me!
Does the woman who spins ever reject a spindle?
Does the woman who dyes ever reject a cloth?
Does the eye that sees ever reject a sight?
Ogun, do not reject me! [Ogun needs his worshippers.][1]

In spite of these elaborate religious praises, however, the most frequent subjects for panegyric are humans, especially kings and chiefs. Sometimes these are self-praises, like the personal recitations of the Hima noble class of Ankole in which a man celebrates his military achievements, building his poem on a sequence of praise names:

> I Who Am Praised thus held out in battle among foreigners along
> with The Overthrower;
> I Who Ravish Spear In Each Hand stood resplendent in my cotton
> cloth;
> I Who Am Quick was drawn from afar by lust for the fight. . . .[2]

Praises of kings are the most formal and public of all, ranging from the relatively simple Ganda praise of the powerful nineteenth-century king Mutesa cited by the Chadwicks

> Thy feet are hammers,
> Son of the forest [a comparison with a lion]
> Great is the fear of thee;
> Great is thy wrath;
> Great is thy peace;
> Great is thy power.[3]

to the more allusive and figurative praise of another powerful ruler, a man who had seized power for himself in Zaria and was deposed by the British when they occupied Northern Nigeria:

> Mahama causer of happiness, Mahama *yenagi yenaga*,[4] Mahama slab
> of salt who handles it tastes pleasure
> — though thou hatest a man thou givest him a thousand cowries

---

[1] Gbadamosi and Beier 1959, pp. 21–2.    [2] Morris 1964, p. 42.
[3] Chadwicks iii, 1940, p. 579.    [4] Meaning uncertain.

— thou hatest a naked man's blood but if thou dost not get his garment thou slayest him

— Mahama the rolling flight of the crow, O boy cease gazing and seeing first white then black . . .[1]

— the wall of silver that reaches the breast of the horseman

— the tying up that is like releasing[2]

— son of Audu thy help (is) God

— son of Audu, the support of God which is more than the man with the quiver, yea more than his chief on his horse

— hammer of Audu

— salt of Kakanda that is both sweet and bitter[3]

— son of Audu, O sun thou dost not look askance and slightingly[4]

— storm on the land, medicine for the man with the mat-cover

— elephant with the red loins, medicine for the standing grass,[5] with thy trunk thou spiest into every man's house

— the beating of the rain does not stop the jingling of the bell[6]

— the swelling of the palm-stem that fills the embrace of the (climbing) boy[7]

— black dafara tree there is labour before thou breakest.[8]

The frank assessment of the emir's character which accompanies the lauding of his power and achievements is not unparalleled. 'Praise' poems of people frequently include derogatory remarks, veiled or otherwise, or give advice as well as panegyric. Thus the praises of two Hausa emirs of Zazzau run

> Look not with too friendly eyes upon the world,
> Pass your hand over your face in meditation,
> Not from the heat of the sun.
> The bull elephant is wise and lives long.

and

> Be patient, and listen not to idle tales
> Poisoned chaff attracts the silly sheep—and kills them.[9]

[1] Reference to crow with a white band which shows intermittently in flight— i.e. do not expect consistency from this powerful ruler.

[2] i.e. we ought to enjoy even ill treatment from such a great man.

[3] We must bear his will whatever it is.

[4] He is as overpowering as the sun dazzling in the sky.

[5] You trample it down as you trample your enemies.

[6] No efforts of ours will curb his will.

[7] As formidable to his foes as the swelling in the palm-tree to one trying to swarm up it.

[8] His power is compared to that of a tough climbing plant. Fletcher 1912, pp. 38–9. On Hausa praise poetry see also Prietze 1918; Smith 1957.

[9] F. Heath (ed.), *A Chronicle of Abuja*, Lagos, 1962, pp. 27, 32.

Self-praises, created and performed by the subject himself, are not uncommon. Among the Sotho all individuals (or all men) are expected to have some skill in the composition and performance of self-praises, and the composition of formalized praise poetry among the Ankole is expected to be within the capacity of every nobleman: he must find inspiration in a particular episode, compose a personal and topical praise poem based on it, and add it to his repertoire.[1] Again, among the Ibo the taking of a title is sometimes followed by a string of self-praises.[2] As we saw in Chapter 4, a certain amount of private enterprise praising of individuals is also wide-spread. In northern Sierra Leone and other parts of West Africa it is not uncommon for expert Mandingo singers, sometimes accompanied by drummers or xylophonists, to wander through the streets or attend festivals on their own initiative. They pick on some outstanding or reputedly wealthy individual for their praises; and even those who refer to them contemptuously as 'beggars' are in fact glad to reward them with gifts and thanks, and thus hope to send them on their way content, avoiding the possibility of public shaming for lack of generosity. Praises by women sometimes occur too. In the kingdom of Dahomey choruses of wives are expected to perform in praise of the king and chiefs,[3] and professional Nupe singers include a women's group.[4]

The most formal state praises, however, are usually made by official male bards. Thus every Zulu king had one or more specialists who both recited the praises of previous rulers and composed new ones to commemorate the achievements and qualities of the present king. Similarly there were specialist praise poets, ranging from the Ashanti state drummers and singers to the Rwanda dynastic poets described in an earlier chapter. Where accompaniment is important whole teams may sometimes be responsible for official praises; among the Hausa a District Head's *maroka* (praise) team normally contained several drummers (to play the different types of drum), eulogists, two or more pipers, and sometimes a horn-blower.[5] Lesser chiefs tended to have bards who were less skilled and less specialized, modelled on the king's but performing in a less complex and more limited way.

[1] Morris 1964, p. 13.
[2] Egudu 1967, pp. 9–10.
[3] M. J. Herskovits, *Dahomey*, New York, 1938, vol. ii, p. 322.
[4] C. Bowers, 'Nupe Singers', *Nigeria Magazine* 84, 1965, p. 54.
[5] Smith 1957, p. 29.

The style of recitation varies between the unaccompanied forms characteristic of the Southern Bantu praises, those with fairly minimal accompaniment on some stringed instrument (apparently typical of Eastern Bantu poetry[1] and of some peoples in West Africa such as the Bambara),[2] and that in which the accompaniment is stressed (usually percussion or wind). This last type is wide-spread in West African states and its precise form is sometimes a significant aspect of the attribution of status implied in the praise. Among the Hausa the amount or type of musical accompaniment is clearly laid down for the praises of each grade of ruler in the hierarchy; wooden gongs, for instance, may not be used to praise anyone below a certain level, and there are special instruments that can only be used for praising kings and leading vassals.[3] In West Africa the whole praise may take place on the drum or on horns, without the use of the human voice at all, a particularly common form in southern Ghana, Dahomey, and Nigeria but also recorded in some more northerly areas.[4]

Most praise poetry, above all the official type, seems to adopt a more or less obscure and allusive style. The language may be archaic and lofty, there are often references to historical events or people which may need interpretation even to local listeners, and figurative forms of expression are common. Especially frequent are comparisons of the person praised to an animal or series of animals. His strength may be conveyed by referring to him as a lion, a rhinoceros, or an elephant, and, particularly in Southern Bantu praise poetry, the actions and qualities of the hero may be almost completely conveyed in metaphorical terms, only the animals to which the hero is implicitly compared being depicted in action. Comparisons to natural phenomena are also fairly frequent—the hero is likened to a storm, a rock, a downpour of rain. Other figurative forms of expression occur, sometimes reaching a high degree of complexity. In one Rwanda poem the royal name, 'Ntare, suggests to the poet the term *intare*, lion; he does not make a direct substitution of one name for the other, but 'veils' the royal lion by talking about the qualities of the animal, and so refers to the king by such terms as 'Hunter of zebras', 'Clamour of the forests', 'Mane-carrier'.[5] Not all praise poetry takes allusion quite

---

[1] Chadwicks iii, 1940, p. 577.
[2] V. Pâques, *Les Bambara*, Paris, 1954, p. 108.    [3] Smith 1957, p. 28.
[4] On drum poetry see Ch. 17.    [5] Kagame 1951*b*, p. 17.

so far, but in general panegyric seems to exploit allusion and imagery to a higher degree than other forms of poetry in Africa. Praise of a person (or a thing) is not something to be expressed in bald or straightforward language.

Much panegyric is unusually formalized, less variable than many other types of oral literature. Unlike self-praises and the more informal and topical praise poems there seems to be a marked tendency for the state praises of present (and particularly past) rulers to be handed down in a more or less received version. Word and stanza order is, indeed, sometimes varied from recitation to recitation, or follows the particular version approved by an individual bard (as in the case, for instance, of Southern Bantu panegyric), but the changes seem to be minor; stress is laid on conformity to tradition. In Ruanda, with its powerful corporation of bards, the exactness of wording seems even more close. In one case there were only very slight variations in four versions by four different bards of a 365-line praise poem attributed to a poet of about 1820.[1]

The occasions for the performance of praise poetry have already been touched on in the discussion of its authors and reciters. Praise names are used when formal address is required. Among the Southern Bantu the praise name of an individual's clan was used on formal occasions, while among the Yoruba praise names, sung or drummed, are to be heard widely on festive occasions when the drummers go about the streets formally addressing the passers-by and receiving a small reward in return. Among many West African peoples drummers at a king's gate play not only the king's praise names, but announce and honour important guests by drumming or piping their names as they enter the palace. A man's status is recognized and reaffirmed by the use of these formalized praise names, particularly when, as in the announcement of visitors, this is a matter of public performance.

Among peoples to whom the concept of praise names or praise verses is common, there are many informal occasions when praises are used in the same way as speeches or commentaries in other contexts. Thus among the Kele of the Congo wrestling matches are often accompanied by a form of praise on the talking drum: the contestants are saluted as they enter the ring ('the hero, full of pride'), there is comment and encouragement from the drums as

---

[1] Kagame 1951*b*, pp. 24 ff.

the match continues, and at the end praise for the victor.[1] On festive occasions among many peoples—the Yoruba are one example—singers and drummers often welcome those who attend with songs or chants of praise, usually led by a soloist who improvises to suit the individual, accompanied by a chorus. The popularity of praises means that they can be used for profit, a possibility frequently exploited by the roving Hausa soloist described in the last chapter.[2] But they can also stir people to genuine excitement: gifts are showered on the praise poets from enthusiasm as well as fear. Among the Soninké, writes Meillassoux,

> leur maniement du langage, les chaleureuses louanges dont ils couvrent leurs auditeurs, la beauté de leur musique ou de leurs rythmes suscitent d'authentiques émotions, une sorte d'ivresse enthousiaste qui entrâine à donner sans compter.[3]

Praise poetry often plays an essential part in rites of passage: when an individual (or group) moves from one status to another in society, the transition is celebrated by praises marking the new status or commemorating the old. The eulogies involved in funeral dirges are described elsewhere, but in a sense they also fall into this category. Again, self-praises by boys at initiation, as among the Sotho or the Galla, are an important aspect of their claim to adulthood, which is heard and accepted by their audience. Among many peoples, weddings are also an obligatory occasion for praises of bride and groom either by their friends and relations or by professional bards. Accession to office is another common context for praise poetry, usually in public and in the presence of those who take this opportunity to express their loyalty. Sometimes self-praising is used on such occasions; the Hima of Ankole recited praises when a man was given a chieftainship by the king or when he dedicated himself to the king for service in battle.[4] Even when a new status is not being formally marked, praise poetry is often relevant in the analogous situation of publicizing an individual's recent achievements, particularly those in battle or the hunt.

Most spectacular and public are the frequent occasions on which

---

[1] Carrington 1949a, pp. 63–5.　　　　　　　　　　　　　　[2] pp. 94–5.

[3] C. Meillassoux *et al.*, *Légende de la dispersion des Kusa (épopée Soninké)*, Dakar, 1967, p. 14.

[4] Morris 1964, p. 12. For similar self-praises among the Ibo on the occasion of taking an *ozo* title see the instance quoted in Ch. 16, pp. 474–5.

rulers are praised. Sometimes this takes a very simple form—as on the bush paths in northern Liberia or Sierra Leone when a petty chief, carried in his hammock, is accompanied by praises as he enters villages and the local dwellers are thus instructed or reminded of his chiefly dignity. Or it may be a huge public occasion as in the Muslim chiefdoms in Nigeria—Hausa, Nupe, Yoruba— when at the 'Sallah' rituals (the Muslim festivals of Id-el-Fitr and Id-el-Kabir) the subordinate officials attend the king on horse- back, accompanied by their praise-singers. Their allegiance is shown by a cavalry charge with drawn swords outside the palace; the official praise-singers take part in the gallop, piping and drumming the king's praises on horseback. Any sort of public event (the arrival of important visitors to the ruler, the installation ceremonies of a chief, a victory in battle) may be the occasion for praises by official bards or other experts; the ruler's position is commented on and recognized by the stress laid both on the dignity of the office and, more explicitly, on the achievements of its present incumbent. Periodic praises are often obligatory. Among some of the Yoruba the praises of the king, with the com- plete list of his predecessors and their praises, must be recited once a year in public. In many Muslim kingdoms the ruler is celebrated weekly by teams of praisers (reciters, drummers, pipers) who stand outside the palace to eulogize his office, ancestry, and power, sometimes including at his request those of his friends or patrons. In return the ruler acknowledges their praise by gifts or money which are often given publicly.

The manifold social significance of praise poetry is clear. It can validate status by the content of the praise, by the number and quality of the performers, and by the public nature of the recitation. This validation is often acknowledged by gifts. Praise poetry stresses accepted values: the Hausa praise their rulers in terms of descent and birth, the Zulu emphasize military exploits, and the Nupe voice their admiration for modern achievement in their praises of the ruler's new car.[1] This kind of poetry can also act as a medium of public opinion, for up to a point praisers can withhold praise or include implicit or explicit derogatory allusions as a kind of negative sanction on the ruler's acts. Further social functions are publicizing new status or achievements in a non-literate culture, flattering those in power or drawing attention to one's own

[1] S. F. Nadel, *A Black Byzantium*, London, 1942, pp. 140–1.

achievements, preserving accepted versions of history (particularly the exploits of earlier rulers), serving as an encouragement to emulation or achievement, and, not least, providing an economically profitable activity for many of those who engage in it. But consideration of the obvious social functions of praise poetry must not obscure its very real literary qualities. It was also appreciated for its intellectual and aesthetic interest, and for the fact that on some occasions it was recited purely for enjoyment—in the evening recitations of the Hima, or in the salons of important Hausa prostitutes where there was nightly praise-singing and witty conversation.

Many of these general points will emerge more clearly in a detailed discussion of the praise poetry of the Southern Bantu, the praise poetry which has been most fully documented and described. Obviously the details of occasion, tone, performance, and, most of all, style are peculiar to the societies which practise them. But the importance of praises in Bantu society has something in common with praises of other aristocratic or kingly societies in Africa, and a consideration of Southern Bantu praise poetry during the remainder of this chapter can throw further light on the general aspects that have been discussed so far.[1]

## II

The praise poems of the Bantu peoples of South Africa are one of the most specialized and complex forms of poetry to be found in Africa. Many examples have been published in the original or in translation (though as yet these are probably only a fragment of what could be found), and there is a large literature about them by scholars in South Africa. Elsewhere, in general studies of African oral literature, they have tended to be ignored, or, in the most recent general account,[2] mentioned only in passing under the heading of 'Briefer Forms', which is an odd way of classifying such elaborate and lengthy poems.

These praise poems have been described as intermediary between epic and ode, a combination of exclamatory narration and laudatory apostrophizing.[3] A certain amount of narrative is involved—the

---

[1] Besides references to panegyric cited elsewhere in this chapter, see also the collection of Kanuri praise poems in J. R. Patterson, *Kanuri Songs*, Lagos, 1926.

[2] Bascom 1965.          [3] Lestrade 1937, p. 295.

description of battles or hunts, and the exploits of the hero. But the general treatment is dramatic and panegyric, marked by a tone of high solemnity and a lofty adulatory style. The expression is typically obscure and intense, and the descriptions are presented in figurative terms, with allusions to people and places and the formalized and poetic praise names of heroes.

This poetry occurs widely among the Southern Bantu cluster of peoples in South Africa where it is regarded by the people themselves as the highest of their many forms of poetic expression. It has been particularly well documented among the Nguni-speaking peoples (a group which includes Zulu, Xhosa, and Swazi as well as the offshoot Ngoni of Malawi) and the Sotho groups (including, among others, the Lovedu and Tswana); and it also occurs among such people as the Venda and the Tsonga-speaking groups. Although at different periods and among different peoples there are differences of tone and form which would have to be considered in a detailed account of this poetry,[1] in general they share the same form and here they will be treated together. Besides these famous Southern Bantu forms, similar poems occur elsewhere among the Bantu, notably among the cattle-owning aristocrats of East Central Africa. The poems of the Bahima in Ankole, described by Morris[2] as 'heroic recitations', and the 'dynastic poetry' and 'historical poems' of Ruanda[3] have something in common with Southern Bantu praise poetry and they could perhaps be classed together.[4]

Although normally addressed to distinguished human beings, praise poems can be concerned with almost anything—animals, divining bones, beer, birds, clans. Even a stick may be apostrophized in high-sounding terms:

[1] See in particular the detailed analysis of different periods of Zulu poetry in the unpublished thesis by Kunene (1962) summarized in Cope 1968, pp. 50 ff. Also detailed studies by Cope, Schapera, Mofokeng, and others. There is a brief description of some different styles which contrast with 'the main stream of Zulu praise-poetry' in Cope 1968, pp. 61–3.

[2] 1964.  [3] Kagame 1951*b*; Coupez 1968.

[4] Besides other references in this chapter see also J. C. Chiwale, *Central Bantu Historical Texts III, Royal Praises and Praise-names of the Lunda-Kazembe of Northern Rhodesia*, Rhodes–Livingstone Communication 25, 1962; the brief description of Shona praise songs by G. Mandishona in Fortune 1964 (also the Rozi praise poem quoted in G. Fortune, 'A Rozi Text with Translation and Notes', *Nada* 35, 1956); H. F. Morris, 'The Praise Poems of Bahima Women', *Afr. Language Studies* 6, 1965; B. Gbadamọși, *Oriki*, Ibadan, 1961 (Yoruba only).

Guardsman of the river fords,
Joy of adventurers reckless![1]

Praises of animals are very common, usually of the male. Among the pastoral Zulu cattle are a particularly popular subject, but wild animals also appear. The lion is referred to as the 'stone-smasher', or 'awe-inspirer', or 'darkness', and the crocodile is the

Cruel one, killer whilst laughing.
The Crocodile is the laughing teeth that kill.[2]

Some animal praises are more light-hearted and humorous than the solemn panegyrics of prominent people. Consider, for example, the following Southern Sotho praise poem with its vivid and concise description of a pig:

Pig that runs about fussily,
Above the narrow places, above the ground;
Up above the sun shines, the pig grows fat,
The animal which grows fat when it has dawned.
Pig that runs about fussily,
With little horns in its mouth.[3]

But even praises of animals are often marked by solemnity and allusiveness. Indeed there is often an intentional ambiguity in the poems between animal and person, and some poems can be interpreted as sustained metaphors. The following Northern Sotho poem appears to be about a, leopard; but the allusion is to the chiefs of the Tlokwa, whose symbol was a leopard:

It is the yellow leopard with the spots
The yellow leopard of the cliffs
It is the leopard of the broad cheeks
Yellow leopard of the broad face, I-do-not-fear
The black and white one, I-get-into-a-small-tree
I tear off the eyebrows[4]
Clawer am I, I dig in my claws
My people (adversaries) I leave behind
Saying: this was not one leopard, there were ten.
Mr. Claws, scratch for yourself
Even for a big man it's no disgrace to yell if scratched
Leopards of the Tlôkwa country
Of Bolea, where the Tlôkwa came from

---

[1] Dhlomo 1947, p. 6 (Zulu).
[2] Lekgothoane 1938, p. 201.    [3] Lestrade 1935, p. 9.
[4] The leopard sits in a tree over the path and claws at the head of a passer-by.

Wild cat with the broad face
Both *impala* buck we eat and cattle
You died in Botlôkwa
In the Tlôkwa-land of Mmathšaka Maimane
Tlôkwa-land of the sons of Mokutupi of Thšaka
Where do you go in Tlôkwa-land (to seize cattle)?
It is full of blood, it has got the liver
Leopard of Bolea.
Yellow leopard of the clan Malôba the great
Yellow spotted one
Poor nobody, active smart fellow that summons together a huge
    gathering
My victim goes away with his scalp hanging down over his eyes
Leopard of the many spots
Leopard of the very dark spots
Leopard grand old man (formidable one)
Even when it can no longer bite, it still butts its adversaries out of the
    way with its forehead.[1]

The most developed and famous forms, however, are those in
which people are directly praised and described. In some areas
these include self-praises, such as those composed by boys on
their emergence from traditional initiation schools or by warriors
on their return from battle. Others occur in the relatively informal
context of a wedding when a woman may be praised (which is
otherwise unusual). Most ambitious and elaborate of all are the
praises composed and recited by the professional bards surrounding a king or chief. The following extract from one of the many
praises of the famous Zulu king, Shaka, illustrates the use of
allusion, metaphor, and praise name which are combined with
some narrative to convey the bravery and fearsomeness of the
king as he defeated his enemy Zwide:

His spear is terrible.
The Ever-ready-to-meet-any-challenge!
The first-born sons of their mothers who were called for many years![2]
He is like the cluster of stones of Nkandhla,
Which sheltered the elephants when it had rained.[3]

---

[1] Lekgothoane 1938, pp. 193–5.
[2] i.e. Shaka's courage is contrasted with the cowardice of those who did not
answer the call.
[3] A reference to a famous battle between Shaka and Zwide which took place
in the broken country near Nkandhla.

The hawk which I saw sweeping down from Mangcengeza;
When he came to Pungashe he disappeared.
He invades, the forests echo, saying, in echoing,
He paid a fine of the duiker and the doe.
He is seen by the hunters who trap the flying ants;
He was hindered by a cock in front,
By the people of Ntombazi and Langa.[1]

He devoured Nomahlanjana son of Zwide;
He devoured Mdandalazi son of Gaqa of the amaPela;
He was lop-eared.
He devoured Mdandalazi son of Gaqa of the amaPela;
He was lop-eared.

The Driver-away of the old man born of Langa's daughter!
The Ever-ready-to-meet-any-challenge!
Shaka!
The first-born sons of their mothers who were called for many years!
He is like the cluster of stones of Nkandhla,
Which sheltered elephants when it had rained. . . .

The Eagle-which-beats-its-wings-where-herds-graze!
He drove away Zwide son of Langa,
Until he caused him to disappear in the Ubani;
Until he crossed above Johannesburg and disappeared;
He crossed the Limpopo where it was rocky;
Even though he left Pretoria with tears.
He killed the snake, he did not kill it in summer,
He killed it when the winter had come.[2]

In more purely panegyric vein is the briefer praise poem to
Moshesh, the famous Southern Sotho chief:

Nketu (frog) of the regiment, companion of Shakhane and Ramakh-
wane,
Stirrer-up of dust, you came from the centre of the plateau of
Rathsowanyane,
The child of the chief of Qhwai saw you,
You were seen by Ratjotjose of Mokhethi;
Cloud, gleaner of shields,
When Nketu is not there among the people,
The leaders of the regiment cry aloud and say,
Nketu and Ramakhwane, where are you?[3]

---

[1] Mother and father of Zwide.
[2] Grant 1927, pp. 211–13.   [3] Lestrade 1935, p. 10.

The main topic tends to be the chief's military exploits. However, other subjects are also introduced. Among the Swazi a leader's praise poems are always known by all his followers, and include references not only to his actions in war but also to acts of generosity and to his skill and achievement in hunting. Comments on personality,[1] and criticism which can provide a kind of social pressure on an unpopular chief, are not uncommon, and sometimes sarcastic or even insulting remarks are included which, among the Ngoni at least, are said to represent a high kind of praise—such comments are so ludicrous that they could not possibly be true.[2] Praises composed more recently may include references to, for instance, winning a case in the High Court,[3] travelling abroad to work in European areas, or dealing with tax collectors.[4] But it remains true that the most outstanding and beautiful of the traditional praises are those to do with war (and often more peaceful exploits are expressed in military terms).

Various stock topics about the hero's military actions are described in, for example, most Sotho praise poems.[5] These include the leader's temper before the battle, his journey to the field, his fighting, his victims, the booty, and finally his return home, all portrayed in emotional and high-flown terms. The basis of the events mentioned is authentic, but the emphasis is on those incidents in which the hero excelled. Thus even if reverses are mentioned, they are expressed euphemistically. Even if a war was lost, the hero won one of the battles. Or a rout may be admitted to throw into greater contrast the hero's second and more vigorous offensive. The opponents are frequently referred to in contemptuous terms, compared, for instance, to a small and despicable ox, or to a bull without horns fighting against a conquering and triumphant bull. In these praises it is usually the chief himself who is the centre of attention, but his companions and relatives may also be mentioned and their support is seen to add to the hero's prestige and success.

The wars in which these heroes are depicted as fighting are varied. Many of them are against neighbouring peoples in South Africa and involve not only pitched battles but more mobile

---

[1] See the examples of this in Zulu panegyric in Cope 1968, p. 34.
[2] Read 1937, p. 22.
[3] Morris 1964, pp. 84 ff.
[4] Schapera 1965, pp. 4, 229.
[5] The following account is mainly based on Mofokeng, 1945 part III, ch. I.

cattle raiding. Others are between rival contenders for power in one area, such as Shaka's hostilities with some of his rivals. Wars against European invaders are also frequent occasions for praise poems—and, as Norton puts it, one may wonder whether the exploits of the conquerors were celebrated in as poetic and elevated a manner as some of those of the conquered.[1] Here, for example, is a poem praising the bravery of a Swazi king, Mavuso, who was involved in fighting with the Afrikaaners:

Mavuso of Ngwane,
Dangazela [i.e. Mavuso] of Ngwane of Sobhusa.
News of war eats the child still in the womb.
If a person can walk he would have run away.
Flee ye by all the paths,
Go and tell the news to Mpande of the Zulu:
Say one elephant ate another,
And covered it with dress material and quantities of beads.
Those who ran away swore by Lurwarwa,
Saying, 'Mswazi[2] will not return, he is killing'
He fights in the darkness, when will the dawn come?
O chief that fights with the light of burning grass until the dawn
    comes.
They were saying that Mswazi was a boy herding calves;
We shall never be ruled by the hoe stood in the door of Majosi-
    kazi.
He will rule Mkuku and Msukusuku.
O one who comes in and goes out of sandy places,
O bird of Mabizwa-sabele
You are called by Shila of Mlambo,
For him you asked cattle from Mhlangala,
You are asked by Mawewe to ask cattle from Mzila of Soshan-
    gane.
Dutchmen of Piet Retief, we do not approve of you,
We blame you
By stabbing the chief who was helping you.
You cry at the grave of Piet Retief,
You cry at the grave of John.
O one alone without an advocate
Although Ntungwa had one:
Our chief who can stab,
I never saw a man who could stab like him.
He stabs with an assegai until he tires.

---

[1] Norton 1950, p. 23.          [2] Early king and prototype.

Mngqimila who bears a headdress of feathers,
Mababala who arms on a bad day,
Lomashakizela [one-who-goes-quickly], Lomashiya impi [one-who-
leaves-his-army-behind],
Bayete, Bayete.[1]

III

The Southern Bantu praise poems are largely built up of a
series of praise names and praise verses. These praise names can
be either category terms—a cock is 'the aggressive one', the class
of cattle 'the horned one' or 'God of the wet nose' (Sotho)—or
individual terms, as when a particular bull is 'biggest in the herd'.
Clan praise names are used in formal address to clan members;
a Tswana clan, for instance, has the praise name *Mokwena* (from
*kwena*, a crocodile, the symbol of the clan), so an individual of the
clan may be called by the general praise name of *Mokwena*. In
addition many individuals have their own laudatory epithets
which refer to their character or their deeds; these epithets are
usually bestowed on kings, leaders, and outstanding warriors. Thus
we meet the Zulu 'Sun-is-shining', 'Fame-spread-abroad', or the
Venda 'Devouring Beast', 'Lord of the Lands', or 'Huge Head of
Cattle'. Sometimes the praise name is expanded so that it takes up a
whole line (as in the Zulu 'Herd-of-Mtsholoza-he-escaped-and-
was-killed'), and certain prominent people are praised with a whole
string of names: Shaka, for instance, is said to have had several
dozen.[2] Sometimes the hero is also referred to by the name of his
clan's symbol or other animal—as, for instance, a crocodile, lion,
rhinoceros, or elephant—and much of the poem is thus built up
on a sustained metaphor, almost allegory, about the animal which
represents the hero. Some poems seem to make special use of these
praise names, but in all of them the inclusion of these colourful
epithets adds both grandeur and imagery to the verse.

Besides individual praise names (often just one word in the
original) there are praise verses or praise lines in which one
laudatory phrase takes up at least a whole line in the poem. One
of the Sotho praise verses about the class of cattle runs: 'The
beast lows at the chief's great place; if it lows in a little village—
belonging to a commoner—it is wrong', while Dingane's silent

---

[1] Cook 1931, p. 193.
[2] Several occur in the poem about Shaka quoted on pp. 124–5.

and cunning character is referred to by 'The deep and silent pool is calm and inviting, yet dangerous', a Venda chief is 'Light of God upon earth', and Shaka is described as 'The play of the women at Nomgabi's'.

A praise poem is in general built up of these smaller units which are often loosely linked together into stanzas.[1] These stanzas follow in varying orders in different versions. The order is variable because the different stanzas are often linked not by specific meaning but by their general application to the hero of the poem; it is often as important to convey a general picture of his actions and character as to present his exploits in a narrative within a chronological framework. The whole composition is extremely fluid, with given stanzas sometimes appearing, sometimes not, or some versions combining into one poem what others give as two or even three distinct praises.[2] Thus each type (praise name, verse, stanza, and poem) is an extension of the previous kind, and the literary significance which is attached to each finds its fullest expression in the complex and extensive poem.

Any discussion of the formal structure of praise poems must include some reference to prosody.[3] This is a difficult topic, but it seems that there is some kind of dynamic stress which, in addition to other stylistic features mentioned below, is one of the main characteristics which distinguish this art form as 'poetry'. The division into lines is in most cases indicated fairly clearly by the reciter's delivery, so that certain groups of words are pronounced together in the same breath, followed by a pause, and fall together in terms of sense, sometimes consisting of a formalized 'praise verse' of the kind already described. Within each of these lines there are normally three or four groups of syllables (or 'nodes', as Lestrade terms them), each group marked by one main stress but containing any number of other syllables. This 'node' sometimes consists of just one word (or is dynamically treated as one word). The main stress is sometimes on the penultimate syllable of the 'node', followed by a brief break; the stress on the last 'node' of

---

[1] There may be some exceptions to this. The pre-Shakan Zulu praise poem is said to be short and simple and not always made up of stanzas (Cope 1968, pp. 52–3).

[2] See the detailed examples of this in Schapera 1965, pp. 11 ff.

[3] See especially Lestrade 1935, 1937: Grant 1927 p. 202; Mofokeng 1945, pp. 136 ff.

the line is usually the strongest, and is followed by a more pronounced break. A stanza—and, ultimately, a whole poem—is thus made up of a succession of these lines, each consisting of three or four 'nodes' following each other indiscriminately. There seems to be no attempt at regular quantitative metre, for the stanzas are made up of irregular numbers of lines each with varying numbers of syllables, but the variety in syllable numbers (by some considered a mark of richness in itself) is bound together not only by the over-all pattern of this strong stress rhythm, but by repetition, parallelism, and other devices to be discussed below.

The over-all pattern is also brought out by certain melodic features in the actual recitation. This has been studied in some detail in the case of Southern Sotho and especially in Zulu praise poetry.[1] In the delivery there is some musical use of pitch, even though the actual tones are too close to the tones of normal speech for the poems actually to count as 'songs'. The melodic aspect centres round a limited series of notes, enough to provide a contrast with the less formalized speech of ordinary prose. The ends of stanzas in particular are brought out by the lengthening and special pitch (often a glide) of the penultimate syllable. This amounts to a kind of concluding formula, melodically marked, for each stanza.[2]

The example quoted by Lestrade may serve to bring out more clearly the effect of the penultimate stress (marked by an acute accent) in the 'nodes' and at the end of each stanza. This is a praise poem of Moshesh:

| | |
|---|---|
| Ngwána/Mmamokhathsáne/Theséle, | Child of Mmamokhathsane, Thesele (praise-name), |
| Thesélé/pháru/e teléle/teléle, | Thesele, deep chasm, |
| 'Kxómo/di kéne/ka yóna,/di sa íle, | Cattle enter into it on their way, |
| Le bátho/ba kéne/ka yóna/ba sa íle. | Also people enter into it on their way. |
| Hlabísi/ya BaKwéna, | You who give the BaKwena cattle to kill, |
| Ák'O/hlabísê/nkxóno/'áo, | Please give your aunt cattle to kill, |

---

[1] Mofokeng 1945, pp. 136 ff.; D. Rycroft, 'Melodic Features in Zulu Eulogistic Recitation', *Afr. Language Studies* 1, 1960; D. Rycroft, 'Zulu and Xhosa Praise-poetry and Song', *Afr. Music* 3. 1, 1962.

[2] A detailed description is given in Rycroft 1960, op. cit. See also the discussion below, pp. 137–8.

Ák'O/hlabíse/Mmasetenáne/ak'a     Please give Mmasetenane cattle
rwálê.     to kill, that she may carry the
    meat away,
Á re/ke mehléhlo/ya dikxómo/le ya     That she may say, These are the
bátho.     fat stomachs of cattle and of
    people.[1]

The poetic style of these poems emerges more fully when one considers the language and form of expression in some detail.[2] The language differs from that of ordinary prose (and to a large extent from that of other poetic genres among the Southern Bantu) in its archaic quality as well as the introduction of foreign words which add colour to the poem. Alliteration and assonance are both appreciated and exploited by the poet.[3] As well there are many syntactic constructions peculiar to the poems: the use of special idioms and of elaborate adjectives and adjectival phrases means that there is a special style which has to be mastered by a composer of praise poetry. Long compounds abound, many of them in the form of the praise names mentioned already, and built up in various ways: from a predicate and object ('Saviour-of-the-people'), predicate and adverb ('The-one-who-sleeps-in-water'), noun and adjective ('The-black-beast'), noun and copulative ('The-cliff-white-with-thick-milk'), and several others. In Southern Sotho praises, prefixes and concord also appear in characteristic ways, with certain rare omissions of prefixes, and with contractions. There are special prefixes suitable for praising, for example *se-*, which indicates the habitual doing of something and is common in praises to suggest the hero's habit or character, and *ma-*, which appears in names with the idea of doing something extensively or repeatedly.

Parallelism and repetition are marked features in praise poetry. These take various forms, and can be illustrated from the praise of Moshesh just quoted. In the third and fourth lines of the first stanza there is parallelism of meaning as well as, in part, of the words, with the second half of the line repeated identically the second time and in the first half a repetition of the same verb but

---

[1] Lestrade 1935, pp. 4–5.
[2] On style and language see especially Lestrade 1935, Grant 1927, pp. 203 f., Schapera 1965, pp. 15 ff., Cope 1968, pp. 38 ff.; the following account is based particularly on Mofokeng's unpublished thesis (especially part III, chs. 1, 3) on Southern Sotho praise poems.
[3] See the instances of this in Zulu praise poems in Cope 1968, pp. 45–6.

with a different noun. Parallelism by which the same person is referred to by different names can be illustrated in the second and third lines in the second stanza, where the proper name Mmasete-nane refers to the same person mentioned earlier, with, again, identical repetition of other parts of the line. Both these forms of parallelism are common elsewhere in praise poetry. There are also many other forms: sometimes the repetition is not exact but the repeated phrase has something added to it, thus leading to progress in the action:

> He has taken out Ntsane of Basieeng
> He has taken out Ntsane from the cleft in the rock[1]

a motif which is frequently used in describing someone's exploits; when placed like this side by side it adds to the impression of achievement. Or the thought may be repeated in following lines even when the wording is different:

> Watchman of derelict homes,
> Caretaker of people's ruins,
> Guardian of his mother's deserted house.[2]

The many other forms that occur include chiasmus (cross parallelism), deliberate change of word order in the second of three parallel lines, and the practice of linking, by which a phrase at the end of a line is taken up and repeated in the first half of the next.

The use of ideophones and interjections in praise poetry is another way in which its poetic quality can be enhanced. In Southern Sotho, for instance, the interjections *hele* (expressing surprise), *he* (of a wish), or *pe* (a recognition of something overlooked) are frequently used to convey emotion. Ideophones too can add to the descriptive quality with vivid conciseness: *qephe*, for instance, conveys a sound picture of the last drop of milk during milking, occurring in such a line as 'There is not even the sound of the last drop, there is no milk'.

The characteristically obscure nature of the language in praises is partly due to its figurative quality, as we shall see. But it also arises from the great emphasis on allusion in this form of poetry, to historical events, places, and peoples. As will be obvious from some of the examples quoted, the use of proper names is often extensive and at times stanzas consist mainly of a catalogue of names and places.

---

[1] Mofokeng 1945, p. 132.　　　　　　[2] Schapera 1965, p. 17.

The imagery in this form of poetry provides a striking contrast to the much more straightforward expression in prose. By far the most common form is that of metaphor. The hero is associated with an animal, often the animal symbolic of his particular clan: a chief belonging to the clan associated with the crocodile may appear as 'The crocodile of crocodiles' or, as in the Southern Sotho praises of Lerotholi, the hero's nature may be indicated in terms of the animal:

> The crocodile looked in the deep pool,
> It looked with blood-red eyes.[1]

Where the comparison is to domestic animals, it is often with the suggestion that they are too wild for their enemies to manage— cattle may refuse their milk, kick mud into the milk, tear their milker's blanket, and in the case of a bull (a common image) his sharp horns are dangerous to those around him. Most frequent of all are comparisons to wild animals, to their bravery, wildness, and fearsome appearance. Thus a hero may appear as a lion, a spotted hyena, a big vulture, or a buffalo. In some praises the hero speaks in his own voice and himself draws the parallel with an animal or a series of animals:

> I am the young lion!
> The wild animal with pad-feet and black back!
> Whose father has given up hope from the beginning and whose mother has wept for a long time.
> I am the fine elephant of the Mathubapula, the finest elephant in the Matsaakgang.[2]

Though animal metaphors are the most common, heroes are also compared to natural phenomena like lightning, wind, or storm, or to other objects like a shield, a rock, flames of fire:

> The whirlwind [i.e. the hero] caused people to stumble
> The people were swept by the downpour of spears
> The heavy rain of summer, a storm,
> The hailstorm with very hard drops.[3]

Sometimes there is a whole series of metaphors by which the hero is compared, or compares himself, to various different objects:

---

[1] Mofokeng 1945, p. 128.
[2] V. Ellenberger, 'History of the Ba-Ga-Malete of Ramoutsa', *Trans. Roy. Soc. S. Africa* 25, 1937, p. 19.  [3] Mofokeng 1945, p. 129.

The rumbling which is like the roll of thunder,
Ox belonging to the younger brother of the chief . . .
I am the wind that raises the yellow dust,
I am the rhinoceros from the Badimo cattle-post,
Son of Mma-Maleka and nephew of Lesèlè.[1]

Similarly in the Transvaal Ndebele lines:

The hail that came down in the middle of winter,
And came down at *emaKhophana*.
The elephant that took fire in a pot-sherd,
And went and set the kraals of men alight,
And burned down those of all the tribe.[2]

Special grammatical forms are also used to introduce a metaphorical impression. In Southern Sotho, for instance, there is
sometimes a change in the course of a poem from class 1 concords (the personal class) to others, a device which both conveys
a metaphor and leads to variety, a change from the monotony
of class 1 throughout;[3] and 'wrong' concords in Zulu similarly
suggest a metaphorical idea.[5]

Similes are much rarer than metaphors, but a few occur in
descriptions. Someone may be said to be

. . . like a stone hammer
Like a round boulder, the hero[3]

or the chief may be 'as shapely as the full moon' or 'as straight as
a sandalwood tree'.[6]

Hyperbole appears in emotional description, adding to the
vividness of the picture. The confusion and fierceness of the battle
may be indicated by

A cow should run carrying her calf
A man should run carrying his child

or

The small herbs were frost-bitten in the middle of summer . . .
The trees lost their leaves,
The sparrows, the birds that lay eggs in the trees, forsook their nests[6]

---

[1] Ellenberger, op. cit., p. 6.
[2] Van Warmelo 1930, p. 77.
[3] Mofokeng 1945, p. 129.
[4] Vilakazi 1938, p. 117.
[5] Schapera 1965, p. 21.
[6] Mofokeng 1945, pp. 130, 124.

while a man's feelings may be conveyed by

> He left grieved in his heart
> He left with the heart fighting with the lungs,
> Heaven quarrelling with the earth.[1]

It is largely through this figurative and allusive form of description that actions and qualities of people are conveyed in the praise poems. There is little stress on personal emotions, lyrical descriptions of nature, or straightforward narration. Rather a series of pictures is conveyed to the listeners through a number of laconic and often rather staccato sentences, a grouping of ideas which may on different occasions come in a different order. In this way impressions are communicated with economy and vividness. Vilakazi comments, for example, on the 'emotional shorthand' of such a passage as this:

> The thunder that bursts on the open
> Where mimosa trees are none.
>
> The giant camouflaged with leaves
> In the track of Nxaba's cattle
>
> He refuses tasks imposed by other people.[2]

Here the figurative language conveys the action. First the hero's temper is described as like a sudden thunderstorn, then his force is indicated by comparing it to a giant elephant hidden by the leaves of the trees. His strength is then brought out further by the way he is able to win back the cattle taken away by one of the headmen (Nxaba) who fled north in Shaka's reign; finally the fact that not even Shaka can impose his commands on him proves his hardihood and strength of mind.

This loose ordering of stanzas by which a series of pictures of a man's qualities and deeds is conveyed to the listener is typical. Nevertheless there are also vivid descriptions of the action itself in a way which fits the partly narrative aspect of praise poetry. Thus there are many examples of battle scenes in Southern Sotho praise poems. Here the sounds of the words, as well as the meaning, sometimes serve to heighten the effect:

> Cannons came roaring, the veld resounding
> Sword came tinkling from all sides
>
> (Kanono tsa tla li kutuma thota e luma.
> Lisabole tsa tla li kelema kahohle)[3]

---

[1] Ibid., p. 131.  [2] Vilakazi 1945, p. 45 (Zulu).
[3] Mofokeng 1945, p. 120.

The hero's attack and the fate of his victims are favourite topics:

> Maame, the whirlwind of Senate,
> Snatched a man off his horse
> The European's horse took fright at the corpse
> It took fright at the corpse without a soul

and

> The lion roared when it saw them near.
> It jumped suddenly, wanting to devour them
> They ran in all directions the people of Masopha,
> They ran in all directions and filled the village,
> They scattered like finches.[1]

When the victim falls on the ground, dead, and lies motionless this is described in one poem as

> He lay down, the grass became taller than him
> While it was finally dead quiet on the ground[2]

while the effect of battle, its many deaths, can also be shown indirectly in a description of the general scene:

> A foul smell came from the ridge,
> They no longer drink water the people of Rampai
> They are already drinking clods of human blood.[3]

It has frequently been remarked that the stress in praise poetry is on action and on the building up of a series of pictures about the deeds and qualities of the hero, rather than on lyric descriptions of nature; and in a general way this is certainly true. A few passages can be singled out as Dhlomo and Vilakazi have done, to represent a more lyrical approach to the beauty of nature. In a Zulu praise poem we have

> The greenness which kisses that of a gall bladder!
> Butterfly of Phunga, tinted with circling spots,
> As if made by the twilight from the shadow of mountains,
> In the dusk of the evening, when the wizards are abroad.[4]

Another picture which seems to be expressed for its own beauty is the brief praise of the blue-throated lizard in the Northern Sotho

---

[1] Mofokeng 1945, pp. 123, 124.    [2] Ibid., p. 123.
[3] Ibid., p. 120.    [4] Dhlomo 1947, p. 6.

Blue-throated lizard of the Lizards
A blue chest (or throat) I have put on
Brown I also have put on
I, father-of-clinging of the hillside.[1]

But while such instances can fairly easily be found, in general the stress is far more on the hero and his character, so that what pictures are given of the scene and surroundings are subordinate to the insight they give into the hero's activity. The weather, for example, may be described not for its own sake but as a kind of formalized indication that some important event is about to be depicted or to show the determination and perseverance of the hero whatever the conditions. This comes out in the following Southern Sotho passage:

When he is going to act the mist thickens;
The mist was covering the snow-clad mountains,
Mountains from which the wind blows.
There was a wind, there was snow, Likila,
There was a wind, there was snow on the mountains,
Some were attracted by pillows and remained.[2]

Here, as in all these praise poems, the first interest seems to be the laudatory description of the hero rather than descriptions of natural phenomena or the straightforward narration of events. It is to this panegyricizing end that both the general form and the detailed style of these poems all tend.

IV

As these poems are very much *oral* compositions, intended to be heard rather than read, they demand also some consideration of the way in which they are delivered and composed and the kinds of occasions on which they tend to be heard.

Although again the details vary, there seems to be general agreement that praise poems are delivered much faster, and in a higher tone, than ordinary prose utterances. The reciter pours forth the praises with few pauses for breath and at the top of his voice. Often there is growing excitement and dramatic gestures are made as the poem proceeds. Grant describes a well-known Zulu praiser

---

[1] Lekgothoane 1938, p. 213.     [2] Mofokeng 1945, p. 121.

whom he heard in the 1920s. As the poet recited, he worked himself up to a high pitch of fervour, his face was uplifted, and his
voice became loud and strong. The shield and stick that he carried
were, from time to time, suddenly raised and shaken, and his
gestures became more frequent and dramatic, so that he would
suddenly leap in the air or crouch with glaring eyes while praises
poured from his lips—until at last he stopped exhausted.[1] The
audience too play their part and often shout out encouragingly in
support of what the praiser is saying or to cheer him on, adding
to the emotional, even ecstatic mood that is induced by the
delivery of these poems.

Something has already been said about the metrical and quasi-
musical form of the delivery. Even in the mood of excitement
described by Grant there is a clear emphasis on the penultimate
syllable of certain words, and, in a more marked way still, on the
word just preceding a pause at a line- or stanza-end. Praise poems
have no musical accompaniment, nor, apparently, are they
actually sung. Rather, they are semi-chanted, in the sense that a
special stylized intonation is expected during the recitation. In
Zulu the tonal and melodic movement is not a separate musical
creation, but arises directly out of the words of a given line; and
at the ends of lines and stanzas there are certain formalized cadences
and glides, used as concluding formulas.[2]

The power of a praise poem seems to depend partly on the
delivery and the personality of the reciter. It is said, for instance,
that when the great general Ndlela kaSompisi recited the whole
audience became awestruck,[3] and Lekgothoane expresses the
same view in an extreme form when he writes that 'a man whilst
praising or being praised can walk over thorns, which cannot pierce
his flesh which has become impenetrable'.[4] However, with this
complex and sophisticated form of poetry, unlike the simpler
prose tales, the literary effect does not seem to have been dependent primarily on the skill of the reciter, but rather on the art
of the poet as composer—in his use of the traditional forms
described above, such as figurative expression, allusion, and the
various stylistic devices which, quite apart from his delivery,
served to heighten the effectiveness and power of the verse.

[1] Grant 1927, p. 202.
[2] D. Rycroft, 'Melodic Features in Zulu Eulogistic Recitation', *Afr. Language
Studies* 1, 1960.        [3] Bang 1951.        [4] Lekgothoane 1938, p. 191.

The composition of praise poetry was traditionally both a specialist *and* a universal activity. All men seem to have been expected to have a certain skill. Commoners composed their own praises or those of their families and their cattle while those of high birth or outstanding prowess had their praises composed by others, the chiefs by specialist bards. The poems about earlier chiefs were handed down and probably known by the chief's followers as well as by the specialist reciters; but it was the particular responsibility of the official bards to recite them on appropriate occasions. Though the older poems were preserved in this way, this is not to say that each recitation of a single poem was verbally identical. Indeed several versions of the 'same' poem have sometimes been recorded, differing in, for instance, the order of the stanzas, their length, or the detailed wording or order of lines. The form of praise poetry makes it easy for poems to become telescoped without radically altering the sense; this is what seems to have happened with many of the earliest poems which tend to be considerably shorter than those about more recent chiefs. The recitation itself can also lead to additions by the performer, in the sense that a stanza or line may be introduced in that particular performance from his knowledge of the stock language and imagery. In these ways each separate performance of the traditional poem may involve a certain amount of 'composition' in the sense of introducing variant forms into a poem which has a clear outline but is not fixed into an exact verbal identity. Composition also of course takes place in the more familiar way with original creation by a single poet, notably by the professional bards of the chief. Using the conventional forms the poet produces a new poem, perhaps designed to commemorate a particular occasion like the coming of distinguished visitors, perhaps in general praise of the chief's deeds and character. The poem may then become famous and be added to the repertoire of praise poems of that particular chief, to be handed down to the court poets even after the chief's death. Among some peoples at least these original praise poems are the property of the composer in the sense that until his death no one may recite them in public,[1] and the names of the original poets may be remembered for some time.

During the nineteenth and earlier part of the twentieth centuries, one of the main occasions for the composition of praise poems,

---

[1] Schapera 1965, p. 6 (on Tswana).

among the Sotho-speaking peoples at least, was at the initiation ceremonies of boys.[1] During their period of seclusion at the age of fifteen or sixteen the boys were required to compose and recite poems in praise of themselves, of their chief, and of their parents, and they had to recite these praises publicly on their emergence from seclusion. In this way the art of composition was insisted on as a necessary accomplishment for every man, involving some acquaintance at least with the various stylized forms of expression and historical allusions mentioned earlier.

Self-praising also takes place on many other occasions. The most famous situation is after a battle when a warrior composes his own praises to celebrate his exploits or, if he is outstanding in bravery or birth, may have them composed for him by others. In this way every soldier had his own praises (in addition, that is, to the praise names possessed in virtue of his membership of a particular clan) which he either recited himself or, among the Zulu at least, had shouted out to him by his companions while he danced or prepared for war.[2] War was the main occasion for such praises, but many other events may inspire them—exploits in hunting particularly, and the experience of going to work in European areas which, as Schapera notes, forms a new type of adventure to be celebrated among the Tswana.[3]

Whatever the initial occasions and subjects of their composition, the situations when recitations are made are basically the same— some public gathering, whether a festival, a wedding, a beer drink, or the performance of some public work. The chanting of praise poetry takes its place among the singing of other songs, and it is frequent for someone to walk about reciting praises of himself or his leader, while those present become silent and attentive. Among the Sotho peoples, the situation of divining also provides a formalized occasion for praises of both the bones used in divination and the various 'falls' which the diviner follows in his pronouncements. Weddings too are very widely regarded as another stock situation in which praises are not only possible but required, for the bride or bridegroom is lauded in praises which include references to the fame of their family and its ancestors.[4]

---

[1] Laydevant 1930, p. 524; Mofokeng 1945, p. 136; Schapera 1965, pp. 2-4.
[2] Tracey, 1948*b*, p. vii; J. K. Ngubane, 'An Examination of Zulu Tribal Poetry', *Native Teachers' Journal* [Natal] 31, 1951.
[3] Schapera 1965, p. 4.
[4] Ibid., pp. 4-5; Vilakazi 1945, p. 58.

However, the prototypical situation for reciting praise poetry arises when a chief and his ancestors are praised by the specialist bards who form part of the chief's official entourage. These praise poets (Zulu *imbongi*, Tswana *mmôki*) were much respected members of the chief's official retinue and had the function of recording the praise names, victories, characteristics, and exploits (or expected exploits) of the chief to whom they were attached. The office was still recognized in the 1920s,[1] although it seems that later on these functions were performed by poets without official positions. One of the traditional occasions for the recitation of praises of the chiefs was in the early morning when the praiser shouted them out. Formal praises were delivered on ceremonial and public occasions when the bard recited a whole series of eulogies, starting with the famous praises of the king's or chief's ancestors—praises handed down to him by word of mouth—and finally reaching the praises, often composed by himself, of the present chief.[2] Such praises were also declaimed on special occasions such as after a victory by the chief, on the advent of distinguished visitors, at the installation of a new chief, or at the distribution of royal bounty.

V

The social significance of these praise poems is bound up with the aristocratic nature of the Southern Bantu societies, traditionally based on a hierarchy of rank dependent on birth, and linked by an emphasis on the institutions of kingship and chiefship. The pastoral emphasis was also important, for even in those groups for whom agriculture formed the basis of the economy, cattle-holding was particularly esteemed as a mark of status and pride, an attitude which the many praise poems to cattle express clearly. The marked military tradition of all these societies, in particular the Zulu, is also relevant, together with the emphasis on competition, whether in military exploits, in hunting, in vying with other members of the same age-set, or for the favour and notice of the chief or king. This desire for fame and praise was something considered relevant not only in life but also after death: a man's memory was kept alive in his praises.

[1] Grant 1927, p. 202.
[2] C. L. S. Nyembezi, 'The Historical Background to the iziɓongo of the Zulu Military Age', *Afr. Studies* 7, 1948, p. 111.

In societies where status and birth were so important, the praise poems served to consolidate these values. As so often with panegyric, the recitation of the praises of the chief and his ancestors served to point out to the listeners the chief's right to the position he held both through his descent from those predecessors whose great deeds were commemorated and through his own qualities so glowingly and solemnly depicted in the poetry. As elsewhere, however, praises could contain criticism as well as eulogy, a pressure to conform to expectations as well as praise for actual behaviour. In this way, praise poetry could also have the implicit result of exerting control on a ruler as well as the obvious one of upholding his position.

These praise poems were, furthermore, not only a result of but in some cases a means towards acquiring position and power. The effective earning of praises was one way in which a man could recommend himself to his chief for honour and advancement. Praises meant support from others and, in Zulu society at least, a man's influence was closely correlated with his praises; the more a man achieved in battle and in council, the more and better his praises. Further, in a culture in which dancing was so important, a man could only dance publicly according to the number and quality of his praise poems.[1] The poems also acted as an inducement to action and ambition. A young man's promise and his future heroic deeds were described in the praises he and his fellows made up, particularly on the occasion of his initiation when the ideals implied in the poems could fire the imagination. A chief who had only recently succeeded to office and whose reign still lay before him could be roused to activity by the exploits expected of him as by the knowledge that the praise poets could, however guardedly, sometimes blame as well as praise. Thus in youth a man was reminded in praises of the measure of his promise; in maturity his praises presented an inspired record of his deeds and ambitions; in old age he could contemplate the praises of his achievements and adventures; while after death the poems would remain as an ornament to his life, an inspiration and glory to his friends and followers, and a worthy commemoration to keep his name alive as one of the ancestors:

People will die and their praises remain,
It is these that will be left to mourn for them in their deserted homes.[2]

[1] Dhlomo 1947, p. 48; Cope 1968, p. 21.
[2] From a Zulu praise poem (Cope 1968, p. 67).

The praise poems thus express pride in the possessions and values of the peoples among whom they were recited—pride in cattle, in family and clan, in chiefship, and in military achievement. It was war in particular that filled people with pride and emotion about their own actions or those of their friends; above all, about those of their chiefs and leaders. And the memory of such actions 'fills the praiser with emotion, excitement, joy mingled with sorrow'.[1]

Praise poetry is also a vehicle for the recording of history as viewed by the poets. There is little straightforward cataloguing of genealogies, for a knowledge of these is assumed in reciter and listener and merely touched on allusively. It is the great deeds and characters of earlier heroes which are commemorated rather than their mere names or ancestry, and national glories are thus recounted and relived. How far back these historical poems can go can be illustrated from the Ngoni praise of Ngwana, the hero who led one group of the Ngoni northwards to their present home in Malawi in the early nineteenth century, in flight from Shaka's wars:

> You who cut the trees and who cut the mouths,
> You the locust, the grasshopper who fixed in your hair the feathers of the locust.
> Who went below, and climbed up, and went to bring the morning star of the dawn.
> You go, since you are rejected; you go and bring the armlets of wild animals; those of cattle will be much disputed.
> You who remember the fault of long ago.
> In descending, you descend together with the mountains.
> You who drank the blood of cattle.
> You who separated from the people of Shaka, Shaka of Mßeleßele kraal.
> You who separated from the people of Nyathi the son of Mashoßane; it thundered, it was cloudy.
> Thou resemblest cattle which were finished by wolves.
> You who originated with the people of Mzilikazi.
> You who originated with the people of Mpakana son of Lidonga.
> You who originated with the people of Ndwandwe.[2]

In spite of the great social importance of praise poetry in the aristocratic and military society of the nineteenth century, it

---

[1] Mofokeng 1945, p. 136.　　　[2] Read 1937, p. 25.

would be wrong to overemphasize the *social* functions of this poetry at the expense of its literary and artistic significance. As is clear from a detailed consideration of their conventional form and style, Southern Bantu praise poems represent a complex form of art, and one which, while in the hands of the second-rate it can lead to mere bombast and pompous repetition, can also give rise to poems of great imagination and power. It would be wrong to suppose that a people capable of developing such an art form were unappreciative of its artistic qualities whether as listeners or as reciters. And praise poems continue to be composed. Although the aristocratic and military basis of society has gone and the content of these poems has been transformed by new interests and preoccupations, nevertheless the form and tone of praise poetry remain. The style has been influential as a basis for written poetry, and such well-known writers as Nyembezi, Mangoaela, Vilakazi, and Dhlomo have made studies or collections of traditional praises in which they find inspiration for their own writings. In some areas praise poetry may no longer be so popular as in earlier years, but local newspapers still abound with written praise poems on important occasions, on the installation of a new paramount chief, for instance, or the arrival of some famous visitor. Interest in praise poetry is not confined to written forms either. Of Zulu panegyric, Rycroft writes:

> Its oral composition continues to be a living art among illiterate and semi-literate people. Young Zulu men from country areas who take up manual work in towns nowadays have the habit of interspersing long strings of their own self-praises between the verses of their guitar songs, despite the firm tradition that no Zulu should ever praise himself.[1] (Guitars are a *sine qua non* and are played while walking in the street.)
> Self-praises here serve to re-assure and raise morale in an unfamiliar environment. They seem to be found particularly useful as a stimulant when proceeding on a courting expedition, besides being used to impress the ladies, on arrival.[2]

Some of the subjects treated in these modern praise poems are analogous to the traditional ones—new types of adventures, distinguished visitors, wedding feasts, self-praises in modern terms— and such topics can be treated with the same kind of solemnity and imagery as the traditional ones. Other new poems concentrate on

---

[1] Though see Cope 1968, p. 21.
[2] D. Rycroft, personal communication.

praises of inanimate things and of animals (race-horses, for instance). The following brief oral poem about a bicycle seems typical of modern interests and treatment; it was recorded from the Hurutshe living in the native reserve and location of Zeerust:

> My frail little bicycle,
> The one with the scar,[1] my sister Seabêlô,
> Horse of the Europeans, feet of tyre,
> Iron horse, swayer from side to side.[2]

From the same source comes this extract from the praises of a train. It includes the traditional motifs of metaphorical comparison to an animal, parallelism, allusion, and adulatory address:

> Beast coming from *Pompi*, from *Moretele*,
> It comes with a spider's web and with gnats[3]
> It having been sent along by the point of a needle and by gnats.
> *Swartmuis*, beast coming from *Kgopi-Kgobola-diatla* [bumping]
> Out of the big hole [tunnel] of the mother of the gigantic woman . . .
> Team of red and white pipits [the coaches], it gathered the track unto itself,
> Itself being spotlessly clean.
> Tshutshu [noise of engine] of the dry plains
> Rhinoceros (*tshukudu*) of the highlands
> Beast coming from the South, it comes along steaming,
> It comes from *Pompi* and from *Kgobola-diatla*.[4]

The same kind of style is also evident in modern written forms. One can compare, for instance, the following lines from another praise poem about a train, this time written by a Sotho student at a training institute:

> I am the black centipede, the rusher with a black nose
> Drinker of water even in the fountains of the witches,
> And who do you say will bewitch me?
> I triumphed over the one who eats a person (the sun) and over the pitch black darkness
> When the carnivorous animals drink blood day and night.
> I am the centipede, the mighty roarer that roars within.[5]

Thus in spite of new interests and the inevitable changes of outlook consequent on the passing of the old aristocratic order,

---

[1] i.e. the bag of tools attached.      [2] Merwe 1941, p. 336.
[3] A reference to the smoke.      [4] Merwe 1941, p. 335.
[5] H. J. Van Zyl, 'Praises in Northern Sotho', *Bantu Studies* 15, 1941, p. 131.

the literary form of praise poetry still flourishes, in however modified a form, and the ancient praises still bring inspiration and a formal mode of literary expression to modern artists. Praise poetry still performs its old functions of recording outstanding events, expressing praise, and recalling the history of the people.

Praise poetry, and in particular the Southern Bantu form, is among the best-documented types of African oral poetry. Nevertheless, much remains to be studied. Further collections could be made or published—so far only a fragment has appeared in print. There are other general problems too. There is the question, for instance, of how far this form, apparently so closely connected with kingly and aristocratic society, also occurs in non-aristocratic areas or periods.[1] Many detailed problems arise too about style, prosody, and, in particular, composition. Though many texts have been collected,[2] particularly from South Africa, full discussions of these are less common,[3] and further detailed accounts are now needed of specific forms in particular areas.

[1] See forthcoming work by W. Whiteley on praise songs among the Kamba; also instances among the Ila and Tonga of Zambia (A. M. Jones 1943, pp. 12 f.).

[2] Including some published in the original only, e.g. C. L. S. Nyembezi, *Izibongo zamakhosi* (Zulu), 1958 (not seen; reference in Cope 1968); Z. D. Mangoaela, *Lithoko tsa marena a Basotho* (S. Sotho), Morija, 1921 (not seen; reference in Schapera 1965).

[3] Though see Schapera 1965 (Tswana); Morris 1964 (Ankole); Cope 1968 (Zulu); Coupez 1968 (Ruanda); and Mofokeng 1945 (as yet unpublished) on Southern Sotho. Otherwise detailed discussion tends to be in the form of short articles.

# 6

# ELEGIAC POETRY

General and introductory. Akan funeral dirges: content and themes; structure, style, and delivery; occasions and functions; the dirge as literature

## I

ELEGIAC poetry is an exceedingly common form of expression in Africa. We hear of it from all areas and in many different forms. However it is usually less specialized and elaborate than panegyric poetry, and, perhaps for this reason, it has attracted less interest.[1] More private and normally lacking the political relevance of panegyric poetry—to which, nevertheless, it is closely related—it tends to be performed by non-professionals (often women) rather than state officials. It shades into 'lyric' poetry and in many cases cannot be treated as a distinctive genre. However, lamentation so frequently appears in a more or less stylized and literary form in Africa that it is worth treating on its own in this chapter. Furthermore, some account of Nketia's detailed work on Akan funeral dirges—a study not widely enough known[2]—may serve as a stimulus to further similar work, and at the same time illustrate some of the complex artistic conventions that can be distinguished in one type of non-professional oral poetry in Africa.

The most obvious instances of elegiac poetry are those poems or songs performed at funeral or memorial rites. In this sense elegiac poetry ranges from the Islamic funeral song sung by Hausa mallams and reduced to writing in the nineteenth century,[3] or the short but complex Akan funeral dirges chanted by women soloists, to the simple laments with leader and chorus which are sung among the Limba and others, laments in which the musical and balletic elements are as important as the words.

[1] I know of only two analyses in any detail (Nketia 1955 and Anyumba 1964), though there are many brief accounts and passing references.
[2] It is not mentioned, for instance, in Bascom's bibliographic survey of African oral literature, 1964.
[3] C. H. Robinson, *Specimens of Hausa Literature*, Cambridge, 1896, pp. 2–13.

The occasions for these laments differ from people to people. Often dirges are sung round the corpse (or round the house in which the corpse lies) while it is being prepared for burial. Sometimes, as among the Akan, this is followed by a period of public mourning, during which the corpse lies in state and dirges are sung. The actual burial may or may not be accompanied by elegies: among the Akan it is not,[1] while among the Limba all normal burials should be accompanied by singing. Deaths are also often celebrated by memorial ceremonies later and these too are usually accompanied by songs which sometimes include strictly funeral songs, and sometimes panegyric of the dead.

On these occasions women are the most frequent singers. Among the Yoruba women lament at funeral feasts,[2] Akan dirges are chanted by women soloists,[3] and the *zitengulo* songs of Zambia are sung by women mourners.[4] The fact that these songs often involve wailing, sobbing, and weeping makes them particularly suitable for women—for in Africa as elsewhere such activities are considered typically female. Also common are laments sung by a chorus of women, sometimes led by one soloist, and often accompanied by dancing or drumming. Occasionally men too are involved. Among the Limba, for instance, the initial mourning over the corpse is invariably by women, in either chorus or antiphonal form; but in the case of an adult male the burial itself is by the men's secret society and the accompanying songs are by men. Specialists too are sometimes conventionally mourned by their peers. Thus an expert hunter may have special songs sung at his funeral by fellow hunters (men) who come to attend the rites. Occasionally too one hears of professional or semi-professional singers. Thus the Yoruba sometimes invited professional mourners to their funerals to add an extra embellishment to the usual laments of the bereaved women.[5]

Many of these songs are topical and ephemeral. That is, they are composed for use at the funeral of one individual and relate to him only, though they naturally use the accepted idioms and forms. Thus among the Ila and Tonga of Zambia, the *zitengulo* mourning songs are sung only once: they are very short and composed by a woman who mourns and thinks over the life's work of

[1] Nketia 1955, p. 15.                    [2] Ellis 1894, pp. 157 f.
[3] Nketia, op. cit., p. 8 and *passim*.    [4] Jones 1943, p. 15.
[5] Ellis 1894, p. 157.

the deceased; she bases her song on this, starts to sing little by little, and adds words and melody until the song is complete.[1] Other funeral songs, perhaps particularly the choral ones, seem to have a set form repeated more or less exactly at all funerals, or all funerals of a certain category—though on this point the evidence is often not very precise. There are also instances of songs or poems said to have been composed initially for some other occasion but taken over for regular use at funerals. The Chadwicks speak of elegies in Ethiopia said to have been preserved 'for several centuries' and instance the famous and much sung elegy for Saba Gadis.[2] Another case is the Ibo song originally sung by warriors to their leader Ojea as he lay dying at the moment of victory, but now used as a generalized funeral dirge:

> Ojea, noble Ojea, look round before you depart,
> Ojea, see, the fight is over;
> Fire has consumed the square and then the home,
> Ojea, see, the fight is over.
>
> Ojea, Brother Ojea, ponder and look,
> Ojea, see, the fight is over;
> If rain soaks the body, will the clothes be dry?
> Ojea, ah! the fight is over.[3]

The content of these elegies varies. At times—as in this Ibo example—there is no direct reference to the deceased. But often he is specifically addressed, and praise is one of the most frequent motifs. Among the Yoruba praise poetry is recited or played on drums at funerals as well as on other occasions,[4] and in Akan dirges the singer calls on the deceased by his praise names and lauds his great deeds and ancestry. Occasionally the personal reference or address to the deceased is deepened by more general allusions. This is well illustrated by the Yoruba funeral song from Ede:

> I say rise, and you will not rise.
> If Olu is told to rise, Olu will rise.
> If Awo is told to rise, he will rise.
> The newly wedded bride gets up at a bidding,
> Although she dares not call her husband by name.
> The elephant on waking gets up,
> The buffalo on waking gets up,
> The elephant lies down like a hill.

[1] Jones 1943, p. 15.  [2] Chadwicks iii, 1940, p. 517.
[3] Osadebay 1949, p. 153.  [4] Gbadamosi and Beier 1959, p. 50.

> Alas! The elephant has fallen,
> And can never get up again!
> You say you have neither wealth nor children,
> Not even forty cowries with which to buy salt.
> You muffled head, rise![1]

We also find resignation and acceptance of the inevitable. These are, for instance, mentioned as frequent characteristics of much Sudanese funeral poetry.[2] Other poems dwell on the personal feelings and experience of the mourner. Ellis quotes from a Yoruba example:

> I go to the market; it is crowded. There are many people there, but he is not among them. I wait, but he comes not. Ah me! I am alone. . . .[3]

The same note of personal grief is heard in the Acholi funeral dirge:

> I wait on the pathway in vain
> He refuses to come again
> Only one, beloved of my mother oh,
> My brother blows like the wind
> Fate has destroyed chief of youth completely
> I wait on the pathway in vain[4]

or again in an Ngoni lament:

> I have stared at the setting (death) of my husband.
> They say, show me the pool that has a crocodile.
> Let me throw myself away.
> What can I do? Alas![5]

We are not, unfortunately, told the details of the occasion on which the much quoted Bushman lament, 'The broken string', was composed or performed, but in this too we see that the main concentration is on the singer's feeling: he is mourning his friend, a magician and rain-maker:

> People were those who
> Broke for me the string.
>    Therefore,
> The place became like this to me,
>    On account of it,
> Because the string was that which broke for me.

[1] Gbadamosi and Beier 1959, p. 51.    [2] Tescaroli 1961, p. 9.
[3] Ellis 1894, p. 157.    [4] Okot 1963, p. 209.    [5] Read 1937, p. 16.

Therefore,
The place does not feel to me,
As the place used to feel to me,
 On account of it.
 For,
The place feels as if it stood open before me,
Because the string has broken for me.
 Therefore
The place does not feel pleasant to me,
 On account of it.[1]

The elegies so far discussed have been those specifically connected with funeral rites of various kinds, or, at least, poems or
songs mourning the death of some individual. There is also,
however, a sense in which elegiac poetry also includes poems
which take death or sorrow as their general themes without being
connected with funerals or actual mourning. In this sense, elegiac
poetry in Africa does not often seem to be a distinctly recognized
genre. Although certain dirges (such as those of the Luo or the
Akan) are sometimes performed in other contexts and with other
purposes, funerals remain their primary and distinctive occasions,
and death is merely one—and not apparently a very common one—
of the many subjects that occur in lyric poetry generally. In this
sense, then, elegiac poetry does not seem a type that demands
extensive discussion here.

The sort of way, however, that the theme of death is occasionally
used outside a dirge is worth illustrating from the impressive
Ngoni song recorded by Read. This is a very old poem, originally
intended for performance at a marriage, but now sung on other
occasions (including church meetings). The refrain, 'the earth does
not get fat', is a reference to the way the earth is always receiving
the dead, but is yet never satisfied:

The earth does not get fat. It makes an end of those who wear the
 head plumes [the older men]
We shall die on the earth.
The earth does not get fat. It makes an end of those who act swiftly
 as heroes.
Shall we die on the earth?

 Listen O earth. We shall mourn because of you.
 Listen O earth. Shall we all die on the earth?

[1] Bleek and Lloyd 1911, p. 237.

The earth does not get fat. It makes an end of the chiefs.
Shall we all die on the earth?
The earth does not get fat. It makes an end of the women chiefs.
Shall we die on the earth?

    Listen O earth. We shall mourn because of you.
    Listen O earth. Shall we all die on the earth?

The earth does not get fat. It makes an end of the nobles.
Shall we die on the earth?
The earth does not get fat. It makes an end of the royal women.
Shall we die on the earth?

    Listen O earth. We shall mourn because of you.
    Listen O earth. Shall we all die on the earth?

The earth does not get fat. It makes the end of the common people.
Shall we die on the earth?
The earth does not get fat. It makes an end of all the beasts.
Shall we die on the earth?

    Listen you who are asleep, who are left tightly closed in the land.
    Shall we all sink into the earth?
    Listen O earth the sun is setting tightly.
    We shall all enter into the earth.[1]

Rather than generalizing further about elegiac poetry or reproducing further isolated examples, it seems best to concentrate on
one example, the Akan funeral dirge. From this something of the
social context of the form and its complex conventions will
emerge. It will also show how some of the familiar questions of
literary criticism can be pursued with profit in the case of oral, as
of written, poetry.[2]

II

The funeral dirges of the Akan have been intensively studied by
Nketia who published his collection and analysis in 1955. Among
the Akan-speaking peoples of southern Ghana dirges form just one

---

[1] Read 1937, pp. 14–15.
[2] Further references to elegiac poetry include Anyumba 1964 (Luo); Beaton
1935/6 (Bari); Tescaroli 1961, part 2 (Sudan); B. Gutmann, 'Grußlieder der
Wadschagga', *Festschrift Meinhof*, Glückstadt, 1927; L. Stappers, 'Kimoshi, de
rouwzang van de BaaMilembwe', *Zaïre* 4. 10, 1950; G. Hulstaert, 'Een rouwzang
van de Mongo', *Africa-Tervuren* 7. 1, 1961; B. Gbadamosi, 'Yoruba Funeral
Songs', *Black Orpheus* 22, 1967; E. Littmann, *Abessinische Klagelieder*, Tübingen,
1949. See also G. Moore, 'The Imagery of Death in African Poetry', *Africa* 38,
1968 (mainly but not exclusively on written forms).

among their many types of poetry. They are sung or intoned by
women as part of the public mourning during funerals. In them
'speech [is] inlaid with music, sobs and tears and conjoined to
bodily movement'.[1] Unlike some of the lyric poetry to be discussed
later, however, the emphasis is on the words rather than the
music, and the poems are performed by soloists without the
accompaniment of either musical instruments or a chorus of supporting singers.[2]

Here in introduction are two examples from Nketia's collection.
The first is sung by a woman for her dead son, Gyima (poetically
referred to as her 'grandsire'):

> Grandsire Gyima with a slim but generous arm,
> Fount of satisfaction,
> My friend Adu on whom I depend,
> I depend on you for everything, even for drinking water.
> If I am not dependent on you [i.e. if there is any doubt that I depend
>     on you], see what has become of me.
> Although a man, you are a mother to children,
> A man who takes another's child for his own,
> Who builds mighty but empty houses,
> Who is restive until he has fought and won,
> Osibirikuo, Gyane the short one,
> Dwentiwaa's husband, and a man of valour.[3]

In the second example the mourner is singing about her dead
mother:

> Grandchild of grandsire Kwaagyei of Hwedeɛmu that drinks the water
>     of Abono,
> Daughter of a spokesman, who is herself a spokesman,
> Mother, it may appear that all is well with me, but I am struggling.
>
> Nyaakowaa of Anteade and grandchild of Ɔsafo Agyeman,
> O, mother, I am struggling; all is not as well as it appears.
> Mother, if you would send me something, I would like a parcel and
>     a big cooking pot that entertains strangers.
>
> The god ɔpem has failed; the gourd of charms has won.
> O, mother, there is no branch above which I could grasp.
> Mother, if you would send me something, I would like parched corn
> So that I could eat it raw if there was no fire to cook it.

---

[1] Nketia 1955, p. 118.

[2] In addition to the dirges described here the Akan also have choral laments
sung by groups of women in solo and chorus form (not discussed here).

[3] Nketia 1955, p. 195.

Mother, the parrot will catch a skin disease from the fowls and die!
Grandchild of grandsire Kwaagyei of Hwendeɛmu that drinks Abono,
Grandsire, the mighty pot, saviour of strangers,
O, mother, I am struggling; all is not as well with me as it appears.
Mother who sends gifts, send me something when someone is coming
    this way.

Mother, there is no fire in the deserted dwelling
From which I could take a brand to light my fire.
My helpful Wicker Basket that comes to my aid with lumps of salt,[1]
O, mother, I would weep blood for you, if only Otire's child would
    be allowed to.

Grandsire, the crab that knows the hiding place of alluvial gold,
What is the matter, child of the spokesman?
Mother has allowed this death to take me by surprise.
O, mother, I am struggling; all is not as well with me as it appears.[2]

Nketia describes in some detail the conventional language and themes of dirges—themes which throw light on features which might otherwise seem puzzling or banal. The deceased is the focal point. He may be addressed, his individual qualities described, or he may be identified with one or several ancestors. To refer to him the mourner often uses a series of different names which vary the language as well as honouring the dead. Besides proper names the Akan also have corresponding 'by-names' and these often occur in dirges for affective reasons. The same applies to praise appellations, terms which 'describe in a convenient short or gnomic form the qualities or expected qualities, accomplishment or status of a holder of the corresponding proper name'.[3] Thus in the first dirge quoted above, Gyima's praise names include *Anko-anna* ('one who is restive until he has fought and won') and *Dwentiwaa kunu barima Katakyie* ('Dwentiwaa's husband and a man of valour'). Other instances of praise names can be translated as 'The beetle that eats away raffia' or 'Noble Apea Kusi, feller of Odum trees'.[4] They may in fact have been won by an earlier individual of the same name, but are used for contemporaries who are imaginatively pictured in the dirge as possessing the same qualities or status as their famous namesakes. The poetry is also further embellished by another type of reference to the deceased—the 'dirge names'. These are sometimes made up of a string of

---

[1] Salt in the past was a very precious and scarce commodity.
[2] Nketia 1955, p. 196.    [3] Ibid., p. 31.    [4] Ibid., p. 32.

by-names, praise names, and other words, but also have less usual forms according to which a person of a given proper name can be addressed by any one of several dirge names. Many of these names cannot be translated—for example, one of the dirge names of a man called Apea: *Nyenenkye Asamanwoma Apeantummaa*[1]—but used in a dirge they introduce an elevated and high-sounding effect.

Beside these specialized names, the deceased is also addressed by kinship terms and terms of endearment. In the second dirge quoted, the dead woman was addressed throughout as 'mother' and other such terms ('father', 'uncle', etc.) are frequent. The relationship to some third person is also used; the deceased may appear as, for instance, 'The Drummer's child', 'Father of Ɔbempɔn and Ayirebiwaa', or 'Grandchild of Wealth'. Finally, a name of reference may be used to associate him with his clan or group—'Child of the Biretuo clan of Sɛkyerɛ', 'Grandchild of the Buffalo' (i.e. of the *Ɛkoɔna* clan), or 'The white fowl spotted by the roving hawk' (i.e. of the Bosomtwe Ntorɔ group).[2]

Besides these ornamental names, qualities are often dwelt on. Benevolence in particular is frequently lauded in the dirges. It is referred to in such stock phrases as 'The slender arm full of benevolence', 'Grandmother, the big cooking pot that entertains strangers', 'You are a mighty tree with big branches laden with fruit. When children come to you, they find something to eat', or 'Fount of satisfaction'.[3] Sympathy and kindness are also picked out: 'He is a father to other people's children', 'He was like the tree of the plantain planted behind the house, that gave shade and coolness'; and frequent references to the wisdom of the dead are expected, expressed by the singer lamenting that she no longer has anyone to give her advice. Fruitfulness is also commonly described, and one of the conventional comparisons is between a fruitful woman and the okro fruit with its many seeds: 'Mother the okro, full of the seeds of many issues and proven.' These stock ways of referring to the deceased both elevate his good points and bring home to the community the loss it has suffered.

While the person of the deceased is the focus of attention, there are other themes. One of the most frequent is that of the ancestor. Among the Akan, ancestry is important, both through the mother (significant for most social purposes) and through the father who represents the 'spiritual' side. In dirges both types of ancestry are

[1] Ibid., p. 33.    [2] Ibid., pp. 33–4.    [3] Ibid., p. 35.

commemorated, and the fact brought out that a member of two social groups (the father's *and* the mother's) has been lost. Thus the paternal ancestry of the deceased is often referred to in special name-clusters which indicate the *ntorɔ* (paternal group) of the person being mourned, names such as 'Nwanwanyane, offspring of the Leopard', or 'Gyebiri Siaw Anim, the nobleman'. References to ancestors in the female line are even more common, and the kinship of the deceased to a series of ancestors is emphasized. Some dirges concentrate almost completely on this theme. One opens

> Kotoku man and grandchild of the Vanguard of Kotoku,
> Grandchild of Ampoma: our lineage originates from Kotoku.
> Grandchild of Baabu: our lineage hails from Kade . . .[1]

and then continues through the various relationships of the deceased. Particularly in royal dirges one of the ancestors may be singled out for praise. An ancestor's bravery, skill, or leadership may be mentioned. His use of power, for example, is dwelt on in one dirge:

> In the olden days, when you were
> On your way to Akora Kusi's house,
> You would stumble over skulls;
> Vultures got up to greet you;
> Blue bottle flies buzzed round you,
> As if to say, Alas![2]

In this way the deceased can be praised indirectly through his ancestors' great deeds. At funerals the Akan remind themselves both that their ancestors too were once human beings and that they themselves, as well as the deceased, are not without an ancestry and a historic tradition of which they can be proud. As a mourner sings:

> We are from Creation.
> It was my people who first came here,
> And were joined later by the Fante Hosts.
> It was my grandfather that founded Komenda.
> I am the grandchild of the Parrot that eats palm nuts.
> It was my grandfather that weighed gold
> And the scales broke into pieces under its weight.
> Grandchild of Apea Korankye hails from Abooso.[3]

---

[1] Nketia 1955, p. 22.    [2] Ibid., p. 23.    [3] Ibid., p. 26.

Rather similar to the theme of ancestors is that of places. The identity of the deceased (or his ancestors) is clarified by adding the name of his home or place of origin. (The link between the dead and their mourners is often brought out by the fact that they share a common home.) This convention often introduces historic evocations into a dirge. It also adds colour to the words, for it is common for a descriptive phrase to be added to the name itself: 'Asumegya Santemanso, where the leopard roars and comes to town for its prey' or 'Hwerebe Akwasiase, where the Creator first erected a fireplace and placed a beating stick by it'.[1] References to places can either be interspersed throughout the poem or, in combination with the theme of the ancestor, form the main framework on which the whole dirge is built up.

While the main focus of the dirge is on the deceased—his nature and qualities, his ancestors, his historic home—the mourner also makes certain reflections. There are certain stock ways in which these are expressed. The dead man is often pictured as setting out on a journey, so that part of what the mourner is doing is bidding him farewell—'Farewell, thou priest' or 'Receive condolences and proceed on'.[2] The sorrow of parting is brought out in stock phrases like 'I call him, but in vain', 'I would weep blood' (if only that would bring you back), or, with more passionate emphasis on the mourner's sense of loss, 'I am in flooded waters. Who will rescue me?' and 'There is no branch above which I could grasp'. The mourner wishes for a continued friendship with the dead man even when he reaches the world of spirits, and speaks of wishing to go with him, or to exchange gifts or messages; this is why the singer so often asks the dead to 'send me something when someone is coming'—an imaginative rather than a literal request. The mourner expresses her sorrow and loss through particular concrete images rather than through general statements about death. Instead of speaking of death taking away her support, she sings 'The tree that gives shade and coolness has been hewn down'; and, when she alludes to the shortness of life, she uses the conventional metaphor in which the duration of life is compared to the time a market woman takes to sell her goods—'What were your wares that they are sold out so quickly?'

Among all these various motifs and conventions of content and expression the individual mourner can select her own. The use of

[1] Ibid., p. 41.　　　[2] Ibid., p. 44.

many of the stock forms of expression does not necessarily mean a lack of sincerity on her part or that she creates little artistic impact. As Nketia puts it, the 'traditional forms of expression [are] still pregnant with emotion to the Akan, expressions which are not considered outworn in spite of frequent use'.[1]

### III

Four main types of dirge can be distinguished. All are built up on the conventional themes and forms of expression already described, but they vary both in the arrangement of the material and in the scope given for the spontaneity of the mourner.

The first, type 'A', is the most stereotyped and dignified. This kind of dirge is short and marked by unity of subject. Besides mention of the deceased, reference is normally made to just one ancestor, one of his qualities, and one single place. Many different dirges of this type can be built up about the same person; the same ancestor can be brought in but with a different quality described; or all the references could be changed, with a different ancestor introduced and a different place of domicile, forming the framework for another set of dirges round that theme. In spite of the stereotyped structure, then, the possibility of variation according to the singer's choice in a particular situation is manifold.

Such dirges open with a name, usually of an ancestor, and this theme is then taken up in the next portion of the poem, referred to as the subject, in which the ancestor's qualities are mentioned. He may be associated with some historical event, or with some message or observation. This portion of the dirge can be short or long according to the theme chosen. This is followed by a break, a point at which the dirge name of the deceased is inserted. In other words, until this point the dirge can be used for any member of the group associated with the ancestor, but the insertion of the dirge name ties the poem to a particular individual. After the dirge name, the formal part of the poem can be ended, often with the theme of the place of origin and domicile. By linking them both to the same place, the ancestor mentioned in the opening and the deceased just referred to by his dirge name are brought together. The dirge may stop at this point, but if the mourner

---

[1] Nketia 1955, p. 49.

wishes she can extend it by adding her own reflections in rather less conventional style.

Type 'A' dirges, then, can be seen to fall into four sections— (*a*) opening, (*b*) subject, (*c*) insertion, (*d*) close, followed by an optional addition, (*e*) the extension. The structure can be illustrated in the following example:

(*a*) Karikari Poti of Asumegya.

(*b*) When I am on the way, do not let me meet
Gye-me-di, the terror.
It is Karikari Poti, Gye-me-di, the terror
That spells death to those who meet him.

(*c*) Pampam Yiadɔm Boakye Akum-ntɛm.

(*d*) Grandchild of Karikari Poti hails from
Asumegya Santemanso
Where the leopard roars and comes to town for its prey.

(*e*) O, mother,
(What of) Your children and I.
O, mother,
Your children and I will feed on the spider,
The mouse is too big a game.[1]

Though dirges of the other three types are somewhat less stereotyped, similar detailed analyses could be made of their conventional structure. Type 'B' is made up of a series of short stanzas which can follow each other in any order and are themselves structured according to certain conventional patterns. An example of this type is the three-stanza dirge:

Grandchild of Boampɔn of Asɔkɔre clan
That walked in majesty amid flying bullets:
Child of a leading Spokesman.

He was an elephant tusk which I was going to use
for carving out a trumpet,
Ofori, child of Konkonti.

Father Apau that overpowers bullets:
Offspring of Nkwamfo Abrɛdwom.
Alas! Death gave me no warning
so that I might get ready.
Mother will go: she has not come back yet.
I shall follow her.[2]

[1] Ibid., pp. 57–8.    [2] Ibid., p. 200.

Type 'C' dirges are constructed on cumulative linear stanzas, sometimes marked off by a reflection or statement—a simple style often used for ordinary people. Such a dirge might open

> Grandchild of Minta that hails from Dunkɛsease.
> Grandchild of Ɔbɛɛko Asamoa that hails from Bɔnkaben.
> Grandchild of Obiyaa that hails from Aborɔdesu[1]

and so on through a dozen lines or so. Even in these very simple dirges emotion is aroused through the connotations of the names introduced. Some women, however, do not consider this type to possess much appeal or depth and instead prefer type 'D' dirges. This type, while not possessing the dignity of the first two, has the attraction of giving more scope to the mourner's individual emotions and reflections. The conventional themes are included but may be woven into the dirge as the individual singer wishes. 'Grandchild of grandsire Kwaagyei' quoted earlier is one example of this type. Another is part of a dirge sung by a Cape Coast woman for her mother, a poem which begins lightly and gains depth as the sorrow of the mourner grows in intensity:

> Mother! Mother!
> Aba Yaa!
> You know our plight!
>
> Mother! you know our plight.
> You know that no one has your wisdom.
> Mother, you have been away long.
> What of the little ones left behind?
>
> Alas!
> Who would come and restore our breath,
> Unless my father Adom himself comes?
> Alas! Alas! Alas!
> Quite often it is a struggle for us!
>
> It is a long time since our people left.
> Amba, descendant of the Parrot that eats palm nuts, hails from the Ancestral chamber.
>
> I cannot find refuge anywhere.
> I, Amba Adoma,
> It was my grandfather that weighed gold
> And the scales broke under its weight.

---

[1] Nketia 1955, p. 65.

I am a member of Grandsire Kɛse's household:
We are at a loss where to go:
Let our people come, for we are in deep distress.
When someone is coming, let them send us something.
Yes, I am the grandchild of the Parrot that eats palm nuts.[1]

A final example of this type illustrates how the conventional themes and stock terms of address can be woven together into an original piece by the mourner in which she can dwell at length on the deceased and her own state. It was sung for a Mass Education Officer who died in 1952, and is in the form of a continuous poem with two slight breaks after 'father on whom I wholly depend':

Valiant Owusu,
The stranger on whom the citizen of the town depends,
Father, allow my children and me to depend on you
So that we may all of us get something to eat,
Father on whom I wholly depend.

When father sees me, he will hardly recognize me.
He will meet me carrying an old torn mat and a horde of flies.
Father with whom I confer,
My childen and I will look to you.
Father on whom I wholly depend.

Killer-of-hunger,
My saviour,
Father the slender arm full of kindness,
Father the Rover whose footprints are on all paths.[2]

Certain types of dirges are considered suitable for particular occasions—types 'A' and 'B', for instance, are held to be more dignified and thus appropriate for royal funerals—but at any funeral the mourner is free to sing whichever kind she prefers.

The detailed linguistic style and delivery of dirges are also discussed by Nketia.[3] The diction is marked by the great frequency of key-words throughout the poems, terms closely associated with the main themes already mentioned. Thus there is constant use of personal names, names of places and sources of drinking water, kinship terms and terms of address, and, finally, terms referring to an individual's clan or paternal group. Certain verbs of identification are also particularly common, for example,

[1] Ibid, pp. 69–70.  [2] Ibid., p. 71.
[3] Especially chs. 5, 7.

*ne* (to be) and *firi* (to come from), which occur in conjunction with
the theme of the ancestor and of the place of domicile. Besides
these key-words, all part of the mourner's stock-in-trade from
which she constructs her dirge, there are also conventional expressions used to describe someone's attributes or express farewell or
condolence. The deceased or his ancestor may be described and
praised by such set phrases as 'fount of satisfaction', 'the big
cooking pot', 'large breast', or 'friend Adu: one on whom someone
depends'. The mourner may also refer to her despair and sense of
loss by using verbs which mean 'to get dark', 'to be flooded', 'to be
homesick or hungry for a person', or nouns like 'coolness', 'darkness' or 'empty house'.

Many conventional arrangements form part of the artistic style.
These include name clusters, repetitions of key-words, and such
combinations as, for instance, 'Asim Abenaa's grandchild-and-my-
mother comes from Ahensan', which follows the common pattern
by which the term *nana* (grandchild) is combined with personal
names, kinship terms, and the verb *firi* (come from).[1] Similar conventions can be observed in the structure of sentences. Of the
varying patterns, the most common is a construction with a front-
placed nominal, that is, sentences opening with a name or name
cluster—as in 'Anɔ Yaa Kani whose kola tree bears fruit out of
season' or 'Asim Abenaa of Ahensan, the Queen of old in whose
vessels we grind millet'. This placing of names at the start of
sentences is a characteristic feature of the language of Akan dirges
and forms a conventional basis on which chains of reference can
be built up.

Apart from these specialized syntactical forms and certain
obscure names and figurative expressions, the language of dirges
is relatively straightforward. Indeed the style as a whole is often
simple and the main units within the dirge (the stanzas) tend to
be short, in keeping with the circumstances of the performance.
The compressed and allusive expression can also be connected
with this; names and historical events, for example, are referred
to briefly rather than described or narrated in full. By these
means, in spite of the ordinary language and short span of the
poem, a whole range of highly charged impressions can be conveyed.

[1] Many other examples of such conventional collocations are given in Nketia
as part of his detailed picture of linguistic conventions in dirges, pp. 86–93.

When the prosody of Akan dirges is considered, it is clear that there is no even beat in a piece as a whole, though there is a scattered use of prosodic patterns of various kinds throughout the poem. Stress is not significant and there is no systematic use of tones or syllables. There is, however, a diffused occurrence of tonal and phonological patterns. These depend on the nature of the lines or linear units in dirges. These units are relatively easily identified through a number of phonological and grammatical forms which mark them off, such as a concluding particle (*ee, oo*), pause, or sob; parallel formation within a line; break in sequence marked by repetition or pronoun referring back; and occasional end-patterning (frequently tonal). Within linear units there is often repetition of single phonological terms (as, for instance, the *s* in the line Ɔsoro *se* mere*s*en a*sas*e), of syllables and groups of syllables in words (e.g. Sakra*butu*, ɔnyɛ *butu*foɔ), or of words or segments (e.g. Yɛse yɛnni ntɔn, yɛnni abusua). Repetitions of tone patterns also occur within lines; for example, in the line ɔdèhye dámfòɔ́ bɔ́ɔ dám, the high tone *dám* is in each case preceded by a low tone, and the repetition of the low–high sequence is noticeable. Within groups of lines similar repetitions can be observed: whole lines may be repeated, the first or second halves of succeeding lines may be identical, or there may be cross repetitions with the word or words in the end position appearing again at the beginning of the following line. This 'prosody of repetition', which is copiously illustrated by Nketia,[1] fulfils some of the functions of rhythm and brings out the poetic style conventionally associated with Akan dirges.

This poetic flavour is further marked by the musical features of the dirge. It is true that, for the Akan, the *verbal* content of the dirge is paramount; Nketia quotes the remark that 'it is not so much the beauty of the voice as the depth of the verbal forms, in particular the range of the praise appellations that counts'.[2] However, musical aspects of form and performance also play some part in the artistry of the dirge as actually heard.[3]

There are two different ways of singing dirges. The first is to adopt a type of wailing voice in which the words of the dirge are 'spoken' and the contours of the melody reflect the speech contours of the performer, sometimes accompanied by a few tuneful

---

[1] Nketia 1955, pp. 77 ff.  [2] Ibid., p. 113.
[3] Ibid., especially ch. 7.

fragments. There are special musical conventions for the treatment of interjections, and this type of delivery also gives scope for the use of the sob, which is often uttered on the syllable *hi* and rapidly repeated perhaps five or six times. The other form is more purely musical. A fairly normal singing voice is used, with melodic contours resembling those of songs. However, there is a general tendency for dirge melodies to begin high and move down to a low resting point at the close. There are some traditional tunes associated with fragments of dirges, but in the main, whichever musical mode she employs, the singer makes up her own tunes as she goes along. Unlike many other types of songs, the rhythm of Akan dirges is free in the sense that there is no handclapping or percussion accompaniment to the singing, nor is it intended for dancing. This, in conjunction with the fact that the mourner herself acts as both soloist and chorus, gives the individual mourner greater scope to treat the subject in her own manner, without reference to others present, and to express her own feelings in the words and melodies she chooses.

## IV

The occasions of the Akan dirge are easily described. It is a literary form expressly composed and performed for the occasion of a funeral and it takes its place alongside such other social expressions as drumming, the firing of guns, singing, wailing, and speaking. Indeed, some of Nketia's informants were unwilling or unable to reproduce their dirges apart from the stimulation of an actual funeral; as they frequently explained, 'they could not utter the words of the dirge without shedding tears or fasting'.[1]

Funerals are important and memorable events among the Akan. They usually open with the preparation of the corpse, a stage at which no dirges are sung. In the second phase of public mourning, however, dirge singing is a central part of the proceedings. As Nketia describes it:

From among the confused noises will be heard the voice of many a woman mourner singing a dirge in pulsating tones in honour of the dead or his ancestors or some other person whose loss she is reminded by the present death, for 'One mourns one's relation during the funeral of another person'. . . . The dirge is made the culminating point of the

---

[1] Nketia 1955, p. 2.

preparation for the funeral as well as the beginning of public mourning. Grief and sorrow may be personal and private, nevertheless Akan society expects that on the occasion of a funeral they should be expressed publicly through the singing of the dirge.[1]

During this stage the women who sing the dirges pace about among those attending the funeral, pausing before the corpse or the chief mourners. Though there is no dancing to dirges, the singer makes gestures and gracefully rocks her head to add to the pathos of what she sings, and, like the chief mourners, she too is expected to fast as a sign of the sincerity of her anguish. There is great freedom as to how and what any performer sings, for dirges are not normally an organized performance, so that the individual can draw on her own resources and originality to express and evoke the emotion she is expected to feel. As the funeral ceremonies go on, the dirges tend to become fewer and fewer, partly because the singers become worn out by the physical and emotional strain of fasting, anguished lament, and pacing about the public gathering. Nevertheless, occasional dirges are heard from time to time until the end of the funeral:

The funeral dirge is heard with diminishing frequency and from fewer and fewer mourners, though it rarely ceases until the funeral is over. A sudden outburst is heard from time to time from a relation while all others may be resting. And so the funeral goes on until after the third day of the event of death when fasting and mourning cease.[2]

The funeral is sometimes followed by remembrance ceremonies some weeks after the death; some dirges are sung on these occasions, but they play a relatively minor part.

Very occasionally dirges are heard outside the context of a funeral. But funerals remain the conventional setting, and at them dirges are obligatory. In this context the dirge is, above all, a means of praising the dead person. He is honoured and mourned, and, as well, the general links between the past and present, the living and the dead, are brought out in stock themes. The sorrow felt by the mourners at the funeral is not only expressed in this conventional form, but can actually be heightened by a skilled singer who evokes the pathos of the situation through her passionate utterances. These dirges, in fact, form the mainstay of any funeral particularly at the outset; it is only towards the later stages that

---

[1] Ibid., p. 8.  [2] Ibid., p. 15.

the dirges of the women are reinforced and finally replaced by music and dancing.

The Akan funeral dirge is a conventional medium of expression, with its own canons of form, theme, and delivery as well as its own traditional occasion when it is performed. There are certain stock forms of phraseology which are regarded as obligatory, and errors in these are quickly corrected. Nevertheless, within these limits both variations and scope for individual creativeness are possible. Traditionally all Akan girls were expected to learn how to sing and compose dirges. They had to master the traditional themes and language, but when performing they were free to exercise their individual tastes and express their own sentiments. The dirges are thus both fixed *and* flexible. For the Akan the funeral dirge is a form recognized not only for its clear social importance but also for its aesthetic merit. Far from being random or wholly spontaneous, the Akan dirge has its own complex and sophisticated conventions, a literary tradition at the service of the individual composer.

# 7

## RELIGIOUS POETRY

Introductory. Didactic and narrative religious poetry and the
Islamic tradition; the Swahili *tenzi*. Hymns, prayers, and
incantations: general remarks; the Fante Methodist lyric.
Mantic poetry: Sotho divining verses; *odu* Ifa (Yoruba).
Conclusion

THERE is a great variety of religious poetry in Africa. There are
hymns, prayers, praises, possession songs, and oracular poetry, all
with their varying conventions, content, and function in different
cultures. They range from the simple one- or two-line songs of
Senegalese women in spirit possession rituals[1] or the mystical
songs of Southern Rhodesia with their many nonsense words[2] to
the specialized hymns to West African deities or the elaborate
corpus of Ifa oracular literature which is so striking a phenomenon
among the Yoruba of Southern Nigeria. We should also take
account of the prevalence in certain areas of the religious literature
associated with the influence of the world religions in Africa. There
is the Arabic-influenced poetry of the Swahili in East Africa and
of Islamized peoples such as the Fulani or Hausa in the northern
portions of West Africa; the ecclesiastical poetry, associated with
the Coptic Church, of the *dabteras* of Ethiopia; and, from less
ancient origins, hymns and lyrics arising from the recent impact
of Christian missions in many parts of the continent.[3] In these
cases it is common for a written tradition of religious literature to
coexist, and to some extent overlap, with an oral tradition.[4]

There are three main ways in which poetry can be regarded as
being religious. Firstly, the content may be religious, as in verse
about mythical actions of gods or direct religious instruction or
invocation. Secondly, the poetry may be recited by those who are

---

[1] G. Balandier, 'Femmes "possédées" et leurs chants', *Présence afr.* 5, 1948.
[2] Tracey 1929, p. 99.
[3] On Ethiopia see Chadwicks iii, 1940, pp. 503 ff. and further references
given in Ch. 3, p. 51. On Islamic and Christian poetry see below.
[4] It is because of this overlap that I have not thought it inappropriate to
include some consideration of the largely written religious poetry in Swahili.

regarded as religious specialists. Thirdly, it may be performed on occasions which are generally agreed to be religious ones. These three criteria do not always coincide. Hymns, for example, may have definite religious content and be sung on religious occasions, but they may or may not be performed by religious experts; oracular poetry may be recited by priests (as in Yoruba divination) but neither the content nor the occasion be markedly religious; and didactic verse, like that of the Swahili, may have a theological content and be recited by specialists but not, it seems, be performed on particularly religious occasions. I do not want to propose any strict definition of religion here; the reader may exclude any examples that seem to him to be only marginally religious or include certain types of poetry such as 'lyric' or 'dirges' that have been treated in other chapters. However, I am not including here poetry that is religious *only* in the sense that it is performed on 'ritual' occasions such as the ceremonies to do with initiation,[1] marriage, or death.[2]

## I

Though didactic and narrative elements are sometimes found in a rudimentary form in the invocations and divination literature that will be discussed later, they do not typically appear in Africa as developed poetic forms. 'Myths' tend to appear in prose rather than verse[3] and the songs embedded in them are not usually independent enough to count as narrative religious poems in themselves. Histories sometimes appear in verse with certain religious overtones—as, for instance, the Akan drum history quoted in Chapter 17—and praise and elegy for dead ancestors may in a sense be both religious and narrative; but the religious aspect does seem to be somewhat secondary in terms of content, occasion, and performer. The same is true for the poems associated with initiation and other rituals—when these are religious in content they are more concerned with invocation or praise than any explicitly didactic interest.

Islamic verse is the exception. In the areas where Arabic models have been influential through the tradition of Islam, religious

[1] See, for example, some of the initiation texts given in Dieterlen 1965.

[2] Dirges are considered in Ch. 6, marriage and initiation songs, etc., mentioned in Ch. 9; some further references on initiation songs are given in Ch. 8, p. 206.

[3] Though see the discussion in Ch. 13, pp. 361 ff.

poetry, often in written form, occurs with a pronounced homiletic and sometimes narrative emphasis. Such religious poetry occurs, for instance, among the Hausa and others in West Africa. Although written in the local language, it is often directly influenced by the Arabic models and contains many Arabic words and sentiments.[1] These poems typically open with some such invocation as

> In the name of God, the Compassionate, the Merciful; and may the peace of God be upon him after whom there is no prophet

and continue in a didactic fashion about, for example, the deceitfulness of this life, Heaven, Hell, pilgrimage to Mecca, exhortations to follow Mohammed, or prayers for divine assistance. This religious literature is a specialist form, often with named authors learned in Islam, and for its composition and propagation it relies primarily on the written word. Nevertheless, it is not totally divorced from the oral tradition, and there are instances of these religious poems being transmitted both orally and through writing; it is not always clear how they began. An example is 'The song of Bagauda'. This is a long Hausa poem said to be of great antiquity which runs to over twenty pages in the Hausa text. It includes a prelude (doxology and eulogy of Mohammed), a list of Hausa kings, and a long homily on the frailty of this world, expressed in a form typical of Islamic tradition with eschatological material from the Koran and the conventional stock of images; it closes with rulings on points of Muslim law. The whole is set in a free form of a classical Arabic metre and rhyme system (*qaṣīda* form, *wāfir* metre and rhyme throughout in *wa*). In spite of its length and form, this primarily religious poem seems to have flourished in both oral and literate forms. Hiskett, its recent editor, was able to collect a text from an old Hausa woman and reports that it is also sung by beggars.[2]

---

[1] Migeod ii, 1913, ch. 18. On Hausa, see C. H. Robinson, *Specimens of Hausa Literature*, Cambridge, 1896; Tremearne 1913, pp. 70–2; Paden 1965; A. Mischlich, 'Religiöse und weltliche Gesänge der Mohammedaner aus dem Sudan', *Afrika* [Berlin] 2. 3, 1943 (not seen). On similar Fulani instances in various parts of West Africa see e.g. Ba 1950; Pfeffer 1939; Monod 1948; E. F. Sayers, 'In Praise of the Faith of Futa and a Warning to Unbelievers—a Fula Poem with Introductory Note and Translation', *Sierra Leone Studies* o.s. 13, 1928; Lacroix 1965; Mohamadou 1963. On Songhai, B. Hama, 'L'esprit de la culture sonrhaïe', *Présence afr.* 14/15, 1957, p. 153.

[2] M. Hiskett, 'The "Song of Bagaudu": a Hausa King List and Homily in Verse', *BSOAS* 27–8, 1964–5.

The same sort of phenomenon appears in Swahili in East Africa. Here too there is a strong written tradition which includes religious poetry. It can be traced directly to Arabic models.[1] This literary tradition goes back something like three hundred years and was a medium of expression which had its origin in the Muslim religion, although it was later used for secular verse. Both Islam and the Arabian models used for its expression may have had their origin outside the area: but the tradition came to be a national Swahili one, influenced and moulded by the genius of the Swahili language and culture. 'Verse composition after the Arabian pattern involved the question of pride in Swahili origins; it revealed knowledge of Arabian life and of Islam, a sure guarantee for the highest prestige among the Swahili people.'[2]

There are many different types of Swahili verse, but they can roughly be divided into the shorter lyric forms and the much longer didactic or narrative poems called *tenzi* (sing. *utenzi*; northern dialect *tendi/utendi*). The first form is closely related to oral traditions and appears sometimes in written, sometimes in oral form: it is 'not easy to classify definitely into "literary" and "popular" sections'.[3] The *tenzi*, however, depend much more on a written form; sometimes indeed they are said to be written as much for the eye as for the ear, and there seems to be less of an overlap between the written and oral forms of such Swahili poems than with the corresponding forms in Hausa. Nevertheless, though in the first instance the *tenzi* were written, they were designed for public performance; they were chanted aloud, sometimes by the composer himself, to musical accompaniment.[4] And it seems clear that the existence of such a wide-spread and valued tradition must have had a profound effect on the whole Swahili literary tradition, oral as well as written.[5]

[1] A great deal of work has been done on this written literature. There is a general discussion with examples (original and translation) in the recent books by Harries (Harries 1962, supplemented by the bibliographic material in the review by J. Knappert in *Afr. Studies* 23, 1964), and Knappert (1967*b*), as well as in earlier writings by Büttner, Velten, Werner, Allen, Dammann, and others (see bibliography under 'Swahili' in IAI *Bibliography* (A) by R. Jones, East Africa, 1960; and M. van Spanndonck, *Practical and Systematical Swahili Bibliography*, Leiden, 1965).   [2] Harries 1962, p. 2.

[3] Werner 1917–20, p. 119.   [4] Harries 1962, p. 24.

[5] See, for instance, the modern Swahili ballad published in P. Lienhardt 1968, which, though purely oral, is in the traditional *utenzi* form. In some areas, e.g. Pemba, the connection with oral tradition seems to have been even closer (see Whiteley 1958).

Swahili *tenzi*[1] are long religious poems containing either homiletic material or a narrative treatment of the deeds of Muslim heroes, including the deeds of war. More recently other secular material has also been included, but the main emphasis is still strongly Islamic. The poems are marked by deep religious inspiration, and the conventional opening, whatever the subject, is a praise of God and his prophet. The narratives are based, more or less closely, on Arabian traditions; however, the models do not seem to have been followed exactly, and in the case of *tenzi* based on the general prose accounts of events relating to the Prophet, the poets were free to treat this material as they wished. To mention just a few, such narrative *tenzi* include accounts of the deeds of Job, Miqdad, or Joseph, a dispute between Moses and Mohammed as to which is the greater, the 'epic of Heraclios' depicting the legend of a Holy War against the Byzantine Christians, and a popular version of the death of the Prophet.

A typical example of the way in which a religious tone pervades the narrative can be seen in the *Utendi wa Ras al-Ghuli*, the story of Ras al-ghul. This deals with the adventures of the Prophet's Companions when they were avenging a Muslim woman whose children had been killed by a pagan king. The events are set in Arabia and the poem opens in characteristic form with praise of God and a description of the copyist's materials and methods. It continues:

> Take down the beginning of the story / One day, we understand, / there appeared the Beloved / Our Prophet the Bringer of News.
>
> At his coming forth, the Trusted One / went to the mosque / there inside the building / at the time of dawn.
>
> After he had arrived / He called for Bilali / He called for him to call the people to prayer quickly / for the time had come.
>
> And Bilali called them to prayer / sending out the cry / and the people heard / from the elders to the children.
>
> And the Companions met together / all of them together / both Ali and Othman / as well as Shaikh Umar.
>
> The leading Helpers / they were all present / with no one absent / and so Abu Bakr was there also.

[1] This section is mainly based on Harries 1962, ch. 3, which contains a convenient synthesis and collection of much of the earlier work on this form of verse. See also Knappert 1966, 1967.

When all had arrived / the Prophet came forward / to lead the people in prayer / with a high voice.

After they had prayed / giving thanks to the Glorious God / the Companions with Shaikh Ali / and the congregation of the Helpers.

They were inside the mosque / studying the holy books / when almost at once / they discerned a cloud of dust.

The Companions watched / and saw people coming / all riding camels / the number of them being ten.

They were coming in a hurry / and on arriving at the mosque / they proceeded to dismount / watering the camels.

And the leader of the party / a woman of distinction / giving greeting / and asking for the Prophet.

She spoke straightway / saying, Where is the Prophet / the Beloved of the Glorious God? / Show me without delay.

She said, Where is the Prophet / the beloved of the Beloved / our Prophet Muhammad / who sets at nought the infidels?

Show me the Exalted One / the Prophet of the Bountiful God / I have come an oppressed person / that I may give him my news.[1]

The woman gives a long account of her suffering, then the miraculous events of the story are recounted, ending with the victory of the Prophet and his friends over the pagans.

Popular epics of this kind were intended for public performance. They 'were meant to amuse and elevate the uneducated masses who liked to see their religious, social, and political ideals realized in the history of former times', and 'occasionally it is still possible to find a *utendi* being intoned in public on the veranda of a house. Public recital ensured that at least the gist of the story would reach the ears of the ordinary man'.[2]

The shorter homiletic *tenzi* were intended for a more limited audience and were often directed at younger members of the community as instruction in religious and social behaviour. The most famous of these is the seventy-nine-line *Inkishafi*, 'Revelation', a poem composed in the early nineteenth century on the theme that all men must die, the glory of this world passes away, and we await judgement in the next world. The poet meditates on the transitoriness of life and the danger of eternal damnation, and looks into his own heart—for the title really implies the revealing

---

[1] Harries 1962, pp. 29–31.　　[2] Ibid., pp. 27, 24.

or uncovering of his own heart and soul. Another well-known didactic poem is *Utendi wa Mwana Kupona*, a mother's instructions to her daughter about her wifely duties. Even such household instructions are permeated with religious sentiments:

> Attend to me my daughter / unworthy as I am of God's award / Heed my last instructions / for it may be that you will apply yourself to them.

> Sickness has seized upon me / and has now lasted a whole year / I have not had a chance to utter / a word of good advice to you.

> Come forward and set yourself / with ink and paper / I have matters at heart / that I have longed to tell you.

> Now that you are near / Write, In the Name of God / name of Him and the Beloved / together with his Companions.

> When you have thus acknowledged / the Name of God the Mighty / then let us pray for His bounty / as God shall deem fit for us.

> A son of Adam is nought / and the world is not ours / nor is there any man / who shall endure for ever.

> My child, accept my advice / together with my blessing / God will protect you / that He may avert you from evil.

> Take this amulet that I give you / fasten it carefully upon a cord / regard it as a precious thing / that you may cherish it with care.

> Let me string for you a necklace / of pearls and red coral / let me adorn you as a beautiful woman / when it shines upon your neck.

> For love let me give you a clasp / a beautiful one without flaw / wear it upon your neck / and you shall perceive benefits.

> While you shall hold to my counsel / my child, you shall escape trouble / you shall pass through this world / and cross over to the next.[1]

After this affectionate opening, the mother goes on to instruct her daughter as to her religious duties, her duties to her husband, household management, and kindness to the poor, followed by her own confession of faith as a Muslim. It concludes:

> Read, all you women / so that you may understand / that you may bear no blame / in the presence of God the Highest.

> Read, you who are sprouts of wheat / obey your menfolk / so that you may not be touched by the sorrows / of the after-life and of this.

---

[1] Ibid., pp. 73–5.

She who obeys her husband / hers are honour and charm / wherever she shall go / her fame is published abroad.

She who composed this poem / is one lonely and sorrowful / and the greatest of her sins / Lord, Thou wilt her forgive.[1]

In form the *tenzi* are modelled on Arabic poetry. Each line is divided into four parts (sometimes written as separate lines), of which the first three rhyme and the fourth acts as a terminal rhyme throughout the poem. This terminal rhyme is often a double vowel, and though these do not always rhyme to our ears (they may be -iya, -eya, -ua, -owa, etc.), added length can be given to both of the vowels in actual reading or recitation. There is a conventional dialect in which *tenzi* are written, but, unlike the involved syntax of lyrics, the narrative is expressed in a straightforward manner. The stock themes and form—in particular the opening prayers and invocations to God, the great emphasis on the frailty of this world, exhortations to religious duty, and the torment of the wicked—are strikingly similar to the corresponding Hausa ones from the other side of the continent.

This *tenzi* form has by no means lost its popularity in East Africa. It frequently appears in the vernacular press, now mainly written in the Roman as distinct from the traditional Arabic Swahili script. It is now also sometimes employed as a vehicle for Christian rather than Islamic doctrine, as in the *utenzi* reported by Knappert in which passages from the Gospel have been cast in the traditional epic style,[2] or for political expression as in the *utenzi* about Nyerere's life, recited in his presence following his inauguration as President in 1965.[3] As has frequently been pointed out, this form of verse, with its conventional prosody and themes, 'lends itself to indefinite *longueurs*'[4] in the hands of a poetaster; but, treated by a master, it can result in magnificent epic poetry.

Though the extent and antiquity of the Swahili tradition of religious verse is probably unparalleled in subsaharan Africa, it

[1] Harries 1962, pp. 85–7.

[2] J. Knappert, 'The First Christian Utenzi: a New Development in Swahili Literature', *Afr. u. Übersee* 47, 1964.

[3] Z. Himid, 'Utenzi wa Muheshimiwa Rais wa Tanzania 28.9.65' [Epic of the Hon. the President of Tanzania, 28 Sept. 1965], *Swahili* 36, 1966.

[4] Werner 1928, p. 355.

is proper to remind ourselves that the influence of Islam, unlike that of Christianity, has a long history in several parts of the continent. The literary tradition that accompanied it, to a greater or lesser degree in different areas, may be particularly evident and well documented among such peoples as the Swahili, Somali, Hausa, Fulani, or Mandingo and have resulted there in many well-known compositions in the local languages. But it may well have had an even wider literary impact to an extent that still remains to be explored.

## II

Apart from Islamic verse the most common type of religious poetry in Africa seems to be the hymn. A common feature of this form is that the religious content consists of invocation or supplication rather than narrative, and is sometimes closely allied to panegyric.[1] The detailed subject-matter and context, however, vary greatly with the differing religious beliefs and institutions of each people.

It is among certain West African peoples that hymns are developed in their most specialized form. This is in keeping with the elaborate pantheon of divinities recognized by such peoples as the Yoruba, Fon, or Akan. Among the Yoruba, for instance, each divinity has not only his own specialist priests and customary forms of worship, but also his own symbolic associations, his iconography, and his literature, including both myths and hymns.

Thus, for example, the Yoruba divinity Eshu-Elegba (the messenger deity and 'god of mischief') has his own cult of worshippers with their special rituals and organization. He is represented sculpturally in shrines according to special conventions which also appear in the insignia worn by his worshippers and in bas-relief representations, with the recurrent motifs of a club, whistle, high head-dress, cowries, and the colour black. The praises of Eshu chanted by his particular worshippers and priests bring out his paradoxical nature: he is shown as big and small, youngest and oldest, black and white, 'one who defies boundaries

---

[1] In some cases (e.g. Yoruba *oriki*) the same term and conventions are used for praises of both deities and humans; in others (e.g. South African Bantu) praise poetry is confined to humans.

and limitations with gay abandon'.[1] His hymns (or praises) are expressed as a series of paradoxes:

When he is angry he hits a stone until it bleeds.
When he is angry he sits on the skin of an ant.
When he is angry he weeps tears of blood.

Eshu, confuser of men.
The owners of twenty slaves is sacrificing,
So that Eshu may not confuse him.
The owner of thirty 'iwofa' [pawns] is sacrificing,
So that Eshu may not confuse him.
Eshu confused the newly married wife.
When she stole the cowries from the sacred shrine of Oya.[2]
She said she had not realized
That taking two hundred cowries was stealing.
Eshu confused the head of the queen—
And she started to go naked.
Then Eshu beat her to make her cry.
Eshu, do not confuse me!
Eshu, do not confuse the load on my head . . .[3]

Eshu slept in the house—
But the house was too small for him.
Eshu slept on the verandah—
But the verandah was too small for him.
Eshu slept in a nut—
At last he could stretch himself.

Eshu walked through the groundnut farm.
The tuft of his hair was just visible.
If it had not been for his huge size,
He would not have been visible at all.

Having thrown a stone yesterday—he kills a bird today.
Lying down, his head hits the roof.
Standing up he cannot look into the cooking pot.
Eshu turns right into wrong, wrong into right.[4]

The obscure and poetic nature of these Yoruba hymns, concerned more with praise and allusive imagery than with intercession, can be further illustrated by another example taken from Verger's great collection of Yoruba hymns.[5] This is the hymn to

[1] J. Westcott, 'The Sculpture and Myths of Eshu-Elegba, the Yoruba Trickster', *Africa* 32, 1962.
[2] Goddess of river Niger, wife of Shango.     [3] Metaphor for 'relatives'.
[4] Gbadamosi and Beier 1959, p. 15.                    [5] Verger 1957.

Shango, the powerful and violent god of thunder, praised in the poem under many different titles. Only about half of the full text is given:

Logun Leko ne me donne pas tort, que ma parole soit correcte
Lakuo peut brûler toutes les terres
Le tonnerre a brisé la maison de Are père du chasseur Mọkin
La mort a amené l'éléphant dans la ville . . .
Mon Seigneur qui d'une seule pierre de foudre a tué six personnes
Logun Leko qui fait beaucoup de bruit sans rien faire
Très sale et très têtu, gifle le propriétaire de la maison et empoigne
    l'amala
Il le coupe en morceaux, il fait de la tête un remède
Il prend l'enfant têtu et l'attache comme un mouton
Ceint d'un tablier d'argent il entre dans la ville
Sur la tête d'un *oṣe* il monte et part
Il se bat comme la tornade dans la ville, il monte en spirale sur un
    arbre Odan et part
Lorsqu'il a tué quelqu'un il accroche sa jambe dans un arbre *arere*
Amugbekun rit sans ouvrir la bouche
Baba Ojẹ Ibadan pénètre dans la brousse et poursuit le danger
Mon seigneur qui coupe une tête comme un régime de noix de
    palme
Contrariété venue comme le signe Oyeku sur le plateau de Ifa
Mon seigneur qui fait lutter le mari et la femme ensemble . . .
Mon cœur n'est pas perdu, j'irai avec lui Shango
Roi qui prend celui-ci et qui prend celui-là
Il est difficile d'être en sa compagnie
Il dit que pour le propriétaire tout est fini
L'enfant mange tout ce qu'il trouve
Il rit lorsqu'il va chez Oshun
Il reste longtemps dans la maison d'Ọya
Ni Ogun ni Shango ne révèlent aucun secret
Revenant puissant pour lequel nous roulons le mortier
Léopard qui tue le mouton et se lave avec le sang
Il lorgne brutalement vers le menteur
Le Sorcier Lakin Sokun chauffe la maison avec son souffle (?)
Mon seigneur qui fait se sauver celui qui a raison
Le menteur se sauve avant même qu'il ne lui parle
Léopard père de Timi
Il attend ce qui nous a fait peur
Il les brise par centaines
Il verse tous les gens dans la forge
Mon seigneur, la forge devient le lit de tous les grands

Il se bat sans avoir tort

Il détruit la maison d'un autre et y met la sienne derrière

Il a battu deux cents personnes dans la forêt et brisé la forêt autour
avec son dos

Il y a beaucoup de débris au-dessus

*Oriṣa* qui ayant déjà tué Efun Doyin, veut encore se battre

Lagun se ferme comme une calebasse d'huile

Il monte sur le mouton sans tomber

Résistant comme la racine de *tipe*

Il monte sur le kapokier et le fait tomber déraciné

Il est sombre, calmement comme l'enfant d'une femme qui prépare
l'indigo.

Seulement quelqu'un qui ne touche jamais terre

Il n'y a pas d'os qui ressemble aux dents

*Balogun* Ẹdẹ tue les gens

Asusu Masa est amer comme la feuille d'*ẹgbẹsi*

Il rit et ne crie pas

Il n'y a pas de danger pour moi en présence de Olukoso

Il va en dansant *gbangu* de Ibadan jusqu'à Oyo . . .

Père de honneur (Nom de Shango)

Propriétaire talisman (Nom de Shango)

Il grille les intestins et les mange

Même dans les jours de détresse il y a des récoltes et Shango mange
de la pâte

Il tue le père, l'a mis sur l'enfant

Enlève son pénis et le met sur son pantalon

Sa poitrine est brûlante comme la brousse du pied du palmier

Entortillé comme la jambe de l'animal *ṣemi*

Il transforme le pilier d'une maison et le fait devenir immense comme
Olokun

Si Olokun est immense Shango également est immense

Il fait brûler le fils de Olumọn (Egba) dans le feu de Aragunan

Il écrase le talisman de mon chef de maison

Il prend auprès de ceux qui ne possèdent pas ce que nous lui souhai-
tons

Il est très sale comme Eshu et se tient, une jambe tendue et l'autre
pliée

Éléphant qui marche avec dignité

Regardez l'éléphant lever aisément une patte guerrière, léopard père
de Timi . . .

Il menace le mâle, il menace la femelle, il menace l'homme important,
il menace le riche

L'indiscret qui veut découvrir le secret de Olukoso ne restera pas au
monde

Celui qui respecte le secret, mon seigneur lui facilitera les
  choses
Il prend quelqu'un, il tue quelqu'un
Il danse avec précision en regardant vers le ciel à la dérobée
Aki Rabata danse avec les gens
Il saute hors de la maison si elle brûle
Si la maison brûle il sort et rit après . . .
Si la pluie tombe il dit qu'il n'y a pas de feu
Si l'auto arrive que les gens accroupis se lèvent de la route
S'éloigner du serpent dont on n'a pas coupé la tête
Le feu brûle celui qu'il connaît
La pluie mouillant l'ortie, éteint son feu.[1]

The hymns of some other African peoples are very different
from these elaborate praises of Yoruba gods. Praise may be replaced by an emphasis on prayer, supplication, or consideration
of the relations of man to god(s). This seems to be true, for instance,
of many of the hymns of the Dinka, a people of the Nilotic group
famous for its special type of monotheism, emphasis on Spirit, and,
at the same time, general lack of any developed priesthood. We
can see the reflective nature of the first of two short hymns quoted
by Lienhardt and, in the second, the tone of complaint and demand characteristic of Dinka hymns. In each 'Divinity' is approached directly and simply, and the poetic effectiveness is
created partly through the use of vivid visual images from the
everyday world:

Great DENG is near, and some say 'far'
O Divinity
The creator is near, and some say 'he has not reached us'
Do you not hear, O Divinity?
The black bull of the rain has been released from the moon's byre.[2]
Do you not hear, O Divinity?[3]

I have been left in misery indeed,
Divinity, help me!
Will you refuse [to help] the ants of this country?[4]

[1] Verger 1957, pp. 342–8, 354–5.
[2] The image is of the clouding over of the penumbra of the moon.
[3] G. Lienhardt, *Divinity and Experience, the Religion of the Dinka*, Oxford,
1961, p. 38.
[4] In religious contexts the Dinka often speak of themselves as 'ants' in the
sight of Divinity, thus looking at themselves as they may be supposed to appear
in the eyes of Divinity.

When we have the clan-divinity DENG
Our home is called 'Lies and Confusion'.[1]
What is all this for, O Divinity?
Alas, I am your child.[2]

When we come to the hymns of the Bushmen of southern Africa
we find the aspect of supplication taken still further. There are
no priests among the Bushmen and, for certain northern groups at
least, invocations to their gods are said to take place spontaneously
when the thought comes to them.[3] Consonant with the continual
difficulties and scarcities of Bushman life, the topics of their
invocations are the day-to-day material needs with which they are
preoccupied:

You have created me and given me power to walk about and hunt.
Why do you lead me in the wrong way so that I find no animals?[3]

In these examples, often characterized by a mixture of mild im-
precation and pleading, the prayer is more marked than the praise
or worship often associated with 'hymns'. The same emphasis on
praying and the demand for daily needs also comes out in the prayers
of some southern Bushman groups, where there is a conventional
form into which such prayers are thrown. Each poem, or each of
its verses, opens with an invocation to the moon, sun, or stars: 'Ho
Moon lying there' or 'O Star coming there', and so on. This is
followed by a prayer for life (that is, a prayer for food), made
the more intense by the repetition and parallelism of the
expression:

Ho Moon lying there,
Let me early to-morrow see an ostrich,
As the ostrich sits on the eggs,
Let me whisk out the yolk
With a gemsbok tail hair (brush)
Which sits together upon a little stick
Upon which the gemsbok tail sits.[4]

[1] Meaning that everything is going wrong, since people deceive and distrust
each other.
[2] Lienhardt, op. cit., p. 45. This is only part of a complete hymn, but most
Dinka hymns seem in fact to be short, a few lines only.
[3] L. Marshall in J. L. Gibbs (ed.), *Peoples of Africa*, New York, 1965, p. 276.
[4] D. F. Bleek 1929, p. 306.

A similar pattern can be seen in the famous 'Prayer to the young moon':

> Young Moon!
> Hail, Young Moon!
> Hail, hail,
> Young Moon!
> Young Moon! speak to me!
> Hail, hail,
> Young Moon!
> Tell me of something.
> Hail, hail!
> When the sun rises,
> Thou must speak to me,
> That I may eat something.
> Thou must speak to me about a little thing,
> That I may eat.
> Hail, hail,
> Young Moon![1]

The same emphasis on intercession is evident in some of the songs associated with rain ceremonies in the central African area. Here, however, the musical and dramatic aspects are more pronounced than in Bushman prayers. As with many antiphonal songs, the refrain is assigned to a chorus while the verses are extemporized by a soloist according to a conventional pattern—a marked contrast to the lengthy and specialist hymns to West African deities. This can be illustrated from a Ndau rain song from Portuguese East Africa, a song in which the antiphonal form is expressively used to indicate the personal plight of both singer and chorus:

> Thunder-of-the-East, we're dying,
> *E we iye yo we*
> And the race will die this season!
> *E we iye yo we*
> O ye Highland folk, we perish!
> *E we iye yo we*
> O ye Sea-Side folk, we're dying!
> *E we iye yo we*
> Ye Mamboni folk, we perish!
> *E we iye yo we*

[1] Bleek and Lloyd 1911, p. 415.

Ye Mashangna folk we're dying:
*E we iye yo we*
Ye Nyalinge folk, we perish!
*E we iye yo we*
Thunder-of-the-East, we're dying!
*E we iye yo we.*[1]

It is sometimes supposed that one of the most common forms of conventional utterance in non-literate society is the spell or incantation—a verse or formula believed to be magically effective in manipulating people or things. In fact the evidence from Africa does not seem to suggest that this is often a particularly significant form of literature. It is true that magical incantations of a kind do occur—perhaps particularly in the areas most influenced by Islam—and in some societies are distinguished by a special term from other religious poetry such as hymns or prayers.[2] But even in these cases this form does not seem to be developed as a lengthy and specialized form in its own right as it is, for instance, in Melanesia.[3] Even among a people like the Azande who are so famous for their emphasis on magic and on witchcraft, verse incantations or spells do not seem to be highly developed: invocation to the poison oracle, for instance, appears to be in a prose form which, though marked by its own conventionally elliptical phraseology, is apparently not a set word-perfect formula. And the songs sung at Zande 'witch-doctors' seances', where we might expect to find such incantations, are in fact short and relatively simple (like, for instance, 'Brush away tears oo eee, we will sit down with her and brush away tears');[4] they deal with a variety of social events unrelated to magic, just as do songs sung at dances or beer-parties, and they are performed in the normal antiphonal form with leader and chorus.[5]

[1] Curtis 1920, p. 30.

[2] e.g. Songhai *zamu* (hymns) are distinguished in terminology, intention, and form from *gyindize* (magical formulas) (J. Rouch, *La Religion et la magie songhay*, Paris, 1960, p. 83).

[3] Or in some literate societies. One of the largest collections of African 'magical' texts is in fact taken from the written tradition of Ethiopia (D. Lifchitz, *Textes éthiopiens magico-religieux*, *TMIE* 38, 1940).

[4] E. E. Evans-Pritchard, *Witchcraft, Oracles and Magic among the Azande*, Oxford, 1937, p. 182. The songs have more latent meaning than may appear on the surface.

[5] Ibid., pp. 180–2. The use of prose for prayers and magical spells and the lack of a rigid word-perfect pattern also occur among the Ibo (Green 1948, p. 841). Some comments on prose prayers, curses, etc., can be found in Ch. 16. Divination literature is discussed later in the present chapter.

A further general point is that even where there is some element of what might be termed 'magic', this does not necessarily lead to a definite type of 'magical incantation'. Just as the previously assumed distinction between 'magic' and 'religion' is now questioned by many students of African beliefs and practices, so too it emerges that it is often not feasible to differentiate a clear-cut category of 'magical' incantations, spells, and charms as distinct from 'religious' poetry involving prayer, praise, invocation, or ritual announcement.

The following two examples may help to illustrate this point. Both are characterized by the kind of rhythmic and expressive diction, further brought out by the use of repetition, that in fact appears in many forms of literature but is often thought to be particularly typical of 'magical' utterances. The first is taken from the Songhai, a people, long in contact with Islam, who do distinguish between religious praises and magical formula. It is a spell used in hunting magic—and yet even here there is mention of God and of his messenger and prophet, Ndebi:

Je parle avec *Ndebi*.
*Ndebi* n'a qu'à parler avec Dieu
Les hommes d'avant ont donné à *Saley*.
*Saley* a donné à son petit frère.
*Ndebi*, laisse-moi passer par le trou avec mes captifs et mon poison.
*Ndebi*, ouvre le trou et referme le trou.
*Ndebi*, ferme le trou aux *Zin*.
*Ndebi*, ferme le trou au lion méchant.
*Ndebi*, ferme le trou à la hyène méchante.
*Ndebi*, ferme le trou aux antilopes méchantes.
*Ndebi*, ferme le trou aux êtres méchants.
*Ndebi*, ferme le trou aux langues méchantes.
*Ndebi*, ferme le trou aux frères méchants.[1]

In the second example, from the Kongo, the ancestors are being thanked for their help in curing a patient, and are being ritually shown the animals brought for a feast in their honour; these animals are to be in good condition and not attacked by hostile forces:

> May the leopard coming from the forest
> Have his teeth on edge for these animals.

---

[1] Rouch, op. cit., p. 275. *Ndebi* also appears in many of the other texts cited in idem., ch. 7 ('La magie').

May the weasel coming from the forest
Be unable to take these fowls.
May the witch who twists his belongings,
Fail to fascinate our goats.
May the thief on the look-out
Sprain his feet in his course.
Let all these animals prosper
And multiply,
Then the feast will be beautiful.

So far, this might seem to accord with the picture of a typical 'magic incantation'; but the speaker continues, addressing the ancestors in whose honour the whole is uttered:

I have held out my hands to you (in prayer),
And he who holds out his hands dies not.
I have shown you the animals of the feast,
And I have brought you no other presents,
Except palmwine,
That you may favour the procreation of (human) wealth.
And here are the kola nuts I brought for you.[1]

I am not intending to suggest that references to personal supernatural beings (such as deities or ancestors) *always* appear in such utterances, but that they appear frequently enough to make a general distinction between 'magical charms' and hymns or prayers a difficult one to draw. As a result it is not easy to find many specialized instances of purely 'magical' verses. It seems that the popular picture of all-important and word-perfect magical formulas, intended to manipulate impersonally through the force of the words alone, is one that does not often have a real counterpart in any developed or specialized form in subsaharan Africa.

Another common supposition is that with the advent of Christianity and its associated literate traditions, the importance of *oral* religious utterances will necessarily diminish. The contrary, however, would seem to be true. It is precisely in the religious sphere that there has been a marked development of oral forms in lyrics, prayers, and testimonies, each with its own conventions and techniques. This goes hand in hand with the great proliferation of native Christian churches and other separatist religious movements that is so well known a feature of contemporary Africa.

[1] J. Van Wing, 'Bakongo Incantations and Prayers', *JRAI* 60, 1930, pp. 418–19.

Sometimes these utterances are subsequently reduced to writing or even make an early appearance in written form: but even in these cases their spread and significance among their largely non-literate patrons is often primarily oral. Instances could be drawn from Mau Mau hymns, from the 'very Zulu' modern hymns of the Church of Nazareth, and from testimonies in various separatist churches in South Africa, which, even when 'spontaneous', have their own conventions and appear as rhythmic and liturgical chants.[1] One example that has been described is the lyric in the Fante Methodist Church in Ghana,[2] and I will discuss this briefly here.

The Methodist Church in Ghana is Western in organization, worship, and ethos. Nevertheless, certain aspects have been developed which appeal particularly to non-literate members, above all the Fante lyric which appears so often in services. There are two main types. In one, words and music are more or less fixed, though there may be minor variations by the congregations who actually sing them. The second type falls into the form of an individual recitative accompanied by a relatively fixed chorus. It is this second form that gives scope to the highest degree of im-provisation. Though the lyrics sometimes become stereotyped in context, a competent singer can improvise. He may wind his theme, for instance, round some reference that has struck him in the sermon just delivered or in a prayer or reading. Sometimes he will even break into the sermon with a lyric which is then taken up by others present. In a way typical of much oral literature, the rest of the congregation also play their part, for they sing the responses in chorus and are quick to anticipate what is required. Not all members of a church are themselves competent lyric singers.

[1] L. S. B. Leakey, *Defeating Mau Mau*, London, 1954, chs. 4–5; B. G. M. Sundkler, *Bantu Prophets in South Africa*, London, 2nd ed., 1961, p. 192; Tracey 1948*b*, pp. 48 ff. See also e.g. R. Kauffman, 'Hymns of the Wabvuwi', *Afr. Music* 2. 3, 1960; B. Kingslake in ibid. 1. 4, 1957, p. 18 (improvised church chants by Yoruba women); E. G. Parrinder, 'Music in West African Churches', ibid. 1. 3, 1956; P. Jans, 'Essai de musique religieuse pour indigènes dans le vicariat apostolique de Coquilhatville', *Aequatoria* 19, 1956. These developments tend to be a feature of the separatist sects rather than of the orthodox mission churches, and also, it is frequently said, arise from the way in which European hymn-tunes in mission churches violate indigenous tonal patterns, thus stultifying further developments.

[2] S. G. Williamson, 'The Lyric in the Fante Methodist Church', *Africa* 28, 1958; see also A. A. Mensah, 'The Akan Church Lyric', *Internat. Rev. of Missions* 49, 1960.

It is common for there to be one or two individuals in the congregation, usually from among the older men and women, who are recognized as song leaders. A good singer must possess two qualities: an extensive repertoire of the more familiar lyrics, and a capacity to improvise successfully within the canons of accepted musical and verbal styles. He thus requires poetic and musical ability as well as considerable verbal skill. Such lyrics are important devotionally to the non-literate Fante Methodists and play a significant part in their religious services. Williamson considers them as 'simple and sincere expressions of religious belief and experience' and contrasts this with the attitude to Western hymns which, even in translation, are stilted and un-Fante.[1]

The background to these modern lyrics lies not in the specialist hymns to deities but rather in certain lyric forms of the oral Akan tradition, particularly those associated with the *asafo* military companies, with the female *mmobome* and *asrayere* songs, and perhaps with the *adenkum* (calabash) music associated with older rituals. They also recall the practice in traditional Fante stories of the narration (like the sermon) being interrupted by a song which acts both as diversion and as commentary. As with the Methodist lyrics, such songs appear either in regular metrical form or as recitative with response from the audience. The lyrical aspect of the church songs comes out particularly in the frequent use of apostrophe and affirmation linked with the idea of a personal proclamation or recital. Most of the lyrics are brief and fairly stereotyped in content, as in the following example of one of the relatively fixed forms. The image of a shower of blessing suggested in the second line of the Fante text is a traditional one:

> Open the windows of heaven,
> Give us thy blessing!
> Open the windows of heaven,
> Give us thy blessing!
>
> Our Father, *Onyame* [God]!
> Sweet Father of us, the Church membership.
>
> Open the windows of heaven,
> Give us thy blessing.[2]

Although such lyrics are short and simple and tend to be despised by literate church members, they nevertheless represent

---

[1] Williamson, op. cit., p. 127.      [2] Ibid., p. 129.

a vigorous oral tradition, and one that has parallels elsewhere. It is one, furthermore, that is now gaining wider currency in a series of voluntary associations outside the church as well as through the increasing emphasis on such lyrics in broadcasts by Radio Ghana. Altogether, this kind of development is one likely to prove a fruitful field in the future study of oral literature.

### III

Mantic poetry represents a different type of religious literature. It can take several forms. One consists of the utterances of mediums believed by themselves and/or others to be possessed by some spirit. When oracular utterances take the from of poetry, they have their own conventions. However, although possibly widespread in Africa, there have been few detailed studies of them,[1] perhaps because they tend to be obscurely expressed in oracular language (sometimes even in a special language of their own) or in a fragmentary or repetitive form. On the other hand the poems that accompany certain divining procedures are of a more systematized and specialized type and, accordingly, have been more accessible to collectors. This type of mantic poetry tends to be highly conventional, with little emphasis on the individual creativity of the performer; a common pattern is for it to be the preserve of specialist diviners who have undergone training and/or special initiation to master the techniques of divination and its interpretation, as well as to develop the ability to recite the requisite poetry. And, finally, there are combinations of these two types, when both possession and more conventional forms of divination are involved.[2]

Two examples of the more specialized divination literature will be illustrated here. The examples come from opposite ends of the continent: the praises associated with divining bones among the Sotho of southern Africa, and the highly elaborate Ifa corpus of literature from West Africa.

---

[1] Though see A. V. King, 'A Bòoríi Liturgy from Katsina', *Afr. Language Studies* 7, 1966 and Supplement, 1967; G. Balandier, 'Femmes "possédées" et leurs chants', *Présence afr.* 5, 1948; and work in progress by F. Topan on spirit (pepo) songs and their role in a spirit mediumship cult in Mombasa, Kenya.

[2] I am not proposing to discuss here the specialized invocations sometimes made to oracles *before* the results of the query are declared. Further remarks on prose prayers, etc., are to be found in Ch. 16.

### (i) *Praises of divining bones among the Sotho*[1]

In Sotho divination an integral part is played by the ritual
chants or praises (*lithoko*; *direto*) associated both with the bones
used in divination and with each of the special combinations
formed by these bones when thrown by a diviner. Mastery of these
oracular poems depends on long training and initiation, and the
diviner must know a large number of them before he can practise
his art.

The general pattern of divination and its associated literature
seems to be constant throughout the Sotho area, though the actual
poems differ according to the locality. The divining apparatus
itself consists of a set of bones from various animals including
cattle. As the diviner begins his session, he handles the bones and
praises them, saying, for instance:

> You my white ones, children of my parents,
> Whom I drank from mothers' breasts!
> And you many coloured cattle
> Whom I knew when still on mother's back,
> From whose hoofs these chips were cut;
> Hoofs of cattle black and red and yellow.[2]

Each of the four principal bones in the set (four to twenty in all)
has special significance as well as its own name and praises.
After praising his bones the diviner makes a throw and notices
how the four principal bones have fallen; the first two have four
sides each and can thus fall in any of four ways; the second pair are
counted as having only two each. Each of these many combinations has a special 'praise' associated with it which the diviner then
recites. This consists of a title, a poem which is interpreted as
alluding to the questioner's problem, and a direct or indirect suggestion as to the remedy that should be employed. After the
recitation, the questioner is led to agree that the verse recited fits
his case.[3]

The enigmatic and allusive nature of these oracular poems can
be illustrated from the praise entitled 'The swimming (fall) of the
sunbird', a poem which illustrates a particular 'fall' of the four

[1] Based on W. M. Eiselen, 'The Art of Divination as Practised by the
Bamesemola', *Bantu Studies* 6, 1932; F. Laydevant, 'The Praises of the Divining
Bones among the Basotho', ibid. 7, 1933; A. W. Hoernlé in I. Schapera (ed.), *The
Bantu-speaking Tribes of South Africa*, London, 1937.

[2] Eiselen, op. cit., p. 11.                    [3] Laydevant, op. cit., p. 344.

principal bones. It can be seen how the symbolic expression is susceptible of several interpretations and is not concerned with direct literal prediction:

'Sunbird, secret and daring.
When you take a bit of straw,
And say you imitate the hammerkop.
The hammerkop nobody can imitate.
It is the bird of those who take a new garment in the deep waters.
It is taking bits of straw one by one.'
It is building above the pools.
The little sunbird should not fall.
It falls and makes *phususu* in the pools.
It is the patient one sitting at the drift.
The sins are passing and you see them.
The reed of the river is mocking at the reed of the plain.
It says: When the grass is burning.
The reed of the plain is laughing at the reed of the river,
It says: When the rivers get full.[1]

One interpretation of the verse is that people are trying to kill the questioner by lightning because of his wealth and good luck; they accuse him of imitating a chief and say he must fall. To protect himself he is told to get a feather of a hammerkop, sunbird, or one of the yellow sparrows living in the reeds, 'a feather of the lightning', which will guard him. Further allusions are suggested to a Sotho listener, not all of them directly connected with the diviner's interpretation: the hammerkop is not only commonly associated with lightning, but is also an accepted symbol of power, while the reeds symbolize the common people quarrelling together because of jealousy; the image of the sunbirds falling into the water is an allusion to the circumcision rites of Sotho girls.[2]

Jealousy and discord are very common themes. In the fall named 'The Fame of the Lamp' the diviner alludes, through the image of an elephant, to a chief who is spreading enmity between his sons while even the nation takes part in the quarrel. It is suggested that the people must be treated with medicine from the horn:

O female elephant,
O elephant, I have become blind,
O elephant, I have entered secretly.

[1] Ibid., pp. 349–50.    [2] Ibid., p. 351.

The path of the enemy was red;
There was blood, there was disorder.
Shake the ear, you running elephant.
That the others should grow and remember your name.[1]

The next verse briefly and effectively pictures the hatred between a man's co-wives. One of them feels she is persecuted on account of the others, and she is given medicine to help her by the diviner:

Child of the tortoise, I am burning,
I suffered in my heart,
On account of my smallness of being a tortoise.[2]

Again, 'The Famous *Masibo* (a plant) of the Swimming':

Swim on the deep waters, lie upon them.
They have no hippo and no little things.
They have no beast of prey biting whilst it moves,
And coiling itself in a corner.
Only the little hippos are swimming.
The big ones do not swim any more.
They rip open and throw out their backs.
Why are the crocodiles quarrelling in the water?
They are quarrelling on account of an old crocodile,
Of many talks in the water.
Which says: I do not bite, I only play;
I shall bite the year after next.
When the mimosa and the willow tree are growing.[3]

The crocodile and hippopotamus symbolize the important people who are spreading misunderstanding between their children. The remedy prescribed is to use certain plants, among them the willow tree and the mint.

Other topics introduced are: problems about going on a journey; hunting; illness; signs of good or bad luck. But the obscure and symbolic character of the poems is noticeable in every context, and there is a tendency for both poems and interpretations to be concerned less with definite predictions than with commenting allusively on some facet of personal relationships. Thus illness is usually dealt with not by predicting a cure or its opposite, but by suggesting the possible enmities and witchcraft that may have given rise to it, alluding to this in poetic and figurative terms.

---

[1] Laydevant, op. cit., pp. 369–70.     [2] Ibid., p. 371.     [3] Ibid., p. 361.

The poems themselves play a central part in the whole divination process, for it is through the imagery of the poetry that the sufferer can recognize his own case. In spite of the conventional nature of the poems there is wide scope for personal interpretations of them in a particular case, a possibility closely connected with their obscure and allusive nature. The flexible application of this oracular literature is added to by the fact that though the poems as a whole seem to be orally transmitted and memorized (with but slight variations) by the diviners, each diviner is also free, if he is able, to compose new praises for the various falls, and 'is only too glad to show his artistic ability in that kind of poetry'.[1] Mantic poetry among the Sotho is developed for its own sake as an artistic form of poetic expression governed by its own conventions as well as for the light it throws on people's ills and hatreds.

## (ii) *Odu Ifa*[2]

The final example of religious poetry is the oracular literature associated with divination among the Yoruba of Southern Nigeria. Although this includes prose as well as poetry, it is worth considering here both for its intrinsic interest and for the way it illustrates the complexity there can be in African religious literature.

Before discussing Ifa literature, it is necessary to describe something of the mechanism and beliefs of the Yoruba divination system.[3] Ifa, the Yoruba oracle, is one among the pantheon of Yoruba gods, and as such appears in many (and sometimes contradictory) stories and myths, often under his alternative title of Orunmila. In one myth, for instance, the gods are depicted as hungy because they received few sacrifices. The trickster god, Eshu, then showed Ifa the system of divination so that as a result men could be helped through the diviners' skill, while, at the same

---

[1] Ibid., p. 341.

[2] The main sources used are G. Parrinder, *West African Religion*, London, 1961, ch. 13; R. C. Abraham, *Dictionary of Modern Yoruba*, London, 1958 (under *Ifá*); Bascom 1941, 1943; Abimbola 1964, 1965; Gbadamosi and Beier 1959, pp. 25 ff.; R. Prince, *Ifa*, Ibadan, 1964; and Morton-Williams *et al.* 1966. Full bibliographies can be found in Maupoil 1961 (who discusses in detail the very similar Fa divination system in Dahomey) and Bascom 1961.

[3] Similar or identical systems are found among the Fon of Dahomey and Ewe of Togo as well as some other Nigerian peoples. Its elaborateness has led some to speculate about possible external origins, but it is now generally agreed that Ifa has a long history in West Africa and that, for recent centuries at any rate, the centre of distribution has been Yoruba country in Southern Nigeria.

time, the gods would benefit through the sacrifices and thank-offerings that human beings would be commanded to make by their diviners. Ifa has a special position among the gods. He is both the deity who acts as the intermediary between men and gods, and also in a sense is the impersonal principle of divination by which mankind has access to what is otherwise hidden from them. Ifa thus, as god and as oracle, plays a central part in Yoruba religious and everyday life:

> Ifa is the master of today;
> Ifa is the master of tomorrow;
> Ifa is the master of the day after tomorrow;
> To Ifa belongs all the four days
> Created by Orişa into this world.[1]

The Ifa divination system is a highly elaborate one. It rests on a series of mathematical permutations, the principle of which must be grasped in order to understand the way in which certain pieces of literature are associated with each of these. The permutations of figures (*odu*) are based on two columns of four units each, and the different combinations which these eight units may form between them. The total number of figures is 256, each with its own name and associated literature. It is only after obtaining one of the figures to form the basis of his utterance that the diviner can proceed to the divination itself.

There are two main ways of obtaining the figures. The first, less elaborate mechanism consists of a chain or cord of eight half-seeds (often split mango stones), divided into two portions of four half-seeds each. When this is thrown down by the diviner, the resultant figure makes two columns of four units each, the exact combination depending on whether the seeds have fallen convex- or concave-side-up. The other way of obtaining a figure, a longer method used in important consultations, is with a set of sixteen palm-nuts and a small board. The diviner throws or passes the nuts rapidly from one hand to the other. If either one or two nuts are left in the right hand, the throw is valid and he makes a corresponding mark on his board: a double mark for one nut, a single for two. The process is repeated eight times and eight marks are thus made in the dust on the tray; these start from the bottom right-hand side and are laid out in the form of two parallel

[1] Abimbola 1965, p. 4.

columns of four sets of marks each. This gives the same result as the eight-seed chain, the double mark corresponding to a seed convex-side-up, a single mark to the concave.

*Table showing the Names and Structure of the Columns which form the Basis of Ifa Figures* (odu)

(from Parrinder, op. cit., p. 141; Abraham, op. cit., p. 276)

| 1. *ogbe* | 2. *ọyẹku* | 3. *iwori* | 4. *odi* |
|---|---|---|---|
| I | II | II | I |
| I | II | I | II |
| I | II | I | II |
| I | II | II | I |

| 5. *irosun* | 6. *ọwara* | 7. *ọbara* | 8. *ọkọnrọn* |
|---|---|---|---|
| I | II | I | II |
| I | II | II | II |
| II | I | II | II |
| II | I | II | I |

| 9. *ogunda* | 10. *ọsa* | 11. *ika* | 12. *oturopọn* |
|---|---|---|---|
| I | II | II | II |
| I | I | I | II |
| I | I | II | I |
| II | I | II | II |

| 13. *otuwa* | 14. *irẹtẹ* | 15. *ọsẹ* | 16. *ofun* |
|---|---|---|---|
| I | I | I | II |
| II | I | II | I |
| I | II | I | II |
| I | I | II | I |

*Note.* The order of the *odu* figures also has some significance in the full divination process. That given here is the order most commonly found, but there are regional variations (see Bascom 1961).

It is the figure thus produced that determines the diviner's utterances to his client. As can be seen from the table, each column of four can fall in any of sixteen permutations. When the two columns are considered together, as they are by Ifa diviners, the total number of different figures that can be produced is 16 × 16 = 256. Of this number, 16 are the leading figures or *odu* proper: these are the combinations of two identical columns. Thus the double figure based on the column called *ọyẹku* and known as *ọyẹku meji* appears as

| | |
|---|---|
| II | II |
| II | II |
| II | II |
| II | II |

while the double figure *iwori meji*, based on the *iwori* column, is

$$
\begin{array}{cc}
\text{II} & \text{II} \\
\text{I} & \text{I} \\
\text{I} & \text{I} \\
\text{II} & \text{II}
\end{array}
$$

The remaining 240 figures, those in which the two columns differ, are considered secondary, and, though often referred to by the same term as for the principal figures (*odu*), are strictly *ọmọ odu*, 'children of *odu*'. An example of one of these secondary *odu* would be that name *iwori ọbara*, a combination of the *ọbara* and *iwori* columns (the right-hand one being named first in the Yoruba title):

$$
\begin{array}{cc}
\text{I} & \text{II} \\
\text{II} & \text{I} \\
\text{II} & \text{I} \\
\text{II} & \text{II}
\end{array}
$$

Once the diviner has thrown his figure, the divination proper can begin. Each figure has several pieces of literature (*ẹsẹ*) specifically connected with it, and it is in the words associated with the figure thrown that the answer to the client's query must be found. There is no definite number of pieces for each *odu*, but a diviner would not normally begin to practise unless he knew at least four for each (thus involving mastery of at least one thousand in all); good diviners are said to know about eight of the pieces for each of the 256 figures and many more for the important figures.[1] It is commonly believed that the number of pieces for each figure is ideally sixteen, in keeping with the mathematical symmetry of the system as a whole. But there seems to be no such fixed correspondence in actual practice, and the number and to some extent the content of the verses vary with individual capacity and with the locality.

The practical point of these pieces is to guide the inquirer by suggesting a sacrifice or type of worship, by indicating his likely fortune, and by referring to a precedent from which he can judge his own case. Since more than one piece can be quoted for whatever figure is thrown, these are recited at random one after the other, and it is for the client, not the diviner, to select which applies to his particular case. The consultation thus proceeds through

[1] Bascom 1941, pp. 43, 50.

poetic allusion and analogy rather than through straight answers to specific questions—and it is this quality which leads to its development as a corpus of literature and gives depth and meaning to the bare injunctions with which the divination may open.

The pieces associated with each figure fall into a general pattern. Each usually opens with a mention of the sacrifices and other actions the client must carry out to have success. This first part is relatively prosaic; it may run, for instance:

> This person is intending to marry a new wife. He is warned to make sacrifice to Ọṣun so that the wife may be prosperous. He is warned never to flog the wife if he wants peace in his home. He should make sacrifice with fifteen cowries and a big hen. Ifa says that if he observes all these warnings, success will be his.[1]

This is followed by the main part of the piece, expressed in poetic language and sometimes chanted all through. This part is concerned with setting out a precedent in terms of a previous divination. First often comes the name of the priest of Ifa who is said to have made the prophecy in the precedent cited, and the name of the client(s) for whom he was divining—these may be people, deities, animals, plants, inanimate objects. Thus the client may be told that on the previous occasion

> The-big-and-terrible-Rainbow[2]
> Cast Ifa for the Iroko tree
> Of the town of Igbo.[3]

Another diviner is referred to as 'Oropa Niga; to fight and stir up dust like Buffalo; parched dust on the top of a rock'[4] or as 'I-have-no-time-to-waste'.[1] It will be seen that this section often involves elaborate and poetic names which may have symbolic meaning. Second in this main part of the piece there usually comes a poem (sometimes elaborated in a prose story) which describes the occasion of the previous divination. As will emerge from the examples given below, the subject-matter of this part is most varied. There are variations in length: sometimes there is only a fragmentary allusion (perhaps not much more than a poetic proverb), while at others there is a long and dramatic narration. Finally, the client is told the result of the previous divination described and thus,

---

[1] Abimbola 1965, p. 15.
[2] Praise name of the diviner.
[3] Abimbola 1965, p. 16.
[4] Bascom 1943, p. 128.

indirectly, what he can expect himself. Very often the conclusion pointedly shows that on the previous occasion the one who performed the due sacrifices prospered, while the negligent met disaster. Sometimes the whole recitation is then closed by a chorus which is chanted in unison by the diviner, his pupils, and the client.

Within this general pattern there is plenty of scope for variation in the actual pieces recited. They differ greatly in length. Abimbola reports several that can be recited for more than half an hour, while others take only one or two minutes.[1] The plots and the people involved in them are also of many different kinds. They include just about all the topics that can be met in narrative stories throughout the continent. This great variety is hardly surprising when one considers that even a mediocre diviner must know at least a thousand of these precedents with their accompanying verses and stories. They can be about animals, gods, legendary humans, natural phenomena like rivers or hills, plants, and even inanimate things like metals or shells, and they may take the form of a simple story about a man going on a journey, an account of the founding of a town, a philosophical discussion of the merits and demerits of monogamy—'there is . . . no limit to the subject-matter which ẹsẹ Ifa may deal with'.[2] The outcome often takes an aetiological form with the present nature of some plant or animal traced to its imaginary actions in the story—in particular its obedience or disobedience to the injunctions laid on it by the oracle; its characteristics in the world today thus provide a kind of imaginative validation of the truth of the story.

The sort of plots involved can be seen from a few brief synopses:[3]

1. It is because Maizebeer, Bamboo-wine, and Palm-wine refused to sacrifice that a person who has been intoxicated recovers from his stupefied condition after sleeping.

2. Lizard was told to make a sacrifice, part of which was to enable him to marry, and part of which was to ensure that his wife would continue to love him. Lizard sacrificed only the first part, and after he had married, his wife left him. It is because he is looking for his wife in the tree-tops that he raises himself on his forelegs and peers from side to side.

3. When Brass, Lead, and Iron were told to sacrifice, Iron said that the diviners were just lying, that events had been predestined by

---

[1] Abimbola 1965, p. 13.                    [2] Ibid., p. 14.
[3] Quoted from the convenient summaries in Bascom 1941, pp. 46, 48, 45.

Olorun [God], and that their course could not be altered by sacrificing. Only Brass and Lead sacrificed, and because of this they can be buried for many years without rotting, while Iron rusts away in a short time.

4. When the 165 kinds of trees in the forest were told to sacrifice, only three did as they were told. The others replied that they did not have enough money. When Eshu [a god] reported this to the gods, a storm was sent to the forest. It pulled up the larger trees by the roots, or broke them down; but the *atori* bush and the *ariran* and *esun* grasses, who had sacrificed, simply bent down while the storm passed over them.

5. Orunmila [another name for the god Ifa] was told to include a knife as a part of a sacrifice, lest he be taken as a thief on a journey he was considering. He postponed the sacrifice, and when he stole some kola-nuts on the way, he escaped capture only after having been cut on the palm of his hand. The owner of the nuts asked the king to gather everyone together so that he might identify the thief by this cut. Frightened, Orunmila went to the diviners, who doubled the sacrifice. While everyone slept Eshu took one of the knives and cut the palms of everyone, including the unborn children. (It is because of this that people have lines on their palms.) When the owner of the nuts demanded that Orunmila open his hand, Orunmila showed that everyone, including the king himself, had the same scars; and because he had been falsely accused, he was given a great deal of wealth.

6. Stout Foreigner was told to sacrifice so as to find good fortune; he sacrificed, and everything to which he turned his hand became good.

The actual poems and prose narratives which give full expression to these plots are of course much more lengthy and elaborate than the bald summaries just quoted. The last one, for instance, seems to be the piece quoted in full in another source, and is associated with the fourth of the sixteen principal *odus*. The allusive verse is, as often, explained and expanded in the straightforward prose narrative whcih follows it.

Ifa sees the prospect of greatness for this person in a strange land. He should make sacrifice with four pigeons, a good garment of his, and a shoe.

I arrived in good time,
I travelled in good time,
I am the only man who travels in time of fortune
When valuable objects of wealth are being deposited I entered unannounced like the heir to the wealth
I am not the heir to the wealth, I am only good at travelling in time of fortune.

(These people) divined for the fat stranger[1]
Who would enter unannounced
On the day the property of the dead king of Benin was being shared.[2]

The fat stranger was going to Benin in search of a suitable place to practise his Ifa. He was told that he would prosper in Benin but he was warned to make sacrifice. After making the sacrifice he made for Benin. He entered Benin just as the King of that city died. He thought that it would not speak well of him—a renowned diviner (*babaláwo*)—if he did not say his condolences to the people of Benin. But he did not know that whenever the properties of a dead king were being shared out in Benin a good portion usually goes to the fortunate stranger who entered just in time. On arriving at the place where the properties were being shared, the fat stranger was given a good portion of the property.

After gathering the materials given him, he made for his native land. He started to sing in praise of his diviners (who divined for him before he went to Benin) while in turn his diviners praised Ifa. He made a party for his neighbours. There the *àràn*[3] was beaten, and it gave its pleasant melodies. Unconsciously, as he stretched his legs, he started to dance. On opening his mouth the song of the diviners was already on his lips.

He said it happened, just as his Ifa priests said it would.

I arrive in good time,
I travelled in good time,
I am the only man who travels in time of fortune
When valuable objects of wealth are being deposited I entered un-
     announced like the heir to the wealth
I am not the heir to the wealth, I am only good at travelling in time
     of fortune.
(These people) divined for the fat stranger
Who would enter unannounced
On the day the property of the dead king of Benin was being shared.
Who will help us reconstruct this city?
Only the fat stranger will help us reconstruct this city.[4]

Additional examples can give a further idea of the poetic quality and variety of much of this Ifa literature. It will be remembered that each is only one of several pieces belonging to a particular throw and that the allusive poems are often accompanied by explanatory prose narrative. To a Yoruba listener their obscurity

---

[1] *Gòdògbò*—fat or bold, and at the same time tall and stately.
[2] Benin has the reputation of great wealth among the Yoruba—'Benin the place of money'.
[3] Drum connected with Ifa.      [4] Abimbola 1964, pp. 7–8.

is also lessened by the fact that they conventionally deal with common and recognizable themes: the consequences of sacrifice (often to be seen in the present characteristics of things); praise of a particular Ifa figure or a particular god (often suggesting that he should be worshipped); and indication of the client's present fortune or misfortune.

In the first, the questioner is allusively told to worship Obatala:

> The sky is immense, but grows no grass.
> That is what the oracle said to Obatala,
> To whom the great God gave the reins of the world.
> God of the Igbo, I stretch out my hands.
> Give the reins of the world to me.[1]

The next extract from a long Ifa poem is about Ifa under his title of Ela, and is remarkable for its effective use of tones. Whenever there is a pause the phrase ends with a low tone, and the whole poem concludes with the word Ela, which 'fittingly comes in on a low monotone, giving the whole extract a sense of gravity':[2]

> He made the 'Odundun' King of leaves,
> And the Tete its deputy;
> He made the Sea King of waters,
> And the lagoon its deputy;
> Still Ela was accused of the mismanagement of the world,
> Whereupon, Ela grew angry,
> And climbed to heaven with a rope.
> Come back to receive our homage,
> O, Ela![3]

In the next two examples the listener can, if he decides they apply to him, draw inferences about his future fortune. The first, if told to a woman, suggests she may bear a child; the second, in narrative form, alludes to death:

> I am blessing two, not one.
> This was prophesied to the sea lily
> Which reaches down into the mud, the origin of creation.
> The time of creation has come.[1]

> This is the oracle of a hunter
> Who went hunting in the forest of Onikorogbo.
> They asked him to sacrifice,
> So that he might not meet his death.

[1] Gbadamosi and Beier 1959, p. 26.  [2] Laṣebikan 1956, p. 46.
[3] Ibid., pp. 46–7.

They asked him to sacrifice eggs,
All the eggs in his house.
But he refused to sacrifice.
He came into the forest,
But found no animals to shoot.

After he had wandered about for a long time
He met Death.

For a while they were hunting together.
At last they found two eggs.
Death said to the hunter:
You may take them home.
The hunter proposed to divide them,
But Death refused.
The hunter went home lonely.
Soon after that famine came.
The hunter cooked the eggs
And ate them with his children.
Then Death arrived and said:
I have come for my share.
There is famine in heaven.
And we have nothing to eat.
The hunter said: Alas,
We have already eaten the eggs.
Then Death killed the hunter and his children.[1]

Particular divination figures are also mentioned in the Ifa poems. One praises the figure *eji ogbe* which is the first and senior figure in all systems of Ifa divination:

The might of all rivers in the world is not to be compared with that
of the sea; the dignity of rivers which rise on a hill is not as that
of the lagoon.
There is no Ifa that can be compared with Eji-ogbe;
To command is the privilege of a commander;
Eji-ogbe, you are the king of them all.
I asked for honours from the Lagoon, for he is greater than the River.
I received them, but I was not satisfied. I asked them at the
hands of Olokun Jeniade, the God of the sea and father of all
rivers, but still I was not satisfied.
Who does not know that only the gifts of Olorun, the God of Heaven,
are sufficient till the day of one's death?[2]

[1] Gbadamosi and Beier 1959, p. 28.
[2] J. D. Clarke, 'Ifa Divination', *JRAI* 69, 1939, p. 248.

The poem about the figure *iwori wotura* also alludes to good fortune:

Iwori Wotura
Anybody who meets beauty and does not look at it will soon be poor.
The red feathers are the pride of the parrot.
The young leaves are the pride of the palm tree. Iwori Wotura.
The white flowers are the pride of the leaves.
The well swept verandah is the pride of the landlord. Iwori Wotura.
The straight tree is the pride of the forest.
The fast deer is the pride of the bush. Iwori Wotura.
The rainbow is the pride of heaven.
The beautiful woman is the pride of her husband. Iwori Wotura.
The children are the pride of the mother.
The moon and the stars are the pride of the sun. Iwori Wotura.
Ifa says: beauty and all sorts of good fortunes arrive.[1]

The final example expresses once more the constant theme that one must sacrifice to obtain success:

The lord of the Forest and the lord of the Savannah,
Wanted to seduce Beloved, the wife of Fire.
They were asked to sacrifice broomsticks, a hen and Ifa leaves.
But the lord of the Savannah refused. He said:
'And why should I, chief of the Savannah bring sacrifice
Merely because I seduced a woman?
Have I not an army of poisonous yams and thorny shrubs
All ready to protect me?'—But the lord of the Forest sacrificed.
The day came when Beloved, Fire's wife, had gone to the house of
    Savannah
The Fire ran burning to the lord of the Savannah and cried:
Beloved, Beloved, Beloved.
And he burned the poisonous yams and the thorny shrubs, and all the
    Savannah was burned.
But when Fire returned to the forest, they sprinkled Ifa leaves on it
    and it died.[2]

Those who memorize and recite such poems are members of a highly trained and respected profession. The Ifa diviners (*baba-lawo*, lit. 'father of mysteries') spend several years learning the literature for their profession. The minimum seems to be three years: the first is often spent learning the names and structure of the *odu*, the second and third learning some of the literature of

[1] Gbadamosi and Beier 1959, p. 30.      [2] Ibid., p. 27.

each as well as the actual practice of divination and its rituals.[1]
But sometimes seven or ten years are spent in apprenticeship to
a qualified diviner, and the general opinion is, not surprisingly,
that an Ifa diviner continues to learn as long as he lives. In some
areas at least it is also a strictly organized profession with a head
diviner (*olori-awo*) in each quarter of a town or village and several
grades of diviners under him.[2] It is clear also that both they and
others regard their skill seriously. Though it is presumably possible in principle for dishonest individuals to exploit the system,
there seems to be no question of the system as a whole being a
piece of calculated trickery. As will be clear even from the few
examples cited (see p. 196, no. 3), however, the Yoruba themselves
admit the existence of individual scepticism on the subject.
Nevertheless, the general belief is not only that the diviners themselves are genuine but that what they say represents the accumulated
wisdom of generations, a belief strengthened by the fact that diviners
themselves approach their own problems through Ifa consultation.

That Ifa divination and its literature should be regarded as
seriously as this is not surprising when one considers the nature of
the consultation. Only one point need be repeated in this connection.[3] For each figure that is thrown the diviner does not repeat
just one poem (and associated story), but at least four or so, either
in outline or in full. Not only are these mostly expressed in allusive
and poetic language, but the diviner himself does not know in
advance the specific problem the questioner has in mind, and it is
left to the client to make his choice among the several verses
recited; there is always likely to be at least one which will appear
relevant to him, particularly in view of the fact that what is described is not an exact prediction for the future but a poetically
described precedent. 'The diviner's role is to recite and explain,
the supplicant's role is to discern the precise canto in which *Ifa* is
speaking to him, and *Ifa* may speak in veiled ways.'[4] In view of
this literary and thus in a sense unfalsifiable nature of Ifa, the
respect given to diviners and the continued popularity of Ifa
divining among Christians and Muslims as well as pagans is not
any cause for surprise.

[1] Parrinder, op. cit., p. 145.
[2] Clarke, op. cit., p. 250; Abraham, op. cit., p. 277.
[3] For further factors involved in the continuing faith in the validity of Ifa
divination procedures see Bascom 1941.
[4] Prince, op. cit., p. 9.

Ifa, then, covers a whole corpus of literature consisting not only of straightforward injunctions to sacrifice, of meaningful and elaborate names and (sometimes) prose stories, but also of a body of allusive and complex poetry. This literature cannot be said to form a definitive and fixed canon. Not only does the number of pieces associated with each figure differ from diviner to diviner, but there are also regional differences in the pieces themselves[1] as well as in the formal order of the figures. Each piece is separate and complete in itself, and may contradict other comparable pieces. The literature itself is fluid in the sense that there may be changes in the pieces, with new material merged and added by individual diviners which is then accepted as authoritative by their followers. But in spite of this lack of fixity and comprehensiveness, it remains true that the Ifa utterances form part of a conventional and vast scheme, hugely conceived, one that is known and recited by serious and highly qualified specialists but which has not yet been systematically collected in written form in anything approaching the scale of its conception.[2]

IV

One of the main points to emerge from this brief account of African religious poetry is its variety. Just as the theory and practice of religions vary in different parts of Africa, so too does religious poetry. Similarly, even in one society there may not only be religious variations with corresponding effects on literature, but different poetic genres, many of them connected with religion, are likely to be recognized. Furthermore simplistic assumptions which attribute cultural unity of various kinds to African religion or to religious expression turn out to be highly questionable. Thus the picture of African religious expression

[1] Bascom 1943, p. 130.
[2] The largest published collection is in Maupoli 1961 (of the more or less identical Fa system of Dahomey), but even he does not attempt to cover all the 256 *odu*. Abimbola has collected much of the literature pertaining to the sixteen principal *odu*, but writes that it will probably take thirty or forty years to record the pieces associated with the remaining *odu* which are less well known—'for if it takes about two sessions to work on 16 Odus, it will take 32 years to work on the remaining 256!' Abimbola 1964, p. 12. A number of recordings have also been made more recently by the Institute of African Studies, University of Ibadan, but not yet fully transcribed.

dominated by magical spells and incantations can be seen to have little evidence to support it. Certain other generalizations also seem uncertain. It is asserted, for instance, in one recent collection of religious texts that when authors of these pieces do exist they are always anonymous, and that such texts possess no *literary* character for their users who are interested only in their religious functions.[1] There are in fact far too many variations to sum up the matter so simply. Sometimes there are official priests and religious specialists, people who tend to be authoritative and conservative and lay great stress on the idea of preserving the ancient text. In other cases there is little interest in authority and more scope for improvisation and originality. Moreover, the literary appreciation of religious pieces varies with culture, context, genre, and even individual—there is certainly no *a priori* reason to suppose that it cannot coexist with religious sentiments or situations.

Another misleading generalization is the idea of the 'intense religiousness' supposed to characterize the peoples of Africa and their religious texts.[2] On the basis of their oral literature this seems doubtful. In any one culture religious poetry is not necessarily the most developed or valued—one need only mention the instance of the Southern Bantu among whom panegyric of human beings (not gods) is the most specialized and prized. Ifa divination literature might perhaps be cited as a counter-example, being the most largely conceived scheme of Yoruba literature. But, quite apart from the question of whether this means it is necessarily the most complex or valued type, one could hardly say, in view of much of its content and context, that it really offered definite proof that the Yoruba were therefore a highly 'religious' people in any obvious sense. In any case the religious significance of a poetic product can only be assessed with a detailed knowledge of its social and literary background, for only then can one grasp its meaning (or meanings) for composer, reciter, and listeners.

It is true that a few general remarks can be made about African religious poetry: the prevalence of the hymn in various forms; the relative lack of significance (apart from Islamic verse) of didactic and narrative religious poetry; and the spread of recent forms influenced by Christianity. But apart from such obvious generalizations few general points can be established. Indeed perhaps they are not worth searching for at this stage. What is now needed is

[1] Dieterlen 1965, pp. 17–18.                    [2] Ibid., p. 20.

much more detailed collection and analysis of religious poetry (including recent Christian-inspired forms). The whole subject deserves far more study than it has as yet received. In particular it needs to be analysed in terms of *literature* (and not just social function) and presented not as isolated snippets but in relation to its proponents, listeners, and social context.

# 8

## SPECIAL PURPOSE POETRY—WAR, HUNTING, AND WORK

Military poetry: Nguni; Akan. Hunting poetry: Yoruba *ijala*; Ambo hunters' songs. Work songs

SOME subjects are of particular significance in African poetry. Besides the subjects already elaborated there are others that could be discussed. There is poetry associated, for example, with secret societies,[1] various types of associations,[2] initiation,[3] begging,[4] masquerades,[5] and there are also the very common songs to do with cattle and cattle herding.[6] But war and hunting are topics of particular interest for many African societies, and have frequently given rise to specialized poetry; while songs to accompany work are so common throughout Africa as to demand treatment by their sheer quantity.

In treating these genres we are faced with one difficulty. Some of them, at first sight at least, seem so closely tied to the actual occasions on which they are performed—whether war, hunting,

---

[1] e.g. songs of various Limba societies.

[2] e.g. the songs of the various associations in Dahomey which extol their own worth and the aid they give to members (M. J. Herskovits, *Dahomey, an Ancient West African Kingdom*, New York, 1938, vol. ii, p. 321).

[3] e.g. H. E. Lambert, 'Some Initiation Songs of the Southern Kenya Coast', *Swahili* 35, 1965; Driberg 1932, pp. 14–15, 29–30 (Didinga and Lango); M. Schulien, 'Il "Muambo" degli Acciuabo. Testi e note sul vero significato della iniziazioni della gioventu', *Annali Istituto Universitario Orientale di Napoli*, N.S. 3, 1949; Mayssal 1965, pp. 59 ff. (Cameroons Fulani); K. Alnaes, 'Nyama-yingi's Song: an Analysis of a Konzo Circumcision Song', *Africa* 37, 1967; Dieterlen 1965, part II; E. J. Krige, 'Girls' Puberty Songs and their Relation to Fertility, Health, Morality and Religion among the Zulu', *Africa* 38, 1968; H. Von Sicard, 'Lemba Initiation Chants', *Ethnos* 2/4, 1943 (*AA* 18.645).

[4] e.g. Fletcher 1912, pp. 62–3 (Hausa).

[5] e.g. Gbadamosi and Beier 1959, pp. 38–49 (Yoruba); B. Gbadamosi and U. Beier, 'The Poetry of Masquerades', *Odù* 7, 1959 (Yoruba); Egudu 1967 p. 9 (Ibo).

[6] e.g. Ba 1950, pp. 175–9 (Fulani); Kagame 1947 (Rwanda); T. O. Beidelman, 'Some Baraguyu Cattle Songs', *J. Afr. languages* 4, 1965; see also Ch. 9, p. 251.

or work—that they seem to approach a fixed formulaic utterance
with little room for variation, and change and innovation are thus
at a minimum. How far then can they be treated in the same way
as other, more innovatory, genres of oral literature? We are reminded here of the difficulty of making a clear-cut distinction
between literature and non-literature in oral cultures.[1] One needs
to remember, however, that this distinction is clearly only a matter
of degree; some of the examples mentioned here are evidently as
much 'literature' as examples in earlier chapters. Even if we make
a rough division between innovatory and non-innovatory genres,
with hunting and work songs in the second category, lyric or
topical songs as pre-eminently in the first, we still find that even
within these categories there can be distinctions on these same
lines. Among hunting poems, for instance, Yoruba *ijala* poetry
clearly provides much scope for variation and composition, whereas
Ambo songs, it seems, do not. The same might be said of work
songs, depending on the amount of variation by the leading soloist.[2]
A second point is that our attitude to such examples must depend
not least on the *local* evaluation of these pieces. Too often this is
something we are not told about, so that in the meantime all we
can do is to present the pieces and hope that more research will
elucidate their background. Finally, some of these poems are not
nearly so closely tied to their occasions as they might seem at first
sight: detachment and insight, so crucial for literary expression,
are also involved.

All in all there is no real solution to the problem—except to
point to it and to suggest further research. What we particularly
need to know about are both local attitudes to these forms
and the amount of innovation and variation that *actually* take
place.

I

Poetry about both hunting and war seems to involve the same
ideas of romance and glory. Sometimes the same genre of poetry
is even used to deal with both, like the Galla *gheraera* or boasts,
universal among warriors and hunters,[3] or the Adangme *tegble*
poetry used both for war and to honour a man who had killed a

---

[1] Ch. 1, pp. 22 ff.  [2] On this point see Ch. 9, pp. 259 ff.
[3] Chadwicks iii, 1940, p. 548.

leopard with a spear.[1] But even where there is no such direct
association, the two subjects seem to be related. Both involve
action which is out of the run of ordinary every-day pursuits; in
both there is danger, triumph, or heroism; and boasting, challenge,
and specialized ability (sometimes supplemented by magic) are
frequent elements in both.

The sorts of occasions on which war songs were sung are not
very thoroughly documented—I suppose one of the conditions for
the collection and study of such songs was in fact the ending of
wide-spread warring—but it is clear that they were by no means
confined to the field of battle. The excitement and emotion associated with military exploits are often expressed in poetry before-
hand. In this way both poet and audience can be stirred up to
declare war or to prepare for battle. So we have:

*Solo.* King be-not-persuaded-by-other-people-not-to-fight-your-
enemies ho! ho!
*Chorus.* So long as the regiment agree, ho! ho![2]

Delafosse, when an administrator in West Africa, was similarly
addressed by an Agni chief and his warriors who came to offer him
their help against a rebel, urging on him and on themselves the
attractions and urgency of war:

Donne-moi de la poudre et des fusils: je partirai demain.
Je veux leur couper la tête: je partirai demain.
Ils ont des femmes qui sont jolies: je partirai demain.
On dit qu'ils ont de l'or: je partirai demain.
Aujourd'hui il faut que je fasse des balles: je partirai demain.
Aujourd'hui il faut que j'offre un sacrifice: je partirai demain.
Je veux leur couper la tête: je partirai demain.
Donne-moi de la poudre et des fusils: je partirai demain.[3]

Such war songs in fact are sometimes more an expression and
reinforcement of the militant strength of a group than a direct
incitement to the fight or a part of the battle itself. Several of the
military poems recorded for the warlike Nilotic peoples seem to
be of this kind. They involve glorification, the expression of high
morale, and, very often, refer to cattle—among the Nilotes there
is a very common association between war and cattle raiding:

[1] D. A. Puplampu, 'The National Epic of the Adangme', *Afr. Affairs* 50,
1951, p. 241.
[2] G. A. Taylor, 'Some Mashona Songs and Dances', *Nada* 4, 1926, p. 39.
[3] M. Delafosse, *Essai de manuel de la langue agni*, Paris, 1900, pp. 180-1.

Great bull with testicles has been killed
It is Divinity
The dark clouds and the morning rain blow up
My mother ABUK, Divinity my father, help me
My father GARANG, help me Divinity my father
If we sleep abroad,[1] the white cow of my father
Will bring us cows
Avoid the spear, my age-set Mayom, avoid the spear
An affair of the great spear (a great fight)
O my club!
The spear-haft in the man's back quivers
DENG KUR is a powerful divinity.
If we sleep abroad, it brings cows
White cow of my father, I did not start the fight
The bulls meet head to head!
Cow which gave peace to my father
Cow bringing cows
Make peace as the Kongor tribe did with the Agar
Last year's fighting is ended
Last year's fighting thus is ended.[2]

The same associations with cattle come out in another Dinka war song where the 'feast' or sacrifice implies war and hostility to enemies:

Though the tribe holds a feast against me
I shall not fear,
Though all the people hold a feast against me
I shall not fear,
O my tribe, I am a bull with sharpened horns,
I am a maddened bull. . . .[3]

Some war poetry, then, is rather the expression of the general values relating to war than an immediate part of an actual military expedition. But other poems involve more direct participation, at least in the preliminaries and aftermath of war. The Ngoni of Malawi, for instance, had two main branches of war songs: first *imigubo*, those specifically intended for singing before going out to fight; and secondly *imihubo*, sung on their return. The first type was still being sung in the 1930s, danced in full war dress with

---

[1] i.e. as warriors on a cattle raid.
[2] G. Lienhardt, *Divinity and Experience, the Religion of the Dinka*, Oxford, 1961, pp. 88–9. Cf. also war poetry of Shilluk and others in Tescaroli 1961, ch. 3.
[3] Lienhardt, op. cit., p. 282.

shields and spears, and performed in the Paramount Chief's village, the traditional place of mobilization. The women too join in the dance, and the tempo works up and up to inspire the men with the lust for battle. Many of these songs seem brief, but much of the tune was sung to meaningless though rousing sounds—*inyo ho, oya ye yayo* and so on—and they were added to by the varied accompaniment of stamping feet and the clashing of spears and shields.[1] Similar war songs from Malawi are mentioned by Kidney. When sung they are accompanied by small drums, by the brandishing of spears, and by bodily movements signifying courage and defiance which stir up warlike feelings:

> Fight now! Come and fight now!
> Slay them! We'll brandish spears!
> Straight forth doth speed your arrow.
> Tremble! Yes! *They* tremble!
> > When *we* draw near,
> > And *far* they'll flee as we approach them!
>
> Sharpen keen your arrows!
> Brave heads upraised and shouting
> > Loudly our defiance.
> All they who oppose us.
> > Quickly our spears
> Shall pierce their breasts. They will be scattered.[2]

It is common for songs celebrating military success to become highly developed after the return home. For example, the Kamba of Kenya make the return into a triumphal procession. Special honour is ceremonially given to a Kamba man who has earned the high title of *mutiaetumo*, i.e. one who has personally killed a Masai warrior. Such a man leads his triumphant band round the villages. When they approach a village, they strike up their songs of victory. The hero is praised but his comrades' help is not forgotten:

You wonder: he who sings the song of victory, who is he? He is *mutiaetumo* X (here follows his real name), who has fought with the men of cattle [Masai], but if we had not helped each other, he should not have come out of it successfully. *aaaaah!*[3]

The women play their part by greeting the warriors with shrill cries—*lili, lili, lili, lili!*—their normal way of expressing joy and

[1] Read 1937, p. 29.  [2] Kidney 1921, p. 126.
[3] G. Lindblom, *The Akamba in British East Africa*, Uppsala, 2nd ed., 1920, p. 199.

delight, thus adding to the display and to the men's sense of heroism.

The use of war poetry in the actual face of the enemy is best documented for certain peoples of North-West Africa. The Galla *gheraera*, warriors' boasting, is often in the form of a challenge, sometimes hurled between two armies.[1] The Somali *geeraar* also played an active part in war. Challenges to another clan to fight at an appointed place used to be delivered in this form, and it was also used to insult the enemy before the battle, at the same time raising the singer's morale. The *geeraar* is characterized by a note of urgency and rapid movement and was traditionally recited on horseback.[2] Among other groups, however, such as some of the Southern Bantu, the convention was to utter certain set war cries rather than songs at the time of the actual charge.

War songs are possibly also sometimes sung in triumph on the victorious field of battle. This is supposed—perhaps speculatively —to have been the case with an old Bemba war song more recently sung only round the camp fire, but originally, it is said, it was sung by warriors dancing round the slain brandishing their spears. In it the chief is described sending out his warriors; on their return they

Sing songs of victory, saying,
'Sompa, sompa, sompa, sompa, sompa', with the heads of the slain.[3]

But there are not, in fact, many references to singing at the actual moment of victory. The most frequent occasions seem to be as the war parties depart or return home, at later celebrations after victory, or, occasionally, as challenge and insult before an actual battle.

Also common are poems in which the events of war are touched on in retrospect. The exploits of war, together with religious topics, are the most common themes of poems associated with the Islamic tradition, as among the Swahili or the Hausa. It has already been said that, apart from Islamic influence, narrative poetry is not a typical form in African oral literature, and it is not surprising to find that in many of the poems about war the element of narrative is overshadowed by that of glorification, so that one cannot always

[1] Chadwicks iii, 1940, pp. 548–9.
[2] Andrzejewski and Lewis 1964, p. 49.
[3] R. O'Ferrall, 'An Old War Song of the Bebemba', *BSOS* 4, 1926/8, p. 841.

draw the line between war poetry and panegyric (including praise at funeral celebrations). The praise poems of the Southern Bantu, discussed in an earlier chapter, have war and military prowess as one of their main themes, and the same blend of praise and interest in battle heroism can be seen in the 'heroic recitations' of the Ankole Hima.[1] In Ruanda, Kagame describes military poetry as taking two main forms.[2] The heroic *ibitekerezo* (the conquests of Ruanda) are preserved by the court bards as a type of 'classical' military poetry. When young men are being trained in the military arts, they have to learn these poems and try to compose others in the same style. In these, it seems, the narrative element is the more marked. The second type, however, is much more in the form of panegyric. These are the lyric odes termed *ibyivugo*, composed by the court bards to exalt the exploits of heroes. There is no exact correspondence with real acts, for the point is to celebrate high and often fictitious deeds rather than to record ('c'était de la Poésie; œuvre d'imagination'),[3] and the descriptions of battles are decorated by the frequent use of praise names glorifying the hero and his companions—'Prodigue-de-blessures', 'Chagrins-des-pays-étrangers', and so on. Contemplation and description of battle after the event seem inevitably to be expressed as glorification and praise.

These then are some of the occasions on which poems described in the sources as 'military' or 'war songs' were (or are) actually performed. It seems clear that the romantic picture of the 'natural' occasion for savage war songs—as mainly confined to the actual heat of battle, or its immediate prelude or aftermath—is an exaggerated one.

How over-simplified this popular picture is will emerge further from a glimpse of the military poetry of the Nguni and the Akan peoples. These peoples, in particular their sub-groups the Zulu and the Ashanti, were well known to their European opponents of sixty or seventy years ago for their military qualities. The Nguni case must be pieced together from various passing references to their military poetry in the past. For the Akan we can look at the equally interesting way in which a type of poetry regarded as military survives in the contemporary situation.

[1] Morris 1964.
[2] Kagame 1956/7; cf. also Coupez and Kamanzi 1962.
[3] Kagame 1956/7, p. 119.

The Nguni-speaking peoples of southern Africa are famous for their military organization and warlike ethic. The best known of all are the Zulu,[1] welded together into a great military system by Shaka in the early ninteenth century. But others too of this group have also been noted for the same all-pervading military spirit— the Swazi, neighbours of the Zulu, the Ndebele, and the Ngoni of Malawi who formed part of the great Nguni dispersal of peoples moving north as a result of Shaka's expansion.

From Shaka's time the whole nation was organized into a kind of military camp, and war was the main centre of interest.[2] The stress on military glory, on triumph, and on the possibility of attaining honour and position through achievement in war comes out both in the praise songs discussed in an earlier chapter, and also in the Zulu war songs (*iziquɓulo, amahuɓo*):

> Oye oyeye!
> Seek out the cowards,
> The lion-conqueror strikes.
> Come, let's march into battle;
> No more the time for boastful arguments.
> What, sayest thou the time for boastful argument is over?
> Begone!
> Who told the news that wranglings have ceased?
> The house of Qolwana set we on fire.
> We make no jokes, no lies tell we.
> He is full of hate, full of hate.
> Oyeyiya wo!
> Come, see us set aflame the house of Qolwana.
> On whom will you make war
> If you wipe out all the nations thus?
> Ho! Ho! . . .
> You who defeat the foes
> And conquer the nations.
> If you wipe out the nations thus,
> On whom will you make war?
> Yea, what will you do?
> You have subdued the kings;
> You have wiped out the nations.
> Where and what next, O Conqueror?
>            E!     E!     E![3]

[1] The most convenient summary is that in E. J. Krige, *The Social System of the Zulus*, 1936, Pietermaritzburg.

[2] Ibid., pp. 261 ff.                                    [3] Dhlomo 1947, p. 6.

Under Shaka, the Zulu were reorganized into regiments of 800–1,000 strong, making up an army of perhaps 20,000, maybe more.[1] There was a centralized standing army, an unusual feature in Africa, and unlike the Nilotes and similar peoples, the Zulu showed an interest in conquest and territorial expansion as well as mere raiding for cattle and other movables. Internally there was rivalry between the different Zulu regiments, expressed in competitiveness in battle and in dancing and singing at the royal kraal. Each regiment had its own regimental songs, dress, and war-cry, which distinguished it from others, and it was only in the actual heat of battle that the national war-cry was used; before that, as they set off, only the regimental war-cries were shouted. Each regiment also often had its military kraal, separate from others and under its own captain. Even in normal conditions the men were expected to serve for at least two to three months a year, and, if there was no war, they were engaged in various communal tasks. Even in peace, the military spirit was paramount. There was stern discipline, and military dances and songs fulfilled the function of drill.[2] Many of these dances were based on military manœuvering and amounted to a kind of sham battle. The desire for glory, the excitement of war, and national and regimental pride could be instilled within the military kraals even in peacetime.

War songs were also sung on more colourful occasions. The most striking of all was the annual first fruits ceremony held in the presence of the king, when the army of the nation gathered, regiment by regiment, to display its might in public. Several of these nineteenth-century displays are described in early sources, summed up by Krige:

> The most spectacular and imposing of all Zulu dancing was . . . that of the regiments of warriors in full regimental dress; and the annual dances at the royal kraal, just after the Feast of the First-fruits, must have presented a most brilliant and colourful sight. . . . The king first of all reviewed the army, seated in his chair of state. On the occasion witnessed by Delegorgue, the regiments of young warriors came, grouped in six great masses of about 1000 each, made a rapid charge, then became orderly again and began to dance a war chant, the ground resounding under their feet. They marched to within five paces of the king, and formed a kind of serpent which unrolled itself from three rings.

---

[1] Krige, op. cit., p. 262.

[2] Similar Swazi chants to accompany military drill (still being sung) can be heard on a recording in the 'Music of Africa' series (GALP 1041).

Each regiment had its own particular dance and song, and each man, on passing the king, bent low and hurled him a greeting with an air of anger. These evolutions lasted many hours. . . .

The king, on one such occasion, took his position at the head and centre of a line of several thousand men, with an equal number opposite them. They began to sing and march, reinforcing their foot movements with gestures of the arms in all directions with wonderful uniformity. Then, chanting and dancing, the column following, the king slowly advanced and the two horns united to form a circle, the warriors finally sitting down in a ring with shields raised yet heads showing. . . .[1]

The excitement and pride engendered by such ceremonial displays come out too, although perhaps with rather lesser intensity, in the war songs sung before going out to battle, or in triumph after it. The desire for glory and the sense of competitiveness were incited by the stirring war songs and dances, where the words, the melody, and the movement all helped to create a warlike atmosphere. These, like other war songs, were often highly rhythmical and onomatopoeic. An example can be given from the Ngoni of Malawi, a Nguni offshoot who preserve war songs of the same types as do the more southerly Nguni groups. They are known as *imigubo* (songs for setting out to war) and, though short and onomatopoeic, mount up to a high pitch of intensity as the men dance, stamping their feet and knocking their shields:

> Ee, ee, ee
> What are we contending for?
> What are we contending for
> In this way in the sky?
> Ee, ee, ee,
>     Oyi, oyi, oyi!
> The sun is setting.
>
> Ee, ee, ee
> What are we contending for?
> What are we contending for
> In this way in the sky?
> Ee, ee, ee,
>     Oyi, oyi, oyi![2]

These songs, once so appropriate to the warlike spirit of Nguni society, are not totally forgotten today. In the 1930s some were still being sung in Malawi; others have been recorded more

[1] Krige, op. cit., p. 342.     [2] Read 1937, p. 30.

recently in South Africa by the African Music Society. However, nowadays they are used mainly for ceremonial display or, at times, to pander to romantic ideas about the savage and tribal past of the Bantu. Some of the songs are now sometimes adapted for faction fighting,[1] and modifications of the old military forms have been used, it is said, for political intimidation.[2] But these survivals are of less interest than the purposeful development of military literature in the nineteenth century. These earlier Nguni war songs can only be fully appreciated in relation to their complex and specialized military organization. They are not attached primarily to the circumstances of actual battle, but to the routine and the ceremonies of military activity, developed among a people for whom, even in peacetime, the military ethic was predominant.

The Akan peoples, with their multiplicity of specialist associations, are very different from the Nguni. The Akan have a tradition of warrior associations or 'war companies' which possess their own characteristic form of drumming and poetry.[3] It is true that these associations no longer flourish as in the past (the Ashanti associations, for example, were suppressed after the events of 1896–1900). But in the southern Akan area, particularly among the Fante, they are still active, and even elsewhere their poetry is still performed. There is an over-all homogeneity in their patterns of music and organization which makes it possible to generalize about their poetry.

There are two main types of Akan warrior associations: companies of the court comprising the highest war leaders under the control of the rulers, and the company of commoners, *asafo*, a term now used indiscriminately for all warrior associations. These war companies consist of all able-bodied men combined under a leader in external or internal disputes. They also act as a group for certain types of communal work and in the enthronement and deposition ceremonies of rulers. In the Fante area where these *asafo* companies are most important, there may be as many as seven or ten companies in a single town; elsewhere one village or group of villages shares one company. All these companies are highly organized bodies with their own captains who act as intermediaries between themselves and the political rulers of the state.

[1] See Tracey 1948*b*, pp. vii–viii.
[2] *Afr. Music* 2. 4, 1961, p. 117 (Southern Rhodesia).
[3] Described in Nketia 1963*b*, ch. 9.

They are headed by the 'captain of the host' or war leader who is helped by various other officials, among them the *frankaatufɔɔ* or standard-bearer who regulates the march, the *asafo kyerɛma*, the master drummer who calls the warriors to action, urges them on, and keeps up morale, and the *nnawutabɔfoɔ*, player of twin gongs.

Drumming plays an important part. Drums and gongs are played with a few members of the company leading the song, the rest acting as chorus. Among the most important songs are the calls. These are rousing cries to the company which, nowadays at least, precede or interrupt a cycle of songs but show clear marks of their once fully military character:

> Fire![1] Fire!
> Fire! Asafo Kyiremu.[2]
> Fire!
> We are not afraid.
> No, not a bit.
> Asafo Kyiremu,
> We are not afraid of anybody.[3]

Different companies often have their own special calls and responses, sometimes partly 'spoken' by the drummer, and these mark out their identity as distinct from others and 'engender the mass feeling that is so important in the activities of *asafo*'.[4]

This feeling is further intensified by the frequent songs celebrating particular companies, combining boastfulness with insults to their enemies. Thus one song about Apɛntɛ (a court company) runs:

> Ɔsɛe, man of Apɛntɛ.
> Ɔsɛe, man of Apɛntɛ,
> We shall fight battles for our nation,
> There was a battle brewing; Ɔsɛe,
> But the army of the enemy never arrived.
> We did not feel their presence.
> You are children of ghosts, and nocturnal fighters.
> Night fighters,
> You have laid them low.
> Ɔsɛe has laid you low.
> The night fighter has laid you low.[4]

---

[1] Sign of danger; hence = alarm.
[2] The name of an association; any other such name may be substituted.
[3] Nketia 1963*b*, p. 107.          [4] Ibid., p. 108.

Another such song refers to the Ashanti wars with the British and praises the deeds of Apagya, a royal military company among the Ashanti:

> Hirelings adamant to rain and scorching sun,
> Members of the Apagya company,
> There was a cannon mounted vainly on top of the fort.[1]
> The cannon could not break us,
> The trusted company that engages in battle.
>    Hail the helper![2]

The Apagya company is also exultantly praised in

> He has killed the Southerners.
> He has killed the Northerners,
> It is Asafo Apagya,
> The Umbrella tree.
> The Umbrella tree has branches above and below,
> The crafty Umbrella tree.
>    King,
>    Hail the helper![3]

Not all military songs explicitly glorify war, however. Some also exhibit an awareness of the dangers and cost of war. There are always casualties, for 'battle never goes hungry'. The warrior leaves in the knowledge that he may not return but that he goes to do his duty courageously:

> Kwaakwaa[4] accompanies me to the front.
> Man of Apagya, if I die in the morning, no-one should mourn for me.
> Yes if I fall in the morning,
> Ɔkoromansa accompanies me to battle, no-one should weep on my account.[5]
> Yes if I fall in the morning,
> If I fall in the morning do not cry.
> Yes if I die in the morning.[6]

Members of the association are also summoned to battle by a drum-call giving the association's name, praise name, and other characteristic marks which distinguish it from others. One of these

> Bodyguard as strong as iron,
> Fire that devours the nations . . .

---

[1] Refers to Ashanti wars with the British.    [2] Nketia 1963*b*, p. 108.
[3] Ibid., pp. 108–9.    [4] The god of a certain Apagya company.
[5] As interpreted by a member of the company: 'If I fall in the morning of my life, do not cry.'    [6] Nketia 1963*b*, p. 109.

is quoted in full in Chapter 17.[1] In another the various names associated with the company are given, then the ordinary members are stirred up for the fight:

> Members of the Advance Guard,
> I mean you.
> The leopard goes hungry
> If it pounces on a tortoise.
> The leopard should never be considered old and feeble.
> The leopard walks in the thicket:
> The thicket trembles and shakes violently.
> Come hosts; come hosts; come hosts!
> Come in thick numbers.[2]

There are also 'songs for conveying a dead member to a place of burial, songs for parading in the street, songs of insult, songs of incitement and so on'.[3] Besides these there are also some characteristic types belonging to particular companies or groups of companies. The No. 1 Company of Cape Coast, for example, has several styles of drumming, each used with a set of songs designed to accompany different kinds of action. A high-spirited style accompanies a display of bravery in leap-dancing and strutting action, and a gentler style is used for normal dancing. Associations also sometimes create their own recreational music and dance as well as the more traditional types. All the regular songs are characterized by their emotional quality and by the specially stirring effect of the drumming, achieved largely by the peculiar timbre of the leading drums. Within this general spirit of the military songs

the leading role is . . . played by the cantors who may vary their styles. Sometimes they sing long sustained notes while the chorus is held in suspense; sometimes they use a recitative style, interpolating pauses in the chorus responses with calls, short phrases or shouts, while others animate the performance with occasional whistling and catcalls. Everybody lets himself go, singing at the top of his voice and with great feeling.[3]

Are these military songs still significant? Obviously the directly military functions of warrior associations have been superseded, and in Ashanti at least, in the present century, they have not even acted as very pronounced corporate groups. Yet it seems that not only are the companies active on certain occasions (particularly in

---

[1] p. 486.   [2] Nketia 1963*b*, p. 111.   [3] Ibid., p. 110.

the south) and seize the opportunity to perform their own songs
and music, but in some contexts they preserve their warlike and
forceful spirit. As Nketia writes:

In the past, the most important context in which Asafo groups
drummed and acted was during wars. Although this is no longer opera-
tive, there is always a resurgence of the war spirit during major political
disputes, particularly disputes over constitutional issues in which Asafo
groups act as political pressure groups. Thus in Ashanti, where Asafo
companies are practically dormant, political crises often bring a
temporary awakening of such groups who are kept together by drums
and songs which promote the type of action required by the situation.[1]

*Asafo* music also still occurs in other contexts.[2] In rural areas
in the south *asafo* companies are called on to perform certain
communal tasks and to organize search-parties for missing persons,
in the forest and at sea. Such searches create a particularly emotional atmosphere if the missing person is a member of the company, and many *asafo* songs are sung. Funerals of a member are
also occasions for the performance of these songs. In the southern
Akan states there are sometimes special annual ceremonies when
members renew their loyalty to their association and to the chief,
in which the most important feature is the performance of music
and dancing, sometimes accompanied by the firing of guns,
exhibition of the association's standards and emblems, and the
installation of new officers. Annual festivals of the community as
a whole are often the most common occasions for corporate public
activity by warrior companies.

In all these contexts the spirit of enjoyment as well as of emotional intensity is now evident. The military companies are distinguished by their specialized artistic conventions—the military
mode of song, music, and drumming—and, in adapting to changing situations, retain the military subject-matter and warlike
fervour which before was of more practical immediate relevance.[3]

---

[1] Nketia 1963*b*, p. 115.

[2] Or apparently did when Nketia was writing. His book appeared in 1963,
based on field research in the 1950s.

[3] Other references on military songs include: A. Munonga, 'Chants historiques
bayeke', *Bull. des jurisdictions indigènes* [Elisabethville] 20, 1952 (*AA* 5. 345;
includes eight war songs); E. Cerulli, 'Poesie di guerra e di amore dei Galla',
*Arch. antrop. e etnol.* 5, 1942 (reference in *IAI Bibl.* (*A*) by R. Jones, North-
East Africa, 1959, p. 33); G. C. Savard, 'War Chants in Praise of Ancient Afar
Heroes', *J. Ethiopian Studies* 3, 1965; H. Gaden, 'Un chant de guerre toucouleur', *Ann. et mém. Com. ét. AOF* 1, 1916; D. Westermann, *Shilluk People:*

Hunting poetry can be discussed more briefly. It shares many of the characteristics of military poetry, particularly its association with the ideas of danger, pride, and glory, its common appearance as a more or less specialized branch of poetry, and, finally, its frequent preoccupation not just with action but with the contemplation of action, in prospect or (more often) in retrospect.

It is not surprising that hunting, with its associated hazards and heroism, is a frequent topic in the songs of many peoples. It is, for example, one of the most common themes of Bushman songs,[1] in a way that fits their harsh struggle for existence. This is well expressed by Marshall:

Women bring the daily food, but there is nothing splendid about returning with vegetables and wood. Many of the vegetable foods, furthermore, are rather tasteless and harsh and are not very satisfying. The return of the hunters is vastly different. The intense craving for meat, the anxiety that goes with the hunt, the deep excitement of the kill, finally the eating and the satisfaction reach to the very core of the people, engaging powerful emotions. Once a young man, /Qui, who was said to be the best hunter in the region, had been charged by a magnificent cock ostrich on a big open pan where there was no refuge. He knelt, facing the creature, until it was within close range and shot an arrow straight into its heart. Back in the werf, while the meat was being cut up and distributed by /Qui's wife's brothers, he slept exhausted on the mound of black and white plumes and the women—some of the plumes in their hair—danced a dance of praise around him. This is the role of !Kung [Bushman] hunters.[2]

The romance and excitement associated with hunting is vividly depicted in the Zulu song about a buffalo hunt:

> Iyeyahe! Iyayayi!
> A whirlwind! the buffalo!
> Some leave and go home;
> Some pursue and obtain;
> We shoot the rising,
> But leave the wounded.
> Iyeyahe.[3]

*their Language and Folklore*, Philadelphia, 1912, pp. 237–8; P. B. Dahle, 'Eine Siegeshymne der Ama-Zulu', *Festschrift Meinhof*, Glückstadt, 1927, pp. 174–95.
[1] Kirkby 1936, p. 245.
[2] L. Marshall in J. L. Gibbs (ed.), *Peoples of Africa*, New York, 1965, p. 255.
[3] Dhlomo 1947, p. 6.

Perhaps the most common occasion for hunting songs is a successful kill. As in military celebrations, they often take place some time after the event. We do, it is true, occasionally hear of a solitary hunter or group of hunters bursting into more or less immediate song over some outstanding kill. Among the Akan, for instance, a hunter is expected to climb on to the body of an elephant and burst into song:

> The violent shaker that shakes down living trees it by-passes [the
> elephant],
> Duedu Akwa,
> Father Duedu Duben,
> Ɔben and Dankyira, trier-of-Death,
> Father [the hunter] deserves to be congratulated.
> Father has achieved something:
> The hunter has done well![1]

But even among the Akan, hunting songs are most frequently performed on public and festive occasions. In general the most commonly mentioned occasion is when the hunter has returned to the village: he is often welcomed and congratulated. The Ethiopian hunter returning from killing an elephant is received by a double chorus:

> *1st chorus.*  He has slain, he has destroyed him.
> *2nd chorus.*  Whither went he when he slew him?
> *1st chorus.*  As he went hence did I see him at all?
> *All.*  Perhaps on the bank of the river he has stricken him down.
> Destroyer and slayer art thou called,
> Hurrah, Hurrah, doubly a slayer.[2]

Among other peoples a later and more organized celebration is the usual pattern. Thus among the Limba of northern Sierra Leone, the killing of a bush cow is regarded as the occasion for a special celebration (*madonsia*). But this never takes place on the actual occasion of the hunt. Instead, a special date is fixed, several days later. Then, in the night, the hunter comes out, accompanied and watched by others, and the special hunters' songs and dances are performed. The occasion necessarily involves many people as

[1] Nketia 1963*b*, p. 81. See Junod 1897, p. 55, for a Ronga song in similar circumstances.
[2] Chadwicks iii, 1940, p. 514.

participants and spectators, and is in striking contrast to the actual process of the hunt, typically pursued, among the Limba, by the solitary individual, followed only by his faithful dog.

Praise and celebration is often reserved for the killing of game considered to be particularly outstanding or dangerous. According to the area, these may be such animals as elephant, lion, leopard, or buffalo. The risks and the achievement of the hunter(s) are further magnified by the terms used to refer to these beasts—like, for example, 'Elephant praisenamed He-who-uses-his-hand-as-a-trumpet, Elephant called He-who-remains-mountainous-even-when-seated'.[1] The hunter himself also sings boastfully of his exploits and retells his heroism in poetry designed for an audience rather than for the exigencies of the hunt itself. Among the Akan he announces his return after a major kill by firing his gun on the outskirts of the village, and when people come to meet him he relates his success in recitative, a set refrain denoting the sex of the elephant killed—for example:

> I am stalking an animal.
> I am stalking an animal stealthily,
> That I might kill it.[2]

Such songs of triumph and recollection are common and are often mentioned as separate forms. In some societies they are particularly specialized. Hunters may be expected to undergo special training, often involving magical and artistic as well as practical skills, and are sometimes formed into organized associations with their own rules, hierarchy, and initiation. Such organizations are not uncommon in West Africa and often have their own songs. Among the Akan the professional association of hunters uses hunting songs to assert their pride and their dominance over even the political authorities—or so they wish to suggest:

> Is the chief greater than the hunter?
>   Arrogance! Hunter? Arrogance!
> The pair of beautiful things on your feet,
> The sandals that you wear,
> How did it all happen?
> It is the hunter that killed the duyker:
> The sandals are made of the hide of the duyker.

---

[1] From a Yoruba hunters' chant (*ijala*), Babalǫla 1965, p. 51.
[2] Nketia, op. cit., p. 84.

Does the chief say he is greater than the hunter?
Arrogance! Hunter? Arrogance!
The noisy train that leads you away,
The drums that precede you,
The hunter killed the elephant,
The drum head is the ear of the elephant.
Does the chief say he is greater than the hunter?
Arrogance! Hunter? Arrogance![1]

Hunting songs are also often sung at the funerals of skilled hunters.[2] Hunting associations also sometimes have special festivals when, for example, they admit hunters to new ranks in the hierarchy or celebrate a major kill.[3] At these celebrations the episodes of the hunt are often dramatically re-enacted, with the members of the association singing and declaiming the traditional hunting songs.

In some cases, hunting poems have become a specialized and independent branch of poetry, no longer related to the actual hunt at all. Yoruba *ijala* chants, for example, are sometimes associated specifically with hunting and performed at gatherings of specialist hunters. But *ijala* artists are also highly regarded by the public as general entertainers and are invited to perform on social occasions that have no specific association with hunting at all.[4] This genre of Yoruba poetry has its own conventions and themes.[5] It is delivered as a kind of recitative—'a type of speech utterance with rudimentary musical characteristics, rather than a species of song'[4] —which is accentuated by certain rhythmic and tonal devices. Often there is no very clear central theme, but the poem rambles from one topic to another in a way which distinguishes these poems from certain of the other specialist branches of Yoruba poetry and also demonstrates how far removed this species of hunting poetry is from direct involvement in action. One dominant theme is verbal salute and praise in such phrases as 'Son of a fighter at Ilala, offspring of warriors carrying many arrows', or 'In my very person I have come, / Atanda He-whose-face-is-usually-cloudy-like-the-sky-before-a-storm, / He-who-fatigues-his-opponent-like-

---

[1] Nketia, op. cit., p. 76.
[2] e.g. among the Dogon, Limba, Akan, Ambo, and many others.
[3] See Nketia, op. cit., pp. 85 ff.
[4] Babalọla 1964, p. 33.
[5] On which see the excellent discussion in Babalọla 1966.

a-person-soaked-and-exhausted by rain'.[1] But there are also many chants about the animals and plants of the forest, particularly about monkeys, antelopes, elephants, or the much feared buffalo. Various comments on social life are also typical and many of the poems are noted for their vitality and humour, in particular their treatment of sex. These points can be illustrated from three *ijala* poems from Gbadamosi and Beier's examples:

### *Tuku—Wild Pig*

The fat one of the thick bush.
The animal that carries scissors in its mouth.
Although we do not marry his daughter
Yet he demands to be treated like our father-in-law.
(For the one who wants to shoot it
Must prostrate to it.)
An animal that enlarges its nose
In order to better smell the vagina.[2]

### *Erin—Elephant*

Elephant who brings death. Elephant, a spirit in the bush.
With his single hand he can pull two palm trees to the ground.
If he had two hands—
He would tear the heavens like an old rag.
The spirit who eats dog, the spirit who eats ram.
The spirit who eats a whole palm fruit with its thorns.
With his four mortar legs—he tramples down the grass.
Wherever he walks, the grass is forbidden to stand up again.
An elephant is not a load for an old man—
Nor for a young man either.[3]

### *Cassava*

If you eat me and call my praises at the same time
You teach me to be dangerous.[4]
Plant me like a good planter—and I will grow fat even like yam.
Throw me away—and I will still develop well.
But the one who hangs me on the branch of a tree—he is really my
    enemy.

---

[1] Babalọla 1965, pp. 52, 54. The last two sections of the second passage consist of three words only in the original.
[2] Gbadamosi and Beier 1959, p. 33.
[3] Ibid., p. 34.
[4] It is forbidden to say the *oriki* (praises) of cassava while eating it.

I do not fight the one who holds the stick—
Only the one who holds the pot.[1]
It causes the lips of the wife to swell.
It enlarges the penis of the husband.
The mouth of Lambare becomes large like a drum.
If you ask him: What is the matter?
Are you eating so much cassava?
He will reply: Oh, occasionally, occasionally,
You just wait: cassava will deal with you.
Tete Bere! Now you have dysentery!
Now you start worshipping Oshun!
This is not a matter for the gods:
Even if you pray to Obatala himself
Cassava will carry you away!
When people see you on the road they argue:
Is it a new wife? Ha, it is cassava.
See how it rubs its body with red camwood.[2]
Cassava with a rough skin to its back.[3]

These *ijala* poems are far removed from simple and more direct hunting songs. The Yoruba hunter is expected to possess intellectual skills beyond those to do with the hunt and to sing of other topics than his own bravery. Yet these poems are locally classed as the poetry of hunters and ultimately are connected with the same root idea as in other hunting poems—the idea of hunting as a heroic and memorable activity.[4]

This cursory discussion of hunting poetry will be concluded by a somewhat fuller account of the hunting songs (*cinseŋgwe*) of the Ambo of Zambia which have been treated in some detail by Stefaniszyn.[5]

For the Ambo the hunter—and above all the elephant hunter—is traditionally surrounded with a halo of romance and hero-worship. Though there seem to be no associations of the West African type, nevertheless, hunters are experts and have their own rituals, feasts, and songs. The Ambo hunter seems to be typically a solitary practitioner, but in certain respects he is helped and guided by other

[1] When making gruel out of cassava flour the one holding the pot may burn his fingers.
[2] Cassava has a reddish colour like camwood. New brides rub their bodies with camwood.　　　　　　　　　　　　[3] Gbadamosi and Beier 1959, p. 34.
[4] For further discussion and examples of *ijala* poetry, see Babalọla 1966 *passim*; also F. S. Collier, 'Yoruba Hunters' Salutes', *Nigerian Field* 18, 1953.
[5] Stefaniszyn 1951.

members of the community and has obligations to them when he kills meat. He usually receives his gun—the mark of a hunter—from one of his mother's relations in accordance with the matrilineal inheritance pattern of the Ambo, and, both after his acquisition of the gun and before certain of the hunts, private and joint rituals are carried out to ensure success. A hunter also has a special relationship with the spirit of one of his dead kinsmen, often his father, who guards and guides him as a hunter. The emotional relationship with his father is of a much more personal nature than the legal bond with his matrilineal kin and comes out in several of the hunting songs. The son praises his father's exploits as a hunter and mourns his loss:

> I had a father,
> The wailing is great.
> Father, it's dawn . . .
> I remember the great hunter.
> They are bursting into tears . . .
> I, a poor fellow, I shall wail,
> I, who had been dividing the meat.[1]

Or, again, he sets out delighting in his gun. Then his thoughts are drawn back sorrowfully to when his father was alive—but he brings himself back to the present, to look at the tracks of his quarry:

> How fine is my gun,
> How fine is my gun,
> Ah, when my father was alive.
> I mourn for Siliyolomona,
> But I must see the tracks.[1]

When an Ambo hunter is wandering alone and unsuccessful he sometimes sings to cheer himself up. But by far the most frequent occasions for performing the hunting chants are communal ones. The hunting chants are sung with other songs at ordinary beer parties. A hunter also joins with others in singing on the night before a hunt, and at the sacrificial beer for a successful hunt. A special 'hunting feast' may also be prepared by a hunter who has killed, say, four animals. He invites his friends and feeds them from the meat he has killed. After the meal the men sing about the hunt.

[1] Ibid., p. 6.

They reminisce, for example, about how the game is being cut up or how a canoe is called for after a hippopotamus has been killed:

> Chop it, chop it, chop it,
> Do take it and chop it;
> Do take it and chop it yourself.[1]

> Chipishya, bring the boat,
> Have you killed it, hunter?
> Chipishya bring the boat,
> Chipishya bring the boat,
> Have you killed it, hunter?[1]

Stefaniszyn states that the hunting songs sung on these occasions are all traditional ones, and that no new songs are composed. They are all relatively short and fairly directly involved with the actual process of hunting and its consequences. In other words, Ambo hunting poetry does not seem to have developed into a complex and flexible branch of poetry which can be turned to many subjects and occasions in the way we have seen in some of the Akan or Yoruba 'hunting poems'. Nor are there lengthy narratives. 'This is lyrical poetry. There are no long descriptions of events, but a short recalling of events of rather sentimental value, always very realistic.'[2]

Their artistic conventions come out partly in the mode of delivery. Though they are sung antiphonally, the melody is not of great importance and the main tone is recitando with strongly marked rhythm. The accompaniment consists of percussion (gourd drums, rattles, and axe-blades struck against stones), and sometimes the hunter himself dances with a gun, horns, and animal trophies. There are also stylistic and verbal conventions. A special poetic vocabulary is used in the songs, including borrowed and perhaps archaic words. This poetic effectiveness is heightened by the frequent use of ideophones and of what Stefaniszyn refers to as 'Homeric epithets'—praise terms like 'The uprooter of *mweŋge* trees' (of an elephant) or 'The pursuer of game. . . . The pursuer of tails' (the hunter). The use of various types of parallelism is also common, compared by Stefaniszyn to that in the Hebrew psalms. This may involve more repetition or the type of development through parallelism exemplified by

---

[1] Stefaniszyn, p. 4.   [2] Ibid., pp. 11–12.

> Off he went to the veld,
> Off he went to the veld, the great hunter.[1]

Parallelism is also used to lead up to a climax at the very end of the piece—a marked tendency in these poems:

> Heavens, my heart is throbbing,
> While I see them standing.
> Heavens, my heart is throbbing,
> While I see them standing,
> While I see the game standing.

> *Nafwa mutima kubamba,*
> *Pakusaŋga silimakene.*
> *Nafwa mutima kubamba*
> *Pakusaŋga silimakene,*
> *Pakusaŋga silimakene nama.*[2]

This song, expressing the hunter's thrill at the sight of game, leads up to an effective climax when the final word 'game' (*nama*) 'is at last uttered as if with awe'.[2]

Besides the conventional forms of delivery and verbal expression there are also stock themes, all directly concerned with hunting. Several of these have been illustrated already: the triumph and excitement of a successful kill and its aftermath; family feelings, especially the emotions of pride and grief felt by a son for his father; and the thrill of pursuit. But the hardships and dangers of hunting are not forgotten, and these too are common subjects. The Ambo hunter's grim tenacity and perseverance in face of hardship are often extolled:

> Let the hunter take out the thorn,
> Let the hunter take out the thorn,
> Then cursing and roving.
> You love it, you will die of the thorn.
> Off he went to the veld.
> Off he went to the veld, the great hunter.[3]

Worse than physical hardship is the disappointment when the hunter is unsuccessful, and this too is a frequent theme in song:

---

[1] Ibid., p. 11.      [2] Ibid., p. 10.      [3] Ibid., p. 4.

> I shall taste the mark of the game,
> When I find them where they lie.
> Abundant is the spoor of game,
> But the game has slipped away—
> It is gone.[1]

and

> We are tired of this bush;
> There are no shadows in it,
> There are no shadows in it, mind you,
> There are no shadows of game.[1]

Success is sometimes tinged with jealousy when the hunter compares his own achievements with those of others. One song, for instance, describes the success of a hunter's companions:

> It's boiling and boiling,
> The hunters are cooking in a big pot.
> It's boiling and boiling,
> The hunters are cooking in a big pot.
> Truly it's boiling hard,
> I'll kill two head to-morrow.[2]

These Ambo hunting songs are more simple and direct than, for example, some of those from West Africa. Yet like them they involve the glorification of the hunter, the expression of his hopes and fears, the activities of the chase, and reminiscence and reflection at a time removed from the actual hunt. They are most frequently performed on public occasions—for in hunting, as in war all members of the community, and not just the individual hero, are involved in both its results and its poetic distillation.[3]

III

Songs to accompany rhythmic work seem to occur universally in African societies. They are extreme examples of 'special purpose' poetry in that they have a direct connection with a specific occasion and with action itself, to an extent not found in most hunting and war chants. The sort of work which these songs

---

[1] Stefaniszyn 1951, p. 4.　　　　　　　　　　[2] Ibid., p. 9.
[3] Further references to hunting songs include A. Bouillon, 'La corporation des chasseurs Baluba', *Zaïre* 8, 1954; G. Paulay, 'Historique de la danse des chasseurs de Touba', *Notes afr.* 55, 1952.

accompany usually consists of routine tasks such as paddling, threshing, or hauling—which are not in themselves regarded as glorious or romantic. Unlike hunting and military poetry the work thus provides the occasion rather than the subject-matter, and the song depends on the rhythm of the work rather than an audience for its point of departure.

The occasions for these work songs include almost all contexts in which monotonous labour is involved; though conventions as to their use vary in different societies.[1] There are co-operative songs for hoeing, weeding, mowing, launching a boat, sawing, hauling in fish-nets, pounding, floor-beating, throwing water up from deep wells in a human chain, carrying a chief in his hammock, hanging up beehives, or rubbing animal skins to make them soft; there are domestic and solitary songs for women grinding corn or pounding rice; there are gang songs for pulling trucks, for road work, for factory hands, and for miners.

It is well known that manual workers often sing such songs to accompany their hard physical labour. The dock hands at Beira have a song

> Dawn—with freight,
> Yes, Yes!
> Dawn—with freight,
> Look for the label.[2]

while the men pushing heavy truck-loads of hides down the Kilindini road in Mombasa used to sing in Swahili

> *Namna hii—macho juu!*    This way—eyes up!
> *Senti hapana—macho juu!*    There are no cents—eyes up![3]

Many other similar songs are popular among labouring gangs. There are, for instance, the songs by South African road workers and miners, by the men working on the Kariba dam, or by builders in Nigeria.

In rural areas, agricultural work provides the occasion for work songs. For instance, in Southern Rhodesia, maize threshing is a popular time for songs. The men and boys do the singing while the women stay in the background, yodelling at intervals with a staccato effect. As often with work songs, the words themselves are

---

[1] On the conventions in different parts of Ghana, for example, see Nketia 1962, p. 7.
[2] Curtis 1920, p. 32.                    [3] Werner 1927, p. 102.

simple, with many nonsense words to fill up the rhythm effectively, and there is alternation between leaders and chorus. This is evident in the following three Zezuru threshing songs from Southern Rhodesia:

*1st.* Leave me to die, they have gored me, Nwechafaka.
*All.* Yes, yes (*he he ha he ha*) the priest, oh, plenty of trouble.

*1st.* Do not trouble me—
*All.* Trouble, trouble
Let the women dance in our honour, do not trouble me
My wife do not come to trouble me.
*1st.* Wife
*All.* Trouble
*1st.* To the spring
*All.* Trouble
We love each other friend, is she not friend.

*1st.* Woe is me, we have grown up
*All.* Those who have cattle, let them gather them, we do not know
*1st.* *Woiye iye iye* you must thresh like mother
*All.* Oh, they cry for a fruit tree.[1]

The way such songs can at once lighten, co-ordinate, and embellish agricultural labour can be briefly illustrated from two types of work songs among the Limba. For them, songs accompany many of their agricultural activities. Two only are singled out here: hoeing the rice near the start of the farming year, and the threshing that follows harvesting.

One of the most demanding occasions of the Limba farming cycle is hoeing in the rice after it has been sown, and this, if undertaken by individuals, is regarded as involving wearisome and exhausting labour. The most common practice is to form special 'companies', each with a drummer, to go round to the farms to hoe. The occasion is turned into a festive one. The drummer stands in front, beating his drum and leading the song. Next follow those who are scattering the seed. And finally the hoers come, perhaps sixteen or twenty of them, sometimes fifty or more, stretched across the hillside in a long line singing in reply to the leader. The whole line raise their hoes simultaneously, then strike together at the ground three times before the up-stroke and pause as the hoes are

[1] W. G. Stead, Zezuru threshing songs, Enkeldoorn, 1937 (manuscript in Doke Collection, University College Library, Salisbury, Southern Rhodesia).

raised once more—a marked rhythm of *dig*, dig, dig, up; *one*, two, three, pause, with strong emphasis on the first down-stroke. The beat and song keep the line exactly together, and there is a feeling of competition and excitement which keeps all in their places with no falling behind or faltering. In this way the huge farm gets hoed with incredible speed, and the Limba themselves point to the importance of the songs in adding both efficiency and pleasure. Their joy in the songs is very obvious (they even look forward to this season of exhausting work), and many of them make.semi-dancing steps as they progress with their hoes up the hill.

Many Limba consider the songs used for threshing even more attractive. In these—normally sung by rather smaller groups—the words are more developed, more variation seems to be encouraged and many different songs are sung on one occasion. There is no drumming and usually no specialist singer, for even the leader takes part in the work, albeit a little less vigorously and regularly than the others. The occasion of threshing is a happy one: the harvest is on the way to completion, there is plenty of food once again, and the moment that has been looked forward to throughout the year has arrived. The rice is piled up on the threshing area, and the young men gather round with their sticks, raising them in a ring of a dozen or so at a time. Another ring may form at the other end of the threshing floor, and, led by the most expert singer, the two groups begin by answering to each other's song in turn, repeating the verse inaugurated by the leader. Later they join together in the chorus. Again a fourfold rhythm forms the framework of the music and the work, this time with the stress on the third beat, followed by a pause as the sticks are raised and the men take a step together, kicking up the straw, to move down the floor—beat, beat, *beat*, pause; one, two, *three*, step. With heavy sticks about three feet long, brought down with great force, the co-ordinated timing given by the rhythm of the music is indeed necessary to avoid accidents as well as to encourage and delight both workers and bystanders. They may sing, for example:

| | |
|---|---|
| *Soloist.* | Don't reproach me about (not having) children! |
| | I had a child long ago but God did not let him live. |
| *1st chorus.* | Don't reproach me about children! |
| | I had a child long ago but the witches ate him. |
| *2nd chorus.* | *Laima o laima.*[1] |

[1] Meaningless but (to the Limba) pleasing syllables.

| | |
|---|---|
| *1st chorus.* | Yes! |
| *2nd chorus.* | *Laima o laima.* |
| *Double chorus.* | Don't reproach me about children! |
| | I had a child long ago but the witches ate him. |
| *Soloist.* | Don't reproach me about (not having) a wife! |
| | I had a wife long ago, but the chief took her. |
| *1st chorus.* | Don't reproach me about a wife! |
| | I had a wife long ago, but the chief took her. |
| *2nd chorus.* | *Laima o laima.* |
| *1st chorus.* | Yes! |
| *2nd chorus.* | *Laima o laima.* |
| *Double chorus.* | Don't reproach me about a wife! |
| | I had a wife long ago but the chief took her . . . |

and so on and on with constant repetitions of the soloist's verses. This time the dancing is quite explicit. The step onwards is a dance step, the movements are thought beautiful in themselves, and sometimes the rice is beaten only twice so that the dance can be elaborated in the time of the third beat. The work is exhausting and the men run with sweat—but the dominant feeling is of a festive and artistic occasion.[1]

Canoeing songs are common among many riverain and coastal peoples. They are especially well known in the Zambesi area. The Chikunda people, for instance, are known as excellent watermen along the Zambesi from its mouth to Feira, and their boat songs are excellently designed to accompany the rhythm of their paddling:

> The outside hand holds the paddle shaft below the bulwarks and over the side. The shaft is then tapped on the boatside during the stroke and again as it is being withdrawn from the water. Then there is a pause before the new stroke. The rhythm is one of four beats, thus— instroke, tap, tap, silent, in, tap, tap, silent. This gives the effect of triple time, and so a cross rhythm results when combined with the singing. The speed of stroke varies between 40 and 44 to the minute.[2]

The songs are usually sung by a soloist, often encouraged by shouts from his companions, while the chorus comes in with meaningless words like *aye, oyo, ndende*. Sometimes they are sung antiphonally, one side of paddles answered by the other.[3] The

[1] Data taken from field notes made in 1961.
[2] S. R. Denny, 'Some Zambesi Boat Songs', *Nada* 14, 1936–7, pp. 35–6. Denny quotes thirty-eight songs, in some cases including the music.
[3] Kidney 1921, p. 119.

actual words are simple, and the attraction of the songs seems to lie in the music and the rhythm that accompany the steady stroke of the paddle. There is also some interest in the subject-matter, which, however sketchy, distracts from the labour of the moment:

> Let the horn sound!
> Sound the trumpet;
> Yes, let it sound.[1]

This is a song about drinking: the beer is finished, so now let us dance, to drums and horns. Or again:

> Leave the drum, leave the drum,
> Leave the dance.
>
> I wear clothes
> Because I am clever.[2]

The background to the third song is said to be a husband's asking his wife where she had got extra clothes beyond what he himself had given her. She replies with this song repeated over and over by the paddlers. The next song is also about love, the song of the cunning Don Juan who has only to look at a woman and speak for her to come—but he never marries properly and is always in trouble with the parents:

> I have married a wife with my eyes,
> The dowry was my mouth, ye ye;
> I have married with my eyes.[3]

Many of the other songs too are about everyday matters—love and marriage, leaving and returning home, dancing, eating, family life. About the only one that refers to the river at all is about the hippopotamus (poetically called a rhinoceros), which is a favourite dish along the river:

> O rhinoceros, O man rhinoceros,
> Rhinoceros of the river banks
> Is good to eat with tomatoes.[4]

The same type of subject-matter also occurs in songs by some of the Congo river boatmen. The Mabale paddle songs recorded by Tanghe[5] are more often about local events, death, the ancestors,

---

[1] Denny, op. cit., p. 41.     [2] Ibid., pp. 43, 38.
[3] Ibid., p. 38.     [4] Ibid., p. 42.
[5] J. Tanghe, 'Chansons de pagayeurs', *BSOS* 4, 1926/8.

or the local chief than about the monotonous and protracted labour of propelling the canoes. The rhythm of the paddles provides the framework of the song. The binary measure in the song matches the twofold structure of the paddle strokes—first a strong beat corresponding to the tension of the muscles and sweep of the paddles, further marked by the beat of an accompanying gong or drum; and secondly a relatively feeble beat while the paddles rest. These paddle songs are sometimes by a soloist echoed by a chorus but, unlike the Chikunda examples, they are more often sung by the whole crew, preceded and accompanied by the beat of a drum. Consonant with this pattern the words are short and simple in the extreme. The song

> Ekouloulou, qui rames incessamment;
> Ekouloulou, qui rames incessamment;
> Ekouloulou, qui rames incessamment . . .
> (Ekululu jaboluka ntɛk' . . .)

repeated over and over in unison is one of the few to refer to the actual work—the crew compare themselves to the little *ekululu* fish that is always swimming.[1] Even simpler are the words which alternate between solo and chorus:

> *Solo.* Les herbes    *Chorus. Oye*
> *Solo.* Les herbes    *Chorus. Oye.*[2]

or:

> *Solo.* Chef, o,    *Chorus. Waza waza*
> Chef, e,    *Waza waza*
> Ventre, e,    *Waza waza*
> Fusil, e,    *Waza waza*
> Malle, e,    *Waza waza*
> Sel, e. . . .    *Waza waza. . . .*[3]

The structure is also simple, and, like many such songs, depends fundamentally on various types of repetition: repetition of the same formula (with or without a pause); repetition with a slight variation the second time through; and alternation and repetition of two different phrases, sometimes with variation. They are sung in a slow, monotonous, and plaintive way, repeated over and over in uniform and regular measure, with the low and constant accompaniment of gong or drum in the background. Each song is brought

---

[1] Tanghe, op. cit., pp. 830, 832.    [2] Ibid., pp. 830, 836.    [3] Ibid., p. 830.

to an end by a long-drawn-out final note, followed by a long low note, not really part of the song itself.

While most of these Mabale paddle songs are sung in unison, occasionally led by one of the paddlers, there is also sometimes a specialist singer. This is a young man with a reputation for both his voice and his repertoire of songs who comes specially to sing and is exempt from paddling. He may sing in alternation with chorus, but sometimes performs freely on his own, a situation which is held to lead to the best songs of all. Yet even here, it seems, the words themselves are relatively unimportant. What matters is the regular repetition that stimulates and eases the effort of paddling:

> Hélas, mon enfant;
> Hélas, je le pleure;
> Hélas, avec douleur;
> Saurais-je l'oublier, hélas.[1]
>
> Hélas, mère;
> Hélas, mère;
> Un homme est tombé;
> Un homme est mort. . . .[2]

The occasions mentioned so far all involve rhythmic work by a group of people in co-operation. But there are also solitary work songs. Grinding corn, for instance, though sometimes done by several women, is also often performed by one woman alone. This is a situation that gives scope to the expression of more personal feelings, uttered at greater length, than in the group songs. Thus a Kamba woman's grinding song is concerned with her own experiences. She was married to a man employed at a German Leipzig Mission Station, a place with large whitewashed buildings which she compares to the hills. She had once said she never wished to set foot in a mission station, but even so she has now left her parents and come to live here at the 'master's' (missionary's) place:

> Let me be! Let me grind my flour in peace and recover from my grief!
> You tell me that I have now neither people nor mother.
> Although I once said that I would never come to these 'hills',
> Yet I have come here to build my hut at the master's (place).
> These high hills, they shine like the seeds of the *kivuti*[3] tree, or like coins.
> I am tending my father's roaming bull.[4]

---

[1] Two soloists. Ibid., pp. 831, 838.  [2] One soloist. Ibid., p. 830.
[3] Large red seeds with black spots.  [4] Lindblom iii, 1934, pp. 48–9.

A similar personal comment is evident in a Sotho domestic song, the lament of a woman whose man is away:

> Far, far away at Molelle's place,
> Where is the train going?
> He has been away at the mines too long.
> I, poor child, always say that.
> I have lost my relatives
> And have no one to tell me what to do.[1]

The various types of work songs can be seen to shade into songs for dancing, for in each case the singing accompanies rhythmic movement. The difference, obviously, is that dance movements are not regarded as monotonous or laborious. But even so there is some overlap between the two, with 'work songs' also functioning as, or following the pattern of, dance songs. Thus the Swahili truck-pushing song quoted above has all the characteristics of an up-country *ngoma* (dance) song.[2] Some tasks, furthermore, are carried out in a half-dancing manner, so that, as with the Limba threshing songs, the work becomes attractive and artistic rather than merely laborious, and the song a background to a kind of dance as well as to labour.

This discussion of work songs has already involved some mention of their style. Since they typically accompany collective rhythmical movement, it is not surprising that a common form is that of leader and chorus. The chorus words tend to be particularly simple, often meaningless—*iyo*, *ayo*, *ye ye*, etc.—or involve repetition from the solo part. The soloist has more scope to develop or improvise his words, particularly when, as sometimes happens, he is not expected to take part in the work directly but can concentrate on his singing (and on the musical accompaniment or even dancing that he is also at times responsible for). But even so, the wording of these songs is usually simple. Typically the leader only sings a line or two of his own before his words are taken up by the chorused refrain brought in by the rhythm of the work, and there is little opportunity for elaboration of the verbal content. The structure of a Southern Rhodesian work song recorded by Tracey is characteristic in this respect. The poetry of the words results in a carefully balanced piece of verse, but the words themselves have little significance:

---

[1] *Afr. Music* 2. 2, 1959, p. 76.      [2] Werner 1927, p. 102.

*Chorus.*  Herende hi ho hi haiwa, hiho gore we hi haiwa (no meaning)
*Solo.*    The girls have got their dancing beads on (i.e. this is a joyful
           occasion)
*Chorus.*  Ye wo ye (oh, yes!), they've got their dancing beads on. . . .[1]

It is the rhythm and the melody, not the words, that are the
most striking aspects of these songs. The rhythm of the work
provides the fixed framework within which the song must be
developed, a framework which is likely to continue for a long
period of time during which the song (and the work) is repeated
again and again. The importance of the rhythmical aspect is
brought out further by the cases—which are beyond our scope
here—where complicated percussion is the main element of
interest in accompanying the work. This sometimes takes precedence over or even altogether replaces the words, and may be by
drums, hammers, or even the regular sequence of blows used by
shipworkers in Dar-es-Salaam as they hammer the rust off the
steel sides of the ships—'producing a pleasant effect which no
doubt assists them in the performance of their monotonous task'.[2]
In the songs the words are punctuated and framed by rhythmical
effort—by hauling at the net in Ewe fishing songs, strokes of the
hoe or flail in Limba farming songs, paddle strokes in canoe songs.
It is this that provides their main structure and conditions their
style.

Work songs stand out from others in their directly functional
relationship to the activity they accompany. Occasionally they
appear as a separate art form for sophisticated audiences,[3] but
normally they are inextricably involved with the work itself. This
is particularly true of songs accompanying collective work. The
joint singing co-ordinates the action and leads the workers to feel
and work as part of a co-operating group, not as separate individuals. Such co-operation may be essential to the job in hand
(e.g. in hauling, paddling, and other tasks which depend on exact
joint timing), but even where this is not essential, as in hoeing or
road work, the rhythm of the song still encourages collaboration
and control within the group, a pressure on all to take part equally
within the given rhythmic framework. The function of rhythmical
music in encouraging people to work harder, faster, and with more

[1] Tracey 1929, p. 100.   [2] Tracey in *Afr. Music* I. 4, 1957, p. 82.
[3] e.g. the Ganda paddle songs performed at court (J. Roscoe, *The Baganda*,
London, 1911, p. 37).

enjoyment has frequently been noted. Work songs can also comment on life in general, on local events, or on local characters, and can express ideas of love, friendship, or even obscenity.[1] In short, work songs lighten the labour and give an opportunity, however limited, for poetic and musical expression in the midst of work.[2]

Such songs seem to occur throughout Africa. Their detailed words and form, however, have not been extensively recorded by either linguists or sociologists who have tended to leave this field to musicologists.[3] However, it may be that the same characteristics which have led to this partial neglect—their relatively slight verbal element, their close association with work, and their musical quality—are precisely those which encourage the continuing development of such songs so that they fit new as well as older types of work. This kind of song, probably unlike military and hunting poems, is likely to remain a continuing source for the student of oral literature.

[1] A point made in connection with work songs in E. E. Evans-Pritchard, 'Some Collective Expressions of Obscenity in Africa', *JRAI* 59, 1929.

[2] For a further general discussion of work songs, see T. C. Brakeley, 'Work Song', in M. Leach (ed.), *Standard Dictionary of Folklore, Mythology and Legend*, New York, 1949. Also A. M. Jones i, 1959, pp. 39 ff. (Ewe) and C. B. Wilson, *Work Songs of the Fante Fisherman*, unpub. thesis for Diploma in African Music, Institute of African Studies, Legon, University of Ghana (not seen; reported in Institute of Afr. Studies, Legon, *Research Review* 2. 3, 1966, p. 77).

[3] Musicologists have made many recordings of such songs, particularly in Central Africa; the words, however, are often not published with these recordings.

# 9

## LYRIC

*Occasions. Subject-matter. Form. Composition*

I N the sense of 'a short poem which is sung', lyric is probably the most common form of poetry in subsaharan Africa. It is not always recognized that these songs, in which the musical element is of such obvious importance, are in fact poems. It is true that the verbal aspect sometimes appears less developed than in the lengthy poems which are delivered in spoken or recitative style, like some of the praise poems, hymns, or hunting chants that have already been described. But this should not prevent us from calling them poems. We should remember that classical Greek or Elizabethan lyrics were equally designed to be sung. Indeed, in its original form of a poem in a musical setting, lyric is one of the most important kinds of African oral literature.

So far, with a few exceptions,[1] the poetry we have considered has mainly been associated with relatively formal events. The lyric songs discussed here are for more informal occasions. Whereas much other poetry depends on a specialist and even esoteric tradition, these involve popular participation. The verbal content of these songs tends to be short (though the actual performance may be lengthy) and is often ephemeral. There is usually plenty of improvisation. Unlike the general pattern of Western European folk-songs, the individual singer does not tend to stand out in a dominant position as against a passive audience,[2] but instead interacts with a chorus. Yet these lyric songs still provide wide scope for individual expression.

I

Songs appear in an almost unlimited number of contexts. In words that might be applied more widely than to the Ibo of whom he was writing, Osadebay speaks of the 'wealth of culture and fine

---

[1] In particular the work songs, which could well have been treated under the present heading.

[2] See A. Lomax, 'Song Structure and Social Structure', *Ethnology* I, 1962 on the general contrasts in this respect between Africa, Europe, the Orient, etc.

feelings which find expression in our music and poetry. We sing when we fight, we sing when we work, we sing when we love, we sing when we hate, we sing when a child is born, we sing when death takes a toll'.[1]

*Rites de passage* are very common occasions for singing. There are songs associated with birth, with initiation and puberty, betrothal, marriage, acquiring a new title or status, and funeral and memorial celebrations. The most serious of these songs, in which the verbal element is elaborated at length, cannot be called lyrical. But often such ceremonies are in fact more an occasion for festivity, which includes song, than a solemn ritual with specially designated music, and the gatherings normal at these times are a reason for singing for its own sake.

Weddings, for example, are popular occasions for comment in song—by no means always involving praise of the newly wedded pair:

> Serpent que tu es!
> Chien que tu es!
> Tu fais: oua-oua![2]

sing the bride's friends about her husband among the Ronga, amid a series of songs cheerfully warning her of the ill-treatment she will without doubt receive at the hands of his parents. In more reflective and personal style is the Ganda song of farewell by the young girl about to be married, with the repetitions typical of this form:

> Oh, I am gone,
> Oh, I am gone,
> Call my father that I may say farewell to him,
> Oh, I am gone.
> Father has already sold me,
> Mother has received a high price for me,
> Oh, I am gone.[3]

It is likely that advantage will be taken of this opportunity to sing songs on many other topics.

Many of these songs are for dancing. A particular song type is sometimes inextricably tied up with a particular dance. Thus the

---

[1] Osadebay 1949, p. 154.  [2] Junod 1897, p. 46.
[3] Sempebwa 1948, p. 18. For other examples of marriage songs see e.g. Beaton 1935 (Bari); W. Leslau, 'Chansons harari', *Rass. studi etiop.* 6, 1947; F. Dufays, 'Lied und Gesang bei Brautwerbung und Hochzeit in Mulera-Ruanda', *Anthropos* 4, 1909.

Swahili used to have a special *gungu* song for the 'pounding figure' of the dance:

> Give me a chair that I may sit down and hold (the guitar)
> Let me sing a serenade for my Palm-daughter
> Let me sing for my wife
> She who takes away my grief and sorrow.[1]

This occasion for song is, if anything, increasing, and many examples could be quoted like the Zulu 'town dancing songs' quoted by Tracey, where the words are subordinate to the dance:

> This is the girl that jilted me,
> The wretch of a girl that jilted me.
> At Durban, the dance leaders are afraid of us![2]
>
> Zululand, my home, I love you.
> Goodbye, Willie I like you too.
> We are the boys.[3]

The same kind of mood, of recreation and light-hearted enjoyment, is evident in many of the 'drinking songs'. These too, for all their lightness, may express the thought in true lyric manner, with economy and grace. In a Shona drinking song, the original is only seven words in all:

> Keep it dark!
> Don't tell your wife,
> For your wife is a log
> That is smouldering surely!
> Keep it dark![4]

There are sometimes more formalized occasions for the singing of lyrics. One could mention the recent interest in the short *balwo*

---

[1] Knappert 1966, p. 130. Cf. Steere 1906, p. 473.

[2] i.e. a boast by the (Johannesburg) dancers that no one can dance better than they—their reputation has even reached Durban! Tracey 1948*b*, p. 61.

[3] Ibid., p. 66. Nearly all collections of poems include some dance songs. See also L. Stappers, 'Vijftig motieven uit de dansliederen van de Baamilembwe', *Kongo-Overzee* 20, 1954; E. Emsheimer, 'Drei Tanzgesänge der Akamba', *Ethnos* 2, 1937 (not seen); A. C. Beaton, 'Fur Dance Songs', *Sudan Notes* 23, 1940; idem., 'The Poetry of the Bari Dance', ibid. 21, 1938; E. v. Funke, 'Einige Tanz- und Liebeslieder der Haussa', *ZES* 11, 1920/1; J. P. Clark, 'Poetry of the Urhobo Dance Udje', *Nigeria Magazine* 87, 1965; M. Traoré, 'Une danse curieuse: le moribayasa', *Notes Afr.* 15, 1942; E. Littmann, 'Amharische Tanzlieder der Galla', *Z. f. Semitistik* 4, 1926; J. Vansina, 'Làam, gesongen kwaadsprekerij bij de Bushong', *Aequatoria* 28, 1955; J. H. Nketia, 'Possession Dances in African Societies', *Internat. Folk Music J.* 9, 1957; also the references given in Ch. 10, pp. 276–7.    [4] Tracey 1933, no. 9.

lyric[1] among the Somali. Special *balwo* parties became fashionable in the towns. People would recite the lyrics they knew or compose new ones, and the recitations would be interrupted for tea and conversation.[2] Popular and occasional bands among the Akan also sometimes perform on specifically recreational occasions.[3] Again, in many areas the radio nowadays frequently creates opportunities for lyrics to be performed.

All over the continent it is a common pattern for stories to be interrupted from time to time by a song, usually led by the story-teller, while the audience act as his chorus.[4] Sometimes these songs amount to quite long poems, and are then often in recitative. Short verses are also very common, sometimes with many non-sense syllables to fill in the rhythm and tune, with repetition over and over again between leader and chorus. One Limba story, about 'The clever cat', has a verse of this kind:

The story is about a cat who proposes to initiate the young rat maidens into the *bondo* (women's society). They, like all young girls, are eager to enter—but the cat's one desire is to have a chance of eating them! The cat pretends to act in the usual way of a *bondo* senior woman. She lines them all up and leads the singing, telling them not to look round. She sings:

> When we go,
> Let no one look behind oh!
> When the cat is free, *fo feŋ*.

The chorus of young rats take up the same words:

> When we go,
> Let no one look behind oh!
> When the cat is free, *fo feŋ*

in the way young initiates do in real life. The rhythmic and melodic song is repeated in the story perhaps eight or ten times, first by the cat (the narrator), then by the rat initiates (the audience) who have quickly picked up the tune. But while the singing is going on, what the cat is really doing is to quietly pick off the rats one by one as they sing with their backs to her. At last only one is left, still singing the song. Just in time, she looks round, and throws herself out of the way and escapes.[5]

A story like this appeals to its audience partly because of the amusing form of words and the parody of the usually very serious

[1] On which see below, pp. 254 ff.  [2] Andrzejewski 1967, p. 11.
[3] Nketia 1962, pp. 16–17; 1963*b*, chap. 6.
[4] On the function of songs in stories see Ch. 13, pp. 385. Also Belinga 1965, pp. 55 ff.  [5] Full story is given in Finnegan 1967, pp. 333–4.

initiation ceremony, but perhaps most of all because of the attractive song which, in terms of the time spent repeating it over and over, took up as long as the prose narrative. Simple as the words were in themselves, the audience all joined in enthusiastically, overlapping slightly with the leader's last note and half dancing as they sang; they would, it seemed, have continued indefinitely had not the leader finally broken into their response to continue his narration.

The same song is sometimes repeated at different points in the story, a kind of signature tune with slight variations on the words to fit the development of the plot. The structure of the story is thus marked by the recurrence of the song in each new episode. Another Limba example can make this plain:

The plot is the intentionally fantastic and humorous one of the hero Sara and his endeavours to kill and eat a guinea-fowl he had caught without sharing it with any of his friends. But the bird is a magical one and the more Sara tries to kill and eat it, going through all the usual preparations and cooking procedures, the more it sings back at him. At last he eats it—but even in his stomach the bird sings and demands to be excreted; and in the final effort, Sara dies.

Each of the many parallel stages of the plot is marked by the same song, with variations to suit the event, the last phrase and response being repeated several times by narrator and audience with the same tune throughout. First, the guinea-fowl is discovered in the snare, and it sings:

> Sara is coming to loose me,
> Sara is coming to loose me.
> Here he found a path, a night passed,
> Here he came and put a snare for me,
> The guinea-fowl,
> The guinea-fowl,
> *Ko de ba ko naligbe*[1]
> What is your name?
> What is your name?
>
> (Response) *Tambarenke, Tambarenke.*
> What is your name?
>
> *Tambarenke, Tambarenke.*
> What is your name?
>
> *Tambarenke, Tambarenke . . ., etc.*

[1] Apparently nonsense words.

Sara looses the bird from the noose, and brings it home to prepare for eating. Again the bird sings:

> Sara is coming to pluck me,
> Sara is coming to pluck me.
> Here he found a path, a night passed,
> Here he came and put a snare for me,
> The guinea-fowl,
> The guinea-fowl,
> *Ko de ba ko nagligbe*
> What is your name?
> What is your name?
>
> > *Tambarenke, Tambarenke.*
>
> What is your name?
>
> > *Tambarenke, Tambarenke. . . .*

As the story continues, new first lines appear:

> Sara is coming to cut me up . . .
> Sara is coming to pound me . . .[1]
> Sara is coming to mould me . . .
> Sara is coming to put me in (to the pot) . . .
> Sara is coming to take me out . . .
> Sara is coming to eat me . . .
> Sara is going to lie down. . . .

And, finally,

> Sara is going to excrete me. . . .[2]

The linguistic content of songs in Limba stories, as in some others, is relatively limited, and for the audience their main interest lies in the rhythm and melody and the fact that they can participate in the singing. In some other cases, however, such as some Akan stories, the words are more developed. The following is a variation on a very common theme:

Elephant and Antelope are said to have made very good friends in the forest. Elephant being the stronger and wealthier of the two was able to lay on sumptuous meals every day to which he invited Antelope. One day he expressed the desire to visit Antelope in his house. This embarrassed Antelope for he also wanted to give him a good meal. It occurred to him after failing to get any meat that Mother Antelope was

---

[1] Meat is often pounded in a mortar, then moulded into balls.
[2] Full story in Finnegan 1967, pp. 284–6.

the answer, so he caused her to be killed and used. When Elephant arrived he was greatly surprised by the declicious meal and asked to see Mother Antelope. But Antelope succeeded in putting this off. After the meal however, Elephant again asked for Mother Antelope and Antelope replied in a song as follows:

Elephant, please don't worry me.
Have you ever seen a poor man
And a wealthy man exchange things equally?
Elephant Akwaa Brenkoto that commands his destiny,
Elephant that plucks the tops of trees on his right,
King of musketry, father and king,
Birefi Akuampon, mighty one to whom all stray goods are sent to be used.
Yes; let us proceed,
Mother Antelope, I have stewed her.
Yes, let us proceed.
Mother Antelope, I have used her to redeem myself.
Yes, let us proceed.[1]

## II

The subjects of the many different songs sung on these various occasions include just about every topic imaginable. There are songs about wives, husbands, marriage, animals, chiefs, this year's tax, the latest football match, a recent intrigue, the plight of a cripple dependent on his family, an amusing incident, a friend's treachery or an enemy's vices, the relationship between variety in the human and the natural world—and so on according to the genre of song involved, the context of performance, and the poetic inspiration of the singer.

It has frequently been remarked that African poems about nature are few and far between, and there is truth in this assertion. Certainly there seems to be little in common between most African lyrics and the romantic interest in 'Nature' typical of certain epochs of the English poetic tradition, and lyrics about people, events, and personal experience are more common. But observation of the natural world, especially the animal world is often significant. Take the simple little song about a brook recorded in Malawi in the nineteenth century. The effect is an imitation of the sound of the brook and it is sung 'softly and soothingly' in a subdued voice; the main point is to reflect the tune of the water,

[1] Nketia 1958*b*, p. 19.

rather than describe in words, though a picture is given of the bank of the little stream (*chiko*) and the prickly bush that grows by it (*likwanya*):

| 1st voice. | *Likwanya likunyanya ku chiko.* |
| Response. | *Anyanyale.* |

simultaneously $\begin{cases} \text{1st voice.} & \textit{Likwanya likunyanya ku chiko.} \\ \text{2nd voice.} & \textit{Anya-nya-nya-le e.} \end{cases}$

Then the two voices interchange the lines twice, with the final response:

*Anyanyale.*[1]

Again, we could mention the case of Somali poetry which 'is imbued with a consciousness of the beauties and cruelties of nature'.[2] For instance, the simple lyric 'O Distant Lightning! Have you deceived me?'[2] gains its emotive tone from the inspiration of rain and its life-giving and beautiful results. Lightning often presages rain, and this symbolizes hope. But sometimes the hope is disappointed and the rain-clouds move away. So here the poet is writing of love, but calls the girl 'Distant Lightning', expressing his disappointment in love in terms of natural forces.

Songs associated with birds are very common.[3] Sometimes the song is envisaged as sung by the bird itself, and at least part is then in onomatopoeic representation of the call. We could instance the many lyrics supposed to be sung and exchanged by birds among the Beti of the Cameroons. The *ngiai afan* (genderme silvatique) sings of the insecurity of life:

Point de sécurité en forêt. (Mviè e se a fiè.
Point de sécurité en forêt. Mviè a se fiè.)[4]

The female *kolvodo ban nga* (magpie) in one of her songs praises the virtues of work:

| Va au travail. | (Kel' esié o. |
| Va au travail. | Kel' esié o. |
| Si tu entends dire: | O wog na: |
| 'C'est une fille d'homme' | 'Ngôn mot' |
| C'est grâce au travail. | H'esié. |

---

[1] Macdonald i, 1882, p. 49.   [2] Andrzejewski 1967, p. 9.
[3] e.g. Pokomo (A. Werner in *Africa* i, 1928, p. 253); Lamba (Doke 1934, pp. 365–6); Cameroun (Belinga 1965, pp. 28 ff.); Lango (Okot 1963, pp. 157 ff.); Nkundo (Boelaert 1949, p. 5); Limba (Finnegan field notes); and the instances mentioned below.   [4] Anya-Noa 1965, p. 129.

| | |
|---|---|
| Si tu entends dire: | O wog na: |
| 'C'est une fille d'homme' | 'Ngôn mot' |
| C'est grâce au travail. | H'esié. |
| Le pays serait-il généreux, | Nnam akab, |
| Ne sois pas quémandeur. | Te bô zaq. |
| Le pays serait-il généreux, | Nnam akab, |
| Ne sois pas quémandeur. | Te bô zaq.)[1] |

The Zulu songs attributed to birds attempt to represent something of the nature and appearance of the bird as well as its cry—and cast a sly glance at humanity too. The bird called *uthekwane* (hammerkop or heron) is pictured strolling gracefully by the waterside, with his fine-looking crest and shapely thighs—symbolizing vanity:

I myself, have often said:—*Thekwane*! You, with your crest, your leisurely strolling when frequenting the spring, at the time it has been opened up—mark you as a very fine fellow. You have large thighs.[2]

Other Zulu bird songs involve interchange between the hen and the cock, the male in deep bass, the hen higher. The song of the *insingizi* (hornbill or turkey-buzzard) is really a comment on married life, particularly the last line of the cock's exhausted rejoinder to his wife's constant nagging:

*Hen.* Where, where is (the) meat? Where, where is (the) meat?
*Cock.* There's none, it's up in the trees above (*bis*)
*Hen.* Where, where are the worms? (*bis*)
*Cock.* There are none, there are no worms (*bis*)
*Hen.* Are there none, are there none over there? (*bis*)
*Cock.* Oh! get away with you! Where will I get them from? (*bis*)
*Hen.* Look for them, look for them over there (*bis*)
*Cock.* There are none, there are none over there (*bis*)
*Hen.* I am going, I am going, I am going home to my people (*bis*)
*Cock.* Go, go, you have long since said so (*bis*).[3]

Most elaborate of all is the song of self-assertion attributed to the *iqola*, the fiscal shrike. In it the cock utters his proverbial cries of '*Goshi! Goshi! Dadi! Dadi!*', cries which are supposed to describe the sounds made by the movements of his wings and feet as well as the ejaculations he utters as part of his great display. He is pictured as turning his head to the right, then to the left, surveying himself in self-admiration. His cry really amounts to saying 'I am

[1] Ibid., pp. 124–5.    [2] Dunning 1946, p. 44.    [3] Ibid., p. 33.

the personification of everything that is Majestic and Powerful and my ornaments jingle and rattle in perfect rhythm.' He sings:

> *Goshi! Goshi! Dadi! Dadi!*
> Who do I kill (stab)? Who do I kill? Who do I kill?
> I kill the relations of these (indicating his victims) outright! outright!
> I kill the relations of these outright! outright!
> I kill the relations of these outright! outright!
>
> Sanxokwe, Sanxokwe (addressing her Majesty)
> I'll pay your bridewealth (lobola) with a red beast
> I'll pay your bridewealth with a red beast
> I'll pay your bridewealth with a red beast.
>
> When men drink beer, they become intoxicated,
> They take up their sticks
> And they (the sticks) clashing together sound *xakaxaka, xakaxaka, xakaxaka.*
>
> I have been across the Umdawane[1]
> Where I ate up the big dance.[2]
>
> I caught a small bird, I fixed it on the end of a slender twig very early this morning.
> I repeated this by catching a Fantail Warbler early this morning
> And fixed it on the end of a slender twig.
> I drank the blood of a bird early this morning.
> I struck its little stomach, it became red with blood at that very moment,
> Because I am the King of Birds.
>
> *Goshi! Goshi! Dadi! Dadi!*
> *Bayede! Bayede!* (Salute me royally) *Khuleka! Khuleka!* (Make obeisance to me) *Nkosi! Nkosi!* [Address me as] King![3]

Finally, in a rather different style, is the brief but pathetic Nyanja song of the unloved night-jar:

> Moon, you must shine, shine that I may eat the tadpoles;
> I sit on a stone, and my bones all rattle.
> If it were not for my big mouth,
> The maidens would be crying for me.[4]

Songs about, or attributed to, animals seem to be less common than those associated with birds. But some certainly exist, particu-

---

[1] A fabulous river.    [2] i.e. won all the prizes.
[3] Dunning 1946, pp. 45–6. The line division is not quite clear in the text and I may have interpreted it incorrectly in places.    [4] Rattray 1907, p. 164.

larly in South and Central Africa. The brief Hottentot song about a baboon gives a vivid little picture of his typical occupation:

> There, I've got you, I've got you, I've got you . . .
> Crack, crack, what a louse . . .
> It bit me, what a louse . . .
> Crack, crack, what a louse . . .
> It bit me, what a louse . . .[1]

and is cast in the typical form of a sung lyric, with plenty of scope for repetition and, apparently, for chorus responses. Among the South African Bantu the tradition of praising seems still strong, and recent praises (although strictly of a different order from the songs quoted in this chapter) are much more simple and lyrical in concept than the lengthy and grandiose praises of traditional culture. Thus Hurutshe men describe a hare:

> *Ga-re-ya-gaa-koo!*[2]
> Son of the little dark brown one with spots,
> Little yellow one, leaper from the stubbles,
> Yonder is the son of the little dark brown one
> Leaper from the treeless plain
> Leaper from the trunks of trees;
> It leaps up, and stretches its tail
> And it places its ears on its shoulders
> *Ga-re-ya-gaa-koo!*[3]

Among pastoral peoples, songs are often composed and sung in praise of individual beasts. Cattle come to mean far more to their owners than mere economic sustenance, and are accepted as emotional and evocative topics for deeply felt expression. This can be seen in the songs collected by recent investigators from the Nilotic cattle-keeping people, and also from a Dinka song published early in the century. The individual singer typically praises his own bull in an outpouring of personal pride:

> My Bull is as white as the silvery fish in the river; as white as the egret on the river bank; as white as new milk.
> His bellowing is like the roar of the Turk's cannon from the great river.

[1] Stopa, 1938, p. 101.
[2] The shout given when the hare jumps up from its lair.
[3] Merwe 1941, pp. 328–9. Animal songs also occur in Central Africa (Lamba) where they bear some resemblance to Southern Bantu praises (Doke 1934, p. 365).

My bull is as dark as the rain-cloud, that comes with the storm.
He is like Summer and Winter; half of him dark as the thunder-
cloud; half of him as white as sunshine.
His hump shines like the morning star.
His forehead is as red as the arum's [hornbill] wattles.
His forehead is like a banner; seen by the people from afar.
He is like the rainbow.
I shall water him at the river, and drive
My enemies from the water with my spear.
Let them water their cattle at the well;
The river for me and my bull.
Drink, O Bull, of the river. Am I not here with
My spear to protect you?[1]

But songs describing animals, or even birds, are apparently far
less common than those in which the main interest is human life.
In fact this can be seen even in many of the songs ostensibly about
birds, for the bite of the comment is often its veiled relevance for
human action, character, aspiration, or absurdity. There are lyrics
about every facet of human activity. Love and marriage are
probably the commonest themes, and the remainder of this section
will illustrate some of these songs.

Marriage is a topic that can be treated many different ways.
Not only its attractions are indicated in song, but also its difficulties or absurdities. Thus one of the Ganda songs connected with
marriage lightly warns young suitors:

> When he sees a pretty girl he falls for her,
> 'I will go with you, let us go.'
> Not knowing that he is going with a girl with a fiery temper.[2]

Among the Shi of the Eastern Congo, again, marital relationships are the most common single subject in songs, many of them
concerned with marital and pre-marital strife. One of the popular
forms is a song describing a girl's rejection of her suitor because
she thinks him too poor:

> 'You want to marry me, but what can you give me? A nice field?'
> 'No, I have only a house.'
> 'What? You have nothing but a house? How would we live? Go to
> Bukavu; there you can earn plenty of money. You can buy food
> and other things.'

[1] S. L. Cummins, 'Sub-tribes of the Bahr-el-Ghazal Dinkas', *JRAI* 34,
1904, p. 162.      [2] Sempebwa 1948, p. 17.

'No, I won't go. I don't know the people there. I have always lived
   here, and I know the people and want to stay here.'
'You are a stupid man. You want me to marry me but you have
   nothing. If you don't go to Bukavu and earn money to buy me
   things then I won't marry you.'[1]

A different point of view is expressed in one of the many Chopi
songs on this subject. Here the girl is pictured as sad and solitary
without her husband; like so many others he has gone off many
hundreds of miles to work in the mines. And yet there is something
in common—a comment on a woman's demand for material
possessions:

> I am most distressed,
> I am most distressed as my man has gone off to work,
> And he does not give me clothes to wear,
> Not even black cloth.[2]

The number of love songs recorded is surprising—at least to
those brought up to the idea that the concept of personal love is
bound to be lacking in African cultures. Even the idea of courtly
and romantic love is not always absent. It seems, for instance, to
occur to some extent among the Hausa, whose rich tradition of
love poetry is now influencing surrounding people.[3] Fletcher
quotes a simple Hausa song of love, 'To Dakabo, a maiden':

> Dakabo is tin!
> Dakabo is copper!
> Dakabo is silver!
> Dakabo is gold!
> Where greatness is a fortune
> The thing desired is (obtained only) with time.
> Thy things are my things,
> My things are thy things,
> Thy mother is my mother,
> My mother is thy mother,
> Thy father is my father,
> My father is thy father!
> Be patient, O maid!
> Be patient, young maiden![4]

---

[1] A. P. Merriam, 'Song Texts of the Bashi', *Afr. Music* 1. 1, 1954, p. 45.
[2] Tracey 1948*a*, p. 46.
[3] Cf. Mayssal 1965, p. 81, on Hausa influence on the Cameroons Fulani.
[4] Fletcher 1912, p. 65.

The Somali *balwo* (later called *heello*) are even more striking examples of romantic and emotional love poetry.[1] These are short lyric love poems which have become popular recently and are particularly associated with the new urban generation. The *balwo* is characterized by extreme brevity—it usually consists of only two lines—and a condensed and cryptic imagery expressed in 'miniature' form. It is sung to a distinct tune with syncopated rhythms, but there are relatively few of these tunes and thousands of different poems. There are two, related, themes in these lyrics: first, those addressed to a beloved woman, in hope of marriage; and secondly those to a woman admired from afar off, even one seen only once whom the poet can have little hope of seeing again. This theme of romantic and frustrated love gives rise, it seems, to genuine and deeply felt emotion, expressed in a condensed and symbolic form arising from one central image:

> Woman, lovely as lightning at dawn,
> Speak to me even once.

> I long for you, as one
> Whose dhow in summer winds
> Is blown adrift and lost,
> Longs for land, and finds—
> Again the compass tells—
> A grey and empty sea.[2]

> If I say to myself 'Conceal your love!'
> Who will conceal my tears?

> Like a tall tree which, fallen, was set alight,
> I am ashes.[3]

> My heart is single and cannot be divided,
> And it is fastened on a single hope; Oh you who might be the moon.[4]

The romantic love poem is not just confined to the coast. The Nyamwezi of central Tanganyika around Tabora can sing:

> My love is soft and tender,
> My love Saada comforts me,
> My love has a voice like a fine instrument of music.[5]

[1] See especially Andrzejewski 1967; also references given below.
[2] Laurence 1954, p. 31 (and general discussion on pp. 6–12).
[3] Andrzejewski 1967, p. 13.
[4] Andrzejewski and Lewis 1964, p. 146 (and general discussion, pp. 49–51).
[5] Tracey 1963, p. 20.

Not all African love songs, however, are in the romantic, even ecstatic vein perhaps more typical of areas like Hausa country or the East Coast, long influenced by Arabic culture. There are many ways of describing this fertile theme. The Kuanyama Ambo of South West Africa have a series of brief antiphonal love poems used in courtship, with call and response between man and girl. Usually some analogy of a general rather than a personal kind is made between nature and human relationships:

> Where one sees birds in their flight, there is water;
> Where one hears the sound of women's laughter, there is a kraal.

> A palm stick bow does not like the rainy season (it warps);
> A woman fond of a man does not like to be among people.[1]

An analogy with nature is also made in a very light-hearted love song by a young Soga in East Africa:

> All things in nature love one another.
> The lips love the teeth,
> The beard loves the chin,
> And all the little ants go 'brrr-r-r-r' together.[2]

Zulu love poetry seems often to be by women, a feature that has parallels elsewhere in Africa. Dhlomo gives one girl's song that is both realistic and romantic:

> Never shall I fall in love with a suckling.
> Joy, joy, O mother, this one sleeps unrealising.
> Never shall I fall in love with one who is no ladies' man.
> Joy, joy, O mother, this one sleeps unrealising.
> I would like to fall in love with a dashing he-man.
> Joy, joy, O mother, this one sleeps unrealising.
> Would love him-who-appears-and-causes-heart-aches!
> Joy, joy, O mother, this one sleeps unrealising.
> Yes, I would like a whirlwind of a man!
> Joy, joy, O mother, this one sleeps unrealising.[3]

In much more disillusioned vein is another Zulu love song, this time by an older woman living in Durban, where she runs her own small group of singers. The song expresses all her despair and the mundane yet heart-breaking aspects of parting:

[1] E. M. Loeb, 'Courtship and the Love Song', *Anthropos* 45, 1950, pp. 847, 848. (The general interpretation by Loeb is, however, highly doubtful.)
[2] Tracey 1963, p. 20.        [3] Dhlomo 1947, p. 7.

I thought you loved me,
Yet I am wasting my time on you.
I thought we would be parted only by death,
But to-day you have disappointed me.
You will never be anything.
You are a disgrace, worthless and unreliable.
Bring my things. I will put them in my pillow.
You take yours and put them under your armpit.
You deceived me.[1]

Among the Luo of Kenya, too, love songs are sung by women. The final examples of love poetry will be taken from their *oigo* lyrics, one of the many types of songs in Luo country.[2] These are love songs in a slightly different sense from the ones already quoted.

The *oigo* are songs sung by young girls on their way to visit the young men they are courting. The girls walk to the hut where they are to be entertained by the men, by the light of the full moon. As they go, they sing these songs, individually or in groups, taking it in turns to sing the whole way. 'There was no formal order of singing; the more musically gifted girls or the more effusive took the leading part according to their mood.'[3] Meanwhile the young men are waiting, straining their ears for the first sounds of the song. When it is heard, one of them announces to the rest, at the top of his voice: 'The landing has taken place, they have arrived.' The girls come and are welcomed with gifts. And then the evening's entertainment proceeds, the men playing on reed flutes while the girls sing their *oigo* songs.

These songs have their own special form. The tunes are simple and rather repetitive with an insistent rhythm. The most striking aspect is the singer's vocal style. 'The singer trills in a bird-like voice and conveys an impression of being possessed by the stream of song within her, breathless and helpless. The emotions expressed are often sorrowful and almost hysterical, yet the singer exults in her ability to sing endlessly like a bird.'[4] This distinctive style comes out, even in translation, in the following poem. The characteristic refrain, *doree ree yo*, is far more repetitive and appealing than can be represented in an English text:

[1] Tracey 1948*b*, p. 41.

[2] I write in the present though in fact these songs are now a thing of the past. The description is taken from Owuor 1961.

[3] Owuor 1961, p. 51.                         [4] Ibid., p. 52.

I am possessed,
A bird bursting on high with the *ree* lament
I am the untiring singer.
Dear bird, let's sing in rivalry
Our *doree ree yo . . .*;
It is my wayward self,
Singing in rivalry
The *doree ree yo*;
I am the untiring singer
That rocks far-off Mombasa
With the *aree ree yo*;
It is the voice crying the *doree*

That rocks far-off Nakuru;
I am the compelling *Ondoro* drum,
The bird bursting with the *doree*'s plaintive tones;
I am the untiring singer
Choking herself with the *doree ree yo*.[1]

Sometimes the emphasis of the song is on the sorrow of the singer, or the way she is possessed by the song. At other times we are given a picture of another side of her nature—wilful and unpredictable, her impulsiveness breaking through the ordinary rules of behaviour. This comes out in one song which is arranged round the image of a family setting out, led by the favourite bull who symbolizes their unity. Impulsively, the girl runs ahead to keep up with the animal, in spite of the pain in her chest from her exertion:

Our bull is starting off for Holo,
The Kapiyo clan have fine cattle.
Our bull is starting off for Holo,
The Kapiyo clan have fine cattle.

Then the giggling one said,
Then the playful one said,
(How amusing)
The impulsive *ree* singer
Is a forest creature lamenting the pain in her chest;
The forest creature lamenting the pain in her chest,
The spirited one lamenting the pain in her chest,
The giggling *ree* singer
Is a forest creature lamenting the pain in her chest,
The *Nyagwe Gune* lamenting the pain in her chest,
The impulsive *ree* singer
Is a forest creature lamenting the pain in her chest.

[1] Ibid., p. 53.

Our bull is starting off for Holo,
The Kapiyo have fine cattle;
The Kadulo clan is a bull which starts off for Holo,
The Kapiyo have fine cattle.[1]

In these songs, a special picture of girlhood is presented. It is one which does not necessarily correspond in all ways to the reality, but forms a conventional part of this particular form of art:

She lives in a dreamland, though much tempered by the idealised role she longs to fill in the community. . . . As with a bird, singing appears to be the natural outpouring of the life force itself. The prestige of clan and family depended not only on the prowess of its young men but also on the zealous way in which its women represented its interests in song and dance. For a group of girls the oigo was a means of announcing their presence and of differentiating themselves from the older married women; for an individual a way of expressing her idiosyncrasies.[2]

I'm still complaining,
Crying the *ree ree ree*,
I'm still complaining,
Ever tearful with the *ree ree ree*,
I'm still complaining;
The redo-singer's unceasing complaint,
Scion of young women
Still complaining,
Ever tearful with the *ree ree ree*,
I'm still complaining.

I am in love with the oigo;
I cry the *ree ree ree*
Infatuated with the oigo;
The redo-singer's unceasing complaint
Blasting Amimo's hearth
With constant complaining;
Ever tearful with the *ree ree ree*,
I'm still complaining.[3]

---

[1] Owuor 1961, p. 54.     [2] Ibid., p. 52.

[3] Ibid., p. 53. Other references on love songs include Tracey 1963, pp. 19–20 (examples and general discussion); Knappert 1967a (Swahili); G. Schürle and A. Klingenheben, 'Afrikanische Liebeslieder' (Duala and Zaramo), *ZKS* 3, 1913/14; Chadwicks iii, 1940, pp. 668 ff. (Tuareg); E. Von Funke, 'Einige Tanz- und Liebeslieder der Haussa', *ZES* 11, 1920–1; Tescaroli 1961, ch. 4 (Sudan); E. Cerulli, 'Poesie di guerra e di amore dei Galla', *Arch. antrop. e etnol.* 5, 1942 (reference in *IAI Bibl.* (*A*) by R. Jones, North-East Africa, 1959, p. 33); D. Earthy, 'A Chopi Love-song', *Africa* 4, 1931. For other discussions or examples of 'lyrics' see J. Vansina, 'La chanson lyrique chez les Kuba', *Jeune Afrique* 27,

III

Songs in Africa are very frequently in antiphonal form. That is, there is response of some kind between soloist and chorus, and the song depends on the alternation between the two parts. The role of the soloist (or 'cantor') is crucial. It is he who decides on the song, and when it should start and end. Even more important, he can introduce variations on the basic theme of the song, in contrast to the part of the chorus which is more or less fixed. In other cases, the soloist has complete scope to improvise his part of the verse as he chooses (apart perhaps from the very first line). This type of composition results in many impromptu and often ephemeral lyrics.

Within the general antiphonal form, which has often been mentioned as one of the main characteristics of African song, there are several possible variations. This is partly a question of who the performers are. Sometimes, for instance, there is more than one cantor; two or even three may interchange verses with each other as well as with the accompanying chorus. In other special musical types, the singers take turns in leading the singing, or two answer each other's song. But, as will appear, even in the most basic type (one leader/one chorus) there is scope for variety and elaboration.

One of the simplest forms, and one that seems to occur widely in Africa, is repetition of two phrases between soloist and chorus. Nketia terms this pattern the 'call and response' form and shows how even this type of antiphony can be elaborated in actual performance.[1] At its simplest level, one that occurs, for instance, in children's games or other action songs, there is merely a repeated interchange between leader and group, the first singing his own phrase (A), the chorus coming in with theirs (B).[2] But there are also more complex forms:

1958; T. Tsala, 'Minlan mi mved (chants lyriques)', *Recherches et études camerounaises* 2, 1960 (Beti); L. Longmore, 'Music and Song among the Bantu People in Urban Areas on the Witwatersrand', *Afr. music Soc. Newsletter* 1. 6, 1953; and references in following sections. For written Swahili forms see Knappert 1966, pp. 128 f., 136.

[1] Nketia 1962, pp. 28 ff. I draw heavily on Nketia's analysis here: though he is working primarily on Ghanian music, his analysis has a wider application. See also the useful article by D. Rycroft, 'Nguni Vocal Polyphony', *J. Internat. Folk Music Council* 19, 1967.

[2] The children's singing games quoted in Ch. 11 include some examples of this basic form.

Various techniques of elaboration of the basic A–B form may be employed. Variations in text, in melody or both may be introduced in the cantor's phrase (A) while the balancing responsive phrase (B) sung by the chorus remains the same. Interest may be further enhanced by varying the beginning and ending point of the cantor's phrase in such a way as to make this part overlap with the chorus response. In addition to these, a little elaboration in the form of a short introduction based on the words of the song may be sung by the cantor or by a member of the chorus who wishes to start a new song before the leading phrase (A) is begun. Examples of this will be found in the music of *kple* worship of the Ga people. It is also greatly exploited in Adangme *klama* music.[1]

Songs founded on this type of repetition are basically short, though the actual repetitions may be drawn out almost indefinitely. Further extensions of the basic principle are also common. One might be built up on a kind of sequential pattern so that A and B are repeated at different levels, resulting in a form of A B $A^1$ $B^1$. The complete unit (now of four sections, or even of six, eight, or more) can be repeated several times over. In this type too the cantor is at liberty to introduce slight variations, melodic or textual. The words of the chorus usually remain the same, though in some elaborations they are changed while the cantor's part stays the same. As can be seen, many other combinations are also possible—like, for instance, the $A^1$ B, $A^2$ B, $A^3$ B pattern of many Limba songs.

All these elaborations of the 'call and response' pattern basically involve the balance of sections sung by leader and chorus against each other, and depend essentially on repetition. This raises the problem of how the song is ended. Sometimes the end is abrupt and the leader simply stops; but at other times he joins in the chorus response, often with a prolonged final note. In other songs there is a special closing refrain.

Another type of antiphonal collaboration between leader and chorus is the 'solo and chorused refrain'.[2] In songs of this pattern there is not the same balanced alternation between the two parts. Instead the soloist merely introduces the song. The cantor might sing the entire verse of the song right through once, and this is then repeated by the chorus. An example of this is the simple but effective Ghanaian song:

[1] Nketia 1962, p. 29.   [2] Ibid., pp. 30–1.

I sleep long and soundly;
Suddenly the door creaks.
I open my eyes confused,
And find my love standing by.
Mother Adu, I am dying.
Adu, kinsman of Odurowa,
What matters death to me?[1]

In the Ewe *nyayito* dance songs, in which new words are continually being composed, the first cantor sings the whole song through unaccompanied. By singing in a dramatic tone he can encourage people to join the dance.[2] In other cases, the cantor sings only a short introductory phrase, and the chorus then sings the main song. The form is highly flexible:

When the cantor has sung through, he may sing a short leading phrase before the chorus comes in. This leading phrase may also be added to a cantor's introduction. Further, the main chorus refrain can be interrupted by a cantor at appropriate points. . . . Furthermore a number of cantors may take turns at leading the chorus. Either of them may sing an introductory phrase before the chorus comes in, or they may take turns at leading each new verse. Sometimes cantors singing in twos are encountered. All these show that this form is flexible, and that there is room for building up complex sectional patterns on the basis of the singing roles taken by the participants.[3]

There are other possible variants. There are various combinations of the two main types described, including songs like the well-known Adangme *klama* which open with an introductory section by the cantor sung in free rhythm, followed by a section in strict tempo with a solo lead and chorus refrain (or overlapping solo and chorus parts), repeated three or more times; each new stanza can then be treated in much the same way as the song proceeds.[4] Sometimes basically solo songs in declamatory style are supplemented by a chorus or instrumental addition.[5] In other songs the antiphony is between two soloists rather than solo and chorus. Thus the Kassena-Nankani of northern Ghana have a special type of song in which a young man who wishes to sing the praises of a girl conventionally asks the assistance of a friend: this results in a kind of duet by the two men, accompanied by gourd

[1] Nketia 1963*a*, p. 37. The emotion of love is, as often in Akan poetry, likened to that of suffering and death.    [2] A. M. Jones i, 1959, p. 75.
[3] Nketia 1962, pp. 30–1.    [4] Nketia 1958*a*, p. 28.
[5] Nketia 1962, p. 31.

percussion.[1] Alternatively the antiphony may be between two choruses. This is the common pattern, for instance, in the Limba women's song which accompanies the boys' *gbondokale* dance and involves almost endless repetition of only a few phrases. Another example is the Zulu wedding song where, after the leader has stated the theme, it is taken up first by the chorus of women, and then by the men who answer with a contrasting theme, overlapping with the women's singing.[2]

It is clear that the antiphonal form provides scope for far more flexibility, rich elaboration, and varied interpretation than is immediately apparent from the bald statement that this is the characteristic structure of African songs. It is also a most suitable form for the purposes to which it is put. It makes possible both the exploitation of an expert and creative leader, and popular participation by all those who wish or are expected to join in. The repetition and lack of demand on the chorus also make it particularly appropriate for dancing. Finally the balanced antiphony both gives the poem a clear structure and adds to its musical attractiveness.

We must not, however, exaggerate the significance of this very common antiphonal type of song and thus overlook the fact that some songs are primarily for soloists only. Thus one of the song types recorded from Zambia, the *impango*, seems to be designed primarily for solo singing;[3] men among the Bushmen sing personal and plaintive songs as solos;[4] and certain types of songs—such as lullabies and sometimes love and herding songs—always tend to be sung by individuals. Such songs can develop the verbal content, unlike the antiphonal songs which normally seem to involve a lot of repetition. It is by no means always clear in the sources how far a song is in fact sung by chorus and leader and how far just by one person, because those taking down texts tend to avoid repetitious phrases and to transcribe the song as if it were sung by one person only. The Akan 'maiden songs' are a good example of how one could easily assume that there is only one singer. Nketia in fact, with characteristic precision, explains that these are sung by groups of women, each taking it in turns to lead the verses of the song; in the case cited here the last three lines are sung by the

[1] Nketia 1962, p. 27.
[2] T. Cope, '"African Music", a lecture given at Natal University', *Afr. Music* 2. 2, 1959, p. 35.     [3] A. M. Jones 1943, pp. 11–12.
[4] A. Lomax, 'Song Structure and Social Structure', *Ethnology* 1, 1962, pp. 438–9.

chorus. But in most other sources this explanation would not be added and the words would have suggested a single singer. The song is in honour of a loved one:

> He is coming, he is coming,
> Treading along on camel blanket in triumph.
> Yes, stranger, we are bestirring ourselves.
> Agyei the warrior is drunk,
> The green mamba with fearful eyes.
>> Yes, Agyei the warrior,
>> He is treading along on camel blanket in triumph,
>> Make way for him.
> He is coming, he is coming.
> Treading along on sandals (i.e. on men).
> Yes, stranger, we are bestirring ourselves.
> Adum Agyei is drunk.
> The Green Mamba, Afaafa Adu.
>> Yes, Agyei the warrior,
>> He is treading along on camel blanket in triumph,
>> Make way for him.[1]

The musical side of these lyrics, unlike spoken or semi-chanted poetry, is of vital importance. The verbal expression and the melody of the song are interdependent. So much is clear—but beyond this there are many areas of uncertainty. For one thing, the relative weight given to melody and to verbal content seems to vary in different areas and between different genres of song. For instance, the work songs designed to accompany and lighten rhythmic labour lay little stress on the words, and much more on the melody and rhythm, while in love songs the words take on greater interest. Further, there seems to be no firm agreement among musicologists about how far, when discussing African lyrics, one can generalize about such matters as scale, melody structure, rhythm, and harmony;[2] few detailed studies have been published for particular areas.[3]

---

[1] Nketia 1958*b*, p. 20; cf. Nketia 1963*a*, p. 51.

[2] For recent general discussions, see Merriam 1962, 1965; A. M. Jones 1959, ch. 9; Rouget 1961; Tracey 1964; A. Adande, 'L'évolution de la musique africaine', *Notes afr.* 54, 1952; J. H. Nketia, 'Unity and Diversity in African Music: a Problem of Synthesis' in L. Bown and M. Crowder (eds.), *Proceedings of the First International Congress of Africanists*, London, 1964.

[3] Though see Tracey 1948*a* (Chopi); A. M. Jones 1943, 1949 (Zambia), 1959 (Ewe); Nketia 1962 (Ghana); Brandel 1961 (Central Africa); also further references in Merriam 1965 and L. J. P. Gaskin, *A Select Bibliography of African Music*, London, 1965.

One point of interest is the question of the exact connection between spoken and sung tone, especially in the highly tonal languages characteristic of parts of Africa. Again, there is some controversy on this score, but it seems clear that there is often a relationship between the tones of speech and the melody, so that the melodic pattern is influenced by linguistic considerations. This is well documented for some West African languages. The relationship seems to be flexible, with the possibility of variation and tone modifications. Nketia sums up the position for the several Ghanaian tone languages:

> What the intonation of a song text provides . . . are tone *patterns* or syllable relationships and not the actual melodic notes that are to be employed. We would not, in traditional Ghanaian music, expect a high tone always to be sung in the upper or middle compass, or a low tone in the middle or lower compass. Within each compass we would only expect the melodic working-out of high, mid and low tone relationships. The verbal intonation would not provide us with the beginning or ending tone, but it may guide the immediate direction of movement from the beginning tone or movement towards the ending tone. . . . The tonal relationship between words and melody is not rigid. It is flexible. While it is important to take the intonation curve into account so that the words of a song may be readily recognised, it must be emphasised that the 'art' of the song lies in the departures that are made from this guide where appropriate, on purely melodic grounds. Thus the use of ascending interlocking patterns or pendular movement where the intonation shows a descending trend, or the use of rising seconds where intonation is level belongs to the 'art' of the song. However, it would be as wrong to assume rigid relationship as it would be to conclude that because such deviations occur, the tones of words are unimportant in the construction of melodies.[1]

Thus, although tone/melody relationships in these languages allow a certain degree of freedom, the link between the two is a complex

[1] Nketia 1962, p. 52. Similar points have been made by other writers: e.g. on Ewe 'tone and tune' see A. M. Jones i, 1959, ch. 10; Igbo, Green 1948, p. 841, and R. W. Wescott, 'Two Ibo Songs', *Anth. Ling.* 4, 1962; Yoruba, A. King, *Yoruba Sacred Music from Ekiti*, Ibadan, 1961, pp. 38 ff.; Bantu generally, E. Westphal, 'Linguistics and the African Music Research', *Afr. Music Soc. Newsletter* 1. 1, 1948; West Africa, M. Schneider, 'Tone and Tune in West African Music', *Ethnomusicology* 5, 1961; Chopi, Tracey 1948*a*, pp. 4–5; Ngala, J. F. Carrington, 'Tone and Melody in a Congolese Popular Song', *Afr. Music* 4. 1, 1966/7 (reference in *Africa* 38, 1968, p. 110); also general discussion in H. H. Wängler, 'Über Beziehungen zwischen gesprochenen und gesungenen Tonhöhen in afrikanischen Tonsprachen', *Jahrbuch für musikalische Volks- und Völkerkunde* [Berlin] 1, 1963.

one, and composition and extemporization demand a high degree of skill.

A further vexed question is that of rhythm. The fundamental importance of rhythm in vocal as in other African music is widely accepted, but there is little agreement as to its exact structure. One helpful distinction is between songs in 'free' and those in relatively 'strict' rhythm.[1] In the former songs (or portions of songs) the singing is not co-ordinated with any bodily rhythmic activity such as work or dancing. The very common songs to strict time, however, have a beat that is articulated with dancing, rhythmic movement, percussion by instruments, or hand-clapping, all of which contribute to the form and attractiveness of the song. These rhythms are worked out in many different ways in various types of song, but one commonly recurring musical feature seems to be the simultaneous use of more than one metre at a time, as a way of heightening the rhythmic tension.[2]

The accompaniment takes many different forms, depending, among other things, on the geographical area and its resources,[3] on the genius of the particular people, and on the different genres within a single culture. It is common, for instance, to find some types of songs regularly without accompaniment, others with just clapping and/or dancing, others again with many different kinds of instrumental accompaniment, conventionally graded according to the song, the singers, or the occasion.

When we come to the verbal style of these poems, it is almost impossible to generalize. As would be expected in poetry, there is a tendency to use a language somewhat different from that of everyday speech. This is particularly evident in the case of sung lyrics, where the melodic line imposes its own requirements, and in tonal languages, where there is the additional complication of the relationship between tune and tone. Connected with the importance attached to the musical aspect in these relatively short, sung lyrics is the frequent occurrence of meaningless words and onomatopoeic sounds which fill in the line, add length to the song as actually performed, and are used especially in chorus responses. Some songs, too, tend to be verbally fragmentary rather than fully

[1] Nketia 1962, p. 64.

[2] On rhythm, see Merriam 1965, pp. 455–6 (and further references given there); Nketia 1962, ch. 9; A. M. Jones 1954, 1964.

[3] See Tracey 1954*a*, pp. 8–9, on the effect of the environment on the choice of instruments.

developed poems as far as the words are concerned, though the fragments themselves may have a terse poetic interest.[1] But there are many variations between different types of songs, each with its own style and diction, and, indeed, in contrast to comments on the subject-matter and contexts of songs, there is relatively little published work available.[2]

IV

How far can these lyrics be said to be truly personal expressions of experience? This raises the difficult question of composition—difficult mainly because so little interest seems to have been shown in this aspect of African poetry. Many commentators, even when they try to take this into account, content themselves with labelling specific songs as 'traditional' or 'improvised' without considering in what senses these words are used. But even this is better than the other still common approach of apparently explaining away the problem by classifying the lyrics as 'folk-songs' which can, it is then assumed, be happily attributed to 'the folk', so that the question of composition does not arise at all.

It is certainly clear that some songs retain their popularity for many years. This may happen less to incidental and recreational songs (like most of the lyrics described here) than to songs definitely tied to particular solemn occasions such as initiation or religious ritual. A common pattern—demanding further research—may be for the music to remain basically the same while the words change.[3] But even with light-hearted dance songs it does seem that some (words as well as music) remain popular for so long that they might with some justice be termed 'traditional'. Others, however—and this is much more commonly mentioned in recent sources—are ephemeral only. The Ibo, for instance, are said to create impromptu poems all the time and forget them.[4] Again, among the Kamba most songs are 'improvised' (with the exception of circumcision songs which reappear in the same form again and again), and

---

[1] e.g. the instance given in Nketia 1958*b*, pp. 15–16.

[2] One exception is the consideration of the Somali *balwo* in Andrzejewski 1967.

[3] In Tanganyika, for example, the poet seldom composes the tune, but is free in his choice of the text; thus it is rare for a tune to be associated with one text only (Koritschoner 1937, p. 51). I noticed a similar pattern with certain types of songs—particularly dance songs—in Limba; see also A. D. Helser, *African Stories*, New York, 1930, p. 65 (Bura), and above, p. 254, on Somali.

[4] Green 1948, p. 842.

with dance songs the leader of the singing and dancing must make a new one when the old one is worn out—about every month or so.[1] Similar comments have been made about songs among many African peoples.

Even with a familiar song there is room for variations on words or tune in actual delivery so that each performance in a sense may be a 'new' song. It must be remembered that these variations on a basic theme are more likely in societies which do not share our stress on the fixing nature of the written word, the concept of a single 'correct' form attributed to a single author. Even such obvious points as the number of repetitions used by a particular leader, the order of the verses, the variations by instruments in an accompanied song, and the varied movements of dancers—all these contribute to the finished work of art as a unique performance of which the verbal text of the song is only one element.

There is one further aspect. The leader of the song adds new verses arising from the basic themes recognized by him and the chorus. Tracey describes this process in Southern Rhodesia. The chorus parts of a song are expected to remain the same, but the soloist (*mushauri*) introduces the song and is allowed full scope for originality during its performance. If he is not able to compose his new verse swiftly enough to keep his initiative, he either repeats the last verse several times to allow himself time for thought or, if necessary, yodels the tune, and finally sings to his neighbour to replace him in the lead.[2] This pattern by which the antiphonal form is exploited through improvisation by the leader and relatively unvaried support by the chorus seems to be very common indeed. Unless there are definite reasons for retaining sanctioned words, it seems generally rather rare for such songs to be repeated *exactly* from performance to performance—there is always scope for some variation by the leader. (This is apparently also sometimes extended to the improvised performance of quite 'new' songs in terms of the melody and the form of the words. At least in some cases, choruses are quick to pick up the melody and words, often after having heard them just once or twice from the leader, and to sing them enthusiastically even though they were previously unknown to them.)

But one must not be so impressed by the excellences of African improvisation that everything is attributed to spontaneous creation.

[1] Lindblom iii, 1934, p. 40.     [2] Tracey 1929, p. 97.

There is, first, the obvious point that improvisation takes place within certain conventional artistic forms known both to the soloist and also, perhaps equally important, to the chorus. More significantly, certain commentators make it clear that serious and conscious composition also takes place.

One of the more detailed accounts of such composition is given by Tracey in his description of musical composition among the Chopi. The Chopi *ŋgodo* is an orchestral dance in nine to eleven movements which certain skilled and known musicians compose anew every two years or so. The stress is on the music and its elaboration. It is worth quoting his description at some length here, for this dependence of the words on the music is by no means unparalleled:

A description of how Katini and Gumukomu set about composing a new orchestral dance will show how musically advanced these men are. Both of them say that the first thing they do is to find appropriate words for their song and compose the verses of the lyric before the music.[1] The subject-matter may be gay, sad, or purely documentary. In every case it is highly topical and appropriate to the locality, so much so, in fact, that most of the allusions would be caught only by those in close touch with the villagers and the district. . . .

To return to the composer: when he has decided upon the words of his poem, or, in the case of a long poem, the opening verse, he must now find his melody. *Chichopi*, in common with other Bantu languages, is a tone language, and the sounds of the words themselves almost suggest a melodic flow of tones. This is developed rhythmically, as Gilbert and Sullivan did in their light operas, in one or other of the well-defined patterns which characterize their national verse, with clever use of repetition and offset phrases. The verses are not always metrically alike, as one would naturally expect of a tone language, but all bear a family relationship to the prototype lines. As often as not, the final verse sung to the coda is a repeat of the statement or first line of the poem. In this they follow a well-recognised trick of the trade which is exploited so frequently in our own popular songs. . . .

The verse and the leitmotive now fixed in the composer's mind, he sits at his instrument [xylophone], over which his hands wander with expert deftness, and picks out the melody. . . . After a while, during which his right hand becomes accustomed to the new tune, his left will

---

[1] This is not necessarily the most common method of procedure. Contrast, for instance, Ngoni composition where 'it is always a single inspiration which leads the composer to find the right words and the right music' (Read 1937, p. 3) (R.F.).

begin to fill in the harmonies or contra-melody with well-understood sequences, punctuated with rhythmic surprises suggested by the ebb and flow of the words. Now the right hand will wander away from the melody, *mapsui*, into a variation, *kuhambana*, and as he sings the words over to himself the contrapuntal accompaniment will begin to form under his hands. . . .

They now have the *primary* melodic line of the poem—the subject or leitmotive—and the *secondary* melodic accompaniment—the orchestral sentence—which fits the words contrapuntally, with a number of variations and sequences. . . .[1]

Though the lyrics and their music are topical and relatively ephemeral, they are certainly not totally impromptu; in describing the process of their creation we can more suitably speak of artistic inspiration coupled with studied technique than of 'improvisation'.

Something of the same process occurs with several song types in Zambia.[2] Among the Ila and Tonga there is commonly an interest in the personal ownership of songs: individuals are often expected to sing one of their own songs—a young man on the day of his marriage, for instance, a young girl on the day she is allowed to wear adult dress. Among their many types of songs are those called *impango*. These are sung by women only, at beer drinks or at work, and each woman must have her own personal repertoire of *impango* songs to sing as solos. One woman stands up at a time and sings her song in a very high and fast style. Meanwhile her intimate friends or her relatives may get up from time to time and interrupt the song with praise and small gifts. *Impango* composition is known to be difficult, and in every village there are a few women who are specially skilled in this art. What happens when a woman wants to make an *impango* is that she first thinks out the rather lengthy words—it may be praise of herself, her lover, or her husband—and then calls in some of her women friends to help her. Together they go to a well-known maker of *impango* songs. After hearing the woman's ideas, she then, often over a period of several days, composes the complete tune for the whole song. She calls a party of women to practise it each evening after supper, and they continue until the *impango* is complete and has been mastered by the whole party. The group is then disbanded and the woman who 'owns' the song continues to sing it on her own, knowing that if she

[1] Tracey 1948*a*, pp. 2–3, 4–5.    [2] A. M. Jones 1943.

forgets at any point she can ask one of the practice party to help her. She is now fully mistress of her *impango* and proud of her accomplishment. Whenever she is invited to a festival she keeps 'singing it in her heart' until it is finally time for her to stand up and sing it in public.[1]

The composition of another type of song, the *inyimbo*, is a simpler matter. The same sort of procedure is followed, but as these songs are shorter and simpler, the process is quicker. There are three main forms of this type of song, and the correct one must be used. The typical occasion of performance is for people to gather and sit down, and then start clapping or beating with sticks. A man or woman then stands up and dances; and as the owner of the song sings it right through, people pick it up and then sing it through themselves several times, followed by the owner again, then back to the group. There are also other types of song: the *mapobolo* song is characterized by brief words and a short tune which a woman first composes herself (working out at least the words or the tune), her friends then helping her to complete it before the actual performance in antiphonal form; while the *zitengulo* or women's mourning songs are composed completely by the individual, with no help from others; she starts to sing little by little and gradually adds the words and melody until the song is complete.[2]

There are, then, many different forms of song among the Ila and Tonga, and each has its own recognized mode of composition. What is striking is the emphasis on the care involved in composition and on the idea of personal ownership.

Song composition in non-literate cultures almost necessarily involves co-operation, particularly where there is an accompaniment by chorus, instruments, or dancing, and where, as so often in African lyrics, there is an emphasis both on performance and on participation by the audience. But that there can also be a purely personal element of the greatest significance in moulding the song is clear from the Chopi and Zambian examples.[3] How far this personal contribution is recognized by the people themselves seems to vary; even within one group certain songs may be

[1] A. M. Jones 1943, pp. 11–12.
[2] Ibid., pp. 13–15.
[3] Cf. also the Luo *nyatiti* songs mentioned in Ch. 4, pp. 99 ff., and the Somali poets who spend hours or days composing their works (Andrzejewski and Lewis 1964, p. 45).

regarded as the property of named individuals, while others are not.[1] But it is quite possible that further investigation of a topic that has hitherto been ignored will show that many other African peoples besides those mentioned engage not only in the art of improvisation but also in a process of long-considered and re-flective individual creation.

[1] e.g. Hurutsche (Merwe 1941, p. 307). For some other discussions of the process of composition and attitudes to it see Babalọla 1966, pp. 46 ff. (Yoruba); de Dampierre 1963, pp. 21 ff. (Nzakara); Read 1937, p. 3 (Ngoni); Nettl 1954*b*, 1956, pp. 12–19 (general).

# 10

# TOPICAL AND POLITICAL SONGS

Topical and local poetry. Songs of political parties and movements: Mau Mau hymns; Guinea R.D.A. songs; Northern Rhodesian party songs

IT has been well said that oral poetry takes the place of newspapers among non-literate peoples. Songs can be used to report and comment on current affairs, for political pressure, for propaganda, and to reflect and mould public opinion. This political and topical function can be an aspect of many of the types of poetry already discussed—work songs, lyric, praise poetry, even at times something as simple as a lullaby—but it is singled out for special discussion in this chapter. It is of particular importance to draw attention to this and to give a number of examples because of the common tendency in studies of African verbal art to concentrate mainly on the 'traditional'—whether in romanticizing or in deprecating tone—and to overlook its topical functions, especially its significance in contemporary situations.[1]

The political role of poetry is not just of recent origin in Africa. It is true that the present wide-spread occurrence of political songs directly associated with modern political parties and national politics did not antedate the founding of such organizations and their relevance in the contemporary political scene. But it would be a very narrow view of politics which would confine it only to the affairs of political parties or the formal institutions of modern nation states. In the wider sense it is certain that there were many political songs and poems in the past. Panegyric is an obvious example, involving propaganda and support for the authorities, taking its extreme form in the mouth of the official court poet

---

[1] There have been a few admirable exceptions to this attitude to African oral literature, notably Tracey and others associated with the African Music Society (see esp. Rhodes 1962). Other references are given throughout this chapter. For a useful general account and bibliography (not specifically related to Africa) see R. S. Denisoff, 'Songs of Persuasion: a Sociological Analysis of Urban Propaganda Songs', *JAF* 79, 1966.

responsible for propagating the versions of historical events authorized by the rulers. Poetry can also be used to pressurize those in authority or to comment on local politics. Songs of insult, challenge, or satirical comment also have a long history, and can function not only on a personal level but also as politically effective weapons.[1] Though such satirical and topical poems will be treated separately from party political songs here, it would be a mistake to assume too easily that there is necessarily a complete break in continuity between 'traditional' political poetry and that of 'modern politics'. It would be more accurate to say that the long-standing interests in oral literature and in politics have, not surprisingly, proved adaptable to the particular political circumstances of the mid-twentieth century.

I

At a local level public singing can take the place of the press, radio, and publication as a way of expressing public opinion and bringing pressure to bear on individuals. This has been particularly well documented of the Chopi people of Portuguese East Africa.[2] Tracey speaks of the 'democratic purpose' of their poetry and the way 'poetic justice' can be said to be achieved through public singing. Established chiefs can be criticized in this way—the medium of song being used for what cannot be said directly:

> You, Chugela, you are proud of your position, yet you are only a chief made by the white man.
> Oh, the chieftainships of Nyaligolana and Chugela!
> Oh, the chieftainships of Nyaligolana and Chugela!
> It is a shame that should be hidden from Wani.[3]
> Chugela is always asking presents from his brother.
> Sitiki is excluded from the council. They say they don't know him.
> The country of Mawewana is full of troubles.[4]

The lines are from a poem attacking the young chief Chugela who, though only of the junior branch of the family, was being supported by the authorities after their deposition of previous (senior) chiefs. The poet is also seeking to publicize the view that Sitiki, the

---

[1] For an interesting description of Swahili political songs and lampoons in the nineteenth century see M. A. Hinawy, *Al-Akida and Fort Jesus, Mombasa*, London, 1950, pp. 33 ff.　　[2] Tracey 1945, 1948a.
[3] Paramount chief of the district.　　[4] Tracey 1948a, p. 68.

best brain of the district and so by rights a councillor, is being ignored by Chugela.[1]

Another Chopi poem is designed to put an ambitious man in his place, an instance of mild political propaganda. Fambanyane had tried to throw his weight around and exaggerate his claims to the chiefship. He was regarded as a public nuisance because of his threats against the other candidate, Manjengwe, and was eventually arrested:

> We are saying,
> We have reason to say we believe
> Fambanyane would have liked to be Chief.
>
> Fambanyane was brought before the judge,
> So now he can't threaten Manjengwe.
> He has lost his chance of wearing chief's uniform.
>
> We are saying,
> We have reason to say we believe
> Fambanyane would have liked to be Chief.[2]

The Chopi are not alone in the use they make of song to attack unpopular public figures. Among many other instances one can quote the effective Somali poem addressed to a sultan who was ignoring the clan assembly and trying to assume dictatorial powers. The sultan—no match for the poet—was deposed:

> The vicissitudes of the world, oh 'Olaad, are like the clouds of the seasons
> Autumn weather and spring weather come after each other in turn
> Into an encampment abandoned by one family, another family moves
> If a man is killed, one of his relatives will marry his widow
> Last night you were hungry and alone, but tonight people will feast you as a guest
> When fortune places a man even on the mere hem of her robe, he quickly becomes proud and overbearing
> A small milking vessel, when filled to the brim, soon overflows.[3]

Pressure on those with or aspiring to positions of power can also be offered in the guise of flattery. Some instances of this have already been noticed in Chapter 5 on panegyric. Again, one could

---

[1] As interpreted in Tracey 1945.  [2] Tracey 1948a, p. 18.
[3] Andrzejewski 1963, p. 24.

cite the piece of Yoruba advice to a pretender to the Alafin's throne:

> Be the king at once my lord,
> Cease acting *like* a king[1]

or, in a rather different context, a poem praising Olorum Nimbe, then Mayor of Lagos. Cast in the form of a piece of popular dance music, it yet proffered advice and instruction:

> I am greeting you, Mayor of Lagos,
> Mayor of Lagos, Olorum Nimbe,
> Look after Lagos carefully.
> As we pick up a yam pounder with care,
> As we pick up a grinding stone with care,
> As we pick up a child with care,
> So may you handle Lagos with care.[2]

This indirect means of communicating with someone in power through the artistic medium of a song is a way by which the singers hope to influence while at the same time avoiding the open danger of speaking directly. The conventionality of the song makes it possible to indicate publicly what could not be said privately or directly to a man's face. To take only one example: when Merriam was collecting song texts among the Shi of the Kivu area in the Congo some were sung to him while he was with a plantation owner. It turned out that the girls working on the plantation were using these songs to express their dissatisfaction with the owner. They felt it impossible to raise this directly with him, but were seizing the opportunity to convey it indirectly. They sang, for instance, of the way the employer had recently stopped giving them salt and oil:

We have finished our work. Before, we used to get oil; now we don't get it. Why has Bwana stopped giving us oil? We don't understand. If he doesn't give us oil, we will all leave and go to work for the Catholic Fathers. There we can do little work and have plenty of oil. So we are waiting now to see whether Bwana X will give oil. Be careful! If we don't get oil, we won't work here.[3]

Not all criticisms of superiors are equally indirect. One could mention the increasingly harsh and direct innuendo of the

---

[1] Beier 1956, p. 26.                                    [2] Ibid., p. 28.
[3] A. P. Merriam, 'Song Texts of the Bashi', *Afr. Music* 1. 1, 1954, pp. 51–2.

unsatisfied Hausa praise singer[1] or Hahn's description of the Hottentots in the nineteenth century. He reports how unpopular chiefs were lectured by women in sarcastic 'reed-songs' (a habit ruefully commented on in the Hottentot proverb about women—'They cannot be as long quiet as it takes sweet milk to get sour') and describes one occasion when the young girls sang into the chief's face telling him

that he was a hungry hyena and a roguish jackal; that he was the brown vulture who is not only satisfied with tearing the flesh from the bones, but also feasted on the intestines.[2]

In all these cases the oblique and limited nature of the attack is maintained by its limitation to a medium with its own artistic conventions or to specially privileged singers, sometimes allowed to perform only on particular occasions.

Songs are also directed against opposing groups or individuals. These can take many forms. There are, for instance, the half-joking 'moqueries de villages' among the Dogon, exchanged between individuals of the same age, between villages, or between different quarters of the same village. Some of these are only short phrases, but there are also longer texts, and, within the conventional form, 'l'imagination fertile et l'ironie acérée des Dogon ne se font pas faute d'inventer sans cesse de nouvelles plaisanteries'.[3] The faults and customs of others are ironically commented on or their accents parodied and ridiculed. Of a more serious and poetic nature are the songs reported from the Ewe of Ghana. There, when two villages quarrel, they compose abusive songs against each other, usually directed against the offending elder of the opposing village. Some of these are very elaborate and can last, without repetition, for as long as half an hour.[4]

Similar self-assertive songs by groups can equally take place in an urban environment. Mitchell has analysed the songs of *kalela* dance teams on the Copperbelt in the early 1950s.[5] Each team boasts of its own distinctiveness as against other tribes and jokingly

---

[1] Above, Ch. 4, pp. 94–5.

[2] T. Hahn, Tsuni-‖Goam, *The Supreme Being of the Khoi-Khoi*, London, 1881, p. 28.

[3] G. Calame-Griaule, 'Les "moqueries de villages" au Soudan français', *Notes afr.* 61, 1954, p. 13.

[4] P. Gbeho, in *Afr. Music* 1. 1, 1954, p. 62.

[5] J. C. Mitchell, *The Kalela Dance*, Rhodes–Livingstone Paper 27, 1956.

derides the customs and languages of others. Yet the content of the songs themselves not only reflects the preoccupations, events, even language of life in the towns, but also, paradoxically, by its very attacks on other ethnic groups recognizes their significance for the singers.[1] Again, songs can be used to assert the unity of trade union groups. The following examples from Tanganyika bring out the distinction between employer and employee:

We regret that the employers should trifle with us.
We are deprived of our rights, indeed we know nowhere to eat.

We do their work, bring them in their money,
Clothes sprout on them through the efforts of the workers.

Give the workers' organisations freedom
We don't want the law to break our Unions
In a free Tanganyika may the Unions be strong
We don't want to be despised
    So let us unite and triumph over (crush/overthrow) the employers.[2]

Lampoons are not only used between groups but can also be a means of communicating and expressing personal enmity between hostile individuals. We hear of Galla abusive poems, for instance,[3] while among the Yoruba when two women have quarrelled they sometimes vent their enmity by singing at each other, especially in situations—like the laundry place—when other women will hear.[4] Abusive songs against ordinary individuals are also sometimes directly used as a means of social pressure, enforcing the will of public opinion. Among the Chopi, for instance, we hear of a verse directed against a young man who was trying to seduce a very young girl:

We see you!
We know you are leading that child astray.
Katini[5] sees you but keeps quiet.
Although he knows it all right he keeps quiet, Katini, the leader of
    *Timbilas*.[6]
We know you![7]

---

[1] For a parallel with the *kalela* dance see H. E. Lambert, 'The Beni Dance Songs', *Swahili* 33, 1962/3.

[2] W. H. Whiteley, 'Problems of a Lingua Franca: Swahili and the Trade-unions', *J. Afr. Languages* 3. 3, 1964, p. 221.

[3] Chadwicks iii, 1940, p. 549.

[4] A. Mabogunje, 'The Yoruba Home', *Odù* 5, 1958, p. 35.

[5] The composer.     [6] Local xylophones.     [7] Tracey 1948a, p. 29.

A group of Hottentots took the same line against an old man who married a young girl: her friends sang 'The first wife is dismissed, his only great thought is the second wife'.[1]

Such songs can even be said on occasion to form part of semi-judicial proceedings against individuals. This is particularly clear in the case of the Ibo. For instance, in one area (Umuahia) *oro* songs are sung at night by groups of young men and women who go to the houses of those they agree have offended, and sing against them as well as causing physical damage to their possessions. A notoriously lazy man is lampooned:

Ibejimato, Ibejimato, it is time now. Woman asks you to wrestle with her but you carry your cutlass and walk about; it is time now.[2]

Ibejimato is so lazy and fearful that he does not even dare to fight a woman; in fact they remind him that when he did once get involved in a quarrel with a woman, he actually ran away, his cutlass on his shoulder. The song is to make him realize his laziness, and make him feel ashamed and turn over a new leaf—and is supplemented by damage to his possessions. On another occasion abusive songs by women formed part of the procedure of collecting a fine already imposed on a woman for false accusation—'the execution of justice'.[3] The women went in a body to the house of the offender to sing and dance against her. Both songs and dances were quite explicitly obscene and the episode had the effect of making the victim undertake to pay her fine.[4]

It is possible to exaggerate the functional aspect of such lampoons. Sheer enjoyment plays a part too. As Green writes of the episode just mentioned:

As for the women, I never saw them so spirited. They were having a night out and they were heartily enjoying it and there was a speed and energy about everything they did that gave a distinctive quality to the episode. It was also the only occasion in the village that struck one as obscene in the intention of the people themselves. Mixed with what seemed genuine amusement there was much uncontrolled, abandoned laughter. There was a suggestion of consciously kicking over the traces about the whole affair.[5]

[1] Hahn, op. cit., p. 29.
[2] A. Madumere, 'Ibo Village Music', *Afr. Affairs* 52, 1953, p. 64.
[3] M. M. Green, *Igbo Village Affairs*, London, 2nd ed., 1964, p. 200.
[4] Ibid., pp. 199–205.                    [5] Ibid., pp. 202–3.

Even without the extra appeal of unaccustomed obscenity as in these derisive Ibo songs, this enjoyment may be just as significant as social control. Thus the Hottentots sing satirically but with humour of a childless couple:

> We love each other as the goats that have no kids love
> We love each other as the goats that have no kids love[1]

and in Tanganyika the Asu *nyimbo za kugana*, songs sung in huts just before sleep, provide an opportunity for improvisation and humour as well as attack. One man starts up the song, then others reply in solo or chorus—for example, in address to a grumbler:

> Ndi-ndi! Ndi-ndi! [expletives used in complaining]
> Grandfather of Mruma,
> He hasn't a cow,
> He hasn't a goat,
> He hasn't a chicken,
> No not (even) a rat (in his house)[2]

—and so on, continued at great length, with plenty of scope for humour, until almost every conceivable possession has been named, while the chorus reply in unison *ndi-ndi!* after each line. Similar enjoyment is evident in the public dances and singing in Abomey (Dahomey) witnessed by Herskovits, when unpopular individuals are ridiculed and attacked in songs. Though no names are mentioned, everyone knows who is meant and rejoices in the occasion. For example:

> Woman, thy soul is misshapen.
> In haste was it made, in haste.
> So fleshless a face speaks, telling
> Thy soul was formed without care.
> The ancestral clay for thy making
> Was moulded in haste, in haste.
> A thing of no beauty art thou,
> Thy face unsuited to be a face,
> Thy feet unsuited for feet.[3]

These derisive songs directed against specified individuals or groups shade into topical and satirical songs in general. Thus the Tiv, among many others, sing about the events of the year: they

[1] Stopa 1938, p. 110.
[2] A. F. Bull, 'Asu (Pare) Proverbs and Songs', *Africa* 6, 1933, pp. 326–7.
[3] Herskovits 1934, p. 78.

comment on the present position of chiefs or express their reactions
to a recent deposition or this season's road work. They also improvise about recent incidents and people—like the song about selling
their soya beans to only one of the rival firms:

> We are not going to sell our soya beans to Mallam Dama
> we are going to sell them to Alhaji Sali.[1]

Domestic affairs also come into such songs. The Ndau dancer
comments ruefully on his father's new wife:

> My father, he married
> A crocodile wife,
> > That bites, that bites.
> > I-ya, I-ya-wo-ye![2]

while a Baule woman sings lightly:

Je commettrai volontiers l'adultère. Les maris de mes camarades
seront tour à tour mes amants. Mais qui d'entre elles aura l'audace de
se plaindre?[3]

These topical songs often give a vivid personal picture of a
general situation and the attitude to it, as well as of the specific
events they comment on. Thus in Malawi, in the late 1950s, the
wives of men detained for opposition to government showed their
pride in their 'Prison Graduate' husbands, and used to sing as they
pounded their maize:

> My husband is a man:
> He's away in Kanjedza.
> The men who are here
> Are women like us.[4]

Again an Acholi girl married to a soldier sings effectively of their
separation: they can write letters—but what can letters do?

Writing writing writing so many letters.
Those letters can they be changed into a child?
Wives of soldiers are barren [have to wait for years before they get
    a child].
Wives of soldiers are truly barren.[5]

[1] M. G. M. Lane, 'The Music of Tiv', *Afr. Music* 1, 1, 1954, p. 14. Cf. also
H. R. Phillips, 'Some Tiv Songs', *Nigerian Teacher* 6, 1936.
[2] Curtis 1920, p. 39.
[3] G. Effimbra, *Manuel de baoulé*, Paris, 1952, p. 297.
[4] Quoted in C. Sanger, *Central African Emergency*, London, 1960, p. 320.
[5] Okot 1963, p. 312.

Or a Chewa woman thinks about her husband who is away working in the copper mines:

> When I get a letter from Masula
> I read it with all my heart.[1]

The same experience—from the man's viewpoint—is touched on in a Sotho dance song in the country areas:

> Basutoland is my fatherland,
> At Bushman's Nek, near Machacha, in the mountains.
> I joined up for work on the mines,
> But when I arrived I found myself in trouble.
> I was with Molelekoa, son of Smith.
> So I crossed the Vaal very early in the morning
> That was when I was nearly swept down with the river.
> Perhaps it was because I was running away,
> Running away and leaving my passes on the veld.
> I left mine in the western Transvaal,
> I left both my pass and my tax receipt![2]

The urban experiences of Africans in the towns of South Africa are commented on in many of the Zulu songs about police and passes recorded by Tracey.[3] These can be illustrated from three of his examples. In the first, the scene is the pass office where all male Africans had to go to get their Registration Certificates, involving a wait of hours, even days, before being interviewed:

> Take off your hat.
> What is your home name?
> Who is your father?
> Who is your chief?
> Where do you pay your tax?
> What river do you drink?
>
> We mourn for our country.[4]

Arrest by the police for not having the correct papers, and imprisonment in 'Blue Sky', the popular name of the gaol at Boksburg near Johannesburg, are the themes of the next two songs:

> There comes the big van.
> All over the country
> They call it the Pick-up Van.

[1] Tracey 1963, p. 19.  [2] *Afr. Music* 2. 2, 1959, pp. 72–3.
[3] Tracey 1948*b*.  [4] Ibid., p. 53.

There is the Pick-up.
There, there is the big van.
'Where's your pass?'
'Where's your tax?'[1]

They caught him!
They caught him and handcuffed him!
They sent him to 'Blue Sky'.[2]

The last type of topical song to be mentioned here comprises those which particularly express the aspirations and self-appreciation of groups, songs which often have at least some political relevance. These merge into the songs already discussed, and also recall some of the military poems which reflect and reinforce the militant unity of a given group. An example would be the Akan hunting song which asserts the power of the hunter's group against that of the chief:

Does the chief say he is greater than the hunter?
Arrogance! Hunter? Arrogance![3]

and the trade union and *kalela* dance songs could be seen to be fulfilling something of the same function. So too in the Congo the followers of the prophet Matswa expressed their protest and their allegiance in song:

Nous autres qui n'avons pas de soutien.
Nous autres qui n'avons pas de défenseur.
Dieu le Père-tout-puissant, veille sur nous.
Père Congo, Père, qui pensera à nous?
A nous autres, qui y pensera?
Matswa, Père-tout-puissant, veille sur nous.
Matswa, Père-tout-puissant, envoie-nous un défenseur.[4]

Even in South Africa a certain amount of fairly explicit political protest seems to be expressed through song if we can assume that certain of the 'South African freedom songs'[5] were of wide circulation. In one, for instance, the singers appeal to Chief Luthuli (President of the African National Congress) in conjunction with Dr. G. M. Naicker (President of the Indian Congress):

---

[1] Tracey 1948*b*, p. 55.                          [2] Ibid., p. 54.
[3] Nketia 1963*b*, p. 76; and see full song in Ch. 8 above, pp. 223–4.
[4] Balandier 1955, p. 1557.
[5] Folkways Records Album EPC-601, New York, quoted in Rhodes 1962, p. 22.

God, save the volunteers,
God, save Africans.
God, save the volunteers,
God, save Africans.

We say yes, yes, Chief Lut'huli,
And you, Doctor Naicker, liberate us.
                    (Bass voices) *Daliga chek.*

We say yes, yes, Chief Lut'huli,
And you, Doctor Naicker, liberate us.
                    (Bass voices) *Daliga chek.*[1]

In certain circumstances hymns can have similar overtones. Some of the religious verses of the South African separatist churches founded by Shembe express political aspirations and ideals that are difficult to communicate through more formal political channels —the idea of Africa for the Africans, or of the value, despite the contemporary political situation, of African customs and leadership:

Africa, rise!
And seek thy Saviour.
Today our sons and daughters
are slaves.[2]

More explicitly political are some of the performances of the originally Methodist-inspired hymn *Nkosi Sikele' iAfrica . . .* ('God bless Africa . . .'), which is used as a political song in meetings of the African National Congress and other political contexts,[3] the Mau Mau 'hymns' discussed in the next section, and the way in which, during Nkrumah's imprisonment by the colonial authorities, political protest was expressed by the singing of Christian hymns like 'Lead kindly light, amid the encircling gloom'.[4]

The social functions of the various types of songs mentioned here are particularly obvious, more strikingly so than most of those discussed in earlier chapters. They can be a way of exerting pressure on others, whether equals or superiors; of expressing often indirectly or in a limited and conventional manner, what could not be said directly, or through a different medium, or on

---

[1] Rhodes 1962, pp. 18–19.
[2] B. Sundkler, *Bantu Prophets in South Africa*, London, 2nd ed., 1961, p. 196.
[3] Rhodes, op. cit., pp. 16–17.                    [4] Ibid., p. 16.

just any occasion; of upholding or suggesting certain values and interests which cannot be expressed in other ways, particularly when there is no direct access to political activity. Like Dogon villagers or *kalela* dancers, the singers may both assert the solidarity of their own group and at the same time recognize their close relationship with others. The songs may even—as Herskovits and his followers remind us—provide a means for the psychological release of otherwise repressed enmities and tensions through a socially permissible form. But besides these obvious social functions we can point equally to the related literary roles of these songs—to the way in which such socially sanctioned occasions are used for artistic purposes, to the humour and enjoyment expressed, to the satirical, meditative, or resigned comment on the circumstances of life, and, finally, to the way in which even enmity or social pressure can be viewed with a certain detachment through the artistic and conventional medium of the song.[1]

II

It is perhaps not generally recognized how widely political songs are used in Africa. Songs are now accepted by African political parties as a vehicle for communication, propaganda, political pressure, and political education. Their exact nature and purpose vary, but they have in common the fact of being *oral* rather than visual propaganda. It is true that some of these songs at times appear in writing, even print, and written collections of party songs circulate in some areas; none the less their propagation among the largely non-literate masses is almost purely oral. As such they are a powerful and flexible weapon in many types of political activity.

One of the advantages songs may have as vehicles of political expression is their apparently innocuous nature. This is particularly true of those songs used at a relatively early stage in African nationalist movements when concealment of organized political activity was felt desirable. In a colonial situation in which political power was ultimately in the hands of foreigners, many of whom could not speak the local language, songs and poems had the

---

[1] For other instances of topical songs see D. C. Simmons, 'Ibibio Topical Ballads', *Man* 60, 1960; J. Roberts, 'Kenya's Pop Music', *Transition* (Kampala) 4. 19, 1965; Ogunba 1967, pp. 370–422 (Ijebu Yoruba).

double advantage of being ostensibly nothing to do with politics
at all (unlike, say, newspapers) and of being unintelligible to
many of those in authority. Rhodes cites an early example of
this from West Africa, in a drum poem used by the Ashanti after
their submission to British rule in 1900. When the Governor
appeared at a public gathering, he was ceremonially, and apparently honorifically, greeted with drum music; what the drums
were repeating, however, were the words of an old war song,
'slowly but surely we shall kill Adinkra'; while the local audience
understood quite clearly that by 'Adinkra' the drums meant the
British, it is doubtful if the Governor was aware of any political
significance at all, let alone a hostile one.[1] Somali love poems,
or apparent love poems, have been used in the same way. They
could safely be performed in public or even on the government-
controlled radio, the obscurity of their language concealing their
meaning for the independence struggle, except from their intended
audiences (the people in the independence movement).[2] Again,
there was the occasion of the Queen's Birthday Festivities in
Nyasaland (as it was then called) in the early 1950s, when official
policy was to encourage the idea of federation against local opposition. The school-children marched innocently past the presiding
District Commissioner singing anti-federation songs taught them
by their schoolteacher—and the District Commissioner did not
understand a word.[3]

One of the best examples of the use of songs for secret propaganda is the hymns used by the Mau Mau movement in Kenya
in the early 1950s.[4] This movement, part political, part religious,
was banned by government, and yet, largely by means of these
songs, was able to carry out active and wide-spread propaganda
among the masses in Kenya. Leakey describes vividly how this
could be done:

> The leaders of the Mau Mau movement . . . were quick to realise the
> very great opportunity which the Kikuyu love of hymn singing offered
> for propaganda purposes. In the first place propaganda in 'hymn' form
> and set to well-known tunes would be speedily learned by heart and
> sung over again and again and thus provide a most effective method of

[1] Rhodes 1962, pp. 14–15 (based on a personal communication by J. H.
Nketia).
[2] Andrzejewski 1967, p. 13.                          [3] Tracey 1954*a*, p. 237.
[4] The present account is taken from the description in L. S. B. Leakey,
*Defeating Mau Mau*, London, 1954, esp. ch. 5.

spreading the new ideas. The fact that such 'hymns' would be learned by heart, by those who could read them, and then taught to others, meant that they would soon also become well known to the illiterate members of the tribe. This was very important, for there were many who could not be reached by ordinary printed propaganda methods.

More important still, these propaganda messages could safely be sung in the presence of all but a very few Europeans, since the vast majority could not understand a word of Kikuyu and if they heard a large, or a small, group singing to the tune of 'Onward Christian Soldiers', 'Abide with Me', or any other well-known hymn, they were hardly likely to suspect that propaganda against themselves was going on under their very noses. They would be more likely to consider that a Christian revival was on its way. . . .

There is no doubt at all that these hymns, which were being sung at K.A.U. [Kenya African Union] meetings, at Independent Schools and Churches, in the homes of thousands in the Kikuyu Reserve, in squatter villages on European farms, and even in the staff quarters and kitchens of European homes, were one of the most powerful propaganda weapons of the whole Mau Mau movement.[1]

Some examples of these Mau Mau hymns (in English translation) will illustrate these points more clearly. The first is praise of Jomo Kenyatta, who is represented as the great leader and saviour, the focus of unity and loyalty:

God makes his covenant shine until it is brighter than the sun, so that neither hill nor darkness can prevent him coming to fulfil it, for God is known as the Conqueror.

He told Kenyatta in a vision 'You shall multiply as the stars of heaven, nations will be blessed because of you'. And Kenyatta believed him and God swore to it by his mighty power. . . .

Kenyatta made a Covenant with the Kikuyu saying he would devote his life to them, and would go to Europe to search for the power to rule, so as to be a judge over the House of Mumbi. I ask myself 'Will we ever come out of this state of slavery?'

He went, he arrived there and he came back. He promised the Kikuyu 'When I return M—— shall go in order to arrange for the return of our land'. May God have mercy upon us.

When the day for his return comes he will come with the decisions about our land and the building which he said he would come to erect at Githunguri ya Wairera shall be the one in which our rule shall be established.[2]

[1] Leakey, op. cit., pp. 53–4, 75.          [2] Ibid., p. 57.

The next two vividly express and encourage hatred of Europeans for their actions and presence in Kenya, particularly their control of land:

> There is great wailing in the land of the black people because of land hunger, you fools and wise people alike, is there any among you who is not aware of the over-crowding in our land.
>
> You Europeans you are nothing but robbers, though you pretended you came to lead us. Go away, go away you Europeans, the years that are past have been more than enough for us. . . .
>
> You of Kikuyu and Mumbi[1] fight hard, that we may be given self-government, that our land may be given back to us. The corn is ripe for harvest, if we are late the harvest will be lost. . . .
>
> Long ago the Europeans came upon us with weapons of war and they drove us out and took our land. Go away, go away you Europeans. . . .[2]

> When the Europeans came from Europe they said they came to give us learning and we accepted them gladly, but woe upon us, they really came to oppress us.
>
> Those who hate the house of Mumbi and say they prefer the Europeans, will have great trouble in Kikuyu land when we achieve self-government.
>
> When the house of Mumbi meets in order to recruit others to the house of Mumbi[3] there are some who side with the enemy and are like Judas of old.
>
> You house of Mumbi even if you are oppressed, do not be afraid in your hearts, a Kikuyu proverb says 'God help those who help themselves'.
>
> You who side with Europeans when they go back to Europe, you will kneel down before us and weep, claiming that you did not realise what you were doing.
>
> When the Europeans return to Europe you who sell the land of the house of Mumbi we will answer you, by saying, 'We disown you even as you disowned us'.
>
> When Kenyatta came back from Europe he came with a spear and sword and shield and a war helmet on his head as a sign for the Kikuyu.
>
> M—— will return with spear and shield to uplift the house of Mumbi and avenge the oppression which they have suffered from the Europeans.

[1] The traditional 'Eve' of the Kikuyu.     [2] Leakey, op. cit., pp. 63-4.

[3] This means that when members of Mau Mau (who always refer to themselves as the house of Mumbi) meet for an oath ceremony at which others are formally enlisted into the movement, there are some who go and report to the police and take on themselves the role of traitor.

Let those who go and report on our doings be accursed by their reports and if they get pay for what they do, let the pay be a curse upon them too.

Oh, house of Mumbi let us exert ourselves to get our land returned, the land which was ours and stolen from us by the deceitful Europeans.[1]

Many other similar threats were expressed against Kikuyu 'loyalists' who supported the government. The effect was a direct incitement to violence, which resulted in the deaths of many of these suspected traitors:

As for you who side with the Europeans, on the day when God hears us, you will be wiped out.

Let every man ask himself, let everyone ask himself, 'How do I stand with the black races?' for the time is soon coming like the days of long ago when the evil people will be burned.[2]

These hymns appeared in books as well as in oral form and were frequently distributed through the offices of the K.A.U. (which operated as a front organization for Mau Mau). Little notice was taken by the authorities of these publications. This was in contrast to the Kikuyu newspapers which were closely scrutinized by the Intelligence Branch of the police and thought to be potentially subversive by European employers. The hymn-books appeared safe from such suspicion, and those in charge were able to become bolder and more blatant in their incitements to violence. One of their triumphs was the setting of new words to the tune of the British National Anthem—calling, in various versions, for blessing on the land of the Kikuyu, on Jomo Kenyatta, and on those agitating for self-government. This ploy was immediately successful. Supporters of Mau Mau were seen enthusiastically standing up for the National Anthem, in reality praying for the return of their own land to them; while Europeans merely remarked on the apparent increase among the Kikuyu of loyalty to the Crown.[3] Calls to violence against Europeans as well as Kikuyu 'traitors' could also become more open. Thus, to the tune of 'Here we suffer grief and pain':

Here we suffer thumb-printing and grass planting. 'T'won't be so when the land is ours.

The warrior hut is set up, one brave leader is already here, the other is on his way.

---

[1] Leakey, op. cit., pp. 65–6.
[2] Ibid., pp. 65, 62. Many 'loyalists' were in fact burned alive.
[3] Ibid., pp. 72–3.

Let the Europeans exert themselves now for the time has come to separate what is theirs and what belongs to others.

Those who were our friends, but who have become spies will be cast into the sea.

What is making you hesitate when you hear the call to prepare? You were born to be warriors.

Their ears are shut, their hearts are shut, Now let us march to war.

Support your just words with strong deeds that you fall not by the wayside.[1]

The results of these hymns as propaganda can be seen in the spread and tenacity of Mau Mau as a political movement. Because the ideas expressed were considered subversive by the government they could not be publicized openly. But the hymns could speak quite explicitly to the audience for whom they were intended. Hymns had the further advantages that they were felt to be a specially effective and personal way of reaching the people's hearts, and could be claimed to result from a special revelation, giving them a religious as well as a political sanction.

Although basic to the Mau Mau situation, secrecy is not always necessary. In other circumstances in fact songs can form a part of a political movement which expressly intends to publicize its aims. A good example of this is given in Schachter's description of the confrontation between the R.D.A. and the local French administration in French Guinea (as it was then) in 1954–5.[2]

The R.D.A. (Rassemblement Démocratique Africain) had the support of a large majority of people in French Guinea, and was led locally by Sékou Touré. This leader had succeeded in capturing both the support and the imagination of his followers. Many myths were woven around him, and in songs and poems he, the R.D.A., and its symbol 'Sily' (the elephant) stood as symbols of the political aspirations of the people:

> Sily is too strong.
> He does not retreat
> When he is provoked.[3]

One of the main weapons used by the R.D.A. was political songs praising Sékou Touré and attacking or advising his opponents. Unlike Mau Mau hymns, these do not ever seem to have

---

[1] Ibid., p. 68.
[2] R. Schachter, 'French Guinea's R.D.A. Folk Songs', *West Afr. Review* 29, 1958 (which see for further details).     [3] Ibid., p. 673.

appeared in written form, but they nevertheless became popular throughout Guinea, mostly in the Susu language. Where less than ten per cent of the population could read or write the French language taught in schools, the effectiveness of these orally transmitted songs as political propaganda is obvious. It was further strengthened by the linking of Sékou Touré and the R.D.A. with Islam, the main religion in Guinea.

The political songs played an important part in the incidents of 1954–5. A deputy for Guinea to the French National Assembly died in 1954 and new elections were held. Sékou Touré, the R.D.A. candidate, was supported by the urban workers and many of the farmers, but his opponent, Barry Diawadou, was backed not only by the officially appointed chiefs but by the French administration. So, when Diawadou was declared elected, the popular belief was that the results had been falsified by the administration to secure the election of their own candidate. Diawadou was abused in song for his opposition to the elephant (the R.D.A.):

> Diawadou you are a thief.
> You stole not only from Yacine,[1]
> You stole from the people.
> There will be a fatal reckoning
> When you face your God.
> You, Diawadou!
> You stole from the elephant.
> You stole a voice.
> One of those voices sings.
> You cannot steal a voice.
> You will pay.
> The elephant is the strongest.[2]

People continued to believe that Sékou Touré was the rightful deputy, their real chief, and when he travelled round the country he was given a hero's welcome and greeted in songs of praise:

> You came into your land.
> You came into your capital.
> You chose your hour for coming.
>
> A chief commands.
> He speaks his will.

[1] The previous deputy.  [2] Schachter, op. cit., p. 673.

> Lift up your head!
> Look at the sea of faces.
> It is your world.
>
> It is your people:
> Which sits
> When you say sit;
> Which rises
> When you say rise.
>
> You are a new chief.
> You are chosen as chief.
> The people is with you.
> The barriers are cut.
> We must follow,
> For all will follow.
>
> You are a new chief.
> Lift up your head!
> Look at the sea of faces,
> That answers when you call.[1]

The official declaration that Sékou Touré had been defeated thus led to general anger in both Conakry and the interior, and there were many demonstrations, riots, and protest meetings in which songs played their part. This mass indignation was used by the R.D.A. leaders to demonstrate their following to the French administration and local political opponents. The following shows how the R.D.A. militants preached unity and solidarity to the people: they must stand united, for even Sékou Touré can do nothing alone against the authorities. The opponents of R.D.A. are called on too: they should accept the 'chiefship' of Sékou Touré and the French National Assembly should refuse to validate the election:

> Listen to the story of Sékou.
> Sékou alone can do nothing,
> Just as no one can act alone.
> All the councillors are against him,
> As are all their henchmen.
> All the important people hate him.
>
> Listen carefully,
> The elections are not yet validated.
> If you want the trouble to end,
> Give the chiefdom to him who merits it.

[1] Ibid.

> So that the trouble ends.
> For the trouble has long antennae
> Which will cross your path
> When least you expect them.[1]

The local French administration attempted to hold the situation. Repressive measures were tried, among them the expulsion of many unemployed in Conakry who were thought responsible for some of the recent incidents. The results of this, however, were not altogether as expected. Schachter describes the removal of these 'vagrants': 'They were piled into trucks, and sent back to the villages. R.D.A. militants tell of their delight at these free rides. The overloaded open trucks carried many R.D.A. supporters on impromptu propaganda tours. This is what they chanted on their trip:

> They say that the elephant does not exist.
> But here is the elephant,
> The elephant no one can beat.'[1]

The French National Assembly's acceptance of the election results added further fuel to the movement. Throughout the land Sékou Touré and his policies were praised in many contexts—in religious terminology:

> God is great.
> It is hard
> To bring unbelievers
> Into the brotherhood of believers.
> But we need the die-hards
> To spur us on
> To make life complete[2]

or in compositions by the women:

> Here is the light
> Of the chieftaincy of Sékou Touré.
> It rises,
> Inextinguishable,
> Immeasurable,
> Glorious.
> Those who are of good faith
> Speak in our way.

---

[1] Schachter, op. cit., p. 675.  [2] Ibid., p. 677.

Those who are of bad faith
Qualify what they say.
One single thing is true.
When the sun rises
The palm of the hand
Cannot hide its light.
It is visible;
It is gigantic.
You cannot stand its heat.
Even in a shaded place.
It is like the light
Of Sékou's chieftaincy.[1]

So effective was this R.D.A. mass opposition that the administration was forced to reconsider its policy and the French Colonial Minister came out to explore the possibility of a different approach. The R.D.A. seized the opportunity to demonstrate its wide support and turned out huge crowds in welcome. R.D.A. militants took charge of public order, giant placards were paraded, and R.D.A. songs were performed all the way along the route from the airport to the town.

This visit marked the turning-point. Though popular protests continued, the R.D.A. considered it a confession of their success and of the metropolitan French government's repudiation of the local administration's policy. More elections were finally held in January 1956 (and yet more songs were composed). The R.D.A.'s candidates, including Sékou Touré, won two of the three Guinea seats to the French National Assembly. This final triumph was summed up in their songs of triumph over their now powerless opponents. They sang:

You prepare food,
The most exquisite food to be found.
You are ready with your spoon
To spoon out the first spoonful.
And lo! a drop of violent poison
Falls into the food.
The water is dirtied
It becomes undrinkable.
All is finished.
All is over.[2]

[1] Ibid., pp. 675–7.   [2] Ibid., p. 681.

The campaign had finally been successful and the propaganda had fulfilled its purpose.

By the late 1950s and early 1960s political songs in Africa seem to have become a standard accompaniment of recognized political parties and the election campaigns that were by now becoming more and more a feature of political activity in African colonies and ex-colonies. Songs formed part of election campaigns in, for example, Sierra Leone and Senegal in 1957, Nyasaland in 1961, and Northern Rhodesia in 1962. Some politicians managed to exploit oral propaganda even further and, like the Western Nigerian leader Adelabu, organized the circulation of gramophone records of songs supporting them.[1] Altogether there is still great reliance on oral means of propaganda—speeches, mass meetings, and songs —in keeping with the still largely non-literate or semi-literate mass electorate for whom the written word is of relatively lesser significance.

Northern Rhodesia (later Zambia) seems to have been particularly rich in organized political songs in the vernacular, sometimes specially composed and written for the party, and often sung by official mass choirs. Several have been published among those written for the African National Congress (A.N.C.) in the late 1950s. One, cast in the form of a praise song, honouring Nkumbula, President of the A.N.C., had the familiar purpose of attempting to project a leader's image to the mass of followers:

> Mr. Nkumbula, we praise you.
> You have done a good work.
> Look today, we sing praising you,
> For you have done a good work.
> We praise, too, all your cabinet
> And all your Action Group.
> You have done good work.[2]

Two other songs can be quoted which were used to promote the A.N.C.'s policies and to educate as well as incite the masses. Ill-defined popular grievances are taken up and focused into definite political aims associated with the party programme. The first is in

[1] See R. L. Sklar, *Nigerian Political Parties*, Princeton, 1963, p. 300, cf. p. 313; also the detailed description of the use of such songs (and others) in electioneering at a local level in Western Nigeria in U. Beier, 'Transition without Tears', *Encounter* 15, Oct. 1960.

[2] Rhodes 1962, p. 18.

the form of a meditation with chorus, suitable for the whole audience to echo:

> One day, I stood by the road side.
> I saw cars passing by.
> As I looked inside the cars
> I saw only white faces in them.
> These were European settlers.
> Following the cars were cyclists
> With black faces.
> They were poor Africans.
>
> > *Refrain.* The Africans say,
> > Give us, give us cars, too,
> > Give us, give us our land
> > That we may rule ourselves.
>
> I stood still but thinking
> How and why it is that white faces
> Travel by car while black faces travel by cycle.
> At last I found out that it was that house,
> The Parliamentary House that is composed of Europeans,
> In other words, because this country is ruled by
> White faces, these white faces do not want
> Anything good for black faces.[1]

Sharp political comment and demand can also be conveyed:

> When talking about democracy[2]
> We must teach these Europeans
> Because they do not know.
> See here in Africa they bring their clothes
> But leave democracy in Europe.
>
> > *Refrain.* Go back, go back and
> > Bring true democracy.
>
> We are no longer asleep
> We are up and about democracy
> We have known for a long time.
> We are the majority and we demand
> A majority in the Legislative Council. . . .[3]

[1] Ibid., p. 19.      [2] The English word is used.
[3] Rhodes 1962, p. 20.

How far removed these songs are from the Mau Mau emphasis on
secrecy can be seen from the fact that a few of these A.N.C. songs
are in fact in English—a way of applying pressure on Europeans.

The open and public nature of Northern Rhodesian party songs
also comes out in the election campaign fought in 1962. Songs,
usually in Bemba, were a recognized part of mass meetings.
Mulford describes a typical rally:

Thousands were packed in an enormous semi-circle around the large
official platform constructed by the youth brigade on one of the huge
ant hills. Other ant hills nearby swarmed with observers seeking a
better view of the speakers. Hundreds of small flags in UNIP's colours
were strung above the crowd. Youth brigade members, known as
'Zambia policemen' and wearing lion skin hats, acted as stewards and
controlled the crowds when party officials arrived or departed. UNIP'S
jazz band played an occasional calypso or jive tune, and between each
speech, small choirs sang political songs praising UNIP and its leaders.

Kaunda will politically get Africans freed from the English,
Who treat us unfairly and beat us daily.
UNIP as an organization does not stay in one place.
It moves to various kinds of places and peoples,
Letting them know the difficulties with which we are faced.
These whites are only paving the way for us,
So that we come and rule ourselves smoothly.[1]

These UNIP songs were not confined to statements of policy and
aspiration ('These whites are only paving the way for us . . .'),
but also sometimes gave precise instructions for the actual voting,
a matter of great importance in campaigns among an inexperienced
electorate. One particularly infectious calypso sung in English gave
the necessary instructions:

Upper roll voting papers will be green.
Lower roll voting papers will be pink.

*Chorus.* Green paper goes in green box.
Pink paper goes in pink box.[2]

These three examples of the use of political songs, drawn from
very different political situations, show something of the flexibility
of this particular medium. Songs can be used to veil a political

---

[1] D. C. Mulford, *The Northern Rhodesia General Election 1962*, Nairobi,
1964, pp. 133–4.      [2] Ibid., pp. 134–5.

message from opponents, to publicize it yet further, to whip up popular support, or to pressurize its enemies. In different contexts, songs can have the effect of intensifying factional differences, or of encouraging national unity.[1] They can focus interest on the image of the leader (or of the opponent) and on the specific political aims of the party. Their effectiveness in reaching mass audiences in countries without a tradition of written communication cannot be exaggerated. Songs can be picked up and learnt by heart, transmitted orally from group to group, form a real and a symbolic link between educated leader and uneducated masses—in short, perform all the familiar functions of political propaganda and comment.

Little has been written about the literary quality and form of these political songs; most of them have been collected by those interested primarily in their political content. But it does not necessarily follow that, just because they have a clear political function, there are therefore no artistic conventions observed by composer or singers, or that they can necessarily be dismissed as of no serious artistic interest. It seems that in some cases the songs are based on traditional literary forms of one kind or another. Praise of political leaders fits with the traditional interest in panegyric,[2] and among some peoples (e.g. Kikuyu or Ndebele) old war songs are sometimes used in new contexts for political pressure or intimidation;[3] while among the Somali the traditional and serious *gabay* form is now commonly used for political propaganda.[4] In other cases one of the dominant models would seem to be that of the Christian hymn, an influence apparent not only in the case of Mau Mau but also, among others, with the C.P.P. in Ghana or the Nigerian N.C.N.C.[5] But how far the artistic conventions of the originals are carried over into the political adaptations is by no means clear.

[1] Cf. G. Nurse, 'Popular Songs and National Identity in Malawi', *Afr. Music* 3. 3, 1964; J. Sachs, 'Swahili-Lieder aus Sansibar', *Mitt. Inst. Orientforsch.* 12. 3, 1966. On rebel songs in the context of an independent African state see forthcoming work on Uganda by K. Alnaes.

[2] Cf. the Shona praise poems with modern political overtones (Fortune 1964, p. 108), and the use of 'griots' for electioneering in Senegambia (D. P. Gamble, *The Wolof of Senegambia*, London, 1957, p. 80).

[3] Leakey, op. cit., p. 56; *Afr. Music* 2. 4, 1961, p. 117.

[4] Andrzejewski and Lewis 1964, p. 48.

[5] See e.g. T. Hodgkin, *African Political Parties*, Harmondsworth, 1961, p. 136.

What does appear certain is that there will remain plenty of opportunity to study the literary quality of the songs, for they show no signs of dying out. Indeed their contemporary relevance is demonstrated—if demonstration is needed—in the action of the Nigerian military rulers in 1966 in banning political songs as part of their attempt to curb political activity, or the Tanzanian government's appeal to musicians in 1967 to help to spread its new policies of socialism and self-reliance to the people through song. It is too easy to assume that this means of oral propaganda is bound to disappear with increasing literacy and 'modernization', as if newspapers and written communications were somehow the only 'natural' and 'modern' way of conducting political propaganda. On the contrary it is possible that the spread of the transistor radio may in fact add fresh impetus to political songs.

# 11

## CHILDREN'S SONGS AND RHYMES

*Lullabies and nursery rhymes. Children's games and verses;
Southern Sudanese action songs*

LITTLE systematic interest has been taken in children's verse in Africa, and though isolated instances have been recorded this has been done without any discussion of context or local significance.[1] On the published evidence it is not clear, for instance, how far the previous lack of a distinct body of schoolchildren in most African societies affected the specificity of children's verse as distinct from that of other groups, or how far the oral compositions now current in the increasing number of schools parallel similar phenomena recorded elsewhere. Nevertheless, some remarks on what is known to occur in Africa may be relevant here, not least if its shortcomings provoke further research or synthesis.[2] I shall discuss first lullabies (and other songs designed for children but primarily transmitted by adults) and secondly the rhymes and songs which tend to be for a slightly older age-group and are regarded as belonging to the children themselves in their own play.

I

Lullabies provide a good example of the way in which what might be expected to be a simple, 'natural', and spontaneous expression of feeling in all societies—a mother singing to her child—is in fact governed by convention and affected by the particular constitution of the society.

[1] Though see Tucker 1933; Griaule 1938*a*, pp. 205–75; Adam 1940, pp. 131–4; Gbadamosi and Beier 1959, pp. 53–8; Béart 1955; Blacking 1967.

[2] Further material can almost certainly be found which so far has achieved only local circulation, e.g. U. Beier and B. Gbadamosi (eds.), *The Moon Cannot Fight*, Ibadan, n.d. (Yoruba children's poems), and collections made by local teachers and others. Children's songs are also sometimes included on recordings published by the International Library of African Music (e.g. five Tswana children's singing games TR 111).

One major factor is the question of who has the main responsibility for looking after a child. Among the Ngoni, for instance, a kind of upper-class group in Malawi, there were few lullabies: most Ngoni women employed nurse-maids from other groups to look after their children. Something similar was true among the rank-conscious Nyoro of Uganda. There, however, the nurses commonly sang their own lullabies to their charges, expressing their feelings about the mothers' attitude:

> Ha! that mother, who takes her food alone.
> Ha! that mother, before she has eaten.
> Ha! that mother she says, 'Lull the children for me'.
> Ha! that mother when she has finished to eat.
> Ha! that mother she says 'Give the child to me'.[1]

One of the main *raisons d'être* of such lullabies among Nyoro nurses would in fact seem to be, not primarily the lulling of the child at all, but an indirect comment on their own position, 'for they were afraid of making direct requests to their masters and therefore they always expressed what they wanted in lullabies'.[1]

Other African lullabies fit more easily into our common picture of a mother concentrated on the needs of her child; but even in these the tone and purpose may vary. Some lay the greatest emphasis on the idea of rocking the child to sleep, often brought out by the rhythm and liquid vowel sounds of the original. Here, for instance, is the first verse of a long Swahili lullaby:

> Lululú, mwana (wa) lilañji,
> Lululú, mwana (wa) kanda!
> Lululú, mwana (wa) lilañji,
> Lululú, mwana (wa) kanda!
>
> (Lululu, Kindchen, warum weinst du?
> Lululu, verwöhntes kleines Kind!
> Lululu, Kindchen, warum weinst du?
> Lululu, verwöhntes kleines Kind!)[2]

and the same soothing repetitive sounds come in one of the commonest Zulu lullabies:

[1] Y. Bansisa, 'Music in Africa', *Uganda J.* 4, 1936, p. 110.
[2] Von Tiling 1927, pp. 291–2.

Thula, thula, thula, mntanami,
Ukhalelani na?
Ushaywa uβani?
Thula mntanami, umam'akekho

(Peace, peace, peace, my child,
Why weepest thou?
Who annoys?
Peace, child, mother is not home.)[1]

Other songs seem to represent more the mother's delight in playing with her child than a desire to soothe it,[2] or a detached and good-humoured comment as in the lullaby a Dogon mother sings to the child on her back:

Où est partie la mère du petit?
Partie puiser de l'eau.
Pas revenue de puiser l'eau.
Partie piler la feuille de baobab
Pas revenue de piler la feuille
Partie préparer les plats
Pas revenue de préparer les plats
Sur la falaise, sur la falaise, un œuf de poule est suspendu!

where the last line vividly pictures the way the little child's bottom is perched like an egg on his mother's steep back.[3] The Kamba mother also pictures her own absorption in her child and her neglect of other things for his sake, viewing her own attitude with a certain detachment:

Mother,[4] mother of the child, leave off crying, poverty!
You have come, you have surpassed me in crying.[5]

---

[1] Dhlomo 1947, p. 7. (See also slightly different versions in Curtis 1920; Vilakazi 1938, p. 120.) The reference to the mother's absence may be just a conventional part of the song, or may, if taken literally, indicate that this lullaby too was much sung by nurses. Some other Zulu lullabies (*isihlaβelelo*) are made up specially by the mother for individual children with whom they are intimately connected, so that each individual has his *isihlaβelelo*, 'the song of his childhood, regarded as something essentially his own' (E. J. Krige, *The Social System of the Zulus*, Pietermaritzburg, 1936, pp. 338–9).

[2] e.g. the Swahili song given by Von Tiling, op. cit., p. 290.

[3] Griaule 1938a, p. 226.

[4] Kamba children are often called 'mother' by their own mothers.

[5] i.e. I am glad that you came to me, but I never cried so much when I was a baby.

And even if it is the rain which rains,
I put away the tree,[1] I shall call my mother.
And even if it is the Masai,[2]
Who carries spear and shield, I put away the tree.
I shall call you, I shall lull to sleep on my arm, mother.
I shall not hear the goats who are bleating.[3]

Like many other lullabies, those of the Rundi are characterized by rhythm and cadence as well as the use of onomatopoeic words. But they also seem notably meditative in tone. The mother expresses and comments on her own feelings and on her expectations of the attitudes of others:

O ce qui me donne du travail, je t'aime.
Demain de bonne heure nous causerons.
De très bonne heure, dès qu'il fera clair.
Viens que je te caresse (en te donnant de petits coups).
Endors-toi, mets fin à ma solitude.
Ecoutons s'il y a des ennemis.
Mon roi, mon roi.

Tranquille! que je te frotte d'odoriférants
Qui t'accompagnent chez le roi (qui te font arriver jusque chez le roi).
Tranquille! sommeille sur le dos.
Ta belle-mère est stérile.
Elle te donnerait du tabac (au lieu de nourriture).
Même si la bouillie ne manque pas.[4]

There are also rhymes or songs for grown-ups to recite to children, distinct both from lullabies and from ordinary adult songs. The Zulu are said to have many 'nursery songs' in both rural and urban areas, among them one made up of an amusing combination of clicks to teach children the correct pronunciation (*Qhuweqha weqhuweqha, / Qhingqilithi qh!* etc.).[5] Several examples of these

---

[1] i.e. digging stick. Women are usually very busy in their gardens at the start of the rainy season, but this mother is thinking only of her child.

[2] Much feared warriors.

[3] Lindblom iii, 1934, p. 51.

[4] B. Zuure, 'Poésies chez les Barundi', *Africa* 5, 1932, p. 352. For some further references to lullabies, besides those already mentioned, see e.g. Nketia 1958*b*, p. 18 (Akan); A. de Rop, 'Berceuses móngo', *Anthropos* 60, 1965; A. Coupez, 'Rythme quantitatif dans les berceuses rundi', *Folia Scientifica Africae Centralis* 5. 3, 1959; Béart 1955, pp. 60 ff. (various lullabies from West Africa); Sempebwa 1948, p. 20 (Ganda); 'Berceuse', *Jeune Afrique* 6, 1949; L. Anya-Noa, 'Berceuses beti', *Effort camerounais* 1962/3; Belinga 1965, pp. 23 ff.

[5] Vilakazi 1938, p. 121.

rhymes for children are included in Griaule's comprehensive study *Jeux dogons*. One is for finger play:

> Le petit doigt a dit; oncle j'ai faim
> L'annulaire a dit: nous allons recevoir (à manger)
> Le majeur a dit: demandons
> L'index a dit: volons
> Le pouce a dit: je n'en suis pas (pour voler).
> Depuis ce temps, le pouce s'est écarté des autres doigts.[1]

The next song is to stop a small child crying by tickling up his arm—

> Singe noir
> Dans la main de mon fils
> Ai mis un pélyé [fruit] cassé
> L'a enlevé puis l'a mangé
> Puis çà, puis çà, puis çà.
> Çà, gêrgêrgêr. . . .[2]

There does not seem to be evidence of a large body of specialized nursery rhymes in any African society to the same extent as in English tradition, for example. However, it is hard to believe that it is only in Zulu and Dogon—two of the most comprehensively studied African cultures—that rhymes of the kind quoted can be found, and it is very possible that further research will reveal similar nursery-rhyme forms in many other African societies.[3]

II

Like children elsewhere, African children seem to have the familiar range of games and verse for their own play—nonsense songs, singing games, catch rhymes, and so on. They also engage in riddle-asking[4] and in other games and dances which cannot be treated here.

---

[1] Griaule 1938*a*, p. 224.
[2] Ibid., p. 225.
[3] They are sometimes mentioned in passing for other peoples, e.g. Tracey 1929, p. 97 (nursey rhymes among Kalanga, Southern Rhodesia); Béart 1955, ch. 6 (West Africa); Adali-Mortti 1958, p. 39 (nursery rhymes among the Ewe and other West African peoples); S. Hillelson, 'Arabic Nursery Rhymes', *Sudan Notes* 1. 1, 1918; D. C. Simmons, 'Specimens of Efik Folklore', *Folklore* 66, 1955, pp. 420–1; H. E. Lambert, 'A Note on Children's Pastimes', *Swahili* 30, 1959, p. 78.
[4] See Ch. 15.

Before quoting instances of such children's verses, one has to sound a note of caution. Obviously, what is to count as 'children's verse' in a given society depends on the local classification of 'children', and one cannot necessarily assume that the 'children's songs' of another society are directly comparable with those of one's own. In English society, for example, the contemporary concept of 'a child' is closely connected with the idea of a school population, a partly separate community of school children with their conventions and lore to some extent opposed to those of adults. It was suitable therefore that the main sources for the Opies'[1] classic work on children's verse should have been the schools. But this close association of children and formal schools does not hold true in all areas of Africa—and was even less true in the past—and one cannot necessarily assume the same clear-cut separation between the interests and orientations of children and those of adults.

This is not to say that there are no local or traditional ways of marking off the age-group of children from that of the adult world, merely that these do not necessarily parallel those of Western Europe. It is common for a ceremonial initiation to mark a clear dividing-line between childhood and maturity, often taking place at around the age of puberty, but in some societies (or with some individuals) this may be much earlier or much later. In some cases, initiation may be as young as, say, seven or eight years old, and the special initiation songs which are so often a feature of this ceremony might seem to parallel songs sung by similar age-groups in other societies. In fact they may be quite different in intention; they are to be sung by the children *qua* initiates (i.e. officially no longer children) and are often taught them by their elders. They cannot then be regarded as children's songs in the sense we are using the term here. In some African societies, again, there is strong pressure from children, as they get older, to prove themselves ready to enter the adult world. This means that, besides having their own verse and games, they are likely to try to master certain of the songs and other activities regarded as suitable for adults, and, indeed, may be encouraged to do so. Among the Ila and Tonga of Zambia, for instance, *ziyabilo* songs in praise of cattle and other possessions are sung by grown-up men; but many of these adult *ziyabilo* were in fact composed by

[1] I. and P. Opie, *The Lore and Language of Schoolchildren*, Oxford, 1959.

their singers when they were still young boys minding their father's cattle in the bush. The child thus models himself and his verse on his father and other adult men rather than concentrating on a special type appropriate to children.[1]

One way in which children are often separated from other groups is in the kind of work they are expected to do, and there are sometimes special songs associated with such tasks. These include the light-hearted songs sung by the young Limba boys who spend long weeks in the rainy seasons in farm shelters scaring away the birds and animals from the ripening rice, or the children's song among the Dogon, sung to discourage various birds from plundering the millet:

> Oiseau, sors!
> goro sors!
> bandey sors!
> Pour vous le mil n'est pas mûr.
> Il n'est pas l'heure de manger le mil vert
> Diarrhée du ventre.
> Où est parti le guérisseur de la diarrhée?
> Il est parti à Banan[2]
> Il est parti à Banan; ce n'est pas le moment de venir.
> Oiseau sors!
> Tourterelle sors!
> Pigeon sors.[3]

If the exact nature of 'children's verse' must be seen as depending partly on the particular ideas of each society about age structure, assignment of tasks, and behaviour expected of the various age-groups, it does nevertheless seem that in most African societies children do to some extent separate themselves off from adults in at least some play activities and have at least some rhymes and songs of their own. This is encouraged by the fact that many of them live in large family groupings, with much time spent outside their own homes in the open air rather than in small, enclosed family circles. Nowadays, too, there is the additional factor of the increasing number of schools.

Nonsense songs, tongue-twisting rhymes, and trick verses are all documented. Ibo girls, for instance, sing a nonsense rhyme which could be translated as 'Oh, oh, oh, oh, / girls agree / tall girl,

---

[1] Jones 1943, pp. 12–13.      [2] A nearby village.
[3] Griaule 1938*a*, p. 220.

Iruka / koko yams, / sour, sour koko yams, / he goat sour',[1] and
tongue-twisters are recorded among the Mbete of West Central
Africa and others:

> *Kusa le podi kudi* — Le liseron enlace le poteau.
> *Kudi le podi kusa* — Le poteau enlace le liseron

and

> *Mva o kwadi ńama* — Le chien attrapa l'animal.
> *ńama o txwi mva* — L'animal mordit le chien.[2]

The nonsense frequently takes the form of a kind of follow-up
or progressive rhyme, usually in dialogue. In one form or another,
this type of verbal play has been recorded from several parts of
the continent.[3] The sequences may be just for fun or may also
include a definite competitive content making up a kind of game.
This is true of the Moru of the Southern Sudan where the children
divide into two sides, one of which asks the questions. The answer
depends on remembering the right sequence of words quickly
enough, and those who get it wrong are ridiculed:

| | | |
|---|---|---|
| *A.* | A'di ru doro maro ni ya? | Who has taken my bowl? |
| *B.* | Kumu au. | Kumu has. |
| *A.* | Kumu a'di? | Who's Kumu? |
| *B.* | Kumu Ngeri. | Kumu son of Ngeri. |
| *A.* | Ngeri a'di? | Who's Ngeri? |
| *B.* | Ngeri Koko. | Ngeri son of Koko. |
| *A.* | Koko a'di? | Who's Koko? |
| *B.* | Koko Lire. | Koko son of Lire. |
| *A.* | Lire a'di? | Who's Lire? |
| *B.* | Lire Kide. | Lire son of Kide. |
| *A.* | Kide a'di? | Who's Kide? |
| *B.* | Kide Langba. | Kide son of Langba. |

---

[1] *Iyòo, ó | Abǫ, kwękwe, | ihwu, Iruka | ęde | bwaloka, okabwalęde, | ńkpi
bwaloka.* N. W. Thomas, *Anthropological Report on the Ibo-speaking Peoples of
Nigeria*, London, 1913, vol. iii, p. 51.

[2] Adam 1940, p. 133.

[3] e.g. the West African Dogon (Griaule 1938*a*, pp. 212–14) and possibly
Fulani (if the examples of 'chain-rhymes' cited by Arnott 1957, pp. 393 ff. are
intended for children, which seems not improbable), as well as the instances
from the Swazi (South Africa), Mbete (West Central Africa), and Moru
(Southern Sudan) mentioned below. Cf. also D. P. Gamble, 'Chain-rhymes in
Senegambian Languages', *Africa* 29, 1959, pp. 82–3 (Wolof, Mandingo, and
Fula), Blacking 1967, p.p. 101, 102, 116–17 (Venda), and catchword com-
positions (for adults) in Malawi (Macdonald 1882, vol. i, pp. 50–1).

| *A.* Langba a'di? | Who's Langba? |
| *B.* Langba Kutu. | Langba son of Kutu. |
| *A.* Kutu a'di? | Who's Kutu? |

(ending up *fortissimo*)

| *B.* Kutu temele cowa | Kutu's a sheep in the forest |
| Dango udute nyorli. | The bulls are fast asleep.[1] |

Sometimes the verbal parallelism is less exact, as in the Swazi 'children's part-song' in which the children are divided into two groups which take turns in singing a line, then join together at the end. It is not an action rhyme, but depends on the words and tune alone for its attraction:

*A.* Yē woman beyond the river!
*B.* Wē! (responding to the call).
*A.* What are you dusting?
*B.* I am dusting a skin petticoat.
*A.* What is a skin petticoat?
*B.* It is Mgamulafecele.
*A.* What have they killed?
*B.* They have killed a skunk.
*A.* Where did they take it?
*B.* To Gojogojane.
*A.* Who is Gojogojane?
*B.* He-who-eats-cowdung-when-hungry.
*A.* For whom would he leave (some of) it?
*B.* He would leave (some) for Shishane.
*A.* and *B.*
    Shishane is not to blame,
    The blame is for Foloza,
    He who says he alone is handsome.
    The hoes of Mbandzeni
    They go knocking against him,
    The knocker of Njikeni.
    Magagula, Magagula keep the clod of earth tightly squeezed in
        your ——.[2]

A more complicated form is quoted from the Mbete where the rhyme builds up in a cumulative way. Two children take part:

[1] T. H. B. Mynors, 'Moru Proverbs and Games', *Sudan Notes* 24, 1941, p. 206.

[2] Given as quoted in J. A. Engelbrecht, 'Swazi Texts with Notes', *Annals of the Univ. of Stellenbosch* (*B*) 8. 2, 1930, pp. 10–11. Several of the references are obscure.

| | |
|---|---|
| *A.* Sedi a nde? | La gazelle où est-elle? |
| *B.* Sedi miye nkwi. | La gazelle est allée au bois. |
| *A.* Omo a nde? | La première où est-elle? |
| *B.* Omo milono sedi o nkwi. | La première a suivi la gazelle au bois. |
| *A.* Oywole a nde? | La deuxième où est-elle? |
| *B.* Oywole milono omo, | La deuxième a suivi la première, |
| Omo milono sedi o nkwi. | La première a suivi la gazelle au bois. |
| *A.* Otadi a nde? | La troisième où est-elle? |
| *B.* Otadi milono oywole, | La troisième a suivi la deuxième, |
| Oywole milono omo, | La deuxième a suivi la première, |
| Omo milono sedi o nkwi . . . | La première a suivi la gazelle au bois . . . |

and so on up to the tenth which involves the answerer repeating the whole sequence.[1]

Other types of rhymes and songs are also recorded. There is the kind of catch rhyme exemplified by the Yoruba:

| | | |
|---|---|---|
| Who has blood? | *Chorus.* | Blood, blood. |
| Has a goat blood? | ,, | Blood, blood. |
| Has a sheep blood? | ,, | Blood, blood. |
| Has a horse blood? | ,, | Blood, blood. |
| Has a stone blood? | ,, | — — |

in which the point of the game is to try to get some child to say 'blood' after an inanimate object. A mistake results in laughter and sometimes a friendly beating.[2] There also seem to be plenty of songs enjoyed for their own sakes or for their usefulness in mocking other children. A Dogon child with his head recently shaved will be greeted with

> Crâne nu, lonlaire!
> Viens manger un plat de riz,
> Viens manger un plat de potasse,
> Viens manger un plat de mil[3]

while a Ganda child who has not washed may hear

> Mr. Dirty-face passed here
> And Mr. Dirtier-face followed.[4]

---

[1] Adam 1940, pp. 132–3. He also gives an example where the response directly echoes the second half of the query (p. 132).

[2] Gbadamosi and Beier 1959, pp. 55, 67.

[3] Griaule 1938*a*, p. 230.     [4] Sempebwa 1948, p. 20.

Or again, a kind of general comment may be made as in the humorous and rueful song by a Yoruba child:

> Hunger is beating me.
> The soapseller hawks her goods about.
> But if I cannot wash my inside,
> How can I wash my outside?[1]

So far we have concentrated on rhymes and songs that are mainly valued for their words or music rather than their relation to action. But there are also many examples of songs sung to accompany games or dances, or forming an integral part of them. A minor example would be the counting-out rhymes of the Dogon where those partaking are gradually eliminated according to whose leg the last syllable falls on at each subsequent repetition.[2] Yoruba children similarly use a rhyme as part of a hide-and-seek game. The searcher faces the wall singing his nonsense song while the others hide. When he reaches the question part of the song the others must reply in chorus, giving him a clue to their hiding-places:

> Now we are playing hide and seek.
> Let us play hide and seek.
> Hey, tobacco seller,
> This is your mother here,
> Whom I am wrapping up in those leaves.
> I opened the soup pot
> And caught her right inside
> Stealing meat!
> Who nails the root?
> > *Chorus.* The carpenter.
> Who sews the dress?
> > *Chorus.* The tailor. (etc.)[3]

Other action songs are more complicated in that they are based on imitation or on definite set dance patterns. Shona children, for instance, have an imitative song in which they circle round and round imitating an eagle catching small chickens.[4] Again, there are the Hottentot action songs based on the common principles of a ring or of two rows facing each other.[5]

---

[1] Gbadamosi and Beier 1959, p. 54.
[2] Griaule 1938a, pp. 214–15. Some of these are in the 'chain-rhyme' form.
[3] Gbadamosi and Beier 1959, pp. 55, 68.
[4] G. A. Taylor, 'Some Mashona Songs and Dances', *Nada* 4, 1926, p. 38.
[5] Stopa 1938, pp. 100–4.

A more detailed account of action songs is given by Tucker, drawing on his observation of children at mission schools in the Sudan in the 1930s.[1] His conclusion is that the songs and games were not introduced by the missionaries themselves (or at least not consciously), but whatever the truth of this, it is in any case suitable to end by quoting from this account in some detail. Schools are becoming increasingly important in the lives of more and more children in Africa, and it is likely that similar singing games— from whatever source—are now wide-spread (and thus accessible to study) among school groups.

The children whose round games were studied were mostly boys from various Southern Sudanese peoples (Nuer, Shilluk, Dinka, Bari, and Lotuko). The games are played on a moonlit night in the dry season and the singing, mostly in strophe and antistrophe, is led by one of the boys and accompanied by hand-clapping, foot-thumping, or the action of the game. Often the words themselves count for little. Sometimes the meaning is almost slurred out of recognition, and in this 'the Shilluks and Nuers are the greatest offenders, some of their songs consisting of mere nonsense syllables, which they themselves do not pretend to understand. (In such cases they usually give out that the words are "Dinka".)'[2] The translations are therefore rather free.

Most of the singing games are based on the principle of a ring, the players squatting or standing in a circle. In one, the equivalent of 'Hunt the slipper', the players sit in a circle with their feet under them. The leader in the middle of the ring has to find a bracelet which is being passed surreptitiously round the ring. He sings, answered by the others as they slap their knees in time to the song:

> *Leader.* Bracelet of my son's wife,
> *Chorus.* I want I want now, bracelet of poor Bana,
>      It is lost

repeated over and over until the leader successfully challenges one of the circle who, if caught with the bracelet, has to take the leader's place in the centre.[3] Another action song based on a ring is a type of counting-out game:

The boys sit in a circle, or, it might be, a right-angle, with their feet stuck out straight in front of them. An elder boy squats on his haunches before them and chants a queer formula, much longer than any

---

[1] Tucker 1933.        [2] Ibid., p. 166.        [3] Ibid., pp. 166–7 (Shilluk).

European equivalent, tapping the feet as he chants, till the last word is said. The foot last touched is 'out' and the owner must sit on it. He goes on in this way till everybody is sitting on both his feet, i.e. practically kneeling. He then begins with the first boy of the line. There is a formula and response, and then he bows down in front of the boy with his eyes shut and his head almost touching the boy's knees. The boy has to stand up without touching the man's head with his knees. (He may use his hands to help himself, if he wishes.) If the man hears the boy's knees creak as he rises, the boy is made to stand on one side. If his knees do not creak, he stands somewhere else. Soon we have two groups —creaky and non-creaky knees. (Of course, the longer one is forced to sit on one's feet, the greater the likelihood of creaky knees!) . . . The game ends with the non-creaky knees pursuing the creaky knees and punishing them.[1]

Another ring game is the Lotuko one in which a boy in the centre, 'the ape', has to try to grab the leg of one of the boys dancing round him in a ring and to upset him. If he succeeds, they change places:

> Here he goes around to steal
> Break away
> > *Bad ape.*
> Break away
> > *Bad ape.*[2]

There are also a number of games based on the idea of the arch or the line. In one the boys line up in two opposing ranks and one line advances slowly towards the other, which retreats, both sides singing:

> The foreigner
> Chin of a goat
> The foreigner comes striding haughtily
> With his red skin.

This is repeated several times, the two lines taking it in turn to advance. Suddenly the pace and verse change. Those advancing now run stiff-legged and try to kick the others' shins, again singing over and over:

> Why does the stranger hurry so?
> Ha! ha! hurry so.
> Why does the stranger hurry so?
> Ha! ha! hurry so.[3]

[1] Ibid., pp. 169–70.　　　[2] Ibid., p. 176.　　　[3] Ibid., p. 182.

Tucker comments that 'this game is definitely a hit at the white man. The "chin of a goat" in the first song refers to the beards of the R.C. missionaries (beards being considered unseemly among the Nilotic tribes); while the kicking in the second song is thought to be a skit on the average official's use of his boots when angry or impatient.'[1]

Chasing and following games also take place to sung words. In the Acholi version of 'Follow my leader' the boys stand in single file, holding each other's waists, and the leader takes them in a closing circle to the words of the song 'close in', then worms his way out again, singing 'open out'. The words of the song form the background. The verse 'A dula dul dula na dula dul. A dula ye. Dula na dula dul. A dula kuk! Dula na dula dul. A dula ye' means 'close in', while the same tune, with *gɔnya* instead of *dula*, means 'open out'.[2]

Finally there are imitations of animals. Some of these occur in chasing games like the Shilluk 'Lion and sheep', but in others the imitations seem to be taken more seriously. In one a boy doubles himself up to represent a frog and tries to jump backwards in a circle without falling over, in time to his companions' song:

> Jump up and down,
> *Up and down.*
> Jump up and down,
> *Up and down.*
> I shall jump again,
> *Up and down.*
> I shall jump again,
> *Up and down.*[3]

In 'Bush-buck in a trap' the success of the game depends on the exactness of the leader's imitation of the animal:

The boys stand in a ring, holding hands. One boy is in the middle, and he is 'Gbodi', the bush-buck. He sings suiting his actions to the words, and the others reply, copying him.

Thus, for example:

> Gbodi shake your head, Gbodi shake your head.
> *Kango.*
> Gbodi crouch down, Gbodi crouch down.
> *Kango.*

[1] Tucker 1933, p. 183.  [2] Ibid., p. 179.  [3] Ibid., p. 185.

Gbodi scratch your ear, Gbodi scratch your ear.
*Kango.*
Gbodi stamp your foot, Gbodi stamp your foot.
*Kango.*
Gbodi snort and snuffle, Gbodi snort and snuffle.
*Kango.*
Gbodi break away now, Gbodi break away now.
*Kango.*

At the words 'Gbodi break away now', he makes a wild dash for safety, and tries to break through the circle. If he fails, he has to act 'Gbodi' again.[1]

These are only a few of the singing games recorded by Tucker,[2] and he himself claims to give only a random selection. But even this, he considers, 'picked up casually from different corners of the Southern Sudan, and covering primitive races with mutually unintelligible languages, should serve to show the main foundations on which the great majority of children's singing games are built. . . . These foundations are, to all intents and purposes, identical with those that underlie the forms of European children's games, viz. the *ring*, the *arch* and the *line*.'[3]

It seems clear that many such singing games and other types of children's songs remain to be collected or analysed.[4] At the moment little can be said about the distribution of different types, the transmission of these forms among the children themselves, the degree of individual originality as against conventional forms,[5]

[1] Ibid., p. 184.
[2] He gives twenty-four in all, fully illustrated with the music, original, and (usually) translation.
[3] Tucker 1933, p. 187.
[4] They are mentioned (or, in a few cases, described) for e.g. Kamba (Mbiti 1959, p. 259); Ganda (Sempebwa 1948, p. 20); Ewe (A. M. Jones i, 1959, pp. 16–39); Ashanti (Nketia 1962, p. 67); Tswana (*Bantu Studies* 7, 1933, p. 80); Mpama-Bakutu (A. Windels, 'Jeux et divertissements chez les Mpama-Bakutu', *Aequatoria* 1, 1939, p. 19); children in Leopoldville (S. Comhaire-Sylvain, 'Les jeux des enfants noirs à Léopoldville', *Zaïre* 3, 1949, and 'Jeux congolais', *Zaïre* 6, 1952); Ibo (B. Nettl, 'Ibo Songs from Nigeria, Native and Hybridized', *Midwest Folklore* 3, 1954, pp. 238–9); Efik (D. C. Simmons, 'Efik Games', *Folklore* 69, 1958); Hausa (K. Krieger, 'Knabenspiele der Hausa', *Baessler-Archiv* N.F. 3, 1955).
[5] The Dogon examples collected by Griaule suggest the same kind of variations on a single theme for some of the verses as is evident in the many variants of the 'same' rhyme in the Opies' collection of English school children's rhymes.

or the incidence of topical or other comment. What does seem certain is that the growing numbers of school children in contemporary Africa are likely more and more to develop their own distinct and conventional songs and games—increasingly it is in the schools that these can most easily and fruitfully be studied.

# III · PROSE

## 12

## PROSE NARRATIVES I. PROBLEMS AND THEORIES

Introductory. Evolutionist interpretations. Historical-
geographical school. Classification and typologies.
Structural-functional approach. Conclusion

THE existence of stories in Africa is widely known. One of the
first things any student of African oral literature or of comparative
literature generally discovers about Africa is the great number of
so-called 'folktales'. He will hear above all of the many animal
tales that so vividly and humorously portray the tricks of the
spider, the little hare, or the antelope, or exhibit the discomfiture
of the heavy and powerful members of the animal world through
the wiles of their tiny adversaries. Less well known, but still
familiar, are the many African tales set in the human world,
about, say, the trials of a young man wooing a wife, the self-
sacrifice of two friends for each other, or the triumph of the
youngest, despised member of a family; and the famous 'myths'
of the various African peoples about such subjects as the origin
of death, of mankind, or of authority.

In fact, all this is if anything *too* well known. So much has been
published of and about this one literary form that its relative
importance in the general field of African oral literature has been
radically misjudged. Far from being 'the great form' in African
literature, as even the author of a recent and well-informed work
on Africa has asserted,[1] tales and other prose narratives in fact
generally appear to be markedly less important than the majority

[1] P. Bohannan, *African Outline, A General Introduction*, Harmondsworth,
1966, p. 137.

of poetic forms, in terms of complexity, of the relatively lesser specialism of their composers, and of the assessment of the people themselves. This, however, is seldom recognized. Owing to a series of secondary characteristics like the greater ease with which prose can be recorded and the way the nature of the tales (particularly those about animals) seemed to fit certain preconceptions about African mentality, these stories have been published in large numbers and have caught the public eye to the almost total exclusion of the often more intrinsically interesting poetry.

So much, indeed, has been published in this field that it would be easy to write not a chapter but a book surveying the present state of knowledge of this form of African literature. But to include too lengthy a description here of this single form of verbal art would inevitably present an unbalanced picture of African literature. These two chapters therefore will give only a brief summary of what is known about African prose narratives and the problems of analysis, and will concentrate on pointing to gaps in our knowledge rather than repeating what is already known.[1]

[1] Most of the general accounts of African oral literature devote much or most of the space to a consideration of prose narratives, cf. e.g. Herskovits 1961; Bascom 1964 (includes a most useful list of collections of African stories); Berry 1961; Balandier 1956. Of the large and varied number of general anthologies of African stories, one could mention Seidel 1896; Basset 1903; Cendrars 1921; C. Meinhof, *Afrikanische Märchen*, Jena, 1921; Frobenius 1921–8 (12 vols.); Radin 1952; K. Arnott, *African Myths and Legends*, London, 1962; Whiteley 1964. Special studies of various aspects of African stories include Klipple 1938 and M. J. and F. S. Herskovits, *Suriname Folk-lore*, New York, 1936 (both dealing with comparative study of motifs); Mofokeng 1955; Von Sicard 1965; H. Tegnaeus, *Le Héros civilisateur*, Stockholm, 1950; H. Abrahamsson, *The Origin of Death: Studies in African Mythology*, Uppsala, 1951 (studies mainly in the 'Scandinavian' tradition); Werner 1925, 1933 (surveys content of stories, including myths). Of the innumerable collections of stories from single societies or areas, the following may be mentioned as of particular interest either because of the collection itself or (more often) because of the accompanying discussion: Roger 1828 (Wolof); Theal 1886 (Xhosa); Chatelain 1894 (Kimbundu); Cronise and Ward 1903 (Temne); Jacottet 1908 (Sotho); Junod ii, 1913, pp. 191 ff. (Thonga); Tremearne 1913 (Hausa); Equilbecq 1913–16 (3 vols.) (West Africa); Smith and Dale ii, 1920, ch. 28 (Ila); Torrend 1921 (Zambia); Travélé 1923 (Bambara); Doke 1927, 1934 (Lamba); Lindblom 1928 (Kamba); Rattray 1930 (Akan); Herskovits 1958 (Fon); Stappers 1962 (Luba); Hulstaert 1965 (Mongo); Mbiti 1966 (Kamba); Finnegan 1967 (Limba); Evans-Pritchard 1967 (Zande). See also the excellent article by Crowley (1967) which, though specifically about the Congo, is of wider relevance.

For further references see General Bibliography and the useful analysis of collections plus bibliography in Bascom 1964; it must be pointed out that the most recent collections (often very much in popular form) are by no means all necessarily improvements on earlier collections from the same peoples.

Because so much has been written and published over many years, this field of study has been particularly subject to the vicissitudes of anthropological theories and has reflected only too faithfully the rise and fall of fashions in interpretations of African (and 'primitive') cultures. As a result there are considerably more misconceptions and misunderstandings to clear away in the case of African prose than with poetry. Indeed, when one considers the vast amount published it is surprising how poor much of it is. Poor, that is, in the sense that so much is based on unquestioned assumptions and so little is said about many topics in which a student of literature would naturally be interested, like, for instance, the art or originality of the individual composer, the nature of the audiences reached, the local assessment of the relative worth or seriousness of stories against other forms, or the position of the story-teller himself. So for all these reasons—the ready accessibility of some aspects, the misunderstandings or gaps in other respects—this section, unlike most others in the central part of this book, will tend to be argumentative and critical rather than descriptive and illustrative.

I

Something has already been said in Chapter 2 about some of the many different approaches to the study of African oral art. These will not all be recapitulated here, but, even at the cost of some repetition, something further must be said about the special case of prose narratives; it is in this field—sometimes regarded as 'folklore' *par excellence*—that these various theories have found their most fluent and extreme expression. The end result has too often been to play down the literary aspect or even to explain it away completely.

One of the most influential of these theories, dating from the nineteenth century but casting a shadow even today, is the type of evolutionist interpretation of human history and society put forward, in various forms, by writers like Morgan, Tylor, or Frazer. Besides their application to the supposed unilinear evolution of institutions such as religion or marriage, these speculative historical generalizations could also be brought to bear on the nature and history of literature. In this field the word 'folklore' became popular as a term to describe the supposed customs, beliefs, and culture of both 'early' man and his presumed equivalents today: contemporary 'primitive' peoples and the modern peasant, i.e. the 'folk' among whom could still, supposedly, be found traces of the earlier stages of unilinear human evolution. When apparently similar customs or beliefs could be detected in societies otherwise considered 'advanced' (in the opinion of the analyst), then they could be explained as 'survivals', remnants of the cruder, barbaric stages of the past. 'Folklore' even came to be defined as 'the study of survivals', with the implication that its subject-matter (which included 'folktales') was basically crude, primitive, 'early', and, in many cases, due to old ideas passed on from previous generations. It was thus—to quote Frazer's words—'due to the collective action of the multitude and cannot be traced to the individual influence of great men'.[1]

The implication of these approaches for the study of oral literature is plain. Any type of oral prose narrative from whatever society could be, and was, referred to as 'folktale' and thus treated as a kind of 'survival' from an earlier and even more primitive state. In this way, the aspect of individual originality and authorship could be played down—or rather, the question of authorship not even raised; for once the word 'folktale' was used, collective tradition could be assumed and no question about individual creation could arise. A further relevant assumption was the still commonly mentioned 'fact' that all 'folktales' (and thus all oral narratives) have been handed down through generations from the remote past, most probably in a word-perfect form. Again, this questionable assumption drew attention away from problems of authorship or of contemporary relevance and variations, and from questions about the actual situations in which these stories are actually told. Moreover, because the tales could be treated as 'survivals', there was felt to be no need to apply to them the normal procedures of literary criticism or to relate them to the contemporary social and literary background, for this, it was assumed, was often alien to the real content of the stories. This approach also lent encouragement to the amateur collection and publication of isolated unrelated snippets of tales and proverbs; for when the whole idea of the subject of 'folklore' was that these 'folktales' were only scraps (survivals), there was no inducement to try to collect them systematically. So it is that, even recently, the

[1] J. G. Frazer, *Folk-lore in the Old Testament*, London, 1919, vol. i, p. vii.

journals are full of such articles as 'Four proverbs and one folk-story from the Bongo Bongo', 'Two folktales and a riddle from the XYZs', and so on, with no attempt to relate the specimens to any background whatsoever or even to have collected anything more than the barest synopsis of the plot.

By now the evolutionist framework from which these approaches sprang has been rejected in professional anthropological circles. Yet in spite of this, these assumptions about oral narratives still linger on. We read, for instance, in a recent collection of Hausa stories of the 'callousness or . . . macabre type of humour' in some stories being 'residues from the past', or the way in which their 'animal and fairy stories are probably as old as the language and perhaps even older';[1] and many other similar instances could be cited.

That these attitudes should still be attractive is not altogether surprising. The hidden implications of the term 'folktale' lead one astray at the outset—a good reason for giving up this otherwise quite useful word. It is also pleasant enough to be able to concentrate on confident assertions about the great age of certain stories without needing to produce evidence (the bland 'probably' of the statement just quoted is typical here). This whole approach absolves one from any systematic treatment of the more difficult and interesting problems.

In fact the question of originality in oral literature is by no means a closed one. Contrary to the assumptions of many writers, the likelihood of stories having been handed down from generation to generation in a word-perfect form is in practice very remote. This whole concept, in fact, is much more plausible in the case of *written* than of oral literature. As already remarked in an earlier chapter, one of the main characteristics of oral literature is its verbal flexibility (even more marked, perhaps, with prose than with some types of verse). So that even if the basic plot did, in a given case, turn out really to date back centuries or millenia—and in one sense it is a truism that all stories (written or unwritten) have already been told—this would be only a very minor element in the finished work of art produced in the actual telling. The verbal elaboration, the drama of the performance itself, everything in fact which makes it a truly *aesthetic* product comes from the contemporary teller and his audience and not from the remote past.

[1] Johnston 1966, pp. xxxi, xxxix.

In any case, how significant is it if some of the content is old or derivative? Does this tempt us to ignore the literary significance of, say, Shakespeare's *Othello* or Joyce's *Ulysses*? The explaining away in terms of origin of subject-matter has really no more justification for oral than for written literature. To suppose otherwise is to assume that in non-literate cultures people accept passively the content in the narratives told them and are not tempted to add or embroider or twist—an assumption which, as will be clear already, there is no evidence to support.

## II

Evolutionist approaches, then, with their accompanying assumptions about the nature of oral prose narratives, both drew away attention from significant aspects of oral literature (including its literary value) and at the same time disseminated unfounded ideas about authorship and transmission. The second group of approaches to be discussed here has done no more than focus attention on certain questions to the exclusion of other equally interesting ones. These are the problems treated by the so-called historical-geographical or diffusionist school which originated in Finland but which also has much influence in America and elsewhere.

This school asks questions about the exact historical and geographical origins of a particular story with the idea of tracing its journeys from one area to another. Unlike the evolutionists, these scholars take little interest in *generalized* questions about origin, or in the relative primitiveness of different categories of tales. They aim to reconstruct the 'entire life history of the tale', working back to the first local forms, hence to the ultimate archetype from which they were all originally derived, in much the same way as literary scholars trace back a series of manuscript traditions to their first original. As an aid to the more effective carrying out of this aim, various classifications have been made to facilitate the recognition of the 'same' tale in many areas so that its biography can more easily be plotted.[1] Various classifications and indexes have been compiled, the best-known being Stith

[1] See particularly Thompson 1961.

Thompson's monumental *Motif-index of Folk-literature* in which the various 'motifs' of 'folktales' are listed for easy reference and comparison.[1]

This general emphasis on questions about the life history of specific tales has been one of the dominating influences in the recent study of oral prose narratives (most often referred to by this school as 'folktales'). Many interesting similarities have been discovered in the plots of stories to be found in Africa and elsewhere—in Europe, in Arabia (notably in the *Arabian Nights*), in India, and, finally, in the New World, where they probably travelled with African slaves. Attempts have also been made, following this approach, to trace the historical and geographical origin of tales found in Africa. Certain plots, it has been concluded, can be reckoned as being indigenous to Africa. An example of this is the famous tale based on the idea of a tug of war in which two large animals (often the hippopotamus and the elephant) are induced by a smaller animal to pull against each other believing that their opponent was really the small weak animal, which had thus tricked them.[2] Another allegedly African motif is that of 'death' from a false message, in which the wrong message is given to mankind so that they have to undergo death instead of living forever.[3] Other motifs, it has been argued, come from outside Africa. The path of one of these—the 'root motif' in which a crocodile is misled into releasing his victim's foot when told it is a root—has been traced through India and Europe by various South African writers.[4] Other African motifs have been given a polygenetic origin or still remain to be analysed. In fact, in spite

[1] Thompson 1955. 'Motifs' include plots, subject-matter, types of character and action, etc. A fairly wide definition is taken of 'folk literature' to cover folktales, myths, ballads, fables, medieval romances, fabliaux, exempla, local traditions, but not riddles or proverbs. Some African material is included. Similar works primarily concerned with Africa (though conceived on a much smaller scale) include M. J. and F. S. Herskovits, *Suriname Folk-lore*, New York, 1936; Klipple 1938; Clarke 1958. See also references given in Ch. 2, p. 39, and, for collections of stories which include much comparative material along these lines, Lindblom 1928, vols. 1–2 and Von Sicard 1965.

[2] K 22 in Thompson's classification (Thompson 1955). A full comparative treatment of this motif using the historical-geographical method is given in Mofokeng 1955.    [3] Klipple 1938, pp. 755 ff.; cf. Abrahamsson, op. cit.

[4] See Mofokeng 1955, following up the D.Litt. thesis by S. C. H. Rautenbach, *Die Wording van 'n Siklus in die Afrikaanse Diersprokie*, Witwatersrand University, 1949 (not seen; reference in Mofokeng 1955). Unfortunately most of this detailed analysis of African material by scholars working at the University of Witwatersrand apparently remains as yet unpublished.

of the general influence of this approach, not many systematic studies of the life history of motifs in African tales have yet been completed. Yet plenty of preliminary material has been collected in that many editors of collections of African stories have said something about comparable motifs in Africa or elsewhere.

The fascination of this approach, however, has sometimes blinded commentators to the significance of other aspects of African prose narratives. There has again been a tendency to play down the significance of the contemporary verbalization and performance of the story as a whole in favour of an attempt to trace back the detailed history of certain elements of its subject-matter. Local artistry, inventiveness, and meaning are minimized, and the concentration focused on external origins.

The unbalanced nature of this approach can be illustrated by a specific example. This is a story taken from the Limba of Sierra Leone. It is quite obvious to any reader that the basic plot is a biblical one; in fact the outline plot was told to the narrator only a few years earlier. It is the tale of Adam and Eve, and even the names of the characters in Limba have remained more or less the same. Yet in its interpretation and telling by a Limba story-teller, the tale has become in almost every sense a truly *Limba* one.

This is the story as told by a skilful Limba narrator in 1964. He opens by asking a friend to 'reply' to him—that is to lead the audience participation that is so essential a part of the whole process of Limba story-telling.

## ADAMU AND IFU

Suri—reply to me. I am going to tell a story, about when the earth came out, how after long we were brought out, we Limba, how after long we came to do work, how we lived. I am going to tell it this evening. You Yenkeni [R. F.], by your grace, you are to reply to me.

You see—Kanu Masala (God), he was once up above. In the whole world then there were no people. So Kanu Masala thought; he said, 'I will take people to there.' What he brought out were two human beings—one man; one woman. What were their names? The man—he was Adamu. The woman—she was Ifu. (Ifu.)[1] Ifu.

When he had brought them out, they came and lived [here]. They spent two days and nights—but they found nothing to eat. So they went to Kanu Masala then.

---

[1] Suri, one of the listeners, repeats the name.

'We have come here to you.'

Kanu asked 'Any trouble?'

'No. We—the reason we have come is this: you brought us out, you went and put us on the earth here; but we—hunger! Nothing for us to eat. Will we not die tomorrow?'

Then Kanu said, 'I will give you food.' Kanu came down. He came and showed them the trees in fruit. He showed them every tree in fruit for them to eat.

'This is your food.' He showed them one—'Don't eat this one oh!' It was like an orange; when it is in fruit it is red. 'Don't eat this one oh! This is a prohibited one. You are not to eat it.'

Adamu said 'All right.'

They lived there for long—they ate from those trees. They did no work. They did nothing except just live there, except that when they were hungry they went and ate.

Then a snake got up there. He came and made love with the woman, Ifu. They travelled far in that love.

Then the snake came near, the *baŋkiboro* snake.[1] He came and said to the woman, Ifu,

'Do you never eat from this tree?'

Ifu said, 'No. We do not eat it. We were told before that we should not eat it, it is prohibited.'

Then the snake said, 'Oh you! That tree—eat from it.'

Ifu said, 'We do not eat it.'

'Eat it! Would I lie to you? We share in love you and I. Just eat it. There is nothing wrong about it.'

Ifu said, 'We do not eat it. If we eat it we are doing something wrong.'

The snake said, 'Not at all. Just eat.'

Ifu said, 'All right.'

He picked it, he the snake. He went and gave it to Ifu.

Ifu said, 'You eat first.'

He the snake—he ate. Ifu took it. She ate one. The other one she kept for Adamu.

When Adamu came, she came and gave it to him.

Adamu said, 'I will not eat this oh! We were told before that we should not eat it.'

'Not at all', said Ifu.

'Just eat it. There is nothing wrong about it.' Adamu refused. She implored him there. Adamu took the fruit, he ate the fruit.

Now Kanu Masala—he saw this. He knew. 'Those people have broken the prohibition I gave them.'

---

[1] A very long, red, and spotted fatal snake.

When they had eaten it, Adamu—his heart trembled. 'When Kanu Masala comes here tomorrow, this means we have done something wrong.'

When Kanu Masala came down, Adamu was hiding now when he saw Kanu coming. He hid himself. Both of them were by now hiding themselves (seeing Kanu Masala).[1] When Kanu arrived he came and called, calling the man.

'Adamu! Adamu!'

Now Adamu was afraid to reply—for he had eaten from the tree. He called him again.

'Adamu! Adamu!'

He was just a bit afraid to reply. He called

'Ifu! Ifu!' Both of them were afraid to reply.

He called Adamu again. Adamu replied. Adamu came. He came and asked him—

'Adamu.' 'Yes?'

'What made you eat from that tree really? I told you you were not to eat it. You took, you ate it just the same. What made you eat it?'

Then Adamu said, 'Ah, my father. It was not me. It was the woman. She came and gave it to me—Ifu. I said, "I do not eat this." She said, "Just eat it." She has brought me into trouble.'

Then Kanu called Ifu.

'Ifu! Ifu!'

Ifu replied, 'Yes?'

'Come here.'

Ifu came near.

He asked her, 'What made you give him from that tree for him to eat?'

Then Ifu said, 'It was not me, my father; it was the serpent who came and gave me from the tree. He said "Eat it. It is food." I refused for long oh! He said "Just eat it. There is nothing wrong about it." I ate it. What I left I came and gave to Adamu.'

He called the serpent, the *baŋkiboro* snake. The *baŋkiboro* snake came. When he had come, he asked him.

'What made you give those people from that tree for them to eat?'

The *baŋkiboro* snake said, 'I gave it to them, yes; there was nothing wrong about it at all.'

Then Kanu said, 'For you, you have not done well. I told them they were not to eat from this tree. You came and gave it to them. You do not want them to prosper.[2] It looks as if you—you will be parted from them. You will go into the bush once and for all. You will never again come out [to live] among human beings.[3] When you meet a human, you will be killed. For you have not done well.'

---

[1] Another interjection by Suri.
[2] Lit. 'do not like their life'.                [3] Or 'Limba'.

Since the *baŋkiboro* snake went off into the bush—if you see a *baŋkiboro* snake now with human beings, whenever they see each other, they kill him. That is why they hate each other.

When the *baŋkiboro* snake had gone into the bush, then Kanu Masala said,

'Ifu.'

'Yes?'

'You, because you were lied to today and agreed to it, and I told you before that you were not to have suffering but you did not agree to this— now you, you will have suffering. You will now stay behind Adamu. All you women now, when you are married to a man, you will live in his power. That is what I say. When you give birth, when you do that, you will have suffering. That is what I say. When you work now, after the man has cleared and hoed, you will weed. The rain will beat on you there. The sun will burn you there—as you think about your husband's sauce.[1] For that is what you chose. That is what you will do.'

Then he said,

'Adamu'.

'Yes?'

'Because you were lied to by the woman and you agreed to it, you will begin to work. You will work now. When you want to get a wife you will have to woo her. Every man will have to give wealth for long to get her. When you have married several [wives] you will look for a house—you must build, you the man. You will have to get a farm for them to go to. That is what I give you. For you refused to live in the good fortune you had.'

If you see now—we Limba we live now to work; the sun burns us; the rain soaks us; ha! we endure that suffering; if you want to get something to eat you have to struggle for long—that began from the serpent, the *baŋkiboro* snake. If you see that we hate each other, him and us— that is the only reason. Now the *baŋkiboro* snake, when he sees a human, says, 'That man is coming to kill me'; and if you do not strengthen yourself, you the human, he will catch you, biting you. For he was driven out from among us. If you see how we live, we Limba, working— that was where it began.

That is it, it is finished.[2]

To explain in detail how typical a Limba story this now is would involve a lengthy description of the types of content, style, and expression characteristic of the genre of oral literature the

---

[1] The wife has the responsibility of growing or gathering the vegetables for the 'sauce'.

[2] Recorded on tape from the Limba narrator (Karanke Dema) in February 1964, and published (in translation) in Finnegan 1967, pp. 267-70.

Limba call *mbɔrɔ*.[1] We can only note one or two points here. There is the way in which the relationship between the snake and Eve is assumed to be that of love: as in so many other Limba stories a wife betrays her husband for the sake of her lover and brings disaster both to him and to mankind as a whole. This idea is by no means confined to the Limba, it is true. But the characteristic way in which it is expressed and appreciated and fits with *Limba* literary conventions is so very interesting that it seems dull to spend much time on the question of where the content first came from. The same could be said of other characteristically Limba points in the story: the use of dialogue; the expression of the action through a series of parallel episodes; the way in which, as so often in Limba stories, a character is at first too fearful to emerge from hiding; the stock description of human beings left by Kanu on earth without food and having to go and ask him for help; and, finally, the reference at the end to the present hard fate of the Limba, about which (in certain moods) they are much preoccupied —the way they have to labour long hours in the fields, season after season, in sun or in rain, to produce the rice which is their basic sustenance. All these points, bare as they may seem on the surface, are in fact of profound meaning to the Limba who hear and tell the story, and possess a whole range of connotations and allusions which would be unintelligible to one unacquainted with their culture.

If this point can be made about a story based on a plot introduced as recently as only two years ago, how much more is this likely to be true of plots and motifs which have supposedly spread in the more remote past. Whatever interest the diffusionists' investigations of origins may have—and they are at least more verifiable than generalized evolutionary theories—it is clear that too great a preoccupation with this can lead, and indeed has led, to a neglect of other equally interesting questions about the present literary and social significance of this genre of oral literature.

### III

Another aspect of the historical-geographical school of 'folklorists' has been the interest in classification. The original motive of this is obvious. Until the various elements in folktales are

[1] See Finnegan 1967, esp. pp. 49–103.

classified for easy reference, it will not be possible to collect and analyse comparatively the data necessary for tracing the life history of the various plots and motifs in question. Other influences from anthropology and sociology generally have increased this desire for classification, so that those now preoccupied with this are not all necessarily outright adherents of the Scandinavian school.

This approach is excellent up to a point. Every subject needs some general agreement about terminology, not least the study of oral prose narratives. Clarification of the general terms here can be most helpful, for instance the recent article by Bascom[1] directed towards a definition of 'myth', 'legend', and 'folktale' as sub-types of the single category 'prose narrative'. Other classifications are more detailed, and include such 'types' as, say, 'dilemma tale', 'aetiological tale', and so on, many of these deriving ultimately from Stith Thompson's categorization.[2] Such typologies have helped to focus our attention on certain facets of prose narratives, to make comparisons and contrasts, and generally to become more aware of the potential differences in structure, content, or outlook in various kinds of stories.

However this can have its dangers. One point is that, in the case of the African material, it may be rather too early to produce helpful typologies of the more detailed kind. This at first sight seems ridiculous when so much has been published in the field of African prose narratives. In fact, however, much of this published material is of questionable quality. Often we are given summaries or synopses of the plot or structure, the texts themselves have frequently been written down by schoolboys or others with little skill in the actual artistry of the genre, and the final versions have often appeared in none too dependable translations with no comment at all on local classifications or attitudes. None of this suggests that classifications based on such data are likely to be very precise or helpful. Too often, indeed, the collections which appear to illustrate particular classifications have themselves been recorded and presented by collectors who have assumed in advance that these categories have universal and 'natural' validity.

One simple example of this is the general category of 'myth'.[3] In most European cultures, it seems natural to assume a distinction

---

[1] Bascom 1965*b*.
[2] Though he himself was not trying to establish a typology.
[3] Discussed further below, pp. 361 ff.

between 'myths' (narratives, believed in some sense or other to be true, and concerned with the origins of things or the activities of deities) and 'folktales' or ordinary stories (fictional narratives, taken much less seriously). This rough classification also applies, more or less, to the narratives of certain non-European peoples. But—and this is the point—there are also societies in which this distinction between 'myth' and 'folktale' is not observed. The local people themselves may not recognize this classification but rather, as in the case of several African peoples, regard both as belonging to the same general genre of oral literature. In some of these cases, one may be able to detect *some* such general distinction, even though the people themselves are not conscious of it, even deny it. But in others, even that basis for categorization is lacking, and it is not possible to find any local or empirical distinction between different groups of narratives. Yet European students often insist that there *must* be some such distinction, and impose their own categories by assuming without question that they can group together all those stories which have any superficial resemblance to what they have been brought up to regard as 'myth'. This sort of naïve assumption is not made by the leading scholars in the field; indeed, writers like Thompson and Bascom have specifically warned against it. But many more popular adherents of this approach have been swayed by a combination of this kind of typology, and of their own cultural traditions, so that they do not stop to ask even whether there is any local basis at all for such a distinction from other narratives. There may be—but there just as well may not be. When facile assumptions about classification take the place of actual investigation (about, for instance, such questions as the attitudes of teller and audience to the narration, or the detailed subject-matter of the different 'types' of stories and how they compare), we have reached the point where easy classification should be replaced by more modest research into the facts.

A further point about too much dependence on typologies here is that this under-emphasizes one of the most striking characteristics of much oral literature—its flexible and unfixed quality. This applies particularly in the case of prose. In the actual narration of stories—and the actual narration is what matters in oral literature—there is very often no fixed wording, and the narrator is free to bind together the various episodes, motifs, characters, and forms at his disposal into his own unique creation, suited to the audience, the occasion, or the whim of the moment. The same point has been well made by Ruth Benedict in the context of American Indian (Zuni) stories when she speaks of the need for more intensive studies:

> The usual library-trained comparative student works with standard versions from each locality; in primitive cultures, usually one from a tribe. This version arbitrarily becomes 'the' tribal tale, and is minutely compared with equally arbitrary standard tales from other tribes. But in such a body of mythology as that of Zuni, many different variants coexist, and the different forms these variants take cannot be ascribed to different historical levels, or even in large measure to particular tribal contacts, but are different literary combinations of incidents in different plot sequences. The comparative student may well learn from intensive studies not to point an argument that would be invalidated if half a dozen quite different versions from the same tribe were placed on record.[1]

It is true that many collections of African stories give the impression of fixity just because they have been written down and printed. But in fact, in most African cases that have been fully examined, this variability of tales according to the teller and the occasion is one of their most apparent characteristics.[2] There is no one *correct* version or form. What on one occasion looks like, say, a 'dilemma tale' or a moralizing parable (to mention two well-known types) may on another, though otherwise similar in subject-matter, look like an aetiological explanation or just a humorous joke. Form, plot, and character may all equally, therefore, provide only a shifting and impermanent foundation for classification, and any attempt at making typologies on this basis can only result in misconceptions about the nature of the stories as actually told.

Altogether, then, the current interest in classification can give a rather one-sided view of the significance of many prose narratives in Africa. This is particularly true when, as so often, they are based on what turns out to be only superficially analysed material. Largely owing to the past preoccupations of evolutionists, of linguists,[3] of educationalists, and of diffusionists, an amazingly

---

[1] R. Benedict, *Zuni Mythology*, New York, 1935, vol. i, p. xiii.

[2] See e.g. Stappers 1962, pp. 14–15 (Luba); Theal 1886, pp. vii–viii (Xhosa); Finnegan 1967, pp. 28–31 (Limba); Evans-Pritchard 1967, pp. 32 ff. (Azande); Junod ii, 1913, pp. 198 ff. (Thonga).

[3] Who have in the past been naturally more interested in the provision of texts for grammatical and syntactical analysis than in the variations of the spoken versions.

large number of these collections have appeared without any rigorous commentary to elucidate their contemporary and local meaning, being presented as just bare 'texts', often no more than synopses of the outline plots. Detailed studies in depth of the literary and social significance of the various stories in any one society are notably lacking. It is time more attention was focused on these aspects, and less on the comparative classification of stories, the tracing of the history of their plots, or the enumeration, however impressive in itself, of the quantities of texts that have so far been collected.

## IV

The approaches discussed so far have mainly been those of recent American and Scandinavian scholarship, or the earlier British approach. The emphasis in more recent British work is very different. If the diffusionist and evolutionist schools concentrated on a few limited elements in their studies of African stories, the recent approach in Britain has been to ignore such stories altogether as an independent field of study. The 'structural-functional' approach of Radcliffe-Brown and others, which has until very recently dominated British social anthropology, is interested in local narratives only in so far as they can be seen to have a clear 'social function'.

Various functions have been stated or assumed. Stories, for instance, are told to educate and socialize children, or, by drawing a moral, to warn people not to break the norms of the society. Other narratives—in this connection always persuasively called 'myths'—are 'charters' which serve to uphold the present structure of society in general, and the position of the rulers in particular. Others again are said to fulfil the function of providing a model through which people can verbalize the relationships and constitution of their society. Throughout, it is the utilitarian aspect of oral narratives that is brought to the fore, and little or nothing is said, even in passing, about verbal or artistic aspects. The prime concern is with the functioning of society; the narrations are assumed to be of no serious interest in themselves.

We owe to this school an awareness of the social significance of certain stories. And we are also rightly reminded of a point overlooked by evolutionist and diffusionist writers: that the stories should be seen as part of their own social context and not just as survivals. But for someone also interested in the stories in themselves, particularly in their literary impact, such an approach in practice offers little further insight.

Obviously a literary critic is interested in social function. But this, paradoxically, is not made much clearer for us by the strict functional interpretations adopted by many recent scholars. In such writings we are seldom told much about, say, how widely known certain 'myths' really are, when they are told, how far (if at all) they differ in tone, context, or telling from the more 'fictional' tales, how far people themselves regard stories as educative, what opinions are held by the tellers on the relative importance of the utilitarian purpose, the attractiveness of subject-matter, and skill in delivery, etc.

In fact the functionalists stress the utilitarian aspect so much but, when one comes down to it, with so little detailed evidence that one begins to wonder whether their confident assertions about a given narration's function have in fact much evidence behind them. Doubtless certain of these functions of educating, upholding, mirroring, etc., are fulfilled by African stories at times (just as they are, directly or indirectly, by many other types of literature); but what is needed now is further study of the detailed ways in which these functions in some cases are, and in others presumably are not, fulfilled (with an awareness that there may well be other aspects to stories besides the utilitarian one).

On the one hand, then, this functional approach has not been very illuminating for many aspects of African stories. It can also, on the other, be positively misleading. For one thing it implicitly insinuates the assumption that, to put it crudely, 'primitive peoples' (i.e. Africans) have no idea of the aesthetic, and therefore the only possible explanation of an apparent work of art, like a story, is that it must somehow be *useful*. And, of course, an assumption of this sort usually turns out to be self-verifying when the evidence is collected and analysed according to it. As will be clear from the whole tone of this book, I believe the evidence can be interpreted differently.

Again, the functional approach focuses attention on the stable and stabilizing nature of both the stories and the society in which they occur. This overemphasis on the *status quo* has been a common criticism of the 'structure and function' school, and it is obviously particularly unsuited to an analysis of the living and creative art of the story-teller.

Furthermore, the functionalist publications have tended to perpetuate the kind of misconception discussed earlier—the assumption that it is always possible to make a clear-cut distinction between 'myths' and other tales. These writers tend to assume that any story which looks at all as if it could be interpreted as a 'charter' for society can be labelled a 'myth'; the impression is thereby neatly given to the reader that this story is widely known, deeply believed, held different from other stories, and, perhaps, part of some systematic and coherent mythology. In fact, it is possible in a given case that none of this may be true at all; but just by using the little word 'myth' these connotations can be conveyed without being stated—or, therefore, questioned by either reader or writer.

Let me give an example from my own field-work to illustrate this point. When I first heard a Limba story about how in the old days Kanu (God) lived with mankind but then withdrew in impatience to the sky, I at first automatically classed this in my mind as a 'myth'. It was easy to see its function (explaining and justifying the present state of things) and, like other 'myths', it was presumably well known and taken seriously. This was, it seemed, the Limba myth which could be treated as the basis of their religious philosophy just as similar 'myths' have been elsewhere. It was only after recording several dozen more Limba stories that I realized that this particular story was no different in style, outlook, or occasion of telling from the clearly 'fictional' and light-hearted narratives about, say, a man wooing a wife or a cat plotting to eat a group of rats. Far from being widely known and believed, I only, in fact, ever heard it told by one man, who was using it as a setting (like other stories) for his own idiosyncratic tricks of style and content; other people did not know it or treat it particularly seriously on the occasions they did hear it. The story still, of course, has its own significance. But it certainly has not the clear-cut separate status that I had wrongly assigned to it before I had a more thorough knowledge of Limba oral literature. One wonders how many of the narratives so easily referred to as 'myths' have in fact been misclassified owing to too superficial an assessment of the data.[1]

---

[1] There is some further discussion of the applicability of the term 'myth' to African narratives in Ch. 13, pp. 361 ff.

The same point could also be made about analyses using a similar approach, though without recourse to the favourite term 'myth'. Take, for instance, Beidelman's interpretations of Kaguru stories as Kaguru representations of social reality, a kind of sociological model of their society through the medium of a story.[1] One tale describes how Rabbit (or Hare) tricks Hyena, and is interpreted, at first sight plausibly, as a Kaguru representation of matrilineal relationships. This may be so—but we are in fact given no solid evidence. As far as *plot* goes, much the same story occurs among other African peoples, so that for this interpretation to stand up we need to be given some discussion about, say, the indigenous and conscious interpretation of the story itself, the Kaguru attitude to this story (and stories in general), the contexts in which it is told, and perhaps some assessment of its relations to the general corpus of Kaguru oral literature. No attempt whatsoever is made to provide this information and it is fairly clear that Beidelman felt no need to consider these points. Because of the general attractiveness of the neat structural-functional framework (of which this is just one variety) the limitations and naïvety of this and similar approaches have been overlooked.

The predominance of this approach in British social anthropology is passing. Scholars are now realizing that, quite apart from the actual mistakes disseminated by this school, a concentration on just social functions and alleged contributions to social structure means treating only one limited aspect of oral narratives. Prose narratives (and oral literature generally) are once again becoming a field of interest in their own right. The influence of the older approach still lingers, however. For many years in Britain it was social anthropologists with this interest who appeared to hold the monopoly in the academic assessment of the role of oral narrative in Africa, and, as so often happens, their views are gaining popular acceptance just as they are becoming less influential in professional circles. It is partly to this influence that we owe the proliferation of collections of stories with the emphasis on bare synopsis or the moralizing element, and on references to, rather than full statements of, the 'myths' and 'legends' which stabilize society.

To end this discussion of the various approaches of the past to

---

[1] Beidelman 1961; also a series of other articles on similar lines by the same author.

the study of oral narratives, there is one general point that can be made. This is, that all these approaches seem to have in common an implicit assumption that oral narratives in Africa (and other non-literate cultures) can be treated in a fundamentally different way from the literature of more familiar peoples. The normal questions asked by literary critics in the case of written literature are brushed to one side in favour of pursuing historical reconstructions or assumptions about utility. No evidence is given that such narratives *are* fundamentally different from literary narratives elsewhere—this is just assumed; and the assumption made to look plausible because it is dealing with the literature of unfamiliar cultures. And yet, amazingly, the crucial way in which such narratives in fact really are different—their *oral* quality—is scarcely taken serious account of at all.

In conclusion, it is clear that many of the earlier approaches to the study of oral narrative in Africa have in fact obscured many points of interest. In addition they have popularized various misconceptions about their nature or role. This has been done to such good effect that unproven or totally false speculations have been taken as truisms. There is still too general an acceptance of such questionable concepts as verbal fixity, dominating significance of subject-matter, lack of native imagination or inventiveness, handing down narratives unchanged through the generations, or the basically pragmatic role of African stories. It is because of the wide prevalence of such misleading but often implicit theories that this rather destructive chapter has seemed a necessary prelude to any direct discussion of African narratives.

# 13

## PROSE NARRATIVES II. CONTENT AND FORM

What is known: content and plot; main characters. Types of tales: animal tales; stories about people; 'myths'; 'legends' and historical narratives. What demands further study: occasions; role of narrators; purpose and function; literary conventions; performance; originality and authorship. Conclusion

AGAINST this background of earlier theoretical speculations and misunderstandings, we can now survey the present position in the study of oral prose narration in Africa. What points have been established so far? And what aspects now need further investigation?

I

First, the basic material. Of actual texts, synopses, and translations of African narratives we have a vast amount. Bascom, in his indispensable survey,[1] lists forty-one peoples for whom collections of fifty or more tales with vernacular texts had been published by 1964. He adds a further list of forty-nine groups for which collections of at least fifty tales have appeared in translation (with fewer African texts), and further collections are appearing all the time.[2]

These collections are of very variable quality. It is often not made clear how they were recorded—on tape, from dictation, by

---

[1] Bascom 1964.

[2] The question of the total number of African stories is sometimes canvassed. Numbers like 5,000, 7,000, or (for unrecorded as well as recorded tales) even 200,000 have been mentioned (Herskovits 1960 (1946), pp. 443–4). But this is hardly a fruitful question; it is not even in principle possible to count up items of oral art when it is the actual narration that matters and there are thus an infinite number of ways in which the 'same' plot can be presented and varied to become a 'new' and unique narration. Similarly, those who aim at the complete recording of all the oral literature of a given people—'every little bit of this vernacular' as Mbiti for one hopes (Mbiti 1959, p. 253)—are setting themselves an impossible goal.

the tellers themselves, or even written by hired schoolboys who are often unskilled in the local arts of story-telling and certainly not experienced in the near impossible task of transforming the oral art form into the medium of the written word. The resulting texts are often little more than abstracts or summaries of the plots—a perfectly adequate source when all one wants to consider is the origin of the plot or its relevance for social structure or education, but clearly quite inadequate for analysis in depth. When only translations are given, there are additional difficulties. The problems involved in any translation, let alone from a totally unfamiliar culture, are of course notorious—not that this has deterred some collectors from going through a double process of translation prior to the publication of their collections.[1] But quite apart from this there is the added point that when none of the original texts is provided it is not possible even for someone who knows the language to check the basic trustworthiness of the translation in the most literal terms. It is often quite impossible to assess how close these translations are to the original texts or whether, as perhaps happens rather often, they are only paraphrases or even touched-up and rewritten versions. What is really needed by now is less emphasis on collecting more and more texts and much more on rigorous and explicit standards in recording and translating.

Using these many available texts, however, it has at least been possible for scholars to establish the very great similarities in African stories from all parts of the continent.[2] This includes similarity in plots, in motifs, and to some extent in characters. Only a few instances can be quoted, but these can be followed up in general works on African stories.[3]

As far as the outline of the plot goes, many of the resemblances are striking. Beyond this, however, there are many differences both of detail and of general treatment. Thus one of the most

---

[1] e.g. Herskovits's Dahomean stories which were apparently first translated (during the actual flow of the story) from Fon into French by local interpreters, taken down on typewriters by the Herskovitses, and finally published in English (see Herskovits 1958, p. 6). How much of the indefinable literary qualities of the stories could survive such treatment can be left to the reader to imagine.

[2] And not just from Bantu Africa as sometimes suggested.

[3] e.g. Berry 1961; Lindblom 1928 (see 'comparative notes' in vols. i and ii); Herskovits 1960 (1946) and M. J. and F. S. Herskovits, *Suriname Folk-lore*, New York, 1936; Wright 1960 (a short and specialized but useful article); Werner 1933 (Bantu). Also (unpublished) Mofokeng 1955; Klipple 1938; Clarke 1958.

common plots is the tug of war into which a small animal induces two larger ones to enter in the belief that they are pulling against him. The small animal involved, however, is not everywhere the same. It may be—to mention only a few instances—a hare (e.g. Ila, Shona, Bemba, and many other peoples of Central Africa), a spider (Limba, Temne, and others in parts of West Africa), a mouse ('Tetela in Congo), a tortoise, (Mpongwe and others in West Equatorial Africa and coastal area of West Africa), or, in the related American version, Brer Rabbit. The two large animals who are tricked are most commonly an elephant and a hippopotamus, but a rhinoceros is also sometimes mentioned.[1] Another common plot describes the aggressor out-tricked: an animal tries to kill his rescuer but is outdone by a third character who persuades him to re-enter the trap as a demonstration of the truth of the story, and leaves or kills him there. Among the various characters involved are: for the aggressor—a snake, leopard, or crocodile; for the rescuer (the potential victim)—a child, baboon, gazelle, water antelope, rat, or white man; for the wily character who foils the aggressor—a jackal, hare, pygmy antelope, or spider.[2] Similar points could be made with many other plots, by no means all of them to do with animals. There is the story also familiar from the *Arabian Nights*: three men co-operate to revive the girl they all love, each with magic objects to help them; in the various versions these include, for instance, a casket of dreams, a mirror, or a telescope to see her danger from afar; a magic arrow, a skin, or a hammock to travel instantly to her side; and a snuff-box, switch, or magic medicine to bring her back to life.[3] Again, there are the many tales about the origin of death which centre round the message sent by God endowing mankind with life, the right messenger being superseded or outstripped, and a second messenger bringing the wrong message—that of death. But the actual messengers named, the title of God, and even the exact framework take different forms in different areas.[4] Another common

---

[1] On the distribution of this tale see Herskovits 1960 (1946), p. 448; Mofo-keng 1955, ch. 2.

[2] The actual instances cited are from the Hottentot, Kgatla, Yao, Tetela, Limba, and Ghana—i.e. from South, Central and West Africa respectively. For further instances see Klipple 1938, pp. 178 ff.

[3] On the distribution of this plot see e.g. Werner 1960, p. 249; Berry 1961, p. 10; Klipple 1938, pp. 490 ff.

[4] See, among other sources, H. Abrahamsson, *The Origin of Death: Studies in African Mythology*, Uppsala, 1951, esp. ch. 2; Klipple 1938, pp. 755 ff.

motif is what could be called a build-up story in that the hero, sometimes a young boy, sometimes an animal, gradually acquires more and more valuable objects by, say, trading, exchange, or refusal to fight unless given his wish. Finally he reaches the pinnacle of any man's desires, in some versions followed by the anti-climax of losing the precious object and being back where he started.[1]

Rather than prolonging this list indefinitely, two versions of the 'same' plot may be quoted to illustrate how much they may in fact differ in tone and character even when the subject-matter seems very close. The plot offers explanations for the way birds of prey swoop down and carry off chickens from the mother hen. According to the story, this is in return for a debt the hen owes from the old days. In both cases the version given is chosen for its brevity; many longer stories have been recorded from each society.

First, a version from the Kikuyu of East Africa, recorded by Cagnolo who had spent many years in the area.

## THE VULTURE AND THE HEN

Long ago the hen and the vulture used to live on excellent terms, helping each other at any time they needed a hand to procure their domestic necessities.

One day the hen thought of borrowing a razor from the vulture, to shave the little ones. The shaving was already much overdue, but it couldn't be helped, because she had no razor, and was depending on the kindness of her neighbours. So the hen went to see the vulture and said: 'Dear vulture, I should like to borrow your razor; mine was lost months ago. My little ones are looking very ugly, and also very untidy, with their long unkempt hair overgrown.'

The vulture listened to the hen with great concern and, after a short silence, said: 'Dear hen, I cannot refuse you this favour. To-morrow perhaps I might need your help as well, and we must help each other. However, you must remember one thing. You know what that razor means to me. I have no other income except the rent of that razor; that is to say, that razor is my field, whence I get my daily food. I do not

---

[1] Klipple 1938, pp. 688 ff. Examples and discussion of other variants of the accumulation or *ritornelle* story in Africa are given in A. Werner, 'A Duruma Tale of "The old woman and her pig"', *Bantu Studies* 2, 1923; cf. also Berry 1961, p. 9.

intend to ask you any fee as I do with others; but please be careful to return it to me, as soon as you have finished your shaving.'

'Thank you, brother vulture, I quite understand what you say, and I am very grateful to you. I'll bring it back very soon.'

The hen was very glad of the favour, and as soon as she arrived home, made arrangements to be shaved by another woman. The following morning she also shaved her two little ones, so that the whole family was now shining like the moon. The work over, instead of immediately returning the razor to the owner, she put it in a leather purse, which was hanging in a corner of the hut.

The days passed, and passed away like the water under the bridge, but the hen never thought again of returning the razor to the vulture. She forgot it completely. The vulture grew impatient, and deeply resented in his heart the unkindness, nay, the ingratitude of the hen. Pressed by necessity, he decided to go personally to the hen and demand his razor.

'Oh dear vulture,' said the hen with confusion and great regret, 'forgive me; I am so sorry for this my negligence. I really intended to return your razor very soon, but I put it in my leather bag, and forgot it completely. Let me go and take it; you will have it in half a minute.'

'Yes, I know you are a forgetful creature; but look at the damage you have caused me. You have deprived me of my sustenance for many days. Mind you, if you have lost it, you will pay for it and very dearly', said the vulture. The hen rushed into the hut to fetch the razor. She plunged her hand into the leather bag, but alas! it was empty; there was no razor in it. She was very shocked at the unpleasant discovery. She started searching on the floor to see if by chance it had dropped from the bag, but there was no finding it. She looked under the children's bed, near the fire stones, in the store; but there was no sign of it. Tired and defeated, she came out and, imploring, said: 'O dear friend and master, I can't find it. Have mercy on me! I will search better; I am ready to demolish my hut altogether, and search diligently until I find it and return it to you.'

'I told you to be very careful, and I repeat it again: I want my razor back! But mind, I want the very one I gave you, and no substitute.'

The poor hen spent all the day searching and searching, but nothing came to light. She demolished her hut, and started searching in the roof-grass, among the rubble of the walls, between the poles, in the ashes, and even in the rubbish pit; but nothing was found.

The following day the vulture came to see the results of the searching. He found the hen still scratching the ground among a heap of dry grass and ox dung; but no razor was yet discovered.

'I am very sorry, dear hen,' said the vulture, 'but now I cannot wait any longer without compensation for my razor. For to-day you must give me a chicken. To-morrow I will return and see what has happened in the meantime.'

So the vulture flew away with a chicken gripped within his talons under its breast. The following day he returned to the hen. She was still scratching the ground; but she could not see any razor. Another chicken went with the vulture. And the same happened in the following days until to-day. That is the reason why the hen is always scratching the ground, and the vulture swooping on chickens even in our days. The hen is still searching for the razor, and the vulture compensating himself for its loss.[1]

The second instance is one of the stories I recorded among the Limba of Sierre Leone.[2]

## THE FINCH, THE EAGLE, AND THE HEN

The finch, a small bird, once borrowed money from the eagle's grandfather. He borrowed that money.

Now the eagle—(he died) leaving his children alone. But he left a message with them: 'Your grandfather had money borrowed from him by the father of the finch.'

Since he (i.e. his family) had lent the money, the (young) eagle spent a long time looking for the finch. He looked and looked; but he could not find him.

One day he went and sat down where they pound the rice. He was sitting there. When he saw the hen standing there, eating the rice, he asked her:

'Oh, hen.'

'Yes?'

'What are you doing here?'

'I am getting my food.'

'Do you know whereabouts the finch is? He's the one I'm looking for. He made use of my father's property. I want him to return it. . . .[3] Do you think I will be able to find the finch?'

'Yes, you can find him.'

[1] From C. Cagnolo, 'Kikuyu Tales', *Afr. Studies* 12, 1953, pp. 129–31.

[2] Recorded on tape from the public telling of the story in February 1961 and given here in a fairly close translation. The original text is given in R. Finnegan, *The Limba of Sierra Leone*, D.Phil. thesis, University of Oxford, 1963, iii, pp. 488–9.

[3] The speaker, apparently by mistake, interpolated a few sentences about the hen which should clearly have come later and are omitted. This particular narrator was by no means distinguished as a story-teller.

'Well, how can I find him?'

'When people get up to go and pound the rice, if you go there and you hide you will find the finch there.'[1]

The eagle got there. He went and hid. The finch alighted and began to pick at the ground, searching for his food. The eagle swooped down.

'Ah! you! What a long time I have spent looking for you. Now here you are today. Today you will have to give me back the property your family took.'

'What?' asked the finch. 'Eagle?'

'Yes?'

'Who told you where I was?'

'The hen.'

'It was the hen that told you?'

'Yes.'

'Oh! dear!' (said the finch) 'We have both been having trouble then. I—ha! I have been looking for the hen here but could not find her. And all the time you have been looking for me and could not find me! Since the hen was the reason you found me, that's why I am going to give her to you now.'

(The eagle did not believe the finch.)[2]

'Haven't you seen my house (then)?'

He (still) did not believe.

'Eagle' (said the finch).

'Yes?'

'Come on.'

They went. They went and stood near the wall (where the finch lived).

'Here is where you can tell that my grandfathers owned her (the hen) as a slave. As for the hen-family—just look here at where my children sleep. You can't find any leaves there, can you, only feathers.'[3]

When they got there the eagle went and looked. He saw the hen's feathers. He turned them over—and over—and over. He could only see feathers.

'Yes, finch. You spoke the truth. Well then let there be no quarrel between us (two).'

'I will give you the hen-family, my slaves.'

That is why hens are carried off by eagles. That is the story. It is finished.[4]

---

[1] The finch, like the hen earlier, goes to pick among the grain.

[2] This was clear in the actual narration, though not in the words.

[3] The finch 'proves' that the hen is his property by showing that his nest is lined with hen's feathers for his children to sleep on.

[4] The same general framework is used in several other Limba stories, e.g. two included in Finnegan 1967, pp. 334–6.

The difference between the two stories is more than merely a matter of translator's style. Both tales give an aetiological explanation of the present misfortunes of chickens and trace this back to a debt (or alleged debt) by the hen; but the framework, the detailed course of the plot, even the implied evaluations of the characters are very different. The subject-matter and literary structure of each story can only be fully appreciated (as distinct from appearing as a catalogue item) with a detailed knowledge of the social and literary experience from which it springs. Indeed, the treatment and impact of stories based on the 'same' plot or motif can vary considerably, even in the same society, if told by a different individual or even, in some cases, by the same individual on different occasions.[1] All this, too, is not to mention the aspect of actual performance which, it is worth repeating, cannot come across at all in a written version, but may appear on the actual occasion of telling as the most noticeable distinguishing characteristic of the story.

Even if the great similarity in plots gives a slightly misleading impression of the degree of cultural uniformity actually involved, this information does throw some light of a limited kind on the sorts of plots which have wide popularity and the continually recurring situations which are the subjects of so many African stories throughout the continent.[2]

Characters of African stories also recur throughout the continent. Most familiar of all are the animals, particularly the wily hare, tortoise, spider, and their larger dupes. But there are also many stories about people, ordinary and extraordinary, some about legendary heroes or ancestors, and a few which recount the actions of various supernatural beings. They are also occasionally woven round other personified objects like, say, the parts of the body, vegetables, minerals, the heavenly bodies, or abstractions like hunger, death, or truth. These various characters do not usually appear in strictly separate cycles, but in many cases are depicted as interacting among themselves: thus a story mainly about animals may introduce a human being or even God as one of the

---

[1] See e.g. Finnegan 1967, pp. 93 ff. and 347 ff., for instances of the effects of different narrators and occasions among the Limba; and E. E. Evans-Pritchard, 'Variations in a Zande Folk-tale', *J. Afr. Languages* 3, 1964 for versions of the 'same' story among the Azande.

[2] For further references see p. 336 n. 3. On plots in Bantu stories, see especially Werner 1933.

figures, or a human hero can be shown as succeeding through his magical powers in speaking with and enrolling the help of various animals. The same general plots may be centred round different types of characters in different areas, or even on different occasions in the same society. In Lamba stories, to cite just one instance, 'the exploits of the little-hare and of a curious little human being, Kantanga . . . are very much the same'.[1] In other cases it may be rather ambiguous whether the central figure is really animal or really human, and it may appear in different guises on different occasions. The Kikuyu Wakahare, for instance, appears sometimes as a squirrel, sometimes as a human, the Zande trickster is called 'spider' but envisaged as a man, while the famous Zulu equivalent of Tom Thumb and Jack the Giant Killer rolled into one, *uHlakanyana*, is usually a tiny clever boy, but in other contexts appears as a weasel.[2]

In spite of such overlapping between the appearance of these various characters, it is convenient to discuss the various types of stories by differentiating them roughly in terms of their main characters. We will thus discuss in turn stories based mainly on animal characters, on human characters, and finally on historical and on supernatural beings of one kind or another ('myths'). That it is not possible to regard these general types as clear-cut categories will be clear both from the way the characters overlap and from the general remarks in the previous chapter on the difficulties of producing clear typologies in the case of such flexible and variable material. This indeed is why the material has been presented in a single chapter here rather than as separate chapters under the popularly acceptable headings of 'animal stories', 'myths', 'legends', etc. However, in view of the nature of the sources available and for mere convenience of discussion, we can speak of animal tales, tales about people, and so on, at the same time insisting that in view of the overlapping and impermanence of any given story, these must not be regarded as categories in any generally valid typology of African narratives.

[1] Doke 1934, p. 358.

[2] C. Cagnolo, 'Kikuyu Tales', *Afr. Studies* 11–12, 1952–3; Evans-Pritchard 1967, p. 23 (and cf. A. Kronenberg, 'JoLuo Tales', *Kush* 8, 1960, p. 237, on characters in Nilotic tales); E. J. Krige, *The Social System of the Zulus*, Pietermaritzburg, 1936, p. 346 (cf. Jacottet 1908, p. xxvii).

II

When we consider the many animal tales that have been collected from Africa, the main factor that has struck most observers is the great emphasis on animal tricksters—small, wily, and tricky animals who cheat and outdo the larger and more powerful beasts. They trick them in a pretended tug of war, cheat them in a race, deceive them into killing themselves or their own relations, gobble up their opponents' food in pretended innocence, divert the punishment for their own misdeeds on to innocent parties, and perform a host of other ingenious tricks.

The actual author of these exploits varies in different areas. Among most of the Bantu peoples it is the little hare, an animal that also occurs as a main character in some of the savannah areas of West Africa; as 'Brer Rabbit' he also appears in similar stories in the New World.[1] The spider[2] is the main character in most of the forest regions of West Africa, particularly in the westerly parts including Ghana, Ivory Coast, and Sierra Leone; he also comes into Hausa stories to the north, Luo and Zande tales in Central Africa, and corresponds to 'Annancy' in the West Indies, a name that directly recalls the Ghanaian *Ananse*, the Akan spider. The tortoise predominates in the easterly regions of the west coast, in an area extending at least from the Yoruba of Nigeria across to the Fang and others of West Equatorial Africa. The tortoise also comes into other areas in a lesser way; among the Ila of Zambia, to give one example, the main cycle of tales are about Sulwe, the hare, but there are also a number about Fulwe, the tortoise. There are also a few other favourite trickster characters who occur often enough in stories but without any clear-cut geographical domain: the little antelope, often portrayed as innocently ingenious; the squirrel (e.g. in many Limba, Kikuyu, and Luba stories); the wren (in Luba tales); and a few with more purely local reference: the small weasel who appears among the Zulu and Xhosa, most often apparently personified as a small boy; and the jackal trickster in Hottentot animal stories, as well as in some Zulu, Xhosa, and Sotho tales.[3]

---

[1] On the hare, see L. Frobenius, *Das unbekannte Afrika*, München, 1923, p. 131.

[2] On the distribution of spider stories see, among other accounts, V. Maes, 'De Spin', *Aequatoria* 13, 1950.

[3] On the jackal, see Bleek 1864, part 1; Jacottet 1908, p. xxvii. The jackal may also occur in stories in some northerly areas of Africa, but the older assumptions,

Though all these trickster figures tend to get up to the same kinds of tricks in story after story, they cannot altogether be assimilated to each other. The spider, for instance, though often wily, is also, in some areas at least, depicted as stupid, gluttonous, boastful, and ineffective, not infrequently outdone by his own wife. There are also instances of the same image being applied to the tortoise.[1] On the other hand, the sly effectiveness of the hare is what we notice in most Bantu tales. All these tricksters, however, are adaptable. They are able to turn any situation, old or new, to their advantage. The tortoise, we are told, now aspires to white collar status in Southern Nigeria and attends adult education classes,[2] while the spider *Ananse* referees football matches among the Ashanti in Ghana.[3]

Besides the leading animal figures, there are also many others who come into the tales in secondary roles. Some of the stock characters associated with them are common to many areas: the lion, strong and powerful but not particularly bright; the elephant, heavy, ponderous, and rather slow; the hyena, *the* type of brute force and stupidity, constantly duped by the little quick animals; the leopard, untrustworthy and vicious, often tricked in spite of his cunning; the little antelope, harmless and often clever; the larger deer, stupid and slow—and so on. (Not all these occur in all regions or all stories in exactly the same way.) Surprisingly, other animals—the zebra, buck, or crocodile—seldom occur, or, if they do, tend to come in just as animals and not as the personified characters presented by those already mentioned.[4] One final and rather different animal character that must be mentioned is the mantis in Bushman tales. He is the favourite hero in Bushman narratives, and though he shares some of the qualities sometimes attributed to tricksters (powerful and foolish, mischievous and kind), his supernatural associations and the unusual type of action

which saw this as part of a wider scheme in which the jackal was the typical trickster among the so-called 'Hamites' (supposed to cover Hottentots as well as certain North Africans), are no longer tenable, and the significance of the jackal in the north may have been exaggerated to fit the theory.

[1] e.g. among the Kalabari. See the analysis of this in Horton 1967.

[2] Berry 1961, p. 14.

[3] J. H. Nketia, 'Folklore of Ghana', *The Ghanaian* 1, 1958, p. 21.

[4] This is pointed out by W. James in her unpublished B.Litt. thesis, *Animal Representations and their Social Significance, with Special Reference to Reptiles and Carnivores among Peoples of Eastern Africa*, Oxford, 1964, p. 215.

in these stories set him rather apart from leading animal characters in narratives elsewhere in Africa.

With few exceptions, these animals are portrayed as thinking and acting like human beings, in a human setting. This is sometimes brought out by the terminology, like the personal prefix used in Sotho to turn the ordinary form of, say, lion (*tau*) into a personal form (*motau*—Mr. Lion),[1] or the class of honorific plural in Lamba which makes an ordinary animal term into a personal name—'Mr. Blue-Snake'.[2] In other cases no grammatical change is or needs to be made. The animals act like human characters, experiencing human emotions. And yet the fact that they are also animals is not altogether lost sight of. This can be exploited either through grammatical forms, like the alternation in Zande stories between animal and personal pronouns,[3] or through allusions to the animal's characteristic cry, appearance, or behaviour to add to the wit or incongruity of the presentation. In a Limba tale, for instance, a spider is shown taking off his cap, gown, and trousers in a vain attempt to placate his magic pot; in the story he is unquestionably like a man—albeit an absurdly foolish man—with a house, wife, and human garb, but the fact that he is, nevertheless, a *spider* struggling with all these clothes adds just the extra understated touch in the telling which makes the whole story very funny.

Many of these stories are light-hearted, even satirical, and centre round the tricks and competitions of the hare, spider, or their friends, set in a wide range of adaptable and adapting situations. But there are also more serious themes. One common form is a story ending up with a kind of moral, sometimes in the form of a well-known proverb. The listeners are told that they can learn a lesson from the experiences of the animals in the tale—that, say, one should not be rude to one's mother-in-law, that men's words are more weighty than women's, that strangers should be treated well, that it is ill-advised to oppress the weak, or even that determination sometimes triumphs over virtue. In some places too, Christian morals are specifically introduced.[4] In such narrations the moral element sometimes seems to form the core of the story, so that we could appropriately term it a parable rather than a

---

[1] Smith and Dale ii, 1920, p. 339.
[2] C. M. Doke, 'Lamba Folk Tales Annotated', *Bantu Studies* 13, 1939, p. 95.
[3] Evans-Pritchard 1967, p. 26.
[4] e.g. among the Luba (Stappers 1962, p. 14).

straightforward story. But in other cases, sometimes even those from the same area or teller, the moral seems no more than a kind of afterthought, appended to give the narration a neat ending.

Another very common framework is that in which an explanation is given for some present behaviour seen in the world, or a known characteristic of some animal or bird. For example, to cite a few titles at random from one society (Ila of Zambia), we have stories about how the Ringdove came by its ring, how Ringdove got her name, how Squirrel robbed Coney of his tail, how Squirrel and Jackal became distinct, how Skunk came to be a helper of man, why Duiker has a fine coat and particoloured tail, why Zebra has no horns, why there are cracks in Tortoise's shell—and so on.[1] These aetiological themes are not just confined to animal stories but can occur in all types of African tales. However, they seem to be a particularly popular and fertile theme when the main characters are animals, and some striking animal characteristic, well known to the listeners from their own observation, can be wittily 'explained' in the story. Not all the aetiological tales are equally humorous and light-hearted. A few explain more serious matters: in these cases the animals are often depicted as interacting with humans or with God as well as with other animals; they explain, for instance, the origin of murder, of death, or of chiefship.

An explanatory ending, in fact, can apparently be tacked on to almost any plot as a pleasing framework and conclusion fitting in with current literary conventions—once again, we see that animal trickster stories, aetiological tales, or even 'myths' are not mutually exclusive types but merely favourite themes which may or may not be combined in any one story. An example of the non-essential nature of the aetiological conclusion can be seen from the following Kikuyu tale where the explanation at the end sounds very much like an afterthought.

## THE HYENA, WAKAHARE, AND THE CROW

One day a Hyena went together with Wakahare to collect honey in the forest, where men used to hang their beehives from the trees. Wakahare climbed the tree, extracted big lumps of combs full of honey from a beehive, and when he was satiated, said to the Hyena: 'Open your mouth and I will drop some honey into it.' The Hyena did so and

[1] Smith and Dale ii, 1920, ch. 28.

swallowed the honey with great pleasure several times, until she was also satisfied. Then Wakahare left the tree and returned to the ground. He asked the Hyena: 'How did you enjoy the honey?'

'Very, very much, what bliss, my dear friend.'

'But remember,' said Wakahare, 'this is a kind of sweetness that must not be evacuated from your body.'

'Yes, I think it must be so; but how can one prevent it from going out?'

'I'll tell you what to do. I will stitch your orifice together with your tail and you may be sure that no sweetness will come out.'

'Good, my friend, do it for me, please.' Wakahare fetched a few sharp thorns and stitched the orifice with the tail of the Hyena and went off. After some time the Hyena felt a terrible urge to evacuate. She looked around for help, but nobody was to be found. At last a Jackal happened to pass thereat. 'Oh, dear friend Jackal,' said the Hyena, 'come please, and help me.'

'What can I do for you, dear friend?'

'Please, release a little bit the stitches which are at the neck of my tail. I cannot bear it any longer.'

'Sorry, my friend, I am unable to do that. I know you have diarrhoea habitually, and don't want to be splashed with a discharge of that kind.' And so saying, he went on. After some time a Serval arrived on his way to the forest. The Hyena beseeched him for help.

'Sorry, Mrs. Hyena, you are very prone to discharge violently,' said the Serval, 'I don't want to be buried under your excrements.' He too went his way without looking back. Later on a Hare passed by. The Hyena asked again for help, but to no avail.

'I am very sorry,' the Hare said, 'don't you see how clean I am? I am going to a feast. I don't want to soil my dress and get untidy for your dirty business.' He too went his way leaving the Hyena groaning and tossing on the ground on account of the pain she was suffering. At last, a Crow perched on a tree nearby. Looking down at the Hyena lying still on the grass, he thought she was dead, and began to foretaste a good meal: but as he was planning what to do next, the Hyena opened her eyes and seeing the Crow on the tree, said: 'Oh dear Crow, dear friend of mine, help! help! please.' The Crow left the tree and approached the Hyena. 'What is the matter with you?' he asked.

'Oh please, release a bit the stitches in my tail. I am dying of the urge of my body and I cannot evacuate.'

'You say dying; dying?'

'Yes, help me please.'

'But you see, I am only a bird with no paws. How can I help you with that business?'

'Oh dear, try as much as you can and you will succeed.'

'I doubt very much, and besides that I am very hungry. I have no strength to do any work.'

'O nonsense! My belly is full of meat. You will eat to-day, to-morrow, and the day after to-morrow and be satiated.' On hearing that, the Crow set himself to think and after a little while decided to see what he could do. With his strong bill he succeeded in extracting the first thorn, and truly, two small pieces of meat fell on the ground. The bird devoured them very greedily, and encouraged by the success, began to tackle the job seriously. After great effort he succeeded in extracting the second thorn, but alas! a burst of white excrement gushed forth with such vehemence, that the poor Crow was cast back ten feet and was buried head and all under a heap of very unpleasant matter. The shock was so great, that he remained buried for two days, until a great shower of rain washed the ground, freeing the Crow of the burden. He remained a full day basking in the sun and regaining strength. He was so weak that he could not fly. The Crow was washed by the heavy rain, but his neck remained white. That is the reason why crows to-day have a white collar in their plumage. The Crow very much resented the alteration of his plumage and decided in his heart to take revenge.

One day he heard that the hyenas had arranged for a great dance in a thicket he knew very well. He cleaned himself with great care in the morning dew, put on a beautiful string made of scented roots and proceeded to the meeting place. On his arrival he was greeted by the hyenas and several of them asked him to give them some of those little pieces of meat he wore around his body. They took his ornamental beads to be meat. He refused to give any of the beads away, but rising on his feet with an air of dignity, he said: 'My dear friends, forgive me this time, I cannot give away this kind of meat, which is specially reserved for our kinship, but I promise you a great quantity of good meat and fat if you follow me to the place I am going to show you.'

'Where is it?' they asked very anxiously.

'You see, we birds fly in the air and our deposits of food are not on earth, but on high for safety's sake. Look up at the sky and see how many white heaps of fat we usually store there. That's where you will find meat and fat in great quantity.' The hyenas gazed up to the sky and asked: 'But how can we get there?'

'I will show you. You can reach there very easily. Now, let us make an appointment. The day after to-morrow we will meet here again. Tell your people, old and young, men and women to come here with baskets and bags; there will be meat and fat for all.' On the day appointed the hyenas came in great numbers. I think the whole population was there. The Crow arrived in due time. He started by congratulating the crowd on their punctuality, and with great poise said: 'My dear friends, listen now how we are going to perform the journey to the place of meat and plenty. You must grapple one another by the tail, so as to form a long chain. The first of the chain will hold fast to my tail.'

There was a general bustle among the hyenas, but after a few moments all were in order. At a given sign, the Crow began to fly, lifting the hyenas one by one till they looked like a long black chain waving in the air. After some time he asked: 'Is there anybody still touching ground?' The hyenas answered: 'No, we are all in the air.' He flew and flew up into the sky for a long time and asked again: 'What do you see on earth? Do you see the trees, the huts, the rivers?'

'We see nothing but darkness', they answered. He flew again for another while and then said to the hyenas nearby: 'Now, release for a while, that I may readjust my ornaments.'

'But dear friend, how can we do it? We will surely fall down and die.'

'I can't help it. If you don't release me, I will let go my tail, I am sure the feathers will grow again.'

'Oh dear friend, don't, please don't for your mother's sake, we would die, all of us.' The Crow would not listen at all. He thought the time had come for his revenge. With a sharp jerk he turned to the right. The feathers of his tail tore out, and with them the long chain of hyenas. They fell heavily on the ground and died. One of them escaped with a broken leg. She was pregnant and so saved the kinship from total destruction. That is the reason why hyenas these days limp when they walk.[1]

One of the obvious points in these stories is just the sheer entertainment afforded by the description of the amusing antics of various animals, and they are often told to audiences of children. The fact that most of the animals portrayed are well known to the audience—their appearance, their behaviour, their calls, so often amusingly imitated by the narrator—adds definite wit and significance that is lost when rendered for readers unfamiliar with this background. The gentle, shy demeanour of the gazelle, the ponderous tread of an elephant, the chameleon's protuberant eyes, or the spider's long-legged steps are all effectively conveyed and provide a vivid and often humorous picture for those present. It is true that the imagery associated with the animal figures in tales hardly matches that implied in other contexts (praise songs, for instance).[2] But on a straightforward and humorous level the

---

[1] C. Cagnolo, 'Kikuyu Tales', *Afr. Studies* 11, 1952, pp. 128–9. Even clearer instances of the sometimes peripheral nature of aetiological conclusions is provided by Limba stories where, even in the 'same' plot, an explanation sometimes appears, sometimes not.

[2] As pointed out by James, op. cit., p. 216.

animals that appear in the stories can be appreciated and enjoyed for their amusing antics or their vivid portrayal by the narrator.

But there is more to be said than this. On another level, what is often involved in the animal stories is a comment, even a satire, on human society and behaviour. In a sense, when the narrators speak of the actions and characters of animals they are also representing human faults and virtues, somewhat removed and detached from reality through being presented in the guise of animals, but nevertheless with an indirect relation to observed human action. As Smith writes of the Ila, in words that can be applied far more widely:

> In sketching these animals, not Sulwe and Fulwe [Hare and Tortoise] only, but all the animals in these tales, the Ba-ila are sketching themselves. The virtues they esteem, the vices they condemn, the follies they ridicule—all are here in the animals. It is a picture of Ba-ila drawn by Ba-ila, albeit unconsciously. . . .[1]

There is no need to try to explain the occurrence of animal stories by invoking out-dated theories about totemism or the unfounded notion that 'primitive man' could somehow not clearly distinguish between himself and animals. Nor need we refer to literalistic interpretations of the stories, and assume that in each case they present clear-cut moral messages, like the protest of weakness against strength, or a direct one-to-one reflection of human or local society, or specific references to definite individuals —though there are occasional instances of the last category.[2] Rather we can see these animal stories as a medium through which, in a subtle and complex way, the social and literary experience of narrators and listeners can be presented. The foibles and weaknesses, virtues and strength, ridiculous and appealing qualities known to all those present are touched on, indirectly, in the telling of stories and are what make them meaningful and effective in the actual narration. In contexts in which literary expression is neither veiled by being expressed through the written word nor (usually) voiced by narrators removed from the close-knit village group, comment on human and social affairs can be expressed less rawly, less directly by being enmasked in animal characters.

---

[1] Smith and Dale, ii, 1920, p. 341.

[2] e.g. in Acholi and Lango tales where the story is ostensibly about, say, the hare, or 'a certain man', and set in the past, but is in fact designed to ridicule someone who is present (Okot 1963, pp. 394–5).

Some of the plots and explanations in the stories may appear puerile and naïve—and so no doubt they are when stripped of the social understanding and dramatic narration that give them meaning. But the background to, say, some little story about a competition between two animals for chiefship, or a race between two birds to the colonial secretariat for the prize of local government office, renders it meaningful to an audience fully aware of the lengths to which political rivalry and ambition can lead men. If we cannot say that such events are represented *directly* in the stories, we can at least see how the tales strike a responsive chord in their audience. In a way common to many forms of literature, but doubly removed from reality in being set among animals, the animal tales reflect, mould, and interpret the social and literary experience of which they form part.

There is a further point about some of the animal stories. This is the effective use that can be made of the image of the trickster (usually but not invariably an animal). This figure can be adapted to express the idea of opposition to the normal world or of the distortion of accepted human and social values. This applies particularly when the trickster figure is made not only wily but also in some way inordinate and outrageous—gluttonous, uninhibited, stupid, unscrupulous, constantly overreaching himself. Here, the trickster is being presented as a kind of mirror-image of respectable human society, reflecting the opposite of the normally approved or expected character and behaviour.[1] Again, the trickster can be used to represent traits or personalities which people both recognize and fear. This aspect has been particularly well described for Ikaki, the tortoise trickster figure among the Kalabari. He appears in both masquerade and story as

the amoral, psychopathic confidence trickster—the type who accepts society only in order to prey upon it . . . the intelligent plausible psychopath, that universal threat to the fabric of the community.[2]

More than this. Not only does the trickster figure stand for what is feared, his representation in literature also helps to deal with these fears. In the first place, he is represented in animal guise which allows narrator and listener to stand back, as it were, and contemplate the type in tranquillity. Further, by portraying him

[1] A point brought out in Evans-Pritchard's account of the Zande trickster (Evans-Pritchard 1967, pp. 28–30).　　　[2] Horton 1967, p. 237.

in stories, people can show the trickster as himself outwitted and overreached, often enough by his own wife. Again, by exaggerating and caricaturing him to the point of absurdity, they in a sense 'tame' him. In these various ways

the disturbing real-life experience of plausible psychopaths is controlled, confined, and cut down to size. People laugh from out of their depths at the ravening forest beast, because for once they have got him behind bars.[1]

These animal tales have been the most popular and well-known type of African narrative among many European collectors and readers. The stories are often amusing in themselves, they fitted in with certain preconceptions about, say, totemism or the supposed 'childlike mentality' of Africans, and they provided pleasing parallels to the Uncle Remus stories of America which they had ultimately fathered.[2] The result is that many more animal stories have been published than those about other characters, and the impression has often been given that animal tales form the main type of prose narrative in Africa or even of oral literature altogether. This in fact is far from being the case. The proportion of animal stories seems to have been much exaggerated, and in some areas at least stories mainly about people or supernatural beings seem to be preferred or to be more elaborate, lengthy, or serious. It is not easy to work out the numerical and qualitative relationship between animal and other stories in different areas. One or two suggestions have been made along these lines—postulating, for example, that animal tales are the most popular form in Central and East Africa, but not at all conspicuous in parts of South Africa.[3] But the evidence is hard to assess. Quite apart from the overlapping between animal and other tales, one does not usually know what principles of selection have been adopted in any given collection of tales: even commentators working in the same areas at the same date may differ widely about the relative significance of different types of tales. Perhaps all that can be concluded for the moment at least is that, for all their popularity in Europe, animal

---

[1] Ibid., p. 239.

[2] Or so it is usually assumed; it is not in fact certain that all the Uncle Remus tales came directly from Africa via the slaves.

[3] See e.g. Jacottet's remarks on this (1908, p. xxvi). The once mooted idea (of Bleek's) that animal tales did not occur among the Bantu is now recognized to be untenable.

tales are not the only or even the most important type of African oral narratives.

Stories about people are, in some areas at least, probably the most important group of narratives. These stories are of many kinds. Some are concerned with marvellous events and personages, some exhibit marked Arabic influence (particularly in the long-established Islamic areas), some deal with everyday events in village life, some with a combination of all these. Like animal stories, some stories contain an aetiological aspect or a moralizing conclusion, others centre round a series of tricks or a competition. There is a definite overlapping in subject and structure, both between various categories of stories about people and, as already remarked, between all these stories and animal tales as a whole.

Less need be said about narratives set in the human world than those about animals. This is not because they are less important, but because, being less well known, they have been less theorized over and confused by Western scholars. It is obvious to most readers that these narratives can be treated as a form of literature comparable to the more familiar types of written fiction rather than analysed as some strange product of a totemistic or as yet childish mentality. After some brief comments on the range of these stories, the narratives can be left to speak for themselves as self-evidently a form of literature.

Many of these stories are about everyday events and characters. They concern such well-known problems as the relations of two co-wives and how these affect their children or their husband; wooing a wife; jealousy between two equals or between chief and subject; the extremes of friendship and affection shown by two companions; or a series of clever tricks by some outrageous but in essence recognizably human character. But even more often, it seems, the story is set back a little further from reality by the introduction of some marvellous element in setting, event, or character. The man who goes to woo a woman, for instance, may have to undergo a series of far-fetched or even magical tests before he can win her—perhaps sowing and harvesting some crop in a single day, or guessing his beloved's closely guarded and amazing secret, or avoiding death only through the magical help of animals or spirits. Similarly the cunning of the central character may rest on enchanted powers and lead the listener into some far-away world of fantasy. The imagination of both teller and audience can rove freely and the exploits of the hero become the more romantic and exciting for being enacted against this imaginary background.

Other stories could be called thrillers. The hero struggles against ogres and monsters who are trying to devour him. These fearsome ogres are stock characters in many stories in Bantu Africa. There are the one-legged, two-mouthed cannibalistic ogres of East African tales, for instance, the *Di-kishi* cannibal of Angolan stories (sometimes appearing as a named 'hero', Dikithi[1]) with his one eye and a single leg made of beeswax, or the half-man, half-animal monsters of some tales in Malawi or the Congo.[2] We also meet various powerful monsters, giants, and spirits in West African stories, many of them man-eating but apparently less often physically deformed; a number of them are clearly closely related either to animals[3] or to the djinns and genies familiar from Islamic sources. In all these cases, the basically non-human and asocial character of these figures comes through clearly either by reason of their deformities or through their association with non-human creatures.

Even without the appearance of exotic characters and settings, an element of fantasy is often apparent. In one Sierra Leonean story, to give just one instance, a pregnant woman's belly grew 'as big as Sierra Leone and Great Britain put together'.[4] All over the continent kings are represented as possessing exaggerated wealth and power, heroes are revived from death, girls are wooed by hundreds and thousands of suitors, young men win whole kingdoms for themselves by force of arms or politic love, or hunters kill and capture fabulous beasts who bring them all their desires. In the areas strongly influenced by Islam, particularly on the East

---

[1] T. J. Larson, 'Epic Tales of the Mbukushu', *Afr. Studies* 22, 1963.

[2] It has been suggested by F. Posselt ('Mashona Folk-lore', *Nada* 5, 1927, p. 36) that the emphasis on ogres and cannibals is rare among Central African groups compared to the warlike South African peoples (Zulu, Sotho, etc.). However, even if this is so with the Shona it certainly does not apply to other Central African peoples: we hear, for instance, of ogres in Lamba stories, cannibalistic 'goblins' in Nyanja, Thonga ogre stories, etc. On the various related Bantu terms for these ogres in stories see A. Werner's review of Lindblom's *Kamba Folklore* in *BSOS* 5, 1928/30, p. 433, and Werner 1933, pp. 174 ff.

[3] Cf. the half-man, half-animal figure that occurs in many West African stories discussed in G. Calame-Griaule and Z. Ligers, 'L'homme-hyène dans la tradition soudanaise', *L'Homme* 1. 2, 1961.

[4] Innes 1964, p. 18.

Coast, we also hear of sultans with wealthy and glittering entourages and of the miraculous assistance given to a hero by genies.

The actual way in which the story-teller's imagination can combine fantastic elements with his knowledge of the real varies not only from society to society but also from narrator to narrator. Each has his own contribution to make of wit, satire, elegance, or moralizing. It is too simple to pick on just one element, like 'realism and lack of sentimentality' or 'placid serenity', and extrapolate this to apply to African narratives in general.[1] Some are realistic; some very definitely are not—unless by 'realism' one merely means that a narrator builds on his own experience of reality to add point and vividness to his literary inspiration, in which case assertions about 'realism' become meaningless. Similarly some stories may give an impression of serenity; others most definitely do not. It is better to say that the opportunities for various kinds of literary effect are exploited differently in different contexts, and that even when some of the themes are the same, the actual tone and impact of the story itself may vary in different areas and according to different narrations.

Two brief stories can illustrate this point. In both there is an element of fantasy and a concentration on human action—but the stories are very different in tone.

## ONE CANNOT HELP AN UNLUCKY MAN
### (Hausa)

There was a certain Man, a Pauper, he had nothing but husks for himself and his Wife to eat. There was another Man who had many Wives and Slaves and Children, and the two Men had farms close together.

One day a Very-Rich-Man who was richer than either came, and was going to pass by on the road. He had put on a ragged coat and torn trousers, and a holey cap, and the People did not know that he was rich, they thought that he was a Beggar. Now when he had come up close, he said to the Rich-Man 'Hail to you in your work', but when he had said 'Hail', the Rich-Man said 'What do you mean by speaking to me, you may be a Leper for all we know!' So he went on, and came to the Poor-Man's farm, and said 'Hail to you in your work.' And the

---

[1] As e.g. Johnston 1966, p. xli; Dadie 1964, p. 207.

Poor-Man replied 'Um hum',[1] and said to his Wife 'Quick, mix some husks and water, and give him to drink.' So she took it to him, and knelt,[2] and said 'See, here is some of that which we have to drink.' So he said 'Good, thanks be to God', and he put out his lips as if he were going to drink, but he did not really do so, he gave it back to her, and said 'I thank you.'

So he went home and said 'Now, that Man who was kind to me I must reward.' So he had a calabash washed well with white earth,[3] and filled up to the top with dollars, and a new mat[4] was brought to close it. Then the Very-Rich-Man sent his Daughter, who carried the calabash, in front, and when they had arrived at the edge of the bush[5] he said 'Do you see that crowd of People over there working?' And she replied 'Yes, I see them.' He said 'Good, now do you see one Man over there working with his Wife?' And she replied 'Yes.' 'Good', he said, 'to him must you take this calabash.' Then she said 'Very well', and she passed on, and came to where the Poor-Man was, and said 'Hail', and continued 'I have been sent to you, see this calabash, I was told to bring it to you.'

Now the Poor-Man did not open it to see what was inside, his poverty prevented him,[6] and he said 'Take it to Malam Abba, and tell him to take as much flour as he wants from it, and to give us the rest.' But when it had been taken to Malam Abba, he saw the dollars inside, and he put them into his pockets, and brought guinea-corn flour and pressed it down in the calabash, and said 'Carry it to him, I have taken some.' And the Poor-Man [when he saw that there was some flour left] said 'Good, thanks be to God, pour it into our calabash,[7] and depart, I thank you.'

Now the Very-Rich-Man had been watching from a distance, and [when he saw what had happened] he was overcome with rage, and said 'Truly if you put an unlucky Man into a jar of oil he would emerge quite dry.[8] I wanted him to have some luck, but God has made him thus.'[9]

[1] The correct reply, the intonation making it a sound of pleasure and not merely a rude grunt.

[2] A woman always kneels when handing food to a man.

[3] This can be used like whitewash, and the calabashes are coated outside. Here a mark of favour.

[4] Little round grass mats which act as covers or lids.

[5] The farms are the only clearings in many parts where the population is not too plentiful.

[6] He was so hungry that he would have been unable to resist eating the whole, for he thought it contained food.

[7] So that she could take her own away again.

[8] A proverb, meaning that whatever you do for a man who is fated to be unlucky he will not profit by it.

[9] Tremearne 1913, pp. 242–3.

## WACICI AND HER FRIENDS
(Kikuyu)

Wacici was a very beautiful girl, admired by many people for her elegance and charm. Her girl friends were very jealous of her and always ill-treated her.

One day her friends were going to visit a *mwehani*[1] to have their teeth filed, spaced, and beautified as girls used to do. Wacici joined them. He was a man of great fame who was highly reputed for his skill. They all had their teeth well done and the girls looked very attractive and charming, but no one looked as pretty as Wacici. The expert praised Wacici's teeth and beauty and added that she had natural beauty and charm in everything. This annoyed her girl friends very much.

On their way home they stopped and talked to young men from time to time. They laughed as they spoke to the boys, 'Aha-aaa! Uuuuuu! Eia!' This is the most romantic laughter which was artificially employed by Gikuyu girls specially when speaking to boys. 'Aha-aaa! Uuuuuu! Eia!' They continued to laugh repeatedly as they spoke to young men and the boys would admire their teeth and their charm and sense of humour.

'You have been to the tooth expert, have you not?' the boys inquired.

'Aha-aaa! Uuuuuu! Eia!' The girls continued to laugh.

'Wacici is looking most attractive,' one boy remarked kindly, 'she is really gorgeous and wonderful.' And all the boys agreed and repeated this remark to Wacici. This infuriated the girls, who were very jealous of Wacici's beauty and many of them wanted her out of their company.

The girls continued their journey towards their homes and on the way they all conspired to bury Wacici alive in a porcupine hole which was somewhere in the forest near the road.

It was suggested that they should all enter the forest and gather some firewood to take back home as it was the custom that girls should return to their homes with some firewood after a day's outing. They all agreed to do this and Wacici particularly was very eager to take home some firewood. She was not only a beauty but also a very good girl who upheld the respect expected of Gikuyu girls, and her mother loved her dearly.

When the girls reached the porcupine hole in the forest, they grabbed Wacici and pushed her down the hole and quickly buried her alive. She was taken by surprise and she did not have a chance to scream as she thought that they were playing with her. They did not beat her or do anything harmful to her body. They sealed the hole very carefully on top, quickly left the forest and returned to their homes; they did not speak to anybody about Wacici.

[1] An expert in beautifying teeth.

That evening Wacici did not return home. Her parents waited and waited. When she did not come they went about asking Wacici's friends if they had been with her that day or whether they had seen her anywhere. They all denied having been with her or seeing her anywhere that day. All this time Wacici was crying in the bottom of the porcupine hole in the forest while her parents were wandering all over the villages looking for her.

'Where has she gone to?' her mother asked. 'Could a young man have eloped with her?' Her disappearance caused so much concern that her father had to go to consult witch-doctors and seers and ask what had become of his daughter.

Next morning Wacici's father met somebody who had seen his daughter in company of the other village girls going to the tooth expert. He reported this to his wife and without wasting any time he went to see the dentist in order to verify this information. The dentist confirmed that Wacici and her friends had been to see him and that he had done their teeth on the day she was reported missing. Also on his way home Wacici's father met some young men who had seen and spoken to his daughter with the other village girls. He returned home and reported to his wife and the family all the information he had gathered.

Wacici's brother, who knew most of the girls who were said to have been seen with his sister, had known for some time that most of the girls had been jealous, and hated Wacici. He suspected foul play.

He left home quickly and tracked the route through which the girls had returned from the expert. He knew that if they gathered some firewood, they must have entered the forest on the way. He went into the forest to check if his sister had been killed there.

When he came near the porcupine hole he noticed that it was freshly covered and that there were many footmarks which suggested that many people had been there. He examined them very carefully. He also saw a bundle of firewood which had been abandoned. This time Wacici could hear some noise and footsteps above her. She was crying and singing and calling her brother's name.

| | |
|---|---|
| *Cinji! Cinj!* | Cinji! Cinji! |
| *Nondakwirire-i! Cinji,* | I already told you, Cinji, |
| *Nothiganagwo-i! Cinji;* | I have been hated and spied on, Cinji; |
| *Cinji! Cinji!* | Cinji! Cinji! |

When he listened carefully he heard the voice of Wacici clearly and he had no doubt that she had been buried there by her girl friends who were jealous of her beauty.

He called out, 'Wacici-i! Wacici!' Wacici heard him and she felt so happy that he had come to liberate her. She answered quickly, 'Yuu-uuu!'

At once her brother started digging and removing the soil. He dug and dug until he came to where she was sitting and crying. He carried her to the surface and examined her: she was in good shape except that she had weakened because of hunger and fear. He took her home and her parents were so happy to see her again. She was given a good bath and a lamb was slaughtered to offer thanksgiving to Mwene-Nyaga who had preserved her life.

Wacici reported what her friends had done to her. The following morning the evil girls were arrested and sent to a trial before the elders in a tribunal court and their fathers were heavily fined. They had to pay many heads of cattle and many rams and bulls were slaughtered and a lot of beer had to be brewed for the judges and the elders to eat and drink. The bad girls were exposed and they were all shunned in society and were unable to get husbands for a long time. Wacici was widely respected and she got married and became a mother of many children and lived happily ever after.[1]

The characters in these tales are sometimes given names. Some societies have their own favourite named heroes, often of a trickster type, for instance the Lamba Kantanga (a little mischievous fellow), the Zanda Ture or Tule (an amusing rogue), the Zulu Uthlakanyana when appearing as a human (a deceitful and cunning little dwarf), the Fon Yo (a glutton with various supernatural powers), and so on. As with animal tales it would be misleading to assume that all these stories about named characters fall into clear-cut cycles in an attempt to give an over-all and in principle unitary history of the hero. In some cases at least there seems to be no attempt at consistency or chronology, the stories are told as short independent narrations on different occasions, and their inclusion into one united narrative may represent the outlook of the Western systematizing scholar rather than the intentions of the narrators.[2] Other characters in African stories are named but totally independent in that they occur in only isolated stories. The names are merely taken, it seems, from everyday names in current use and given to a character for ease of reference. Or, alternatively, the name itself has meaning and contributes to the effect of the story, though without necessarily carrying on into other similar stories, like the Zande 'Man-killer' and 'One-leg', or the Limba brothers 'Daring' and 'Fearful'.

---

[1] N. Njururi, *Agikuyu Folk Tales*, London, 1966, pp. 86–9.
[2] e.g. Callaway's presentation of the Zulu tales about Uthlakanyana (Callaway 1868).

In very many cases, however, the characters are not given names. They appear just as 'a certain woman', 'a chief', 'a small boy', 'a hunter', 'two twins', and so on. Each literary culture has its own stock figures whose characteristics are immediately brought into the listeners' minds by their mere mention. Thus the Ila are particularly fond of stories about fools,[1] the Kamba especially like tales about those 'chosen from the extreme bracket of society' like the one-eyed, sickly, orphan, widow, very poor or despised,[2] and the Hausa, among others, make great play with the theme of the unfaithful wife. Some stock characters have wide application and appear in various contexts in the stories of many African peoples. We often hear of the actions of a jealous husband, a boaster, a skilful hunter, an absurdly stupid person, a despised youngster making good, a wise old woman, an oppressive ruler, twins, good and bad daughters, or young lovers. The basic human dilemmas implied by so many of these figures have clearly brought inspiration to hundreds of story-tellers practising their otherwise diverse skills throughout the continent.

When we come to consider the types of African stories usually termed 'myths' we run into some difficulty. This is partly because 'mythology' is sometimes loosely used to cover all kinds of prose narratives, including ordinary animal tales and stories about people.[3] More important, however, is the point that if we accept either the popular or the scholarly distinction of 'myth' from 'fictional' narrative, this does not seem to fit much of the African material. As it is not possible to touch on every single case it may be helpful to make some rather general comments about the problem of delimiting and discussing African 'myths'. This will involve recapitulating several points touched on earlier.

One recent account of what is meant by 'myth' is that put forward by Bascom, based among other things on his assessment of how this term has been used by students of oral literature. This provides a convenient starting-point. He writes:

*Myths are prose narratives which, in the society in which they are told are considered to be truthful accounts of what happened in the remote past.*

---

[1] See Smith and Dale ii, 1920, pp. 404 ff.     [2] Mbiti 1959, p. 257.
[3] As in e.g. A. Werner's *African Mythology* which includes chapters on 'Hare and Jackal Stories', 'Tortoise Stories,' etc., or K. Arnott's *African Myths and Legends* (London, 1962) in which the largest single group consists of animal stories.

They are accepted on faith; they are taught to be believed; and they can be cited as authority in answer to ignorance, doubt, or disbelief. Myths are the embodiment of dogma; they are usually sacred; and they are often associated with theology and ritual. Their main characters are . . . animals, deities, or culture heroes, whose actions are set in an earlier world, when the earth was different from what it is today, or in another world such as the sky or underworld. . . .[1]

This account fits well with the everyday connotations of the term 'myth' in terms of the content, the authoritative nature of these narratives, the way in which they are believed, and their special context and characters, often consciously distinguished from other less serious narratives.

When this sense of the term is taken, it seems evident that myths in the strict sense are by no means common in African oral literature. This is in spite of the narratives presented as myths in many popular collections.[2] It is true that many of these have an aetiological element, refer to supernatural beings, or are concerned with events set in some remote time in the past. But they do not necessarily also possess the other attributes of 'myths'—their authoritative nature and the way in which they are accepted as serious and truthful accounts. It is seldom, also, that we seem to find narratives depicting the activities of deities or other supernatural beings alone or even as the central subject:[3] much more frequently the interest seems to be centred on human or animal characters with supernatural beings only appearing in secondary roles. Radin's remark in 1952 that cosmological myths are rare in Africa compared to their significance among, say, the Polynesians or American Indians[4] has not been invalidated by evidence produced since then. And one could go further and say that myths in any strict sense do not seem, on the evidence we have, to be a characteristic African form at all.

It is worth pointing out the actual classifications made in several African societies between different types of narrative. Though these may not amount to a distinctive category of myth, they do

[1] Bascom 1965b, p. 4. The whole of this passage (and the article as a whole) is worth consulting.

[2] e.g. H. U. Beier, *The Origin of Life and Death: African Creation Myths*, London, 1966. It is highly doubtful whether these stories were really locally regarded as 'myths' in any full sense of the term.

[3] There are some exceptions to this in West Africa, where religious ideas sometimes find expression in a belief in pantheons of deities.

[4] Radin 1952, p. 2.

provide a somewhat analogous though less marked contrast between more fictional tales and those said in some sense to be 'true'. This can be illustrated from three or four of the better-studied African cultures.

First, the Fon of Dahomey. They generally distinguish in terminology between *hwenoho* and *heho*, a distinction only at first sight corresponding to 'myth' as against 'fiction'. *Hwenoho* is literally 'time-old-story' and includes, to use Herskovits's terms, 'myths' (stories of the deities and the peopling of the earth), 'clan myth-chronicles' (telling of the origin and adventures of the powerful families), and 'verse-sequences' (sung by professional poets to memorize genealogies and events incorporated into ritual or law).[1] These narratives are not presented with the same art and dramatization as more fictional tales, and tend to be told by specialists (priests, diviners, etc.) or within a small family group, particularly a family council. The elements of entertainment and of conscious artistry seem relatively unimportant. The second group of Fon narratives, the *heho*, covers more light-hearted stories. There are tales about various supernatural, human, and animal characters: about hunters, women, twins, orphans, or children-born-to-die; about the trickster-deity Legba or the mythical Yo with his gross appetites; and various kinds of explanatory and moralizing tales. All these latter stories are normally told at night. Some of them also occur in the context of divination[2] where they may appear on the surface to be obviously 'myths'—yet they are locally classified as *heho*. In fact, as Herskovits points out,[3] the classifications are not absolutely clear-cut ones; there is overlap between them in terms of symbolic characterization, plot, motif, and function.

In these and some other West African cases the local classifications bear some resemblance to the general distinction between 'folktale' (or ordinary fictional narrative) on the one hand and a blend of myth-legend on the other.[4] In other cases, however, either no such distinction is made at all, or else what there is makes rather different, sometimes more complicated groupings. The Kimbundu classifications, for example, divide narratives into three

---

[1] Herskovits 1958, p. 17.
[2] The Fa or Ifa divination system described in Ch. 7.
[3] Op. cit., pp. 25–6.
[4] For some further examples see Bascom 1965*b*.

main groups (excluding the closely related proverbs, *jisabu*). There are, first, the stories regarded as fictitious, *misoso*, arising from imagination. 'Their object', writes Chatelain, 'is less to instruct than to entertain, and to satisfy the aspirations of the mind for liberty from the chains of space and time, and from the laws of matter.'[1] This class includes animal tales and stories about the marvellous and supernatural. Secondly there are the *maka*, reputedly true stories or anecdotes. These are instructive as well as entertaining, and are socially didactic, concerned with how to live and act. Finally there are the 'historical narratives'—*malunda* or *misendu*—the chronicles of the tribe and nation transmitted by headmen or elders. They are considered to be state secrets and 'plebeians get only a few scraps from the sacred treasure of the ruling class'.[1]

Another local classification which does not exactly fit the standard folktale/myth/legend typology is that of the Dogon. Their oral literature is divided into several categories.[2] There is, first, *so nanay*, 'true saying'. This includes the genealogies, back to the supposed time when all Dogon descended from the three sons of a common ancestor. It also includes accounts—how far appearing in narrative sequence it is not clear—about the deeds of the first ancestor and his descendants, and about the ancestors of each clan and the founding of the various contemporary villages. Then there are the *tanye* or *tanye nanay* (literally impossible or unbelievable but true). These are the 'true' fantastic tales which are believed by the teller to have happened; they took place, he holds, in the ancient times when things could happen which would now be impossible. These include what Lifchitz calls 'myths'—i.e. tales about, say, the origin of death or stories explaining the origin of various animal characteristics and so on. She goes on to point out, however, that it is only when told by elders or adult men, usually to educate the young, that these tales can really be called myths or 'true'; if they are told by the young among themselves they become just ordinary stories (*elume*). 'Untrue' fantastic tales are termed *tanye nanay la*, i.e. incredible things which are not true. These are tales about events which not only could not but in fact, according even to the teller, never did take place, and take

[1] Chatelain 1894, p. 21.
[2] This follows Lifchitz's account in *Africa* 13, 1940. See also Calame-Griaule 1965, pp. 447 ff.

the form of fantastic stories often ending up with a dilemma. Distinct from all these are the stories (*elme* or *elume*) told to entertain children, often by the children themselves. These include stories about animals and can, at will, always be transformed into aetiological narratives by changing just one or two phrases and adding some such conclusion as 'and since then people have done that'. These tales are not usually told by adults but by young people while in the fields or during their time as herders.

Other instances of complex indigenous classifications could also be cited. All of them make it difficult to draw any clear distinction between a 'myth' and a 'folktale' if this is to have any basis in local terminology.

There are also many cases in which no distinctions at all in the terminology seem normally to be made between different types of narrative. The West African Limba, for instance, mostly use the single term *mbɔrɔ* to cover all kinds of narratives, the Yao of Malawi similarly use *ndano* of tales in general,[1] the Azande have no distinct term for 'myth',[2] while for the Hunde of the eastern Congo *migani* equally covers 'contes, fables, légendes'.[3]

What light does this discussion of terminology throw on the occurrence or nature of 'myths' in African oral literature? Amid the variety of classifications a few general points emerge.

First there is the frequent absence of any specific term which would exactly translate our term 'myth'. It is true that the absence of the word need not imply the non-occurrence of the thing. But it is certainly suggestive if the local terminology either makes no distinction at all within narratives or a distinction on different lines from those of the foreign theorist.

Then there are the cases where there are local distinctions analogous to the familiar one between folktale and myth (or perhaps more often between folktale and myth-legend). Here it often appears that the crucial differentiating factors are not so much the content or the characters of the narratives but the context in which they are told. Thus among the Fon and the Ashanti the serious and 'true' narratives, the 'myths', are told within circumscribed groups or are limited to a select group of elders who guard them with care. They are used in serious discussion during the day, as

---

[1] Macdonald i, 1882, p. 48.    [2] Evans-Pritchard 1967, pp. 31–2.
[3] L. Viaene, 'Coup d'œil sur la littérature orale des Bahunde (Kivu)', *Kongo-Overzee* 21, 1955, p. 212.

distinct from the entertaining stories of the evenings. Certain of the same factors recur in the otherwise rather different cases of the Kimbundu and the Dogon. Among the former the *malunda* (historical narratives that might by more superficial commentators have been classed as 'myths') are secret, known only to the politically influential; and the Dogon *tanye nanay* are regarded as 'myths' when told in one type of context and merely as stories in another.

It emerges that in trying to distinguish different categories of African oral narrations, in particular potential 'myths', it may be more fruitful to look not primarily at subject-matter but at context. Questions about the circumstances in which the narrations take place, their purpose and tone, the type of narrator and audience, the publicity or secrecy of the event, and, finally, even the style of narration may be more crucial than questions about content and characters. Unfortunately it is precisely about these former factors that we are often least well informed: subject-matter is so much more easily observed than the more significant and more subtle aspects of narrations. We know, for instance, of the many aetiological tales or of those including references to certain supernatural beings or events. But without also being informed about the context of narration, there is no justification for glibly assigning them to the class of 'myths'. Indeed, all we do know about the contextual aspect leads to the impression that these are probably ordinary stories, not authoritative myths. The point is that we cannot decide by subject alone, we *must* know about context.

A further point that stands out is that with the probable exception of certain West African narratives, religious beliefs seem often not to be regularly enshrined in narrative sequence at all. This emerges partly from the local terminologies which, in East, South, and Central Africa, seldom have a word to cover the *literary* formulation of these beliefs. The published narratives apparently relating to religious phenomena seem (in the cases where they are not just ordinary stories) to be elicited narratives: it is not clear that they would have been expressed in narrative and literary form were it not for the request of the collector. If, however, we knew more about the contexts and circumstances of narration in general, this assessment might in fact turn out to be mistaken. But it is noticeable that it is particularly among those collectors who have had the closest knowledge of the peoples they are writing about that we find a telling absence of any reference to or inclusion of religious narratives, or even an explicit denial that these play any significant role at all in the local oral literature.[1]

It is probably possible to find some exceptions to this general lack of literary expression of religious ideas in much of Africa. The Bushmen may perhaps provide one instance of this, and the Pygmies or some of the Nilotic or West African peoples may provide others. It is possible that other exceptions may also emerge, particularly when more is known of the contexts in which religious beliefs are expressed. But at the moment the general impression remains of the lack of formulated religious narratives among most African peoples. Herskovits summed this up well in 1946 (though, because of his preconceptions, it led him to the different conclusion that the commentators had just inexplicably failed to record the religious narratives that he presumed must have existed). He observed:

Except for West Africa, narrative myth sequences appear only rarely in the literature. . . . From the point of view of the student who approaches mythology as a literary phenomenon, what is lacking is the presentation of the narrative sequences, as told by natives, of events in the supernatural world that are believed to have brought about the situations described. . . .[2]

Publications since the time of his remark give no cause to revise that general statement.

This lengthy discussion has been necessary because of the way it is presumed that myths *must* exist and play a part in African oral literature, and the consequent inclusion in many collections of stories that are claimed to be myths. However, with a few exceptions there is an absence of any solid evidence for myth as a developed literary form in most areas of Africa. It is possible that further research, particularly into the local classifications and the contextual background of oral narratives, may reverse this conclusion. But from what has been published to date it seems clear that myth in the full sense of the term has not developed as a typical art form in African oral literature.

This discussion leads us on naturally to the question of legends and historical narratives generally in African oral literature. The

[1] e.g. Lindblom and Mbiti (Kamba), Doke (Lamba), Junod (Thonga and Ronga), Cagnolo (Kikuyu), Chatelain (Kimbundu), Theal (Xhosa), Jacottet (Sotho).    [2] Herskovits 1960 (1946), pp. 447–8.

two terms are really synonymous in their denotation, although 'legends' seems to have become the commoner term when describing *oral* historical narratives or, sometimes, those in whose truth the commentator himself has little faith. This general class of narratives covers those which are regarded locally as true, particularly by the narrator himself and his immediate audience, but differ from 'myths' in being set in a much less remote period when the world was much as it is today. They depict the deeds of human rather than supernatural heroes and deal with, or allude to, events such as migrations, wars, or the establishment of ruling dynasties.[1]

In discussing this group of narrations, some of the same points should be made as were made earlier about myths. The local classifications, for one thing, do not always coincide with our analytical distinction between historical and fictional narratives. Again, the degree of 'belief' in a particular narrative is one of the hardest of things to assess. Even in a familiar society this is notoriously difficult—but it is even more difficult in unfamiliar cultures; it is made more difficult still in that investigators have taken very little interest in this question.[2] It is clear that the recorded words by themselves or the mere description of the deeds of various human heroes often give us no inkling about the authority or lack of authority locally attached to these descriptions. Questions about the context, circumstances, purpose, and personnel involved, all of which could throw more light on the problem of credence, are usually all ignored. Finally, one must repeat the point already made that well-known and agreed beliefs need not necessarily find their expression in narrative or literary form at all. Genealogies, origins, lines of succession, the famous deeds of past rulers—all these can be known and recognized in a society without necessarily being found in any literary genre. Or, if they do find

---

[1] See the definition of 'legend' in Bascom 1965*b*, pp. 4–5, from which the above account is largely drawn. My discussion here is not concerned with the large question of the historical accuracy of legends and oral narratives in general and thus leaves aside the much discussed problem of the dependability of oral traditions for historical research (on which see e.g. Vansina 1965 and references given there); I might add, however, that in view of the inherent variability of oral expression and the significance of the literary aspect, I am rather doubtful how far we can regard oral literary forms as providing much evidence for actual events in earlier periods.

[2] There is a good discussion of this in Evans-Pritchard 1967, pp. 24 ff. Cf. also Lindblom's comment on the difficulty of deciding whether Kamba explanatory tales are serious or humorous (Lindblom ii, 1935, p. iii).

literary expression, this may take the common African form of panegyric poetry rather than prose narrative.

It has been necessary to sound this note of caution because of the facile assumptions on which so many collections and references in this field are based. We are not infrequently given examples of 'legends' in published collections without any evidence about whether the narratives are regarded as true in any sense.[1] Sometimes even the minimum formal requirements for classifying a tale as a 'legend' are lacking.[2] Again, it is too often assumed that any knowledge of the past must always find expression in literary form. The result is that the content of 'oral traditions' is constantly referred to, without evidence, as being expressed in sustained literary form, or such traditions are elicited and recorded by the historian or anthropologist in narrative form without any consideration for whether this is an indigenous type of formulation, and, if so, in what contexts and forms it spontaneously appears. We are, in short, so often given either just the narrative with no reference to its context, or else just a reference to the context and content without any indication of how far this knowledge is crystallized in narrative form, that one is sometimes tempted to wonder whether historical narrative is in fact anything like as important as is usually assumed as a form of oral literature in the non-Islamic areas of Africa.

This said, we can go on to consider the real instances of legends and historical narratives (or, at least, the clear elements of this form that appear in association with other literary genres). There seems generally to be far more literary interest in historical narrative—in the deeds of historical heroes in the not so remote past—than in myths (in the sense of the actions of deities in the furthest past or of cosmological speculations).

---

[1] e.g. K. Arnott, op. cit., 1962; Werner 1933; J. Maes, 'Mythes et légendes sur l'allume-feu', *Africa* 9, 1936 (Congo); Vanneste 1949 (Alur); A. Werner, 'Two Galla Legends', *Man* 13, 1913; A. de Clercq, 'Quelques légendes des Bena Kanioka', *Anthropos* 4, 1909, and 'Légendes des Mongwandi', *Revue congolaise* 2, 1912; D. St. John-Parsons, *Legends of Northern Ghana*, London, 1958; A. Terrisse, *Contes et légendes du Sénégal*, Paris, 1963.

[2] e.g. C. M. Turnbull's collection entitled 'Legends of the BaMbuti' (*JRAI* 89, 1959) in which, even on his own account, the great majority are ordinary imaginative stories about people, animals, spirits, and the various tricks used among them. The same applies to M. I. Ogumefu's *Yoruba Legends*, London, 1929, the 'legends of the tortoise' in Werner 1933, and many other similar references.

It is particularly in the areas deeply influenced by Arabic cultural traditions that historical narrative seems to emerge most clearly as a sharply differentiated and distinctive art form, sometimes even referred to by a term derived from the Arabic.[1] But in other areas too more serious narrations concerned with historical events may be distinguished as a separate literary form.

Thus we have the Yoruba *itọn* (or *itan*) which refers mainly to historical narratives and seems to include both creation stories (which are sometimes classed as 'myths') and conquest legends about how Oduduwa, the legendary ancestor of the Yoruba, and his descendants spread out through the various contemporary kingdoms, towns, and lineages of the Yoruba.[2] These histories, it appears, were told among those most closely concerned—the people of the particular town or lineage—and were not presented in as formalized or detailed a form as the corresponding praise poems.[3] But they do seem to have had a fairly clear literary framework, which is exploited by the fashion for published Yoruba histories of towns in written form.

Strong historical traditions which are expressed in narrative form are also of marked importance among many of the interlacustrine Bantu kingdoms of East Africa. Again, this tradition has flowered recently with many versions of such historical chronicles now appearing in vernacular written forms.[4]

The narratives of the Congolese Nkundo about the life and exploits of their national hero, Lianja, are remarkable for their length and detail.[5] In fact, the sustained forms in which these Nkundo narrations have been published probably give a misleading impression: collectors have pieced together many different tales to make up one written 'epic' account, and it is highly doubtful

[1] e.g. the *habaru* and *gisa* forms of the North Cameroons Fulani (Mohamadou 1963, p. 71).

[2] See e.g. P. C. Lloyd, 'Yoruba Myths: a Sociologist's Interpretation', *Odù* 2, 1955 (mainly a discussion of what would normally be classed as legends); H. U. Beier, 'The Historical and Psychological Significance of Yoruba Myths', *Odù* 1, 1955; J. Wyndham, *Myths of Ifè*, London, 1921; S. Johnson, *The History of the Yorubas*, London, 1921, chs. 1, 2, and *passim*.

[3] Lloyd, op. cit.

[4] e.g. Kagwa 1934*a* and the chronicles associated with various kingdoms and places published in several issues of the *Uganda Journal* and elsewhere.

[5] Among the large literature on various aspects of this 'epic' see e.g. Boelaert 1949 and 1957; de Rop 1964; and for discussion of a written version based on it A. de Rop, 'L'épopée des Nkundo: l'original et la copie', *Kongo-Overzee* 24, 1958. See also discussion in Note to Ch. 4, pp. 109 f. above.

whether in fact these tales were really narrated and conceived as part of one vast design. The degree of belief involved is also not very clear. Still, there are indications that these narrations were fairly frequent and that the occasions on which they were told were dramatic ones, the main narrator being helped by a chorus. The narrative relates the deeds of Lianja's parents, his mother's pregnancy, and the birth of the hero and his sister Nsongo, Lianja's battles with his father's murderer, his wanderings in search of a place for his people and his settlement of them there (a section very subject to variation and endless, often fantastic elaboration), and, finally, his ascent into the sky. A brief extract can illustrate the type of narration involved:

Un jour, au temps de Wai, sa femme, Bolúká devient enceinte . . . Et voilà que la grossesse de Bolúká dépasse le terme: accoucher, elle ne le peut; grossir, elle ne le fait; elle reste comme avant. Les gens ne font que se moquer d'elle.

Un jour Bolúká prend des calebasses et va puiser de l'eau au ruisseau. Pendant qu'elle y va elle ne cesse de pleurer:

> Depuis que Wai est parti,   ma
> que fait cette grossesse,   ma
> qui n'avance pas.   ma

Et pendant qu'elle puise comme ça de l'eau au ruisseau elle entend comme si un homme bougeait dans les herbes. Elle s'effraie et dit: 'Qui est là?' Elle voit une vieille femme. La vieille dit: 'Ne fuis pas. Car je viens chez toi parce que tu pleures sur ta grossesse et que tu n'accouches pas. Viens que je te touche au ventre.' Bolúká s'approche d'elle; la femme touche son ventre et un œuf est là, comme un œuf de perroquet. La vieille dit: 'Bolúká, regarde, ta grossesse c'était cet œuf. Donne-le moi, que je le garde pour toi, et demain matin apporte-moi à manger.' Bolúká lui donne l'œuf.

Le lendemain Bolúká prépare des vivres, les prend et vient à la place convenue: elle voit la vieille arriver avec un très bel enfant. Elle dit: 'Bolúká, voici ton enfant.' Bolúká le prend et lui donne le sein. La vieille dit: 'Donne-moi l'enfant, cherche ton manioc et pars.' Quand la mère a sorti le manioc de l'eau, elle dit: 'Donne-moi l'enfant.' La vieille: 'Non, non, l'enfant doit rester; toi, retourne et viens encore ici demain avec vivres.'

Bolúká retourne, prépare des vivres et les porte à l'enfant et à la vieille, là-bas au ruisseau. L'enfant qui n'était qu'un nourrisson hier est devenu un grand garçon.[1]

---

[1] Boelaert 1949, pp. 9–10.

Finally, one must mention the clear historical interest that has evidently characterized many of the legends and narratives of kingdoms of the Western Sudan. Here there is a tradition of Arabic culture and of written historical chronicles in either Arabic or local languages—a tradition which has affected oral literary forms.[1]

The examples given so far have mainly been drawn from the powerful kingdoms of traditional Africa. This is no coincidence. It is evident that it is in these kingdoms in particular that there are manifest political advantages in propagating certain historical interpretations of the past whether in the form of 'myths' or of 'legends'. Narratives purporting to recount, for instance, how the ancestors of the present ruling houses first came to the area as saviours, or first settlers, or even victorious conquerors (all common themes) provide a justification for the continued position and power of these houses in the present. The 'mythical charter' thus given by the stories can be an important support for the existing distribution of political power, and it is not surprising that in these conditions there is a marked emphasis on history.[2] (However, even here, panegyric poetry seems often in fact to have surpassed prose history in both literary specialism and political propaganda.)[3]

In the uncentralized societies of Africa, even if historical narratives are less conspicuous they certainly exist. Even in egalitarian communities it is common for various families and villages to have stories about their origins and ancestors, and sometimes these are expressed in narrative form. Among the Lugbara of Uganda, for instance, historical narratives (termed 'myths' by Middleton) justify not the position of ruling houses but present-day social relationships between families and groups.[4] Sometimes such

---

[1] e.g. to cite just a few instances, M. Delafosse, *Traditions historiques et légendaires du Soudan occidental*, Paris, 1913 (Bambara and Arabic); A. Wade, 'Chronique de Wâlo sénégalais', *Bull. IFAN* (B) 26, 1964 (Wolof); R. M. East, *Stories of Old Adamawa*, Lagos, 1935 (Adamawa Fulani); G. Adam, *Légendes historiques du pays de Nioro*, Paris, 1940; E. J. Arnett, 'A Hausa Chronicle', *J. Afr. Soc.* 9, 1909/10; H. Sölken, 'Die Geschichte von Kabi nach Imam Umaru', *Mitt. Inst. Orientforsch.* 7. 1, 1959/60; 9. 1, 1963. For various translations or paraphrases of Arabic chronicles see e.g. O. Houdas and M. Delafosse, *Tarikh el-fettach, par Mahmoûd Kâti*, Paris, 1913 (on Songhai empire); M. Delafosse and H. Gaden, *Chroniques du Foûta sénégalais; traduites de deux manuscrits inédits . . .*, Paris, 1913; E. J. Arnett, *The Rise of the Sokoto Fulani*, Kano, 1922.

[2] As pointed out e.g. by Whiteley 1964, p. 7; see also the references given in Vansina 1965, pp. 155 ff. and biblio.

[3] See Ch. 5 *passim* and Whiteley, loc. cit.

[4] J. Middleton, 'Some Social Aspects of Lugbara Myth', *Africa* 24, 1954.

historical tales are told not so much for their sanctioning effect as for their sheer entertainment value.

All in all there certainly are instances of historical narratives which play a more significant part in African literature than do the 'myths' we explored earlier. But when we look closely at the evidence we have to admit the surprising fact that it hardly sustains the generally accepted view of the great importance of this form as a specialized literary type in non-Islamic Africa. In many cases these narratives appear only as elements in other narrations, or they appear as elicited or pieced-together recordings by foreign collectors rather than as spontaneous art forms. Altogether much more research needs to be done on the indigenous contexts, tone, and classifications of 'historical narratives' before we can make assertions about them.

### III

So far we have been considering the conclusions which, with all their problems and uncertainties, we can still make from the many published collections of African narratives—about their distribution, subject-matter, and, to some extent, literary types. This final section will, in contrast, be devoted to a brief consideration of questions which so far have been hardly explored in published sources.

The first point is an obvious one. In the case of *oral* literature the actual occasions, performers, and purpose of the narrations are obviously of vital importance. As far as the occasions go, we do know a certain amount. It has been made clear in many publications that a very common context for telling stories is in the evening when the day's work is over. In some cases, this general pattern is even expressed as a definite rule. Some imagined sanction is suggested to frighten those tempted to break it—like the Zulu or Transvaal Ndebele threat that anyone who tells stories in the day-time will grow horns, or the parallel assertion among the Kamba that their cattle would perish if tales were told in the day.[1] In other cases the limitation to the evening hours seems to be made merely from convenience, not compulsion. In certain circumstances stories are also told during the day—for instance, when

---

[1] How seriously these statements are taken, at least by adults, is not at all clear, however.

people have to spend long hours on long-drawn-out but not very exacting tasks like herding, mending fishing-nets, or guarding crops from birds and animals.

The normal pattern seems to be for a number of relatively short, self-contained stories to be told during an evening story-telling session. But there are also occasional instances of serial stories. We hear of Mende 'endless stories'[1] or the Kalabari practice of carrying on with the 'same' story—albeit one without a very tight plot or over-all view—night after night, often stopping at an exciting point.[2]

Occasionally we hear of story-telling sessions of a highly specialized kind like the Tuareg evening parties, presided over by some woman famous for her wit, in which story-telling, music, and cultivated conversation all play their part in creating popular and highly valued occasions.[3] Most are less formal, however. They are very frequently started off by the asking of riddles, usually by children. As the evening wears on these are followed by stories delivered with more art and, relatively, more seriousness. Finally people lose interest or are too sleepy to continue. However, not very many detailed accounts have been produced about these and other occasions for story-telling.

The stories are told according to the local conventions about the suitable personnel and order—sometimes by just a few outstanding narrators, sometimes according to a rotation round each participant in turn, sometimes by whoever has the story 'thrown on to him' by the last teller. 'Myths' and 'legends' are more often told during the day, often in the course of solemn discussions or gatherings about serious matters. But in these cases in particular, details about such occasions are usually lacking. For all types of narrative, in fact, further investigation of their contexts is needed.

The position of the story-teller himself is central to any discussion of the context or purpose of the various narrations. But here very little is said by collectors—even less than about the occasions on which they are told. Most editors, indeed, do not even include the names of those who told them the stories, far less give details about their background or position in the local community.[4]

---

[1] Innes 1964, pp. 16–17.

[2] R. Horton, personal communication.

[3] Chadwicks iii, 1940, p. 666.

[4] Among the few exceptions to this one can mention Chatelain 1894, Steere 1906, Equilbecq 1913–16, Hulstaert 1965, Dijkmans 1965, Finnegan 1967.

The degree of specialism conventionally expected of story-tellers is often unclear. In some societies, we are told, there are at least a few 'professional' story-tellers who travel from one village to another, and, presumably, live on their art: this has been asserted of, among others, the Temne, Hausa, and Yoruba of West Africa, Yao of East Africa, and the Bulu, Rwanda, and possibly the Pygmies of Central and West Equatorial Africa.[1] It might perhaps be questioned how far all these men were really professionals in the sense of gaining their livelihood purely from literary activity or, even so, whether this referred merely to the telling of prose stories. Often the references are no more than brief assertions in passing.

What is certain, however, is that story-telling is usually practised by non-professionals. Leading story-tellers are recognized as possessing a certain degree of specialist skill, but this is a spare-time skill only. In most instances there is no evidence that any material reward accrues to the story-teller, however great his expertise. Though some individuals are clearly regarded as more expert than others, story-telling typically tends to be a popular rather than a specialist art. All, it appears, are potentially expert in story-telling and are, with some limitations, prepared to take part in the evening occasions when stories are being told and exchanged in social gatherings. There is thus no African parallel to the specialist privileged class of narrators to be found, say, in Polynesia.[2]

The limitations on this general mastery of the art of story-telling arise from local conventions about the age and sex of the narrators. In some societies, it appears, these are quite free; in others there is a definite emphasis on one or another category as being the most suitable one for a story-teller. In some areas it is the women, often the old women, who tend to be the most gifted, even when the stories themselves are universally known.[3] Elsewhere

---

[1] See, respectively, Cronise and Ward 1903, p. 8 (Temne); Johnston 1966, p. xxx, and S. Leith-Ross, *African Women*, London, 1939, p. 86 (Hausa); Ellis 1894, p. 243 (Yoruba and Ewe); Whiteley 1964, p. 8 (Yao); A. N. Krug, 'Bulu Tales', *JAF* 62, 1949, p. 350; E. Hurel, *La Poésie chez les primitifs ou contes, fables, récits et proverbes du Ruanda*, Brussels, 1922, p. 1; Trilles 1932, p. 235 (Pygmies); cf. also the mention of an 'official story-teller' to the king among the Luba, according to A. C. L. Donohugh and P. Berry, 'A Luba Tribe in Katanga; Customs and Folklore', *Africa* 5, 1932, p. 180.

[2] A point made in Radin 1952, p. 14.

[3] This is a common southern African pattern, e.g. among the Thonga, Ronga, Zulu, and Xhosa; it is also mentioned for the Fjort and, in the case of certain types of tales at least, for the Cameroons Fulani.

it is men who tend to be the more expert,[1] and this applies particularly to the more serious types of narration (myths and legends).[2] In other cases again, certain stories (perhaps particularly animal stories) are felt to be the preserve of children and to be most suitably told by and to them even though adults know them and sometimes join in.[3] Tales told by and for children can scarcely be judged on a par with those by adults, and the particular preoccupations of certain narrations might well be elucidated if we knew whether, say, they were typically narrated by women.[4]

The same point arises from the question of the audiences for whom these stories are intended. In some cases at least it is clear that certain categories of stories are designed primarily for children and are told to them either by other children or by the old women.[5] But in other instances either this is not known or the collector has not thought it worth while to describe the audience. Such topics, which could be crucial for an assessment of the social and literary significance of the texts, are most often left to the reader's uninformed imagination.

This leads directly to the question of the functions and purpose of stories and of the various types of narrations. Since it was argued earlier that under the influence of functionalist anthropology,[6] too much attention has been paid to this question, it might seem contradictory to include it here in a discussion of topics which need more investigation. But the earlier assertions about utilitarian function often depended on very doubtful assumptions. While it is true that the moral, sanctioning, and justifying functions do sometimes form one aspect of the stories which we might otherwise have missed, many questions remain. In studying the oral literature of any particular people, we want to know, for instance, about the views of the people themselves (or, sometimes more significantly, about the views of different groups among them) concerning the purpose and functions of their narrations; about local classifications of different types of narrations and whether these have any relevance for native assessments of their aims and

---

[1] e.g. Limba, Hausa, Fang, Pygmies.

[2] Cf. also the special case of stories introduced into the Yoruba Ifa divination process (Ch. 7) which are delivered by fully professional diviners (male).

[3] e.g. Ibo, Dogon, Galla.

[4] See the treatment of this in M. D. de B. Kilson, 'Social Relationships in Mende *dɔmɛisia*', *Sierra Leone Studies* 15, 1961.

[5] See the instances cited above.     [6] See Ch. 12 above, pp. 330 ff.

nature; about how far individuals, or people in general, are prepared to verbalize their attitude to their stories; about the consistency or otherwise of their stated views (as well as that of the
actual narrations, audiences, and contexts involved); and about
the relative weighting they would give, perhaps varying in different
contexts or at different periods, to the various elements involved
such as entertainment, imagination, education, practice in public
speaking, recording, humour, elegance, ridicule, obscenity, moralizing, etc.[1] Of course, even then we need to remember that, as in the
case of written literature, there can be no final definition of the
purpose and use of oral literature.

Amid all the theorizing about the possible functions of stories
there is one point which, it seems, is too often overlooked. This
is the likelihood that within a culture stories are likely to have
many functions. They will probably vary with the content and
tone—compare, for instance, the three different Kikuyu stories
quoted in this chapter.[2] Even more important are the details of
the occasion on which a story is told—including the audience, the
narrator's state of mind, and recent events in the locality. Again,
intentions affect the possible functions of stories. We could illustrate this with the way in which some Christians now try to turn
stories in the Congo into Christian allegories,[3] or the political
purposes to which origin stories have recently been put in Gabon[4]
or Western Nigeria. This point about varying functions is an
obvious one, but it has often been neglected. It is only too tempting
to pick on just one aspect or one transient function and try to
extrapolate it to apply to all stories on all occasions.

The idea that African stories are above all designed to convey
morals has caught the imagination not only of functionalist
anthropologists but also of some of the *Négritude* writers.[5] This
assumption is made so often that it is worth challenging it in
detail. Certainly some stories do end with a moral or a proverb
(though in some cases this does not seem an integral part of the

---

[1] For useful general discussions of various possible functions of African
stories see Bascom 1965a; Fisher 1963; E. W. Smith, 'The Function of Folktales', *Afr. Affairs* 39, 1940.

[2] Pp. 338–40, 347–50, 358–60.    [3] Stappers 1962, p. 14.

[4] Fernandez 1962.

[5] e.g. Thiam, 'Des contes et des fables en Afrique noire', *Présence afr.* 4, 1948;
B. Dadié, 'Le rôle de la légende dans la culture populaire des noirs d'Afrique',
ibid. 14/15, 1957; Colin 1957 (*Présence afr.* publication); E. A. Adewa, 'Qualities
of African Folklore', *Nigeria* 15, 1938.

tale). Also stories are sometimes told to educate or admonish children, and this class of tales may even have a special local term.[1] But there is no evidence at all to suggest that this is the only or the primary aim of the stories—and plenty of evidence that many African tales contain neither direct nor indirect moralizing. This single Hausa story is merely one of innumerable examples of this. Here a realistic appraisal of the ways of the world outshadows, even ridicules, any attempt to moralize.

## FALSEHOOD IS MORE PROFITABLE THAN TRUTH
### (Hausa)

This is about certain Men, the King of Falsehood and the King of Truth,[2] who started off on a journey together, and the King of Lies said to the King of Truth that he [the latter] should get food for them on the first day. They went on, and slept in a town, but they did not get anything to eat, and next morning when they had started again on the road, the King of Truth said to the King of Lies 'In the town where we shall sleep to-night you must get our food', and the King of Lies said 'Agreed.'

They went on, and came to a large city, and lo, the Mother of the King of this city had just died, and the whole city was mourning, and saying 'The Mother of the King of this city has died.' Then the King of Lies said 'What is making you cry?' And they replied 'The King's Mother is dead.' Then he said 'You go and tell the King that his Mother shall arise.' [So they went and told the King, and] he said 'Where are these Strangers?' And the People replied 'See them here.' So they were taken to a large house, and it was given to them to stay in.

In the evening, the King of Lies went and caught a Wasp, the kind of Insect which makes a noise like '*Kurururu*', and he came back, and put it in a small tin, and said 'Let them go and show him the grave.' When he had arrived, he examined the grave, and then he said 'Let everyone go away.' No sooner had they gone, than he opened the mouth of the grave slightly, he brought the Wasp and put it in, and then closed the mouth as before. Then he sent for the King, and said that he was to come and put his ear to the grave—meanwhile this Insect was buzzing—and when the King of the city had come, the King of Lies said 'Do you hear your Mother talking?' Then the King arose; he chose a Horse and

[1] e.g. the Ila *kashimi* (byword) stories which, unlike other Ila stories, have a definite didactic aim (Smith and Dale ii, 1920, p. 343).

[2] These titles do not refer to the powers of good and evil, much less to God and Satan. King or chief is merely a title, and corresponds somewhat to our captain.

gave it to the King of Lies; he brought Women and gave them to him; and the whole city began to rejoice because the King's Mother was going to rise again.

Then the King of Lies asked the King of the city if it was true that his Father was dead also, and the King replied 'Yes, he is dead.' So the King of Lies said 'Well, your Father is holding your Mother down in the grave; they are quarrelling', and he continued 'Your Father, if he comes out, will take away the chieftainship from you', and he said that his Father would also kill him. When the King had told the Townspeople this, they piled up stones on the grave,[1] and the King said 'Here, King of Lies, go away; I give you these horses', and he continued that so far as his Mother was concerned, he did not want her to appear either.

Certainly falsehood is more profitable than truth in this world.[2]

Other aspects which could be further explored are the various literary conventions in the narrations of particular cultures. By this I mean not so much the larger questions like plot or character, though these too deserve more study, but points like phraseology, stock treatment of certain minor episodes, favourite allusions, and the kind of openings and conclusions that are found satisfying or attractive in a particular culture.

The type of language used often seems to be simple and straightforward. This is, however, at times rendered less prosaic by various devices, including a more frequent use of ideophones, dramatic delivery and dialogues, and the interruption of the prose exposition by songs. The language of the stories shows little of the allusive and obscure quality of some African poetry (except in the interpolated songs). But on this whole subject we have so far merely impressions; much further detailed investigation of the language of narratives *as actually delivered* is still required.[3]

About opening and closing formulas we do know a great deal. In various forms these are common in all areas of Africa (though it is not always clear how far they are obligatory for *all* tellers rather than idiosyncratic to particular informants): they occur too frequently to need detailed references.[4] Thus among the Kamba,

---

[1] So as to keep the father in.　　　　[2] Tremearne 1913, pp. 204–6.

[3] There is a good description of style in Mende story-telling in Innes 1964; see also A. M. Jones and H. Carter, 'The Style of a Tonga Historical Narrative', *Afr. Language Studies* 8, 1967.

[4] Possibly they are not so frequent in southern Africa, but this impression may be due to lack of interest by local collectors or because I have missed this point in the sources.

tellers end their stories with various stylized forms, usually a
wish for narrator and audience to the former's advantage: 'May
you become rich in vermin in your provision-shed, but I in cows
in my cattle-kraal', 'May your cattle eat earth and mud, but mine
the good grass', or, finally, 'You'd better swing with the tail of
a panther while I swing with that of a sheep'—in other words the
teller is to be better off than his listeners (a sheep's tail is fat and
edible) and the audience had better learn to tell stories themselves.[1]
Other closing formulas include the Nigerian Bura 'Do not take
my life, take the life of a crocodile' (notorious for its long life), the
Swahili 'If this is good, its goodness belongs to us all, and if it is
bad, its badness belongs to that one alone who made this story',
the Angolan Kimbundu 'I have told my little story, whether
good or bad', the Hausa 'Off with the rat's head', or the Akan
'This my story, which I have related, if it be sweet, (or) if it be
not sweet, take some elsewhere, and let some come back to
me'.[2] In these closing formulas the narrator hands over, as it
were, to the audience, as well as making it clear that his story is
concluded.

Conversely the opening formulas serve to rouse the interest of
the audience, sometimes eliciting a formal response from them
as well as setting the mood for the start of the narration. Among
the Fjort of West Equatorial Africa the narrator opens with 'Let
us tell another story; let us be off!'; the narrator repeats 'Let us be
off': the audience replies 'Pull away!'; and the narrator can then
embark on the story itself.[3] Similarly, among the West African
Ewe, where a narrator is usually accompanied by a drum, a few
beats are first played to call attention and then the narrator announces his subject: 'My story is of so-and-so'; the audience
replies 'We hear' or 'We take it up' and the recital begins.[4] Many
other formal introductory phrases could be mentioned: the Hausa
'A story, a story. Let it go, let it come', or 'See her (the spider),
see her there' with the reply 'Let her come, and let us hear', the
Central African Nilyamba 'A story. How does it go?', or the
famous Akan 'We do not really mean, we do not really mean [that

---

[1] Lindblom i, 1928, p. xi; Mbiti 1959, p. 255.

[2] A. D. Helser, *African Stories*, New York, 1930, p. 11; Steere 1906, p. 137;
Chatelain 1894, pp. 21, 51, 63; Rattray i, 1913, pp. 48, 66, etc. (and cf. the long
closing Hausa form given in Tremearne 1913, pp. 11–12); Rattray 1930, p. 3, etc.

[3] Dennett 1898, p. 25.

[4] Ellis 1890, p. 269.

what we are going to say is true]'.[1] All such phrases serve to involve the audience directly in the narration and to mark the formal opening or close of the story.

There are also other less obvious phrases which are worth study. These are, so to speak, the internal formulas by which the story is begun and ended. Thus all Limba stories tend to open (after the introductory formulas) with a phrase setting them firmly in the fairly remote past (rather like our 'Once upon a time')— 'A woman once came out (on the earth)', 'A spider once got up and . . .', 'A chief once married a wife . . .', and so on. A Kamba tale often opens with the more dramatic 'How did it happen . . .',[2] the Kimbundu with the generalizing 'I often tell of . . .',[3] while the Luba employ what is perhaps a favourite device for bringing the protagonists directly and vividly on to the stage by an opening like 'That which did—leopard and bushbuck' (or whoever the main actors are).[4] The stock endings, in both phraseology and situation, are also interesting. There is the common Hausa conclusion 'they remained'; the Limba return home, marriage, or formal reporting to some authority of the adventures undergone by the hero; or the frequent conclusion in Ila fool stories about how the events have now become a byword, as 'And to this day it is put on record. When a person looks for a thing he has got, they say: "You are like yon man who looked for the axe that was on his shoulder".'[5] These may seem very trivial points, but in fact the study of them, in the context of a large collection of narratives from one area, can throw light both on the conventional elements involved—the phraseology and presentation thought suitable—and also on the attitude of the narrator himself to the story he is telling.

On a slightly higher level, in studies of stories the literary conventions peculiar to a culture about the treatment of certain motifs and situations could often be more emphasized. Thus when one sees a relatively large selection of Kamba stories, it emerges that one of the stock climaxes is for the monster, about to die, to tell his conqueror to cut off his little finger; when this is done, all the people and the cattle devoured in the course of the story come to life again.[6] Similarly, in Zulu stories a stock way of killing an

---

[1] Rattray 1913, loc. cit., and Tremearne 1913, p. 11; F. Johnson, 'Kiniramba Folk Tales', *Bantu Studies* 5, 1931, p. 340, etc.; Rattray 1930, pp. 49, 53, etc.
[2] Lindblom i, 1928, p. x.          [3] Chatelain 1894, pp. 21, 43, 53, etc.
[4] W. F. P. Burton, 'A Luba Folk-tale', *Bantu Studies* 9, 1935, pp. 69, 75.
[5] Smith and Dale ii, 1920, p. 407.          [6] Lindblom i, 1928, p. ix.

enemy is to give him a bag of snakes and scorpions to open,[1] while the *deus ex machina* in Luba stories is usually a little dirty old woman who lives in the woods and who appears at the critical moment.[2] Similarly we can find many other cases of stereotyped and yet, through that very fact, markedly allusive and meaningful treatments of particular episodes. There is the pregnant but outwardly simple Limba comment in a story 'he sharpened his sword', which at once hints at drama and danger to come, or their economical indication of the horror, finality, and shock of finding a dead body lying on the floor by a brief reference to the flies buzzing round the corpse. Both these motifs occur in several narrations; yet their full impact would not emerge were they not known to be common and yet allusive literary stereotypes.

Even more important than the points mentioned so far is the need for further study of the delivery and dramatic performance of African stories. Since these narratives are *oral* ones, to ignore this aspect is to miss one of their most significant features. The vividness, subtlety, and drama with which stories are often delivered have often been noted in general terms by those who know a lot about the literature they present (as distinct from collectors who merely reproduce texts written for them by employees). One of the best single descriptions of African stories, for example, allied to a full appreciation of the social context, is that of Smith and Dale on Ila stories; when they come to pointing to the difficulties encountered by foreign readers in fully appreciating the literary value of the tales, they concentrate, significantly, on precisely this:

We have to reconcile ourselves to the fact that for us, at least, it is impossible to do justice to these tales, and we doubt if the most skilful hand could reproduce in a translation the quaintness, the liveliness, and humour of the original. . . . They gradually lose flavour as they pass from the African's telling, first into writing and then into a foreign idiom. It would need a combination of phonograph and kinematograph to reproduce a tale as it is told. One listens to a clever story-teller, as was our old friend Mungalo, from whom we derived many of these tales. Speak of eloquence! Here was no lip mumbling, but every muscle of face and body spoke, a swift gesture often supplying the place of a whole sentence. He would have made a fortune as a raconteur upon the English stage. The animals spoke each in its own tone: the deep rumbling voice of Momba, the ground hornbill, for example, contrasting

[1] E. J. Krige, *The Social System of the Zulus*, Pietermaritzburg, 1936, p. 357.
[2] Stappers 1962, p. 17.

vividly with the piping accents of Sulwe, the hare. It was all good to listen to—impossible to put on paper. Ask him now to repeat the story slowly so that you may write it. You will, with patience, get the gist of it, but the unnaturalness of the circumstance disconcerts him, your repeated request for the repetition of a phrase, the absence of the encouragement of his friends, and, above all, the hampering slowness of your pen, all combine to kill the spirit of story-telling. Hence we have to be content with far less than the tales as they are told. And the tales need effort of imagination to place readers in the stead of the original listeners.[1]

Junod too, in describing the stories of the Thonga and of the Southern Bantu in general, stresses the same fact. The story-tellers 'live' and act the tales rather than just telling them. No written version, however accurate in language or translation, could hope to reproduce the real atmosphere of the actual narration.[2] A similar description is given by Doke of the art of the Lamba story-teller:

To reproduce such stories with any measure of success, a gramophone record together with a cinematograph picture would be necessary. The story suffers from being put into cold print. . . .[3]

In my own study of Limba stories, the single characteristic that I found both most striking and most incommunicable in writing was just this—the way narrators could add subtlety and drama, pathos or humour, characterization or detached comment by the way they spoke as much as by the words themselves.

In the majority of published collections of African tales not even a token reference is made to this fact. Detailed studies tend to be lacking. We are practically never told, for instance, about the accepted stylistic devices through which the performer makes his narrations more effective, or of individual differences between various narrators in respect of this skill. I have tried to treat these questions in a preliminary way for Limba story-tellers. Since this account is easily accessible,[4] I will here merely mention some of the general factors often involved in delivery.

First there is the way in which stories are dramatized, the narrator taking on the personalities of the various characters,

---

[1] Smith and Dale ii, 1920, pp. 334–6.    [2] Junod 1938, p. 58.
[3] Doke 1927, p. xiii. For some other good descriptions of the narrator's art see e.g. Roger 1828, pp. 9 ff. (Wolof); Trilles 1932, pp. 234–5, 240 (Pygmies); Tremearne 1913, pp. 27–9.    [4] Finnegan 1967.

acting out their dialogue, their facial expressions, even their gestures and reactions. This point is worth remembering when one is tempted to complain of the shadowy or crude characterization of many personalities in African stories—it is not necessary to formulate all this in words when a good narrator can present it much more economically and subtly in performance. The narrator does not enact the actions of the characters in the full sense: this is dramatized narrative and not actually drama. But even from his seat or when, as happens occasionally, he stands or moves within the circle of listeners, he can vividly suggest the acts and feelings of his characters by the use of dramatic dialogue or through expressions on his face or gestures of hand or body.

Actual mimicry of a humorous and satirical kind seems most common in the case of animal characters. Some attempt at copying the cries and sounds of birds or animals in a stylized form is frequently mentioned as a characteristic of story-tellers. In Hausa stories, for instance, special words are used to imitate the sounds of dogs quarrelling and barking, the wildcat's call, and the crow of the rooster, with the words intoned to resemble the animal sounds. Speeches by animal characters are often sung, sometimes in falsetto, and always with a nasal twang.[1] The Bushmen have a specialized form of this in the speech conventionally attributed to certain animals (and the moon) in stories; the Blue Crane, for instance, adds *tt* to the first syllable of almost every word, whereas the tortoise's lisping makes him change all the clicks and other initial consonants into labials.[2] Though not so complex as the Bushman example, similar stylized and imitative speech attributed to animals occurs widely in African narrations.

The actual delivery and treatment of the words themselves is also relevant. Even when he does not choose to elaborate any extremes of dramatization, the narrator can and does create vivid effects by variations and exaggerations of speed, volume, and tone. He can use abrupt breaks, pregnant pauses, parentheses, rhetorical questions as he watches the audience's reactions and exploits his freedom to choose his words as well as his mode of delivery.

A form of onomatopoeia is often used to add elegance and vividness to the narration. A style plentifully embroidered with ideo-

---

[1] Tremearne 1913, p. 28.

[2] See especially D. F. Bleek, 'Special Speech of Animals and Moon used by |Xam Bushmen', *Bantu Studies* 10, 1936.

phones is one of the striking characteristics of an effective story-teller. We can actually hear the sound of a Limba boy leaping into a lake (*tiriŋ!*), the noise of the Akan spider hitting the ceiling (*kado!*), the Luba onomatopoeic expression of a chase (*kwata-kwata-kwata*), or the tortoise swimming (*seki seki seki*) and pheasant fluttering its wings (*fu fu fu*) in Mabale tales. In this way the action is dramatized by a skilful teller.

In all this the participation of the audience is essential. It is common for members of it to be expected to make verbal con-tributions—spontaneous exclamations, actual questions, echoing of the speaker's words, emotional reaction to the development of yet another parallel and repetitious episode. Further, the audience contributes the choruses of the songs so often introduced into the narration, and without which, in many cases, the stories would be only a bare framework of words.

Songs are characteristic of African tales all over the continent. They do not occur in every story, and in some cases there are local distinctions between 'prose' and 'choric' stories.[1] But songs are infinitely more common than would appear from a cursory reading of the published collections. Since the songs are almost always so much more difficult to record than prose, they are usually omitted in published versions; even when they are included, the extent to which they are repeated and the proportion of time they occupy compared to spoken narration is often not made clear. Yet the singing can at times become the main element of the story—'So much so that in many tales the narrative is to it no more than a frame is to a picture'.[2] Or, as Steere writes of the Swahili:

Frequently the skeleton of the story seems to be contained in these snatches of singing, which the story-teller connects by an extemporized account of the intervening history.[3]

Similar comments could be made on narrations from many areas in Africa, though the emphasis on singing varies not only with the type of tale involved but also, in some cases, with the individual teller. Among the Limba, for instance, I found that certain in-dividuals were particularly fond of songs so that the singing, with much repetition of the choruses, took up more time than the words, and the plot and verbal element were little developed; other

---

[1] e.g. Lamba (Doke 1934, p. 358).
[2] Torrend 1921, p. 3.  [3] Steere 1906, p. vii.

narrators on the other hand only introduced songs or recitative rarely, and then merely as an ornament. But in spite of these variations, it is safe to say that singing is an element that is worth looking for in tales of all kinds (except, probably, specialized historical narratives) all over Africa.

These songs fulfil various functions in the narrative. They often mark the structure of the story in a clear and attractive way. Thus, if the hero is presented as going through a series of tests or adventures, the parallel presentation of episode after episode is often cut into by the singing of a song by narrator and audience. Further, the occurrence of songs adds a musical aspect—an extra dimension of both enjoyment and skill. In some areas (particularly parts of West and West Equatorial Africa) this musical element is further enhanced by drum or instrumental accompaniment or prelude to the narration.[1] The songs also provide a formalized means for audience participation. The common pattern is for the words of the song, whether familiar or new, to be introduced by the narrator, who then acts as leader and soloist while the audience provide the chorus.[2]

Having discussed the significance of the actual performance of stories, we can raise the question of the individual contributions of the various narrators. Even if there are conventionally recognized ways of enhancing delivery, the narrator can exploit these and, in the last analysis, is responsible for all the aspects of performance already mentioned. It is evident then that one way of discovering the extent of the individual artistry involved in the narration of African stories is through the investigation of individual narrators' relevant skills and idiosyncrasies.

Composition as well as performance is involved. The narrator of a story is likely to introduce his own favourite tricks of verbal style and presentation and to be influenced in his wording by the audience and occasion; thus he will produce linguistic variations on the basic theme different from those of his fellows or even from his own on a different occasion. In addition to this, there is the individual treatment of the various incidents, characters, and

[1] e.g. Yoruba, Ewe, ex-French Equatorial Africa, Bulu (Ellis 1894, p. 243; Ellis 1890, p. 269; Nassau 1914, p. 5; A. N. Krug, 'Bulu Tales', *JAF* 62, 1949, p. 350).
[2] For further points on songs in stories (including some examples) and the common modes of antiphony see Ch. 9. See also Innes 1965; Belinga 1965, pp. 55 ff.

motifs; these do not emerge when only one version of the story appears in published form. Finally, there are the occasions when, in a sense, a 'new' story is created. Episodes, motifs, conventional characters, stylistic devices which are already part of the conventional literary background on which the individual artist can draw are bound together and presented in an original and individual way.

This *real* originality, as it appears to the foreigner, is really only a difference in degree, for there is seldom any concept of a 'correct' version. In all respects the narrator is free to choose his own treatment and most stories arise from the combination and recombination of motifs and episodes with which the individual is free to build. Stories are thus capable of infinite expansion, variation, and embroidery by narrators, as they are sewn together in one man's imagination.[1] The subject-matter too on which such artists draw is by no means fixed, and the common picture of a strict adherence to 'traditional' and unchanging themes is quite false. Not only are there multiple references to obviously recent material introductions—like guns, money, books, lorries, horse-racing, new buildings—but the whole plot of a story can centre round an episode like an imaginary race to the Secretariat building in a colonial capital to gain government recognition for an official position (Limba), a man going off to get work in Johannesburg and leaving his wife to get into trouble at home (Thonga), or a young hero winning the football pools (Nigeria). The occupations and preoccupations of both present and past, the background of local and changing literary conventions, and the current interests of both teller and listeners—all these make up the material on which the gifted narrator can draw and subject to the originality of his own inspiration.

The question of the originality of the individual teller, whether in performance or composition, is one of the most neglected aspects of African oral narratives. That so obvious a point of interest should have been overlooked can be related to various constricting theoretical presuppositions about African oral art

---

[1] For further comments on this aspect see e.g. Theal 1886, pp. vii ff.; Finnegan 1967, pp. 94 ff.; Junod ii, 1913, pp. 218 ff.; Stappers 1962, pp. 14 ff. Cf. also Propp's interesting analysis of the 'functions' or stable and constant elements in (Russian) folktales—though his approach seems a little too formalistic for direct application to the African field (V. Propp, *Morphology of the Folktale*, tr. L. Scott, Bloomington, 1958).

that have been dominant in the past: the assumption about the significance of the collective aspect, i.e. the contribution by 'the folk' or the masses rather than the individual; the desire to find and record *the* traditional tribal story, with no interest in variant or individual forms; and, finally, the prejudice in favour of the 'traditional', with its resultant picture of African oral art as static and unchanging through the years and the consequent explicit avoidance of 'new' or 'intrusive' stories. It is worth stressing here yet again that the neglect of this kind of point, one which seems so self-evidently a question to pursue in the case of any genre of literature, is *not* primarily due to any basis in the facts or to any proven lack of originality by African literary artists, but to this theoretical background of by now very dubious assumptions. Now that the dominance of many of these theories is passing, at least in some circles, it is to be trusted that far more attention will be paid to this question of authorship and originality in African oral literature.

This final section on the various aspects of oral prose narratives which, hitherto neglected, now demand further emphasis has had one underlying theme. That is, that the many questions which we would normally expect to pursue in the analysis of any literary genre should also be followed up in the case of these African stories. That this obvious approach has tended to be obscured is largely due to the limiting theoretical assumptions of the past that were discussed earlier. The stories are in fact far more flexible, adaptable, and subtle than would appear from the many traditionally-orientated published collections and accounts; if certain types and themes are dying out, others are arising, with new contexts and themes that provide a fruitful field of study. Once we can free our appreciation of past speculations, we can see these stories as literary forms in their own right. While some of the questions such as the significance of occasion, of delivery, or of audience participation, arise from their *oral* nature, others, such as the literary and social conventions of a particular literary form, its purpose and functions, and the varying interpretations of individual artists, are the traditional questions of literary analysis. These aspects concern both the literary scholar and the sociologist who want to understand the at once subtle and significant role of literature in a given society, and their study would seem to provide the greatest potential for further advance in our knowledge of African oral prose narratives.

# 14

## PROVERBS

*The significance and concept of the proverb. Form and style.*
*Content. Occasions and functions. Specific examples: Jabo;*
*Zulu; Azande. Conclusion*

### I

PROVERBS seem to occur almost everywhere in Africa, in apparent contrast with other areas of the world such as aboriginal America and Polynesia. Relatively easy to record, they have been exceedingly popular with collectors. Particularly well represented are proverbs from the Bantu area (especially the Southern Bantu); the Congo and West Africa have also provided many extensive collections. It is notable, however, that there are apparently few or no proverbs among the Bushmen of southern Africa and the Nilotic peoples,[1] and few seem to have been recorded in Nilo-Hamitic languages. In other areas proverbs seem universal and in some African languages occur in rich profusion. Four thousand have been published in Rundi, for instance, about 3,000 in Nkundo, and roughly 2,000 in Luba and Hausa. In addition Bascom lists about thirty other African peoples for whom 500 or more proverbs have been recorded.[2] Also many editors say that they doubt whether their collections are complete.

The literary relevance of these short sayings is clear. Proverbs are a rich source of imagery and succinct expression on which more elaborate forms can draw. As Nketia puts it in his comment on Ghanaian proverbs

The value of the proverb to us in modern Ghana does not lie only in what it reveals of the thoughts of the past. For the poet today or indeed for the speaker who is some sort of an artist in the use of words, the proverb is a model of compressed or forceful language. In addition to

[1] C. M. Doke, 'A Preliminary Investigation into the State of the Native Languages of South Africa', *Bantu Studies* 7, 1933, p. 6; Evans-Pritchard 1963*b*, p. 109.

[2] Bascom 1964, pp. 16–17; cf. Doke 1947, pp. 115–17; Whitting 1940.

drawing on it for its words of wisdom, therefore, he takes interest in its verbal techniques—its selection of words, its use of comparison as a method of statement, and so on. Familiarity with its techniques enables him to create, as it were, his own proverbs. This enables him to avoid hackneyed expressions and give a certain amount of freshness to his speech.

This . . . approach to proverbs which is evident in the speech of people who are regarded as accomplished speakers or poets of a sort makes the proverbs not only a body of short statements built up over the years and which reflect the thought and insight of Ghanaians into problems of life, but also a technique of verbal expression, which is greatly appreciated by the Ghanaian. It is no wonder therefore that the use of proverbs has continued to be a living tradition in Ghana.[1]

In many African cultures a feeling for language, for imagery, and for the expression of abstract ideas through compressed and allusive phraseology comes out particularly clearly in proverbs. The figurative quality of proverbs is especially striking; one of their most noticeable characteristics is their allusive wording, usually in metaphorical form. This also emerges in many of the native words translated as 'proverb' and in the general stress often laid on the significance of speaking in symbolic terms. Indeed, this type of figurative expression is sometimes taken so far as to be almost a whole mode of speech in its own right. The Fulani term *mallol* for instance, means not only a proverb but also allusion in general, and is especially used when there is some deep hidden meaning in a proverb different from the obvious one.[2] Similarly with the Kamba term *ndimo*. This does not exactly correspond to our term 'proverb' but is its nearest equivalent, and really means a 'dark saying' or 'metaphorical wording', a sort of secret and allusive language.[3]

The literary significance of proverbs in Africa is also brought out by their close connection with other forms of oral literature. This is sometimes apparent in the local terminology, for proverbs are not always distinguished by a special term from other categories of verbal art. The Nyanja *mwambi*, for instance, refers to story, riddle, or proverb, the Ganda *olugero* means, among other things, a saying, a story, a proverb, and a parable,[4] and the Mongo *bokolo* is used of all poetic expression including fable, proverb, poetry,

---

[1] J. H. Nketia, 'Folklore of Ghana', *The Ghanaian* 1, 1958, p. 21.
[2] Gaden 1931, p. vi.  [3] Lindblom iii, 1934, p. 28.
[4] Doke 1947, p. 102.

and allegory.[1] This overlap in terms is fairly common in Bantu languages and also sometimes occurs in West Africa too: the Limba *mbɔrɔ* refers to story, riddle, and parable as well as to sayings which we might term proverbs, while the Fulani *tindol* can mean not only a popular moral story but also a proverb or maxim.[2]

In some languages (such as Yoruba or Zulu) a distinction does exist in terminology between proverbs and other types of literary expression.[3] But even here there is often a practical connection between proverbs and other forms of oral literature. Chatelain pointed out that Kimbundu proverbs are closely related to anecdotes, so much so that anecdotes are sometimes just illustrations of a proverb, while a proverb is frequently an anecdote in a nutshell.[4] Again, the Nyanja proverb 'Pity killed the francolin' is a direct allusion to the story in which the francolin came to the help of a python and was in return eaten by it.[5] Similar connections between story and proverb are mentioned for the Azande, Zulu, Ashanti, and many others, and a moralizing story may end with, or imply, a proverb to drive home its point. As well, proverbs frequently appear in songs and poems. The drum proverbs of Ghana or Dahomey are particularly striking examples here. Among other instances we could mention the Nguni saying 'The earth does not get fat' (i.e. however many dead it receives the earth is never satiated) which also appears as the central theme and chorus in an impressive Ngoni lament,[6] and the Swahili poem about silence based on the proverb 'Much silence has a mighty noise' ('Still waters run deep') but elaborated and drawn out in the verses arising from it.[7] Written forms too sometimes make use of traditional proverbs, as in Muyaka's Swahili poems, and these in turn may give further currency to new or old proverbs.[8] Proverbs are also sometimes connected with riddles[9] or, as among the Liberian Jabo, with praise names.[10] They also frequently occur in general conversation and in oratory to embellish, conceal, or hint.

---

[1] Hulstaert 1958, p. 6.  
[2] Gaden 1931, p. vi.  
[3] There are also several cases where there are both a general term, covering both proverbs and other types of verbal art, and, in addition, a more precise term referring to proverbs only.  
[4] Chatelain 1894, p. 21.  
[5] Gray 1944, p. 102.  
[6] See Ch. 7 above, pp. 151–2.  
[7] Taylor 1891, pp. 32–3.  
[8] Doke 1947, p. 105.  
[9] e.g. the Anang 'proverb-riddles' discussed below, p. 431.  
[10] Herzog 1936, p. 12.

Proverbs, in short, are closely interwoven with other aspects of linguistic and literary behaviour.

As well as these obvious and common ways in which proverbs overlap with other kinds of verbal art, they also appear in certain specialized forms. Their use in the form of 'proverb names' is one. Among the Ovimbundu, to give one example, the woman's name *Simbovala* is a shortened form of the proverb 'While you mark out a field, Death marks you out in life'—in life you are in the midst of death.[1] Another connection is with bird lore, a form particularly popular among the Southern Bantu. The cries attributed to certain birds can be expressed as a proverb or a song. The hammerkop, for instance, can be referred to as a symbol of vanity either in a brief proverb or in the full song in which he is represented as praising himself at length;[2] the songs here are thus inextricably linked with the proverbs. Proverbs are also sometimes connected with other artistic media: they can be drummed (a characteristic form in some West African societies), sung, as with Lega judicial proverbs,[3] or can appear on the flags of military companies, as among the Fante.[4] Most striking of all is the way the Ashanti associate a certain proverb with one or other of their many 'gold-weights'—small brass figures and images originally used to weigh gold dust and worked with great skill and humour. Thus a snake catching a bird represents the proverb 'The snake lies upon the ground, but God has given him the hornbill' (that flies in the sky). Another weight depicts two crocodiles with only a single stomach between them, representing 'Bellies mixed up, crocodiles mixed up, we have between us only one belly, but if we get anything to eat it passes down our respective gullets'—a famous proverb often cited when one individual in a family tries to seize for himself rather than sharing.[5]

Certain of the direct associations between proverbs and other artistic forms such as metalwork or drumming may be peculiar to certain African societies, but the general association of proverbs and other forms of literature is not after all very surprising. These

[1] Ennis 1945, p. 3. On names in general see Ch. 16.     [2] Ch. 9, p. 249.

[3] A. E. Meeussen, 'Aktiespreuken bij de Lega', *Kongo-Overzee* 25, 1959, p. 73.     [4] Christensen 1958, p. 240.

[5] R. S. Rattray, *Ashanti*, Oxford, 1923, pp. 312–13. Cf. also D. Paulme, 'Les poids-proverbes de la Côte-d'Ivoire au Musée de l'Homme', *J. Soc. africanistes* 11, 1941; M. W. Plass, *African Miniatures, the Goldweights of the Ashanti*, London, 1967.

close connections are perhaps particularly characteristic of an *oral* literature without a clear-cut distinction between written and un-written forms, but the sort of way in which proverbial expression and other types of literary art (including the art of conversation) mutually enrich and act upon each other is something which is presumably a quality of most cultures. In this sense, then, pro-verbs in Africa are not so very different from those in any literate culture, in both of which their main impact seems, in fact, to be in an *oral* rather than a written form. In neither case should they be regarded as isolated sayings to be collected in hundreds or thousands on their own, but rather as just one aspect of artistic expression within a whole social and literary context.

The close connection of proverbs with other literary forms raises a difficulty. How, particularly in an oral culture, can we distinguish proverbs from other forms of oral art? or, indeed, from ordinary clichés and idioms, and from such related but different forms as maxims and apophthegms?

Most of the published collections ignore this point of definition and by merely entitling their works 'Proverbs' often give the mis-leading impression that these sayings are clearly differentiated from other expressions or that they are in all ways equivalent to our idea of proverbs. Some of the best collections, such as those of Hulstaert, Nyembezi, Doke, or Chatelain, specifically point out this difficulty, but most have little or no discussion of this point.

The exact definition of 'proverb' is no easy matter. There is, however, some general agreement as to what constitutes a proverb. It is a saying in more or less fixed form marked by 'shortness, sense, and salt' and distinguished by the popular acceptance of the truth tersely expressed in it. Even so general a picture as this contains some useful pointers for the analysis of African proverbs.

First, their form. They are picked out first and most obviously as being short; and secondly by the fact that even where the word-ing itself is not absolutely fixed, at least the main structural pattern is accepted in the society concerned as an appropriate one for this purpose. This question of form has been well noted by collectors and is pursued further in the following section. It will emerge that, in addition to terseness and relative fixity, most say-ings classed as proverbs are also marked by some kind of poetic quality in style or sense, and are in this way set apart in form from more straightforward maxims.

The question of 'popular acceptance' is, however, a more difficult one. If one of the marks of a true proverb is its general acceptance as the popular expression of some truth, we are seldom given the data to decide how far this is indeed a characteristic of the sayings included in collections of 'proverbs'. In many cases presumably the sayings included are proverbs in this full sense. But we have in fact no way of telling whether some of the 'proverbs' included are not just the sententious utterances of a single individual on a single occasion which happened to appeal to the investigator.

The sort of terminology involved can sometimes provide a clue to the local attitude to 'proverbs'. As we have seen, there is sometimes a specialized term, sometimes not. This is not always made clear by collectors. Even more serious is the frequent failure to consider when, how, and by or among whom common proverbs are used.[1] Even where something about the general context is given we are practically never told in detail how a given single proverb was actually used.[2] Yet, as will emerge, this may in fact determine its significance, the way in which it is appreciated locally, even its meaning. This aspect is often crucial, if whether or not some attractive saying is really a 'proverb' depends on the local evaluation of it. This question is made more difficult because proverbs often have no specialized occasions for their use. Unlike such forms as riddles and stories they are not normally set apart as suitable for relaxation after, say, the end of the day's work, but are closely involved with speech and action on every sort of occasion (including general conversation). Therefore to differentiate those sayings which are merely idiomatic from those which *the people concerned* consider to have that special flavour which makes it correct to call them proverbs, we need more precise information about context and attitude than we are usually given.

This said, we can in a general way accept most of the published sayings as falling, more or less, within the general category of proverb. But it is worth making these points about the difficulties inherent in differentiating proverbs if it helps to deter yet more facile collections and to encourage more consideration of their context. In the case of proverbs above all, an understanding of this is essential.

---

[1] A point well made in Arewa and Dundes 1964; cf. also Evans-Pritchard 1963*a*.  [2] For some exceptions to this see pp. 418 ff. below.

II

In discussing the style and structure of African proverbs one of the first things one notices is the poetic form in which many are expressed. This, allied to their figurative mode of expression, serves to some degree to set them apart from everyday speech. This point often does not emerge in collections of translated examples. A more detailed discussion of form in African proverbs is therefore needed here to show these two characteristics more clearly.

The general truth touched on in a proverb can be conveyed in several ways: more or less literally, through a simile, or (most commonly) through a metaphor.

The relatively literal forms of proverbs often contain some allusion or a picturesque form of speech, and among certain peoples at least are marked by some poetic quality such as rhythm. Examples of this type are fairly common. 'The dying of the heart is a thing unshared', 'If the chief speaks, the people make silent their ears', and the humorous description of a drunkard, 'He devoured the Kaffir-beer and it devoured him', are instances from South Africa.[1] Comments on what is considered to be the real nature of people or things often occur in this form, as in the Thonga 'The White man has no kin. His kin is money', the Xhosa description of Europeans as 'The people who rescue and kill' (i.e. they protect with one hand, destroy with the other),[2] or the witty Akan comment that 'An ancient name cannot be cooked and eaten; after all, money is the thing'.[3] General advice is also often tendered in this sort of form, as in the Thonga 'Dis du mal du chef quand tu quittes son pays' or the humorous Ila injunction to hospitality in the form of 'The rump of a visitor is made to sit upon'.[4] It is true that several of these (and similar) proverbs may also conceal deeper meanings as well as picturesque language, but in explicit form, in contrast to the clearly figurative, they present the thought in a simple and straightforward way.[5]

[1] McLaren 1917, pp. 343, 338, 341.
[2] Junod 1938, p. 49; Theal 1886, p. 199.    [3] Rattray 1916, p. 118.
[4] H. P. Junod, *Quelques Proverbes thonga*, Lausanne, 1931, no. 56; Smith and Dale ii, 1920, p. 312.
[5] In these straightforward forms the veiling or allusiveness characteristic of so much proverbial expression is sometimes in fact achieved by devices other than direct imagery. Abbreviation is one common way (e.g. in the Ovimbundu proverb-names); another is to express the proverb in some medium other than verbal utterance, with drums, for instance, or through gold-weights (Ashanti).

More often the proverbs are figurative in one way or another. Direct similes occur fairly often. The Hausa, for example, say that 'A chief is like a dust-heap where everyone comes with his rubbish (complaint) and deposits it'.[1] Among the Southern Bantu the likening of something to dew melting away in the sun appears in many forms: the Zulu suggest that something is only a passing phase by asserting that 'This thing is like the dew which showers down', and the comparison often appears in a more direct and concise form, as with the Thonga 'Wealth is dew' or Ndebele 'Kingship is dew'.[2] Wealth is another stock comparison, as in the Swahili 'Wits (are) wealth', or the vivid saying of the Thonga and others that 'To bear children is wealth, to dress oneself is (nothing but) colours'.[3] Many other examples of these direct comparisons could be cited: the Southern Bantu 'To look at a man as at a snake' (i.e. with deadly hatred), or 'To marry is to put a snake in one's handbag';[4] the Ashanti proverbs 'Family names are like flowers, they blossom in clusters' or 'A wife is like a blanket; when you cover yourself with it, it irritates you, and yet if you cast it aside you feel cold';[5] and the Xhosa 'He is ripe inside, like a water-melon', describing a man who has come to a resolution without yet expressing it publicly (one cannot tell if a water-melon is ripe from the outside).[6]

Most frequent of all, however, and the most adaptable are the proverbs where comparison is evoked metaphorically. In this form proverbs about animals and birds are very common indeed (perhaps particularly in the Bantu areas); here, as in the tales about animals and in certain praise names, a comment is often being made about human life and action through reference to non-human activity. Egotism, for instance, is commented on and satirized in the Sotho '"I and my rhinoceros" said the tick bird' or the Ndau 'The worm in the cattle kraal says "I am an ox"', and among the Ila it is said of squanderers 'The prodigal cow threw away her own tail'.[7] Similarly, generalizations about animals

---

[1] Tremearne 1913, p. 62.

[2] J. Stuart and D. Malcolm, *Zulu Proverbs and Popular Sayings*, Durban, [1949], p. 70; Junod 1938, p. 49; K. D. Leaver and C. L. S. Nyembezi, 'Proverbs Collected from the Amandeßele', *Afr. Studies* 5, 1946, p. 137.

[3] W. E. Taylor 1891, p. 2; Junod and Jaques 1936, no. 450.

[4] McLaren 1917, p. 336; Junod 1938, p. 50.

[5] Rattray 1916, pp. 125, 139.  [6] Theal 1886, p. 194.

[7] McLaren 1917, p. 334; E. B. Jones, Ndau proverbs (manuscripts in Doke Collection, University College Library, Salisbury, S. Rhodesia); Smith and Dale ii, 1920, p. 316.

imply a comment on human affairs. Thus the Thonga 'The strength of the crocodile is in the water'[1] can comment in various ways, implying from one point of view that a man is strong when his kinsmen help him, from another that a man should stick to his own place and not interfere with others. The importance of self-help is stressed in 'No fly catches for another',[2] while the Zulu generalization 'No polecat ever smelt its own stink' alludes picturesquely to man's blindness and self-satisfaction.[3]

Though proverbs about animals are particularly common, generalizations about other everyday things are also used to suggest some related idea about people. The Zulu observe that man is able to manage his own affairs through the metaphor that 'There is no grinding stone that got the better of the miller', and the Ndebele remind one that 'The maker of a song does not spoil it' when wishing to warn that it is not right to interfere with someone who understands his own business.[4] The Lamba 'Metal that is already welded together, how can one unweld it?' can be used in the same sort of way as our 'Don't cry over spilt milk', while the Thonga 'The nape of the neck does not see' alludes to the way people get out of control when the master of the village is away.[5]

Perhaps even more common than the metaphorical generalization is the form in which a general or abstract idea is conveyed not through any direct generalization at all but through a single concrete situation which provides only one example of the general point. Thus the Thonga 'The one who says "Elephant die! I want to eat! I am on the way"' alludes to the way in which some people are over-impatient instead of taking the time to do the job properly, while a different point of view is suggested in the specific Hausa statement that 'The man with deepest eyes can't see the moon till it is fifteen days old'—in other words is so narrowly concentrated that the obvious escapes him.[6] The Zulu express the general idea that people reap the fruit of their own folly by mentioning specific situations: 'He ate food and it killed him' and 'The won't-be-told man sees by the bloodstain'.[7] The frequent effects

---

[1] Junod 1938, p. 47.   [2] McLaren 1917, p. 340.

[3] F. Mayr, 'Zulu Proverbs', *Anthropos* 7, 1912, p. 958.

[4] Stuart and Malcolm, op. cit., p. 17; N. Jones, 'Sindebele Proverbs', *Nada* 3, 1925, p. 66.   [5] Doke 1934, p. 361; Junod and Jaques 1936, no. 352.

[6] Junod and Jaques 1936, no. 2; Whitting 1940, p. 3.

[7] O. Ripp, Newspaper cuttings on Zulu proverbs, 1930 (Doke Collection, University College Library, Salisbury, S. Rhodesia); Dunning 1946.

of over-confidence and officious advice are alluded to in the pointed
Nyanja saying 'Mr. Had-it-been-I caused the baboons belonging
to someone else to escape', while they comment on fools from the
specific case of 'Mr. Didn't-know' who 'took shelter from the rain in
the pond'.[1] Fools are similarly alluded to in the Ewe 'If a boy says he
wants to tie water with a string, ask him if he means the water in the
pot or the water in the lagoon'.[2] This hinting at a general or abstract
idea through one concrete case, either direct or itself metaphorical,
is a common proverbial form throughout the continent.

Hyperbole and exaggeration are also frequent motifs, often in
addition to some of the forms mentioned above. Many instances
could be cited, among them the common Bantu saying that 'If you
are patient, you will see the eyes of the snail', or 'The monitor has
gone dry', which alludes to the fact that even the monitor, famed
for its affection to its young, has come to the end—and that the
guest has outstayed his welcome![3] There is the Fulani proverb
'You will not see an elephant moving on your own head, only the
louse moving on another's'; and the Zulu description of an un-
blushing and flagrant liar, 'He milks also the cows heavy with calf'
—he would actually go as far as saying he could milk cows *before*
they had calved.[4] Paradox is also occasionally used with the same
kind of effect, as in the Hausa comment on the effects of idleness
('The want of work to do makes a man get up early to salute his
enemy'), or the cynical Ila remark 'He has the kindness of a witch'.[5]
The quality of being far-fetched and humorous is used for similar
effect in the Zulu reference to impossibility 'A goat may beget an
ox and a white man sew on a [native] head ring', the Yoruba 'He
who waits to see a crab wink will tarry long upon the shore', the
Nyanja 'Little by little the tortoise arrived at the Indian Ocean',
or the exaggerated Yoruba equivalent of our idea that one reaps
as one sows—'One who excretes on the road, will find flies when
he returns'.[6]

The allusions of proverbs in the various collections are often not
obvious. This is frequently due to our ignorance of the culture,
particularly with proverbs which allude to some well-known

[1] Gray 1944, pp. 112, 117.                    [2] Ellis 1890, p. 260.
[3] Werner 1906, p. 212; McLaren 1917, p. 335.
[4] Whitting 1940, p. 160; Nyembezi 1954, p. 40.
[5] Whitting 1940, p. 121; Smith and Dale ii, 1920, p. 323.
[6] J. G. Stuhardt, 'A Collection of Zulu Proverbs', *Nada* 8, 1930, p. 69; Ellis
1894, p. 237; Gray 1944, p. 110; Gbadamosi and Beier 1959, p. 60.

story or famous individual. A knowledge of the situations in which proverbs are cited may also be an essential part of understanding their implications, and this is complicated further by the fact that the same proverb may often be used, according to the context, to suggest a variety of different truths, or different facets of the same truth, or even its opposite. Some proverbs, furthermore, are obscure even to local individuals or groups. We cannot, then, expect African proverbs to be crystal-clear or to be able to grasp in each case the modes through which they figuratively or picturesquely suggest certain truths. However, it does seem that the main ways in which these are expressed are the ones already mentioned: by a straight, relatively literal statement; by similes; by various types of metaphor (often comparisons with animals or with one particular case suggesting a generalization); and by hyperbole and paradox.

Having considered some of the general forms in which proverbs appear we can now look at the detailed stylistic devices which these mainly figurative sayings employ to make their points effectively. Unlike stories and songs, the *performance* does not generally seem to be of importance. Rather, proverbs rely for their effect on the aptness with which they are used in a particular situation and—the point considered here—on the style and form of words in which they appear.[1]

Proverbs are generally marked by terseness of expression, by a form different from that of ordinary speech, and by a figurative mode of expression abounding in metaphor. The first two characteristics can be treated together here with illustrations from the Bantu group of languages. There are no *general* rules for the formation of Bantu proverbs and particular peoples have their own favourite forms, but certain common patterns are apparent. Pithiness and economy are always noticeable in proverbs, but in the Bantu languages this can be achieved particularly effectively through the system of concord. The subject noun, for example, can be omitted as in 'It is worked while still fresh' (i.e. 'Make hay while the sun shines'), where the concord makes clear that 'it' refers to 'clay'.[2] Economy of wording is also often achieved through elision: not only are whole words left out (often for the sake of rhythm) but vowels are frequently elided, especially the

---

[1] On form and style the best discussion is that by Doke (1947) on Bantu proverbs, and his account is followed closely here.    [2] Doke 1947, p. 106.

final vowel of a word.[1] The terse expression grammatically possible in Bantu can be illustrated from a Tswana proverb, 'Young birds will always open their mouths, even to those who come to kill them', which in the original is only three words.[2] Furthermore, proverbs are often quoted in abbreviated forms; in Bantu languages these are almost always prefered to more drawn-out forms.[3]

The actual wording may take the form of a simple positive or negative proposition, as in the Swahili 'The goat-eater pays a cow' (i.e. sow the wind and reap the whirlwind), or the Zulu 'He has no chest' (he can't keep secrets), or of various types of simple rhythmic balanced propositions (e.g. the Lamba *muŋanda yācitāla, ubwālwa ẃulasasa,* 'In the house of wrangling, beer becomes bitter', where there is exact balance in the two parts, each with three followed by four syllables). Double propositions in which the second portion is explanatory are also common, as in the Lamba 'A male is a millipede, he is not driven away with one driving (only)' (a man does not take a single refusal from a girl). Negative axioms also occur and are a particularly popular form in Xhosa and Zulu: 'There is no elephant burdened with its own trunk' (a comparison which occurs widely with various connotations, among them the idea that a mother does not feel her baby's weight), 'There is no partridge (that) scratches for another' (everyone for himself), 'There is no sun (which) sets without its affairs' (every day has its own troubles). Contrast propositions are a particularly striking and economical form and may be presented in either of two ways: by a direct parallel between the two portions of the proverb, as in the Lamba 'The body went, the heart did not go' (*umuẃili ẃaya, umutima tawile*), or by cross parallelism (chiasmus), as in the Lamba proverb 'One morsel of food does not break a company, what breaks a company is the mouth' (*akalyo kamo takotoẃa—citenje, icitoẃe'citenje kanwa*). Another common form is reduplication, with repeated words or syllables. This usually comes at the beginning, as in the Swahili 'Hurry, hurry, has no blessing' (*haraka, haraka, haina baraka*) or the Ganda 'Splutter, splutter isn't fire' (*bugu-bugu simuliro*).[4]

Among the Bantu, as elsewhere, the use of quoted words attributed to some actual or fictional person is another device for giving

---

[1] Nyembezi 1954, pp. 13 ff.    [2] A. Werner, *J. Afr. Soc.* 16, 1917, p. 184.
[3] Doke in *Afr. Studies* 18, 1959, p. 150.
[4] Examples quoted from Doke 1947, pp. 106–10.

point and sometimes authority to a proverbial saying, the form sometimes known as 'wellerism'.[1] This may be humorous as with the Ganda ' "I'll die for a big thing", says the biting ant on the big toe',[2] but is usually more serious. There are also miscellaneous patterns of fairly frequent occurrence such as the widespread 'If ... then ...' formula, the proverbs opening with 'It is better', particularly popular among the Thonga, the frequent Lamba form 'As for you ...', the Zulu negative axioms opening 'There is no ...' or 'There is not ...', the Nyanja use of special diminutive prefixes (*ka-* and *ti-*),[3] and the 'slang' form in Tumbuka-Kamanga proverbs of *cha-*, referring to the typical behaviour of some animal or thing.[4] Another form that occurs occasionally is the rhetorical question, as in the Karanga 'The swallower of old cows, is he choked with the bone of a calf?' (a chief who settles big cases is not likely to be overcome by a small one).[5] Although not mentioned by Doke a further formal element in the proverbs of certain peoples is that of tones (e.g. in Luba proverbs[6]), and rhyme, in parts of East Africa.[7]

The wording of Bantu proverbs seems to be relatively fixed in outline so that these general patterns are maintained, or recalled, in their various citations. Minor variations, however, not infrequently occur. A proverb may appear in the singular or plural, with various verb tenses, or in the first, second, or third persons.[8] The forms also sometimes vary from place to place. Two sets of Ndebele proverbs, for instance, collected about a hundred miles from each other, differed slightly in form though they were clearly the 'same' proverbs,[9] and over wider areas there may be similar variations due to differences in dialect.[10] As mentioned already

---

[1] For some non-Bantu 'wellerisms' see A. Dundes, 'Some Yoruba Wellerisms, Dialogue Proverbs and Tongue-twisters', *Folklore* 75, 1964.

[2] Doke 1947, p. 110.    [3] Gray 1944, p. 102.

[4] T. Cullen Young, *Notes on the Customs and Folk-lore of the Tumbuka-Kamanga Peoples*, Livingstonia, 1931, p. 266.

[5] C. J. Bisset, 'Some Chikaranga Proverbs', *Nada* 11, 1933, p. 98.

[6] Van Avermaet 1955, pp. 3 ff.

[7] See e.g. J. Knappert, 'Rhyming Swahili Proverbs', *Afr. u. Übersee* 49, 1966; for some non-Bantu rhyming proverbs see H. C. Jackson, 'Sudan Proverbs', *Sudan Notes* 2, 1919.

[8] This, incidentally, makes the alphabetical classification adopted by some collectors an unsatisfactory one.

[9] W. R. Benzies and H. M. G. Jackson, 'Proverbs from the Matabele', *Nada* 2,1924; G. Taylor and N. Jones, 'Sindebele Proverbs', *Nada* 3, 1925.

[10] Hulstaert 1958, p. 8.

there are sometimes two forms, the full and the abbreviated, the second being the one normally cited. Sometimes the saying is cut down even further and merely referred to in one word, a phenomenon particularly common in one-word personal names. Thus among the Ovimbundu a woman may be called *Sukuapanga* ('God willed') from the proverb 'God willed; Death unwilled' (*Suku wa panga*; *Kulunga wa pangulula*), or *Mbundu* from a proverb about customs differing: 'The mist of the coast (is) the rain of the upland' (*Ombundu yokombaka ombela yokonano*).[1] A similar tendency is noted among the Ganda who often prefer to leave a proverb to be completed by the hearer: names are sometimes the first word of a proverb, and even the title of a book appears as just '*Atanayita*' (from the proverb *Atanayita atenda nyina okufumba*— 'The untravelled man praises his mother's cooking').[2] Thus on any particular occasion the actual form of a proverb may vary according to whether it is abbreviated, merely referred to, or cast in one or other of various grammatical forms. But the basic patterns which mark Bantu proverbs tend to recur and be recalled in their various citations.

Bantu proverbs, then, are noted for special patterns which in many cases give a poetic flavour to the saying. They use various devices to express the thought succinctly and sometimes rhythmically, or even in what Chatelain calls 'blank versification'.[3] The effectiveness is heightened by the fact that often, though not always, there are archaic or unusual words and picturesque phrasing.

Similar tendencies probably also occur in many non-Bantu proverbs, although no such detailed synthesis as Doke's has been published for any other language group. There is widespread evidence of balanced propositions. Yoruba proverbs, for instance, are said often to come in couplets with antithesis between the two lines, noun answering to noun and verb to verb: 'Ordinary people are as common as grass, / But good people are dearer than the eye', or 'Today is the elder brother of tomorrow, / And a heavy dew is the elder brother of rain', while repetition also occurs effectively in the form 'Quick loving a woman means quick not

[1] Ennis 1945, p. 3.
[2] R. A. Snoxall, 'Ganda Literature', *Afr. Studies* 1, 1942, p. 59; M. B. Nsimbi, 'Baganda Traditional Personal Names', *Uganda J.* 14, 1950, pp. 204–5.
[3] Chatelain 1894, p. 22.

loving a woman'.[1] Parallelism and chiasmus also occur as in the
Baule praise of mutual help, 'Gauche lave droite, droite lave
gauche',[2] and rhythm may also be evident. Fulani proverbs use
assonance, special grammatical forms such as subjectless verbs or
the subjunctive without specific time reference, and parallel phrasing as in 'An old man does what men don't like, but he does not
do what men don't know' (i.e. his actions may be unpopular, but
they cannot be unnoticed).[3] Related forms sometimes employ
elaborate and studied expression; particularly good examples of
these are the neat Fulani epigrams cited by Arnott or the long
and complex Akan 'drum proverbs'.[4]

In proverbs the actual performance as distinct from apt citation
and picturesque form is not usually significant. Nevertheless, it is
sometimes of interest, perhaps particularly where the words themselves are not so elaborately stylized as in Bantu proverbs. Thus in
Limba, where proverbs are not highly developed in any fixed
form and there is little stress on rhythm or balance, I was told that
in the saying mocking unjustified self-importance ('Do not walk
like a European while wearing a loin-cloth'), part of its attractiveness lay in the way it was said, with a pause before the last word
and the emphasizing of the idea of the loin-cloth by the long-
drawn-out way in which it was pronounced. Herzog says of the
Jabo that proverbs are uttered in a much more rhythmic way
than would be the case with the corresponding words in ordinary
speech.[5] Also a more studied and rhetorical utterance is likely
when, as so often in West African societies, proverbs are used in
formal speeches before law courts. It is possible then that where
the poetic quality of a proverb is not so evident in its verbal content, this is sometimes compensated for by the manner or the
context in which it is said.

The question, therefore, of the actual style of proverbs appears
to demand further research. Whatever the details, however, it is
clear that *some* sort of heightened speech, in one form or another,
is commonly used in proverbs: and that this serves to set them
apart from ordinary speech.

[1] Ellis 1894, p. 238.
[2] G. Effimbra, *Manuel de baoulé*, Paris, [1952], p. 289.
[3] Arnott 1957, p. 389.
[4] Nketia 1958c. See also Ch. 17, pp. 488 ff.
[5] Herzog 1936, p. 8.

III

Since proverbs can refer to practically any situation, it would be impossible to give any comprehensive account of the content of African proverbs. Something of their variety can be gathered from the headings under which they are classed in many collections (in terms either of explicit content or implied allusion), for these headings include every aspect of human affairs. Categories of the manifest content include such headings as 'Animals' (subdivided into, for instance, 'dangerous', 'game', and 'domestic'), 'Birds', 'Insects', 'Mice, rats, and others', 'Strangers, Europeans, and Europe', 'War, fighting, guns, and weapons', and innumerable others; while classifications in terms of the latent reference range from 'Man and woman', 'Efficiency and its conditions', 'Home life', 'Life and death', and 'Passage of time' to 'Conceit', 'Power', 'Cunning', and, of course, 'Miscellaneous'.

Since the actual import depends on the context of use, it is in fact impossible to give any definitive treatment of the allusive content of proverbs without a study of their situations; this material is not usually included in the published collections. A few general points, however, may be worth mentioning briefly and tentatively.

It could perhaps be said that though abstractions in the sense of generalizations are an essential aspect of proverbs, abstract notions are little considered in their own right (except perhaps in some of the more religiously orientated sayings of the Islamic peoples). The stress is rather on comments about human affairs; thus the Thonga 'The heart of a man is a sea' and the picturesque Yoruba saying about the mind confronted with a difficult problem ('As the leper's hand struggles to grip the needle') exemplify the exception rather than the rule.[1] It is noteworthy also that in most Bantu proverbs there are few references to religion; this contrasts with West Africa where this topic is fairly frequent, particularly among Muslim peoples such as the Hausa and Fulani. This may perhaps be connected with the significance of the ancestor cult in many Bantu societies, so that the equivalent of this sort of allusion is made in terms of *human* experience and activity without reference to a transcendent god or specialist religious activity.

There are very many proverbs about authority, government oppression, or the burden of power. Some examples are the Akan

[1] Junod and Jaques 1936, no. 803; Gbadamosi and Beier 1959, p. 60.

suggestion that a king's sons do not need to be taught violence ('No one teaches a leopard's cub how to spring'), or the frequent reminders that even power must bow sometimes, which the Hausa express by 'Even the Niger has an island' and the Yoruba by 'The river carries away an elderly person who does not know his weight'.[1] The Thonga saying 'The centipede's legs are strengthened by a hundred rings' alludes to the chief's dependence on the number of his subjects, while through 'Authority is the tail of a water-rat' they bring out the way power can slip away from its possessor;[2] many other comments on the nature and consequences of power could be cited. Death is another favourite topic, for 'Death has many petticoats' and 'There is no hillside without a grave'.[3] The inexorability of death is often stressed—'There is no ragwort that blooms and does not wither' and 'Death has the key to open the miser's chest'—and resignation and the fact that no one after all is indispensable are also brought out: 'Even there where no cock is crowing, it becomes light.'[4] The conflicts inherent in marriage are very frequently satirized ('Two wives are two pots full of poison', according to the Kikuyu), and self-importance is often picked on—as in the Kikuyu 'Knowing too much is like being ignorant', the Southern Bantu 'No cleverest fellow ever licked his own back', or the Nyanja '"Watch me" was carried off by a crocodile' (the man plunged in vaingloriously instead of patiently waiting for the boat).[5] But a list of popular topics could be prolonged almost indefinitely.

Something has already been said about the sorts of comparisons which appear explicitly in the proverbs. Very often these are to animals or birds, not because Africans have some mystical closeness to nature but because many live in relatively rural and sparsely populated areas where the animal world impinges closely on their lives. But in fact almost anything of which people have experience —not excluding problems of modern government—can appear directly in their proverbs. It is often impossible to grasp the point or attraction of a given proverb without some knowledge of the cultural background and of what the thing mentioned means to those who utter it. Thus the effectiveness of the Zulu saying that

---

[1] Rattray 1916, p. 63; Whitting 1940, p. 5; Gbadamosi and Beier 1959, p. 61.
[2] Junod and Jaques, no. 107.  [3] McLaren 1917, p. 344.
[4] Ibid., p. 343; Rattray 1916, p. 51; Ripp, op. cit.
[5] G. Barra, *1000 Kikuyu Proverbs*, London, 2nd ed., 1960, pp. 2, 40; McLaren 1917, p. 341; Gray 1944, p. 112.

'No proud girl ever had the better of the skin-skirt' is lost to us unless we know that it is customary for only married women to wear skin-skirts and that the proverb therefore refers to the tonic effect of marriage on 'proud cheeky girls'.[1] Similarly the image in the Xhosa likening of a woman to 'a mimosa tree that yields gum all day long' arises from the Xhosa fondness for chewing gum, and the picture in the Mongo proverb 'La marche pendant les eaux hautes, c'est celui qui marche devant qui est intelligent' fits their swampy surroundings where the one in front warns those behind of holes and obstacles underwater.[2] Among pastoral people as preoccupied with cattle as are many of the Southern and Eastern Bantu it is not surprising to find very many proverbs referring to cattle. There is, for example, the warning 'Don't throw away the milk-pails' (your last hope), the common description of a liar ('He milks even cows which are in calf'), and the comment on people's sensitivity and interdependence in terms of cattle, 'It licks the one which licks it, it kicks the one which kicks it'.[3] The interests of each society tend to be reflected in the sort of images through which their proverbs are expressed—like the Ashanti experience of gold ('Wisdom is not gold-dust that it should be tied up and put away'), or the Fulani interest in rank in 'Les vêtements cachent le corps mais ne cachent pas la généalogie'— even a rich and well-dressed man of servile origin will still only be a slave: appearances are not everything.[4]

Similar comparisons sometimes occur over a wide area, often in nearly the same words. This may be partly due to cultural contact between peoples in the present or past. Many Hausa and Fulani proverbs, for instance, are near identical in overt meaning and translation, and the same applies to the Kru and Jabo of Southern Liberia and many others. The Bantu languages provide many examples of this, the more striking owing to their similarity in language as well as sentiment. Thus very similar proverbs are mentioned in many collections from different Bantu societies— 'The eye crosses a full river' (usually referring to man's ambition), 'The buttocks rubbing together do not lack sweat' (friction between those who live together), and 'The sweat of a dog ends

---

[1] Nyembezi 1954, p. 11.
[2] McLaren 1917, p. 333; Hulstaert 1958, p. 412.
[3] Ripp, op. cit.; Nyembezi 1954, p. 6.
[4] Rattray 1916, p. 154; Gaden 1931, p. 103.

in its hair' (a poor man must swallow his wrath or, alternatively, hard work and effort are not always appreciated). Doke gives a detailed example of the way a proverb can take slightly different forms in the many languages in which it occurs (this one is the equivalent of our pot calling the kettle black): the Ila have 'The baboons laughed about one another's overhanging brows', Tswana 'A monkey doesn't see its own hollow eyes', Kimbundu 'The monkey does not notice his tail', Nyanja 'Baboons laugh at one another's buttocks', Swahili 'The ape sees not his own hinder parts, he sees his neighbour's'.[1] The comparisons, then, are close. But the actual application and interpretation may vary from society to society, whatever the wording.

The range of comparisons and applications, then, is enormous. References to the animal world seem particularly frequent everywhere, but they are by no means the only analogies. These include everything with which a given people is preoccupied, and the extent to which any single sphere is stressed depends, as one would expect, on the culture and experience of a particular society.

IV

So far we have been considering the content and formal characteristics of proverbs in Africa. However, it is particularly true of proverbs whose use and application depends so crucially on their context that no full understanding can be reached without some knowledge of the occasions and purposes of their actual use. To consider the myriad different occasions (and hence meanings) would manifestly be impossible—as a Fante elder put it, 'There is no proverb without the situation'[2]—but some comments should be made about the main contexts of proverbs and the functions they fulfil.

There are two themes that one encounters particularly in any discussion of the uses and contexts of proverbs. First, there is the sense of detachment and generalization inherent in proverbs. The speaker stands back, as it were, from the heat of the actual situation and draws attention, for himself or others, to its wider implications. And secondly, there is the oblique and allusive

[1] Doke 1934, p. 360.
[2] Christensen 1958, p. 232; and cf. the story about the Akan attitude to proverbs cited in Evans-Pritchard 1963, p. 7.

nature of expression through proverbs which makes it possible to use them in a variety of effective ways.

Perhaps most often mentioned is their use in oratory, particularly in law cases or disputes. In this situation proverbs are often used by one or other of the parties to get at his opponent or try to make out a good case for himself by drawing some analogy through the image in a proverb. Among the Anang Ibibio, for instance, proverbs are often skilfully introduced into speeches at the crucial moment and are influential in the actual decisions reached.[1] In one Anang law case, the plaintiff managed to stir up antagonism towards the accused (a chronic thief) by alluding to his past record and untrustworthy reputation. He did this by quoting the proverb 'If a dog plucks palm fruits from a cluster. he does not fear a porcupine': if a dog can deal with the sharp needles of the palm fruit, he is likely to be able to face even the porcupine's prickles; similarly a thief will not be afraid to steal again. In this case, however, the thief's guilt was not in fact clear. As part of his defence he on his side used a proverb which was influential in winning over the judge to acquit him, hinting at the way in which he alone had no sympathizers and supporters—'A single partridge flying through the bush leaves no path.'[2]

Counsellors and judges also use proverbs to comment obliquely on the conduct of those involved, often with implied advice or rebuke. A number of these have been recorded among the Nyanja, for whom the court is *the* place for the use of proverbial wit and wisdom and who often refer to such cases in metaphors drawn from hunting. As they put it, ' "Quietly—quietly" doesn't kill game (that which) kills game is "there it is! there it is" '—unless, that is, those who bring the case explain what it is all about, they cannot expect to win any more than a hunt can be successful without noisy beaters driving the game into the net; what is more, the judge should be quiet and listen like the guard at the net. People are rebuked for their wrong behaviour in court and reminded allusively that what they are doing falls into some general category they too disapprove of. Telling lies, for instance, only makes matters worse: an animal caught in a net only entangles itself further with wild struggles, and so a man is told in court that 'It is patience which gets you out of the net'. Again, those who try to excuse themselves before the court by saying that what they did

[1] See the article by Messenger 1959.      [2] Ibid., pp. 68–9.

was only a small thing may be reminded that 'The thing which upsets the porridge-pot is a small piece of *tsekera* grass'.[1]

In court and elsewhere there are also frequent occasions for using a proverb to smooth over a disagreement or bring a dispute to a close. According to the Yoruba proverb, 'A counsellor who understands proverbs soon sets matters right',[2] and a difficult law case is often ended by the public citation of an apt proverb which performs much the same generalizing function as citing legal precedents in other societies. Some of these might be classed as juridical axioms and maxims, but many in fact succeed just because the attempt at reconciliation is oblique and through an analogy rather than a straightforward injunction. The contenders are not only brought to view the dispute in a wider perspective (and thus be more ready to come to terms), but this is conveyed in a tactful and allusive way. Among the Limba, for instance, an elder in court tries to persuade one party to a dispute not to be angry with someone younger by reminding them that one 'does not shoot the chimpanzee for its ugliness'; i.e. one should not go to extremes in punishing a child, however bad, any more than one actually kills a chimpanzee because it is ugly. In pronouncing his decision the president of an Anang court frequently uses the proverb 'If you visit the home of the toads, stoop' to remind those involved that one should conform to the divine moral law, and the Yoruba make the similar point that once a dispute has been brought to an end it should then be regarded as finally settled—'When the face is washed you finish at the chin.'[3] In a less formal context, the Kikuyu bring an interminable and profitless discussion to an end by asking the question, agreed to be unanswerable, 'When new clothes are sewn, where do the old ones go?'[4]

More or less formalized law cases, then, provide many opportunities for proverbs. However, they also occur in less formal situations for giving ordinary advice. Here too their oblique and tactful nature makes them particularly effective. Many examples of this could be given. In Lamba culture, for instance, the young are

---

[1] Gray 1944, pp. 107, 108.       [2] Ellis 1894, p. 218.

[3] Messenger 1959, p. 70; Ellis 1894, p. 231.

[4] M. S. Stevenson, 'Specimens of Kikuyu Proverbs', *Festschrift Meinhof*, Glückstadt, 1927, p. 246. On judicial proverbs, see also A. E. Meeussen, 'Aktiespreuken bij de Lega', *Kongo-Overzee* 25, 1959; E. Van Goethem, 'Proverbes judiciaires des Mongo', *Aequatoria* 10, 1947; I. Schapera, 'Tswana Legal Maxims', *Africa* 36, 1966.

warned in such terms as 'Your mouth will turn into a knife and cut off your lips' or 'You will let the mouse rot in the trap' (i.e. let the opportunity pass),[1] and among the Tetela the proverb 'The palm-tree grows in the tall grass' may be used as a gentle hint to parents that it is best to leave a child alone and to let him play and get dirty—he will grow up.[2] The Oron miser who, with some polite excuse, refuses a request, particularly for money, is told obliquely that the asker knows quite well that he does not really want to do it: 'The child who refuses to go an errand says he does not know the way.'[3]

This function of proverbs to advise, rebuke, or shame another into complaisance has been particularly well described for the Ila of Zambia.[4] A man may be reminded that, as we would put it, Rome was not built in a day—'One day is not sufficient to rot an elephant'—or that pride and contempt of authority are not admired since 'We do not like the pride of a hen's egg': eggs in a nest are all equal, so one of them should not be proud. Practical as well as ethical advice is given: 'If you eat with one chief only, it is because you have no feet', for you should get what you can out of all of them. Ridicule and mockery in proverbs are also effective. As Smith writes of Ila proverbs, wit has a utilitarian aim; laughter is never far away, and because of their susceptibility to ridicule the Ila, like many others, can sometimes be laughed out of a thing more effectively than deterred by argument or force. Thus Pharisees are mocked as those who 'spurn the frog but drink the water': they are the kind of people who object to finding a frog in their drinking water but are perfectly happy to drink once the frog has been removed. Another pressure is through irony, assuming that what *ought* to be done *is* always done; the quickest way to gain hospitality among the Ila is to quote 'The rump of a visitor is made to sit upon'.[5] Indeed, any kind of satirical or penetrating comment on behaviour may be made in the form of a proverb and used to warn or advise or bring someone to his senses. He is reminded of the general implications of his action—and the fact that the reminder

[1] Doke 1934, p. 361.

[2] E. B. Stilz, Otetela proverbs, Wombo Nyama, 1939 (manuscripts in Doke Collection, University College Library, Salisbury, S. Rhodesia).

[3] Simmons 1960*b*, p. 135 (slightly expanded to make the literal English translation intelligible).

[4] Smith and Dale ii, 1920, pp. 311 ff.

[5] Ibid., p. 312.

is cast in apparently innocent and irrelevant terms may make it all the more effective.

There is another aspect of proverbs which is connected with their use for comment or persuasion and which sometimes appears in a specialized and extreme form. This is their oblique and suggestive character. The speaker wishes to convey something, but in such a way that later on he can deny that he actually stated what was implied, or so that only some among his listeners may understand the point. This type of suggestiveness is developed to a particularly high degree in the Zande *sanza* in which a kind of malicious double-talk is used to convey a meaning other than the obvious sense. Again, the Nyanja have a special term which can be translated as 'speaking by opposites' by which they make deliberate mis-statements with an esoteric intention—the older people and *cognoscenti* can understand, but not other listeners.[1] Similarly among the Thonga a proverb may be used with an apparently clear meaning but in practice a completely different intention,[2] while the Kamba *ndimo*, 'dark saying', is a kind of secret language.[3]

Irony or sarcasm as a way of getting at someone is, of course, widespread in many forms, but the proverb is a particularly good way of conveying this. This kind of implicit attack on another, already mentioned in the context of a formal law case, sometimes takes more unusual forms. An example is the elliptical language of names. Through this people can refer to another's fault while at the same time avoiding any direct commitment. Thus, among the Karanga, a dog may be called by the proverbial name 'Things which change from day to day' in allusion to a capricious wife, or a flirtatious woman may be called 'All eyes' as a reproof since she has eyes for all personable males; similarly a dog's name may be 'Home-wrecker', given him by a suspicious husband to warn off his wife's lover.[4]

Certain themes seem to be present in the various contexts of proverbs we have discussed so far. Though proverbs can occur in very many different kinds of contexts, they seem to be particularly important in situations where there is both conflict and, at the

---

[1] Gray 1944, p. 102.
[2] Junod and Jaques 1936 (foreword).
[3] Lindblom iii, 1934, p. 28.
[4] N. A. Hunt, 'Some Notes on the Naming of Dogs in Chikaranga', *Nada* 29, 1952.

same time, some obligation that this conflict should not take on too open and personal a form. Such conflict can occur in many different ways—there may be competition for scarce resources, there may be a stress, as among the Zulu or Ibo, on the idea of personal achievement or, as among the Azande, on the significance of hierarchy, with the competitiveness for advancement and notice so closely connected with these; in all these situations there may also be an idea that the conflict involved should not be allowed to become extreme and explicit. It can be seen how the veiled and metaphorical language of proverbs is particularly relevant in such contexts.[1] Indeed, proverbs may also be specially suitable even in everyday situations of advice or instruction where the hidden tensions that are sometimes inherent in such relationships are controlled through the use of elliptical, proverbial speech. Even in cases of overt and institutionalized conflict—for example, the law cases in the more highly organized African states—proverbs play a part in formalizing and controlling the conflicts involved. In some Western societies, there are provisions in the legal system for minimizing personal clashes involved in lawsuits while at the same time making it possible for each side to present their case effectively by the relative impersonality of the written word, and by the institution of counsels for each of the two parties who, as well as forwarding their clients' interests, impose a kind of veil which prevents direct confrontation. It seems that in certain non-literate African societies the use of proverbs may fulfil something of the same function.

Proverbs, then, may be a particularly suitable form of communication in situations and relationships of potential or latent conflict. This aspect may perhaps serve to throw some light on the fact that whereas some peoples make great use of proverbs, among others, for instance the Nuer, they seem to be of little or no importance.[2] For it may be that it is precisely those societies in which there is marked latent conflict, or in which there is particular need to

---

[1] Proverbs are not, of course, the only way of dealing with such situations and relationships in non-literate societies. There are also, for instance, witchcraft beliefs and accusations; the use of veiled political and satirical songs; or joking relationships. In this last form, the opposite means is, in a sense, being chosen: proverbs may deal with conflict by smoothing it over; joking resolves it by exaggerating the hostility involved and thus, in its way, resolving it.

[2] A point raised by Evans-Pritchard in 1963*b*, p. 109 and, so far as I know, nowhere satisfactorily discussed.

regulate formalized conflicts, that proverbs play an especially large part.

Collectors and commentators frequently mention the use of proverbs in education. Although the details are often not made very clear, it seems that there are several different senses in which proverbs can fulfil educational functions. Sometimes proverbs (and other verbal forms like riddles) are used in a quite specific way in societies which lay great stress on initiation ceremonies. The initiates may be instructed in the proverbs and aphorisms current in the society, just as they are also often taught dances, songs, and other skills. Among the Chaga, for instance, proverbs play an important part in formal instruction during initiation ceremonies and are highly valued;[1] 'the Chaga', it is said, 'have four big possessions: land, cattle, water and proverbs'.[2] This sort of formal instruction may have a certain esoteric intention; the members of the group versed in these proverbs are now, by their very knowledge, marked off from those who have not yet reached this stage. In addition, in a non-literate society instruction through proverbs provides a means for relatively formal education and transmission of cultural traditions. Proverbs with their implicit generalized import are clearly a suitable and succinct form in which to verbalize socially prescribed actions and attitudes.

Proverbs, then, are sometimes used quite formally and consciously as a vehicle to achieve the ends, and in the same sort of contexts, that we associate with formal education. However, when collectors comment on the educational function of proverbs they do not necessarily intend to convey such a specific role as that described above, one which certainly does not occur in every African society. What they often seem to be describing is the *general* educative role of proverbs. Now proverbs often imply some general comment on the way people do, or should, or should not behave. It is clear that the conveying of a people's experience and expectations can be performed in a particularly effective way through the use of proverbs. But proverbs are in practice cited in a whole variety of situations, and only in some of them does there seem to be any intentionally educational purpose. The manifest aim may in fact be to get at an opponent, to defy a superior in a polite and

[1] O. F. Raum, *Chaga Childhood*, London, 1940, pp. 217, 333–4.
[2] Ibid., p. 217.

oblique way, to make an effective and unanswerable point in a speech, etc.—yet at the same time the latent function is performed of transmitting a certain view of the world, a way of interpreting and analysing people and experience, and recognition of certain situations. Among the Ibo, for instance, proverbs fulfil this aim incidentally even though the explicit occasion is that of a dance. As the masked dancer progresses, he has proverbs and aphorisms called out before him, and, as Green writes, 'the chanting in front of the masked figure of these utterances is a way of steeping the members of the society in the traditional values of their culture'.[1] Other quasi-educational results which may come from the frequent use of proverbs seem only incidental, not really distinguishable in kind from the general socialization and education undergone by people just because and in that they are members of a particular society.

In between these two extremes there is the kind of situation in which, without any specific formal occasion for their use, proverbs are yet consciously used from time to time with the intention of instructing or of giving advice. Thus we are told of proverbs in many societies[2] that they are used for 'instruction' or 'child-rearing'. Most authors, however, do not give details of the actual situations of such usage. It is true that the generalizations implicit in many proverbs make them suitable vehicles for this sort of instruction; but the occasions we are told about suggest that what in fact is often being done is to convey the applicability of a proverb to a particular *situation* rather than to teach any actual generalization implied or stated in the proverb. This too is of course a type of education. But it is perhaps not quite that implied by the frequent references to the 'educational purpose' of these proverbs.[3]

Besides these relatively utilitarian aspects of proverbs it is clear that there is also what might be called a purely literary aspect. That this view is not just that of the outside observer is clear from

[1] Green 1948, p. 840.

[2] e.g. Zulu, Lamba, Ila, Nyanja, Kuanyama Ambo, Fante, Anang Ibibio.

[3] Straight generalizations and aphorisms are sometimes included in collections of proverbs and these may be used to instruct in some general sense; but further study may show that several of these satisfy neither the criterion of being a generally accepted truth, nor that of involving allusive, figurative, or otherwise picturesque expression; they are thus strictly only marginal to the analysis of proverbs and of oral literature in general.

the overlap in terminology already mentioned between proverbs and such unquestionably literary genres as stories, parables, or riddles. In the case of certain peoples, indeed, their proverbs (sometimes together with their riddles) appear to be the richest or most interesting part of their oral literature.[1] Of the proverbs in many African societies we are told that they are consciously used not only to make effective points but also to embellish their speeches in a way admired and appreciated by their audiences. It is part of the art of an accomplished orator to adorn his rhetoric with apt and appealing proverbs. The Anang Ibibio reputation for eloquence largely arises from their skilful use of proverbs, and a Zulu orator who can quote aptly, readily, and profusely is particularly admired.[2] Proverbs are also used to add colour to everyday conversation. This aspect seems to be very widespread indeed and in some cases at least to be an art cultivated to a very high degree. Thus among the Mongo, proverbs are said to be continually cited; among the Zulu, someone who did not know their proverbs would be lost in the allusiveness of their conversation; while among the Bambara, proverbs are honoured to such an extent that they tend to use a proverb every two or three phrases even in everyday conversation.[3] The Akan allude to the subtlety in proverbs by their saying 'When a fool is told a proverb, the meaning of it has to be explained to him', and as Nyembezi writes of the Zulu, in words also applicable to many other African cultures, proverbs are essential to life and language: 'Without them, the language would be but a skeleton without flesh, a body without soul.'[4]

This literary use of proverbs in ordinary speech is sometimes taken further and shades into more elaborate forms like the Akan drum proverbs, Fulani epigrams, or Zulu bird songs. Unlike many other prose forms, proverbs are not normally used specifically for entertainment but are more involved in everyday situations. However, we do hear occasionally of contests in proverb telling. Among the Fante proverbs are recited as entertainment both at casual gatherings in the evening and at ceremonies and celebrations

[1] For example the Fang (Tardy 1933, p. 282) and the Anang Ibibio (Messenger 1959, p. 64).
[2] Messenger 1959, p. 64; Vilakazi 1945, ch. 10.
[3] Hulstaert 1958, p. 5; J. Stuart and D. Malcolm, *Zulu Proverbs and Popular Sayings*, Durban, [1949] (introd.); Travélé 1923, p. 35.
[4] Rattray 1916, p. 152; Nyembezi 1954, p. 44.

with a panel of judges to decide between the contestants, while Lestrade writes of the South African Bantu that proverbs are sometimes used in a regular game similar to that of riddle asking—interpretations of proverbs are exchanged and the players 'buy' a new proverb and its interpretation in exchange for one they know.[1] In all these contexts the proverb is a vehicle particularly suited to give depth and elegance through its allusive, figurative, and poetic mode of expression.

Proverbs, finally, are often said to represent a people's philosophy. In proverbs the whole range of human experience can be commented on and analysed, generalizations and principles expressed in a graphic and concise form, and the wider implications of specific situations brought to mind. This aspect has always appealed particularly to collectors. Some editors have taken it rather far and suggested that proverbs make up 'tribal law'[2] or illustrate every belief and prescribed piece of behaviour in a direct and literal way. This is to miss the flexibility and situational aspect that is so striking a characteristic of African proverbs. As has been pointed out by several authorities, the same proverb may be used in a whole range of situations with different applications and meanings. Furthermore, as has frequently been noticed, the occurrence of 'contradictory' proverbs is widespread; thus the Southern Bantu stress both the unruliness *and* indispensability of a man's tongue: 'The mouth has no lid to cover it', yet 'The tongue is a man's tail-switch to drive away the flies';[3] and many other such examples could be cited. If interpreted as literal injunctions or evaluations, clearly there is contradiction. Instead they might be regarded as a way of summing up what is recognized as only one facet of the truth, to be used as and when it applies or appeals; then it is possible to appreciate more fully the flexible and subtle way in which, through a whole series of overtones and depths of meaning, proverbs represent 'the soul of a people'.

In relation to the question of the occasions and functions of proverbs something should be said about the people who cite or listen to proverbs. There is not much evidence on this, but clearly

---

[1] Christensen 1958, p. 239; Lestrade 1937, pp. 293-4.
[2] e.g. G. Barra, *1000 Kikuyu Proverbs*, London, 2nd ed., 1960 (foreword).
[3] McLaren 1917, p. 341.

the details vary from society to society. Sometimes the proverbs are potentially known to everyone and free for all to use on suitable occasions. The actual use, of course, depends on the occasion: thus where proverbs are most common in law cases and men are the chief litigants, proverbs are seldom used by women; and proverbs giving advice are most naturally used by elder people. In other societies there seem to be certain proverbs which are reserved for use only by older people and would not be cited in the presence of youths or uncircumcised adults. Sometimes proverbs as tools in argument are reserved for the elderly alone; thus of the Fon Herskovits tells us that 'one limiting principle governs their use. The young may not presume to press a point with their seniors by using proverbs.'[1] Among the Nyanja proverbs are sometimes used with a definitely esoteric intention,[2] and we may guess that in societies with a fairly high degree of specialization, particularly with regard to religious and artistic affairs, there is likely to be a group who are particularly conversant with the allusions and possibilities inherent in proverbs. The situation described of the Mongo is very likely typical of many societies: that whereas some proverbs are used by the whole population and known very widely, others are rare or reserved for certain specialists.[3] But this whole subject is obscure and the evidence scanty.

There is also the question of individual authorship and originality. Since one of the characteristics of a proverb is that it should be accepted by the community as a whole, the scope for individual initiative is clearly limited. However, the fact that there is a certain amount of variation in form and the great range of varied situations to which proverbs can be applied with greater or lesser aptness and insight give some opening for individual contributions. There is a certain amount of evidence about the way new proverbs are coined by individuals and later taken up by the community. As Nyembezi points out about the Zulu, there are no special people with the job of evolving proverbs, but new ones nevertheless arise through individuals; and we are told elsewhere that many Zulu proverbs were first uttered by famous men or by bards or jesters before the king or at a beer-drink and were then taken up and popularized by others.[4] It is common for proverbs to be attributed to well-known historical personages; this is often conventional but

---

[1] Herskovits 1958, p. 57.   [2] Gray 1944, p. 102.
[3] Hulstaert 1958, p. 5.   [4] Nyembezi 1954, p. xi; Ripp, op. cit.

in some cases may be justified. Similarly new proverbs are mentioned as being taken by individuals from various outside sources, or arising from individual inventiveness and poetic imagination within the framework of the conventional forms and functions in any given society.[1]

We can, then, sum up the various ways in which proverbs are used in African societies by saying that they really occur on *all* occasions when language is used for communication either as art or as a tool—i.e. on every sort of occasion imaginable. In particular societies there may be certain rules or tendencies about the sorts of occasions on which they are most frequent or suitable, or the classes of people who should use them. Some peoples may use proverbs in a particularly sophisticated way as the basis for more elaborate forms of literature, while others stress the useful aspect of proverb-citing or their more literary and artistic purpose. But they are above all used as a form of formalized conflict and its resolution, as an oblique and allusive way of communication, as a form of expression with a certain educational relevance, as an artistic activity in its own right, or as all these at once.

V

So far the discussion has been rather general and comparative. However, some of the points made may emerge more clearly with a discussion of the nature and use of proverbs in three specific societies, ones which differ in language, social organization, and geographical location.

First, the Jabo. These are a Kru-speaking people living in small independent settlements in south-eastern Liberia. Their proverbs were collected and studied in the 1930s by Herzog and his native assistant. They were published in the original and in translation with a full commentary on their various meanings and situations and an illuminating introduction.[2]

Though it is difficult to estimate the number of Jabo proverbs it seems to be considerable; Herzog gives 416 (in addition to related 'sayings') and considers that more could have been collected and that new proverbs were constantly being made. Jabo proverbs shade into other forms: the 'sayings' (which are sometimes merely idiomatic expressions); the 'singers' words' (or 'lying words')

---

[1] Cf. Herzog 1936, p. 7; Hulstaert 1958, pp. 5–6.    [2] Herzog 1936.

which are formalized statements, easily transformed into proverbs, which singers introduce into their songs of praise; and the 'titles' or honorary addresses for characterization and praise. Proverbs are more or less distinct from these forms in their style, being more poetic and symbolic than the 'sayings' but considerably less poetic than the other two forms.

The proverb proper is termed *dále'kpa*, a word also used for a parable or short animal tale rounded out with a proverb which serves as the moral. The term is also said to be connected with an archaic form meaning 'old matters', and this implies the idea of taking an old situation and applying it to the present, coping with it by regarding it in the light of something that has occurred before. It is also connected with the idea of generalization in idioms like 'He quotes stingy proverbs' (i.e. 'He supports his stinginess with generalities'), used of someone who by way of excuse evades a request with stock phrases.

Although the citing of proverbs is not a specialized activity like riddling or story-telling, and occurs freely and informally in every sort of context, there are nevertheless certain stock situations where proverbs are especially frequent. They play an important part in Jabo legal proceedings; indeed at a certain stage the discussion mainly takes place through the quoting of proverbs. In this way the case can be raised from the particular to the general and can be classified according to the generalizations inherent in proverbs. The more proverbs a man can use, the more effective he is considered to be, and 'since almost any act has legalistic aspects, there is hardly a discussion of any consequence (whether or not actually in court) in which proverbs are not employed'.[1] Proverbs are also very commonly used to smooth social friction and help individuals to adjust themselves to their positions; there are a very great number of proverbs implying 'under the circumstances what did you expect?' which are used in these contexts (e.g. 'The butterfly that flies among the thorns will tear its wings' or 'If you marry a beautiful woman, you marry trouble', a comment, among other things, on the dangers attending prosperity). These are often particularly effective in smoothing dissatisfaction because uttered by an older person in a society where seniority is taken seriously. Besides their general use in legal and social life, both formally and informally, proverbs also provide the means

[1] Ibid., p. 2.

by which generalizations can be made explicit, and at times provide an intricate and artistic intellectual exercise for the adept.

The characteristic of proverbs which Herzog brings out most forcefully is their flexibility. The same proverb may be used as advice, instruction, or warning, and may be cited in situations which may seem far removed from the original application, or even in contradictory senses. Thus the saying 'We watch the bird's neck while he is talking' can be used in at least three situations with different meanings: as a retort when someone weak makes a threat, meaning that before taking a threat seriously we should look to see who makes it; as an expression of doubt about the truth of what another is saying; and, finally, as an indication that everyone agrees with a speaker.[1] Jabo proverbs thus have a wide range of applicability, and the ostensible meaning can in certain situations even shade into its opposite.

The form of Jabo proverbs is somewhat removed from that of everyday prose utterance. Many proverbs begin with '... says: ...', as in 'North wind says: if you rise, they will know you are there' (used either to point out something self-evident or to remind that a man must demand in order to get his due). The supposed speaker is often either some natural object, (sea, plant, etc.), people (e.g. the Kru, white people), or, very often, specific animals or birds. Such proverbs can be quoted either with or without this attribution. There are also other introductory formulas used for emphasis which may or may not appear on a given occasion, such as 'I say' or 'It is the truth what they say'. Very many proverbs have the patterns 'If..., then...', 'Where..., there...', or give rule of conduct with the impersonal pronoun 'one'. The ideas of contrast and of limitation are also frequently brought out by the form. Contrast is emphasized in, for instance, 'When the spirits are gone, dogs will serve the wine', a complex proverb which implies among other things the contrast between mature age ('spirits') and careless impetuous youth ('dogs'); and limitation is conveyed by alluding to the immutability of certain laws in 'When it rains, the roof always drips the same way'. Poetic and archaic expressions occur, and the poetic tone is intensified by the symmetrically balanced structure and occasional rhythmic swing which is accentuated in actual utterance. In this way,

[1] Herzog 1936, p. 70.

proverbs are a kind of technical language, with specialized vocabulary, style, and linguistic and logical constructions.

These proverbs and related sayings, then, are described as playing a central role in Jabo society. They characterize and evaluate persons, events, and situations, interpret the particular into general and recognizable experience, and are 'the most important verbal instrument for minimizing friction and effecting adjustment, legal, social, or intellectual . . . they form a vital and potent element of the culture they interpret'.[1]

The Zulu of South Africa are exceedingly rich in proverbs. These have been extensively collected and commented on for many years. The best account is that by Nyembezi who has published over 700 proverbs, gleaned both from earlier collections and from his own field-work.[2]

In Zulu, as in many languages, it is not easy to draw a sharp line between idioms and proverbs proper, but there seems to be a general distinction in form and terminology between 'sayings' or plain prose usages (*izisho*), and *izaga*, proverbs. Consonant with the general Zulu interest in rhythm, music, dance, and poetry, their proverbs are often marked by a certain metrical form which makes a contrast with plain prose. This is often brought out by balanced structure such that contrasted subjects are governed by one predicate (thus presenting two opposed ideas), by contrasted predicates governed by one subject, or by contrast in both subjects and predicates.[3] Word-order is important so that verb contrasts with verb, adverb with adverb, and so on, and cross-parallelism also occurs. In some proverbs the contrast lies in the ideas rather than the words themselves. Economy of expression is particularly marked in Zulu proverbs, often with elision of vowels or whole words and the subject suggested only by the concord. Certain patterns occur frequently and give the proverbs a distinct form even when, as in some cases, they lack rhythm. There are frequent expressions in terms of two, three, or four word-groups, and a specially popular form is that beginning with *akukho* (or its abbreviation *aku*), 'there is no . . .', as in 'No polecat ever smelt its own stink': people fail to recognize their own faults. The

---

[1] Ibid., p. 15.
[2] Nyembezi 1954. Unattributed references are to this work throughout this section.     [3] Vilakazi 1945, ch. 10.

vocabulary used seems to be the everyday one, but the proverbs cease to be ordinary not just because of their special forms but because they are generally accepted as clever and attractive expressions of some truth.

The proverbs gain their significance from the situations in which they are used. If some of the proverbs appear to have contradictory senses, this is merely because there are many possible situations and different angles from which one can look at a problem. Besides their importance in teaching, proverbs are also commonly used in lawsuits and arguments to minimize friction. They are used too in general comment on people and the world, often humorously. Proverbs can be used to enrich and enliven speech at every level, whether of formal oratory or of everyday conversation, and are regarded as essential to the life and language of the Zulu.

The images in terms of which many of the Zulu proverbs are phrased are primarily drawn from observation of human behaviour, of the ways of animals, and of other things in the natural environment. As we would expect of a pastoral people devoted to their livestock, there are very many proverbs connected with cattle and cattle husbandry. Hunting is another popular subject; birds are often referred to, and the proverbs in fact often merge into, or appear in, the songs attributed to many well-known birds.[1] Proverbs may also contain references to historical events, such as those which speak of the famous Shaka, or they may be connected with well-known tales, sometimes gaining their effectiveness through referring to the events in the tale, and sometimes apparently giving rise to the story.

There are a great number of proverbs about hospitality, and about both bravery and caution. Change of fortune is another common theme, and many involve recognition of different types of people, whether within or outside the family—the good and bad, crafty and cunning, honest and truthful, or angry and overbearing—(the last compared to 'a log with a centipede in it'). Through all these topics, and many others, the Zulu are able to comment on and mould their social experience; their proverbs are an important facet of their conversation and literature.

The final example is that of the Azande of Central Africa, a people characterized by their powerful aristocratic class of princes,

[1] See Dunning 1946.

their state organization which gives rise to competition and jealousies among those at court, an authoritarian model for social relationships, and the tortuous and suspicious mentality which goes with all this. They have developed a characteristic mode of speech, '*sanza*', an oblique and ambiguous form of expression of which their proverbs form only one example. This double-talk (including proverbs) has been described by Evans-Pritchard in a series of articles drawing mainly on his own field-work supplemented by published collections of proverbs.[1]

The Zande term *sanza* means both proverb and spite (or jealousy) and, in addition, refers to the whole range of circumlocutory expression in which there is a hidden as well as a manifest meaning, usually malicious. The Azande have many proverbs and these are marked by the same kind of characteristics as those of other peoples. Though they do not rhyme or show much alliteration, there is a certain rhythmic balance between the two halves of the sentence: 'Cautious one was grazed by the spear / it went right through the careless one', or 'The little gazelle stood by the fallen tree / and said he was bigger than it'. Where this balance is lacking the Azande tend to supply it with an introductory half-sentence. Besides the presence or absence of such prefaces there are also other variations in their verbal structure, and it is common for the proverb not to be spoken in full but to be alluded to by only an extract from it.

The content of the proverbs is sometimes derived from Zande folktales and their meaning depends on a knowledge of these. But the metaphors seem most frequently to arise from the intimate Zande knowledge of wild life, connected with the fact that their traditional form of settlement is in scattered homesteads with wild life all around them. Very many of the images are taken from wild creatures, from hunting, and from collecting activities; far fewer are taken from agricultural work and domesticated plants—a fact which Evans-Pritchard thinks may be explained by the relatively recent change from hunting and collecting to agriculture.

Evans-Pritchard has documented fully how the situation in which a proverb is cited affects its import, so that any one proverb may have a wide range of meanings. So, for example, the saying 'The wildcat honoured itself by its cry' can be variously interpreted as a reference to the respect resulting from its cry, with the

---

[1] Evans-Pritchard 1956, 1963*a*, 1963*b*, 1964*a*.

implication that even if someone is not honoured he can manage for himself; to the fact that the wildcat prizes her own cry and that each person talks after his own fashion; and to the idea that 'as there is no one who will exalt me I must exalt myself'.[1] Many similar examples are given of differing interpretations of single proverbs.

Proverbs seem most typically to be used for warning, to bring another to a sense of proportion, and to comment on or ridicule another's action. They are also used, in a connected way, to take the wind out of another's sails in a dispute. Thus if, instead of saying bluntly 'you are bringing trouble on yourself', you express it as the undeniable fact that 'the frog brings down rain on its own head', you have an unanswerable argument, you come out of it uppermost, and you manage to sting your opponent while sounding quite innocent.

Besides its sense of proverb, *sanza* also refers to ambiguous or hidden language in a wider sense. Usually this form of speech is used in a malicious way, often with the intention of speaking *at* someone while seemingly making an innocent remark. It is particularly common between man and wife and between courtiers in jealous competition with each other at a prince's court, but it enters into all Zande social activities. By using this form of speech, as with the narrower class of proverbs, a man can get at another while at the same time keeping himself under cover; the sufferer will not be able to make overt trouble, and in any case the insult, being hidden, can be withdrawn without loss of dignity. This oblique and veiled form of speech is one which, as Evans-Pritchard shows in some detail, fits the suspicious and competitive outlook of the Azande, and can be connected with the authoritarian nature of their relationships and their dominant fear of witchcraft.

This hidden and oblique form of speech, then, with its overtones of playing safe and avoiding direct commitment, is one developed to a high degree among the Azande. However, it seems to be an element in all use of proverbs, one which comes out particularly in situations of conflict or uneasy social relationships and where depths of hidden meaning are sensed or implied.

Proverbs in Africa are effective in a whole range of ways in life and in literature. This might not be immediately obvious from the manifold, usually unannotated, volumes in which African proverbs

---

[1] Evans-Pritchard 1963*a*, p. 6.

have been collected. Their literary significance emerges not only in the beauty of words and form, their sense of detachment and generalization, and their connections with other genres of artistic expression, but also in the aptness and perceptiveness with which they are used in an actual context. Perhaps the most interesting point to emerge from the writings of those who have studied the actual use of proverbs is their *situational* aspect. Proverbs are used on particular occasions, by individuals in a particular context, and their wit, their attractiveness, their insight, even their meaning must be seen as arising from that context.[1]

[1] Like stories and riddles, proverbs are among the most readily collected items of African oral art. Besides references already given here and in the Bibliography, see the useful bibliography and list of collections in Bascom 1964; also references in Doke 1947 and the extensive bibliography in the general article by J. Werner, 'Sprichwortliteratur', *Z. f. Volkskunde* 57, 1961; 58, 1962.

# 15

## RIDDLES

*Riddles and related forms. Style and content. Occasions and uses. Conclusion*

IT may be surprising to find riddles included in a survey of oral literature. However, riddles in Africa have regularly been considered to be a type of art form, albeit often of minor and childish interest, and have long been included in studies of oral literature. There is some reason for this. As will be seen, riddles often involve metaphorical or poetic comment. This indeed was pointed out long ago by Aristotle when he remarked on the close relation of riddles to metaphorical expression.[1]

In Africa riddles are common and have been extensively collected. They are often very closely related to proverbs. Like proverbs they are expressed briefly and concisely; they involve analogy, whether of meaning, sound, rhythm, or tone; and the two forms are sometimes even combined in the 'proverb-riddle'. Riddles also sometimes have close connections with other aspects of literary expression—with such forms as enigmas and dilemma tales, with stories and epigrams, and with praise names. In spite of such connections, however, riddles emerge as a distinct type of literary expression in most African cultures,[2] often one considered to be the special domain of children and, unlike proverbs, to be for entertainment rather than for serious consideration.

### I

In a general way 'riddles' are readily distinguishable by their question-and-answer form and by their brevity. However, a pre-

---

[1] *Rhetoric* iii. 2 (1405ᵇ): 'Good riddles do, in general, provide us with satisfactory metaphors: for metaphors imply riddles, and therefore a good riddle can furnish a good metaphor' (quoted in Georges and Dundes 1963, p. 116).

[2] The local word for riddle sometimes also covers other forms of literature, e.g. Yoruba *alọ* (riddle, story), Efik *ŋke* (story, riddle, tongue-twister, proverb), but it is common for there to be a distinct term (sometimes in addition to a more general one), e.g. in Nyanja, Mbundu, Dogon, Lyele, etc.

liminary point must be made here. The popular European or American picture of a riddle is of an explicit *question* to which a respondent must try to puzzle out the correct answer. African riddles are not altogether like this. The 'question' is usually not an interrogative at all in form but, outwardly at least, is a statement.[1] An answer is expected but very often the listeners are not directly asked to guess but merely faced with an allusive sentence referring analogously to something else which they must then try to identify. The point, furthermore, is normally in some play of images, visual, acoustic, or situational, rather than, as in many English riddles, in puns or plays on words.

There are many different forms. Very often the riddle is in the simple form of a phrase or statement referring to some well-known object in more or less veiled language. Examples of such simple riddles seem to occur all over the continent. There is the Tonga 'Little things that defeat us—Mosquitoes', Makua 'Water standing up—Sugar-cane', Fulani 'Be born; come morning, give birth— Fresh milk' (because milk is left overnight before making butter), Shona 'The little wildcat in the long grass—Scissors', or the Lamba 'The house in which one does not turn round—The grave'.[2] The Nyanja have a characteristic series of riddles in which not only the answer but the question[3] consists of one word only— 'Invisible!—The wind', 'Innumerable—Grass'.[4]

In most of these riddles, what is required is that the answerer should identify the object indicated in these allusive general statements. In fact many riddles need a double process to solve them, for the analogy in the initial statement may not be im- mediately obvious; therefore the solver must first select the salient features of the object or situation mentioned, and then go on to

---

[1] There are a few genuine exceptions to this, but some of the apparently interrogative forms which are sometimes published seem to be due to the European collector's conscious or unconscious imposition of the form more familiar to him. The great majority of these who have explicitly paid attention to the form of riddles in Africa are agreed that the typical pattern is not an interrogative one. (For some exceptions see D. C. Simmons, 'Specimens of Efik Folklore', *Folklore* 66, 1955, p. 422; Bascom 1949, pp. 7 f. (Yoruba).)

[2] J. R. Fell, *Folk Tales of the Batonga and Other Sayings*, London, n.d.; Harries 1942*b*, p. 282; Arnott 1957, p. 382; Fortune 1951, p. 41; Doke 1934, p. 363.

[3] The initial statement which poses the problem will be referred to as 'question' even though this usage is clearly not strictly accurate.

[4] Gray 1939, pp. 258, 261; similar or identical examples are given in Dewar 1900.

identify a similar object. A good example is the Fulani riddle 'I threw a lance, it flew over seven rivers and went and speared the Chief of Masina's bull', where the answer is 'A vulture', the salient features being the fact that it goes far and lands on an animal.[1] Many other examples of such analogies could be cited—for example, the Karanga riddles 'My father's little hill which is easily destroyed —Porridge' because of the way porridge is heaped up on the plate and soon eaten, or 'A flame in the hill—A leopard', and the Zezuru 'The little chap who plays the typewriter—The tongue'.[2]

In these simple riddles, then, some generalization or some image is suggested and the answer involves pointing to the particular object implied. The answer here is the name of the object indicated, often just one word, and the analogy is one of meaning; the respondent must recognize the similarity of situation, character, or behaviour in the statement and its answer.

This type seems to be the most common African form. But there are also other cases in which the analogy involved is not of meaning but of rhythm, sound, or tone, often with a longer reply. These forms must now be considered.

Sometimes there is a rhythm or balance between question and reply. Among the Thonga, for example, one riddle runs 'Over there smoke goes up, over there smoke goes up', to which the reply, in balancing structure, is 'Over there they mourn over a chief, over there they mourn over a poor man'.[3] Junod speaks of many other Thonga riddles in which there is a kind of rhythm in the syllables so that the questions and answers are like 'two little verses, balancing each other in a poetical way',[4] a form of riddle distinguished in the native terminology from the one-word-answer type. Similar 'strophic' riddles are recorded among the Transvaal Sotho,[5] a form reminiscent of the similarly balanced proverbs so common in the same areas.

Besides rhythm, the analogy may take the form of tone resemblance between question and reply. This has been recorded, for

---

[1] Arnott 1957, p. 381. This article is one of the best analyses of African riddles and is drawn on largely here.

[2] N. A. Hunt, 'Some Karanga Riddles', *Nada* 29, 1952, pp. 94, 96; Fortune 1951, p. 39.

[3] Junod and Jaques, 1936.

[4] Junod 1938, p. 41.

[5] C. Endemann, 'Rätsel der Sotho', *ZES* 18, 1927/8; cf. Cole-Beuchat 1957, pp. 144–5.

instance, from the Luvale of Zambia,[1] the Luba of the Congo,[2] and
the Ibibio–Efik group of Southern Nigeria.[3] In these riddles, occurring in languages in which tonality is a significant feature, the
question and answer are marked by identical or similar tonal
patterns. The Ibibio tone riddles described by Simmons are
characterized by their erotic content or allusions, practically all
containing some reference to vagina, clitoris, or coition, as in
the riddles 'Big ships—Big clitoris' and 'Sun shines (and) come
hits ground (and) splits—Vagina opens (and) come takes fly (and)
chews', each characterized by exact or nearly exact tones in each
part.[4] Not all tone riddles have this erotic content (Luvale ones, for
instance, do not[5]). But they all share the characteristic that the
analogy between statement and reply is primarily one of form—
tone and perhaps rhythm—rather than meaning.

So far at least, tone riddles have been infrequently recorded.
Other acoustic images, on the other hand, are very common indeed.
Very often the 'question' consists of just one word or phrase to
suggest the answer through its sound alone. This sound may be
one which gives a direct onomatopoeic impression even to foreigners. In the Kamba riddle '*Seh!*' the answer is 'A needle stabbed
the sand', for the question imitates the sound made by a needle
dropping point first into the sand,[6] a riddle not unlike the similar
Limba one from the other side of the continent, '*Seŋsekede*',
answered 'You cannot put a needle on a rock' (because the sound
of *seŋsekede* suggests the sound made by the needle when it falls
over). More often the acoustic analogy implicit in the question is
not immediately obvious, for ideophones conventionally recognized
in one culture are used to convey an acoustic image to members
of that culture. Thus the Makua riddle '*Ziya eyeya*', an ideophone
representing a state of life, is answered 'An orphan', the Fulani
'*Kerbu kerbu njolla*' represents 'Goats' feet on hard ground',[7] the

[1] C. M. N. White, 'African Tone Riddles', *Man* 58, 1958.
[2] Van Avermaet 1955.
[3] Simmons 1956, 1958. (Not all the so-called 'tone riddles' he gives are, in
fact, characterized by marked resemblance in tone. Efik 'tone riddles' on
Simmons's own showing (1958) include several with 'dissimilar tones', so that
it may be misleading to overemphasize the tonal aspect and ignore other possible
analogies such as, perhaps, rhythm or similarities in structure betweeen question
and answer.)
[4] 1956, pp. 80, 82. Simmons gives only very literal translations.
[5] White, loc. cit.          [6] Lindblom iii, 1934, p. 26.
[7] Harries 1942*b*, p. 287; Arnott 1957, p. 381.

Thonga have '*Shigiligigi shigi*—The rain of early morning', and the Kamba '*Aa*' is answered 'The old man drank a little milk in the dry season'—the sound conventionally suggesting the man's intense thirst and his enjoyment of the milk.[1] In none of these is the connection a 'natural' one which could be recognized by someone unacquainted with the culture.

Besides composing the whole question, there are also ideophones and nonsense-words suggesting some acoustic image which appear as just one part. The Mwera riddle, for example, '*Ndendende* the plaiter of a mat' is answered by 'A hornet'; the ideophone *ndendende* suggests the way the hornet moves its hindquarters rapidly in filling its hole for egg-laying, just as the leaves shake about when someone makes a mat.[2] In Karanga the riddle '*Magiregede* walks as if he were proud' is solved by 'A wagon' because of the onomatopoeic word which imitates the sound of wagon wheels on a road,[3] while the process of going to the spring with an empty pot and coming back with a full one is suggested by the sounds in 'To go u, to return i', where *u* in Shona represents the empty sound, *i* the full one.[4] Sometimes both acoustic and visual images are combined in a riddle, as in the Fulani example explained by Arnott '*Tiisiinii taàsaànaà siradel woogana*—The gait of a large pigeon in sand'; the long-drawn-out words, with a few short syllables in between, correspond to the image of feet dragging through sand with occasional hops; the high-tone and close vowels of *tiisiinii* alternating with the low-tone open vowels of *taàsaànaà* represent the pigeon's gait, swaying from side to side.[5]

The characteristic form of riddles in Africa, then, is for some analogy to be recognized between question and answer, most frequently an analogy of meaning or of sound, with simple one-word reply, but also occasionally longer forms involving tonal and rhythmic correspondence. Though less fully documented than proverbs, many collections of riddles of this form have been made from all parts of the continent.

There are, however, certain other specialized forms which appear to occur only rarely (or else have proved less accessible to collectors) and often overlap to a larger extent with other forms of oral literature. They will only be treated very briefly here.

[1] Junod and Jaques 1936, no. 159; Lindblom iii, 1934, p. 7.
[2] L. Harries, 'Some Riddles of the Mwera People', *Afr. Studies* 6, 1947, p. 24.
[3] Hunt, op. cit., p. 91.     [4] Fortune 1951, p. 42.     [5] Arnott 1957, p. 381.

First, among some peoples riddles may be particularly closely connected with proverbs, so that either the answer or even both parts of the riddle are sayings accepted in other contexts as proverbs. One group of riddles recorded from Leopoldville stands out as being integrally connected with proverbial sayings.[1] Thus change of fortune and the mortality of all men are brought out in the two proverb-riddles 'La terre tourne — Tu possedes, tu seras privé' and 'Toi qui te couches sur un lit et moi qui me couche sur une natte — Nous sortirons (de ce monde) par le même chemin'.[2] Similar instances have been recorded from Southern Nigeria. In a number of the Efik 'tone riddles' the response is said to be a proverb,[3] while the neighbouring Anang Ibibio have a distinct class of proverb-riddles distinguished from their simple riddles which are only to amuse. In these both portions of the riddle consist of a proverb. One example is 'The vine grows along the edge of the pit—He is made to speak in public'. This is explained by the fact that the Anang take a great pride in eloquence and their children are early trained to develop verbal skills; the proverb instructs children to attempt public speaking as early as possible, but at the same time recognizes that this is difficult for them: just as a vine has to struggle to grow along the edge of a hole (and not into it, which would be easier but would cut off the sun), so a child must struggle to overcome his shyness and endeavour to speak.[4] Though proverb-riddles have not been widely reported as a distinct named type, it is possible that proverbs may in fact turn out to occur more frequently than realized in connection with riddles, either explicitly or by allusion, so that in a full analysis of the literature of any one people proverbs and riddles should really be treated in conjunction. Among some of the Central Bantu, for instance, a common riddle that occurs in various forms—'Something I threw over to the other side of the river—Eyes'[5]—recalls the equally common proverb 'The eye crosses a full river', metaphorically signifying that desire goes beyond the possible.

A similar overlap of forms is the way in which praise names occasionally occur in riddles. Thus among the Tlokwa the

---

[1] Referred to as *devinettes-proverbes*, S. Comhaire-Sylvain, 'Quelques devinettes des enfants noirs de Léopoldville', *Africa* 19, 1949.
[2] Ibid., p. 51.     [3] Simmons 1958, p. 125.
[4] Messenger 1960, p. 229. He gives eighteen other examples of these proverb-riddles, with full explanations of each.
[5] The Ila form (Smith and Dale ii, 1920, p. 330).

common praise name for cattle—'God with a watery nose'—is said
also to occur as a riddle, the answer being 'An ox'.[1] The Hausa
riddle referring to a camel is also clearly in the style of a praise
term—'Largest of beasts, devilish property, everyone who loses
you has to look for you'.[2] Again, this sort of connection may turn
out to be widespread.

In South Africa we hear of the 'bird riddle'.[3] This is a kind of
competitive dialogue between two boys or young men in front
of an audience. Each has to prove he 'knows the birds' by making
an assertion about one, then an analogy likening it to a type of
person. Each in turn tries to show that he 'knows' more birds
than his opponent. In this game 'freshness of idea, wit and humour
count more than just the number of birds named'.[4] Thus a com-
petitor with the following was declared the winner with a single
attempt:

*Challenger.* What bird do you know?
*Proposer.* I know the white-necked raven.
*Challenger.* What about him?
*Proposer.* That he is a missionary.
*Challenger.* Why so?
*Proposer.* Because he wears a white collar and a black cassock, and
is always looking for dead bodies to bury.[4]

Song-riddles occur among the Makua,[5] a form said to be unrecorded elsewhere in Africa.[6] These riddles (*ikano*) differ from
ordinary ones in that they are in the form of action songs accompanying a dance and have a didactic purpose closely connected
with initiation rituals. An expert improviser leads the singing,
and the solution of some of the song-riddles are known only to
him; it is forbidden for initiates who have learnt these riddles to
tell them to the non-initiated. Many of these song-riddles include
sexual references or allusions to the initiation rituals. In 'The
handle of the hoe is bent, let him be adze-ed—The seed of the
baobab tree', the seed is compared to a piece of wood which needs

---

[1] Nakene 1943, p. 135.
[2] G. Merrick, *Hausa Proverbs*, London, 1905, p. 80; cf. also praise names in
Lyele riddling (Nicolas 1954, p. 1015) and in Efik (D. C. Simmons, 'Specimens
of Efik Folklore', *Folklore* 66, 1955, p. 422).
[3] Jordan in *Africa South* 2. 2, 1958, pp. 102–3.
[4] Ibid., p. 103.       [5] Harries 1942*a*.
[6] Though see O. F. Raum, *Chaga Childhood*, London, 1940, p. 221; Ghilardi
1966, pp. 183–5 (Kikuyu).

to be straightened so that a hoe can be fixed on (a baobab seed is cleft down the middle); the parallel is to a disobedient person who needs to be straightened by initiation rites.[1] In another, 'A woman smoothly seducing (*ntiya ntiya*), by the grinding, the grinding, the grinding', the answer is 'A helmeted shrike'; *ntiya* is an ideophone for the way in which the woman grinds seductively to attract the man she wants, and she is compared to the helmeted shrike which knows no fear of people.[2] A final example contains an instruction to initiates to avoid incest—'The sweet stalk of millet within the boundary however sweet I shan't break it', answered by 'Blood relationship'.[3]

Besides their occasional connections with songs, praise names, and proverbs, riddles also sometimes shade into other forms of oral literature. They have obvious connections with enigmas, puzzles, and dilemma stories and in some societies the same term refers to all of these. Among the Ila of Zambia, for instance, there is a series of enigmas with the same question, 'You who are (or have grown) so clever!', with a series of possible answers. The point is to be 'a kind of catechism challenging the self-complacency of men who think they know everything'.[4] This is brought out in the responses: 'When the milk of your cows is put together you can't tell which is which', 'You can't tie water in a lump', 'Can you catch hold of a shadow?', 'Can you follow up a road to where it ends?', 'Can you put an ugly person back into the womb to be reborn handsome?'[5] The Ila also have conundrums like, for instance, the puzzle about who should be the one left to perish of a man, his wife, and their two mothers when they reach a river across which only three can be ferried; each possible combination having been found unacceptable, the final answer is that they all had to sit on the bank and die together![6] Similar puzzles, as well as the longer dilemma stories, are widespread. Less common are the epigrams that occur among the Fulani as a form closely connected with both riddles and proverbs. They share the characteristics of grouping together a number of phenomena which have some basic similarity or illustrate some general principle in the same way as riddles. Thus in one example quoted by Arnott a list of similia is given preceded by a statement of the general principle linking them:

[1] Harries, op. cit., p. 33.   [2] Ibid., p. 36.   [3] Ibid., p. 44.
[4] Smith and Dale ii, 1920, p. 330.   [5] Ibid., pp. 330-1.
[6] Ibid., pp. 332-3.

Three exist where three are not:
Commoner exists where there is no king, but a kingdom cannot exist
where there are no commoners;
Grass exists where there is nothing that eats grass, but what eats
grass cannot exist where no grass is;
Water exists where there is nothing that drinks water, but what
drinks water cannot exist where no water is.[1]

Several other examples, including a threefold classificatory epigram, are quoted by Arnott who points out their similarity in certain respects to both proverbs and riddles. They recall the striking
Hausa saying, classified as a riddle by Fletcher but with much in
common with the Fulani epigrams: 'Three things are like three
things but for three things: Sleep is like death but for breathing;
marriage is like slavery but for wifely respect; a guinea-fowl is
like grey cloth but for being alive.'[2]

II

These longer and more complex forms are, however, relatively
rare, and most of the remaining discussion about style and language
will be concerned with the more common simple riddle where some
analogy is drawn, usually of sound or sense, between a brief question and often briefer answer.

There are various approaches to the analysis of style and form
in riddles. Those interested in 'structural analysis'[3] have pointed
to certain basic elements in riddles and the way these are related
to one another. In particular Georges and Dundes pick out the
'descriptive element' in the question, the 'referent' of which has to
be guessed. Many riddles consist of more than one such descriptive element; for example, 'It has a head / but can't think—Match'
has two elements. These two, in turn, may be in opposition to each
other (as in the common European type such as 'What has legs /
but cannot walk?—Chair'). Furthermore, the opening question
may be either literal or metaphorical in terms of its solution. This

---

[1] Arnott 1957, p. 384.

[2] Fletcher 1912, p. 51. A somewhat similar riddle-type classification is found
in the Galla hymn in which six 'wonders' are listed (Chadwicks iii, 1940, p. 553).

[3] Especially Georges and Dundes 1963 (from whom the following examples
are taken) and D. F. Gowlett, 'Some Lozi Riddles and Tongue-twisters Annotated and Analysed', *Afr. Studies* 25, 1966. (For an alternative analysis and
critique of Georges and Dundes see C. T. Scott, 'Persian and Arabic Riddles:
a Language-centred Approach to Genre Definition', *Internat. J. American
Linguistics* 31. 4, Oct. 1965, part II, Publication 39.)

becomes clear with some examples. A riddle like 'I know something that sleeps all day and walks all night—A spider' is to be counted as a literal form; whereas 'Two rows of white horses on a red hill—Teeth' is metaphorical in that the solution (teeth) and the subject of the descriptive element (horses) are different and are only analogous through a metaphor. Following this analysis one can thus distinguish between different types of riddles in terms of (1) oppositional/non-oppositional (further divided into three sub-types), and (2) literal/metaphorical.[1]

This kind of analysis can be applied to African riddles. It seems in general that the typical European oppositional type is not nearly so common in Africa where, if we adopt these 'structural' terms, non-oppositional riddles are by far the most frequent.[2] A metaphorical rather than a literal emphasis too seems to be to the fore. However, when we reach this point we find we have to extend some of these structural elements, in the sense that, as described earlier, analogies of sound, tone, or rhythm have also to be taken into account in many African riddles in addition to analogy in terms of content. This kind of generalized structural analysis, then, can be helpful up to a point in studying African riddles, but beyond that we have to turn to more detailed accounts.

When we come to the precise style in which riddles are expressed, it quickly becomes obvious that this tends to vary from culture to culture according to the favourite forms current at any particular time. Thus in parts of West Africa (e.g. Hausa, Fulani) reference to the number three is common in both proverbs and riddles; among the Makua many of the simple riddles open with 'I went to my friend and . . .' (as in 'I went to my friend and he gave me a black chain—(Black) driver ants');[3] the Kamba have a series opening 'I was about to . . .'; the Zulu apparently like long riddles; while the Thonga make frequent use of the opening *tseke-tseke*.[4]

---

[1] For further details and elucidation see articles cited and further references given there.

[2] See instances throughout this chapter and the discussion in Gowlett, op. cit. For an exception to this, see a number of the Yoruba riddles discussed by Bascom which are based on a pattern of 'two statements which appear to be mutually contradictory, incongruous or impossible' (Bascom 1949, p. 4). There are also a number of scattered exceptions, including some of those cited in this chapter.

[3] Harries 1942*b*, p. 279.

[4] Lindblom iii, 1934, pp. 26–7; Callaway 1868, pp. 364–74; Junod and Jaques 1936.

However, in spite of this great variation in style, there are certain typical stylistic patterns which seem to have a very wide distribution. The initial statement which serves as the 'question' is sometimes preceded by some such phrase as 'Guess what . . .' or by some stereotyped formula which introduces a whole session of riddling.[1] Very often, however, the statement is not itself accompanied by any explicit indication that a solution has to be found. The answer is typically in the form of a single word, but longer phrases and sentences occur even in simple riddles. Among the Lamba, for instance, a characteristic reply is in the form of a question as in their version of a common Bantu riddle 'That which has no ending—What of the path, who has ever come to the end of it?'[2]

Within riddles themselves, there are also some typical patterns. The thing alluded to in the question is often referred to in terms of some other specific (and favourite) noun. This will be clear from some examples. Among the Tlokwa a common form of expression is in terms of cattle, so that the referent is veiled by being called 'our cow' or 'cattle': 'Black cattle which stay in a forest— Lice' and 'My father's cow is green outside and black inside— Reed'[3] are only two of many examples.[4] The Ngala use 'A chief' in a similar way (e.g. 'Un chef avec des boutons sur tout le corps — L'ananas') and the Bambara ask about 'Ce petit homme'.[5] Proper names of people, or sometimes of places, are not uncommon in this context, occurring, for example, among the Lyele of Upper Volta, the Yoruba of Nigeria, and the Shona of Southern Rhodesia where a question about 'The thing of so-and-so' is frequent.[6] The first person singular (pronoun or possessive) also constantly appears. Most common of all is the use of kinship terms in reference. 'Father' or 'My father' seems to be the most popular of all (occurring frequently in the riddles of peoples as far apart as, for example, the Limba, Lyele, and Yoruba of West Africa, the Fang of West Equatorial Africa, the Ngala of the Congo, and the Shona and

[1] See below, p. 439.
[2] Doke 1947, p. 118. On the different forms of questions and answers in Bantu riddles see Cole-Beuchat 1957, pp. 137–42.
[3] Nakene 1943, pp. 136, 134.
[4] Names of other animals are, however, surprisingly uncommon in the question part of riddles, contrasting with their frequent appearance in stories and proverbs.
[5] Comhaire-Sylvain, op. cit., p. 43; Travélé 1923, pp. 50–3.
[6] Fortune 1951, p. 32.

Tlokwa of Central and southern Africa). Other kin, too, frequently appear—mother, children, grandfather, even affines (as in the Shona 'Your staggering, Mr. Son-in-law, where did you drink beer?—The chameleon'[1]).

The language of riddles is sometimes said to be archaic and certainly often contains apparently meaningless words. Puns and word play are not a significant aspect, but appear occasionally, for instance in Yoruba riddles.[2] As will already be obvious from examples cited, the language of riddles is also marked by a frequent use of reduplication, ideophones, and diminutives (occasionally augmentatives) which take the form either of special prefixes, as in Nyanja, or of separate adjectives conveying the idea of smallness, usually applied to the main noun in the question.[3]

In general form riddles seem to represent a relatively fixed type of oral literature. Their stereotyped brevity offers little opportunity for variation or elaboration and there is little if any stress on performance. The creative aspect may in any case be limited, in that simple riddles are so often the domain of children. However, occasional variant forms have been recorded between which individuals can choose,[4] and several authorities mention the fact that new riddles are constantly being made, presumably within the general and particular stereotypes just discussed.[5]

In content, riddles can include just about every sphere of natural and human life, and vary according to the preoccupations and customs of the society in which they are told. An understanding of the point of a riddle thus often depends on a knowledge of the ways of a particular society. The Nuer riddle, for instance, 'Guess what big man it is near whom they have the wedding talk but he never makes a remark—It is a barn' is explained by the fact that among the Nuer, wedding negotiations commonly take place near a barn.[6] Some of the stock comparisons suggested in the questions have already been mentioned—'my father', 'our cow', etc.—and the answers, according to which collections of riddles are often classified, range from the human body, tools and

---

[1] Ibid., p. 34.  [2] Bascom 1949, p. 5.
[3] On linguistic structure see Cole-Beuchat 1957, pp. 142 ff.
[4] e.g. the three versions of the Limba acoustic riddle where the ideophone *kikiri kɔkɔrɔ* suggests the great size of a pregnant woman. (Finnegan 1967, p. 339.)
[5] See e.g. Schapera 1932, p. 217; Smith and Dale ii, 1920, p. 324; Bascom 1949, p. 5.
[6] R. Huffman, *Nuer Customs and Folk-lore*, London, 1931, p. 105.

implements, and domestic life, to examples from the animal and vegetable world, crops, and natural phenomena like the moon or stars. Many riddles give vivid visual impressions, particularly those about the natural world, which often indicate close observation. The Nyanja, for instance, have a riddle about the fly, 'The chief from the north when walking says, where I came from is good, where I go to is good'—because the house-fly's habit of rubbing its front and back legs together alternatively suggests to the Nyanja a feeling of satisfaction.[1] The Kgatla riddle 'Tell me: a green cow which bears white calves—It is the mimosa tree' gives a vivid picture of the white thorns on the green tree, while a Thonga riddle compares the wild apricot's root to 'A red copper bangle'.[2] There is evidence of more imaginative observation in the Makua riddle about the moon—'A very beautiful thing which (if you) say to it, Come on, something inside it refuses'.[3]

There are some stock subjects which occur widely whatever the other variations. One of the most common is that of the various staple crops—maize, millet, yams, etc.—in different parts of the continent. Another is that of the sexual and obscene references which are so common in riddles that Doke, in his general description of Bantu riddles, can say that many of them 'take the place of the lewd joke of other communities'.[4] Many examples could be cited of this. The erotic Ibibio riddles have already been mentioned.[5] The Lamba too have many obscene riddles, while the Shona specialize in riddles characterized by their suggestiveness but to which the real answers are always in fact innocent.[6] Others are more outspoken, like the Bambara 'Ce petit homme se mit en colère, dansa longuement jusqu'à en vomir; lorsqu'il eut vomi, il mourut — Le membre viril'.[7] Besides such stock topics, certain riddles with the same content but different forms sometimes have a wide circulation. Among the Bantu, for instance, Doke notices the very frequent occurrence, in various versions, of a riddle about an egg ('A house without any door') and about hair (e.g. 'I sowed my big field and reaped it, and my hand was not full').[8]

[1] Gray 1939, p. 263.
[2] Schapera 1932, p. 220; Junod 1938, p. 40.
[3] Harries 1942*b*, p. 276.     [4] Doke 1947, p. 118.
[5] Simmons 1956.     [6] Fortune 1951, p. 31.
[7] Travélé 1923, p. 53.     [8] Doke 1947, p. 118.

### III

The occasions for the asking of simple riddles are strikingly similar throughout Africa. There are two main situations in which they occur. Riddle-asking is often a prelude to the telling of stories, typically by children in the evening before the rather more serious narrations commence; sometimes, as among the Fang, riddles are asked between stories, partly to allow the professional story-tellers some respite in their lengthy narrations.[1] The other very common occasion is a game of riddling, usually among children; this is conducted according to special rules and formulas and is often highly competitive. Again it takes place most typically in the evening.[2]

Competitive riddling has been extensively described for many of the Bantu-speaking peoples. In southern Africa it not infrequently takes the form of a contest between two teams. Among the Tlokwa, for instance, the children are divided into two groups as they sit round the fire in the winter when it is too cold to be outdoors, and the first group to start goes on asking until the other side can no longer answer.[3] Among some other Bantu peoples such as the Nyanja the competition is between individuals, not teams. Schapera describes the game as played among the Kgatla: if two children are involved, one begins asking the other, and continues until the other is unable to answer; the second then says 'Let the buyers come' and questions in turn; when the other fails he says 'Tell me yours', and there is an exchange of the riddles each had not known. A similar process is followed when several children are playing, with a division into sides which 'buy' the unknown riddles from each other, the more skilful side taunting their opponents.[4] This fiction of having to 'pay' in return for the unguessed answer is a fairly common theme. Among the Nyanja in Central Africa the pretended recompense is cattle ('We pay up oxen.' 'How many?' 'Such-and-such a number')[5] while in Kenya the one giving up has to name a town ('Give me a town'—

[1] Tardy 1933, pp. 282, 294.
[2] On time and place for riddles in Bantu see especially Cole-Beuchat 1957, pp. 133–5.
[3] Nakene 1943, p. 126.
[4] Schapera 1932, p. 216.
[5] Werner 1906, p. 214.

'Go to Mombasa', etc.).[1] Similarly in West Equatorial Africa Mbete children have to 'pay' a village.[2]

Such riddling competitions are often conventionally preceded by special formulas which are surprisingly alike throughout the Bantu area: in Lamba, for instance, the propounder says *tyo* ('guess') while the other replies *kakesa* ('let it come') or *kamuleta* ('bring it'), and then the riddles are asked;[3] the Nyanja lead off riddle-sessions round the communal fire with *cilape!* ('a riddle!') answered by *nacize!* ('let it come!') and a shout of *wafa* ('he has died') when the right answer is given;[4] and innumerable similar examples could be cited from Bantu-speaking peoples.[5]

Elsewhere, in West Africa for instance, riddles are asked before or during performances of stories or songs. Even where there is apparent similarity to the Bantu pattern with introductory formulas before riddling sessions, the practice is very different because of the absence of the competitive element. Among the Anang Ibibio of Southern Nigeria, for instance, riddle-asking is preceded by special introductory formulas, posed by an individual, then answered in unison by the group. The riddles are not told to baffle the audience or stimulate them to guess, for the answers are all known; even when a new one is invented, the originator adds the reply with the question instead of asking for a solution. The emphasis is very much on communal entertainment rather than competition: 'The enjoyment of a riddle derives from the sharing of it by members of a group rather than from the challenge to the imagination it presents.'[6]

Riddles also occasionally occur in other contexts. Among the Lamba, and perhaps other peoples, riddles are sometimes referred to in speeches as a striking way of holding people's attention, and thus contribute to the literary richness of oratory.[7] In addition to the Makua song-riddles, even simple riddles sometimes have connections with initiation, as among the Tlokwa where the special language learnt in the initiation ceremonies is connected with riddles.[8]

---

[1] A. C. Hollis, 'Nyika Enigmas', *J. Afr. Soc.* 16, 1917, p. 135.

[2] Adam 1940, p. 134; see also Lukas 1937, p. 163 (Kanuri), Calame-Griaule 1965, pp. 471–2 (Dogon), and Berry 1961, p. 16 n.

[3] Doke 1934, p. 362.     [4] Gray 1939, pp. 253–4.

[5] See also Doke 1947, p. 117; Werner in Hollis, op. cit., pp. 135–6; Cole-Beuchat 1957, p. 137.

[6] Messenger 1960, p. 226.     [7] Doke 1934, p. 362.

[8] Nakene 1943, p. 127. See also the use of riddles in initiation schools in

To some extent riddles also appear in various spheres of every-day life. Among the Chaga, riddles can be used to influence some-one's action through irony or indirect suggestion, to imply a threat without actually stating it, or to convey secret information.[1] This kind of usage somewhat resembles that of proverbs and seems more usual with the complex forms than with the more simple riddle mainly used by children. The Anang proverb-riddles, for example, are used, like proverbs, by people of both sexes and all ages in a multitude of social situations and are expected to instruct as well as amuse,[2] while among the neighbouring Efik the complex tone riddles, with their proverbial replies can be used for oblique cursing, humorous greeting, succinct explanation of an action, and to embarrass women through their erotic content.[3]

However, such everyday usages are relatively rare. Conven-tionally riddle-telling is a social pastime, for amusement pure and simple. This aspect of riddling is brought out by two further points about its occasions. First, it tends to be a separate and restricted activity. It is very common in all parts of Africa for there to be a general rule—not always strictly observed, but a rule nevertheless —that riddle-telling should take place in the evening and not during the day; in East Central Africa there is sometimes the further limitation that riddling should not take place during cer-tain phases of the farming year.[4] Riddles are thus, unlike proverbs, regarded as a kind of marginal activity reserved for special times rather than a universal aspect of human activity and communica-tion. Secondly, it is generally children who are expected to take an interest in the light-hearted asking of riddles. There are some exceptions to this: among the Yoruba, for example, both children and adults are said to enjoy riddles although they are especially popular with young children,[5] while Kamba adults, even more than children, compete in riddling; two outstanding riddle experts are described as exchanging 'riddles and answers with a rapidity re-sembling two skilled fencers making thrusts and parries'.[6] How-ever, these situations are not common. More generally, riddles are

Kenya (H. E. Lambert, 'Some Riddles from the Southern Kenya Coast', *Swahili* 33, 1962/3, p. 17).   [1] Raum, op. cit., p. 219.
   [2] Messenger 1960, pp. 225–6.   [3] Simmons 1958, p. 124.
   [4] Fortune 1951, p. 30; E. ten Raa, 'Procedure and Symbolism in Sandawe Riddles', *Man* N.S. 1. 3, 1966, p. 391.
   [5] Gbadamosi and Beier 1959, p. 53; Bascom 1949, p. 7.
   [6] Lindblom iii, 1934, p. 4.

associated with children's amusement in contrast to the more serious use of proverbs by their elders.

The explicit purpose of riddles, then, is almost invariably amusement. Commentators have, however, predictably pointed to many of their incidental functions as well. Besides entertainment, riddles are sometimes claimed to play an indirect educational role by training children in quick thinking, in intellectual skill, and in classification,[1] providing, through their sexual or comic bias, a release from tensions imposed by the moral and social code,[2] or leading to a fuller participation in social life.[3] They are also like proverbs, sometimes used as an indirect means of saying something without the risk involved in stating it explicitly. These points have been frequently mentioned. Less common are the incidental functions of the more complex riddles as a form of communication, an esoteric accomplishment associated with initiation, and the encouragement of either sharing or competitiveness implicit in various forms of riddling. In the various societies these indirect functions of riddle-asking have greater or lesser significance. What all seem to share, however, is the explicit assumption that riddles, or at least the simple form of riddles, are primarily for entertainment and, unlike proverbs, not for any deeper purpose.

IV

Like proverbs, riddles represent a concise form of conventionally stereotyped expression. Though in some ways riddles can be regarded as a relatively minor and crude form of art, suitable merely for children, they nevertheless have some relevance for the general literary background. This comes out partly through the connections of riddles with literary forms like proverbs, epigrams, praise names, and rhetoric. More significantly, the imagery and poetic comment of even the simple riddles are clearly part of the general literary culture. Insight into the nature of people's behaviour can be expressed in a poem or a story—or in a riddle. The Kgatla say 'Tell me: two civet cats which when they fight are not to be separated—It is a married couple', while the Kamba

---

[1] As in the 'structural' interpretation by I. Hamnett, 'Ambiguity, Classification and Change: the Function of Riddles', *Man* N.S. 2. 3, 1967.

[2] Dupire and Tressan 1955.

[3] For an excellent discussion of this last point see Blacking 1961.

show their insight in 'Matters of importance—Children's secrets'.[1]
There is the Ila comment on humankind with 'It is far—And it's
a long way to God!', and the Bambara and Lamba express their
view of man in 'Quelle est la plus rapide de toutes les choses?—
La pensée', and 'That which digs about in the deserted village—
The heart' (which always turns to think of the past).[2] That paradox
too can be conveyed vividly in the brief words of a riddle can be
illustrated from the Hausa 'A prince on an old mat—A kola-nut',
in which we are given a vivid picture of the way the beautiful pink
or white kola-nuts, so valued a commodity, are exposed for sale
in the market on a piece of old matting.[3]

Most of all, riddles, however simple, involve a play of images,
visual and acoustic, through which insight and comment can be
expressed. In this way, even this very minor form of art, with its
own stylistic peculiarities in different cultures, has its part to
play in the richness of oral literature in African societies.[4]

[1] Schapera 1932, p. 227; Lindblom iii, 1934, p. 18.
[2] Smith and Dale ii, 1920, p. 330; Travélé 1923, p. 51; Cole-Beuchat 1957,
p. 146.
[3] Fletcher 1912, p. 51.
[4] Though riddles tend to be recorded in rather smaller numbers than proverbs, there is still a large number of collections, too many to catalogue here.
Useful bibliographies can be found in Doke 1947, Nicolas 1954, Cole-Beuchat
1957, Bascom 1964. See also I. X. de Aranzadi, *La adivinanza en la zona de los
Ntumu: tradiciones orales del bosque fang*, Madrid, 1962, and, among many other
short articles, J. Jacobs, 'Énigmes tetela, espèces et fonction', *Aequatoria* 25,
1962; B. M. du Toit, 'Riddling Traditions in an Isolated South African Community', *JAF* 79, 1966; J. Ittmann, 'Aus dem Rätselschatz der Kosi', *ZES* 21,
1930; J. Bynon, 'Riddle Telling among the Berbers of Central Morocco', *Afr.
Language Studies* 7–8, 1966–7.

# 16

## ORATORY, FORMAL SPEAKING, AND
## OTHER STYLIZED FORMS

Oratory and rhetoric: Burundi; Limba. Prayers, curses, etc.
Word play and verbal formulas. Names

I

The art of oratory is in West Africa carried to a remarkable pitch of
perfection. At the public palavers each linguist [official spokesman]
stands up in turn and pours forth a flood of speech, the readiness and
exuberance of which strikes the stranger with amazement, and accompanies his words with gestures so various, graceful and appropriate that
it is a pleasure to look on, though the matter of the oration cannot be
understood. These oratorical displays appear to afford great enjoyment
to the audience, for every African native is a born orator and a connois-
seur of oratory, a fact that becomes very manifest in the Courts of
Justice in the Protectorate, where the witnesses often address the juries
in the most able and unembarrassed manner; I have even seen little
boys of eight or ten hold forth to the court with complete self-possession
and with an ease of diction and a grace of gesture that would have
struck envy into the heart of an English member of Parliament.[1]

This comment on Ashanti rhetoric in the nineteenth century
could be paralleled by similar remarks about the oratorical ability
of many African peoples. Of the Bantu as a whole a linguist writes
that they are 'born orators; they reveal little reticence or difficulty
about expression in public. They like talking. They like hearing
themselves in an assembly. . . .'[2] We hear too of the significance of
oratory among the uncentralized Anang Ibibio[3] or Ibo of Eastern
Nigeria. Of the Ibo, indeed, Achebe has stated categorically
that 'the finest examples of prose occur not in those forms [folk-
tales, legends, proverbs, and riddles] but in oratory and even in
the art of good conversation. . . . Serious conversation and oratory

[1] R. A. Freeman on his visit to Ashanti in 1888, quoted in F. Wolfson (ed.),
*Pageant of Ghana*, London, 1958, p. 193.
[2] Doke 1948, p. 284.                    [3] Messenger 1959; 1960, p. 229.

... call for an original and individual talent and at their best belong to a higher order.'[1] Similar comments on the relevance of oratory could be multiplied.[2] It is not in fact surprising that many peoples who do not use the written word for formalized transactions or artistic expression should have developed the oral skill of public speaking to perform these functions.

Yet for all the passing references to the significance of oratory, there seems to be little detailed documentation on the actual practice of public speaking as a skill in its own right. It is true that oratory, a form in which oral characteristics are of the essence, does not possess the same easily recognized 'literary' qualifications that can be discerned in, say, panegyric poetry or fictional narrative where parallels in literate cultures are easy to find. Oratory falls between, on the one hand, highly conventional and recognized literary expression and, on the other, informal everyday conversation. But even though the line between rhetorical and informal speech is not easy to draw, oratory in many African societies would seem to deserve further consideration than it has yet received. The speeches of classical antiquity have, in one form or another, long been counted as one form of literary expression with aesthetic as well as purely practical appeal, and it is not ridiculous to regard these as comparable to some of the oratory of African societies. Though little detailed material has been published and the account given here is thus exceedingly thin, it seems worth including a few points and examples, not least if this leads to further investigation.

In Africa, as in antiquity, one of the commonest contexts for public speaking is that of a law case, a formalized occasion which allows both litigants and judges to display their rhetorical skill. Their conscious aims, doubtless, are clearly functional; but aesthetic considerations are also involved, if only to add to the persuasiveness of the speech. Some of these speeches are highly sophisticated and skilled. We often hear of the use of proverbs on such occasions to appeal to the audience or make a point with extra forcefulness. In the case of the Anang Ibibio their famous eloquence arises largely from their skilful use of proverbial

---

[1] Achebe in Whiteley 1964, p. vii.

[2] See e.g. Koelle 1854, p. vii (Kanuri); Tracey 1962, p. 26 (Karanga); Rodegem 1960 (Rundi); Andrzejewski and Lewis 1964, p. 4 (Somali); M. Tew, 'Elicited Responses in Lele Language', *Kongo-Overzee* 16, 1950; E. Jones, 'Krio in Sierra Leone Journalism', *Sierra Leone Language Rev.* 3, 1964, p. 24 (Krio in election speeches, etc., on public platforms).

maxims, particularly in court. Long speeches are given by plaintiff and defendant to explicate their cases, lasting as long as an hour each and listened to with rapt attention. The Ibibio audience is particularly appreciative of a speech which abounds in original or unusual proverbs to capture their interest, or which cleverly introduces an apposite saying at just the crucial moment.[1]

The formalized and literary aspects of legal rhetoric can even take the extreme and unusual form of a portion of the speeches being delivered as song. This is apparently sometimes the case in Mbala litigation in the Congo. The formal interchange between the opponents is partly conducted through spoken argument, but this is then followed by a snatch of allegorical song in which the supporters of each party join with voice and drum, the two sides drawn up to face each other. An extract from one case is quoted as follows:

IST PARTY. I was in my house and would have liked to stay. But he has come and wants to discuss the matter in public. So I have left my house and that is why you see me here.

(*sings*) I am like a cricket. I would like to sing, but the wall of earth that surrounds me prevents me. Someone has forced me to come out of my hole, so I will sing.

(*continues argument*) Let us debate the things, but slowly, slowly, otherwise we will have to go before the tribunal of the white people. You have forced me to come. When the sun has set, we shall still be here debating.

(*sings*) I am like the dog that stays before the door until he gets a bone.

OPPONENT. Nobody goes both ways at the same time. You have told this and that. One of the two must be wrong. That is why I am attacking you.

(*sings*) A thief speaks with another thief. It is because you are bad that I attack you.[2]

Political discussions are also obvious occasions for oratory—indeed the two are often closely related. At the local level at least, there are not infrequently rules about the order in which such

---

[1] Messenger 1959 and Ch. 15 above.

[2] Quoted in Brandel 1961, pp. 39–40, from L. A. Verwilghen, notes to *Folk Music of Western Congo*, Ethnic Folkways Records P 427, 1952, p. 3.

politicians must speak, and accepted conventions of style, content, and set phraseology which speakers more or less follow. Such political speeches often shade into other formal and public occasions involving, say, speeches of welcome, religious injunctions, sermons, harangues, or solemn marriage transactions.[1]

A few of the orators seem to be real professionals, as in the case of the Ashanti 'linguists' described by Freeman in the quotation given earlier. These men were the spokesmen of kings and chiefs among the Akan. Not only were they charged with repeating the words of their patron after him, acting as a herald to make it clear to all his audience and to add to his utterances the extra authority of remoteness, but they were also expected, in the words of Danquah, to 'perfect' the speech of a chief who was not sufficiently eloquent, and to elaborate his theme for him. The linguist should not add any new subject-matter, but

he may extend the phrases and reconstruct the sentences and intersperse the speech with some of the celebrated witty and philosophical reflections for which they are justly celebrated to the credit of both himself and his Chief. . . .[2]

In another description:

When the Linguist rises up to speak in public, he leans upon the King's gold cane, or a subordinate linguist holds it in front of him. He is going to make a speech now, and it is sure to be a happy effort. It will sparkle with wit and humour. He will make use freely of parables to illustrate points in his speech. He will indulge in epigrams, and all the while he will seem not to possess any nerves—so cool, so collected, so self-complacent! He comes of a stock used to public speaking and public functions.[3]

The use of heralds whose sole function is to repeat the words of the speaker and thus endow them with greater dignity or volume is not without other parallels in West Africa, and is a practice which has lent itself well to the situations, under colonial rule at least, where the speeches of administrator or missionary were transferred, sentence by sentence, through the intermediary of an interpreter.

---

[1] The literary aspects of some of these conventionalized utterances are discussed in the following section.
[2] J. B. Danquah, *Gold Coast: Akan Laws and Customs*, London, 1928, p. 42.
[3] C. Hayford, *Gold Coast Native Institutions*, London, 1903, p. 70.

Most speeches, however, seem in fact to be made not by professionals but by experts who acquired their skills in the course of carrying out their various political, religious, or just good-neighbourly duties in the society. Such men—like the Limba 'big men' described below—are recognized by others as skilled in speaking, reconciling, and persuading, and it is partly through such skill that they retain their positions; but this is merely one aspect of their specialized functions as political leaders, judges, or public figures. There are also those who merely possess a general ability to speak well—people skilled more in the art of conversation and the use of proverb and metaphor to enrich their speech than in the more formal arts of public oratory. There is no general rule about the background and training of those regarded as particularly eloquent, for this varies according to the structure of the society in question.

How far oratory varies not only between societies but even in different groups within one state may be illustrated from the kingdom of Burundi, one of the few areas in which some detailed investigation of rhetoric has been carried out. This can be followed by a brief account of the very different society of the Limba of Sierra Leone.

Traditional Burundi (for the time described by Albert[1]) was a highly organized state, marked by an extreme degree of hierarchy between the various ranks in the community—in particular between the cattle-keeping lords (the Tutsi) and the farmer-peasant class (the Hutu). The different classes have their own special speech patterns, and there are also stylized ways of address considered appropriate according to the status, sex, or age of the speaker, and to the particular personal or political relationships of those directly involved. The rules of rhetoric can thus be closely related to the social and political structure.

In Burundi, eloquence is thought to be of the greatest significance, both practical and aesthetic, whether it is used in legal cases, political transactions, petitions, the stylized phrases of polite intercourse, or the art of elegant conversation:

Speech is explicitly recognised as an important instrument of social life; eloquence is one of the central values of the cultural world-view; and the way of life affords frequent opportunity for its exercise. . . .

[1] Albert 1964, based on field-work 1955-7.

Argument, debate, and negotiation, as well as elaborate literary forms are built into the organization of society as means of gaining one's ends, as social status symbols, and as skills enjoyable in themselves.[1]

It is among the upper classes above all that the ideals of oratorical ability are most stressed. The very concept of good breeding and aristocracy, *imfura*, implies 'speaking well' as one of its main characteristics. Aristocratic boys are even given formal education in speech-making from the age of about ten. Albert describes the content of their training:

> Composition of impromptu speeches appropriate in relations with superiors in age or status; formulas for petitioning a superior for a gift; composition of *amazina*, praise-poems; quick-witted, self-defensive rhetoric intended to deflect an accusation or the anger of a superior. Correct formulas for addressing social inferiors, for funeral orations, for rendering judgment in a dispute, or for serving as an intermediary between an inferior petitioner and one's feudal superior are learned in the course of time as, with increasing age and maturity, each type of activity becomes appropriate. Training includes mastery of a suitable, elegant vocabulary, of tone of voice and its modulation, of graceful gestures with hand and spear, of general posture and appropriate bodily displacements, of control of eye-contacts, especially with inferiors, and above all, of speedy summoning of appropriate and effective verbal response in the dynamics of interpersonal relations.[2]

As a result of such formal training and unconscious assimilation of the practice of eloquence, Tutsi men of the upper classes acquire a consciousness of superior education and elegance of speech. The accepted stereotype, quite often lived up to in practice, is that the aristocrat possesses grace and rhetorical ability in speech and bearing, marked particularly by his characteristic dignity and reserve in public address.

The formal speech of peasants is expected to be rather different. Social pressures ensure that peasants are aware of the tactlessness of producing an elegant aristocratic-type speech before a superior. In their own strata, however, they may speak with equal dignity and ability—for instance, as judge, in council, or in funeral orations. There are some set differences. The Hutu use a different accent, and the figures of speech tend to reflect a peasant rather than an aristocratic background and to be drawn from agriculture rather than herding or the courtly life. 'The gestures of the

[1] Ibid., p. 35.      [2] Ibid., p. 37.

muscular arms and heavy set body and the facial expressions will not be like those of the long-limbed, slim-boned . . . Batutsi herders, but they will not lack studied grace and dignity.'[1]

The recognized stylistics in Rundi oratory, marked particularly in the case of the aristocrats, are dignity of bearing and speech, enhanced, on occasion, by effective use of the rhetorical technique of silence. There is also careful attention to stance, gesture, modulation of the voice, and grace and elegance of vocabulary according to the criteria of Rundi culture. The highest ideal of public speaking, in Rundi eyes, is that associated with an *umushingantahe*, a recognized elder and judge. He is expected to be

intelligent, in complete command of the arts of logic, a fine speaker— i.e., he speaks slowly and with dignity, in well-chosen words and figures of speech; he is attentive to all that is said; and he is an able analyst of logic and of the vagaries of the human psyche.[2]

The position of an *umushingantahe* depends both on a prolonged experience of legal cases and on wealth for the expensive initiation party. Others too, however, can use the same type of rhetorical style. It is one considered particularly appropriate in political speeches of advice or persuasion before a superior, or in serious decision-making and problem-solving. On the other hand, rhetorical fireworks are more to be expected when individuals are trying to forward their own interests as litigants in a law case, or in personal petitions to a superior.

A further characteristic of Rundi rhetoric is the premium placed on elegance and appropriateness rather than on literal truth. This has a practical value. It is known that a man is more likely to be able to defend himself on the spot by rapid and plausible falsehood, mixed with a suitable amount of flattery, than by a careful telling of the truth. But there is also an aesthetic aspect—graceful appropriate speech is considered attractive in its own right. Allusiveness, often through figures of speech, is prized in both speechmaking and polite social intercourse. Even a slight request may be addressed to a superior with stylized formality and oblique allusion. Thus a petition by a poor man for a trifling gift like a new pair of shoes to replace his worn-out ones is expressed through circumlocution. 'One does not hide one's misfortunes; if one tries to hide them they will nevertheless soon be revealed. Now, I know

[1] Albert 1964, p. 42.　　　　[2] Ibid., p. 45.

a poor old man, broken in health and ill; there is a spear stuck in his body and he cannot be saved.' By this he indicates his old shoes, so ragged that one is being held together by a safety-pin (the 'spear').[1]

It is not only the style and content that are conventionally laid down for Rundi speeches, but in some cases the general setting as well. The rules of precedence are strictly observed, in keeping with a society in which ranked hierarchy is of such significance. Thus the order in which individuals speak in a group depends on their seniority:

> The senior person will speak first; the next in order of rank opens his speech with a statement to the effect, 'Yes, I agree with the previous speaker, he is correct, he is older and knows best, etc.' Then, depending on circumstances and issues, the second speaker will by degrees or at once express his own views, and these may well be diametrically opposed to those previously expressed. No umbrage is taken, the required formula of acknowledgment of the superior having been used.[2]

The situation of making a formal request is also highly stylized. A special type of bearing is obligatory. If it is a request for a bride or cattle, the normal form is for the petitioner to

> assume a formal stance, often standing during delivery of the formal request. His speech has probably been carefully composed in advance. To follow the general formula, one refers to the gift one has brought, usually several pots of banana beer; one expresses love, admiration, and respect for the excellent qualities, real, imagined, and hoped-for, of the superior; one expresses the hope that the affection is reciprocated; one again refers to the gift, this time as a token of affection; one promises further gifts in the future; one states one's wish; one closes with a repetition of the praise of the superior and an expression of hope that the wish will be granted.[3]

Much remains to be investigated in relation to Rundi oratory. But it is abundantly clear from Albert's publications so far that the skills of eloquence were highly valued and sophisticated in traditional Rundi society, and that they present a literary sphere which, though perhaps marginal, is clearly enough related to literature to deserve fuller critical analysis. Such skills were exhibited in their most extreme form in the elegant formal speeches of Rundi aristocrats. But that they were recognized in some degree

[1] Ibid., pp. 50–1.    [2] Ibid., p. 41.    [3] Ibid., p. 38.

at all levels of society is evident from the explicit aesthetic interest in these arts; even in their everyday conversation which is 'near the bottom of the [aesthetic] scale, elegance of composition and delivery, figures of speech, and the interpolation of stories and proverbs are normally called for and employed'.[1]

A second case where one can observe the significance attached to oratorical ability is that of the Limba people of northern Sierra Leone.[2] These are a people with a very different culture from that of the highly stratified Rundi—farmers living in a relatively homogeneous society, without the marked differences of wealth and birth characteristic of the Rundi state. Their speech-making is correspondingly much less sophisticated and specialized. But they too have their stylized forms of public address, and oratorical ability is regarded as an art as well as a necessity.

To be able to carry out formal speaking pleasingly is one of the first essentials of a Limba local chief and of the sub-chiefs and elders who model themselves on the ideal picture of a chief. There are many occasions when such formal speeches are obligatory. Most important in Limba eyes are the continual law cases. The local chief, assisted by his elders or 'big men', must sift the evidence and, after the more junior judges have spoken, must sum up with an eloquent speech which both analyses the complex rights and wrongs of the case and in addition 'pulls the hearts' of the litigants to accept his verdict and become reconciled. There are also large gatherings where local or, occasionally, national political issues are debated. In these, the leading elders and men of influence, and, increasingly, the younger men, take it in turn to make long speeches marked by great formality and—very often—repetition. Meetings called to deal with an election to chiefship also give opportunity for the candidates to demonstrate their wisdom and oratorical skill in public. Public and formal speeches are also made to welcome visitors or returning travellers, exhort juniors, negotiate marriage arrangements, acknowledge some piece of news formally delivered, and as well are made during the intervals at dances, at initiations and ceremonies, and as stylized thanks for a visit, a gift, or a transaction. Formal speech-making is the characteristic

---

[1] Albert 1964, p. 49.
[2] The account given here is based on field-work among the Limba (1961 and 1963/4).

quality of a Limba chief in his role of reconciling people and thus bringing peace to individuals and to his chiefdom as a whole. But it is also a desired attribute and activity of anyone with any pretentions to authority over others—a father can speak formally among his chilren, a household head between his dependants, a respected senior wife among her co-wives, even an elder boy among his juniors.

Unlike the Rundi, the Limba do not provide any specialist training in rhetoric. It is true that chiefs are sometimes said to be instructed how to 'speak well' when, as in the case of a few of their number, they go into several weeks' seclusion as part of their installation ceremonies. But this represents more the explicit significance attached to oratorical ability than any real attempt at training. In fact all Limba—particularly the men—gradually assimilate the accepted tricks of speaking as they listen to their fathers, the local 'big men', and the chiefs officiating and settling disputes on public occasions. The young boys begin by making speeches among their peers at initiation, farming associations, and play. Then as they grow up they gradually try to speak in more public contexts and (if of the right social background) in legal cases and discussions. Finally they may become, informally but unmistakably, accepted as respected elders, responsible for speaking at the most important gatherings.

The content of formal Limba speeches varies. But sentiments tend to recur. This can be illustrated, for example, in marriage negotiations and legal speeches. To the Limba marriage negotiations are regarded as semi-public transactions. The suitor—represented by a friend—must do far more than just undertake to pay the due bride-wealth and carry out his duties; he must also speak pleasingly to win over the hearts of his future in-laws and impress them with the respect he has for them. The speeches are regarded as something more than mere etiquette by the Limba participating. Rather, they are a form of expression which makes those involved feel pleased and proud and conscious of the deeper meanings in life. The father of the girl too must reply in graceful words and convince his listeners of the sincerity of his appreciation. He thanks the messenger who has come, saying perhaps:

I thank you. I thank you for coming. Greetings for [undergoing] the journey. Greetings for the sun. Greetings for the rain. I, the father of the girl, I have no long words to say. I accept—by grace of the mother who bore the girl. She says that it is pleasing to her. For me too—it is pleasing to me. I accept.

But often the basic content of this is drawn out to very much greater lengths. Other stages in the marriage follow at intervals, each accompanied by similar speeches—of thanks, appreciation, implied undertakings for the future, and tactful moralizing about the nature and obligations of marriage.

In legal speeches the moralizing is often even more explicit as the leaders try to reconcile contenders and soothe angry feelings. Though the litigants themselves state their own cases, their speeches seem to be regarded more as background factual data for the court, whereas the real flowering of oratory is in the speeches of the judges who, one after the other, address the court in turn, finally ending with the senior judge (often the chief) who uses the wisdom given by all (as the Limba put it) to add to the weight of his own final assessment and persuasion. In political speeches too there is a certain amount of moralizing as well as excited rhetoric.

The most elaborate and lengthy of all speeches are the long funeral harangues given on the occasion of memorial rites for some important man several years after his death. This is one of the most important events in Limba social life, and hundreds of people gather from many miles around. One of the highlights is the speeches made by the leading men; they speak in turn, often going on for several hours, and their words are relayed, half-intoned sentence by sentence, by a herald who is specially engaged for the occasion. These orations are even more full of moralizing than the legal and family speeches. They dwell relatively little on the character of the dead man, and instead reflect on the importance of the dead, the duties of the living, the function in life of the various groups listening to them, and the general philosophy and ideals which, they presume, they and their listeners share. A small portion of one of these speeches, this time on the subject of mutual interdependence and the dangers of pride, ran something as follows, with each sentence punctuated by a pause:[1]

. . . If someone has the reputation of being proud—then leave him alone. He is someone who dislikes taking anything from others. He is always working hard—for himself. [Similarly] if you know a child who

---

[1] A summary paraphrase of a speech on which I made notes in 1961 but did not have the opportunity to record word for word.

does not pay attention to his parents—does not pay attention to his chief—does not pay attention to his mother-in-law[1]—then people will never appoint him as chief, he is not good. God will help the man who shows respect to the chief [i.e. authority]. With some young people, when they are asked about their behaviour, they just say: 'Oh, I took presents to my wife's mother, but now I'm tired of giving her things.' Even if someone is a son of a chief, if he doesn't care to work, care for his parents, for his mother-in-law—he mustn't think, even if he *is* a chief's son, that he will ever be made a chief. . . .

If someone works hard, perhaps he will gain power. And if a powerful man opens his hands [i.e. gives gifts freely], then he has gained something. But if he does not give, then his possessions are worthless. Blessings come from children, from the dead people [ancestors], from God. But no one can win a reputation without working for it. . . . If God says goodbye to someone then he shows him the road he must walk on.[2] If you are appointed [to a position of authority] you must not say that because you have been appointed you need not do anything; you must not say that you won't feed [i.e. give gifts to] the people who are working for you. If you do that, things won't grow well [prosper]. Let no one think that he is a big man, more than his companions. It is for others to say if you are a big man. You must think well of your companions. . . .

There are recognized conventions about the diction, phraseology, and form of Limba speeches, although these conventions are not very explicitly stated. Gestures are much used: elders in particular stride about in the centre of the listening group, making much play with their long, full-sleeved gowns, alternating for effect between solemn stance and excited delivery when the whole body may be used to emphasize a point. They are masters of variations in volume and speed: they can switch from quiet, even plaintive utterance to loud yelling and fierce (assumed) anger, only to break off abruptly with some humorous or ironic comment, an effective silence, or a moving personal appeal. Among the best legal speakers figures of speech are common, as well as proverbs, allusions, and rhetorical questions. These men are admired for their ability to express their points by 'going a long way round in parables'. There are also many stock formulas that it is considered both correct and attractive to use in Limba speeches; in addition to the set phrases which introduce and close a formal speech, the speaker's words also regularly include an appeal to

[1] Someone who above all, in Limba philosophy, should receive respect.
[2] i.e. if God disapproves of a man's behaviour, he may send sickness to kill him.

what the 'old people' did, references to what *Kanu* (God) does or
does not like (a convenient channel for moralizing of which some
Limba take frequent, even tedious, advantage), personal appeals
to members of the audience, and the frequent conventional expression of humility through referring to the grace of those present,
of superiors, and of the ancestors. A good speaker, furthermore,
makes sure of the participation of the audience in a way analogous
to story-telling; he expects murmurs of support and agreement,
muttered rejoinders of his rhetorical questions, laughter when he
purposely brings in something amusing or exaggerated, and thanks
and acknowledgement when he has ended.

The whole organization of such speaking is carefully regulated.
The speakers rise in order and are not expected to interrupt another speaker during his oration with any substantive point beyond
the general reactions of an attentive audience. A man stands up to
speak when the last speaker 'passes the word' to him by the recognized formula 'so much (for what I have to say)' (*tindɛ*), adding
the name of the one who is to follow him. The new speaker must
then speak appreciatively of the words of his predecessor (even
if he disagrees with him), acknowledge the leading men present,
then turn to the matter of his speech. Of course, not all live up to
these ideals all the time. But many do, and the Limba are quite
clear that someone who loses his temper or speaks with real and
self-interested anger (as distinct from the occasional assumed anger
of rhetoric) cannot be regarded as the cool and accomplished
orator whom the Limba admire so much.

Much of the content and phraseology of these Limba orations
may appear trite to someone from a different tradition. But it is
certain that to the Limba themselves such speeches, when delivered by a recognized orator, complete with flowing gesture and
all the overtones of accustomed word and sentiment shot through
with the fresh insights of the individual speaker, are an expression,
through a beautiful medium, of some of the most profound truths
of their society.

## II

There are certain types of formal speech which, without being
as lengthy and elaborate as formal oratory, have a tendency to
become stylized. Just as stylized words in, say, the English Book of

Common Prayer have a literary interest of their own, and must have had the same characteristic even before being crystallized into fixed and written form, so prayers in non-literate societies sometimes fall into a kind of literary mode; they may be characterized by a conventional form, perhaps marked by greater rhythm or allusiveness than everyday speech, within which the individual must cast his thoughts. The same is sometimes true of other forms of stylized expression—salutations, curses, oaths, petitions, or solemn instructions.

How far such utterances fall into a more or less fixed and formulaic mode varies according to the conventions of differing cultures. It is always of interest to inquire into this, not least because of the possibility that the fixity of such utterances has in the past been overemphasized.

It is clear that, in some cases at least, there can be both a conventionally recognized over-all form—a literary genre, as it were—and also, within this, scope for individual variation according to speaker and context. This can be illustrated, to take just one example, from the conventional mode of uttering curses among the Limba.[1] In outline these curses are always much the same. The occasion that gives rise to them is when some unknown criminal is believed to have engaged, undetected, in any of the three crimes the Limba class together as 'theft' (actual physical theft, adultery, and witchcraft). Laying the curse is thought to stir up the object known as the 'swear' which pursues and punishes the unknown offender by its mystical power. The content of the curse follows prescribed lines: invocation of the 'swear', explanation of the offence concerned, instructions about the fate that the 'swear' should bring on its victim, and, finally, a provision that confession and restitution should be acceptable, sometimes accompanied by a clause that the innocent receiver of stolen goods should not suffer. Other details as to time and circumstance are also laid down.

The style and literary structure of these curses are clearly understood by speaker and audience. They begin and end with short formulas which are invariable and have no clear meaning beyond their acceptance as necessary adjuncts to ritual utterances. The main body of the curse is more flexible. It is usually spoken in

[1] For some further details see R. Finnegan, ' "Swears" among the Limba', *Sierra Leone Bull. of Religion* 6. 1, 1964.

a semi-intoned voice, particularly in the phrases describing the victim's expected fate, and is partially expressed in balanced parallel phrases which, while not possessing a clear enough over-all rhythm to be classed as poetry, nevertheless from time to time exhibit a definite beat of their own. The rhythm is further brought out by the common accompaniment of much of the curse—a rhythmic beat of the speaker's stick on the ground next to the 'swear', said to arouse it to action and power. The dignity of the occasion is further brought home by the singsong voice of the speaker and his controlled and rather sparse use of gesture. The key-phrases which threaten the victim are repeated in various slightly differing forms, and this repetition, sometimes repeated yet again by an assistant, enhances the serious and intense tone of the curse.

Provided these central points are included, the actual curse can be longer or shorter according to the wishes of the speaker, the heinousness of the crime, or—in some cases—the magnitude of the fee or the audience. The possible fates to which the offender is to fall victim may be only sketched in, or they may be elaborated at great length. The same is true of the phrases which safeguard the position of the innocent and the repentant. Provided the speaker includes the set formulas at start and finish plus the occasional prescribed points within the body of the curse, and covers the main headings mentioned above, the actual words he uses do not seem to be a matter of any very great concern.

The kind of form and content characteristic of these curses can best be illustrated from extracts from two Limba examples. The first concerns the suspected secret theft of a hen:

*Ka harika lɔŋtha, ka harika lɔŋtha.*
So and so bought a hen. He bought a hen at such and such a village. The hen was lost. He came to me. The man who ate it did not confess. I agreed. We are 'swearing' the eater this morning, Thursday.

The one who took the hen,
—If it is an animal in the bush, a wildcat, let it be caught;
    Wherever it goes may it be met by a man with a gun;
    May it be found by a hunter who does not miss;
    If it meets a person, may it be killed.

But when it is killed, may the one who kills and eats it [the wildcat] go free—*fo feŋ.*

—If it is an animal [that stole it],
> Let it be killed in a trap;
> Let it be killed going into a hole where it cannot come out.

—If it is a bird,
> Let that bird be killed by a hunter or by a trap.

—If it was a person that stole and would not confess,
> Let the 'swear' catch him.

—If it was a person,
> If he stands on the road, let him meet with an accident;
> If he takes a knife, let him meet with an accident;
> If he is walking along the road, let him hit his foot on a stone and the blood not stop coming out;
> If he begins farming—when he cuts at a tree with his cutlass, let him miss the tree and cut his hand;
> If he has a wife and she knows about the hen, or two or three wives who helped him, let the 'swear' fall on them;

—If it is a man,
> Let him always walk on a dangerous road, and when danger comes let him think about the hen he has stolen and confess.

If he does not confess,
> Let him spend the whole night weeping [from pain].

When they ask why, let the 'swear' answer:
> 'I am the one who caught the man, because he stole the fowl of the stranger.'

But if he confesses and says 'I stole it', and if the case is brought to me [the speaker] and I perform the ceremony [to release him],
—Let him no longer be ill.
—Quickly, quickly, let him be better—*fo feŋ*.

If he does not confess,
—Let him suffer long, for he is a thief.

The stolen hen—if someone ate it who did not know [that it was stolen], let the 'swear' not catch them. But those who ate knowing it was stolen, let them be caught, for it was the stranger's hen.

*Ka harika lɔŋtha, ka harika lɔŋtha.*

The second example is when a smith speaks over the pile of rice that has just been threshed and fanned in the farm. His words are intended both to prevent the rice from being diminished through quarrels and as a curse against anyone who tries to steal it away through witchcraft. Though much shorter than the first example, the same kind of framework is evident:

*Ka harika lɔŋtha, ka harika lɔŋtha.*

You the [dead] smiths, you the dead.
This is the rice, Sanasi's rice, that we threshed today.
> When we threshed it, it was not much.
> When we fanned it, it was not much.
> But when we gather it together—then let it be much!

—If it happens that someone tries to bewitch it as a big bird,[1] coming for the rice—let it be unsuccessful, let him not be able to take it.

—The ones we are warding off, they are no one else but *them* [i.e. witches].

You the smiths—if any one can say 'since I was born, I have never needed the work of the smiths' [i.e. iron], let that person only [i.e. no one] be able to bewitch the rice.

—If there is quarrelling in the house,
> Let it [the rice] go free, *fo feŋ*,
> Let it not follow the rice.

*Ka harika lɔŋtha, ka harika lɔŋtha.*

Prayers are another very common type of solemn and stylized utterance which tend to manifest the same kind of characteristics as Limba curses. There are often accepted forms within which individuals can extemporize or even develop their own favourite phrases which they then produce on many occasions. Prayers also very often have their own special mode of delivery in terms of tone of voice, pitch, speed, gesture, or even occasionally antiphonal form. This sets them apart from ordinary speech and can bring out a rhythm and balance in the central phrases. Very often too there is intensive use of metaphor, images through which the nature of God or the plight of the living are picturesquely conveyed.

Consider, for example, this prayer by a Milembwe woman after a child's birth, recorded in the Congo:

God almighty creator,
God Mbuuwa Mukungu a Kiayima,
> Created trees, created people, created all in the countries,
> Created the Been' Ekiiye of Kalanda, created the Beena Mpaaza and BaaMilembwe,

---

[1] i.e. in the form of one of the birds that consume huge quantities of rice in the fields.

Created the Beena Musolo and Muelaayi, created the Beena
    Kibeeji of Muteeba,
Created the white and whitish,
Created the Lomami, created the Luamba Kasseya [two rivers],
Created the land where the sun rises,
Created the fish at Msengye,
Created the eldest and youngest of a twin,
Created the guide who leads (child that opens the womb),
Created the eatable and uneatable ants.

God, thou art the lord,
Who cometh in the roar of the whirlwind,
Out of your dwelling place from where the sun rises.
God creator, thou art father and thou art mother.
Oh God I shouldn't offend You as if You were a man;
There is no gratitude for what God bestows upon you,
Although He gives you a wife who grinds maize, a woman is a basket
    [i.e. she leaves her family on marriage],
A man is a refuge, when rain falls I may enter [i.e. a man remains in
    the village and may be a solace for his parents].
God if he hasn't given you a gift, He'll remember when you praise
    Him,
Honour Him and you arrive at Musengye of the Mulopwe (?).
Everyone isn't a welcome guest, only a child is a stranger who comes
    quite new in our midst.
Oh eldest and youngest of a twin, only a child is welcome as a
    stranger.
Friend good-day, friend good-day![1]

The prayer makes striking use of repetition, in the form of parallelisms through which the creative power of God is progressively described, then his relations with mankind meditated on, and, finally, the new-born child is welcomed.

The literary effectiveness of such prayers can be illustrated in some further examples from the Congo. These are taken from one of the largest published collections of prayers and invocations, that by Theuws in his *Textes Luba* (Katanga).[2] These Luba prayers are characterized by their rich use of figurative language, by their rhythm and balance, and by the stereotyped clichés recognized as the appropriate and natural way of praying among the Luba. Luba prayers are said to be particularly formulaic and fixed, but

---

[1] L. Stappers, 'Prayer of a Milembwe Woman after a Child's Birth', *Kongo-Overzee* 18, 1952, pp. 6–7.     [2] Theuws 1954.

new ideas and new formulas are assimilated.[1] It is also clear from
the following examples that a stereotyped form need not necessarily imply lack of variety or literary expressiveness:

1. Toi, qui nous a fendu les doigts dans la main,[2]
   Toi, Créateur,
   Toi, Kungwa Banze,
   Pourquoi nous as-tu tourné le dos?

2. Ainsi la mort vint parmi nous,
   Maintenant nous sommes venus pour t'apaiser.
   Tu étais fâché sur nous,
   Alors nous sommes venus, maintenant nous nous sommes réunis.

3. Et vous, pères et mères, qui êtes morts déjà,
   De votre côté, tenez vos mains sur nous,
   Intercédez pour nous.

4. Toi, qui nous a fendu les doigts dans la main,
   Toi, Créateur des montagnes,
   Toi, Kungwa Banze,
   Tu nous as tourné le dos.
   Fais-nous devenir nombreux, nous tous,
   Que notre race soit nombreuse.

5. Vous, pères et mères qui êtes morts,
   Tenez vos mains sur nous,
   Nous mourons.[3]

1. O Esprit, Seigneur des Hommes, Seigneur de la terre,
   Seigneur des arbres et Seigneur des termitières,
   Aujourd'hui nous venons nous plaindre de notre misère.

2. Seigneur de tous les insectes, c'est Toi,
   Les légumes nous tuent.[4]

The last two examples are on a much more personal note: the
bitter complaint of a man who has already lost most of his family
and has now suffered yet another death, and the rather quieter
prayer for help in infirmity. Both are marked by a similar structure
based on repetition, invocation, and complaint. But there is far
more to each than the mere structure. Colour is added through
imagery drawn from observation of the human and the natural
world. The invocations are in places elaborated to comment on the
divine in relation to the human order and forcibly bring out the

---

[1] Thuews 1954, p. 26.      [2] i.e. created us as men.
[3] Theuws 1954, pp. 87–8 (prayer to appease the Spirit when there have been
many deaths).      [4] Ibid., p. 83 (prayer by a hunter).

contrast between the dead (and the Spirit) and the survivor struggling to grasp the reason for his sufferings. In short, each piece, though in practice a prayer, is in effect a kind of poem expressing and reflecting on the personal plight and insights of the speaker:

1. Hélas, Toi, Esprit, Tu m'as frappé, que ferai-je?
   Debout dans le chemin, je ne vois plus par où aller.

2. Je m'agite comme l'oiseau qui erre,
   L'oiseau même il a son nid,
   Il revient pour y entrer.

3. Moi, ami avec l'Esprit.[1]
   Toi, tu es mort, moi, je reste.
   Je mange à satiété.

4. L'homme qui t'a pris par ses ruses,
   Pars avec lui, ne le laisse pas, du tout.
   Alors il n'y a pas même d'Esprit
   Dont ils disent: l'Esprit existe. Où est-il?

5. Lui seul nous tue. Ils crient continuellement: Esprit! Esprit!
   Nous voudrions le voir.
   Aujourd'hui, nous mourons simplement comme des moutons....

11. La mort a dressé son camp chez moi.
    Dans quelle palabre suis-je pris?
    Les choses que je possède sont à moi,
    Gagnées par mes propres mains.

12. Pleure la misère, pleure la tienne,
    Pleure seulement celle de l'ami qui restait chez toi.
    Pintade de ma mère, assieds-toi sur l'arbre,
    Regarde les enfants de chez toi,
    Comment ils errent partout.

13. Salue les défunts de ma part,
    Bien qu'eux me m'envoient pas de salut.
    Nous ne sommes sur la terre que pour la mort,
    Pour voir des malheurs.

14. Tu es parti,
    Alors qui reste pour moi, pour me pleurer et pour conduire le deuil?
    Cette mort est aussi la mienne,
    Si vous sentez de la pourriture, c'est moi qui périt.[2]

[1] i.e. he had not offended the Spirit or deserved his misfortune.
[2] Theuws 1954, pp. 147–52.

1. Que ferai-je?
   Tous mes amis passent bien portants,
   Moi, je suis ici comme un paralysé.

2. Toi, Père-Créateur, aide-moi,
   Que je marche avec force.

3. J'étais au milieu de mes amis, Tu m'en as fait sortir.
   Maintenant, je suis dans le malheur.

4. Bien, je me fâche contre Dieu, je ne me fâche pas contre l'homme
   qui se moque de moi,
   Lui aussi en verra encore.

5. Si c'est un homme qui m'a tendu des pièges,
   Maintenant, il n'a pas de malheur, mais l'avenir est long.
   L'Esprit m'a regardé, Dieu Tout-puissant,
   Père-Créateur, alors, Tu ne tiens plus Tes mains sur moi?

6. Toi, père, qui m'aimais ici sur la terre,
   Si tu m'aimais tant quand tu étais en vie, tu ne me protèges plus
   maintenant?
   Que je sois avec force.

7. Toi, Père, Père du savoir,
   Qui chassais la petite perdrix au collet et y pris une petite gazelle,
   Le termite mangea la gazelle ainsi prise.

8. Tu ne me tues pas encore, qui que tu sois?
   Celui qui m'a jeté le sort
   Qu'il ne reste pas en vie, qu'il meure à son tour,
   S'il n'est pas difforme, qu'il le devienne.

9. Ai-je mangé quelque chose de lui? L'ai-je volé?
   Lui ai-je jeté le sort? Qu'est-ce que je lui ai fait?
   On me mutile comme un voleur. Je ne vole pas.

10. Vous m'avez mutilé sans plus disant:
    Qu'il ait des malheurs pendant sa vie,
    Après la mort, ils ne sont plus sentis.

11. Vous m'avez brisé par terre,
    Je me recroqueville comme fixé dans le sol.
    Je ramasse les vers.

12. Qui me tendit ses pièges disant: pourquoi existe-t-il?
    Les malheurs ne lui manqueront pas,
    Tôt ou tard.
    Je suis le cochon qui meurt dans les taros.[1]

---

[1] Theuws 1954, pp. 126–9.

Though surprisingly little work has been done on the literary aspect of prayers as distinct from their content or function,[1] this is certainly a fruitful field. There is scope for many studies about the extent of individual variation, style, and content; about the way in which, in pagan, Christian, and Islamic contexts, prayer may be expressed through conventional literary forms; and about the relationship of prayers to the other literary genres of the language.[2]

The same could probably be said of other formalized utterances such as blessings, instructions to a new king or leader,[3] oaths, sermons,[4] lengthy salutations, formulaic speeches of thanks or acknowledgement, and so on. Even so apparently trivial an occasion as that of a beggar approaching a would-be patron may, in certain communities, have its own expected clichés and form. An example of this—a standardized cry by a Hausa beggar—can conclude this discussion:

The name of God we praise, the merciful one we praise; I will praise Mahamad. Alas, alas for the ignorant one! He is doing a sorry thing! He is letting off the world,[5] he knows not that death is approaching. Both morning and evening let him regard the prophets of the great God; there are none in the world save they who follow Isa and Merau and the Creator my Lord. The believer in the prophet who fasts, who has scared charms, who gives alms—he will have his reward in this world, and in the next he will not be without it.[6]

[1] The frequent use of rhythmic phrases, for example, has more often been associated with its function in aiding memorization than with its literary effectiveness in heightening the intensity and tone of the words.

[2] For some further examples or discussions of prayers see, for example, R. Boccassino, 'La preghiera degli Acioli dell'Uganda', *Ann. Lateranensi* 13, 1949; E. E. Evans-Pritchard, 'A Note on Nuer Prayers', *Man* 52, 1952; A. Werner, 'A Galla Ritual Prayer', *Man* 14, 1914; R. Van Caeneghem, 'Godsgebeden bij de Baluba', *Aequatoria* 7, 1944, 10, 1947; A. G. de Pélichy, 'Prières païennes d'Afrique noire', *Rythmes du monde* (Bruges et Paris) 7. 1, 1959 (*AA* 12. 4); J. H. K. Nketia, 'Prayers at Kple Worship', *Ghana Bull. Theology* 2. 4–5, 1963; Calame-Griaule 1965, pp. 408 ff. (Dogon); and the selection given in French tr. in Dieterlen 1965.

[3] e.g. Akan instructions quoted in R. S. Rattray, *Ashanti Law and Constitution*, Oxford, 1929, p. 82.

[4] See H. W. Turner, *Profile through Preaching: a Study of the Sermon Texts used in a West African Independent Church*, London, 1965.

[5] i.e. not treating it sternly as a temptation.

[6] Fletcher 1912, p. 64.

### III

In Africa, as elsewhere, people delight in playing with words and on words. Tongue-twisters, for example, are sometimes popular with children—or even adults—and even these represent one type of awareness of the potentialities of language for more than just conveying information. They have been recorded in particular in parts of West Africa, though doubtless examples can be found elsewhere.[1] Among the Yoruba, for instance, a favourite game, according to Ellis, used to be to repeat certain tricky sentences at high speed; for example:

*Iyan mu ire yo; iyan ro ire ru.*

When there is famine the cricket is fat (that is, considered good enough to eat); when the famine is over the cricket is lean (i.e. is rejected),[2]

and similar instances are recorded from the Fulani and the Hausa. Here are two Fulani examples from Arnott's collection:

*ŋgabbu e mbaggu muuɗum, mbabba maa e mbaggu muuɗum: ŋgabbu firlitii fiyi mbaggu mbabba naa, koo mbabba firlitii fiyi mbaggu ŋgabbu?*

A hippopotamus with his drum, a donkey too with his drum: did the hippo turn and beat the donkey's drum, or did the donkey turn and beat the hippo's drum?[3]

*ŋdabbiimi pucca puru purtinoo-giteewu, e ŋgu aardini kutiiru furdu furtinoo-giteeru, e ndu aardini nduguire furde furtinoo-giteere; nde diwa ndu ɗunya, ndu diwa nde ɗunya, nde diwa ndu ɗunya, ndu diwa nde ɗunya, etc., etc. . . .*

I mounted a pop-eyed dun horse, he was driving before him a pop-eyed dun dog, and *he* was driving a pop-eyed dun duiker; she jumped, he ducked, he jumped, she ducked, she jumped, he ducked, he jumped, she ducked, etc. . . .[4]

Puns are another common form of verbal play. These take various forms. In tonal languages the play is sometimes with words

---

[1] See also example quoted from West Equatorial Africa in Ch. 11, p. 306.
[2] Ellis 1894, p. 241.　　　　　　　　　　　[3] Arnott 1957, p. 391.
[4] Ibid., p. 392; Arnott gives several further instances and also discusses the phonetic bases of these tongue-twisters. For Hausa examples see Fletcher 1912, pp. 56 ff.; Tremearne 1913, pp. 66–7. Also D. F. Gowlett, 'Some Lozi Riddles and Tongue-twisters', *Afr. Studies* 25, 1966; A. Dundes, 'Some Yoruba Wellerisms, Dialogue Proverbs and Tongue-twisters', *Folklore* 75, 1964.

phonetically the same (or similar) but different tonally. This can be illustrated in the Yoruba punning sentence:

The rain on the shoes (*bàtà*) goes patter, patter, patter (*bata-bata-bata*), as on the rock (*àpáta*); in the street of the chief drummer (*ajula-bàtá*), the drum (*bàtá*) is wood, the shoes (*bàtà*) are of hide.[1]

There is also the Swahili word game played with reversed symbols, a special kind of punning.[2] Puns can also be used as the basis of an elaborate game. This is recorded of the Hausa where the second participant in the long punning series finally turns out to be mere 'worthless grain'. An extract can illustrate the kind of exchange, though the subtlety obviously depends on the actual Hausa words which make it possible for B to take up each of A's remarks in a different sense:

> *A.* How art thou?
> *B.* Am I sick?
> *A.* Art thou not reclining?
> *B.* I recline? Am I a king?
> *A.* Does not one beat the drum for the king?
> *B.* Beat the drum for me? Am I a state camel?[3]
> *A.* Does not the camel carry a load?
> *B.* Carry a load! Am I a donkey? . . .
> *A.* Does not the bow inflict a sting?
> *B.* Sting! Am I a scorpion?
> *A.* Does not the scorpion lie flat against a wall?
> *B.* Flat against a wall! Am I a cockroach?
> *A.* Does not the cockroach go into a calabash?
> *B.* Go into a calabash! Am I milk?
> *A.* Does not one imbibe milk?
> *B.* Imbibe me? Am I tobacco?
> *A.* Tobacco is worthless grain.[4]

Besides the use of puns for amusement in ordinary talk, punning can also occur in a quite elaborate, stylized way in cultivated conversation. This can be taken to such an extent that a man can

---

[1] Ellis, loc. cit.

[2] See C. Sacleux, *Dictionnaire swahili–français*, Paris, 1939, t. 1, under *kinyume* (p. 390).

[3] Because large drums are sometimes carried and played by camel riders in processions.

[4] Fletcher 1912, pp. 60–1. Cf. also the similar Fulani 'chain-rhyme', also based on a series of double meanings, quoted in Arnott 1957, p. 394; and the simpler examples in Tremearne 1913, p. 67.

even become famous—as in the case of certain Amharic wits—
for his linguistic gymnastics and philosophical punning. It is worth
quoting Messing's comment on this:

The Amharic language lends itself readily to puns and hidden
meanings, since many verbs can have double or triple interpretations
due to the hidden variations in the basic verbal stem and the absence
or presence of gemination of some consonants. The listener must pay
close attention. If he misinterprets the context and fails to discern the
pun, he is often made the butt of the next tricky joke by those who have
heard it before. The more a storyteller and wit masters the *sowaso*
'grammar' of the Amharic language, the better he can manipulate this
humor.[1]

A few other instances of relatively light-hearted sayings also
deserve mention. There is, for instance, the case of Galla humorous
prose. This was the preserve of the professional jesters who used
to be maintained at the small courts among the Galla. The wittiest
of their sayings were learnt by heart and regarded as a distinct
literary form—*hâsā*. One such piece opens:

In the whole world there are three misfortunes. Of these misfortunes
one is wealth when it is great and increases. The second is thy wife.
The third is God, who has created us . . .

and so on, in expansion and explanation of the same theme.[2]
Strikingly similar are the various examples of Fulani 'epigrams'
collected by Arnott, some in a form of verse, others, apparently,
in a kind of rhythmic prose. Some of these resemble a type of
extended classificatory proverb, often based on a threefold principle. Another common form is for the saying to be opened by a
short general statement followed by trios of particulars in parallel
terms. The effectiveness of these epigrams, marked by repetition
of key-words and assonance from recurring suffixes, is heightened
by the structure of the Fulani language with its practice of concord
in nominal classes and the potentialities of verb tenses. Two
types of epigrams, one based on a stated general principle, one
a crisp classificatory form, can be illustrated from Arnott's
material:

[1] S. D. Messing, 'Ethiopian Folktales Ascribed to a Late Nineteenth-century
Amhara Wit, Aläqa Gäbre-Hanna', *JAF* 70, 1957, p. 69.
[2] Cerulli 1922, pp. 190–1.

Three exist where three are not:

Commoner exists where there is no king,
  but a kingdom cannot exist where there are no commoners;
Grass exists where there is nothing that eats grass,
  but what eats grass cannot exist where no grass is;
Water exists where there is nothing that drinks water,
  but what drinks water cannot exist where no water is.[1]

Beards; three of fire, three of sun, three of shade.
  (These are the nine beards of the world.
  Three fire, three sun, three shade.)

  Chief, shade,
  Teacher, shade,
  Tailor, shade;

  Blacksmith, fire,
  Corn-cob, fire [i.e. roasted in ashes],
  He-goat, fire [i.e. branded?];

  Farm-labourer, sun,
  Pedlar, sun,
  Herdsman, sun;
  These also are three.

These are all the nine beards of the world.[2]

There are many other short stereotyped phrases and sentences
which, in varying cultures, may be worthy of literary study. One
could mention, for instance, various short semi-religious formulas
—such as the Hausa expressions used after yawning, sneezing,
etc.,[3] market cries,[4] or the conventionalized calls sometimes attributed to birds.[5] Formal salutations can also have a literary flavour.
Thus Hulstaert has collected several hundred such salutations
from the Nkundo, which are used formally to superiors or (in certain formal situations) to equals. These Nkundo forms to some
extent overlap with proverbs and, particularly the more stereotyped among them, should in Hulstaert's view be given a place
'dans le trésor du style oral', for they are marked by a certain
rhythmic quality, by figurative expression, and by a use of archaic

[1] Arnott 1957, p. 384.                    [2] Ibid., pp. 386–7.
[3] Fletcher 1912, pp. 68–9.                 [4] Ibid., p. 59.
[5] e.g. among the Yoruba (see Ellis 1894, p. 242), Hausa (Fletcher 1912, p. 58),
Azande (E. E. Evans-Pritchard, 'A Note on Bird Cries and Other Sounds in
Zande', *Man* 61, 1961), Limba (Finnegan, field-notes); for longer forms built
up on such calls, see instances and references in Ch. 9, pp. 248 ff.

language.[1] The salutation 'Les écureuils se moquent du python', for instance, is an oblique way of saying that only a fool provokes the powerful, for this is to risk entanglement, even death; while 'La terre est un fruit' suggests that just as a round fruit rolls and turns, always showing a different face, so too does human fortune.[2] Few formal greetings, perhaps, approach the Nkundo figurative elaboration, but further study of this type of formal wording in other cultures could well be of interest.

## IV

I shall end this miscellaneous list of minor literary usages with a brief account of the significance of names. This is a subject of greater literary interest than might at first appear. In fact it would be true to say that names often play an indispensable part in oral literature in Africa. Such names as 'One who causes joy all round' (Yoruba), 'Its hide is like the dust' (a man's name after his favourite ox whose hide has marks like writing) (Jie), 'He who is Full of Fury' (Ankole), 'Devouring Beast' (Venda), 'God is not jealous' (Bini), or 'It is children who give fame to a man' (Bini) can add a depth even to ordinary talk or a richly figurative intensity to poetry that can be achieved in no more economical a way.

There have been many different interpretations of these names. They have ranged from the psychological functions of names, in providing assurance or 'working out' tensions,[3] to their connection with the structure of society,[4] their social function in minimizing friction,[5] or their usefulness either in expressing the self-image of their owner or in providing a means of indirect comment when a direct one is not feasible.[6] As usual, there is some truth in most of these approaches.

One of the most striking aspects is the way names can be used as a succinct and oblique way of commenting on their owners or on others. Junod gives some good examples of this kind of use of

[1] Hulstaert 1959, pp. 6, 9.                          [2] Ibid., pp. 46, 50.
[3] e.g. J. H. M. Beattie, 'Nyoro Personal Names', *Uganda J.* 21, 1957; J. Middleton, 'The Social Significance of Lugbara Personal Names', *Uganda J.* 25, 1961.
[4] e.g. J. Vansina, 'Noms personnels et structure sociale chez les Tyo (Teka)', *ARSOM Bull.*, 1964 (following Lévi-Strauss).
[5] As e.g. H. H. Wieschhoff, 'The Social Significance of Names among the Ibo of Nigeria', *Am. Anthrop.* 43, 1941, p. 220.
[6] See below.

nicknames among the Thonga. One is the instance of an administrator nicknamed 'Pineapple' or 'The one of the Pineapple'. On
the surface this was a flattering and easily explained name. But it
also had a deeper meaning. The reference was to a custom (said
to be followed by another tribe) of burying someone they had
killed and planting pineapples on the grave—nothing could be
seen but the leaves, and their crimes were hidden. The administrator's name, then, really suggested one who shirked his duty
and tried to bury matters brought to him for judgement—a fitting
designation for a man who avoided responsibility and sought com-
promise. In another case a woman missionary was called *Hlan-
ganyeti*—'The one who gathers dry wood for the fire'. In a way
this was polite—it is pleasant to have a fire and wood gathered
ready. But it also implied the idea of gathering wood for another
to kindle, of bringing information to her husband who kindled the
fire, of being someone who never showed anger herself but stirred
up others. Many other similar nicknames were given to Europeans
by the Thonga, an effective and quiet comment on their characters:
'The fury of the bull'; 'Kindness in the eyes (only)'; 'The little
bitter lemon'; 'The one who walks alone'.[1]

Names can also be used in oblique comment. Thus the Karanga
subtly give names to their dogs as an elliptical way of chiding
another. A dog called 'The carrier of slanders' really alludes to
a particular woman, 'A waste of cattle' reproves a bad wife, while
'Others' and 'A wife after the crops are reaped' are a wife's complaint
that others are more loved than she, that she is only fed in time of
plenty, unlike her co-wives.[2] Somewhat similarly a parent may
choose for his child a name with an oblique or even open comment
on the other parent's behaviour—like the Nyoro *Bagonzenku*,
'They like firewood', from the proverb 'They like firewood who
despite the gatherer of it', a name given by a mother who has been
neglected by the child's father.[3]

Names are also often used to express ideas, aspirations, sorrows,
or philosophical comments. Grief and an awareness of the ills
of life are frequent themes—'Bitterness', 'They hate me', 'Daughter

---

[1] Junod 1938, pp. 54–6.

[2] N. A. Hunt, 'Some Notes on the Naming of Dogs in Chikaranga', *Nada* 29,
1952; some further Karanga examples are given in Ch. 14, p. 411. For a similar
use of dogs' names among the Gbeya of the Central African Republic see W. J.
Samarin, 'The Attitudinal and Autobiographic in Gbeya Dog Names', *J. Afr.
Languages* 4, 1965.                                    [3] Beattie, op. cit., p. 100.

born in Death' are Thonga examples,[1] and many other similar names could be cited expressing suspicion, sorrow, or fear.[2] Among the Ovimbundu a mother can lament a lost child in the more complex form of a name representing an abridged proverb 'They borrow a basket and a sieve; a face you do not borrow', in her knowledge that though she may have other children, there will never be another with that same face.[3] But names can also express joyful sentiments, like the Yoruba 'Joy enters the house', 'The God of iron sent you to console me', 'I have someone to pet',[4] or a sense of personal aspiration for oneself or others, like the Dogon name *Dogono* (from *Dogay*, 'It is finished') which expresses a wish that the son of a rich man may end life as he began it, in wealth,[5] the Fon assertion that the name's owner is not afraid of his rivals, expressed in the form of an abbreviated proverb 'Le crocodile ne craint pas les piquants qui servent de défense aux poissons',[6] or the Bini name 'The palm-tree does not shed its leaves' which claims that its holder is invulnerable, cannot be caught unawares, and, like an old palm-tree, will stand against all opposition[7]—and similar examples abound in the many published collections of names.

Names contribute to the literary flavour of formal or informal conversation, adding a depth or a succinctness through their meanings, overtones, or metaphors. They can also play a directly literary role. We have already considered the studied use of names in Akan dirges; a whole series of different forms (day names, by-names, praise names, and dirge names) together enhance the intensity and high-sounding tone of the poems. The introduction of names in other forms of literature also—perhaps particularly in the case of those with a historical cast—can bring a sense of allusiveness and sonority not easily expressed in other forms. This is strikingly so in panegyric poetry, a genre which is in Africa so often based on an elaboration of praise names like 'He-who-fails-not-to-overthrow-the-foe', 'Transformer-of-peoples', or 'Sun-is-shining'. Names also play a significant part in the drum literature discussed in the following chapter. In such a passage as

---

[1] Junod 1938, p. 53.

[2] See especially Beattie, op. cit.; Middleton, op. cit.

[3] Ennis 1945, p. 5.          [4] Gbadamosi and Beier 1959, p. 6.

[5] D. Lifchitz and D. Paulme, 'Les noms individuels chez les Dogon', *Mém. IFAN* 23, 1953, p. 332.

[6] C. da Cruz, 'Petit recueil des pseudonymes (Fon)', *Etudes dahoméennes (IFAN)* 15, 1956, pp. 23–4.          [7] Omijeh 1966, p. 26.

The ruler of Sɛkyerɛ has bestirred himself.
The great Toucan, has bestirred himself . . .
He has bestirred himself, the gracious one.
He has bestirred himself, the mighty one . . .[1]

the names which describe and refer to the person being addressed are most significant. Names also have a close connection with proverbs; many names are in fact abbreviations or restatements of recognized proverbs and share some of their stylistic characteristics.

The colourful and often figurative quality of many of these names should be brought out.[2] There are, of course, many names which are relatively straightforward, with little overt meaning. Others, however, are richly allusive. Among these, the most interesting are perhaps the abundant proverb names already mentioned. In these a proverb is either stated or, more often, referred to by only one of its words, and all the overtones of meaning and allusion inherent in the proverb can be found in the name. Thus we find several Nyoro names which refer to proverbs—like *Bitamazire* (a reference to the saying *nkaito z'ebigogo bitamazire*) 'The sandals which were made of banana fibre were inadequate' (in other words, small children cannot be expected to survive long), or *Ruboija* meaning 'It pecks as a fowl does'—just as one does not know which exact grain will be picked up next by a fowl, only that *some* grain will be attacked, so one cannot tell who will be struck next by death.[3] Many similar cases occur among the Ganda who are said to have thousands of proverbial names—among them *Nyonyintono* (from *Nyonyintono yekemba byoya*) 'A small bird, to appear big, must clothe itself in many feathers', and the female name *Ganya* which comes from the saying 'When a wife begins to disrespect her husband it shows that she has found another place where she intends to go and live'.[4] In West Africa, Bini proverbs about wealth (among other topics) also appear as names in abbreviated forms that recall the full tone of the proverb. This is so, for instance, in the recommendation to go prudently about

---

[1] Nketia 1963*b*, pp. 148–9.
[2] This is not, however, the place for a detailed description of such questions as who gives names in various societies, how and when they are conferred, or their varying subject-matter, important though these points may be for the meaning and use of the name.    [3] Beattie, op. cit., 1957, p. 101.
[4] M. B. Nsimbi, 'Baganda Traditional Personal Names', *Uganda J.* 14, 1950, p. 205.

gathering property ('It is with gentleness one draws the rope of wealth', i.e. lest it break), or the satiric comment on the lengths to which men will go for money ('If one is seeking wealth, one's head would go through a drainage pipe').[1]

Proverb names that are chosen by their bearers, as among, for instance, the Fon or the Ovimbundu, offer the opportunity for their chosers to express their own images of themselves. One man may choose the name *Cindele* from the saying 'C'est le Blanc aux cheveux bien coupés qui traverse la mer' (*Cindele ca ndumba ci njawuka ca kalunga*), indicating that he too would claim to belong to this superior rank; in another case the choice might be *Kacipiluka* (from 'Le soleil ne danse pas, mais le temps change') claiming constancy and importance for the name's owner, or *Munda* ('Une haute montagne ne peut être mesurée qu'à l'aide des nuages') to show his pride.[2] As Hauenstein describes it:

Le nom est une espèce de condensé, de résumé du proverbe. . . . Dans la coutume de *okulisapa* [assuming a proverbial name] l'intéressé, dans une espèce de dialogue avec lui-même, se dit ce qu'il aimerait être (puissant, riche, respecté, fort, noble), ou alors se confie à lui-même, si l'on peut dire, sa misère, sa pauvreté, ses malheurs.[3]

Strings of proverb names can also be used to praise oneself. This is exploited effectively among the Ibo. When a man takes an *ozo* title he sings aloud a list of the names he now wishes to be addressed by. These are usually a series of proverbs which refer metaphorically to his various exploits and wealth:

I am:
The Camel that brings wealth,
The Land that breeds the Ngwu tree,
The Performer in the period of youth,
The Back that carries its brother,
The Tiger that drives away the elephants,
The Height that is fruitful,
Brotherhood that is mystic,
Cutlass that cuts thick bushes,
The Hoe that is famous,
The Feeder of the soil with yams,
The Charm that crowns with glory,

[1] Omijeh 1966, pp. 28, 29.  [2] Hauenstein 1962, pp. 106–8.
[3] Ibid., p. 106. Similar instances are recorded among the Fon of Dahomey (da Cruz, loc. cit.) and the Bini of Nigeria (Omijeh 1966).

The Forest that towers highest,
The Flood that can't be impeded,
The Sea that can't be drained.[1]

Praise names are a category of great interest for the student of oral literature. This is a convenient term used to cover many honorific appellations and flattering epithets.[2] These names have already been mentioned in Chapter 5 as existing both independently and as a basis for praise poetry where they fulfil something of the same function as Homeric epithets. Thus the Yoruba *oriki*, Zulu *izibongo*, and Hausa *kirari* are praise terms which occur both as names and as elements in panegyric, and come in such metaphorical and evocative forms as, for instance, 'Fame-spread-abroad', 'Thunder-on-earth', 'Father-of-the-people', 'Light of God upon earth', 'Bull Elephant', 'Weaver-of-a-wide-basket-he-can-weave-little-ones-and-they-fit-into-one-another', 'He draws red palm oil from the necks of men', or (one of several praise names referring to Rhodes) 'A powerful bull from overseas'.

The forms which particularly concern us here are the personal praise names applied to individual people. But their effectiveness cannot be fully appreciated without noticing the other, related applications of praise names and epithets. It is not uncommon for these terms to be applied also to non-human, even non-animate objects, and the succinct summing up in this form of the referent's basic characteristics—or, it may be, of just one facet that catches the imagination—is part of the genius of these languages. Thus the Hausa have elaborate praise terms for animals or for general categories of human beings. The hyena, for instance, has its own praise name 'O Hyena, O Strong Hyena, O Great Dancer', the eagle's reputed wisdom is alluded to in 'O Eagle, you do not settle on the ground without a reason' (i.e. without seeing something to eat there), while the general *kirari* of wife and husband is 'O Woman whose deception keeps one upon tenterhooks (thorns), your mouth though small can still destroy dignity. If there were none of you there could be no household, if there are too many of you the household is ruined.'[3] Similar types of praise names

[1] Egudu 1967, p. 10.
[2] For details about their distribution see Bascom 1965a, p. 485; S. de Ganay, 'Les devises des Dogons,' *TMIE*, 41, 1941, p. 1; Lifchitz and Paulme, op. cit., p. 354; to which add the *zǎ-yil* of the Lyele of Upper Volta (Nicolas 1950/4).
[3] Tremearne 1913, pp. 174–6. For further examples of these Hausa *kirari* see Ch. 5, pp. 111–12.

occur in various languages for particular clans, families, villages or regions, trees, deities, natural phenomena like rain or storms, masks, particular professions, or even tobacco. Some of these are expressed in short phrases or compounds only, but others come in fuller form and can be elaborated into a kind of prose poem, closely related both to praise poetry and to the lengthy salutations and the prayers mentioned earlier.

Like the generic praise terms for things, individual personal praise names take various forms, more or less elaborate according to context and area. Besides their use as an element in more lengthy literary forms, they also appear on many ceremonial occasions— terms of formal address to superiors, public and ceremonial announcement of the arrival of some leading personage by the calling or drumming of his praise name (very common in Nigeria, for instance), honorific pronouncement of a dead man's praise name in funeral rituals, or utterance of a praise name as a part of personal aspiration or encouragement of another to live up to the ideals inherent in the name.

How elaborate praise names can be among certain African peoples is well illustrated from the Dogon *tige* of which several accounts have been published.[1] Among the Dogon, every child is given three ordinary names; but in addition each man has his own individual praise name (*tige*), a kind of motto. Those of individual human beings refer less to personal characteristics than to some general truth; Dogon *tige* thus really blend the characteristics of praise and of proverb. One man's name is translated as 'Parole d'homme âgé' (implying the wisdom expected of an old man's words), another '(Il est) inutile (de faire) un cadeau (à celui qui ne remercie jamais)', '(Même si) le plat (est) mauvais, (on peut manger la nourriture qu'il contient)',[2] 'Femme menteuse' (aussi rusé qu'une femme menteuse), or 'Hogon, chef de la communauté, ventre de Hogon' (i.e. 'Les meilleurs champs appartiennent au Hogon, c'est l'homme le mieux nourri').[3]

These praise names are used on a variety of occasions. One is on any rather formal occasion in which polite exchange is expected. They are shouted out during the ritualized combats which take place in public at a certain stage in funeral celebrations; during

---

[1] de Ganay 1941; Lifszyc 1938; Lifchitz and Paulme, op. cit. 1953, pp. 343 ff.
[2] de Ganay 1941, p. 50.  [3] Lifchitz and Paulme, op. cit., p. 346.

other stages of the mortuary ceremonies it is the dead man's praise name that is called—he is addressed by this full title and conjured to leave his people in peace. Praise names are also much used at a time of physical exertion, especially in the farms. When a group of young Dogon men join together to work, as custom demands, in their father-in-law's fields, they cry out each other's praise name to incite them to greater efforts, calling on their *amour propre* and evoking the names of the ancestors from whom the names were severally inherited and of whom each individual must show himself worthy.[1] Though the outward contexts for these names are so different, they have something in common: 'la criée du *tige* présente presque toujours un caractère déclamatoire ou solennel qui diffère nettement de l'énoncé du nom et du ton habituel de la conversation.'[2] These formally used Dogon titles are something far more evocative and meaningful than anything we normally understand from the everyday sense of the term 'name'. As Lifchitz and Paulme sum up its uses, it is clear that the Dogon *tige* has relevance for their literature and could not easily be dismissed as a mere label for some individual: 'il est en même temps formule de politesse, vœu, exhortation, flatterie, remerciement et moquerie.'[3]

Praise names in general, then, evoke more than just their individual referent on a particular occasion. Expressed through a conventionally recognized artistic form, often marked by elliptical or metaphorical language, they can bring a range of associations to mind and put the bearer and utterer of the name in a wider perspective—either placing him within a whole class of similar beings (in the case of category praise names) or (with personal names) invoking some proverb of more general application or referring to some quality which the bearer is believed, or hoped, or flatteringly imagined to possess.

There remain two other forms of names to mention briefly. First, the use of names on drums (or other instruments). By a technique described in the next chapter, long forms of personal names are very popular items for transmission on drums. Elaborate forms appear in this context, many of them very similar to the praise names just discussed. 'Spitting snake whose poison does not

---

[1] Ibid., pp. 343–4; de Ganay 1941, pp. 47 ff.

[2] Lifchitz and Paulme, op. cit., p. 344

[3] Ibid., p. 343.

lose its virulence, sharp harpoon, from the village of Yatuka', 'Chief who takes revenge, who stabs civet-cats, root of the neck of the elephant, son of him who sets his face to war . . .', 'The man who is to be trusted with palavers, son of him who bears the blame . . .', 'Bright light does not enter the forest, elder of the village of Yaatelia'[1]—these are all drum names or portions of drum names used in various areas of the Congo. In savannah areas it is not drums but whistles that are used for this kind of transmission. Nicolas has made a collection of such praise names from the Lyele of Upper Volta, names which in many respects resemble the Dogon *tigę* but with the difference that they are thought most effective when whistled. The names bear some relation to proverbs, though forming a distinct literary genre, and include such colourful phrases as 'Les pas du lézard sont sonores dans les feuilles (sèches)', 'Le vent de la tornade ne casse pas la montagne', 'Le tambour de l'orage fait sursauter le monde entier', or 'On ne prend pas (à pleine main) la petite vipère'.[2] These names add to the prestige of chiefs and leaders when they are whistled by those who surround them or escort them on their journeys.

Secondly, a word about some personal names other than those directly applied to people. Besides the generic praise and drum names already mentioned, personal names are also sometimes attached to certain things which, for the particular people involved, are of special emotional or symbolic interest. Among some Congolese peoples, for instance, the drums themselves have their own names—'Mouthpiece of the village', 'In the morning it does not tell of death', 'Drifting about from place to place (as water in a canoe) it has no father'.[3] Dogs[4] and occasionally horses[5] may be given names, and another frequent object for evocative and metaphorical naming is cattle.[6] In some cases these names reflect back, as it were, on human beings; with dogs' names this is sometimes

---

[1] Carrington 1949*b*, pp. 87, 92, 99, 102.

[2] Nicolas 1950 (pp. 89, 97, 92), 1954 (p. 88).

[3] Carrington 1949*b*, p. 107; see also J. Carrington, 'Individual Names given to Talking Gongs in the Yalemba Area of Belgian Congo', *Afr. Music* 1. 3, 1956.

[4] See examples given above, p. 471.

[5] See instances of *noms de guerre* of horses in M. Griaule, 'Noms propres d'animaux domestiques (Abyssinie)', *J. Soc. africanistes* 12, 1942.

[6] See e.g. Hauenstein 1962, pp. 112 ff. (Ovimbundu); E. E. Evans-Pritchard, 'Imagery in Ngok Dinka Cattle-names', *BSOS* 7, 1934; Morris 1964, pp. 24–5 (Ankole).

with an insulting intention; cattle names are more often used in a laudatory and honorific sense, as, for example, the 'ox-names' given to human beings in many East African areas.[1]

The exact literary value of these names cannot be fully assessed without further research, particularly on their actual contexts of use and on the relationship between these forms and other literary genres in a given culture. But we can certainly find some literary significance in the occurrence of these condensed, evocative, and often proverbial or figurative forms of words which appear as personal names in African languages—sometimes appearing directly as elements in large-scale creations, sometimes affording scope for imagery, depth, personal expressiveness, succinct comment, or imaginative overtones in otherwise non-literary modes of speech.[2]


In this chapter we have worked our way down the scale from the fuller forms like oratory or formalized prayer to small-scale phenomena like puns, tongue-twisters, and, finally, names. It is not claimed that all these forms necessarily present any very profound or polished instances of oral literature. Some are of only marginal interest (at least in most cultures) and are of minor significance compared to the more complex forms discussed in earlier chapters. However, in some cases they provide recognized literary genres in their own right, in others they provide the elements out of which more elaborate forms may be built up, in others again they provide the essential background of a popular interest in words out of which the gifted artist can mould his own individual work of art. It is not only in non-literate cultures that these oral forms take on a literary relevance. Even in literate societies there are such conventions—among them the art of conversation, of sermons, of 'extempore' but stylized witty speeches—which may play an

---

[1] See e.g. P. H. Gulliver, 'Bell-oxen and Ox-names among the Jie', *Uganda J.* 16, 1952; E. E. Evans-Pritchard, 'Nuer Modes of Address', ibid. 12, 1948.

[2] For some further discussion and instances of names in addition to references cited in this chapter and in the Bibliography see, among many other articles, B. Holas, 'Remarques sur la valeur sociologique du nom dans les sociétés traditionnelles de l'Ouest africain', *J. Soc. africanistes* 23, 1953; M. Houis, 'Les noms individuels chez les Mosi', Dakar (IFAN), 1963; C. Spiess, 'Bedeutung der Personennamen der Ewe-Neger in Westafrika', *Archiv. für Anthropologie* 16, 1918.

indispensable, though often unrecognized, part in the flowering of an accepted literature. But it seems to be above all in cultures without our current distinction between formal written literature on the one hand and 'informal' spoken words on the other that the artistic significance of these oral forms can most clearly be seen.

# IV · SOME SPECIAL FORMS

## 17

## DRUM LANGUAGE AND LITERATURE[1]

*Introductory—the principle of drum language. Examples of drum literature: announcements and calls; names; proverbs; poetry. Conclusion*

I

A REMARKABLE phenomenon in parts of West and Central Africa is the literature played on drums and certain other musical instruments. That this is indeed a form of literature rather than music is clear when the principles of drum language are understood. Although its literary significance has been overlooked in general discussions of African oral literature,[2] expression through drums often forms a not inconsiderable branch of the literature of a number of African societies.

Communication through drums can be divided into two types. The first is through a conventional code where pre-arranged signals represent a given message; in this type there is no directly linguistic basis for the communication. In the second type, that used for African drum literature and the form to be considered here, the instruments communicate through direct representation of the spoken language itself, simulating the tone and rhythm of actual speech. The instruments themselves are regarded as speaking and their messages consist of words. Such communication, unlike that through conventional signals, is intended as a *linguistic*

[1] The description in this chapter is mainly based on Rattray 1923; Carrington 1944, 1949*a*, 1949*b*; and Nketia 1963*b*. Nketia's book forms the first part (all as yet available) of his detailed analysis of various aspects of Akan drumming; the second volume is to discuss drum poetry in more detail.

[2] e.g. Bascom 1964, 1965*a*; Berry 1961; Herskovits 1946 (1960).

one; it can only be fully appreciated by translating it into words, and any musical effects are purely incidental.

This expression of words through instruments rests on the fact that the African languages involved are highly tonal; that is, the meanings of words are distinguished not only by phonetic elements but by their tones, in some cases by tone alone. It is the tone patterns of the words that are directly transmitted, and the drums and other instruments involved are constructed so as to provide at least two tones for use in this way. The intelligibility of the message to the hearer is also sometimes increased by the rhythmic pattern, again directly representing that of the spoken utterance.

It might seem at first sight as if tonal patterns, even when supplemented by rhythm, might provide but a slight clue to the actual words of the message. After all, many words in a given language possess the same combination of tones. However, there are various devices in 'drum language' to overcome this. There is, of course, the obvious point that there are conventional occasions and types of communication for transmission on the drum, so that the listener already has some idea of the range of meanings that are likely at any given time. More significant are the stereotyped phrases used in drum communications. These are often longer than the straightforward prose of everyday utterance, but the very extra length of the drum stereotypes or holophrases leads to greater identifiability in rhythmic and tonal patterning.

The principle can be illustrated from the Kele people of the Stanleyville area of the Congo, whose drum language has been extensively studied by Carrington.[1] In the Kele language the words meaning, for example, 'manioc', 'plantain', 'above', and 'forest' all have identical tonal and rhythmic patterns. By the addition of other words, however, a stereotyped drum phrase is made up through which complete tonal and rhythmic differentiation is achieved and the meaning transmitted without ambiguity. Thus 'manioc' is always represented on the drums with the tonal pattern of 'the manioc which remains in the fallow ground', 'plantain' with 'plantain to be propped up', and so on. Among the Kele there are a great number of these 'proverb-like phrases'[2] to refer to nouns. 'Money', for instance, is conventionally drummed as 'the pieces of metal which arrange palavers', 'rain' as 'the bad

[1] Carrington 1944, 1949*a*, and 1949*b*.    [2] Carrington 1949*a*, p. 38.

spirit son of spitting cobra and sunshine', 'moon' or 'month' as 'the moon looks down at the earth', 'a white man' as 'red as copper, spirit from the forest' or 'he enslaves the people, he enslaves the people who remain in the land', while 'war' always appears as 'war watches for opportunities'. Verbs are similarly represented in long stereotyped phrases. Among the Kele these drum phrases have their own characteristic forms—marked by such attributes as the use of duplication and repetition, derogatory and diminutive terms, specific tonal contrasts, and typical structures[1] and it is evident that they not only make for clear differentiation of intended meanings but also, in Carrington's words, are often 'poetical in nature and constitute an important part of the oral literature of the tribe'.[2]

The sort of communication that can be sent using these drum phrases can be illustrated from the Kele drum representation of a simple message. It will be noticed how much longer the drum form is, both because of the repetition necessary to make the meaning clear and the use of the lengthy stereotyped phrases. The message to be conveyed is: 'The missionary is coming up river to our village tomorrow. Bring water and firewood to his house.' The drum version runs:

> White man spirit from the forest
> of the leaf used for roofs[3]
> comes up-river, comes up-river
> when to-morrow has risen
> on high in the sky
> to the town and the village
> of us
> come, come, come, come
> bring water of *lɔkɔila* vine
> bring sticks of firewood
> to the house with shingles high up above[4]
> of the white man spirit from the forest
> of the leaf used for roofs.[5]

[1] Discussed in detail in Carrington 1949*b*, pp. 47–54.
[2] Op. cit., p. 47.
[3] Generic drum name for European. The reference is to the very large leaves used for roof tiles, compared to the Bible.
[4] Common drum phrase for house.
[5] Carrington 1949*a*, p. 54. There are sometimes additional complications in practice: e.g. in Kalabari, a language with three tones, these are abstracted into a two-tone basis for drumming (Horton 1963, p. 98 n.); in Yoruba tonal glides

Expression through drums, once thought so mysterious by visitors who failed to grasp its principles, thus turns out to be based directly on actual words and their tones. In a sense drum language fulfils many of the functions of writing, in a form, furthermore, better suited to tonal languages than an alphabetical script.[1] Its usefulness too is undeniable in regions of dense forest where the only possible way of communicating, apart from actually sending messengers, was by sound.[2]

This type of drum communication is known to occur widely in the Congo, Cameroons, and West Africa (particularly the coastal areas). The same principle—that of representing the tones of actual speech through stereotyped phrases—is also used for 'spoken' communication through other instruments such as horns, flutes, or gongs.[3] Among some peoples such as the Ashanti or the Yoruba, drum language and literature are very highly developed indeed. In such cases, drumming tends to be a specialized and often hereditary activity, and expert drummers with a mastery of the accepted vocabulary of drum language and literature were often attached to a king's court. This type of expression is a highly skilled and artistic one and adds to the verbal resources of the language.

II

The relevance of drum language for oral literature is not confined to utilitarian messages with a marginally literary flavour. As will emerge clearly from some further examples, this type of

are sometimes represented, sometimes not (U. Beier, 'The Talking Drums of the Yoruba', *Afr. Music* I. 1, 1954, pp. 29–30); in the Congo it is the essential word tones that are transmitted and not the modifications of these as they would actually be pronounced in a spoken sentence (Carrington 1949*b*, p. 59). But the basic principle of representation of the tones of words seems to apply throughout.

[1] A point made in J. Jahn, *Muntu, An Outline of Neo-African Culture* (Eng. tr.), London, 1961, pp. 187 ff.

[2] Drum messages can be heard at a distance of between three to seven miles, according to Carrington 1949*b*, p. 25.

[3] Strictly the term 'gong' should be used to refer to the hollow wooden ideophones or 'slit-gongs' typical of the Congo area; whereas 'drum', which I have used in a wide sense here, should be confined to membranophones such as the Ashanti 'talking drums', a pair of hide-covered drums, one sounding a high, the other a low tone. Other media mentioned for this type of communication include horns, bells, yodelling of various types, sticks, a blacksmith's hammer and anvil, stringed instruments, and whistling.

medium can also be used for specifically literary forms, for proverbs, panegyric, historical poems, dirges, and in some cultures
practically any kind of poetry. Something of the range and variety
of this literature can be seen in the following examples, beginning
with relatively simple messages, more typical of the Congo area
and going on to some of the complex poetry found most characteristically in the southern areas of West Africa.

Among the Kele in the Congo, drum communication is used
for formalized announcements. There are drum messages about,
for instance, births, marriages, deaths, and forthcoming hunts or
wrestling matches. A death is publicized on the drum by a special
alert signal and the words, beaten out in drum language,

> You will cry, you will cry, you will cry
> Tears in the eyes
> Wailing in the mouth

followed by the name and village of the dead man.[1] The announcement of an enemy's approach is also transmitted by a special alert
and the drummed tones which represent the words

> War which watches for opportunities
> has come to the town
> belonging to us
> today as it has dawned
> come, come, come, come.[2]

Another stock communication is the announcement of a dance,
again with the drum speaking in standardized and repetitive
phrases:

> All of you, all of you
> come, come, come, come,
> let us dance
> in the evening
> when the sky has gone down river
> down to the ground.[3]

A final Kele message warns that rain is imminent and advises
those in the forest or near the village to take shelter:

[1] Carrington 1949a, p. 58.       [2] Ibid., p. 65.
[3] Ibid., pp. 61–2.

Look out, look out, look out, rain,
bad spirit, son of the spitting snake
do not come down, do not come down, do not come down
to the clods, to the earth
for we men of the village
will enter the house
do not come down, do not come down, do not come down.[1]

Not all the peoples choose the same topics for these standardized drum announcements. Among the Akan, for instance, births, ordinary deaths, and marriages are not normally publicized on drums.[2] However, the use of drums to announce some emergency and, in particular, to call to arms seems very common indeed. In some cases this takes a very elaborate and poetic form. Compare, for instance, the simple and relatively straightforward call to fight among the Tumba of the Congo—

Make the drum strong;
strengthen your legs,
spear, shaft and head,
and the noise of moving feet;
think not to run away[3]

—with the literary and emotional quality typical of the specialized military drumming of the Akan of Ghana, exemplified in one of their drum calls:

Bodyguard as strong as iron,
Fire that devours the nations,
Curved stick of iron,
We have leapt across the sea,
How much more the lagoon?
If any river is big, is it bigger than the sea?
Come Bodyguard, come Bodyguard,
Come in thick numbers,
Locusts in myriads,
When we climb a rock it gives way under our feet.
Locusts in myriads,
When we climb a rock it breaks into two.
Come Bodyguard, come Bodyguard,
In thick numbers.[4]

[1] Carrington 1949*b*, p. 88.                     [2] Nketia 1963*b*, p. 43.
[3] R. T. Clarke, 'The Drum Language of the Tumba People', *American J. Sociology* 40, 1934, p. 39.          [4] Nketia 1963*b*, pp. 111–12.

Besides messages and announcements, drum language is also used for names. This is one of the most common forms of drum expression and occurs even among people who do not seem to have other more complicated drum poetry. Among the Hausa, for instance, praise names and titles of rulers are poured forth on drums or horns on certain public occasions,[1] and the Lyele proverb names (*surnoms-devises*) are commonly performed in the analogous whistle language;[2] in both cases this amounts to special praise and flattery of the individuals named.

Personal drum names are usually long and elaborate. In the Benue–Cross River area of Nigeria, for instance, they are compounded of references to a man's father's lineage, events in his personal life, and his own personal name.[3] Similarly among the Tumba of the Congo, all-important men in the village (and sometimes others as well) have drum names: these are usually made up of a motto emphasizing some individual characteristic, then the ordinary spoken name; thus a Belgian government official can be alluded to on the drums as 'A stinging caterpillar is not good disturbed'.[4] Carrington describes the Kele drum names in some detail. Each man has a drum name given him by his father, made up of three parts: first the individual's own name; then a portion of his father's name; and finally the name of his mother's village. Thus the full name of one man runs 'The spitting cobra whose virulence never abates, son of the bad spirit with the spear, Yangɔndɛ'. Other drum names (i.e. the individual's portion) include such comments as 'The proud man will never listen to advice', 'Owner of the town with the sheathed knife', 'The moon looks down at the earth / son of the younger member of the family', and, from the nearby Mba people, 'You remain in the village, you are ignorant of affairs'.[5]

These drum names often play a significant part in the societies in which they occur. Their use in the conveying of messages is quite clear—the elaborateness of the names in this context has the directly utilitarian function of differentiating the tonal patterns without the possibility of ambiguity. They are also frequently used in the context of dances, entertainments, and festivals: they call on those present to encourage or to praise them by singling

[1] Smith 1957, p. 29.  [2] Nicolas 1950, p. 87.
[3] R. G. Armstrong, 'Talking Drums in the Benue–Cross River Region of Nigeria', *Phylon* 15, 1954, p. 361.
[4] Clarke, op. cit., p. 38.
[5] Carrington 1949*a*, pp. 41 ff.; 1949*b*, pp. 87, 107.

them out. As an Idoma informant told Armstrong, 'when an African hears his name drummed, he must jump up for joy even from his sick bed'.[1] The literary and poetic quality that may be associated with names has been discussed earlier:[2] in the case of drum names these elements are often especially marked because of the very elaboration, convention, and publicity necessarily involved in this particular medium.[3]

In some areas, particularly much of southern West Africa, drum literature takes a more highly specialized form. There are drum proverbs, panegyric, and other poetry for drums, horns, or flutes, and sometimes state history is transmitted.

First, proverbs. These are commonly performed on drums in West Africa, sometimes as an accompaniment to dancing. In the Niger–Cross River area of Nigeria the drums review the philosophy and history of the group at a big dance: 'When a dancer or a mask dances to the intoned proverbs and histories, he may be said to express them with his body. He does so quite consciously. Education in such matters is necessary for membership in the men's societies.'[4] Among the Akan almost every ordinary proverb can be reproduced on drums, and in drum poetry in general there is frequent use of proverbs to provide encouragement and incitement.[5] But there are also extended proverbs specifically intended for performance on the drums. Thus the common Akan proverb 'If a river is big, does it surpass the sea?' can be played just as it is, or appear in the special drum form:

> The path has crossed the river,
> The river has crossed the path,
> Which is the elder?
> We made the path and found the river.
> The river is from long ago,
> From the Ancient Creator of the Universe.[6]

The Akan have a special cycle of proverbs associated with the Akantam dance and especially constructed for performance on drums. These have a regular metrical form and are marked by repetition of words, phrases, and sentences which create metrical

---

[1] Armstrong, op. cit., pp. 360–1.      [2] Ch. 16.

[3] Among the Kele the idea that drum names are part of their oral literature also comes out in their terminology, if Carrington is right in deriving *bombila* (drum name) from the same root as that for 'story' or 'parable' (Carrington 1944, p. 83).      [4] Armstrong, op. cit., p. 360.

[5] Nketia 1958c, p. 49.      [6] Nketia 1963b, p. 47.

and musical effects. In this Akantam series, each piece contains at least two proverbs. It is preceded by special introductory rhythms, and the proverbs are then beaten out in unison by all the heavy drums while the small drums provide the musical 'ground'. As the piece proceeds, the proverbs are repeated as a refrain, and the piece is concluded with special rhythms which merge into the introduction of the next piece in the cycle.[1]

This form can be illustrated from a long example published by Nketia. It consists of about twenty stanzas interspersed with refrains drawn from two proverbs. I give only a short extract from the second half:

> The great Toucan,
> I have bestirred myself,
> Let little ones lie low.

> *Duiker Adawurampon Kwamena,*
> *Who told the Duiker to get hold of his sword?*
> *The tail of the Duiker is short,*
> *But he is able to brush himself with it.*

Kurotwamansa, the Leopard, lies in the thicket.
The thicket shakes and trembles in the dark forest.

> *Duiker Adawurampon Kwamena,*
> *Who told the Duiker to get hold of his sword?*
> *The tail of the Duiker is short,*
> *But he is able to brush himself with it.*

The antelope lies in its thicket-lair,
The hunter lures him with his call.
The hunter deserves to die.
For he will not answer him.

> *Duiker Adawurampon Kwamena,*
> *Who told the Duiker to get hold of his sword?*
> *The tail of the Duiker is short,*
> *But he is able to brush himself with it.*

Wild Bear, Akuampɔn,
How did it happen that the water buck got tied up in cords?
It is because he could not hold his tongue.

> *Duiker Adawurampon Kwamena,*
> *Who told the Duiker to get hold of his sword?*
> *The tail of the Duiker is short,*
> *But he is able to brush himself with it.*

[1] Nketia 1958c, p. 49.

The tall forest palm tree is bent low.
The tall forest palm tree is bent low.
Whether it will fall or not,
The jealous one is mighty anxious, over-anxious, over-anxious;
The jealous one is deeply anxious, over-anxious, over-anxious.

> *Duiker Adawurampon Kwamena,*
> *Who told the Duiker to get hold of his sword?*
> *The tail of the Duiker is short,*
> *But he is able to brush himself with it.*[1]

Panegyric poetry is a genre to which public and ceremonial performance in drum language is particularly suited, whether the actual medium happens to be in fact drums, gongs, or wind instruments. Especially in parts of West Africa, praise poetry on drums and other instruments may take a complex and specialized form and is particularly common on public or state occasions. For Southern Nigeria, for instance, Armstrong quotes the following praise; it is taken from a performance in the royal court of the chief of Igumale, and is spoken by a flute. Throughout the poem the chief is praised in the imagery of a leopard:

Akpa killed those who have horses *coza loga*.[2]
The leopard in power is no toy!
The mouth of him who goes wrongly and pays a fine is what is guilty![3]
*Ogo tikpa logwu gokpaawaga !*[4]
When the land is dry ('strong') they will wait for the rains![5]
When the leopard is on the way, the animals fear.
When the kite calls, it is noon.[6]
The locusts swarm![7]
Big, powerful man *cuna zegba*.
When there is a lion, there is a leopard![8]
The Chief, a full-bodied leopard in the hole!
The horses, here they are![9]
When the Chief did this, did that, they said it is not fitting. The Chieftaincy is not a plaything!

[1] Nketia 1958c, pp. 51–2.  [2] Title of a person present.
[3] i.e. 'keep quiet everybody!'  [4] Meaning unknown; a title?
[5] i.e. 'A patient person'; title of someone present.
[6] i.e. 'A precise man'; title of someone present.
[7] i.e. 'the people have all come together'.
[8] i.e. 'Here is a chief'; chiefly praise.
[9] i.e. 'The royal people have assembled'.

When the girls have no husbands, they say they belong to the Chief!
The girl from the corner with shame in her head, let her take shame
    from her head, for dancing is no plaything![1]
The leopard and the Chief have claws, have claws; the leopard and
    the Chief are coming today!
When the good thing is coming into public, what will the singer do
    today?
He who sits on the (royal) stool, Lion of lions, Chief, it is of him that
    I worry; the leopard and the Chief are no plaything!
He who is fitted for the kingship, let him be king! It is God who makes
    the King![2]

Again, one could quote from the elaborate drum praises so
freely used among the Yoruba. The rulers of the old kingdom of
Ede, for example, are still praised on the talking drum every
month and in the course of all important festivals. These eulogies
are built up on a series of praise verses. Thus in the drum praise
of Adetoyese Laoye, the eleventh ruler, we have the building up of
praises (mingled, as so often, with admonition) with the whole
poem bound together by both the subject (the king) and the recurrent image of the tree:

Adetoyese Akanji, mighty elephant.
One can worship you, as one worships his head.[3]
Son of Moware.
You enter the town like a whirlwind.
You, son of Odefunke.
*Egungun*[4] blesses quickly when you worship him.
*Orisha*[4] blesses more quickly when you worship him.
My father Akanji is an orisha.
The more devoutly you worship him
The greater blessings you receive from Adetoyese Akanji.
Bless, and bless me continuously;
Akanji, and do not leave me unblessed.
Do not attempt to shake a tree trunk.
One who shakes a tree trunk, shakes himself.
One who tries to undo you, you who are as short as death,
He will only undo himself.
A wine tapper cannot tap wine from a coconut palm.[5]

[1] i.e. 'Come on, girls, get out and dance!'
[2] Armstrong op. cit., pp. 362–3.
[3] 'Head' here stands for the Yoruba 'ori' which means: head, good fortune or
luck. People sacrifice to their head as thanksgiving for success, etc.
  [4] Yoruba spirits.         [5] They are trying to do the impossible.

An elephant eats up the entire roots of an oro tree.
Do not behead me, I am not among them
I am not among the conspirators.
Conspirators, the hair on whose heads
Is ugly and ruffled.
A serious case may worry one but it will come to an end.
A serious case worries one, as if it will never be settled.
The case will be settled, and the slanderers and gossipers
Will be put to shame.
You met them in front, and you greet and greet them.
You met them behind you, and you greet and greet them
Your being courteous does not please them, like being insolent.
Keep on being insolent to them and their fathers!
It is unusual for one to greet his father's slave and prostrate.
You Adetoyese Akanji, bend one foot to greet them,
You leave the other unbent![1]
You, a notorious confuser! You confused everybody by your ap-
        pearance![2] Akanji you confused all those
Who tie cloth round their waists, without carrying a child[3]
I beg you in the name of God the great king, confuse me not!
Do not allow me to starve.
The leaves on a tree, do not allow the tree to feel the scorching sun.
You are a lucky person to wear the crown
A person who is on the throne
When the town prospers,
Is a lucky person to wear the crown.[4]

In a rather different style are the many Akan panegyrics for
drums, used for honouring kings and chiefs both of the past and of
the present. They recall their origin, their parentage, and their
noble deeds. The following is an extract from one of these praise
poems, this time on the drum:

> Korɔbea Yirefi Anwoma Sante Kɔtɔkɔ,
> When we are about to mention your name,
> We give you a gun and a sword.

---

[1] Trying to conciliate your opponents, show respect—but not too much
because you are the oba (king).

[2] During the chieftaincy dispute all the contestants were confused by the
sudden appearance of Adetoyese Laoye.

[3] Policemen. The reference is to the cummerbund on the Native Authority
Police uniform. During the contest police had to be transferred from Ede
because they were alleged to favour one of the contestants.

[4] Oba Adetoyese Laoye I, *The Orikis of 13 of the Timis of Ede*, Ede, [1965].

You are the valiant man that fights with gun and sword.
If you were to decide, you would decide for war.
You hail from Kɔtɔkɔ, you are truly Kɔtɔkɔ.

Ɔsɛe Asibe, you are a man,
You are a brave man,
You have always been a man of valour,
The watery shrub that thrives on stony ground,
You are the large *ɔdadeɛ* tree,
The tree with buttress that stands at Dɔnkorɔnkwanta,
A man feared by men.[1]

In another Akan example the chief is saluted and ushered to his seat by the drummer's praise, while all remain standing until he is seated:

Chief, you are about to sit down,
Sit down, great one.
Sit down, gracious one.
Chief, you have plenty of seating space.
Like the great branch, you have spread all over this place.
Let us crouch before him with swords of state.
Ruler, the mention of whose name causes great stir,
Chief, you are like the moon about to emerge.
Noble ruler to whom we are indebted,
You are like the moon:
Your appearance disperses famine.[2]

Among the Akan and the Yoruba, drum poetry also appears in invocations to spirits of various kinds. Longer Akan poems sometimes open with stanzas calling on the spirits associated with the drum itself—the wood and its various components—or invoke certain deities or ancient and famous drummers. Important rituals are also commonly opened or accompanied by the suitable drum poems. 'The Awakening' is one which must be performed before dawn on the day of the Akan Adae festival:

The Heavens are wide, exceedingly wide.
The Earth is wide, very very wide.
We have lifted it and taken it away.
We have lifted it and brought it back,
From time immemorial.
The God of old bids us all
Abide by his injunctions.

[1] Nketia 1963*b*, p. 45.    [2] Ibid., p. 147.

Then shall we get whatever we want,
Be it white or red.
It is God, the Creator, the Gracious one.
'Good morning to you, God, Good morning.'
I am learning, let me succeed.[1]

A final example from the Akan area will illustrate how drums can speak of the history of a community. This is from the drum history of the Mampon division of Ashanti published by Rattray in 1923. This type of poetry is performed on the public occasion of an Adae festival and, as Rattray points out, it has 'a deeply sacred significance. The names of dead kings are not to be spoken lightly, and with the recounting of such a history comes no small sadness to the listener.'[2] The history consists in all of twenty-nine stanzas, and opens with an invocation to the spirits associated with the drum. The actual historical record starts in the fourth of the stanzas quoted below:

(Spirit of) Earth, sorrow is yours,
(Spirit of) Earth, woe is yours,
Earth with its dust,
(Spirit of) the Sky,
Who stretches to Kwawu,[3]
Earth, if I am about to die,
It is upon you that I depend.
Earth, while I am yet alive,
It is upon you that I put my trust.
Earth who received my body,
The divine drummer[4] announces that,
Had he gone elsewhere (in sleep),
He has made himself to arise.
(As) the fowl crowed in the early dawn,
(As) the fowl uprose and crowed,
Very early, very early, very early.
We are addressing you,
And you will understand.
We are addressing you,
And you will understand . . .

---

[1] Nketia 1963*b*, p. 44.
[2] R. S. Rattray, *Ashanti*, Oxford, 1923, p. 264.
[3] A locality on the Gold Coast.
[4] The drummer of the talking drums, a powerful figure, is commonly referred to as the 'divine drummer' or 'Creator's drummer' (Nketia 1963*b*, p. 154).

(Spirit of) the fibre, Ampasakyi,
Where art thou?
The divine drummer announces that,
Had he gone elsewhere (in sleep),
He has made himself to arise,
He has made himself to arise;
(As) the fowl crowed in the early dawn,
(As) the fowl uprose, and crowed,
Very early, very early, very early.
We are addressing you,
And you will understand;
We are addressing you,
And you will understand.

Oh Pegs, (made from) the stump of the Ofema tree,
(Whose title is) Gyaanadu Asare,
Where is it that you are?
The divine drummer announces that,
Had he gone elsewhere (in sleep),
He has made himself to arise,
He has made himself to arise.
(As) the fowl crowed in the early dawn,
(As) the fowl uprose and crowed,
Very early, very early, very early.
We are addressing you,
And you will understand;
We are addressing you,
And you will understand . . .

(Spirit of) Asiama Toku Asare[1]
Opontenten Asi Akatabaa,[2]
Asiama (who came from) the God of the Sky,
Asiama of the Supreme Being,
The divine drummer declares that,
Had he gone elsewhere (in sleep),
He has made himself to arise,
He has made himself to arise.
(As) the fowl crowed in the early dawn.
(As) the fowl uprose and crowed,
Very early,
Very early,

---

[1] The first Queen Mother of the Beretuo clan, said to have descended from the sky. She was head of the clan before they migrated to Mampon.
[2] Strong names (titles).

Very early,
We are addressing you,
And you will understand.

[Oh] Boafo Anwoma Kwakyie,
Kwakyi, the tall one,
Kwakyi Adu Asare,
Whence camest thou?
Thou camest from Mampon-Kontonkyi, the place where the rock
    wears down the axe.
Mampon Kontonkyi Aniampam Boafo Anwoma Kwakyi,
Kon!
Who destroys towns, Firampon,
Alas!
Alas!
Alas! . . .

[Oh] Adu Boahen,
Boahen Kojo,
Whence was it that thou camest?
Thou camest from Mampon Akurofonso,
The place where the Creator made things.
Adu Gyamfi with an eye like flint, (whose title is) Ampafrako.

The Shadows were falling cool,
They fell cool for me at Sekyire[1]
The day dawned,
It dawned for me at Sekyire,
Who is Chief of Sekyire?
The Chief of Sekyire is Kwaitu,
Kwaaye knows Afrane Akwa,
Boatimpon Akuamoa,
Akuamoa,[2] whom we even grow weary of thanking, for his gifts,
Akuamoa, you were of the royal blood since long, long ago,
Thou camest from Mampon Kontonkyi, where the rock wears away
    the axe.

Kon!
Akuamoa Firampon,
Alas!
Alas![3]

---

[1] The name of the wider region which includes Mampon.
[2] The sixth ruler of the Beretuo clan.
[3] Rattray, op. cit., pp. 278–82, stanzas II, IV, V, VIII, IX, XII, XIII. He reproduces the poem in drum language, in ordinary Ashanti, and in English translation.

### III

Drum language, it is clear, is a medium that can be put to a wide range of uses. Its appearance in messages, in names, in poetry, and in the performance of proverbs has been illustrated. It can also be employed to comment on or add to some current activity. Armstrong, for example, describes the actions of a chief drummer at a dance in the Benue–Cross River area, in words that could be applied elsewhere too: he

maintains a running commentary on the dance, controls the line dancers with great precision, calls particular persons by name to dance solo, tells them what dance to do, corrects them as they do it, and sends them back into line with comment on the performance. He does this by making his drum talk, even above the sound of four or five other drums in the 'orchestra'.[1]

In this example, the 'speaking' and comment of the drum form a linguistic complement, as it were, to the musical and balletic aspects of the artistic event as a whole. Among the Kele, the talking drum accompanies wrestling matches, saluting contestants as they enter the ring, uttering comment and encouragement throughout the fight, and ending up with praise for the victor.[2] Similar literary contributions are made by the drums among the Akan even to the otherwise mundane duty of carrying the chief. It is raised to a state ceremonial by the conventions surrounding it and by the drum poetry that accompanies and comments on it: the drums say 'I carry father: I carry father, he is too heavy for me', to which the bass drum replies, in conventional form, 'Can't cut bits off him to make him lighter'.[3] In funerals too, Akan drums play their part, echoing the themes of dirges and heralding the occasion with messages of condolence and farewell.[4] Such comment by drums can take so elaborate a form as to be classed as full drum poetry in its own right. In this case it covers the sorts of drum proverbs, panegyrics, and histories already quoted, forming a specialized type of poetry apparently most characteristic of certain traditional states of West Africa.

Expression by drums or other instruments can also be an alternative medium to the human voice through which ordinary poetry

[1] Armstrong, op. cit., p. 360.  [2] Carrington 1949*a*, pp. 63–4.
[3] Nketia 1963*b*, p. 135.  [4] Ibid., p. 64.

can be represented. Thus among the Yoruba each of their many types of poetry can be recited on the drum as well as spoken, and the *oriki* (praise) poems are as frequently drummed as sung.[1] With the Akan some poems can be drummed or sung, others are designed specifically for voice, drums, or horns respectively.[2]

Many different kinds of communications, then, can be conveyed through the medium of drum language—messages, public announcements, comment, and many types of poetry—and the same sorts of functions can be fulfilled as by the corresponding speech forms, with the additional attributes of the greater publicity and impressiveness of the drum performance. In spite of its wide range of uses, however, drum communication is in certain respects a somewhat limited medium. There are limitations, that is, on the types of communications that can be transmitted; the stereotyped phrases for use in drum languages do not cover every sphere of life, but only the content conventionally expected to be communicated through drums.[3] Furthermore, in certain societies at least (for example, the Yoruba and the Akan), drumming is a highly specialized activity, with a period of apprenticeship and exclusive membership, so that to a greater extent than in most forms of spoken art, drum literature is a relatively esoteric and specialized form of expression, understood by many (at least in its simpler forms) but probably only fully mastered and appreciated by the few.[4] In the case of some peoples the response to such limitations has been the creation of a highly elaborate and conventional mode of artistic expression through drums—with the apparent corollary that in this very specialized and difficult medium the scope for individual variation and improvization seems to be correspondingly limited and the stress laid on technical mastery rather than on verbal originality.[5]

[1] Lasebikan in Osadebay 1949, p. 154; Gbadamosi and Beier 1959, p. 9.

[2] Nketia in Osadebay 1949, p. 156.

[3] Or so it seems. With the exception of some remarks in Rattray, op. cit., 1923, pp. 256–7, the sources do not discuss this point directly.

[4] Not much has been written about the distribution of this skill among the population generally and further study of this question is desirable. Its prevalence in the contemporary scene also demands research; clearly it is at times highly relevant as, for instance, in the use of drum language over the radio during the Nigerian civil war to convey a message to certain listeners, and conceal it from others.

[5] Again, further evidence on this point would be welcome. Of the Akan Nketia makes the point that all drum texts are 'traditional' (apart from the nonsense syllables sometimes included in them which may be invented) and

In conclusion it must be stressed again that what is transmitted in drum language is a direct representation of the *words* themselves. This is worth repeating, because for someone unacquainted with this medium it is not easy to grasp that the drums actually speak words, that from the point of view both of the analyst and of the people involved, the basis is a directly linguistic one. From this it follows that the content and style of drum communication can often be assessed as *literature*, and not primarily as music, signal codes, or incidental accompaniment to dancing or ceremonies. Some of the items of drum language that have been mentioned— the 'proverb-like' phrases of Kele drum language, for instance, or the whistled names in the Upper Volta—are only marginally literary. Other forms, however, in particular the drum poems of southern Ghana, Nigeria, and Dahomey, unmistakably fall into the category of highly developed oral literature. But whatever the assessment of individual examples it is clear that it is both correct and illuminating to analyse drum language in terms of its literary significance. Among the people who practise it, drum literature is clearly a part, albeit through a highly specialized and unusual medium, of their whole oral literature.[1]

that many are known in the same form to drummers in widely separated areas (1963*b*, p. 48).

[1] There is a huge (and very variable) literature on drum language which it is impossible to begin to cover here. Useful bibliographies are to be found in Carrington 1949*b*, and T. Stern, 'Drum and Whistle "Languages": an Analysis of Speech Surrogates', *Am. Anthrop.* 59, 1957. Cf. also, among many other accounts: Witte 1910 (Ewe); J. Jacobs 1959; Schneider 1952 (Duala); E. Van Avermaet, 'Les tons en kiLuba Samba et le tambour-téléphone', *Aequatoria* 1, 1945; R. G. Armstrong, 'Talking Instruments in West Africa', *Explorations* 4, 1955; G. Hulstaert, 'De telefoon der Nkundo', *Anthropos* 30, 1935; H. Labouret, 'Langage tambouriné et sifflé', *Bull. Com. ét. AOF* 6, 1923; G. Herzog, 'Drum Signalling in a West African Tribe', *Word* 1, 1945 (reprinted in Hymes 1964).

# 18

# DRAMA

Introductory. Some minor examples: Bushman 'plays';
West African puppet shows. Mande comedies. West African
masquerades: South-Eastern Nigeria; Kalabari. Conclusion

I

How far one can speak of indigenous drama in Africa is not an
easy question. In this it differs from previous topics like, say,
panegyric, political poetry, or prose narratives, for there it was
easy to discover African analogies to the familiar European forms.
Though some writers have very positively affirmed the existence
of native African drama,[1] it would perhaps be truer to say that
in Africa, in contrast to Western Europe and Asia, drama is not
typically a wide-spread or a developed form.

There are, however, certain dramatic and quasi-dramatic phenomena to be found, particularly in parts of West Africa. Many are
of great interest in themselves, particularly, perhaps, the celebrated
masquerades of Southern Nigeria. Furthermore, some discussion
of such elements of drama helps to throw light on oral literature
in general in Africa.

There are other reasons why some discussion of 'drama' in
Africa is essential. The subject is in many minds inextricably
linked to the question of the origin of drama and to the interpretations of a particular critical school. The existence and supposed
nature of drama, mimetic dances, or masquerades in Africa have
been taken as evidence in discussions of the origin of drama. While
many would now reject the assumptions (often inspired by *The
Golden Bough*) which are inherent in the evolutionist approach,
works built on such assumptions still circulate widely and provoke
an interest in the question of what sort of drama *can* be found in
Africa.[2] It is, in fact, natural that students of the nature and history

[1] e.g. Traoré 1958, Delafosse 1916.
[2] e.g. F. M. Cornford, *The Origin of Attic Comedy*, and A. H. Krappe, *The
Science of Folklore*, which both adopt this line, have each appeared in new
paperback editions in the 1960s.

of European drama should be interested in comparative evidence of analogous forms in Africa. In addition, interpretations of literature in terms of myth and archetype might at first sight be expected to draw particular support from a knowledge of African dramatic forms.

It is clearly necessary to reach at least some rough agreement about what is to count as 'drama'. Rather than produce a verbal definition, it seems better to point to the various elements which tend to come together in what, in the wide sense, we normally regard as drama. Most important is the idea of enactment, of representation through actors who imitate persons and events. This is also usually associated with other elements, appearing to a greater or lesser degree at different times or places: linguistic content; plot; the represented interaction of several characters; specialized scenery, etc.; often music; and—of particular importance in most African performances—dance.

Now it is very seldom in Africa that all these elements of drama come together in a single performance. One or several do of course occur frequently. But which, if any, of such performances are counted as fully 'drama' will depend on which of the various elements mentioned above are considered as most significant (a point, of course, that applies to more than just *African* dramatic performances). What is clear is that while dramatic elements enter into several different categories of artistic activity in Africa and are thus worth consideration here, there are few or no performances which obviously and immediately include all these dramatic elements.[1]

In order to bring out the respective significance of these various elements we will look first at some minor forms. This will be followed by a discussion of the more obviously dramatic forms of West Africa—the comedies of the Mande-speaking area and the complicated masquerades of South-Eastern Nigeria.

II

The emphasis on histrionic ability in story-telling has already been mentioned.[2] Stories are often enacted in the sense that, to a greater or smaller degree, the speech and gestures of their charac-

---

[1] The plays of certain of the Mande-speaking peoples of West Africa, discussed later, are one possible exception.     [2] Ch. 13.

ters are imitated by the narrator, and the action is largely exhibited through dialogue in which the story-teller directly portrays various characters in turn. It is true that such enactment of character is not sustained or complete, that straight narration, as well as dramatic dialogue, is used to communicate the events of the story, and that only one real 'actor' could be said to be involved; thus story-telling can only be spoken of as possessing certain dramatic characteristics, rather than being 'drama' in the full sense. Nevertheless, these dramatic aspects are of the greatest importance in the telling of stories. It has been said of written literature that drama, unlike prose narrative, is not 'self-contained' but depends on other additional elements for its full effect. Precisely the same point could be made of oral narration. As Delafosse writes of certain story-tellers in the Ivory Coast: 'J'ai entendu des griots raconter des histoires au cours desquelles ils faisaient parler leurs héros et qui devenaient dans leur bouche de véritables scènes de théâtre à personnages multiples représentés par un acteur unique.'[1]

This similarity to dramatic performance is heightened by the frequent occurrence of music and sometimes even rudimentary dance movements. It is common for the story-teller to begin a song in the course of the narration—often a song sung by, or representing the actions of, one of the characters—and for this to be taken up antiphonally by the audience acting as chorus, in this way partaking in the dramatic enactment of the story. Occasionally too the story-teller stands and moves among the audience. If most African peoples lack specialized drama, they yet, by the very oral nature of their art, lay greater stress on certain dramatic characteristics of their literature than do cultures which rely primarily on written forms.

A very different side of dramatic art is exhibited by the ǂKhomani Bushman plays described by Doke.[2] Here the linguistic element is apparently non-existent, but the action is portrayed completely through the imitation of several actors. Among the southern Bushmen in particular, there is also some attempt to make themselves up to resemble the animals represented by using paint, or

---

[1] Delafosse 1916, p. 355.

[2] C. M. Doke, 'Games, Plays and Dances of the ǂKhomani Bushmen', *Bantu Studies* 10, 1936; cf. also I. Schapera (ed.), *The Khoisan Peoples of Africa*, London, 1930, pp. 203 ff.

the skins or horns of animals. These 'dramas of the desert'[1] represent the different stages in hunting. Doke describes ten of these plays, and considers that since they depend on imitation and mimicry they have to be considered as drama. In the 'springbok and lion play', for instance, the various animals are portrayed: the girls take the part of the springboks, with the little children as kids, while two or three men act the lions. First the kids, then the springboks are shown as being stalked by the lions with a vividness that makes it into 'a very exciting drama'.[2] 'The gemsbok play' Doke regards as 'probably the Bushman masterpiece of dramatic representation'.[3] In it, one man acts the part of the gemsbok, with a forked stick tied or held to his forehead to represent the horns, and imitates its actions and gait. He is pursued by three or four armed huntsmen and by boys acting as dogs who look out the spoor. The gemsbok is chased, then finally turns at bay. After an exciting fight the play is ended by the death and dispatch of the gemsbok by the hunters and their dogs.

It is possible that similar mimicry and dramatization, particularly of hunting, occur elsewhere in Africa. However, I know of no descriptions of such plays (or dramatic performances of any other kind) from Bantu Africa as a whole, with perhaps the exception of a certain dramatization sometimes found in rituals like initiation and funeral rites.[4] For our other examples of dramatic or quasi-dramatic phenomena we must turn to West Africa, where we can find more elaborate forms ranging from mere puppet shows to the plays of the Mande-speaking peoples of the savannah areas and the masquerades mainly typical of the forest region. These can be discussed in turn.

There are several passing references to puppets in West Africa, though, it seems, few detailed descriptions of their performances. They have been recorded as appearing, in various forms, in the north of the Ivory Coast, in Bornu, Zaria, Bida, and other places in Northern Nigeria and Niger, and occasionally in Southern

---

[1] Doke, op. cit., p. 465.
[2] Ibid., p. 467.                                    [3] Ibid., p. 466.
[4] Cf. especially installation rites and annual ceremonies to do with kingship, such as those described, for instance, by H. Kuper for the Swazi (*An African Aristocracy*, London, 1947, ch. 13, 'The Drama of Kingship'). But the whole subject of the aspect of dramatization and symbolism in ritual (and the various interpretations of this) is too large to enter on here and is not, in any case, directly relevant to a treatment of *literature*.

Nigeria.[1] It is uncertain how long a history they have in these areas.[2]

One detailed description has been given by Ellison of a puppet show in Bornu.[3] Here the puppets consist of rag dolls which fit over the manipulator's hand rather like gloves and are shown through the opening in a kind of tent made by draping a large gown over a stick planted in the ground. The manipulator speaks for the puppets in a special voice produced by half swallowing pieces of ostrich egg-shell; the shrill whistle that results is barely intelligible and the words are therefore repeated by an assistant standing by. In the performance that Ellison witnessed there were eight short scenes, each lasting three to four minutes and complete in itself. Only two puppets could appear at a time, but there were about six in all, and during the intervals while they were being changed inside the tent, the audience were entertained by drummers and singers. The scenes portrayed involved a clear plot, speech, suitable costumes for the parts enacted, and dramatic and exaggerated action. One scene, for example, showed a thief entering a man's house and on the point of making off with his booty when the owner's wife wakes and gives the alarm; the husband appears and dramatically gives the thief a sound beating. Another included a coy Shuwa Arab girl dressed in a long flowing gown with cowries in her hair who sings and dances, and thus captivates a married man; he, inevitably, is caught by his wife and is scolded and beaten; and the scene ends with a realistic fight between the husband and a bystander who has come to see what is happening. A final example is about a rest-house keeper. He is told by the village head that the District Officer is coming—a very particular and fussy D.O., we are informed—and that the rest-house must be very well swept, and wood and water all provided with the greatest care. The D.O. arrives dressed all in white, complete with white pith helmet, and is shown being greeted with exaggerated respect by the village head. But, the story continues, the rest-house turns out to be not exactly spotless and the scene ends with its keeper being severely reproved.

[1] Delafosse 1916, p. 355; R. E. Ellison, 'A Bornu Puppet Show', *Nigerian Field* 4, 1935; Labouret and Travélé 1928; K. C. Murray, 'Dances and Plays', *Nigeria* 19, 1939, p. 218; R. Pageard, 'Travestis et marionnettes de la région de Ségou', *Notes afr.* 93, 1962.

[2] Puppet shows in Bornu are said to have begun in the mid-nineteenth century according to Ellison, op. cit., p. 91.     [3] Ellison, op. cit.

Are such shows to be called drama? Certainly they include most of the dramatic elements we have already mentioned: the enactment of character and events; several actors, albeit in puppet rather than human form; plot; linguistic content; specialized costume; and a limited amount of singing and dancing as well as interval music. In a way it seems unsuitable to call this form drama; and it is worth noting that even in Bornu it seems to have been relatively rarely practised and not regarded as a serious form of art. Still, it must be accepted that the plots and attitudes involved are very similar to some of those in the Mande 'plays' described later, and that even puppet shows can be used to comment comically and dramatically on the events and characters of everyday life.

### III

Of much greater interest are the comedies of certain Mande-speaking peoples in the savannah areas of ex-French West Africa. These, perhaps alone among African enactments, would seem fully to satisfy most of the normal criteria for a truly dramatic play. They have clear plot and linguistic content, as well as music, dancing, costume, definite audience, and the interaction of several human actors appearing at once in the village square that acts as a stage. They are described as 'véritables pièces parfaitement ordonnées et réglées, destinées à exposer une intrigue déterminée, en employant pour interpréter celle-ci des acteurs humains. On peut donc affirmer, dans ces conditions, qu'il existe bien un théâtre soudanais.'[1]

One group of these plays—those of the Mandingo—were described in some detail by Labouret and Travélé in 1928. They are all comic, intended for entertainment and the realistic portrayal of the characters and faults of everyday life. As implied by the Mandingo term *kote koma nyaga*, the plays treat especially of marriage and the various misfortunes of married life, but also involve satirical comment on many other aspects of life. The authors are also actors.

These comedies are said to have been performed every year in the Bamako and Bougouni *cercles* of what was then French Soudan, in the region of the old Mali kingdom. The normal occasion is after the harvest, between October and March. In the evening the

[1] Labouret and Travélé 1928, p. 74.

audience is called to the open village square where, with no scenery or special building, the comedies are presented in the open air, lit either by the moon or by lanterns and candles. Each evening's entertainment follows a fixed order which Labouret and Travélé term respectively the opening ballet (*kote don*), the prologue, the presentation of the players, and, finally, the plays proper.

The proceedings begin with the announcement of the *kote koma nyaga* at about eight in the evening; people hurry to the square and sit ready, with the children running around among the spectators. The drum orchestra enters and takes its place in the centre, and the young men and women start to dance in a slow, circular movement. This makes up the opening ballet. Then the orchestra withdraws to the edge of the square and the choir of women and girls group themselves around it ready to take up the actors' singing. Meanwhile the actors (almost always men) are preparing in a nearby house, dressing and making up by covering the face and body with clay or ash to create a fantastic or ridiculous appearance. They dress themselves for comic effect, with torn clothes and the various implements which they need for their roles.

When the actors are ready, this is made known and the audience fall silent. At first only a cry is heard from an invisible actor calling on the audience in set phrases which are answered, line for line, by the chorus. Then the actor makes a hesitating entry. He presents a strange appearance, partly naked, his body covered with white ash, a short torn cloak on his shoulders, an old turban on his head, and rags hanging down his back. The orchestra persuade him to call the others, so he runs to the entrance and calls his comrades in an exaggerated and burlesque way, miming his impatience, listening for them, and running round the different entrances. At last the other actors enter. Each is dressed according to his role: one is an infirm old man, another is blind, lame, or a leper; other stock characters include an idiot, an unskilful hunter, a brigand, an adulterer, a deceived husband, a thief, and a sorcerer. They go right round the square, singing and dancing, and then retire, marking the end of the prologue and presentation.

These introductory sections are followed by the comedies themselves of which several are performed one after the other. These include titles like 'The boastful coward', 'The adulterous wife', 'The deceived hunter', 'The sorcerer with large ears', and 'Thieves of yams'. The play entitled 'The kola seller and the flirtatious wife', one of seven described by Labouret and Travélé, can illustrate the type of plot and action involved. The dramatis personae are: the seller of kola nuts; Fatimata, a coquettish woman (played by a young man); Fatimata's husband; the chorus; and the orchestra.

Fatimata enters and sits in the centre, simpering, with a mirror on her knees; she is wearing an exaggerated dress with huge pearls in her hair and colossal bracelets. The kola seller comes in hesitatingly with his basket of kolas and asks the orchestra if this is a good place for selling kola nuts. When the musicians reply that it is, and, furthermore, that there is a pretty woman there too, the kola seller protests that he is not concerned with women, and dances in the square calling out 'kolas for sale'. As he dances, he catches sight of Fatimata (still making herself up). He goes up to her, calling out persuasively about his kolas. When asked the price, he offers her a few kolas free, and steals up to her to present them. The scene is repeated several times—and results in his discovery that he has given all his merchandise away! The kola seller bemoans his fate exaggeratedly: all is finished, Fatimata has deceived him. She replies self-righteously: the kola seller for his part, she says, has been interfering with the end of her loin cloth. At first indignant at this charge, he finally decides he might as well be hung for a sheep as a lamb, and tries to pull her cloth right off. Up to now Fatimata has been all complaisance. But—the kolas finished—she now turns defensive and there is a violent tussle between her and the kola seller, with great leaps and vivid representation, prolonged or contracted according to the skill of the actors. Attracted by the noise, Fatimata's husband now makes an imposing entry. When he hears Fatimata's version of the story he attacks and beats the kola seller, and the play ends with him chasing his rival from the stage with Fatimata, all innocent, by his side.

A similar comedy was reported by Delafosse in 1916 from the Bambara[1] who use the same term, *kote koma nyaga*, to refer to their plays. Again the characters are a wife (acted by a man), her husband, and her lover. The action takes place in the village square, surrounded by spectators, and with an orchestra and choir to take up and echo the actors' songs.

[1] Also Mande-speaking.

The man and his wife enter and ask permission from the village elders (the orchestra) to set up house. Then, while the husband is occupied in building their hut, his wife catches sight of the third actor, her would-be lover. For the time being they have no opportunity to be together. But time passes and at last the husband's crops are planted and ready for harvest (the whole process being vividly mimed by the actor). When they have harvested the crop the wife offers to go and pick off the seeds—an excuse, of course, to be with her lover in the fields. But it is not long before her suspicious husband follows them. She sees him first—as she thinks —and hastily buries her lover under a pile of stalks. The husband pretends he has seen nothing and sits down. Then follows a conversation, with the husband on his side pretending ignorance, the wife more and more alarmed as detection seems to approach nearer:

> *Husband.* Have you finished picking off the seeds?
> *Wife.* Yes. Here they are in my basket.
> *Husband.* Well, you carry the seeds, I'll take the ashes.
> *Wife.* (*Taken aback*) What ashes?
> *Husband.* I'm going to burn the stalks.
> *Wife.* (*More and more alarmed*) You can burn them tomorrow. Let's go home now.
> *Husband.* No, I'm in no hurry, I'm going to burn them now.
> *Wife.* (*Very alarmed*) Don't you see the storm coming?
> *Husband.* (*Still pretending not to notice anything*) Yes I see. If it rains I'll cover the ashes with my coat.
> *Wife.* The wind will blow it all away before you can collect it up.
> *Husband.* (*Decidedly*) I'm not going until I have burned that straw.

He sets fire to the pile while his wife dances round it singing. At this the lover pushes his way out and takes to his heels, while the husband rushes after him shouting 'Catch the rat that's escaped from my pile of stalks' (repeated several times). The three actors disappear and the audience bursts into laughter.[1]

From these two examples of Mande comedies, it can be seen that both plot and characterization are simple and depend for their effect very largely on the actors' art: we are told that they display great talent, based on keen observation and the exact imitation of gesture, voice, and intonation.[2] The characters are conventional types. Most popular of all is the deceiving wife, represented (as

---

[1] Delafosse 1916, pp. 352–4.  [2] Labouret and Travélé 1928, p. 92.

in stories from the same locality) as a flirtatious and capricious liar, with both her actions and her husband's jealousy satirically and comically portrayed. Similar stock characters also appear in Mandingo plays: the leper, ridiculed for his lack of fingers and consequent awkwardness, the thief, the coward, the boaster, and the sorcerer represented as an old woman, ugly and infirm, with huge ears and a frightening appearance.[1]

These plays can be counted as comedies, satires on the foibles and ridiculous aspects of everyday life, particularly marriage. In this sense they can be called drama even though it is drama enlivened by music, dance, and mime as well as spoken conversation. However, such comedies, it appears, have only a limited distribution—basically among certain Mande-speaking peoples of Mali, Soudan, and the Ivory Coast.[2] Even within West Africa they are not wide-spread and—on present evidence at least—they provide the exception rather than the rule for full dramatic performances in Africa.[3]

IV

The final class of dramatic phenomena to consider are the masquerades of West Africa. These are wide-spread in this part of Africa[4] and take many different forms, but seem to be especially developed in the southern (forest) areas where the carving of wooden masks has reached such a high degree of artistic development. The masquerades—dances of masked figures of various kinds—probably vary throughout the region in content, purpose, and pattern, but they all seem to include certain elements of drama and are often referred to as 'plays'. There is generally the idea of some kind of enactment or representation by the masked figure with great emphasis on costume (especially masks) and on music and dancing. On the other hand, there seems to be little or no linguistic content, though there is sometimes a rudimentary plot.

[1] Ivory Coast 'animal ballets' are even more burlesque and include more clowning and miming and less linguistic content (Prouteaux 1929).

[2] The plots and tone of some of the Northern Nigerian puppet shows have something in common with these plays and possibly indicate a wider incidence than as yet appears.

[3] On these comedies see also Meillassoux 1964. For the way in which some modern skits in Mali owe much to traditional dramatic forms see N. S. Hopkins, 'The Modern Theater in Mali', *Présence afr.* 53, 1965.

[4] Including, to some extent, the Mande area.

Rather than trying to describe all variations, I will speak of masquerades in South-Eastern Nigeria. It is in the forest (or once forest) regions of this area among the Ibo, Ijaw, and Ibibio peoples that, in the words of G. I. Jones, 'Nigerian masked plays reach their greatest development'.[1]

Even in this fairly circumscribed region there are variants enough. But it is clear from Jones's article ('Masked plays of South-eastern Nigeria'),[2] that they all share certain common features. There is always some religious element, a belief, for instance, that the masked figures are in some sense supernatural, or closely associated with supernatural beings. There is the disciplinary element expressed in the awe in which the masked dances are held by women and the uninitiated: the men who produce the play are initiates of a secret society whose mysteries and rules they are bound to keep. Finally, there is always an element of pageantry and display; 'however secret the society there is always an occasion when the community is inspired by the spectacle of the supernatural beings parading round in public, resplendent in all the finery the society can provide'.[1]

In different areas one or another of these aspects is to the fore. Thus in the Cross River region, where secret societies have such central importance, the element of display and pageantry is relatively undeveloped and the local 'spirit plays' stress the macabre and supernatural 'to a degree unequalled in any of the other masked plays'.[3] Among the Ibo, by contrast, with their democratic and independent traditions, the religious and disciplinary aspects have relatively little significance. There are many Ibo, Ibibio, and Ijaw groups, furthermore, who choose to use these masked plays primarily as vehicles for their artistic talent. 'Here the play itself is the important thing; the supernatural element, particularly the feeling of fear, recedes and comedy and a sense of fun takes its place.'[4] There is much display of fine costumes, masks, drumming, dancing, and singing. Acting too has a place:

Usually this acting is limited to each mask playing its own particular

[1] G. I. Jones 1945, p. 191.

[2] Op. cit. I draw very heavily on this article here; also on J. S. Boston, 'Some Northern Ibo Masquerades', *JRAI* 90, 1960, and Horton 1963. See also Messenger 1962; Horton 1966 and 1967; K. C. Murray, 'Ayɔlugba', *Nigerian Field* 12, 1947; G. I. Jones 'Okorosia' (by 'Daji'), *Nigerian Field* 3, 1934.

[3] G. I. Jones, 1945, p. 196.

[4] Ibid., p. 192. Cf. also Messenger 1962.

role without regard to the other characters, but in a few plays the masks act together in a complete drama. In one Ogoni play, for instance, all the masks appear as a group of decrepit old men and hold a meeting guying the local village elders. In another play the mask called 'Doctor', after boasting greatly of the potency of his medicines, tries them out on the mask called 'Rain Maker' and poisons him; in terror he appeals to Kamalu, the god of the rain, and after much comic byplay and bargaining as to the value of the sacrifice he must make to Kamalu, he succeeds in bringing 'Rain Maker' to life again.[1]

Important varieties of masked plays in South-Eastern Nigeria are the Ibo and Ibibio ghost plays. These are enacted by dancers wearing true masks (i.e. right over their faces) and often elaborate costumes. The Northern Ibo ghost play (*Mau*), for instance, often includes a great variety of characters wearing masks or carved heads (or both). These masks have conventional meanings. Some are represented as masculine, some as feminine; some are fierce, some comic, some (mostly the feminine ones) beautiful. It is the 'beautiful' masks, portrayed according to Ibo ideas of stylized beauty and feminine character (but in fact worn by men), who do most of the actual dancing; first the 'daughter' masks appear and dance, then the 'mothers', and finally the 'grandmother' mask performs her solo dance. The comic masks amuse by clowning, whereas the fierce ones are meant to frighten. Some are so fierce (especially those combining the features of lion, elephant, and buffalo) that they must be kept on a leash by their attendants; others are used to keep the crowd back from the dancers, and threaten them with whips. Miming and sometimes parody seem to be highly developed in these 'plays'. In one instance given by Jones:

When the play has just begun a white-faced mask with a cavalry moustache, wearing white ducks and a spotless sun-helmet, stalks into the arena and casts a supercilious eye over the scene. The play stops, the mask languidly signals them to proceed and strolls over to sit amongst the audience in the seat of honour. This character is Oyibo the White Man.[2]

The importance of miming and even satire is brought out by another writer on Ibo masquerades.[3] In northern Iboland it is

[1] G. I. Jones 1945, pp. 192–3.    [2] Ibid., p. 193.    [3] Boston, op. cit.

apparently the dramatic element that has been developed at the expense of the religious. But even here the element of plot is very undeveloped indeed compared to the emphasis on music and dancing. Boston expresses clearly the Ibo order of priorities when he writes:

Each type of masquerade has a characteristic rhythm, which is produced by a subtle and intricate combination of voices, instruments, and stylized movement, and this rhythm supplies a compulsive force to the performance, as the plot does in European drama. It also creates a dramatic link between the various elements of the masquerade, which are often scattered in different parts of the village.[1]

Though there are several other types of Ibo and Ibibio ghost plays besides those mentioned, all seem to share the characteristic of less emphasis on plot than on miming, music, and dancing.

The third main variety of masquerade in South-Eastern Nigeria comprises the Ijaw water-spirit plays. The plays of one group of Ijaw peoples (the Kalabari) have been discussed by Horton and the outline of his account is followed closely.[2] In these plays too there is an emphasis on music, dance, and costume at the expense of linguistic content.

The plays are staged by the Kalabari *Ekine* Society. This is a religious and artistic association for men, separately organized in each Kalabari community. Each such society stages a cycle of thirty to fifty masquerade plays. The society is divided into grades through which members can progress according to their skill and on payment of a small fee. Each society has its own headman and certain other officials and its own rules of behaviour; one of the strictest of these is the idea of concealment of certain activities from women. The plays themselves are connected with water spirits, and in the myths about their origin we are told how a woman was once abducted by the water spirits and was shown their special plays before she returned home; they were then taken over by the men as an art or recreation, but their religious significance was still remembered.

In these masquerades there are comments and accompanying songs. The subject-matter covers a diversity of social experience; though it is ostensibly concerned with the activities of water

---

[1] Boston, op. cit., p. 55.
[2] Horton 1963; cf. also 1966 and 1967. There is not, unfortunately, space to do justice to the subtlety of his discussion.

spirits, in fact it clearly reflects the everyday life of Kalabari town and village, portrayed in a realistic manner:

Perhaps the commonest theme is that of the ferocious male warrior, laying about him with matchet or spear, his violence set off by the plump, comely, slow-moving figure of his wife. This pair is portrayed by some of the most widely distributed masquerades such as *Agiri*, *Egbelegebe*, *Egbekoro*, and *Seki*. Then there is the dignified, opulent 'house head' portrayed by masquerades like *Gbassa* and *Alagba*. Or the massive, stolid character portrayed by the maskers of *Otobo*—a water spirit who is thought of as part man, part hippopotamus, and who is addressed in song as 'Beast who holds up even the flowing tide'. By way of contrast, there is the cunning, amoral hypocrite portrayed by *Ikaki*—'Tortoise'. Or the sexy, good-for-nothing aristocrat *Igbo*, of whom they sing: 'His father sent him to market to buy yams; but instead he bought woman's vagina. O! *Igbo*, son of a chief! O! *Igbo*, son of a chief!' Or again, there is the native doctor *Ngbula*, grunting around with grim concentration in search of bad medicines and evil spirits: suspicious like all of his profession that people are talking ill of him, and breaking off from time to time to make ferocious charges at his supposed detractors among the *Ekine* members. Female water spirits, too, some-times take the central place in a masquerade. Notable among these is *Igoni*; a garrulous, self-pitying old widow who alternately bemoans her own and everyone else's troubles.[1]

But in spite of the existence of such plots and of some linguistic content in songs and comment, this aspect of *Ekine* masquerading is only of secondary importance. It is worth quoting Horton at some length on this point, for he makes absolutely clear that it is the dancing and the drumming rather than the linguistic element which is the important part of these dramatic performances:

Diverse as they are . . . the verbalized themes of the masquerade are never very elaborate. All that can be said about the characters portrayed in a particular play takes no more than a sentence or two. And the plots of the *Egberi* tableaux are sketchy in the extreme—especially if one compares them with the rich narrative which the Kalabari weave about the water spirits in other contexts. There is, in fact, a good reason for this sketchiness and brevity. For *the masquerade is not intended as the enactment of verbal narrative*. Its dominant symbols are those of rhythmic gesture, dictated by the drum; and in so far as its verbal com-mentaries have a use, it is one of directing attention to the broad area in which the meaning of the dance gestures lies. *Words here provide no*

[1] Horton 1963, p. 97.

*more than a bare, crude outline of meaning, and it is left to the language of*
*the dance to fill in the detail which makes the masquerade rich and satisfying*
*to its audience.*[1]

If an *Ekine* member is asked how he recognizes a particular play, he
does not start to talk about the character portrayed or about the plot of
the *Egberi*. He starts by imitating the rhythm of its drums; and perhaps,
if there are no women about, by dancing a few of its characteristic steps.
By this, he is able to convey the distinctive features of the play: for
every masquerade has its own characteristic set of drum-rhythms,
beaten on a characteristic combination of drums. . . .

The value which *Ekine* sets on the dancer's attunement to the drum
does much to explain why its members consider possession by the
masquerade spirits to be the crowning achievement of the expert
performer. In Kalabari thought, all symbols of the gods are instinct
with their presence. Now the drum-rhythms of each masquerade are
symbols of its spirit 'owner', and as such they too are vehicles of his
presence. So, saying that the spirit 'owner' has taken charge of the
dancer's body is a natural way of describing the ideal state of attunement in which the drum-rhythms seem to have taken over the man's
movements from his conscious will and thought. That these are indeed
two ways of describing the same experience is suggested by the reply
of a gifted dancer whom I asked what it was like to become possessed
during the dance. As he put it: 'One plays until, as it were, the drum
pushes one around.'[2]

Besides verbalized content and rhythm, a third element in
these Kalabari masquerades consists of the costumes, of which the
most distinctive part is the headpiece, sometimes including a wooden
mask. This mask is regarded as distinct from the rest of the costume and is the 'name' of the masquerade, so that even when it
is not in fact visible to the spectators it still plays a part. But even
the masks have only a secondary role compared to the dancing.
'The real core of the masquerade lies in the dance and . . . by and
large other elements are only considered important in so far as they
contribute to it.'[3]

Horton concludes that despite certain functions of *Ekine*
activity (its significance as a status symbol or organ of government)
the essential values 'can only be called aesthetic'.[4] Why then, if
the masquerade is first and foremost an art, does it retain close
associations with religion? 

Horton argues that reacting to a human performance as a work

---

[1] My italics (R. F.).　　　　　　　[2] Horton 1963, pp. 98–9.
[3] Ibid., p. 100.　　　　　　　　　　[4] Ibid., p. 111.

of art seems to involve two main factors: first, an ability to exchange practical workaday reactions to the subject-matter for some sort of attitude of contemplation—'an eye which is engaged yet somehow aloof';[1] and secondly, a suspension of personal reactions to the actor as a known individual in favour of a concentration on his *role* in the performance. Now in modern Western theatre and ballet these requirements are usually fulfilled without much difficulty. The theme of play or ballet is often removed from the first-hand experience of the audience; so too are the actors, so that the problem of suspending personal reactions to them as individuals does not arise. But in a small-scale homogeneous society like that of the Kalabari the situation is very different:

In the first place, the greater uniformity of social experience means that the audience will have had first-hand exposure to the subject-matter of almost any dramatic performance. In their case, the subject-matter is always near the bone. Secondly the performers are always personally known to most of their audience.[2]

The Kalabari solution to these difficulties can be found in the religious context of the masquerades. First, by associating the plays with water spirits, the Kalabari can, in a complex way, disentangle them from the too human and personal context. Furthermore the actors' water spirit disguise makes it relatively easy for the spectators to concentrate on the play itself, on the roles rather than the individuals. This also helps to explain the prohibitions laid on women in connection with *Ekine* activity (as well as with West African masquerades elsewhere). It is not that they are forbidden all knowledge of the masquerades: indeed, they are its principal spectators. What they are forbidden is to know of or suggest any connection between masquerades and an *individual* player. In Kalabari masquerades the masks, the costume, the religious associations and prohibitions all serve to bring about the 'psychical distance' essential in dramatic art.

This discussion of West African masquerades tends to one main conclusion. That is, that though these performances possess certain of the elements we associate with drama, the emphasis is very different from that of most modern European drama. Even where there are some linguistic content and plot, these always seem secondary to drumming and its essential counterpart, dancing. As

---

[1] Ibid., p. 103.    [2] Ibid., p. 104.

Horton suggests it seems that 'at least in certain areas of West Africa, the dance overshadows sculpture, painting, architecture, and literature as the leading traditional art'.[1]

V

How far can the discussion in this chapter be said to be relevant for the study of African oral literature? With a few possible exceptions, there is no tradition in Africa of artistic performances which include all the elements which might be demanded in a strict definition of drama—or at least not with the emphases to which we are accustomed. We can go further and add that what dramatic or quasi-dramatic performances can be discovered never seem to involve tragedy in the normal sense. The events and characters are depicted as comedy, and treated more or less realistically, even cynically. Though costumes and masks are sometimes important, there is no evidence of specialized scenery or of buildings or sites specifically designed for theatrical performances. The players are sometimes skilled experts or belong to artistic associations such as the *Ekine* Society, but there is no tradition of *professional* actors. The audience, finally, is sometimes a 'pure' audience in the sense that it appreciates without itself taking part directly; but, with the significance of the dance and the absence of the 'proscenium barrier', there is often a tendency to greater audience participation than is typical of most recent Western drama.

We can also make other negative points. Little direct light is thrown on the question of the origin of drama by a study of African dramatic forms—except possibly in the vague sense that it might be said to enlarge our general view of the possibilities of drama, or of certain elements in drama. Similarly it adds little support to the kind of interpretation of drama which relies on the idea of tragic archetypes and of rituals ultimately referable to *The Golden Bough*.

However, one positive point does emerge. Though different

[1] Horton 1963, p. 112. For further references to 'drama' in Africa see the bibliographies in *Afr. Studies Bulletin* 5. 2, 1962, pp. 50–3 (by H. L. Shore) and in Traoré 1958. There is a detailed and sympathetic account of Ijebu (Yoruba) masquerades in Ogunba 1967. See also the briefer report in J. P. Clark, 'Aspects of Nigerian Drama', *Nigeria Mag.* 89, 1966, and J. M. Gibbs, 'Aspects of Nigerian Dramatic Tradition', unpub. M.A. thesis, American University, Washington, 1967, esp. chs. 1, 2, and bibliography.

elements of drama are stressed in different African cultures, one theme that seems to run through almost all these African performances is the overriding significance of music and dance and the secondary importance of the spoken word. Even in the Mande comedies, which at first sight seem most to resemble the more verbalized type of European drama, the stress laid on words seems to vary: what is constant is the emphasis on dance, song, and mime. Further research obviously needs to be done on this. But it does appear that, at least in West Africa (the area which provides the most highly developed dramatic forms), we would be mistaken to look only at the verbal content in any discussion of drama and miss the rich traditions in music and dance which form essential elements in dramatic performances.[1] Though there may be no 'plays' in quite the Western sense, these indigenous artistic forms nevertheless possess some of the elements we associate with drama. They present a dramatic representation of life in a detached and yet somehow more direct and active way than can be conveyed through descriptive words alone, and in this way provide a complement to the various forms of oral literature already described.

[1] Traditions exploited in modern literature by, for instance, the 'Yoruba folk operas' described by H. U. Beier, *Afr. Music* 1. 1, 1954, and the musical and balletic emphases in productions by recent West African playwrights.

# CONCLUSION

SEVERAL points emerge from this examination of oral literature in Africa.

The first is an obvious one. This is the relevance of African oral literature for comparative literature in the wide sense. The study of the kinds of instances and genres touched on in this account can enlarge both our literary experience and our concept of 'literature' altogether. It can also throw light on some recent literary experiments (jazz poetry, for instance) as well as on the oral background to literature even in literate cultures. Its significance, in other words, is by no means confined to those with a special interest in the continent of Africa.

The kind of conclusions I myself would draw about the nature of this African literature would be, first of all, to repeat the obvious point of its variety. Not only is generalization difficult, but many of the general conclusions that have been stated to date turn out to be based on relatively little evidence. It now seems obvious, for example, that simple generalizations about the collective nature of art in non-literate cultures cannot hold good in face of the evidence about the creative activity of the individual poet or story-teller, and that the process of artistic composition even in non-literate societies turns out to be more complex than often imagined. Again—and this is perhaps more controversial—I would hold that there is less support than might be expected from the African material for the mythopœic or archetypal interpretation of literature, or the idea that African literature is all marked by 'dark mysticism' or similar catchwords. Finally, the fashionable 'structural' approach of Lévi-Strauss and his followers has not seemed a fruitful one for any detailed study of actual oral genres in Africa in their own context. This type of elegant but at times rather far-fetched analysis turns out, in my opinion, to be less illuminating in the face of the facts than a less ambitious analysis of the obvious meaning and context of actual instances.

Some of these conclusions are no doubt controversial. But the main point that I want to insist on here is that such questions are relevant ones for the study of literature, and ones on which the African material can throw light. It should no longer be acceptable to discuss such problems in the abstract without reference to the actual facts of African literary expression. African oral literature, in short, is part of the literature of the world and should be considered significant as such.

The second main point may not be so obvious. This is the relevance of African oral literature for sociological analysis. It has been well said that a society cannot be fully understood without its songs. But this has sometimes, it seems, been forgotten by the sociologists.[1] In particular, those who have concerned themselves with the sociology of foreign and of so-called 'primitive' societies have too often neglected to take any serious interest in their literary forms.

This aspect is so important that I want to expand on it a little. Traditional African societies have by and large normally been grouped into the general category of 'primitive'. And one of the most important differentiating characteristics of this category is normally taken to be the fact of being 'non-literate'; another is of being 'simple'. People have found it only too easy to slip from this into the assumption that 'non-literate' involved something like our concept of 'illiterate' (i.e. someone who in a *literate* community may be regarded as having failed to master the ways of that particular culture),[2] and, further, that 'simple' implied simple intellectually or artistically as well as simple in technology. Neither of these assumptions is in fact logically or empirically defensible. In particular, there is nothing necessarily 'backward' about a poet in a culture which does not use the written word choosing to express his literary ability through the rich oral medium at his disposal. Furthermore—and this is the pertinent point in this context—it should now be clear from the descriptions and examples given in this book that being non-literate or technologically simple does not mean that such societies are lacking in elaborate artistic forms, in literature, in complex symbolism, in scope for the individual to express his own artistry and insights, or in an awareness of the depths and subtleties of the world and of human life. As a Kongo proverb expresses it: 'The human heart is not a bag into which one can plunge one's hand.'[3] This becomes evident with even a cursory study of oral literature. But it is a facet that is

---

[1] A term in which I include social anthropologists.

[2] A point well made in Andrzejewski 1965, p. 96.

[3] Kongo proverb (J. Van Wing, 'Bakongo Incantations and Prayers', *JRAI* 60, 1930, p. 401).

almost always overlooked when people speak of the 'non-literate' and 'simple' societies of traditional Africa.

This oral literature, furthermore, needs to be taken seriously in its own right. Explaining oral literature away by reference to social or even 'symbolic' function is to miss much of its actual detailed significance, and is as much of a disservice to the sociologist as to the literary critic. The relationship between literature and society is too complex and various to be reduced to such generalized explanations. Even for a sociological analysis literature must be considered first in its own terms before an accurate assessment can be made of its role in society. And if some still prefer not to speak of 'literature' here, it must at least be admitted that whatever the actual term used there exists a complex oral art in African cultures and that this must be taken seriously into account in any balanced assessment of African societies.

This is a point I want to emphasize. The fact of the existence of this oral art—this literature as I would call it—is something which both throws light on the nature of African societies and also helps to undermine the old view of the quality of non-literate societies generally. It is not something peripheral, but basic to their life and thought. It is something, in short, which, too often forgotten, must be taken into full account by the sociologist in his approach to these societies.

This leads on to one final point. It might be supposed that such literature is dying out with the impact of literate, wealthier, and reputedly more 'progressive' cultures. This is not necessarily so at all. Some genres, it is true, are receding; but others—political songs, new versions of dance songs, new religious lyrics—are increasing in importance. Oral literature, in fact, plays its part in developing, not just traditional, Africa.

It is frequently assumed that the only and the natural direction of development for 'undeveloped' countries like Africa must be towards greater reliance on the written word. This assumption, however, may not be justified. People have spoken of the 'revolution' in communications in Western countries in the last few decades which involves a change to a much greater dependence on auditory forms (the radio in particular) at the expense of the visual (the written word). This greater reliance on auditory forms is something which would not seem at all strange to those brought up in the traditions of *spoken* literature characteristic of Africa.

Indeed this reliance on the spoken word—and thus on oral forms of expression—may well increase rather than decrease in Africa in the future. This is not unlikely to follow increasing European influence, both in its general turning towards non-written forms and in some of the particular literary experiments with oral or semi-oral forms. This tendency towards oral forms may also be intensified as the transistor radio spreads still further. Already there is evidence from all over the continent of the radio being used as the vehicle of oral literary forms—the *mvet* songs over Yaounde radio, for example, or the Somali *balwo*, ideal material for broadcasting; and though a medium involving a mass rather than a face-to-face audience must necessarily lead to some changes in the traditional nature of oral art, it is yet clearly related to it. It may be, then, that increasing dependence on the written word may not necessarily be the obvious line of development in the Africa of the future.

Whatever our guess for the future, however, it is clear that oral literature—whether addressed to small family groups, an emir's court, political rallies, or radio listeners—is not just something of the past. It is relevant for the contemporary analysis of African society and not just for those interested in 'traditional culture' or antiquarian researches.

African oral literature, then, is of interest not only for students of literature, but also for sociologists and all those with an interest in African society, past or present. The final note must be, however, to point to the great need for further research into this subject: the present book can provide only an introduction.

# BIBLIOGRAPHY

## I. REFERENCE WORKS

The following have been particularly useful:

*African abstracts*, IAI, London, 1950– .

P. Duignan and K. M. Glazier, *A checklist of serials for African studies*, Stanford, 1963.

*Fiches analytiques* (Sciences humaines africanistes), Centre d'analyse et de recherche documentaires pour l'Afrique noire, Paris, 1966–.

L. J. P. Gaskin, *A select bibliography of music in Africa*, IAI, London, 1965.

IAI, *Africa bibliography series* (*series A*): *ethnology, sociology and linguistics*, compiled by R. Jones.

    *West Africa*, 1958.

    *North-East Africa*, 1959.

    *East Africa*, 1960.

    *South-East Central Africa and Madagascar*, 1961.

IAI, Bibliography of current publications (quarterly in *Africa*).

## II. GENERAL BIBLIOGRAPHY

ABIMBOLA, W., 'The Odù of Ifá', *Afr. notes*, [Ibadan], 1. 3 (1964).

—— 'Yoruba oral literature', *Afr. notes*, [Ibadan], 2. 2–3 (1965).

ADALI-MORTTY, G. 'Ewe poetry', *Black Orpheus* 4 (1958).

—— 'Ewe poetry', *Ɔkyeame*, [Accra] 1 (1960).

ADAM, J., 'Nouvel extrait du folklore du Haut-Ogooué (AEF). Devinettes et fables des Ambede', *Anthropos* 35/6 (1940–1).

ALBERT, E. M., '"Rhetoric", "logic", and "poetics" in Burundi: culture patterning of speech behavior', *Am. anthrop.* 66. 6, pt. 2 (1964).

AMES, D., 'Professionals and amateurs: the musicians of Zaria and Obimo', *African arts* 1. 2 (1968).

ANDRZEJEWSKI B .W., 'Poetry in Somali society', *New society* 1. 25 (21 Mar. 1963).

—— 'Emotional bias in the translation and presentation of African oral art', *Sierra Leone language review* 4 (1965).

—— 'The art of the miniature in Somali poetry', *Afr. language review* 6 (1967).

—— and LEWIS, I. M., *Somali poetry: an introduction*, OLAL, Oxford, 1964.

—— and MESSENGER, J. C., *J. of the folklore institute* [Indiana], 4. 2/3 (June/Dec. 1967), special issue on Africa.

ANYA-NOA, L., and ATANGANA, S., 'La sagesse béti dans le chant des oiseaux', *Abbia* 8 (1965).

ANYUMBA, H. O., 'The nyatiti lament songs', *East Africa past and present* (*Présence africaine*), Paris (1964).

AREWA, E. O., and DUNDES, A., 'Proverbs and the ethnography of speaking folklore', *Am. anthrop.* 66. 6, pt. 2 (1964).

ARNOTT, D. W., 'Proverbial lore and word-play of the Fulani', *Africa* 27 (1957).

BA, A. H., 'Poésie peule du Macina', *Présence afr.* 8/9 (1950).

BABALQLA, S. A., 'The characteristic features of outer form of Yoruba Ijala chants', *Odu* 1. 1 and 2 (1964–5).

—— *The content and form of Yoruba ijala*, OLAL, Oxford, 1966.

BALANDIER, G., 'Littératures de l'Afrique et des Amériques noires' (in R. Queneau, *Histoire des littératures*, Encyclopédie de la Pléiade, t. 1, Paris, 1955).

BANG, D. N., 'In praise of Zulu literature', *Native teachers journal*, [Natal] 30 (1951).

BARKER, W. H., and SINCLAIR, C., *West African folk-tales*, London, 1917.

BASCOM, W. R., 'The sanctions of Ifa divination', *JRAI* 71 (1941).

—— 'The relationship of Yoruba folklore to divining', *JAF* 56 (1943).

—— 'Literary style in Yoruba riddles', *JAF* 62 (1949).

—— 'Verbal art', *JAF* 68 (1955).

—— 'Odu Ifa: the order of the figures of Ifa', *Bull. IFAN* (B) 23 (1961).

—— 'Folklore research in Africa', *JAF* 77 (1964).

—— 'Folklore and literature' (in R. A. Lystad (ed.), *The African world. A survey of social research*, London, 1965) (1965*a*).

—— 'The forms of folklore: prose narratives', *JAF* 78 (1965) (1965*b*).

BASSET, R., *Contes populaires d'Afrique*, Paris, 1903.

BAUMANN, H., *Schöpfung und Urzeit des Menschen im Mythus der afrikanischen Völker*, Berlin, 1936.

—— and WESTERMANN, D., *Les peuples et les civilisations de l'Afrique* (French tr. by L. Homburger), Paris, 1948.

BÉART, C., *Jeux et jouets de l'Ouest africain*, 2 vols. (*Mém. IFAN* 42) (1955).

BEATON, A. C., 'Some Bari songs', *Sudan notes* 18 (1935); 19 (1936).

BEIDELMAN, T. O., 'Hyena and rabbit: a Kaguru representation of matrilineal relations', *Africa* 31 (1961).

—— 'Further adventures of Hyena and Rabbit: the folktale as a sociological model', *Africa* 33 (1963).

BEIER, H. U., 'Yoruba vocal music', *Afr. music* 1. 3 (1956).

—— (ed.), *African poetry*, Cambridge, 1966.

—— (ed.), *Introduction to African literature*, London, 1967.

BELINGA, M. S. E., *Littérature et musique populaires en Afrique noire*, Toulouse, 1965.

BÉRENGER-FÉRAUD, L. J. B., *Recueil de contes populaires de la Sénégambie*, Paris, 1885.

BERRY, J., *Spoken art in West Africa*, London, 1961.

BIEBUYCK, D., '*Mubéla*: een epos der Balèga', *Band* [Leopoldville], 12 (1953).

BLACKING, J., 'The social value of Venda riddles', *Afr. studies* 20 (1961).

—— *Venda children's songs*, Witwatersrand, 1967.

BLEEK D. F., 'Bushman folklore', *Africa* 2 (1929).

BLEEK, W. H. I., *Reynard the Fox in South Africa; or, Hottentot fables and tales*, London, 1864.

—— *A brief account of Bushman folk-lore and other texts*, London, etc., 1875.

—— and LLOYD, L. C., *Specimens of Bushman folklore*, London, 1911.

—— —— (ed. D. F. Bleek), *The Mantis and his friends*, Cape Town, [1924].

BOELAERT, E., 'Premières recherches sur la structure de cinq poésies lonkundo', *IRCB Bull.* 23. 2 (1952).

—— 'De structuur van de Nkundo-poëzie', *Kongo-Overzee* 21 (1955).

—— 'Nsong'â Lianja: l'épopée nationale des Nkundó', *Aequatoria* 12 (1949).

—— *Lianja-verhalen*, I. *Ɛkɔfɔ-versie*, *AMRCB-L* 17 (1957); II. *De voorouders van Lianja*, *AMRCB-L* 19, 1958.

BOWRA, C. M., *Heroic poetry*, London, 1952.

—— *Primitive song*, London, 1962.

BRANDEL, R., *The music of Central Africa: an ethnomusicological study. Former French Equatorial Africa, the former Belgian Congo, Ruanda-Urundi, Uganda, Tanganyika*, The Hague, 1961.

BURTON, R. F., *Wit and wisdom from West Africa; or, a book of proverbial philosophy, idioms, enigmas, and laconisms*, London, 1865.

BURTON, W. F. P., 'Oral literature in Lubaland', *Afr. studies* 2 (1943).

CALAME-GRIAULE, G., 'Ésotérisme et fabulation au Soudan', *Bull. IFAN* (B) 16. 3/4 (1954).

—— 'L'art de la parole dans la culture africaine', *Présence afr.* 47 (1963).

—— *Ethnologie et langage. La parole chez les Dogon*, Paris, 1965.

CALLAWAY, H., *Nursery tales, traditions, and histories of the Zulus*, Springvale, etc., 1868.

CARRINGTON, J. F., 'The drum language of the Lokele tribe', *Afr. studies* 3 (1944).

—— *Talking drums of Africa*, London, 1949 (1949*a*).

—— *A comparative study of some Central African gong-languages*, *IRCB Mém.* 18 (3), 1949 (1949*b*).

CASALIS, E., *Études sur la langue séchuana*, Paris, 1841.

CENDRARS, B., *Anthologie nègre*, Paris, 1921.

CERULLI, E., 'Folk-literature of the Galla of southern Abyssinia', *Harvard Afr. studies* 3 (1922).

CÉSARD, E., 'Proverbes et contes haya', *Anthropos* 23 (1928); 24 (1929).

—— 'Devinettes et observances superstitieuses haya', *Anthropos* 29 (1934).

CHADWICK, H. M. and N. K., *The growth of literature*, 3 vols., Cambridge, 1932–40.

CHADWICK, N. K., 'The distribution of oral literature in the Old World', *JRAI* 69 (1939).

CHATELAIN, H., *Folk-tales of Angola* (Memoir of the American folk-lore society, 1), Boston and New York, 1894.

CHRISTALLER, J. G., *A collection of 3,600 Tshi proverbs*, Basel, 1879.

CHRISTENSEN, J. B., 'The role of proverbs in Fante culture', *Africa* 28 (1958).

CLARKE, K. W., 'A motif-index of the folktales of culture area V, West Africa' (unpub. Ph.D. thesis), University of Indiana (1958).

COLE-BEUCHAT, P. D., 'Riddles in Bantu', *Afr. studies* 16 (1957).

—— 'Notes on some folklore forms in Tsonga and Ronga', *Afr. studies* 17 (1958).

COLIN, R., *Les contes noirs de l'Ouest africain*, Paris (*Présence africaine*), 1957.

COOK, P. A. W., 'History and izibongo of the Swazi chiefs', *Bantu studies* 5 (1931).

COPE, T., *Izibongo–Zulu praise poems*, OLAL, Oxford, 1968.

COUPEZ, A., 'Les rythmes de la poésie rwanda', *Folia scientifica Africae centralis*, [Bukavu], 4. 3 (1958).

—— and KAMANZI, Th., 'Rythmes quantitatifs en poésie rwaanda', *Folia scientifica Africae centralis*, [Bukavu] 3. 3 (1957)

—— —— *Récits historiques rwanda*, *AMRAC* 43 (1962).

CRONISE, F. M., and WARD, H. W., *Cunnie Rabbit, Mr. Spider, and the other Beef, West African folk tales*, London, 1903.

CROWLEY, D. J., 'Folklore research in the Congo', *JAF* 74 (1961).

—— 'The dilemma of Congolese folklore', *J. folklore institute* 4, 2/3 (1967).

CURTIN, P. D., *The image of Africa*, London, 1965.

CURTIS, N., *Songs and tales from the dark continent*, New York, 1920.

CUTTER, C., 'The politics of music in Mali', *African arts* 1. 3 (1968).

DADIÉ, B. B., 'Folklore and literature' (in L. Bown and M. Crowder (eds.), *Proceedings of the first international congress of Africanists*, London, 1964).

DAMMANN, E., *Dichtungen in der Lamu-Mundart des Suaheli*, Hamburg, 1940.

DE DAMPIERRE, E., *Poètes Nzakara*, Classiques africains 1, Paris, 1963.

DE FOUCAULD, C., *Poésies touarègues*, 2 vols., Paris, 1925–30.

DELAFOSSE, M., 'Contribution à l'étude du théâtre chez les noirs', *Ann. et mém. Com. ét. AOF* (1916).

—— *The negroes of Africa. History and culture* (Eng. tr. by F. Fligelman), Washington, 1931.

DEMPWOLFF, O., 'Ein Märchen und 30 Lieder der Dzalamo', *ZKS* 3 (1912/13).

DENNETT, R. E., *Notes on the folklore of the Fjort, French Congo*, London (Folk-lore society), 1898.

DE OLIVEIRA, J. O., *Literatura africana. Moçambique: provérbos, adivinhas, contos e fábulas dos Tongas do Sul do Save, Tongas da Zambézia e Vátuas*, Lisboa, 1944.

DE ROP, A., *De gesproken woordkunst van de Nkundó*, *AMRCB-L* 13 (1956).

—— *Lianja, l'épopée des Mɔngɔ, ARSOM* 30. 1 (1964).

DEWAR, E. H., *Chinamwanga stories*, Livingstonia, 1900.

DHLOMO, H. I. E., 'Nature and variety of tribal drama', *Bantu studies* 13 (1939).

526          *Bibliography*

DHLOMO, H. I. E., 'Zulu folk poetry', *Native teachers journal*, Natal, 27 (1947–8).
DIETERLEN, G. (ed.), *Textes sacrés d'Afrique noire*, UNESCO, Paris, 1965.
DIJKMANS, J. J. M., *Zande-woordkunst*, *AMRAC* 7 (1965).
DOKE, C. M., *Lamba folk-lore*, New York (Memoir of the American Folklore Society, 20), 1927.
—— 'A preliminary investigation into the state of the native languages of South Africa with suggestions as to research and the development of literature', *Bantu studies* 7 (1933).
—— 'Lamba literature', *Africa* 7 (1934).
—— 'Bantu wisdom-lore', *Afr. studies* 6 (1947).
—— 'The basis of Bantu literature', *Africa* 18 (1948).
DOOB, L. W., *Communication in Africa*, New Haven, 1961.
DOOB, W. L. (ed.), *Ants will not eat your fingers: a selection of traditional African poems*, New York, 1966 (not seen).
DRIBERG, J. H., *Initiation: translations from poems of the Didinga and Lango tribes*, Waltham St. Lawrence, 1932.
DUNNING, R. G., *Two hundred and sixty-four Zulu proverbs, idioms, etc. and the cries of thirty-seven birds*, Durban, [1946].
DUPIRE, M., and DE LAVERGNE DE TRESSAN, M., 'Devinettes peules et bororo', *Africa* 25 (1955).
EBDING, F., and ITTMANN, J., 'Religiöse Gesänge aus dem nördlichen Waldland von Kamerun', *Afr. u. Übersee* 39–40 (1955–6).
ECHEGARAY, C. G., 'Un poema épico de los bujebas', *Africa*, [Madrid], 12 (1955).
EGUDU, R. N., 'Ojebe poetry', *Black Orpheus* 21 (1967).
ELLIS, A. B., *The Ewe-speaking peoples of the slave coast of West Africa*, London, 1890.
—— *The Yoruba-speaking peoples of the slave coast of West Africa*, London, 1894.
ENDEMANN, C., 'Sotholieder', *MSOS* 31 (1928).
ENNIS, E. L., 'Women's names among the Ovimbundu of Angola', *Afr. studies* 4 (1945).
EQUILBECQ, F. V., *Essai sur la littérature merveilleuse des noirs, suivi de contes indigènes de l'Ouest africain français*, 3 vols., Paris, 1913–16.
ESTREICHER, Z., 'Chants et rythmes de la danse d'hommes bororo', *Bull. Soc. neuchâteloise* 51 (1954–5).
EVANS-PRITCHARD, E. E., '*Sanza*, a characteristic feature of Zande language and thought', *BSOAS* 18 (1956).
—— 'Ideophones in Zande', *Sudan notes* 43 (1962).
—— 'Meaning in Zande proverbs', *Man* 63 (Jan. 1963) (1963*a*).
—— 'Sixty-one Zande proverbs', *Man* 63 (July 1963) (1963*b*).
—— 'Zande proverbs: final selection and comments', *Man* 64 (Jan. 1964) (1964*a*).
—— 'Variations in a Zande folk-tale', *J. Afr. languages* 3 (1964) (1964*b*).
—— *The Zande trickster*, OLAL, Oxford, 1967.
FERNANDEZ, J. W., 'Folklore as an agent of nationalism', *Afr. studies bull.* 5. 2 (1962).

FINNEGAN, R., *Limba stories and story-telling*, OLAL, Oxford, 1967.
FISCHER, J. L., 'The sociopsychological analysis of folktales', *Current anthropology* 4 (1963).
FLETCHER, R. S., *Hausa sayings and folk-lore, with a vocabulary of new words*, London, 1912.
FORTUNE, G., 'Some Zezuru and Kalanga riddles', *Nada* 28 (1951).
—— *Ideophones in Shona*, London, 1962.
—— (ed.), *African languages in schools*. (Dept. of African languages, University College of Rhodesia and Nyasaland, Occasional paper 1), Salisbury, 1964.
FRANZ, G. H., 'The literature of Lesotho', *Bantu studies* 4 (1930).
FROBENIUS, L., *Atlantis: Volksmärchen und Volksdichtungen Afrikas*, 12 vols., Jena, 1921-8.
—— *Kulturgeschichte Afrikas*, Zurich, 1933.
GADEN, H., 'Proverbes et maximes peuls et toucouleurs', *TMIE* 16 (1931).
GAUTHIER, J., 'La littérature orale des Fali', *Abbia* 7 (1964).
GBADAMOSI, B., and BEIER, U., *Yoruba poetry*, Ibadan, [1959].
GEORGES, R. A., and DUNDES, A., 'Toward a structural definition of the riddle', *JAF* 76 (1963).
GHILARDI, V., 'Poesie-canti kikuyu', *Africa*, [Roma], 21. 2 (1966).
GIDLEY, C. G. B., '"Yankamanci—the craft of the Hausa comedians', *Afr. language studies* 8 (1967).
GOODY, J., and WATT, I., 'The consequences of literacy', *Comparative Studies in society and history* 5 (1963).
GRANT, E. W., 'The Izibongo of the Zulu chiefs', *Bantu studies* 3 (1927/9).
GRAY, E., 'Some riddles of the Nyanja people', *Bantu studies* 13 (1939).
—— 'Some proverbs of the Nyanja people', *Afr. studies* 3 (1944).
GREEN, M. M., 'The unwritten literature of the Igbo-speaking people of South-Eastern Nigeria', *BSOAS* 12 (1948).
—— 'Sayings of the Ọkọnkọ society of the Igbo-speaking people', *BSOAS* 21 (1958).
GREENBERG, J. H., 'A survey of African prosodic systems' (in S. Diamond (ed.), *Culture in history*, New York, 1960).
—— 'Linguistics' (in R. A. Lystad (ed.), *The African world. A survey of social research*, London 1965).
GREENWAY, J., *Literature among the primitives*, Hatboro, Pennsylvania, 1964.
GRIAULE, M., *Jeux dogons*, TMIE 32, Paris, 1938 (1938*a*).
—— *Masques dogons*, TMIE 33, Paris, 1938 (1938*b*).
GUTMANN, B., *Volksbuch der Wadschagga. Sagen, Märchen, Fabeln und Schwänke, den Dschagganegern nacherzählt*, Leipzig, 1914.
—— 'Lieder der Dschagga', *ZES* 18 (1928).
HARRIES, L., 'Makua song-riddles from the initiation rites', *Afr. studies* 1 (1942) (1942*a*).
—— 'Some riddles of the Makua people', *Afr. studies* 1 (1942) (1942*b*).
—— 'Popular verse of the Swahili tradition', *Africa* 22 (1952).
—— 'Cultural verse-forms in Swahili', *Afr. studies* 15 (1956).
—— *Swahili poetry*, Oxford, 1962.

528 *Bibliography*

HAUENSTEIN, A., 'Noms accompagnés de proverbes, chez les Ovimbundu et les Humbi du sud de l'Angola', *Anthropos* 57 (1962).

HERSKOVITS, M. J., 'Freudian mechanisms in primitive Negro psychology' (in E. E. Evans-Pritchard *et al.* (eds.), *Essays presented to C. G. Seligman*, London, 1934).

—— 'Negro folklore' (in J. T. Shipley (ed.), *Encyclopedia of literature*, New York, 1946; reprinted in S. and P. Ottenberg (eds.), *Cultures and societies of Africa*, New York, 1960).

—— 'The study of African oral art', *JAF* 74 (1961).

—— and HERSKOVITS, F. S., *Dahomean narrative*, Evanston, 1958.

—— and TAGBWE, S., 'Kru proverbs', *JAF* 43 (1930).

HERZOG, G., and BLOOAH, C. G., *Jabo proverbs from Liberia*, London, 1936.

HORTON, R., 'The Kalabari *Ekine* society: a borderland of religion and art', *Africa* 33 (1963).

—— 'Igbo: an ordeal for aristocrats', *Nigeria magazine* 90 (Sept. 1966).

—— 'Ikaki—the Tortoise masquerade', *Nigeria magazine* 94 (Sept. 1967).

HULSTAERT, G., 'Style oral', *Aequatoria* 3 (1943).

—— *Proverbes mongo, AMRCB-L* 15 (1958).

—— *Losako: salutation solennelle des Nkundó, ARSC* 20. 1 (1959).

—— *Contes mongo, ARSOM* 30. 2 (1965).

HUNWICK, J. O., 'The influence of Arabic in West Africa', *Trans. Hist. Soc. Ghana* 7 (1964).

HYMES, D. (ed.), *Language in culture and society*, New York, 1964.

INNES, G., 'Some features of theme and style in Mende folktales', *Sierra Leone language review* 3 (1964).

—— 'The function of the song in Mende folktales', *Sierra Leone language review* 4 (1965).

ITTMANN, J., 'Ein Bakoko-Märchen aus Kamerun', *Afr. u. Übersee* 38 (1954).

JACOBS, J., 'Le message tambouriné, genre de littérature orale bantoue (Tetela, Sankuru, Congo belge)', *Kongo-Overzee* 25 (1959).

—— 'Le récit épique de Lofokefoke, le héros des Mbole (Bambuli)', *Aequatoria* 24 (1961).

—— 'Het epos van Kudukese, de "culture hero" van de Hamba, Congo', *Africa-Tervuren* 9 (1963).

—— and VANSINA, J., 'Het koninklijk epos der Bushong', *Kongo-Overzee* 22 (1956).

JACOBS, M., 'A look ahead in oral literature research', *JAF* 79 (1966).

JACOTTET, E., *The treasury of Ba-Suto lore*, London, 1908.

—— *Contes populaires des Bassoutos*, Paris, 1895.

JOHNSTON, H. A. S., *A selection of Hausa stories*, OLAL, Oxford, 1966.

JONES, A. M., *African music*, Rhodes–Livingstone Museum Occasional Paper 2, 1943.

—— *African music in Northern Rhodesia and some other places*, Rhodes–Livingstone Museum Occasional Paper 4, 1949.

—— 'African rhythm', *Africa* 24 (1954).

JONES, A. M., *Studies in African music*, 2 vols., London, 1959.
—— 'African metrical lyrics', *Afr. music* 3. 3 (1964).
—— 'African metrical lyrics', *Afr. language studies* 5 (1964).
JONES, G. I., 'Masked plays of South-Eastern Nigeria', *Geographical magazine* 18. 5 (Sept. 1945).
JORDAN, A. C., 'Towards an African literature', *Africa south* 1–3 (1956–9).
JOUSSE, M., 'Le style oral rythmique et mnémotechnique ches les verbo-moteurs', *Archives de philosophie*, [Paris], 2 (1924).
JUNOD, H. A., *Les Chants et les contes des Ba-Ronga de la baie de Delagoa*, Lausanne, 1897.
—— *Nouveaux Contes ronga transcrits dans la langue indigène avec traduction française*, Neuchâtel, 1898.
—— *The life of a South African tribe*, 2 vols., Neuchâtel, 1912–13.
JUNOD, H. P., *Bantu heritage*, Johannesburg, [1938].
—— and JAQUES, A. A., *The wisdom of the Tsonga-Shangaan people*, Pretoria, 1936.
KAGAME, A., 'Le Rwanda et son roi', *Aequatoria* 8 (1945).
—— 'La poésie pastorale au Rwanda', *Zaïre* 1. 7 (1947).
—— 'Avec un troubadour du Rwanda', *Zaïre* 3. 7 (1949).
—— 'Bref aperçu sur la poésie dynastique du Rwanda', *Zaïre* 4. 3 (1950).
—— 'Une ode guerrière du vieux Rwanda', *Lovania* 20 (1951) (1951*a*).
—— *La poésie dynastique au Rwanda, IRCB Mém.* 22. 1 (1951) (1951*b*).
—— 'La poésie guerrière', *Présence afr.* 11 (1956/7).
KAGWA, A., *The customs of the Baganda* (Eng. tr.), New York, 1934 (1934*a*).
—— (tr. F. Rowling), *The tales of Sir Apolo. Uganda folklore and proverbs*, London, [1934] (1934*b*).
KALANDA, A., 'Bartholomée Dipumba ou les perspectives nouvelles de la poésie congolaise', *Kongo-Overzee* 25 (1959).
KIDNEY, E., 'Native songs from Nyasaland', *Afr. affairs* 20 (1921).
KIRBY, P. R., 'A study of Bushman music', *Bantu studies* 10 (1936).
KLINGENHEBEN, A., 'Zur amharischen Poesie', *Rass. studi etiop.* 15 (1959).
KLIPPLE, M., 'African folktales with foreign analogues' (unpub. doctoral thesis), Indiana University (1938).
KNAPPERT, J., 'Notes on Swahili literature', *African language studies* 7 (1966) (1966*a*).
—— 'Some aspects of Swahili poetry', *Tanzania notes* 66 (1966) (1966*b*).
—— 'Swahili songs', *Afr. u. Übersee* 50 (1967) (1967*a*).
—— *Traditional Swahili poetry*, Leiden, 1967 (1967*b*).
KOELLE, S. W., *African native literature; or, proverbs, tales, fables, and historical fragments in the Kanuri or Bornu language*, London, 1854.
KORITSCHONER, H., 'Some East African native songs', *Tanganyika notes* 4 (1937).
KUHN, G., 'Pedi-Texte', *ZES* 27 (1936/7).
KUNENE, R., 'An analytical survey of Zulu poetry' (unpub. M.A. thesis), University of Natal 1962 (not seen; reference in Cope 1968).

530          *Bibliography*

LABOURET, H., and TRAVÉLÉ, M., 'Le théâtre mandingue (Soudan français)', *Africa* 1 (1928).

LACROIX, P. F. (ed.), *Poésie peule de l'Adamawa*, 2 vols. (Classiques africains, 3 and 4), [Bruges], 1965.

LAMBERT, H. E., 'Swahili popular verse', *Africa* 22 (1952).

LAṢEBIKAN, E. L., 'Tone in Yoruba poetry', *Odù* 2 [1955].

—— 'The tonal structure of Yoruba poetry', *Présence afr.* N.S. 8/10 (1956).

LAURENCE, M., *A tree for poverty. Somali poetry and prose*, Nairobi, 1954.

LAYDEVANT, F., 'La poésie chez les Basutos', *Africa* 3 (1930).

LEKGOTHOANE, S. K., 'Praises of animals in Northern Sotho', *Bantu studies* 12 (1938).

LESTRADE, G. P., 'Bantu praise-poems', *The Critic* [S. Africa] 4 (1935).

—— 'Traditional literature' (in I. Schapera (ed.), *The Bantu-speaking tribes of South Africa*, London, 1937).

LIENHARDT, G., 'The Dinka of the Nile Basin', *The Listener* 69 (16 May 1963).

LIENHARDT, P., *The medicine man. Swifa ya Nguvumali*, OLAL, Oxford, 1968.

LIFCHITZ [Lifszyc], D., 'Les formules propitiatoires chez les Dogon des falaises de Bandiagara', *J. Soc. africanistes* 8 (1938).

—— 'La littérature orale chez les Dogon du Soudan français', *Africa* 13 (1940).

LINDBLOM, K. G., *Kamba folklore*, 3 vols., Uppsala, 1928–35.

LITTMAN, E., *Galla-Verskunst; ein Beitrag zur allgemeinen Verskunst nebst metrischen Übersetzungen*, Tübingen, 1925.

LUKAS, J., 'Sprichwörter, Aussprüche und Rätsel der Kanuri', *ZES* 28 (1937/8).

MACDONALD, D., *Africana; or, the heart of heathen Africa*, 2 vols., London, etc., 1882.

MACKENZIE, A. S., *The evolution of literature*, London, 1911.

McLAREN, J., 'The wit and wisdom of the Bantu, as illustrated in their proverbial sayings', *South African J. of science* 14 (1917).

MADUMERE, A., 'Ibo village music', *Afr. affairs* 52 (1953).

MALCOLM, D. McK., 'Zulu literature', *Africa* 19 (1949).

MATEENE, K., 'Sur un poème kihunde', *Présence afr.* 55 (1965).

MAUPOIL, B., *La géomancie à l'ancienne Côte des Esclaves*, TMIE 42 (1961).

MAYSSAL, H., 'Poèmes foulbé de la Bénoué', *Abbia* 9/10 (1965).

MBITI, J. S., 'Reclaiming the vernacular literature of the Akamba tribe', *Présence afr.* 24/5, special issue (1959).

—— *Akamba stories*, OLAL, Oxford, 1966.

MEILLASSOUX, C., 'La farce villageoise à la ville (le *Koteba* de Bamako)', *Présence afr.* 52 (1964).

MEINHOF, C., *Die Dichtung der Afrikaner*, Berlin, 1911.

MERRIAM, A. P., 'African music' (in W. R. Bascom and M. J. Herskovits (eds.), *Continuity and change in African cultures*, Chicago, 1962).

—— *The anthropology of music*, Evanston, 1964.

Merriam, A. P., 'Music and the dance' (in R. A. Lystad (ed.), *The African world. A survey of social research*, London, 1965).

MERWE, D. F. v. d., 'Hurutshe poems', *Bantu studies* 15 (1941).

MESSENGER, J. C., 'The role of proverbs in a Nigerian judicial system', *SWJA* 15 (1959).

—— 'Anang proverb-riddles', *JAF* 73 (1960).

—— 'Anang art, drama and social control', *Afr. studies bull.* 5. 2 (1962).

MIGEOD, F. W. H., *The languages of Africa*, 2 vols., London, 1911–13.

MOFOKENG, S. M., 'Notes and annotations of the praise-poems of certain chiefs and the structure of the praise-poems in Southern Sotho' (unpub. dissertation for honours (Bantu studies)), Univ. of the Witwatersrand, 1945.

—— 'The development of leading figures in animal tales in Africa' (unpub. doctoral thesis), Univ. of the Witwatersrand, 1955.

MOHAMADOU, E., 'Introduction à la littérature peule du Nord-Cameroun', *Abbia* 3 (1963).

MONOD, Th., 'Un poème mystique soudanais', *Présence afr.* 3 (1948).

MONTEIL, C., *Contes soudanais*, Paris, 1905.

MORRIS, H. F., *The heroic recitations of the Bahima of Ankole*, OLAL, Oxford, 1964.

MORTON-WILLIAMS, P., BASCOM, W., and McCLELLAND, E. M., 'Two studies of Ifa divination', *Africa* 36 (1966).

NAKENE, G., 'Tlokwa riddles', *Afr. studies* 2 (1943).

NASSAU, R. H., *Where animals talk: West African folk lore tales*, London, 1914.

NEBEL, A., 'Dinka-Lieder', *Archiv für Völkerkunde* 15 (1960).

NETTL, B., 'Ibo songs from Nigeria, native and hybridized', *Midwest folklore* 3 (1954) (1954*a*).

—— 'Notes on musical composition in primitive culture', *Anth. quart.* 27 (1954) (1954*b*).

—— *Music in primitive culture*, Cambridge, Mass., 1956.

NICOLAS, F., 'Folklore twāreg: poésies et chansons de l'Azāwarh', *Bull. IFAN* 6. 1/4 (1944).

NICOLAS, F. J., 'Les surnoms-devises des L'éla de la Haute-Volta', *Anthropos* 45. 1/3 (1950); 49. 1/2 (1954).

—— 'Énigmes des L'éla de la Haute-Volta', *Anthropos* 49. 5/6 (1954).

NKETIA, J. H. K., *Funeral dirges of the Akan people*, Achimota, 1955.

—— 'Organization of music in Adangme society', *Afr. music* 2. 1 (1958) (1958*a*).

—— 'Akan poetry', *Black Orpheus* 3 (1958) (1958*b*).

—— 'Drum proverbs', *Voices of Ghana*, Accra (Ministry of Information and Broadcasting, 1958) (1958*c*).

—— 'The music of Africa', *J. of human relations* 8. 3–4 (1960).

—— *African music in Ghana: a survey of traditional forms*, Accra, 1962.

—— *Folk songs of Ghana*, Legon, 1963 (1963*a*).

—— *Drumming in Akan communities of Ghana*, Legon, 1963 (1963*b*).

NORTON, W. A., 'African life and language', *Afr. studies* 9 (1950).

NYEMBEZI, C. L. S., *Zulu proverbs*, Johannesburg, 1954.

OBIECHINA, E. N., 'Transition from oral to literary tradition', *Présence afr.* 63 (1967).

OBUMSELU, B., 'The background of modern African literature', *Ibadan* 22 (1966).

OGUNBA, O., 'Ritual drama of the Ijebu people: a study of indigenous festivals' (unpub. Ph.D. thesis), University of Ibadan (1967).

OKOT, J. p'B., 'Oral literature and its social background among the Acholi and Lango' (unpub. B.Litt. thesis), University of Oxford (1963).

OMIJEH, M. E. A., 'The social significance of Bini personal names' (unpub. essay for B.Sc. (Soc.)), University of Ibadan (1966).

OSADEBAY, D. C., *et al.*, 'West African voices', *Afr. affairs* 48 (1949).

OWUOR, H., 'Luo songs', *Black Orpheus* 10 (1961).

PADEN, J. N., 'A survey of Kano Hausa poetry', *Kano studies* 1 (1965).

PÂQUES, V., 'Mythe et structures dans les sociétés africaines traditionnelles', *Bull. IFAN* (B) 26 (1964).

PAULME, D., 'Littérature orale et comportements sociaux en Afrique noire', *L'Homme* 1. 1 (1916).

—— *et al.* (ed.), 'Littérature orale et folklore africains. Sur un thème de contes africains: l'impossible restitution ou le cadeau prestigieux', *Cah. étud. afr.* 30 (1968).

PFEFFER, G., 'Prose and poetry of the Ful'be', *Africa* 12 (1939).

PHILLIPS, H. R., 'Some Tiv songs', *Nigerian teacher* 6 (1936).

PLAATJE, S. T., *Sechuana proverbs with literal translations and their European equivalents*, London, 1916.

PRIETZE, R., *Haussa-Sprichwörter und Haussa-Lieder*, Kirchhain N.-L., 1904.

—— 'Bornulieder', *MSOS* 17. 3 (1914).

—— *Haussa-Sänger*, Göttingen, 1916 (1916*a*).

—— 'Lieder fahrender Haussaschüler', *MSOS* 19. 3 (1916) (1916*b*).

—— 'Gesungene Predigten eines fahrenden Haussalehrers', *MSOS* 20. 3 (1917).

—— 'Haussa-Preislieder auf Parias', *MSOS* 21. 3 (1918).

—— 'Lieder des Haussavolkes', *MSOS* 30. 3 (1927).

—— 'Dichtung der Haussa', *Africa* 4 (1931).

PROUTEAUX, M., 'Premiers essais de théâtre chez les indigènes de la Haute-Côte-d'Ivoire', *Bull. Com. ét. AOF* 12 (1929).

RADIN, P., *African folktales and sculpture*, New York, 1952.

RATTRAY, R. S., *Some folk-lore stories and songs in Chinyanja*, London, 1907.

—— *Hausa folk-lore, customs, proverbs, etc., collected and transliterated with English translation and notes*, 2 vols., Oxford, 1913.

—— *Ashanti proverbs: the primitive ethics of a savage people*, Oxford, 1916.

—— 'The drum language of West Africa', *J. Afr. soc.* 22 (1923), reprinted in R. S. Rattray, *Ashanti*, Oxford, 1923.

—— *Akan–Ashanti folktales*, Oxford, 1930.

READ, M., 'Songs of the Ngoni people', *Bantu studies* 11 (1937).

RHODES, W., 'Music as an agent of political expression', *Afr. studies bull.* 5. 2 (1962).

RODEGEM, F. M., 'Le style oral au Burundi', *Congo-Tervuren* 6 (1960).

—— *Sagesse kirundi. Proverbes, dictons, locutions usités au Burundi,* AMRCB 34 (1961).

ROGER, J.-F., *Fables sénégalaises recueillies dans l'Ouolof,* Paris, 1828.

ROPER, E. M., 'Poetry of the Haḍenḍiwa', *Sudan notes* 10 (1927).

ROUGET, G., 'La musique d'Afrique noire' (*Histoire de la musique,* 1), Encycl. de la Pléiade, n.d.

RYCROFT, D. K., 'Zulu and Xhosa praise poetry and song', *Afr. music* 3. 1 (1962).

SCHAPERA, I., 'Kxatla riddles and their significance', *Bantu studies* 6 (1932).

—— *Praise-poems of Tswana chiefs.* OLAL, Oxford, 1965.

SCHARFE, D., and ALIYU, Y., 'The tradition of Hausa poetry', *Black Orpheus* 21 (1967).

SCHLENKER, C. F., *A collection of Temne traditions, fables and proverbs, with an English translation, with a Temne–English vocabulary,* London, 1861.

SCHNEIDER, M., 'Zur Trommelsprache der Duala', *Anthropos* 47 (1952).

SCHÖN, J. F., *Magána Hausa: native literature, proverbs, tales, fables and historical fragments in the Hausa language,* London, 1885.

SEIDEL, A., *Geschichten und Lieder der Afrikaner,* Berlin, [1896].

SEMPEBWA, E. K. K., 'Baganda folk-songs: a rough classification', *Uganda J.* 12 (1948).

SENGHOR, L. S., 'La poésie négro-africaine', *Problèmes d'Afrique centrale* 12 (1951).

SIMMONS, D. C., 'Specimens of Efik folklore', *Folklore* 66 (1955).

—— 'Erotic Ibibio tone riddles', *Man* 56 (1956).

—— 'Cultural functions of the Efik tone riddle', *JAF* 71 (1958).

—— 'Tonal rhyme in Efik poetry', *Anth. ling.* 2. 6 (1960) (1960*a*).

—— 'Oron proverbs', *Afr. studies* 19 (1960) (1960*b*).

—— 'Analysis of cultural reflection in Efik folktales', *JAF* 74 (1961).

SMITH, E. W., 'The function of folk-tales', *J. Roy. Afr. Soc.* 39 (1940).

—— and DALE, A. M., *The Ila-speaking peoples of Northern Rhodesia,* 2 vols., London, 1920.

SMITH, M. G., 'The social functions and meaning of Hausa praise-singing', *Africa* 27 (1957).

SOW, A. I., *La femme, la vache, la foi: écrivains et poètes du Foûta-Djalon,* Classiques africains 5, Paris, 1966.

STAPPERS, L., 'Eerste geluiden uit de Luba-poëzie', *Kongo-Overzee* 18 (1952).

—— 'Toonparallelisme als mnemotechnisch middel in spreekwoorden', *Aequatoria* 16 (1953).

—— with VINCKE, J. L., *Textes luba: contes d'animaux,* AMRAC 41 (1962).

STEERE, E., and WERNER, A., *Swahili tales, as told by natives of Zanzibar, with an English translation,* London, 1922 [1st ed. 1870].

## 534 Bibliography

STEFANISZYN, B., 'The hunting songs of the Ambo', *Afr. studies* 10 (1951).

STOPA, R., *Studies on the population and culture of Africa South-West*, Warsaw, 1938.

TAIWO, O., *An introduction to West African literature*, London, 1967.

TARDY, L., 'Contribution à l'étude du folklore bantou. Les fables, devinettes et proverbes fãng', *Anthropos* 28 (1933).

TAYLOR, A., *The proverb*, Harvard, 1931.

—— *A bibliography of riddles*, Helsinki, 1939.

—— 'Some trends and problems in studies of the folk-tale', *Studies in philology* 37 (1940).

TAYLOR, W. E., *African aphorisms or saws from Swahililand*, London, 1924 [1st ed. 1891].

TEN RAA, W. F. E. R., 'Sandawe oral literature' (unpub. D.Phil. thesis), Oxford, 1967.

TESCAROLI, L., *Poesia sudanese*, Bologna, 1961.

THEAL, G. M., *Kaffir folk-lore: a selection from the traditional tales current among the people living on the eastern border of the Cape Colony*, London, 1886.

THEUWS, T., *Textes luba, CEPSI* 27 (1954).

THIAM, 'Des contes et des fables en Afrique noire', *Présence afr.* 4 (1948).

THOMPSON, S., *The folktale*, New York, 1946.

—— *Motif-index of folk-literature*, revised ed., 6 vols., Copenhagen, 1955–8.

—— *The types of the folktale. A classification and bibliography* (2nd ed.), Helsinki, 1961.

TORREND, J., *Specimens of Bantu folk-lore from Northern Rhodesia*, London, 1921.

TOWO-ATANGANA, G., 'Le *mvet*, genre majeur de la littérature orale des populations pahouines (Bulu, Béti, Fang-Ntumu)', *Abbia* 9/10 (1965).

—— and F., 'Nden-Bobo, l'araignée-toilière', *Africa* 36 (1966).

TRACEY, H. T., 'Some observations on native music of Southern Rhodesia', *Nada* 7 (1929).

—— *Songs from the kraals of Southern Rhodesia*, Salisbury, 1933.

—— 'Poetic justice', *Nada* 22 (1945).

—— *Chopi musicians: their music, poetry, and instruments*, London, 1948 (1948a).

—— '*Lalela Zulu*', *100 Zulu lyrics*, Johannesburg, [? 1948] (1948b).

—— 'The social role of African music', *Afr. affairs* 53 (1954) (1954a).

—— 'The state of folk music in Bantu Africa', *Afr. music* 1. 1 (1954) (1954b).

—— 'African music within its social setting', *Afr. music* 2. 1 (1958).

—— 'The arts in Africa: the visual and the aural', *Afr. music* 3. 1 (1962).

—— 'Behind the lyrics', *Afr. music* 3. 2 (1963).

—— 'The development of music in Africa', *Optima*, [Johannesburg], 14. 1 (1964).

TRAORÉ, B., *Le Théâtre négro-africain et ses fonctions sociales*, Paris (*Présence africaine*), 1958.

TRAUTMANN, R., *La littérature populaire à la Côte des Esclaves*, *TMIE* 4 (1927).

TRAVÉLÉ, M., *Proverbes et contes bambara et malinké, accompagnés d'une traduction française et précédés d'un abrégé de droit coutumier bambara et malinké*, Paris, 1923.

TREMEARNE, A. J. N., *Hausa superstitions and customs: an introduction to the folk-lore and the folk*, London, 1913.

TRILLES, H., *Les Pygmées de la forêt équatoriale*, Paris, 1933.

TUCKER, A. N., 'Children's games and songs in the Southern Sudan', *JRAI* 63 (1933).

VAN AVERMAET, E., 'Langage rythmé des Baluba', *Aequatoria* 28 (1955).

VAN DYCK, C., 'An analytic study of the folktales of selected peoples of West Africa' (unpub. D.Phil. thesis), University of Oxford (1966).

VANNESTE, M., *Legenden, geschiedenis en gebruiken van een Nilotisch volk. Alur teksten*, *IRCB Mém*. 18. 1 (1949).

—— *Wijsheid en scherts. Sprookjes van een Nilotisch volk. Alur-teksten*, *IRCB Mém*. 25. 3 (1953).

VAN ROY, H., and DAELEMAN, J., 'Proverbes kongo', *AMRAC* 48 (1963).

VANSINA, J., *Oral tradition, a study in historical methodology* (Eng. tr. by H. M. Wright), London, 1965.

VAN WARMELO, N. J., *Transvaal Ndebele texts*, Pretoria, 1930.

VAN ZYL, H. J., 'Praises in Northern Sotho', *Bantu studies* 15 (1941).

VELTEN, C., *Prosa und Poesie der Suaheli*, Berlin, 1907.

VERGER, P., *Notes sur le culte des Oriṣa et Vodun à Bahia, la Baie de tous les Saints, au Brésil et à l'ancienne Côte des Esclaves en Afrique, Mém. IFAN* 51 (1957).

VIEILLARD, G., 'Le chant de l'eau et du palmier doum: poème bucolique du marais nigérien', *Bull. IFAN* 2. 3/4 (1940).

VILAKAZI, B. W., 'The conception and development of poetry in Zulu', *Bantu studies* 2 (1938).

—— 'Some aspects of Zulu literature', *Afr. studies* 1 (1942).

—— 'The oral and written literature in Nguni' (unpub. D.Litt. thesis), University of the Witwatersrand (1945).

VON FUNKE, E., 'Einige Tanz- und Liebeslieder der Haussa', *ZES* 11 (1920–1).

VON SICARD, H., *Ngano dze Cikaranga: Karangamärchen, Studia ethnographica upsaliensia*, [Uppsala], 23. 1965.

VON SYDOW, C. W., *Selected papers on folklore*, Copenhagen, [1948].

VON TILING, M., 'Frauen- und Kinderlieder der Suaheli', *Festschrift Meinhof*, Glückstadt (1927).

WELLESZ, E. (ed.), *Ancient and oriental music*, London, 1957.

WERNER, A., *The native tribes of British Central Africa*, London, 1906.

—— 'Swahili poetry', *BSOS* 1 (1917–20).

—— *African mythology*, Boston, 1925.

—— 'Swahili poetry', *J. Afr. Soc.* 26 (1927).

536     *Bibliography*

WERNER, A., 'Native poetry in East Africa', *Africa* 1 (1928).
—— *Myths and legends of the Bantu*, London, 1933.
WHITELEY, W. H., *The dialects and verse of Pemba: an introduction*, Kampala, 1958.
—— (ed.), *A selection of African prose*. 1. *Traditional oral texts*, OLAL, Oxford, 1964.
WHITTING, C. E. J., *Hausa and Fulani proverbs*, Lagos, 1940.
WIEGRÄBE, P., 'Ewelieder', *Afr. u. Übersee* 37 (1953); 38 (1953/4).
WITTE, P. A., 'Lieder und Gesänge der Ewe-Neger', *Anthropos* 1 (1906).
—— 'Zur Trommelsprache bei den Ewe-Leuten', *Anthropos* 5 (1910).
WRIGHT, M. J., 'Lango folk-tales—an analysis', *Uganga J.* 24 (1960).
YONDO, E. E., 'La littérature orale douala', *Abbia* 12/13 (1966).
ZEMP, H., 'Musiciens autochtones et griots malinké chez les Dan de Côte-d'Ivoire', *Cah. étud. afr.* 15 (1964).

# INDEX

PRINTED IN GREAT BRITAIN
AT THE UNIVERSITY PRESS, OXFORD
BY VIVIAN RIDLER
PRINTER TO THE UNIVERSITY